ACCLAIM FOR PETER LANCE'S GROUNDBREAKING *1000 YEARS FOR REVENGE*

"An astonishing series of revelations, this book is a must-read for the FBI, the 9/11 commission, Congress, and anyone whose job it is to protect national security. If the FBI is to successfully transform itself from a crime-solving agency to a terrorism prevention force, it must learn from the mistakes described in *1000 Years for Revenge*."
—Senator Chuck Grassley (R-Iowa), Judiciary Committee

"There are a small handful of books that must be read if we are to understand the present threat of Islamic extremists to our way of life— and *1000 Years for Revenge* is one of them. This is a wake-up call to show America how our barn door was left open, and how uncertain we should be that our institutions are capable of closing it."
—Dennis Smith, bestselling author of *Report from Ground Zero* and *Report from Engine Co.82*

"An astounding investigation. The Senate-House Joint Inquiry report said there were no smoking guns on how the FBI missed 9/11. Peter Lance's book is a 500-page smoking gun."
—Kristin Breitweiser, co-chair, September 11 Advocates

"I had not realized there was more material to mine in the story of the first attack on the World Trade Center in 1993 but Peter Lance hit a mother lode in his recounting of the story of FBI agent Nancy Floyd and her relationship with Emad Salem, the FBI informant who could have prevented that attack."
—Peter Bergen, author of *Holy War Inc.*

1000 YEARS
FOR
REVENGE

1000 YEARS FOR REVENGE

INTERNATIONAL TERRORISM AND THE FBI—
THE UNTOLD STORY

PETER LANCE

REGAN

An Imprint of HarperCollinsPublishers

*To the ground troops in the war
on terror: the investigators of first
impression . . . the street agents, the
fire marshals, and the uniformed cops.*

*To the first responders: the fire
fighters and EMS workers who bear
the full impact of the threat.*

*To all the families who support them
and to every innocent person who has
ever died from an act of violence
committed in the name of God.*

Quis custodiet ipsos custodes?
Who is guarding the guardians themselves?

—JUVENAL

CONTENTS

PART III

A NOTE TO READERS

Much of the information in this book was gathered from sources inside the U.S. law enforcement and intelligence communities. The database of research included dozens of first-person interviews, hundreds of pages of declassified documents from the FBI and foreign intelligence services, and more than forty thousand pages of court records and open source material from the print and electronic media. My primary focus was the Federal Bureau of Investigation, specifically the FBI's handling of the original World Trade Center bombing investigation and the hunt for its mastermind, Ramzi Ahmed Yousef. A genius at crafting improvised explosive devices, Yousef fled New York the night of the bombing in 1993 and went on to create the blueprint for the subsequent 9/11 attacks.

The evidence I uncovered established a direct connection between those two events—a dotted line of intelligence that ran like a hot circuit cable from Afghanistan to New York to the Philippines and back to New York again. Each dot on that line represented a lost opportunity for the U.S. intelligence community to stop Osama bin Laden and his al Qaeda juggernaut. While many were culpable, the evidence now suggests that the agency most responsible was the FBI.

As early as 1983, President Reagan designated the Bureau as the lead agency for combating terrorism in the United States.[1] More than any other of the "Big Five" intelligence agencies,[2] the FBI was specifically charged with the responsibility for preventing acts of terror on American soil. Yet in less than a decade, the nation was scarred by the 1993 Twin

Towers bombing, the 1995 bombing of the Murrah Federal Building in Oklahoma City, and the 9/11 attacks. The question is, *Why?*

In my effort to find an answer, much of the material I unearthed was "in the black"—either classified or known to key players unable to speak on the record. Still, I interviewed a number of retired FBI agents and supervisors who were close to the Yousef hunt, including Carson Dunbar, the assistant special agent in charge (ASAC), and Jim Roth, the principal legal officer (PLO), of the FBI's New York office. Both men spoke publicly for the first time about their roles in the investigation leading up to the first World Trade Center bombing and its aftermath.

I conducted multiple interviews with Detective Louis Napoli, who spent twenty years with the NYPD-FBI Joint Terrorist Task Force in New York. On condition of anonymity, I also spoke with a number of special agents and investigators who are still on active duty. One of the key agents in the investigation that led up to the Trade Center bombing was Special Agent Nancy Floyd. I had been personally acquainted with her for some time, but we had never discussed the case. Then, in October 2002, I made a formal application with the Bureau to interview her on the record. The FBI never responded to my request, and Bureau policy restricted Agent Floyd from discussing the specifics of her work. However, because of our past association, she *was* able to talk about her moving personal life in the years before and after the WTC bombing on February 26, 1993. The remaining details surrounding her story came from confidential Bureau sources and retired agents close to the investigation who agreed to speak to me on the record.

The remarkable story of FDNY Fire Marshal Ronnie Bucca was drawn from dozens of interviews with his brother firefighters in Rescue One, the marshals of the Bureau of Fire Investigation, and personnel with whom he worked as a U.S. Army Reserve Warrant Officer in the 3413th Military Intelligence Detachment.

I owe a special debt of thanks to the chief fire marshal of the FDNY, Louis F. Garcia, and another to Jacob L. Boesen, a former intelligence analyst who worked with Ronnie at the Defense Intelligence Analysis Center in Washington, D.C. But without the generous cooperation of the Bucca family, specifically his wife, Eve, and their children, Ronnie and Jessica, Fire Marshal Bucca's extraordinary role in this story could not have been told.

The most enigmatic figure in this mystery was Yousef himself, the brilliant bomb maker who defied the Feds for years as he escaped from New York and plotted one horrific act of terror after another until he was brought to ground in Pakistan in 1995. Yousef's terrifying story was pieced together from dozens of interviews with members of the U.S. intelligence community, sources in the Bureau of Prisons, and officers of the Philippine National Police, as well as Yousef's former lawyer Roy Kulcsar and his current attorneys, Bernard Kleinman and Steven Legon. A particular thanks goes to Frank Gonzalez, a retired federal agent who played a key role as an investigator assigned to the Yousef defense team.

My longtime friend and attorney Jeff Feldman and his associate Ruth Botstein were most helpful in analyzing a number of legal issues relating to the World Trade Center bombing investigation. Private investigator Joe Murphy, with whom I'd worked many years before on an arson investigation for ABC News, gave me hours of assistance. I owe a personal thanks to Richard Arlook of the Gersh Agency, whom I've known since my days as a correspondent for *20/20.* But the book would not have been possible without the tireless support of Judith Regan, who believed in my ability to report this epic and sometimes volatile story. Cal Morgan, the brilliant editorial director at Regan Books, helped me tell it in a way that was both human and journalistically precise. My thanks to his tremendously supportive assistant, Lina Perl, and to Judith's remarkable executive assistant, Angelica Canales.

This is a work of nonfiction, but there are elements in the story as gripping as a spy thriller. I started looking into the origins of the 9/11 attacks in the late fall of 2001, but back then I had only a small piece of the puzzle. Already dozens of books on the aftermath of September 11 were in the works, and though only a few would examine the *cause,* I wasn't sure what I could contribute to the body of knowledge.

I had done a number of investigative stories on the intelligence community, the Pentagon, and the Justice Department while working as a correspondent for ABC News in the late 1980s. I had a law degree, and I'd worked as a trial preparation assistant in the office of the Manhattan DA while in law school, but I'd spent most of the last fifteen years writing fiction, and my most recent book had involved an investigation into whether the CBS television network had violated 1950s FCC game show rules in the alleged rigging of its reality series *Survivor*.[3] While relevant in 2000, when *Survivor* was the third biggest news story of the year,[4] the subject had lost its meaning in the aftermath of 9/11, and after years away from covering intelligence issues, I wasn't sure I was ready to take on the job.

Then, one night in 2002, Chief Fire Marshal Louis Garcia took me to Memorial Park. It was a three-story, white temporary structure tucked down between Bellevue Hospital and the FDR Drive. The structure was surrounded by a high fence topped with the flags of a dozen municipal and law enforcement agencies. Inside, the floor was covered with green Astroturf. An enormous American flag hung from a rafter overhead. Backed into the east and west sides of the structure were eight enormous white refrigerated trailers. Each had a small set of wooden stairs leading up to its back doors. The stairs were surrounded by dozens of funeral wreathes and standing bouquets of flowers. The trucks were covered with purple and black mourning crepe. Along the sides of the trailers, visitors had written their good-byes.

"Our hearts are crying," wrote one. "You're my heroes," wrote another. "No greater love than he who laid down his life—John 15:13," wrote a third. A detective named Moran had written, "God bless all my brothers."

When I realized what this was, I stepped back. All I could say to Garcia was, "My God." We were standing inside an enormous makeshift mortuary.

In those trucks were the eleven thousand body parts of the 9/11 World Trade Center victims who had not yet been identified. Each one had been assigned a DM (Disaster Mortuary) number by the medical examiner's office in the hope that DNA comparison would eventually help identify the victims. Until then, they were being kept in a state of perpetual preservation—eight tractor trailers holding the partial remains of thousands of innocent people.

For many, the horror of the 9/11 attacks hit home when they first saw the awful video pictures of Tower Two collapsing. For others it came after they shuffled past the hundreds of images and moving remembrances posted along the viewing wall by Ground Zero. But I never fully understood the utter cruelty of the 9/11 attacks until that night when Chief Garcia brought me into that sad, white temporary structure. When those planes hit the towers, the people inside weren't just murdered, they were *eviscerated,* and as late as April of 2003 only 1,481 of the 2,819 New York victims had been properly identified and laid to rest.[5]

As we stood at the edge of the first trailer, marked MOS (Members of Service), I turned to Lou. He had narrowly escaped death himself that day, when he rushed down to Church Street to find his men. As a veteran of Manhattan's Rescue One company, Garcia had known dozens of the 343 FDNY victims personally. Now, as he stared at the MOS trailer, almost numb, I asked, "Has this hit you yet? Have you been able to process this?"

Garcia hesitated. A big, strong, gregarious Cuban–Puerto Rican American who'd worked his way up through the ranks of New York's Bravest, he'd sent his son to Harvard and his daughter to Yale. Garcia himself was an embodiment of the American dream, but now he was standing by that trailer almost weak-kneed. I asked him again, but put it another way: "Lou, have you been able to grieve?"

"No. Not really. Not yet," he said. "I just keep working."

And that's when it really hit me—the importance of this story.

On the day of the attack I was on the West Coast. I saw it all second-hand as the news pieces played over and over. By the night of my visit to Memorial Park I hadn't even been down to "the pile" between Church and West Streets. But I knew then and there that I had to make sense of this—to try, as a reporter, to answer the questions that were gnawing at so many Americans. More than three thousand people had died that day in New York, Pennsylvania, and D.C. How could such a monumental act of terror be inflicted against so many civilians—and why couldn't our government stop it?

From that night on, I kicked over one rock, and then another and another, until, after months of interviews and a trip to the Philippines to visit Ramzi Yousef's bomb factory, I reached a kind of bedrock conclusion myself. The mass murders of September 11 were the culmination of a plot that had been in the works for seven years. The pathology that spawned it had begun to infect our country another five years before that. Twelve years. That's how far back I followed the trail to 9/11. With all the dots on that line, why couldn't our government see it coming? For some investigators, that answer was found in a complex analysis of multiagency intelligence failures. But for me, it was buried in the stories of three people whose lives converged in a fireball over Lower Manhattan.

INTRODUCTION

As American Airlines Flight 11 hit the World Trade Center's North Tower and United Airlines Flight 175 sliced through Tower Two, three people who had never met had their day of reckoning. For years, they had been strangely bound on a collision course: a female FBI agent, an FDNY fire marshal, and the bomb-making terrorist an American judge once called "an apostle of evil."[1] Now their paths had crossed in the greatest mass murder on American ground. Their fate might have been altered if the nation's primary law enforcement agency had simply done its job. But in a devastating series of missteps, the FBI *failed*—and its negligence is a metaphor for the danger America continues to face.

This is the story of how the FBI was a hair's breadth away from catching the most dangerous man on earth, and blew it. It was a failure that allowed Osama bin Laden's chief bomb maker to inflict two devastating strikes on our country: the World Trade Center bombing in 1993, and the attacks of September 11, 2001. The terrorist, Ramzi Ahmed Yousef, had set his deadly plan into motion years before, and the FBI had *dozens* of chances along the way to stop it. But like others, the warnings of Fire Marshal Ronald Bucca and the Bureau's own Special Agent Nancy Floyd were ignored. What's worse, Floyd's experience in New York was appallingly similar to the stonewalling encountered by FBI agents in Phoenix and Minneapolis. Ronnie Bucca's efforts were thwarted because he lacked direct access to FBI investigators, who turned him away repeatedly; Nancy Floyd, who was working *inside* the Bureau, shouldn't have had the same problem, but she did—and the Bureau superiors who dismissed her concerns missed an opportunity to bring down the plot years before it was realized.

Since 9/11, the FBI has made significant gains against Osama bin Laden and his al Qaeda terror network. The biggest "get" came in early March 2003 with the arrest of Ramzi Yousef's uncle Khalid Shaikh Mohammed, who helped his nephew plan the strikes on the World Trade Center and the Pentagon. There was some hope that Operation Iraqi Freedom might uncover links to al Qaeda and put the terror network on the run. But even after the fall of Baghdad, Osama bin Laden's cohorts responded with a stunning series of attacks that demonstrated the abiding power of their network.[2]

In early May a top al Qaeda commander, believed to have masterminded the bombing of the U.S.S. *Cole,* was captured; two of his coconspirators were later indicted.[3] But arrests have been made in the past, and FBI predictions of victory over al Qaeda have proven premature. At least three times since 1989, Justice Department officials assumed that the conviction of prominent al Qaeda members had diminished the threat.[4] Each time, however, the danger to America increased exponentially.

The title of this book is drawn from an old expression in the Baluchistan no-man's-land of Pakistan, the homeland of Ramzi Yousef: "If it takes me ten centuries to kill my enemy, I will wait a thousand years for revenge." That pledge underscores the years of planning that went into the 9/11 attacks, and the long-term war that lies ahead. The shock troops of al Qaeda have something Americans don't—time. Time to dig in. Time to wait us out. Time to pick the next target. The odds are that between the date of this book's publication and the date that you read it, another major loss of human life will have taken place somewhere at the hands of bin Laden's network.

This is the work of a single investigative reporter. It was written in the spirit of Justice Benjamin Cardozo, who believed that "sunlight is the best disinfectant."

In examining the intelligence failures leading up to 9/11, at least two books have focused on the role played by the CIA, the Defense Intelligence Agency (DIA), and the National Security Agency (NSA).[5] Another examined the FBI, but told only part of the story.[6]

This book focuses exclusively on the Bureau, because it was the one

U.S. law enforcement agency that had the responsibility and the knowledge to stop both attacks on the Trade Center. Further, the FBI's continuing job of containing the al Qaeda threat is key to the safety of us all.

An attempt by a Joint Senate-House Committee to get at the truth behind 9/11 was limited. The committee, known as the Joint Inquiry, restricted itself to an examination of the intelligence agencies, and left out major components of the government, including the executive branch. After a ten-month investigation, the panel issued twenty-six pages of public "Findings" and "Recommendations," but its full report remained classified for months. While citing multiple acts of negligence by the FBI and the CIA, the Joint Inquiry stopped far short of assessing blame. Its report was considered so restrictive that Republican senator Richard Shelby, vice chairman of the Senate Select Committee on Intelligence, issued his own eighty-four-page minority report chiding the overall Joint Inquiry for its failure to "assess accountability."[7] Later, senator Bob Graham, a Democratic candidate for president and a member of the original investigation, charged that the Bush administration's apparent unwillingness to declassify the Joint Inquiry's full report amounted to a "cover-up."[8] By July 24, the Administration had negotiated a deal with the Joint Inquiry staff to release a heavily redacted version of the 858-page report. But an entire 27-page section dealing with possible Saudi ties to the 9/11 attacks was left blank. One congressional investigator described the report as "a scathing indictment of the FBI...an agency that doesn't have a clue about terrorism."[9] The final report was so incomplete that its co-chairman, Rep. Porter J. Goss (D-FL), admitted, "I can tell you right now that I don't know exactly how the plot was hatched. I don't know the where, the when, and the why and the who.... That's after two years of trying."[10]

In 2002, having given up hope that Congress would get to the truth, the organized families of 9/11 victims called for the creation of an independent panel, similar in scope to the Warren Commission established in 1964 to investigate the assassination of President Kennedy.[11]

After fighting creation of such a commission through the summer and fall of 2002, the White House changed tack in September and agreed to an eleventh-hour compromise with Congress. The deal allowed President Bush to name the commission's chairman and cochairman.[12] But the first two appointees, Henry Kissinger and former Democratic

4 · 1 0 0 0   Y E A R S   F O R   R E V E N G E

senator George Mitchell, resigned within days, citing potential conflicts of interest.[13] In late December the president appointed former New Jersey governor Tom Kean to head the panel, but as hearings got under way in March 2003 serious questions were raised about whether the commission had the proper funding to do the job.[14] Any probative findings relating to 9/11 aren't expected until May 2004, and in its first report, issued July 8, 2003, commission staffers complained that their work was being hampered by the failure of the executive branch (particularly the Pentagon and the Justice Department) to quickly respond in the production of documents and testimony.[15]

The attacks of September 11 represented the greatest failure of intelligence since the Trojan horse. Each of the nation's spy agencies was responsible in part, but after an eighteen-month investigation, the evidence presented in this book shows that the FBI in particular had multiple opportunities to stop the devastation of 9/11 and simply failed to follow through. At first glance, the long road to 9/11 is a tangled conspiracy populated by Islamic shadow figures with multiple aliases. To the Westerner the task of untangling the web can be daunting. It's a labyrinth that stretches for a dozen years across four continents. But the story snaps into focus when one hones in on the real "ground zero," the FBI's New York office—specifically the NYPD-FBI Joint Terrorist Task Force (JTTF). Simply put, the Bureau's failure to stop 9/11 was directly linked to the inability of JTTF agents and detectives to contain the cell surrounding a blind old man: Egyptian cleric Sheikh Omar Abdel Rahman.

The so-called blind Sheikh, spiritual leader of two Egyptian hate groups, remains an ominous presence throughout this story, from the bloody East Side Manhattan murder of right-wing Jewish rabbi Meier Kahane in 1990, up through the moment the nineteen hijackers boarded the American and United flights on the morning of September 11. The Bureau's initial failure to capture Abdel Rahman's followers as they built the Trade Center bomb resulted in the escape of master bomb maker Ramzi Yousef. We now know that as far back as 1994, in Manila, Yousef and his uncle Khalid Shaikh Mohammed had begun to plot the hijacked-airliners-suicide scenario that culminated on 9/11. Yet even after Yousef's capture in 1995, the FBI failed to follow up on key evidence from the Philippines that al Qaeda operatives were training at that moment in U.S. flight schools. One Saudi pilot who began flight lessons in Arizona in 1996 went on to hijack American Airlines Flight 77 and fly it into the Pentagon on September 11.

Then in 1996, having lost Yousef once, the Bureau and federal prosecutors became so concerned that he would promote terror from inside his jail cell in Manhattan, that they recruited the son of a Mafia capo in a desperate attempt to stop him. Perhaps most disturbing, in 1999 the FBI's New York office dismissed probative evidence that an Egyptian-American FDNY employee who was a close confidant of Sheikh Rahman's had obtained blueprints of the World Trade Center, prior to the 1993 bombing.

Examined in light of what the FBI knew about bin Laden's stated intent to make war on U.S. citizens, a full investigation of this man might well have focused the hunt on the al Qaeda cell then working in Hamburg, Germany, to perfect Yousef's 9/11 plan. Evidence now shows that the release of Sheikh Rahman, jailed by the Feds in 1993, was a key goal of Osama bin Laden in launching the September 11 attacks.

Parts of that story have already been told. But this investigation found that the origin of the FBI failure stretches back more than a decade. Previously secret files unearthed in the Philippines and interviews with key intelligence operatives there show that Yousef's suicide hijacking plot was a virtual blueprint of the September 11 attacks. Thus, it can be fairly argued that if the FBI had done its job in the fall of 1992 and apprehended Yousef *before* he set the Trade Center bomb, they might have prevented the tragedy of 9/11.

President Ronald Reagan's CIA director William Casey likened intelligence gathering to the process of building a mosaic. There were thousands of pieces of intel, he observed—little pieces of broken glass consisting of ELINT (electronic intelligence), PHOTINT (spy-satellite imagery), COMINT (communication intercepts), and HUMINT (from on-the-ground spies).[16] Policy could never depend exclusively on any given piece of the mosaic, Casey argued; only by standing back and viewing the assembled pieces together could one get a clear picture of the truth.

In the FBI's attempt to assemble the mosaic on Osama bin Laden, significant pieces of the puzzle were lost, ignored, or minimized in the twelve years between the time the Bureau's New York office first began surveilling members of the blind Sheikh's cell and the moment American Airlines Flight 11 finally slammed into the North Tower. As this book will demonstrate, the weight of the blame sits with the FBI's middle and upper management, which thwarted the efforts of street agents like Nancy Floyd and spurned the outside input of capable investigators like Ronnie Bucca. Further, many of the same SACs and ASACS who were responsible for these failures have advanced in the FBI hierarchy or been rewarded in other ways.

On February 26, 2003, Coleen Rowley, the Minneapolis agent celebrated in December as one of *Time* magazine's "Persons of the Year," sent a second warning to FBI director Robert S. Mueller. In the letter Rowley alleged that the Bureau was continuing to mishandle counterterrorism investigations. She predicted that the FBI would be unable to "stem the flood of terrorism that will likely head our way" after the invasion of Iraq.[17] While the capture of Khalid Shaikh Mohammed promises to yield considerable intelligence, the threat from the worldwide network of cells he directed remains significant![18]

In May 2002, Director Mueller announced a restructuring of the Bureau's counterterrorism program, but there are ongoing doubts about whether reforms can be implemented soon enough to forestall the next disaster.

The growing scandal surrounding the misinformation communicated by the Bush Administration prior to the invasion of Iraq is further proof of the urgent need for honest and precise intelligence in the ongoing war on terror. Given the emerging guerrilla war in Iraq and the continued instability in that country, the danger to America from radical Islam may be more acute than ever.

In examining the intelligence failures that led up to America's first pre-emptive war, two central questions continue to haunt us: how did 9/11 happen, and can it happen again?

It's my hope that, through the stories of Special Agent Floyd and Fire Marshal Bucca, the reader will come to understand the human price of our government's negligence—and from that, true reform will come.

—Peter Lance, August 2003

PART I

1

BLACK TUESDAY

On the morning of September 11, 2001, the greatest would-be mass murderer since Adolf Hitler was locked down in solitary confinement in a Colorado prison. In a seven-by-twelve-foot cell at the Supermax, the most secure of all federal jails, Ramzi Yousef sat waiting like a bird of prey. Small, gaunt, and reed thin, with close-cropped hair and two milky-gray eyes, he looked across his cell at the stainless-steel toilet and sink below a shelf supporting a thirteen-inch TV. It was Yousef's only link to the outside world. As CNN played silently in the background, his eyes darted across the dog-eared pages of his Koran.

Yousef may not have known the precise moment of the attacks, but he was sure they would come. After all, he'd set them in motion seven years before in Manila. The idea of hijacking jetliners laden with fuel, and using them as missiles to take down great buildings, had come to the bomb maker after he'd tried to kill a quarter of a million people with his first Twin Towers device in 1993. He'd gone on to plot the deaths of President Clinton, Pope John Paul II, and the prime minister of Pakistan, while hatching a fiendish plan to destroy up to a dozen jumbo jets as they flew over American cities. But his most audacious plot involved a return to New York to finish the job he'd started in the fall of 1992. In one horrific morning, suicide bombers trained as pilots would take the cockpits aboard a series of commercial airliners and drive them into the Trade Center towers, the Pentagon, and a series of other U.S. buildings.

Now, just before 6:45 A.M. Mountain Time, as Ramzi Yousef sat in the Supermax reading the Koran, he heard muffled noises on the cell block: inmates shouting. One of the prisoners down the corridor had been watching CNN and now he was screaming. A guard rushed to his cell, went inside, and saw the devastation.[1]

He yelled, "Some plane just hit the Trade Center."

Yousef quickly looked up at the black-and-white TV above his head. Eyes wide at the site of the North Tower burning, he turned up the sound and heard the voice of an eyewitness: "I just saw the entire top part of the World Trade Center explode."

Yousef rocked back, amazed *himself* at the execution of his plan. He stared at the news footage of racing FDNY engines, terrified evacuees, and bodies dropping from the towers. Then, from the Battery, a camera captured United Airlines Flight 175 slamming into the South Tower.

Another onlooker described it as "a sickening sight." But Yousef, the master terrorist, saw it as the culmination of a dream and the end to some unfinished business. He dropped to the floor, bent over, and gave thanks. "Praise Allah the merciful and the just, the lord of the worlds. We thank you for delivering this message to the apostates."

Later that morning, Yousef's cell door swung open and a pair of FBI agents from the Colorado Springs office came in. They stood in the three-foot-wide anteroom between the solid steel cell door and the bars to the cell.

The convicted terrorist got up from his bed and approached the bars as the two agents presented Bureau IDs and identified themselves.

"Why do you come here?" he demanded.

One of the agents nodded to the TV behind Yousef, still tuned to CNN.

"Did you have anything to do with that?"

Yousef shot back: "How would I possibly know what was going on from in here? Besides, I am represented by counsel. You have no right to question me without my attorney present."

The two agents eyed each other. Now they were facing Yousef the lawyer, the man who had represented himself throughout the entire three months of the Manila airline bombing trial.

"I have nothing else to say to you," snapped Yousef. He turned up the sound on the TV and sat back down on his bed.

The agents withdrew, but within minutes the steel door swung back open and two Bureau of Prisons guards stormed in.

As one began to unlock Yousef's cell bars, the other one shouted, "Get up and face the wall." Yousef stared at him defiantly for a moment, but then the guard slammed a black box and a belly belt chain against the bars, so Yousef got up. Now, as he faced the wall, one guard came in and quickly put the belt around his waist. The other one bent down and snapped on ankle irons and a chain.

"What is this?" shouted Yousef. "What are you doing?"

"Changing cells," said one of the guards. He turned off the TV. "Hands clasped in front of you." Yousef ground his teeth but complied, as the guard snapped the black box onto his wrist—a six-inch-long solid restraint that rendered the prisoner's hands completely immobile. The guard locked the box onto the belly belt, making it impossible now for Yousef to strike out with his arms or fists. The guards turned him around and shuffled him out of the cell, moving him down the corridor of "D" wing, past the cell of the infamous Unabomber, Ted Kaczynski. (For a time, this so-called bombers row had also housed convicted Oklahoma City bombers Timothy McVeigh and Terry Nichols.)

One of the guards unlocked the door to an empty cell and moved Yousef inside as he continued to rant.

"Why are you moving me? My papers—you have to let me take my Koran!"

But when the guards had him locked behind the cell bars, they slammed closed the steel door and went back to Yousef's cell. There they began to toss it, searching around the mattress and on the shelf beside the bed, throwing Yousef's letters, papers, and drawings into a plastic garbage bag. The units on the maximum-security "D" wing are supposed to be soundproof, but as the guards worked to clean out Yousef's cell, they could still hear him screaming down the corridor.

"Why are you doing this? Why would you think that I could have any knowledge of this thing that happened? I've been in this place locked down for years. *Do you hear me?*"

In fact, Yousef's knowledge of the plot was quite precise. He had designed it with his uncle and his best friend back in 1994. It had now been executed almost exactly as he intended. Only the details of the timing had been unknown to him.

Another thing Yousef couldn't possibly know was that across the country, earlier that morning, a woman who'd almost stopped him had watched the devastation firsthand. She had put all of this behind her years ago, or so she thought. But now the terror she'd been so close to preventing was back. For FBI special agent Nancy Floyd, an old wound had just been ripped open.

The View from the Bridge

She had come within weeks of breaking Yousef's bomb cell in the fall of 1992, but her investigation had been shut down by a Bureau superior in New York. Now, just before 9:00 A.M., as she drove west across the George Washington Bridge on her way to an off-site surveillance assignment, Agent Floyd heard a report on her car radio about an explosion at the Trade Center.[2]

She hit the brakes. Dozens of cars in front of her skidded to a stop, and traffic on both sides of the bridge ground to a halt as the morning commuters heard the news. Nancy shoved her gun into a holster on her belt, threw a jacket on, and got out of the car. She quickly crossed the center median and moved with dozens of other onlookers to the south side of the bridge.

Down the Hudson River at the tip of Lower Manhattan, smoke billowed up from the North Tower. Nancy listened to a radio broadcast from a nearby car. It was still early in the attack, and the onlookers around her were speculating: "Are they sure it's a plane?" "Maybe a gas leak?"

Standing there on the bridge, though, the forty-one-year-old special agent from Texas knew in her gut what it was: an attack by Middle Eastern terrorists—and not just *any* attack, but one hatched in the brilliant but deadly mind of Ramzi Yousef.

Minutes later, United Airlines Flight 175 roared across the river from New Jersey. For a moment it looked as if the 767 was pointed toward the Statue of Liberty in New York Harbor; then it turned to the left, and slammed into the upper floors of the South Tower.

Back in 1992, through Emad Salem, an Egyptian informant she'd recruited, Nancy Floyd had come so close to the men around Yousef that she could almost smell them. By then, Ramzi Yousef was hard at work at an apartment in Jersey City, building the 1,500-pound urea-nitrate–fuel oil device he would soon plant on the B-2 level beneath the two towers.

Now Nancy watched those towers as they burned, knowing that, though he'd been in federal lockup since 1995, this was somehow the fulfillment of Yousef's plan. For Agent Floyd it was a vindication, but she took little comfort in the thought.

Her attempt to expose the first Trade Center plot had almost ended her career. Only now, years later, had she begun to recover. She'd put in for a transfer to a small FBI regional office in the far west; her request had been granted, and now Nancy was only eighteen days away from leaving New York.

Long ago she'd tried to bury thoughts of Yousef and the 1993 bombing, but now she couldn't stop thinking about him—especially after a call she'd received that past August from her old informant Salem. He'd been in the Federal Witness Protection Program ever since testifying against the cell around Yousef and Sheikh Abdel Rahman. Largely on Salem's word, the blind Sheikh had been convicted of a plot to blow up a series of New York landmarks, including the tunnels leading into Manhattan and the very bridge Nancy Floyd was now standing on.[3]

But years before, Floyd had been prohibited by the Bureau from taking Salem's calls, or ever discussing the details of the original bombing with him. In all the years since, even when Salem had been diagnosed with cancer in 1998, Nancy had never broken the silence.

Then, a few weeks before 9/11, she was working an FBI undercover assignment when Salem sent word that he wanted to talk to her.

They never connected. So she never heard what he wanted to say.

Now, as she stood watching the towers burn, Nancy Floyd felt a cold throb at the base of her spine. *Could Emad have been calling to warn me about this?* she wondered. She would never know. Only in the summer of 2002, months after the attacks, did Nancy Floyd become aware that another investigator had been on a parallel course.

Along with the word *tragedy,* September 11 was the day the word *hero* took on new meaning. For the FDNY, the statistics were numbing: three hundred and forty-three members of service lost their lives; ninety firefighters in the Department's Special Operations Command were wiped out; Rescue One, the preeminent heavy rescue company in the world, lost eleven men in a house of twenty-five.[4] September 11 was a day full of terrible ironies, but one of the cruelest involved a man who was already a bona fide legend in the FDNY fifteen years before he ever roared down to Liberty Street and raced up the stairs of the South Tower.

Ronnie Bucca was a forty-seven-year-old fire marshal with the FDNY's Bureau of Fire Investigation. A veteran firefighter himself, Bucca had investigated the original WTC bombing in 1993—and had come away convinced that the perpetrators would return to finish the job.

Over the next six years, as he educated himself on Islamic fundamentalism, Bucca found himself continually frustrated by the FBI's inability to appreciate the bin Laden threat or share the intel. Despite the fact that he had a Top Secret security clearance as a warrant officer in a high-level Army Reserve intelligence unit,[5] Bucca was repeatedly frozen out by members of the NYPD-FBI Joint Terrorist Task Force, one of the key Bureau units hunting Yousef.[6] His frustration reached a fever pitch in 1999, after he uncovered startling evidence that an Egyptian with direct ties to the blind Sheikh was actually working inside FDNY headquarters.

Now, astonishingly, on that morning, as Nancy Floyd watched from the George Washington Bridge, Ronnie Bucca was on the seventy-eighth floor of the South Tower with a hose in his hand, trying to beat back the flames.

2

THE FLYING
FIREFIGHTER

Just after noon on September 16, 1986, Ronnie Bucca was working as an outside vent man on the day tour at Rescue One, the busiest heavy rescue company in New York City.[1] Ronnie, his lieutenant, and four other firefighters had just knocked down an electrical fire in the West Twenties and were "taking up," heading back to the house on West Forty-third Street, when they got the call from Dispatch. A 10-75, the FDNY code calling for backup assistance, had been transmitted for Box 22-1138 at 483 Amsterdam Avenue on the Upper West Side; 40 Engine and 35 Truck had responded. Dispatch indicated that the "fire ground" was on the fourth floor, moving toward "exposure two," the right side of the building.

In the cab of the company's big Mack R truck, Lt. Steve Casani, a blue-eyed Irish-Italian bear, turned to his driver (called the chauffeur) and said, "*Hit it.*"

The siren roared and the enormous "toolbox on wheels" headed up Eighth Avenue to the Upper West Side. Heavy rescue companies like One were created to provide backup for working fire suppression units. Their job was to get inside, help move the hose, help vent the flames, and look for bodies, both civilians and members of service (other firefighters).

"By the time we got there," recalled Casani, "the fourth floor was fully engulfed. Forty Engine needed help, so we went to work."[2]

Hydrants were tapped, hose lines were pulled, and 35 Truck's ladder rose toward the roof of the five-story old-law tenement. As the men from Rescue One jumped off the truck, they quickly pulled their Scott Air Packs over their Nomex turnout coats.

Ronnie Bucca, a darkly handsome ex–Green Beret reservist who'd made dozens of jumps with the 101st Airborne, was known for his attention to the gear. He took an extra second to buckle his harness so that the thirty-five-pound compressed air bottle on his back would stay secure.

It was a move that would soon save his life.

Ronnie grabbed a Haligan forcible-entry tool and took off with firefighter Tommy Reichel into 485 Amsterdam, the tenement next to the fire building. A five-mile-a-day runner, Bucca took the steps two at a time. At five-feet-nine and 165 pounds Bucca was slightly built compared with some of the "beefalos" in the house, but what he lacked in size he made up for in tenacity and heart.

At the roof, Ronnie burst through the door and was immediately pushed back by the heat. Even under his mask he felt it. Next door, the fourth floor at 483 Amsterdam was an inferno. Just then, over the Handie-Talkie radio clipped to his turnout coat, he heard a Mayday from Lt. Dave Fenton from 35 Truck, who was trapped on the fifth floor.[3] There was a fire escape outside, but in a classic New York irony, the windows were covered by security "scissor gates." Designed to keep predators out, the gates had locked the lieutenant in, and he was running out of time.

Ronnie climbed through a gooseneck ladder onto the fire escape. As soon as he hit the rusted metal he slipped. The broken glass on the grid was like ice. Worse, smoke thick as pea soup was coming out of the windows behind the gates. Ronnie tightened his mask and switched on the Scott's bottle. Compressed air filled his lungs. He moved cautiously to the edge of the fire escape and leaned over to smash the glass.

The smoke rushed out. Ronnie leaned over again and made a stab with the Haligan tool, trying to hook the gates and pop them free. But as he swung out, he slipped on the glass and went over the edge, going down past the fourth floor, then the third, falling face up as he dropped.[4]

Miraculously, at the second-floor level, the Scott's Air Pack he'd so tightly cinched hit a metal conduit—a two-inch pipe across the alley that delivered electricity to the building. The force of the impact flipped Bucca 180 degrees and partially broke his fall.

He landed hard in a pile of debris on the ground level. The last thing he remembered was hearing a cracking sound.[5]

At that moment, Lieutenant Fenton broke free. He moved to a fifth-floor window, which he vented to get air. But when he looked down, Fenton saw Ronnie's body lying in the alley. His boots were twisted outward as if his legs had snapped. Bucca wasn't moving.

"Jesus," Fenton thought as he clicked on the Handie-Talkie.

"Mayday. *Mayday*. Man down in the alley." He didn't wait for a response. Fenton took off down the stairs.

Now, as he fought the blaze with firefighter Tom Reilly on the fourth floor, Lt. Steve Casani heard the distress call. The two of them rushed to the window and looked down. "Christ," said Casani, "I just lost my first guy."

Fenton was first to hit the alley. When he saw Ronnie, he was sure he was dead. But he leaned down, felt Bucca's neck, and got a pulse. There was respiration, but maybe not for long. Fenton quickly pulled off his own turnout coat and covered Ronnie as Casani and Reilly burst into the alley from upstairs.

Right away, Casani jumped on the radio. "I need a Stokes basket and a bus," he said, using FDNY-speak for a rescue stretcher and an ambulance. Roosevelt Hospital was closest, but Casani demanded they head to Bellevue, which had a trauma unit. The only problem was, Bellevue was fifty blocks south and clear across town. Reilly didn't think he heard right.

"Lieu, East Thirty-first? At noon on a Tuesday? We're on the fuckin' West Side."

"Then call the fuckin' PD," growled Casani. "Have 'em clear Fifth." He looked down at Ronnie. "I am *not* gonna lose this kid."

Minutes later the siren roared. Casani was in the back of an FDNY rescue unit gripping Ronnie's hand as the ambulance cut through Central Park and did sixty behind Rescue One's Mack R, cutting a swath through the noon traffic down Fifth Avenue. As the chauffeur looked left and right, virtually every intersection had been blocked off by an NYPD sector car, an FDNY ambulance, or a piece of fire apparatus. It was perhaps the greatest single midday hospital run in FDNY history, and soon the radio stations got word.

The anchor on WINS Radio said that traffic was being blocked on Fifth Avenue between Ninety-sixth and Thirty-fourth Streets. Mayor Koch and Cardinal O'Connor were on their way to Bellevue. A firefighter had been badly injured after a five-story fall; his name was being withheld pending notification of next of kin.

Ronnie's brother Robert, a former medic with the 82nd Airborne who was then a cadet at the Police Academy, got the first call. He asked the FDNY to patch him through to Ronnie's wife, Eve, who was in the kitchen of their modest home north of the city. Eve's father, Bart Mitchell, had been an FDNY battalion chief with the 12th in Harlem. Her grandfather was a retired FDNY lieutenant who'd worked the Bronx. Growing up, she'd heard the phone ring dozens of times before, but never for something like this. Robert told her not to worry. He'd pick her up in an NYPD car for the trip downtown.

When they roared up to Bellevue with siren and lights flashing, there was a small crowd of reporters outside keeping the deathwatch. Ronnie's older brother Alfred, who worked for the Transit Authority, was there along with Ronnie's parents, Joe and Astrid, and a few of his buddies from the 11th Special Forces. Together they moved past the press gauntlet.

In the hallway outside the Intensive Care Unit, Eve could feel her heart pounding. Then the door opened and Lieutenant Casani walked out, still in his bunker coat. She hesitated, studying his face. Then he grinned. "It's gonna be all right." He opened his coat and hugged her.

"At that moment I knew we had a miracle," said Eve, thinking back. She moved quickly inside the ICU toward Ronnie's bedside and saw that though he was lying flat, barely moving, he was conscious. She bent down and kissed him. Ronnie lifted a finger and Eve squeezed it. He motioned for her to come close and whispered, "Wasn't my time, hon."

Eve bit down on her lower lip, holding back tears. Just then, a young female resident came up behind her. Dr. Lori Greenwald-Stein was holding a set of X rays. She motioned Eve aside and put the X rays up on a light box. Ronnie had sustained multiple contusions and lacerations. He'd broken his knee and the first lumbar vertebra in his back. It was a compression fracture; otherwise Ronnie would have been paralyzed.

Eve closed her eyes.

"Lucky to be alive," said the doctor. Then she leaned in and whispered, "But if he walks, it'll probably be with a cane."

Grateful as she was, Eve rocked back at the news. Her husband had been a firefighter for nine years, and was planning to go the distance. Her father had done thirty-five, and so had his father before him.

"Ronnie was always first into the burning building," said Eve, thinking back. "As a paratrooper he was the first one out of the plane. The idea that at the age of thirty-two he might spend the rest of his life as a cripple didn't even occur to him."

Later, when some of the family members had left, Eve moved close to Ronnie's bed. Eyeing the monitors measuring his vitals, she tried to cope by using her Irish. "Hmmm," she said, "pretty cheesy way to get out of the house painting."

Ronnie tried to smile, but his face ached. He gestured her closer. Eve bent down next to him and he whispered, "I'm goin' back."

"You mean Rescue?"

Ronnie nodded. Eve was stunned. As well as she knew her husband—how he'd made it out of the Queens projects to qualify for the Green Berets; how he'd earned a position in an elite Screaming Eagles air assault unit; how he'd been cited for bravery by the FDNY—she couldn't quite believe what she was hearing. Rescue One was the Special Forces of the FDNY. They went on seven to nine hundred runs a year. The idea of going back to that house after suffering such trauma was unthinkable. Besides, after a life-threatening injury that was sure to leave him at least partially disabled, Ronnie could retire with a three-quarter tax-free pension. A thousand other men would have opted out. So, looking down at him in the half-body cast, Eve was apprehensive.

"What about light duty?"

"No," said Ronnie. "It's Rescue."

And a year later, almost to the day, Ronnie Bucca was rappelling down a wall at The Rock, the FDNY's Fire Academy on Randall's Island. After months of rehab—he began walking slowly, with a cane, then graduated to a treadmill and moved on to weight training. Ronnie had shed his body brace and completed the "rope course." It was the last phase of retraining, allowing him to qualify back into Rescue One. He had finished each of the course evolutions: moving the hose and working the ladder, proving he could lower himself on a rope down the side of a building or lower an injured victim, even the Mask Confinement Course, where he had to wear a Scott's mask with its faceplate blackened and get through a complicated maze with a limited amount of air in the bottle. That was the one phase of rescue training where most firefighters washed out. But Ronnie did it under the clock, with seconds to spare.

"It's difficult to emphasize what an achievement this was for him," said Paul Hashagen, a big six-foot-five Rescue One chauffeur who had gone through probie school with Ronnie.[6] "You've got eleven thousand men in the department. A few hundred of the most competitive guys make it into Special Operations Command, which comprises the squads and a rescue company in each of the five boroughs. But everybody wants Manhattan, and there are only twenty-five spots in Rescue One. To requalify back into that house after a five-story drop where you broke your back—I've got to tell you, that's astonishing."

But Ronnie Bucca was half Sicilian and half Swedish on his mother's side. Eve always said he got his stubbornness from both of them.

Now, as he rappelled down to the bottom of the wall, a half dozen of his "brothers" surrounded him and let out a war whoop.

One of them pasted a joke shipping label on the back of his helmet. It said "This side up," but the arrow was pointing down.

The men cheered and lifted him up on their shoulders. Ronnie Bucca, henceforth known throughout the FDNY as "the flying fire-fighter," was back.

Months later, Ronnie raced into a burning "taxpayer," a one-story corner building down on Avenue D in Alphabet City. It was a three-alarm response. Heavy flames licked out of the first-floor windows of an abandoned paint store where squatters had come to live in the frigid cold. The old paint cans left in the store were giving off a lethal combination of volatiles, creating a toxic cloud so black that Bucca couldn't see his hand in front of him. He clipped a Nomex search rope with a carabiner onto a metal doorjamb so he could find his way out. He donned his mask and gave himself air from the Scott's pack, feeling his way on his hands and knees. It was the Mask Confinement Course all over again, only this time he was crawling past thousand-degree flames. As he inched his way into the store, Ronnie heard a faint whimper. The sound of a little girl.

Feeling his way along some old shelves, he found a door to a back room. Ronnie reached up and tried the knob but it was locked, so he used a modified Haligan tool to pop it open. Searing heat came out as he crawled inside. He could hear the little girl moaning. Ronnie pushed forward with his light.

There, huddled inside an old storage cabinet, he saw her two little eyes. She couldn't have been more than eight, the same age as his daughter Jessica. She was dressed in a urine-soaked oversized Knicks T-shirt. The little girl was half-dead. So Ronnie reached into the cabinet and grabbed her. She was gagging, coughing.

He took off the Scott's mask and put it around her face, giving her air. The child's respiration was starting to slow, so Ronnie quickly doubled back along the search rope until he could feel the chill from the outside air.

He was barely out the door when a woman screamed and rushed over. It was the girl's grandmother. She threw her arms around Ronnie and hugged him for dear life as he passed the child into the hands of an EMS medic. Ronnie dropped down on the curb. The pain in his back was throbbing, but he'd refused to take any medication beyond aspirin. He didn't want to let on to Lieutenant Casani or the other men how much the broken back still dogged him. He was about to get up and go back inside when the lieutenant came over and motioned for him to stay down. "They're all out," he said, and Ronnie nodded.

He unclipped the buckle on the strap of the Scott's harness—the one that had saved his life. As he watched the old lady jump into the ambulance with the little girl who was alive because of him, Ronnie knew that all the retraining and the rehab had been worth it.

Later, half a world away in a terror camp near the Afghan-Pakistani border, a fierce young jihadi would begin another kind of training. Ronnie Bucca had dedicated his life to putting fires out. Soon, it would be Ramzi Ahmed Yousef's mission to start them.

3

BLOWBACK

Yousef was his nom de guerre. Another alias. Not only his name, but his precise date of birth—even the place—are still subject to question. Most intelligence analysts agree that his roots were in Baluchistan, a radical Islamic no-man's-land the size of France that crosses the frontiers of Iran, Pakistan, and Afghanistan. By his own account he was raised in Kuwait, his father a Baluchistani and his mother a Palestinian.[1] One scholar contends that Yousef was an agent of Iraq who murdered a young Kuwaiti and hijacked his identity.[2]

Whoever he was, with his protruding ears and parrotlike nose, Yousef was a man of a dozen faces, posing in the same period as Arnaldo Forlani, a distinguished Italian parliamentarian; Dr. Abel Sabah, an Egyptian chemical specialist; and Dr. Naji Owaida Haddad, a Moroccan mechanical engineer.[3] At the height of his terror spree, when Yousef was dubbed "The Most Wanted" man on earth,[4] he manufactured his own fake ID and routinely changed his dress, hair, and eye color using contact lenses and skin dye to avoid capture.[5] But cosmetics could never conceal his scars: his fingers were disfigured, there were burn marks on the bottoms of his feet, and he was partially blind in his right eye—all casualties of his years as a bomb maker.[6]

"Cold-blooded" and "diabolical" were the words used by men who had hunted him. "An evil genius," said another.[7] But Yousef was immensely complex. A Sunni Muslim, he maintained a multivolume collection of the Koran,[8] and once reportedly set a bomb that killed twenty-six rival Shiites at a mosque in Iran.[9] Yet he was far from devout: witnesses said he rarely attended Friday prayers at a mosque in Pakistan, and never fasted during Ramadan.[10]

With a wife and two children,[11] Yousef was also a notorious womanizer with a taste for first-class travel and Armani suits. Hours after murdering a young Japanese man with an airplane bomb, he was trolling the karaoke bars of Manila for B-girls.[12] But Yousef also showed a flare for the romantic. During the first of two federal trials in New York, he took Spanish lessons in order to woo an attractive Cuban-American attorney on his defense team. Even while he was in jail, with no visible means of income and the U.S. government financing his defense, he sent the young lawyer a lavish bouquet of flowers.[13] Yousef told FBI agents that he felt guilty about killing, but in the same breath he endorsed a plot to murder two hundred and fifty thousand people in New York in retaliation for U.S. support of Israel.[14]

"A new breed of terrorist" was how one U.S. intelligence operative described him.[15] And apart from his technical skill as an engineer and his ability to think outside the bomb box, what made Yousef so dangerous was his charm and charisma. A master recruiter of young men, he displayed an uncanny knack for convincing them to risk prison or die in the name of Allah. Yet he never even considered suicide for himself.

A growing body of evidence now suggests that, between the first World Trade Center bomb and his construction of the 9/11 plot, Yousef may well have also designed the ammonium nitrate–nitromethane bomb that destroyed the Murrah Federal Building in Oklahoma City on April 19, 1995.[16] Some have even suggested that he had a hand in the crash of TWA Flight 800.[17] The former associate director of the FBI called him "the most dangerous and prolific terrorist since Carlos the Jackal."[18]

The general consensus in the intelligence community is that the man who became famous as Yousef was born Abdul Basit Mahmud Abdul Karim in Kuwait.[19] His father, an engineer named Mohammed Abdul Karim, had emigrated to Fuhayhil, a Kuwaiti oil boom town where young Yousef/Basit came of age.

In 1989 he earned a diploma in electronics from the West Glomorgan Institute of Higher Learning in South Wales. At the three-year technical college, he specialized in computer-aided electronics.[20] Yousef was in Kuwait visiting family and friends in August of 1990 when Saddam

Hussein's tanks rolled in and took the country. His Iraqi connections would be the subject of debate among intelligence analysts for years to come. But sometime after the invasion, the twenty-three-year-old took off for the University of Dawa and Jihad, an al Qaeda training school located at the Jalozai refugee camp thirty miles east of Peshawar in northwest Pakistan.[21]

There, with fifty-five other young jihadis from around the world, Yousef took a six-month course, specializing in explosives.[22] He learned how to make slow-burning fuses using gunpowder rolled into cotton, or linen coated with an insulating layer of pitch. He studied the use of electrical switches, discovering that given the proper accelerant, the spark from a simple nine-volt battery would be sufficient to detonate a device of tremendous killing power.[23]

By one account, the gangly young Yousef sat in the back of a tent in the Jalozai camp as an instructor lectured in Arabic on how to build an effective improvised explosive device from an egg timer, some lamp cord, and an open can of gasoline.[24]

"You must be careful how you set the timer," the instructor said, splitting the ends of the lamp cord and twisting it around the poles of the small device.

He stripped the other ends into a pig's tail and taped them across the mouth of the gas can. "When the timer rings, it will send a charge along the wire which will short, causing a spark to ignite the gas vapors." But he took care to admonish them: "These timers are unreliable. Always set them ahead. Five minutes can mean three." He asked for a volunteer.

Without hesitating, Yousef jumped up. He strutted like a young fighting gamecock toward the device. The instructor told him to get behind the sandbags, remove the pairs, reconnect them, and reset the timer.

Yousef nodded, cold as ice. He quickly examined the live device, then deftly removed the pairs. He reconnected them—then reset the timer for *one minute*. The timer ticked away. But instead of running, Yousef walked slowly back around the sandbags. When the gas tank suddenly blew, Yousef was knocked to the ground.

Raging, the instructor ran up to him.

"*Murtadd!*" he said. "Fool! You might have been killed."

But Yousef eyed him defiantly. "Let the man who lacks the courage to do this for Allah go live with the women."

The instructor winced, then smiled at Yousef's reckless bravery. The other students surrounded him. They fired AK-47s into the air in a blizzard of lead. Abdul Basit savored the triumph, and the legend of Ramzi Yousef was born.

The First Afghan War

The irony was that Yousef acquired his bomb-building knowledge under the tutelage of men who were funded in part by Uncle Sam. In intelligence circles they call it *blowback*, a deadly unintended consequence of a covert op. In this case Yousef learned his deadly skills from men who, for years, had been supported and sponsored by the CIA.

In the late 1980s the Central Intelligence Agency funneled billions in arms and munitions to the Afghan mujahadeen rebels in their war against the invading Soviets. The U.S. price tag for the covert aid reportedly reached three billion dollars. Journalist Mary Anne Weaver noted that the Soviet invasion, begun in 1979, was a kind of Spanish Civil War for Islamics. As many as twenty-five thousand young jihadis like Yousef poured in from around the globe to fight and train in guerrilla tactics.[25]

Though they were all later dubbed "Afghan Arabs," there were blue-eyed Chechens, black South Africans, and Filipinos training along with Kurds, Yemenis, Uzbekis, and Saudis. They studied bombmaking, hijacking, and other covert ops. The difference was that the veterans of the antifascist campaign in the 1930s, like Hemingway, went to Paris to write books, while the Afghan War jihadis decided to focus their attention on the West and blow things up.

During this period, intelligence officials believe that Yousef first hooked up with three men who would one day carve their names in the history of Islamic terror. Abdurajak Janjalani was a Libyan-trained Filipino whose nom de guerre was Abu Sayyaf.[26] Mahmud Abouhalima was a six-foot-two redheaded Egyptian who did two tours in Afghanistan. Known as "the Red," Abouhalima was a disciple of Sheikh Omar Abdel Rahman, leader of the al Gamm'a Islamiya (IG), one of the most virulent Egyptian terror groups.[27]

These Afghan connections would prove crucial to Yousef as his career advanced. Abouhalima would become one of his key operatives as he built the original World Trade Center bomb in 1992. Sheikh Rahman would be at the heart of Yousef's bombing cell, based in Jersey City. Later, the Abu Sayyaf terror group, named for Janjalani, would provide Yousef with the infrastructure he needed when he plotted the 9/11 attacks in Manila in 1995.

But the bomb maker's chief sponsor over the years—the man who funded and guided him—was the seventeenth son of a Saudi construction billionaire named Osama bin Laden. Beginning in the early 1990s, Yousef emerged as the point man for bin Laden's worldwide terror network. Al Qaeda, meaning "the base," sprang directly from a string of refugee centers set up as fund-raising conduits for the mujahadeen rebels.

In short, when probing the origin of the 9/11 attacks, all roads lead back to Afghanistan and Peshawar in the final days of the Soviet invasion.

Working Russians

Back in Texas, the call came early to Nancy Floyd. In the sixth grade, her teacher had asked the students at Inwood Elementary School to write essays on what they wanted to do in life. Nancy thought that she might serve with the CIA, or possibly the FBI. After all, her father, Tom, was an Air Force major. She'd grown up on bases all over Europe and the States, and watched her dad take off on dangerous, sometimes classified missions. One of her older brothers would become an Army captain. To Nancy, a job as an agent or case officer seemed like a sure way to contribute. Her teacher had other ideas.

"She sent a letter home to my parents that they should direct me toward a career in nursing or teaching," remembered Nancy. "At the time there were no female agents." But raised as a Catholic with a military work ethic, Nancy felt drawn toward another form of public service.

"My dad worked for the government my whole life, and he was a very proud patriot," she recalled. "That was what I wanted to do—work for the government in a way where I could help people and lock up bad guys. I was raised that there's good and bad, and the good have to help put away the bad."

That keen Texas sense of justice drove Nancy through the University of Texas at Arlington, where she got her B.S. in criminal justice in 1982. By that point she had her sights fixed on the Bureau. Baby-sitting for the children of an FBI agent in Dallas throughout high school, she had marveled at how much he'd reminded her of her father, who had died of a sudden heart attack at the age of fifty-three. Nancy was shocked by his loss, but rule number one in the Floyd house was, you didn't stay down for long. "We weren't allowed to be moody," said Nancy. "My mother would say, 'This isn't gonna work here, because you have so much to be grateful for. So let's cut it and move on.' And we did."

Three years out of college, Nancy took the test for the Bureau. After a successful interview, she received a letter that she'd been accepted for training at the FBI Academy. There were only eight women in her start-ing class of sixty at Quantico. Right away she made friends with Martha Dixon and Icey Jenkins, two women who went on to distinguish them-selves in the FBI.[28]

After receiving her coveted badge as a special agent, Nancy worked in Savannah, Georgia, where she qualified for the SWAT unit before being transferred to the FBI's "flagship" office in New York. Soon, harking back to that sixth-grade essay, she found herself working in the best of both worlds: law enforcement and intelligence. Special Agent Floyd was assigned to Branch A in the Bureau's Foreign Counter Intelligence Divi-sion (FCI). Located on the twenty-fifth floor at 26 Federal Plaza in Man-hattan, FCI was the unit tasked to gather intel on the GRU (Glavnoe Razvedyvatelnoe Upravlenie), the intelligence unit of the Russian army. In the FBI shadow world that monitored the GRU, Nancy began learn-ing tradecraft from one of the Bureau's top agents, Len Predtechenskis.

For twenty-seven years, from the last frigid days of the Cold War through glasnost and the breakup of the Soviet Union, Predtechenskis was a secret weapon in the FBI's New York Office. Born in Latvia, fluent in English, Latvian, and Russian, the former Leonids Predtechenskis became the FBI's chief counterintelligence agent in Manhattan.[29] In 2001, after holding the record for the longest Russian double agent recruitment in FBI history (twenty-five years), Len reached the manda-tory retirement age. The "brag wall" in his den would rival that of any U.S. senator or congressman, with commendations or letters of praise from Presidents Richard Nixon and George W. Bush and every FBI director since Hoover. But one of his proudest accomplishments was the mentoring and support he gave to a young Texas recruit named Nancy Floyd. "I'm old school," said Len. "Frankly, I'm the type who had no use for female agents in the Bureau. That's until I met Nancy."

Agent Floyd came to the New York office full of piss and vinegar. Driven, bright, and sometimes a tad outspoken, she was hungry to learn.

"I told her, 'We're working Russians,'" Predtechenskis remembered. "'So educate yourself. Go out and find Hedrick Smith's book *The Russians*.' She had it read the next day."

Nancy was ready for more, so Predtechenskis suggested that she reactivate the Hotel Asset Program, an initiative he'd started in the 1970s.

"I used to go to hotels and talk to the front-desk managers," said Len. "I'd give them my card and ask them to be on the lookout for any stray diplomats for the Soviet mission. Let me know if any of them got into trouble. We developed a lot of doubles this way. So I suggested that Nancy work it."

One day, in August of 1991, she stopped off at a hotel in midtown Manhattan. Without realizing it, Nancy Floyd was about to meet a source that would put her next to the most dangerous threat to American homeland security since the Cuban missile crisis.

4

THE FIRST
SHOTS FIRED

Much has been made of the alleged links between the September 11 attacks and two Middle Eastern countries: Saudi Arabia and Iraq. A primary motivation for the U.S. invasion in March of 2003 was the allegation that Saddam Hussein's regime was tied to the terror network that executed 9/11. In fact, as we'll see, the connections between al Qaeda and the old Baghdad regime were limited and tenuous. Saudi Arabia, however, was another story.

Fifteen of the nineteen 9/11 hijackers were Saudis. A miniscandal erupted in November 2002 when it was learned that money from the wife of the Saudi ambassador to the United States found its way through a San Diego–based charity into two of the hijackers' hands.[1] The very same charitable entity that evolved into al Qaeda had begun as a fundraising conduit during the Afghan war, in which the Saudis matched the U.S. contribution dollar for dollar.[2] And though his roots are in Yemen, Osama bin Laden himself is the scion of a family whose multibillion-dollar construction empire built much of Saudi Arabia's infrastructure.[3]

But the record now shows that if the Islamic dissidents of any Arab country had a major role in the attacks of September 11, it was Egypt. After a bitter dispute for control of the multimillion-dollar Afghan rebel fund-raising network, it was an Egyptian bloc that first helped Osama bin Laden cement his position at the top of the jihad power structure. Both of bin Laden's chief lieutenants came from Egypt.[4] The spiritual leader of the two Islamic extremist groups associated with them is Egyptian.[5] In fact, the first known shots in al Qaeda's war on America were fired largely by Egyptian immigrants at a rifle range in Calverton, Long Island, on four successive weekends in July of 1989.

Back then, blasting away with AK-47 assault rifles, 9mm semiautomatic handguns, and .357 magnums was a virtual rogue's gallery of terrorists-in-training. They included:

- Mahmud Abouhalima, the Egyptian émigré said to have interfaced with Ramzi Yousef on the Afghan-Pakistani border. Since coming to New York, Abouhalima had taken a job as a New York City taxi driver.

- El Sayyid Nosair, born in Port Said, Egypt. A thirty-four-year-old Prozac-popping maintenance man, Nosair worked in the basement of the Manhattan Civil Court building.

- Mohammed Salameh, a Palestinian born in Jordan. Salameh was related to Nosair's cousin, an Egyptian contractor named Ibrahim El-Gabrowny.[6]

There were two non-Egyptians: Nidal Ayyad, a young Kuwaiti Rutgers grad and naturalized U.S. citizen, and Clement Rodney Hampton-El, an American Black Muslim who also reportedly fought in Afghanistan. Hampton-El worked as a medical technician and used the name "Dr. Rashid."

But the most enigmatic of the group was its leader, Ali Mohammed, an ex-Egyptian army officer and member of the Egyptian Islamic Jihad. Ali's old unit was linked to the 1981 assassination of Egyptian president Anwar Sadat. Mohammed himself had escaped indictment in the slaying because at the time of Sadat's murder in Cairo he was visiting the U.S. Army's Special Operations Warfare School at Fort Bragg, North Carolina.[7] He later went to work as a CIA "contract" agent, before being dismissed because of his ties to the radical terrorist group Hizbollah. He was put on a State Department Watch List, forbidding him entry to the United States, but he slipped back into the San Francisco Bay Area and married a local woman. By 1986, incredibly, Ali had managed to enlist in the U.S. Army, rising to the rank of supply sergeant and—despite his Watch List status—even earned a security clearance of SECRET.

Perhaps even more astounding, during the late 1980s, while advising the Fifth U.S. Special Forces at Fort Bragg, Mohammed stole away on weekends to New York, where he stayed with El Sayyid Nosair and ran the Calverton paramilitary sessions. He instructed the radical Egyptians in martial arts, small-arms fire, and the proper use of hand grenades.

Three of Mohammed's trainees—Abouhalima, Salameh, and Ayyad—would later be convicted as Ramzi Yousef's coconspirators in the World Trade Center bombing,[8] and another, Nosair, would soon use his Calverton .357 magnum training to ignite the first act of al Qaeda violence on American soil.

But what makes these Calverton sessions so troubling is the fact that the Feds *knew* about them. In fact, they were photographed by agents from the New York office of the FBI.

Beginning on the weekend of July 2, 1989, the FBI's Special Operations Group (SOG) was assigned to watch a series of "MEs" who hung out at the Alkifah Refugee Center in the Al Farooq Mosque on Atlantic Avenue in Brooklyn. MEs, in Bureau parlance, were Middle Eastern men.

Special Agent James P. Fogle, a ten-year Bureau veteran, was the photographer. Working with half a dozen other agents in a five-vehicle team, Fogle photographed a number of MEs loading boxes into vans outside the mosque. Minutes later, a convoy consisting of two vans and a Jeep Cherokee took off and headed onto the Brooklyn-Queens Expressway. Being careful to switch tail vehicles, the SOG team followed the convoy onto the Long Island Expressway. An hour later the suspects turned off at Exit 71, not far from where thousands of New Yorkers were heading south to the Hamptons. The convoy pulled into the Calverton Rifle Range, and the FBI team rolled into a position where Fogle could bang off a series of surveillance shots.

Using a Canon T 70 with a 135mm lens, Fogle watched as the men donned white robes, bowed to pray, and then put on ear protectors to deaden the noise before firing weapons smuggled in from the Afghan front.[9]

While Agent Fogle snapped black-and-white stills of Abouhalima blasting a Kalashnikov, a stray bullet from one of the other AKs hit the ground just a few feet from the shooter's foot. Fogle would later testify that the big redheaded Egyptian came over, "grabbed the weapon and . . . slapped the person for . . . carelessness."[10]

The shooting sessions and the FBI surveillance continued every Sunday until July 23, 1989. The SOG team had been specifically assigned to an investigation of "international terrorism" after reported tips that some Palestinians who visited the Alkifah Center were planning violence at Atlantic City casinos. But by August, when the casino threat didn't materialize, the surveillance ended.[11]

In a saga littered with what-ifs, one can only imagine what would have happened if Agent Fogle's FBI supervisors had taken his surveillance photos seriously. At the height of the Afghan war there had been a winking acceptance in the Bureau of recruitment and fund-raising activities aimed at helping the mujahadeen "freedom fighters." But by the summer of 1989 the war was winding down. In retrospect, the idea of ignoring Islamic men in paramilitary training, firing automatic weapons, at the height of the summer season on Long Island, seems almost criminally negligent—especially in light of what Abouhalima, Salameh, and Ayyad went on to do.

Ali Mohammed later became a triple agent, working for the Special Forces, bin Laden, and even the FBI, informing for the Bureau in California as a way of diverting attention from himself. He got an honorable discharge from the U.S. Army in 1989, then traveled to Sudan, where he personally trained bodyguards for Osama bin Laden.[12] A naturalized U.S. citizen, Mohammed was later dispatched by bin Laden to Kenya, where he took surveillance photographs of the U.S. embassy prior to a pair of deadly al Qaeda bombings in 1998.[13]

Those attacks were almost a decade down the line. But now, in the hot summer of 1989, the FBI was on to Mohammed and his cohorts.

Why they didn't follow up on the shooting sessions at the time is one of the great unanswered questions in this mystery. But back then, twelve years before 9/11, for reasons known only to supervisors in the FBI's New York office, the surveillance of the radical Egyptians was shut down.

The FBI's termination of the Calverton surveillance was the first of many warnings in this story—signals to the FBI that an emerging al Qaeda cell tied to Osama bin Laden was beginning to operate in the New York metropolitan area. There were a number of other incidents that should have put the Bureau on alert before the first Trade Center bombing in 1993, and dozens more before both Towers went down on September 11, 2001. The FBI's surveillance at the Calverton shooting sessions represents the first of these missed signals.*

The next warning came sixteen months later, on a Monday night in early November of 1990.

The First Murder

On the road to 9/11, if there was a single incident that should have rung the cherries at the FBI's New York office it was the bloody slaying of right-wing rabbi Meir Kahane. The founder of the ultraconservative Jewish Defense League, Kahane referred to Arabs as "jackals." He advocated the removal of all Arabs from Israel. After winning a seat in the Israeli parliament, he drafted legislation making it a crime for Jews and Arabs to have sex. Kahane's views were considered so extreme that he was barred from sitting in the Knesset. By 1990, Kahane was advocating the wholesale emigration of Jews from New York to Israel, and on the November night in question he announced the formation of ZEERO (the Zionist Emergency Evacuation Rescue Organization).

Kahane had just left the podium of the Morgan D Room in Marriott's East Side Hotel, where he'd been addressing a group of followers. He had begun to sign books, when suddenly El Sayyid Nosair, wearing a yarmulke and posing as a Sephardic Jew, burst forward and fired two shots from a silver-plated .357 magnum. The rabbi grabbed his throat. One bullet entered his neck and exited through his cheek.

In the chaos and blood that followed, Nosair rushed toward the door of the conference room, but he was stopped by a seventy-three-year-old follower of the rabbi named Irving Franklin. Again Nosair fired, striking the old man in the leg. Then he burst out the front door of the hotel.

Wild-eyed and pumped with adrenaline, Nosair was expecting to find

*To give the reader some perspective on the quantity of evidence missed—and to offer clarification in a story dominated by a number of Islamic figures with similar names and aliases—an illustrated timeline has been included at the center of this book. As the story continues, footnotes will link specific intelligence lapses, warnings, or lost opportunities to this timeline. The result should help readers connect the dots that the FBI itself missed on the road to 9/11. Timeline #03. p. 1.

Mahmud Abouhalima waiting outside, revving his taxi for the getaway. But with heavy security surrounding the rabbi's lecture, NYPD uniforms had waved the big redhead off, and in a panic Nosair mistakenly jumped into the cab of a stranger named Franklin Garcia.[14] The cabbie started to drive off down Lexington Avenue, but when he turned and saw Nosair's revolver, he jammed on the brakes. Nosair jumped out and started to run south, frantically searching for Abouhalima. The plan had been to drive around the corner to Park Avenue, where Mohammed Salameh would be waiting in Nosair's own car. The assassin would then change cars, and Abouhalima's taxi would follow Nosair to his home in New Jersey.

But now, as he approached the post office half a block south of the hotel, Nosair ran into Carlos Acosta, a uniformed U.S. postal inspector. At the sight of Nosair's gun, Acosta drew his own sidearm, but Nosair opened fire. Though Acosta was wearing a Kevlar vest, he was blown back with a wound to the shoulder. Nosair started to run, but the inspector dropped to his knees and capped off a shot that hit Nosair in the neck.

Within minutes, a pair of ambulances screamed toward Bellevue Hospital. In the same trauma center that had treated Ronnie Bucca years before, doctors worked on the two men, shooter and victim, in parallel ER cubicles. Nosair survived. Kahane did not.

Later that night, five detectives and an investigator from the NYPD's 17th Precinct descended on Nosair's house in Cliffside Park, New Jersey, near the George Washington Bridge.[15] There they found Abouhalima and Salameh waiting, and took them in for questioning. In the densely packed rooms of the small rented house, the cops also stumbled onto a mountain of evidence. There were formulas for bomb making, 1,440 rounds of ammunition, and manuals from the John F. Kennedy Special Warfare Center at Fort Bragg marked "Top Secret for Training," along with classified documents belonging to the U.S. Joint Chiefs of Staff.[16] The police found maps and drawings of New York City landmarks like the Statue of Liberty, Times Square—and the World Trade Center.

The forty-seven boxes of evidence they collected also included the recorded sermons of blind Sheikh Omar, in which he exhorted his followers to "destroy the edifices of capitalism."[17] Entries in one notebook, which Nosair apparently copied from another such sermon, called for the "destruction of the enemies of Allah," by "destroying their . . . high world buildings."[18]

The evidence was hauled back to the 17th Precinct.

When word reached the FBI's Joint Terrorist Task Force, two of its members, FBI special agent John Anticev and NYPD detective Lou Napoli, dug back into the Bureau files to find the 1989 Calverton surveillance photos. Right off they spotted Abouhalima, Salameh, and El Sayyid Nosair.[19]

Napoli was a veteran of the NYPD's Narcotics Division. In 1983 he'd joined the Task Force, an elite unit formed originally with twenty-five to thirty investigators. By 1993 the JTTF had grown to include forty investigators and agents from the FBI, NYPD, the INS, the FAA, the ATF, and the U.S. Marshals Service, among other agencies.

The New York JTTF, which partnered seasoned detectives like Napoli with FBI agents like Anticev, became a prototype for sixty-five similar units around the country.[20]

Now, in the hours following the Kahane murder, the two men did exactly what the Task Force was set up to do: they connected the dots. By identifying Nosair with the Calverton training photos of Abouhalima and Salameh, they matched a local murder to a dangerous paramilitary cell. Given the Fort Bragg manuals left behind by the mysterious Special Forces sergeant Ali Mohammed and the recorded rantings of Sheikh Rahman, a cleric tied to two extremist Egyptian hate groups, Kahane's assassination had all the earmarks of an "international conspiracy."[21]

But NYPD's chief of detectives, Joseph Borelli, the man who had made his bones on the notorious Son of Sam case, saw it otherwise. As *Newsday* reporters Jim Dwyer, David Kocieniewski, Diedre Murphy, and Peg Tyre pointed out in their impeccably researched book *Two Seconds Under the World,* "There hadn't been any political assassinations in New York in more than a decade and Borelli didn't want one on his watch."[22]

Within hours, at a news conference, Borelli declared Nosair a "lone deranged gunman." "I'm strongly convinced that he acted alone," said Borelli. "He didn't seem to be part of a conspiracy or any terrorist organization."[23]

A month after the murder the Feds went along, telling the *New York*

Times that they believed "more strongly than ever that Mr. Nosair had acted alone,"[24] Not all of Borelli's men agreed. Lt. Eddie Norris, who ran the Homicide Squad at the 17th Precinct, reportedly saw proof of a conspiracy, but Borelli told him to "shut up."[25] Now problems developed over custody of the evidence.

"The New York City police department had the investigation the first couple of days," said Detective Napoli in an interview for this book. "They were hemming and hawing about whether to go federal or state [with the prosecution]. Then, three or four days in, we got the word that it was going to be given to us, and so we went and picked up the evidence. We had [it] for two, maybe three days, and we were starting to photostat it. Then we got the word that things had been changed . . . that the state was going to do it, and then we had to bring all the evidence back. We didn't get a good look at it until after the [Kahane murder] trial."

In fact, their analysis of the evidence came two years late. It wasn't until *after* the Trade Center bomb exploded in 1993 that the FBI got around to translating the blind Sheikh's threats to the "edifices of capitalism."[26] The Bureau blamed the lapse on the heavy Arabic-language traffic requiring translation at the time of the Gulf War. Incredibly, as late as 1998, the FBI had only two Arabic speakers capable of translating documents like those seized from Nosair's lair.[27]

One of the nuggets missed by Napoli and Anticev was a bomb formula for a device constructed of fuel oil and urea nitrate, the same lethal combination Yousef would use on the Trade Center bomb twenty-five months later.[28] FBI explosives experts would eventually admit that in the thousands of improvised explosive devices examined by the Bureau's lab, they had encountered only one other urea-nitrate bomb.[29]

Coupled with other crucial evidence that would surface in the next few months, the unique signature of the device could have provided another link between Nosair and the Trade Center bomb plot. But Borelli and prosecutors in the Manhattan DA's office wanted to avoid a "show trial," especially after Nosair hired left-wing attorney William Kunstler. The Joint Inquiry that examined intelligence failures leading up to 9/11 concluded that "The NYPD and the District Attorney's office . . . reportedly wanted the appearance of speedy justice and a quick resolution to a volatile situation. By arresting Nosair, they felt they had accomplished both."[30]

But in fact what the police had stumbled onto was the opening act of a massive international conspiracy that would play out slowly for more than a decade. If properly examined by Bureau agents, the bonanza of evidence seized from Nosair's house would have proven, as early as 1990, a *direct* connection between Special Forces army sergeant Ali Mohammed and Osama bin Laden's emerging al Qaeda terror network. If the Feds had simply pressed beyond the NYPD's "lone gunman" theory, they might have sought to question Mahmud Abouhalima and Mohammed Salameh, who had been captured while waiting for Nosair to return. All three men had been caught on film during the FBI's Calverton surveillance. Abouhalima and Salameh would eventually be convicted as coconspirators in the Trade Center bombing plot—but not before six people died, a thousand were injured, and Yousef's bomb punched a hole in Lower Manhattan.

Now, on the day after the Kahane murder, Abouhalima and Salameh were released, set free to plot the next great act of murder to hit New York City. Their proximity to the Kahane murder was another extraordinary dot on the line of terror that the FBI failed to connect.*

---

*Timeline #10. p. 3.

5

AL QAEDA'S
NEW YORK CELL

By the late 1980s, New York City was beginning to feel the early stir-rings of a clandestine movement born out of a war half a world away. An estimated fourteen thousand jihadis had dispersed after the Russians abandoned Afghanistan in 1989,[1] and untold numbers began to settle in New York and New Jersey. Ali Mohammed, the secretive ex-Egyptian army officer who conducted the Calverton paramilitary train-ing, later told federal investigators that al Qaeda sleeper agents called "submarines" were burrowing deep into U.S. cities.[2]

When the Afghan war ended, "we got the hell out of there," said Milt Bearden, the former CIA station chief in Islamabad. "Afghanistan was off the front burner." But America's sudden abandonment of the region, a theater of ops it had invested in so heavily, was a strategic mistake of historic proportions. A few months after the World Trade Center bomb-ing in 1993, Jack Blum, the former special counsel to the Senate Foreign Relations Committee, drew a direct link between the devastation below the Trade Towers and U.S. support for the "Afghan Arabs" in the war against the Soviets.

"Large chunks of our Government don't want to look at the disposal problem at the end of our war," said Blum. "Nobody wants to acknowl-edge this is our glorious victory in Afghanistan coming home to bite us."[3]

At that moment, the man with the sharpest set of teeth was preaching from a mosque located on the third floor above a toy store in Jersey City.

* * *

Born in 1938 in the village of Al Gamalia near the Nile Delta, Sheikh Omar Abdel Rahman lost his sight as an infant. By the age of eleven, driven by a relative who forced him to get up at 4:00 A.M. and study Islamic scripture in Braille, the young Omar had memorized the entire Koran.[4] He went on to distinguish himself at Cairo's Al Azhar, the oldest university in the Islamic world, where he earned a degree in Koranic studies in 1972.[5]

The young Sheikh was hardened by the philosophy of the fourteenth-century Muslim thinker Ibn Taymiyah, who believed that Islam had replaced Judaism and Christianity.[6] He was later radicalized by the teachings of Sayyid Qutb, a modern Egyptian scholar who spent three years in the United States and returned with the belief that Western civilization had led humanity "to corruption and irreligion from which only Islam can save it."[7] In moderate Islamic circles, the word *jihad* means "task" or "calling." To scholars like Qutb it meant "holy war." In 1966 he was executed by Egyptian president Gamal Abdel Nasser, whom the blind Sheikh called "the wicked pharaoh." Abdel Rahman preached that Muslims had a duty to kill political leaders who didn't adhere strictly to the Sharia, the holy law of Islam. He was later jailed for nine months in the notorious Qala prison, and reportedly subjected to brutal torture, which only steeled his resolve.

By the early 1980s, Sheikh Rahman, paroled and on his way to becoming a mythic figure among young Islamic radicals, had become spiritual adviser to a number of members of the Egyptian Islamic Jihad (EIJ). In 1981, when EIJ radicals from an errant Egyptian army squad[8] murdered President Anwar Sadat during a military parade, the Sheikh was imprisoned and tried as a coconspirator. He had blessed the *idea* of Sadat's assassination, but when no proof was presented at trial that the Sheikh had any direct involvement, he was acquitted.

In 1988, having been jailed, tried, and acquitted once again for his alleged role in a wave of terror against Egyptian Coptic Christians, the Sheikh made his way to Peshawar, Pakistan, near the Afghan border.

It was the height of the anti-Soviet war, and Peshawar, a kind of Wild West town near the Afghan frontier, was the staging area for the U.S. supply operation. Here the blind Sheikh soon became allied with the head of the largest Afghan mujahadeen rebel faction backed by the CIA.[9] As billions of dollars poured in from the United States and the Saudis matched the U.S. contribution, the Sheikh reconnected with another former Al Azhar instructor, Sheikh Abdullah Azzam. A Palestinian Ph.D., Azzam was one of the founding fathers of the modern radical Islamic jihad.[10] His slogan was "Jihad and the rifle alone: no negotiations, no conferences, no dialogues."[11] Terrorism analyst Steven Emerson has said that Azzam "is more responsible than any Arab figure in modern history for galvanizing the Muslim masses to wage an international holy war against all infidels and non-believers."[12]

Exhorting Muslims to "unsheathe [their] sword[s]" against the perceived enemies of Islam, Azzam crossed the world from 1985 to 1989. He visited dozens of U.S. cities and began setting up a network of offices designed as recruiting posts and fund-raising centers for the mujahadeen in their battle with the Soviets. Informally they were known as NGOs—nongovernmental organizations—entities that purportedly raised money for charitable purposes.

The first center, established in the early 1980s in Peshawar, was called Alkifah. Over the next decade, Azzam set up branches at mosques in the United States, the United Kingdom, France, Germany, Norway, and throughout the Mideast.[13] The network was formally known as the Services Office for the Mujahadeen, or Makhtab al-Khidimat (MAK). The flagship Alkifah center in the United States was established on the ground floor of the Al Farooq Mosque in Brooklyn. A counterpart was created at the Islamic Center in Tucson. Soon Azzam opened similar offices in Atlanta, Boston, Chicago, Pittsburgh, and thirty other U.S. cities.[14] During the late 1980s the network raised millions each year for the Afghan struggle.

At its height, the Services Office published a magazine called *Al-Jihad* with a circulation of fifty thousand. It was distributed by the centers in Brooklyn and Tucson, Arizona, which became the east-west anchors in Azzam's U.S. network. All this would come to have deadly importance in 1989, when the Services Office was taken over by Osama bin Laden and morphed into his terror network called al Qaeda.[15]

It was Azzam who introduced the blind Sheikh to the young Saudi billionaire. At the age of twenty-two, bin Laden had arrived in Peshawar in the mid-1980s with a military transport plane full of bulldozers and equipment from his family construction conglomerate, the Bin Laden Group. Dubbed "the Contractor," bin Laden quickly used the equipment to build roads, storage depots, and tunnels for the mujahadeen then battling the Soviets.[16] Before long, Azzam convinced bin Laden to help fund his worldwide Services Office network of NGOs.

During the late 1980s, as the Afghan war waged on and the cash poured in, bin Laden became devoted to Azzam. But soon after the Soviets were defeated, a conflict developed between Azzam and bin Laden over the best use of the fortune in aid that still flowed through the centers of the MAK. Azzam wanted the money to help install a pure Islamic government in Afghanistan, in a revolution akin to the one that had swept Iran in 1979.

But bin Laden's plan was much more ambitious. He wanted the Services Office money directed toward a "global jihad" that would carry the war to secular Islamic nations and the West. Like the blind Sheikh, bin Laden was a puritanical disciple of Taymiyah and Qutb, who saw America in particular as a "satanic state."

Azzam argued openly and bitterly with the blind Sheikh,[17] who backed bin Laden along with two other Egyptians: Dr. Ayman Al Zawahiri, head of the Egyptian Islamic Jihad (EIJ), and Mohammed Atef, a former Cairo police official who became bin Laden's right-hand man. Atef was so close to the Saudi billionaire that his son married bin Laden's daughter.

The power struggle for control of the Services Office rivaled the internecine warfare of two Mafia families. Finally, after a violent triple homicide, the Egyptian-backed bin Laden bloc prevailed. On November 24, 1989, Azzam and his two sons were killed by a car bomb in Peshawar as they drove to *juma* (Friday prayers). The murders remain unsolved, and although he expressed public grief at their deaths, some U.S. intelligence officials believe that Osama bin Laden himself gave the order for the hit.

At that moment, one of Azzam's most productive U.S.-based Services Office outposts was the Alkifah Center in Brooklyn. This was the very NGO the FBI had under surveillance during the Calverton shooting sessions in 1989. It was run by Azzam's handpicked representative, an electrical engineer named Mustafa Shalabi. Under Shalabi, the center became a propaganda front and meeting place for aspiring young jihadis in the New York area. It also turned into a cash machine, raising millions of dollars each year. The Egyptian was so successful that Osama bin Laden himself asked for Shalabi's help when he moved from Afghanistan to Sudan.[18]

Now, with the Afghan war over, bin Laden needed financing for his worldwide holy war. While Israel had been radical Islam's primary enemy for decades, bin Laden's new rhetoric encompassed a twin-headed hydra: the "Zionist-Crusader." This new second enemy was a reminder of the Christian hordes who had descended from Europe to crush Islam in the eleventh century.

Eager to take his fight to America, the young Saudi billionaire needed a beachhead. So he turned his attention to the Alkifah center that Azzam had sent Mustafa Shalabi to run. Bin Laden was plotting a coup at the Brooklyn center, and the man he dispatched to stage it was none other than the blind Sheikh.

On his return to Egypt in 1990, Sheikh Rahman was placed under house arrest, but he escaped when his followers used a double to pose for him.[19] By that summer, Rahman had made his way to Sudan. There, even though he'd been on a U.S. terrorism Watch List for three years, the Sheikh was granted a visa to enter America. This was another blunder on the part of U.S. intelligence that became a significant dot on the chart.* Later, the CIA would try to blame his admission on a corrupt case officer who helped Abdel Rahman's lawyer obtain illegal U.S. visas for his clients.[20] But the State Department later determined that, although he was on the list of "undesirables," the Sheikh obtained three sanctioned visas from CIA agents posing as State Department officials at the U.S. embassy in Khartoum.[21] Many intelligence analysts believe that Abdel Rahman's entry was payback by the Agency for his help in the CIA's support of the Afghan "freedom fighters."

Begun under President Jimmy Carter, the mujahadeen covert aid campaign was considered one of the CIA's greatest achievements during the Reagan years, and the Peshawar-based covert supply operation enjoyed broad bipartisan support. By the late 1980s, when the CIA's secret funding of the Contras in Nicaragua had become a foreign policy

---

*Timeline #8. p. 3.

disaster for the Reagan White House, many Democrats saw Afghanistan as "the good war."[22] At the time, no one in U.S. intelligence circles seemed to notice that the chief Afghan warlord, backed by the CIA, was denouncing the United States with the same level of hatred he'd shown toward the USSR.[23]

The night he flew into JFK in July of 1990, Omar Abdel Rahman was picked up by Mahmud Abouhalima, the redheaded Egyptian who had fired AK-47s at Calverton. This was the same man who would drive the aborted getaway cab on the night of Kahane's murder four months later. Also in the welcoming party was Mustafa Shalabi, Abdullah Azzam's representative, who had sponsored the Sheikh's entry.[24] Seemingly unaware that a conspiracy to displace him was afoot, Shalabi installed the Sheikh at a Bay Ridge apartment, and Abouhalima began to serve as his driver. Soon the charismatic Sheikh was preaching at the Al Farooq Mosque in Brooklyn.

An Egyptian in the FDNY

Among the Sheikh's devoted followers at the mosque was a quiet, unassuming accountant named Ahmed Amin Refai. Born in Alexandria, Egypt, Refai had emigrated to the United States in 1970. For the past sixteen years he had worked in the Capital Budget Unit of the New York City Fire Department—or *hardly* worked, according to Kay Woods, an assistant FDNY commissioner who was Refai's boss at the time.

"Ahmed really had the time of his life," said Woods. "He would come in late. He would call in sick. He would take long lunches. He would make phone calls to Egypt. He literally fell asleep at his desk sometimes."[25]

After Sheikh Rahman arrived, Refai would spend hours at the Al Farooq and Abu Bakr mosques, not far from FDNY headquarters on Livingston Street in Brooklyn.

"Every day there was something," said Woods. "Arrive a little bit late. Leave early. Take a long lunch. Wouldn't come in."

But for the most part, Refai kept his head down and acted like a nondescript city bureaucrat. His tenure remained uneventful until one day in the early 1990s when Woods decided to empty out a series of filing cabinets left over from an FDNY unit that had once used the office.

"There were these old beat-up green cabinets," said Woods, "full of files that a former FDNY fire captain had reviewed." The file cabinets were loaded with architectural drawings and the plans of various city buildings. To accommodate the discarded files, Woods brought in two Dumpsters. She was just coming back from lunch one day when she found Ahmed Refai rifling through them. Along with the blueprints, there were pen-and-ink drawings and some architectural renderings. Woods asked what Refai was doing. He smiled and turned to face her.

"Oh, I was just going to keep those. Do you mind if I keep some?"

"No," she told the immigrant Egyptian. "They're going out in the garbage. Keep whatever you want. Why? What are you gonna do with them?"

Refai just smiled and gathered up the files that he wanted. Among them were detailed drawings and blueprints of the bridges and tunnels around Manhattan, and the eight-square-block Port Authority complex between West and Liberty Streets: the World Trade Center.

"I had no idea at the time," Woods said in an interview for this book.

In the years to come, however, the events that unfolded around the blind Sheikh's circle would send a chill through her.[26]

As the summer of 1991 approached, the connections between the players became clearer. Sheikh Omar's circle operated out of three mosques: the dingy al-Salaam in Jersey City, and the two mosques in Brooklyn. The Al Farooq was the location of Mustafa Shalabi's Alkifah Center on Atlantic Avenue. The Sheikh also preached at the Abu Bakr on Forrest Avenue. The second-floor imam's residence there had been renovated by Ibrahim El-Gabrowny, a forty-two-year-old Egyptian immigrant who worked as a contractor.

El-Gabrowny was the cousin of El Sayyid Nosair, the Calverton shooting trainee who was about to stand trial for the murder of Rabbi Kahane. In the months before the trial in 1991, Mustafa Shalabi, emir of the Alkifah, dedicated himself to raising money for Nosair's defense. A reported $163,000 was collected from Arab restaurants and mosques all over Brooklyn. El-Gabrowny even made a trip to Saudi Arabia, where he met with Osama bin Laden himself and solicited twenty thousand dollars for Nosair's legal bills. Years later, after the 9/11 attacks, an FBI agent told a congressional committee that it was in the context of this legal fee contribution that the Bureau heard bin Laden's name for the first time.[27] But in 1991 nobody in the New York Joint Terrorist Task Force thought to put the bin Laden dot on the chart.*

Meanwhile, violence seemed to follow the Sheikh wherever he went. He'd only been in town four months before his follower Nosair gunned down the rabbi. Though the Sheikh's own driver, Abouhalima, had been Nosair's intended wheelman on the night of the hit, the FBI seemed powerless to connect the cleric to Kahane's murder. But that wasn't his last association with a violent homicide. A few months later, a rift began to develop between Mustafa Shalabi and Sheikh Rahman. It would result in a second act of violence that might have led the FBI to another important bin Laden link.

Early in 1991, in a conflict that mirrored bin Laden's earlier dispute with the murdered Azzam, the Sheikh began openly arguing with Shalabi over the best use for the fortune that continued to pour into the Alkifah Center. One account estimated it at over two million dollars a year.[28] Shalabi, like Azzam, wanted the money to go to the Afghanis struggling to build a post-Soviet government in Kabul. But the Sheikh demanded that half the funds be earmarked for his own cause: the removal of Hosni Mubarak as president in Egypt.[29]

The split drove the Sheikh to rage, and he denounced Shalabi—his original sponsor—in a pamphlet circulated to area mosques. "He is no longer a Muslim," the pamphlet read. "We should no longer . . . be manipulated by his deviousness."

The president of the Abu Bakr Mosque's board of directors made a personal appeal to the Sheikh on Shalabi's behalf. "You have been invited into your neighbor's home, and now you are trying to take over that home. How can you say that is just?"

"Shalabi is wrong," the Sheikh snapped back defiantly.[30]

Just after 7:00 P.M. on the night of February 26, 1991, Shalabi was packing at his apartment in the Seagate neighborhood of Brooklyn for a trip to Egypt the following day. He was planning to join his wife and child there, and he was worried. He'd told friends that because of the struggle with the volatile Sheikh, his life might be in jeopardy.[31]

He never made it to Cairo.

*Timeline #13. p. 4.

The next day, when Shalabi's relatives in Egypt began calling his Brooklyn home, the phone went unanswered. Soon, they contacted the police. But on that particular day, February 27, 1991, the attention of most Americans was focused on events halfway around the world: the U.S. forces of Operation Desert Storm were about to close in on Baghdad.

6

OPERATION IRAQI FREEDOM ONE

Across the Saudi Arabian peninsula, the airborne and ground forces of the U.S.-led coalition were driving divisions of Saddam Hussein's elite Republican Guard back into Iraq. It was day three of the ground war. Allied Commander General H. Norman Schwarzkopf was determined to rout the brutal Guard divisions and carry U.S. forces into the Iraqi capital. The "mother of all battles" had been a stunning defeat for Saddam. His regime hung by a thread. Then, a few hours later, General Schwarzkopf received a call from the chairman of the Joint Chiefs of Staff, Colin Powell.

Powell informed him that President George H. W. Bush was considering ending the war in six hours, at 5:00 A.M. Persian Gulf Time. The elder Bush would later tell Gulf War veterans that the decision to pull the plug and leave Hussein in power was made on the advice of Powell and Secretary of Defense Dick Cheney.[1] Schwarzkopf reportedly swallowed hard and said, "I don't have a problem with that."[2]

As soon as the air war broke out on January 16, Ronnie Bucca's reserve unit in the U.S. Army's 242nd Military Intelligence Battalion had been put on alert. Bucca was a first sergeant, and at that moment in late February he was in uniform, up in the bedroom of the family home packing to go. A decorated Special Forces paratrooper, Bucca had maintained his reserve status since his discharge from active duty in 1975.

"Ronnie read everything he could get his hands on about military strategy and history," his wife, Eve, recalled. "Naturally, being Special Forces, one of his favorite books was *The Green Berets*. He started reading the comic strip series when he was in grammar school. By the time he was in high school, the movie starring John Wayne had come out along with that hit song by [Staff Sgt.] Barry Sadler."[3] Ronnie devoured them all.

In 1973 he headed for the recruitment office. "He had to make the Special Forces," said his brother Alfred, a reserve army major. "And he wouldn't stop even after he was jumping with the Screaming Eagles. Our dad had run an LTDP landing craft pulling wounded Marines off the beaches in the Philippines back in World War II. So rescue and the military was in our blood. We studied guerrilla warfare since the time we were fourteen years old. It started with books about the French in Dien Bien Phu. *Street Without Joy* by Bernard Fall. We just started reading and got intrigued with it."[4]

Ronnie's bookshelf was filled with Vietnam memoirs, from *The Secret War Against Hanoi* to *We Were Soldiers Once and Young*. His books on strategy included *How Great Generals Win* and *The Art of War* by Sun Tzu.

"Firefighting was his job, but he loved the Army," said Eve. "After his fall back in eighty-six when he couldn't jump anymore, Ronnie put in for a unit in military intelligence."

In 1989, then a Special Forces first sergeant, Bucca transferred to the 242nd MI Battalion on Staten Island. Eventually he'd rise to the rank of warrant officer in the 3413th MI Detachment of the 800 MPs. This was one of only four reserve units in the entire country assigned to support the Defense Intelligence Analysis Center at Bolling Air Force Base in Washington. Dubbed "The Death Star," the seven-story DIAC building was the nerve center of the Defense Intelligence Agency. And the assignment had one crucial benefit for Ronnie Bucca: it earned him a Top Secret security clearance.

"You have to understand," said Alfred Bucca, "on weekends, when he did his reserve duty, Ronnie wasn't just driving a HMMV around some camp in upstate New York. He was over at Dix or down in D.C. looking at intel at the highest level."

Now, a few days into the ground war, with U.S. forces heading for

Iraq, Ronnie was preparing to ship out when the "stand down" was reported by CNN.

His daughter, Jessica, now thirteen, burst into the bedroom to tell him the news. "Hey, Dad, they said on TV you don't have to go." Little Ronnie, now eleven, jumped up on the bed and grabbed his father, wrestling him down and tickling him. The kids were thrilled.

Eve rushed in to hug him, but Ronnie wasn't smiling. "What's wrong?" she said.

Ronnie asked Jessica and Ronnie Jr. to unpack his bag, and gestured his wife into the den. The TV was still on. CNN was airing video of victorious Allied troops and shots of shell-shocked Iraqi soldiers surrendering with white flags. "We should have finished it," said Ronnie.

"What do you mean?" said Eve. "It's done. Look how few people we lost."

"I know," said Ronnie, "but you leave a guy like Saddam in power, and the next time our kids are gonna have to go." Eve hugged him and nodded toward the TV.

"Come on, Ron. We kicked butt."

"On the battlefield, maybe," said Bucca. "But there are other ways they can get to us." Ronnie pulled her close, whispering so the kids wouldn't hear. "Look at what's been going on in the last ten years— Lebanon, the hostage takings. Pan Am Flight 103. They can find lots of other ways to hit us. This isn't over."

As always, Eve tried to take the edge off with humor. "Yeah, well, just let 'em try something here in New York. Toughest city on the planet." She elbowed Ronnie and winked, but her husband wasn't smiling.

Two days later, on the morning of March 1, a neighbor noticed that Mustafa Shalabi's front door was open. The thirty-nine-year-old electrical contractor, who had raised millions for the jihad, was lying dead inside, in a sticky puddle of dried blood.

He had been bludgeoned, stabbed multiple times, and finished off with a gunshot to the head. More than a hundred thousand dollars in Alkifah funds were missing from the apartment,[5] and at the time, though Shalabi was found with two curled red hairs in his hand, the redheaded Mahmud Abouhalima wasn't even considered a suspect. In fact, it was

Abouhalima who identified Shalabi's body, telling NYPD detectives he was the dead man's brother. Despite no signs of forced entry and indications that Shalabi knew his killer, Abouhalima was let go.*

Now, given their knowledge of the Calverton shooting sessions, the connection of Abouhalima and Salameh to Nosair the night of Kahane's murder, and Abouhalima's presence at a second grisly homicide, FBI Agent John Anticev and his partner, Detective Lou Napoli, got interested again. They traced records of repeated phone calls prior to the Kahane killing from Nosair's phone to a number registered to someone named Weber on Fifth Avenue and Seventy-first Street in Brooklyn.[6] Curious why Nosair would be calling a person with a German name, they went out to investigate.

"We knock on the door," Anticev recalled, "and somebody . . . answers on another floor and we go, 'Who is this Weber?' And the guy goes, 'Him? I think [he's] a terrorist.'"

Anticev and Napoli traded looks and asked why.

The man said that the tenant had Arabs visiting his apartment all the time. He got magazines about bombs in the mail.

Anticev pressed him. "Weber?"

"Yeah," said the neighbor. "But his real name is Mahmud Abouhalima." Weber was the maiden name of the Red's wife.[7]

"Bingo," Anticev said to Napoli—the word he used whenever he connected the dots.

Later, posing as Con Ed workers, the two of them returned to the Fifth Avenue building. When they arrived, the super told them that he'd seen boxes of bomb-making material in Abouhalima's apartment. But the search turned up nothing. Abouhalima was beginning to get a reputation among the Feds as "the Teflon terrorist." Though they would continue to monitor Abouhalima, Anticev and Napoli seemed stymied.

The Arizona Connection

If they had thought to check the visitors' log at Rikers Island, they might have noticed that on March 8, a week after Shalabi's body was discovered, a man tied to an Arizona homicide had been out to see El Sayyid

---

*Timeline #11. p. 3.

Nosair. Wadih El-Hage is another of the shadowy figures who runs in and out of this story. A Lebanese convert to Islam, he had been dispatched from Arizona to watch over the Alkifah money machine while Shalabi was gone. El-Hage worked out of an Arizona Islamic center with links to Ramzi Yousef. He'd met Mahmud Abouhalima at an Islamic conference in 1989. At the Red's request, El-Hage picked up a pair of AK-47s for him. A naturalized U.S. citizen, El-Hage went on to become Osama bin Laden's personal secretary in Sudan in the mid 1990s and was later convicted in the 1998 East African embassy bombings.[8]

Like the mysterious Ali Mohammed before him, El-Hage's name would appear on the dotted line between bin Laden and the 9/11 attacks half a dozen times; yet at this point he was unknown to the FBI. Still, in March 1991, Anticev and Napoli might have tripped to him if they had focused on Shalabi's bloody murder.

If they had visited the Alkifah Refugee Center where Shalabi had raked in millions, they might have learned of the battle royal that had been raging between the dead man and the blind Sheikh. Despite a perfect motive to kill Shalabi, Omar Abdel Rahman wasn't even an official suspect, and the murder remained unsolved. The fact that the Sheikh was preaching at a Brooklyn mosque attended by Nosair and renovated by the assassin's cousin, El-Gabrowny, didn't seem to register with Napoli or Anticev, or the fact that the boxes of evidence they'd started to inventory contained tapes with the Sheikh's threats to "the edifices of capitalism."

It's clear now that if the FBI had fully investigated the Shalabi murder at the time, it could have given the Justice Department another early window into Osama bin Laden's violent plan for a jihad against the United States. It wasn't until years later, when an al Qaeda turncoat named Jamal Ahmed al-Fadl confessed, that the Feds understood why.

Al-Fadl was a young Sudanese who had worked as Shalabi's assistant at the Alkifah Center. As far back as 1988, Shalabi had sent al-Fadl to a series of training camps in Afghanistan and Pakistan, where he was instructed in the use of the AK-47 and RPG-7 grenade launcher. He visited other camps where young jihadis were learning how to do what he called "tricks" with explosives like TNT and C-4.[9] During this period, al-Fadl was at a guest house where he personally witnessed Osama bin Laden lay out his plan for al Qaeda. Soon, like a young Mafia member taking a blood oath, al-Fadl swore a *bayat,* an Islamic pledge, to bin Laden's new organization.

According to this young Sudanese, Sheikh Omar Abdel Rahman had come to New York to take over the Alkifah Center in much the same way bin Laden had assumed control of the Services Office (MAK) founded by his mentor Azzam. Now, following Shalabi's death, with the blind Sheikh in control of the Alkifah, Osama bin Laden had *an effective al Qaeda cell right in the middle of Brooklyn, New York.* A tough look at the Shalabi murder might have ripped the lid off al Qaeda years before the FBI ever heard of the network.

This is no exercise in second-guessing. After all, Al Farooq, the very mosque al-Fadl worked out of, was the scene of that intense four-week FBI surveillance in the summer of 1989, when agents followed the convoys of jihadis to their Calverton shooting sessions. The Shalabi homicide, like the Kahane killing before it, was just the kind of case the NYPD-FBI Joint Terrorist Task Force was established to investigate. The very concept of the JTTF was to pair bright, well-educated FBI agents like John Anticev with seasoned, street-smart detectives like Lou Napoli to investigate local crimes that might have national security implications.

But by the summer of 1991, with evidence of a radical Islamic paramilitary cell training in New York, two bloody murders in the space of four months, and the presence of a radical Muslim cleric who'd slipped past a Watch List to gain entry, the two top Egyptian investigators on the JTTF were apparently dead in the water.

Looking back, the evidence seemed to be screaming at Anticev and Napoli, but it's impossible to say how much support they were getting from their superiors in the FBI's New York office—the Bureau's office of origin for all Islamic terrorism cases.

Still, in the fall of 1991, luck was about to smile on them. The two investigators got another chance, courtesy of Special Agent Nancy Floyd, who worked two floors above them chasing Russians. She was about to hand John and Louie a dot that, if properly connected, would have made their careers.

7

A NEST OF VIPERS

I t was six months after the Gulf War when Nancy Floyd walked into the lobby of the Woodward, an old Beaux Arts hotel on the corner of Broadway and Fifty-fifth. Built in 1904, the Woodward had lost its luster decades before. It was now home to low-rent tourists looking for bargain accommodations within walking distance of Times Square. The rooms didn't exactly rent by the hour, but the Woodward was just the kind of "off Broadway" venue where an errant Russian diplomat might slip away for an assignation.[1]

When Nancy asked the front-desk man for the head of hotel security, she was led into the office of Emad Salem, a barrel-chested forty-one-year-old Egyptian who had immigrated to New York from Cairo in 1987.[2] On this day in August 1991 the goateed Salem was dressed impeccably in a double-breasted suit. Retired special agent Len Predtechenskis described how the encounter went.

"Nancy flashed her badge and gave him her card," said Len. "On the back Nancy wrote down the name of a Russian we were trying to find. We thought he'd slipped into the country and may have stayed at that hotel."

Salem told Agent Floyd that he didn't have all of the hotel records handy. He would check the guest register for the past few months and get back to her.

"Frankly, she didn't expect to hear from him again," said Len. "But sure enough, he got back to her in a few days. It turned out that the Russian we were after *had* been there, but the INS screwed up and failed to let the Bureau know he'd left the country."

Agent Floyd was impressed that Salem had made the ID. She was doubly surprised when he called her back a week later. "There are some more Russians here," he said. "Would you be interested?"

"Nancy said, 'Sure,' and went back," said Len. "Pretty soon, this guy Emad had turned into a really good source. The chemistry between an FBI brick agent like Nancy and a source like Salem is a hard thing to define, but after he'd given her a couple of more leads that panned out, they just clicked."

In the meantime, just as she'd done with the Russians, Nancy began to read up on Egyptians. The homework paid off—because Emad Eldin Aly Abdou Salem turned out to be a complicated figure. Like many Middle Eastern immigrants, he'd left a country where he had some professional standing, only to find disappointment in America.

In the five years since his arrival, Salem had gone through a series of menial jobs. He'd been a stock boy, a cabdriver, and a clothing salesman. He'd only recently begun to move up the food chain in security, working first as a guard at retail stores like Henri Bendel and Bergdorf Goodman, and finally getting a chance to wear plainclothes as a house detective at the Woodward.

Emad Salem had been raised for better things. After graduating from a military technical college in Cairo in 1974, he'd risen to the rank of major in the Egyptian army, and was said to have worked in a prison for a time. His résumé listed "specialized training in plastic explosives." He claimed to be an expert marksman and judo champion.[3] All this gave rise to rumors that Salem was an Egyptian intelligence agent—a fabrication that Salem himself spun to virtually everyone he met.

He also claimed to have been a member of an elite unit that protected Egyptian president Anwar Sadat. He boasted that while traveling in Sadat's security detail he'd met Saddam Hussein in Iraq, Colonel Qaddaffi in Libya, and Jordan's King Hussein. He even lied under oath at a criminal trial, claiming he'd been wounded trying to save Sadat when he was gunned down in 1981.

In reality, Salem was a low-level technical officer with a few acquaintances in Egyptian intelligence. But to everybody he met—including Barbara Rogers, an Avon cosmetics secretary he married six weeks after his arrival—Salem puffed his résumé.

"I tried to maintain myself to be a big shot," he later confessed, and in the beginning he told all the same lies to Nancy Floyd. He showed her a picture of himself on the reviewing stand the day Sadat was murdered, claiming that a scar on his head was from a stray bullet.

Nancy took it all in, but she didn't let it influence her belief in Salem. What mattered to her was whether he could deliver the intelligence he promised, and on the issues that counted—fingering Russians and other diplomats—he delivered time and time again.

In the early days, Salem gave Floyd a lead on an illegal ring selling bogus green cards for two thousand dollars apiece.[4] He also blew the whistle on a number of illegal aliens that the INS had picked up.

"People exaggerate who they are all the time," said an FBI source. "Salem's wife, Barbara, even told him she was a *doctor* when they first met." But considering the way the Egyptian had lived since he'd come to New York, Nancy knew he was no double agent.

"An intelligence agent doesn't sit in a hotel and wait for somebody to come get them," said the source. "They have to be proactive. Their whole purpose is to make contact with other foreign agents so they can get intel. Salem had been in the U.S. since '87 and never made any contact until he met Nancy."[5]

But the meeting with Floyd ignited a spark of ambition in Salem, who'd felt undervalued for years. His wife, Barbara, was quoted as saying that once, while driving a taxi, Salem had been humiliated when an angry passenger threw a two-cent tip in his face. "You have to understand," she said, "this man had his own driver in Egypt."

"One day Salem and Nancy were talking," Len Predtechenskis recalled. "He said to her, 'I know you are working Russians, but there is a man in this city, an Egyptian, who is so much more dangerous than the worst KGB hood.'" Nancy eyed him with some skepticism. Salem had come through before, but now he was upping the stakes. Middle Eastern terrorism wasn't even close to Nancy Floyd's area of assignment.

"Another agent might have played it safe," said Len. "Kept her head down and stayed with what she knew. But not Nancy."

"This Egyptian," she answered, "what's his name?"

Salem leaned forward and motioned her close. Almost in a whisper he said, "The blind Sheikh. Omar Ahmad Ali Abdel Rahman."

The name didn't register with Nancy, but she scribbled it down in a notebook. "That's R-A-C-K—"

"No," explained Salem. "We pronounce the R-a-h like a *k*. You would say it like 'Rackman.' But you might as well write down 'pit viper.'" Nancy asked why, and Salem explained that Sheikh Rahman was head of al Gamm'a Islamiya, an Egyptian terrorist group. He was currently preaching at two mosques in Brooklyn and at the Masjid al-Salaam in Jersey City.

"This means 'the mosque of peace,'" said Salem. "But there is no peace in this place."

Nancy Floyd—the Texan who had dreamed of joining the Bureau to "put away bad guys"—was intrigued. Until now, for all her effort, the most she'd accomplished was getting a few diplomats deported. Now her Egyptian source was talking about a man associated with the death of Anwar Sadat.

"He's here in New York, you're saying?"

Salem nodded.

"And he's dangerous?"

Salem nodded. "He is blind in one eye, with the pupil missing. The other eye is an empty socket. But the Sheikh sees all."

"Be specific."

Salem smiled. After months in a mind-numbing hotel job, he was anxious to show what he knew. He took Nancy into his office and gave her a crash course on the Afghan War, the Services Office network, and the murder of Mustafa Shalabi. From what he had heard, the local police never even questioned the Sheikh in the homicide.

"That is the power of this man," said Salem. "Wherever he goes, there are bodies. I tell you, the Sheikh and his followers . . . it's a nest of vipers."

"Nancy was knocked out," says Len. "She came to see me right after that and asked what I thought she should do. I told her to bring it to the guys who worked the UN. See if they knew any of these players."

So Nancy Floyd approached a pair of agents in her own Foreign Counter Intelligence Division on the twenty-fifth floor at 26 Federal Plaza. These agents dealt strictly with Egyptian diplomats who might be engaged in espionage under UN diplomatic cover.

A source close to the meeting said that the agents decided to give Salem a test. "We just had this new Egyptian officer come in through the Diplomatic Service at the UN," one of the agents told Nancy. "We think maybe he's an intel officer, but we can't get our finger on him. Do you think your boy Salem could take a look at him and let us know?" Nancy said she would see what she could do.

She met with Salem the next day. "Listen, it's not that I'm trying to get you to do anything against Egypt," she said, "but they need to know if this guy is actually a diplomatic corps person or actually—"

"A spy," Salem said, smiling. "This I will do for you."

Nancy took out the man's picture and gave Salem the name she'd received from the two agents. Immediately, Salem shot back, "I know this man. He's *absolutely* a spy and he works for the CIA."

Nancy did a double take. If Salem was right, there would be repercussions: the CIA was forbidden by statute from operating "assets" inside the United States.

A week later, the FBI Egyptian agents called Nancy to a meeting.

"They were floored," said a source who knew what happened. "Not only was Salem accurate, but the information he gave allowed the Bureau agents to shut down an illegal Company operation."

The agents from the Egyptian counterintelligence branch suggested that Nancy bring this newly discovered asset to the attention of one of their agents, who was attempting to infiltrate Middle Eastern terrorist groups. He was located two floors below, in the Joint Terrorist Task Force.

"What's his name?" asked Nancy.

"Anticev," said one of the agents. "His partner's a cop named Napoli."

Given what they knew about Nosair, Abouhalima, and the blind Sheikh, Anticev and Napoli jumped when Nancy Floyd dangled Emad Salem as a possible source.

"Let's meet the guy," said Lou. "See if he's for real."[6]

Right away, Nancy arranged a meeting at Juanita's, a now-defunct Mexican restaurant on the Upper East Side.

"Salem basically blew them out of the water," said a source who attended the meeting. "He had beaucoups of information."

"First of all," Salem said, "I can't believe you allowed Sheikh Rahman in here. He spent ten years in our prisons. His people killed my beloved President Sadat. If the man is here, he's doing nothing but bad."

Anticev and Napoli eyed Salem. They decided to test him with a name.

"Mahmud Abouhalima," said Napoli.

"Cabdriver," the Egyptian shot back. "Big guy. Six two or three. Born with crusader's blood."

"What's that mean?" asked Napoli.

"You know," said Salem. "He is redhead—mixed. A fierce *mujahad*. He fought the Russians. Now he drives the Sheikh around."

Anticev and Napoli traded looks. Salem had described their man to a T.

"Bingo," said Anticev in a muffled voice. He and Napoli had been stalled for months; Salem might well be the answer.

After the meeting at Juanita's, the agent and the detective regrouped with Nancy and asked if she could convince Salem to go undercover. Floyd said she wasn't sure. The Egyptian was making five hundred dollars a week at the hotel. He was in the process of getting a divorce from Rogers, his second wife. He'd met a German jewelry designer with a big apartment on the West Side and already moved in with her. Salem needed a steady income.

"With Nosair's trial coming up, we could use somebody on the inside," said Napoli.

Nancy nodded. "I'm not sure he'll work with y'all."

"Why not?" asked Napoli.

"The trust that's between him and me," she said. "I might be able to talk him into going under, but I'm GRU and my supervisor's not gonna let me go. So how do we work this?"

"Ask him first," said Anticev. "We'll cross that bridge."

So Nancy agreed. It wasn't a very hard sell. If there was ever an eager subject it was Emad Salem. Dangerous as the assignment was, he'd been pining away in back-end jobs, waiting for a chance to regain some of the prestige he'd enjoyed as an officer in the Egyptian army.

"He was an individual who saw an opportunity for fame," said Napoli, "being known as someone who took down the blind Sheikh."

Assuming they could work out the salary, Salem told Nancy he was ready. He would leave his hotel day job and try to infiltrate the Sheikh's cell. The Bureau agreed to match his weekly paycheck so that he could work undercover full-time. "Salem loved this stuff," said a source close to the operation. "He got five hundred a week, the same pay as his hotel salary. But it wasn't about the money."

"He did it for the glory," said Napoli. "A chance to put this Sheikh away who had done so much harm in his country."

Deep Undercover

Salem agreed to go undercover, but he had one crucial condition: he didn't want his identity disclosed. Before coming to the United States Salem had been jailed by the Egyptian intelligence service and reportedly tortured.[7] "He was fearful," Napoli recalled. "In no way, shape, or form did he want to be in a position where his undercover activities against the Sheikh would be known. He was also afraid for his ex-wife and two children back home. He didn't want his family to be the recipient of any fallout in Egypt."

Salem told Floyd and Napoli that he'd be willing to wear a wire if he they could promise he'd never have to appear in open court. But they had to be honest with him. "We said, if you're wired, we cannot guarantee that somewhere down the line you won't have to testify," said Napoli. So the FBI agreed to use Salem purely as an intelligence asset. If he developed information that a crime was about to be committed, agents would then move in and do the necessary surveillance to make a case.

There was a long tradition in the Bureau of maintaining such assets. For decades during the Cold War, Morris Childs, an executive in the Communist Party USA, operated as an FBI double agent, informing on the CPUSA and infiltrating the highest levels of the Soviet government.[8] To the FBI he was known simply as Agent 58. His asset code designation was CG-5824S*. The asterisk meant that he was a source who would never be called upon to blow his cover and testify. From 1952 to 1997, Childs made fifty-two dangerous missions to Moscow and was never suspected.

Even on the criminal side of the Bureau there had been dozens of confidential informants over the years, people who had infiltrated ongoing criminal enterprises from the Ku Klux Klan to the Gambino family. To keep them from having to testify and risk exposure, there was wide body of case law, beginning with the landmark Supreme Court case *Rovario v. the United States* in 1957.

Rovario held that the word of a "reliable informant" was sufficient to grant agents or police officers probable cause to obtain search, arrest, or wiretap warrants without having to name the informant in open court.[9] Given Salem's earlier exposure of the CIA's Egyptian asset, and the number of INS green card arrests he'd been responsible for, he clearly met the reliability test.

At that time in 1991, the Terrorism branch Anticev and Napoli worked for had no immediate supervisor or assistant special agent in charge, so the deal was approved by Jim Sherman, Nancy's supervisor for her GRU work, and his boss, an ASAC named Jack Lowe. Salem would work as an asset of the Foreign Counter Intelligence Branch, with Nancy Floyd as his salary contact and Napoli and Anticev as the formal case agents who would process his intel. He would not wear a wire to record his dealings with the members of Sheikh Rahman's cell. His role would be one of pure intelligence, to warn the FBI of any potential terrorist threats from the Sheikh or his followers.

"We told him to start hanging out at the Nosair trial," said a source close to the operations. "We wanted to see if he had the ability to get close to them. We had given him six weeks to get under. He did it in two days."

The Near Miss

If the NYPD and the Manhattan district attorney's office had wanted to avoid a politically charged show trial by holding to the lone-gunman theory, the plan backfired. For days, as Nosair's murder trial unfolded, demonstrators for both sides stood in the streets outside the Manhattan Criminal Courts Building flinging invective at each other.

"Death to Nosair," chanted a group of JDL supporters and Hasidic Jews on one side. "Allah-u-Akhbar" ("God is Great"), chanted the Egyptians on the other, shaking defiant fists behind their set of barricades. Ironically, the object of the protests, Nosair, had worked as a maintenance man in the basement of 111 Center Street, just across the street from the trial site.

Upstairs, in the thirteenth-floor courtroom, seventy-two-year-old William Kunstler and Nosair's cocounsel, Michael Warren, a tall black Muslim, spun a conspiracy tale for the jury. Rabbi Kahane had been killed, they contended, by divisive factions in his own fractured JDL organization. Without the forty-seven boxes of evidence seized from Nosair's house suggesting a broader terrorist plot, the defense pounded away on the lack of forensic evidence.

For one thing, there hadn't been an autopsy. Orthodox Jewish law forbade the evisceration of bodies, and with the cause of death obvious, the city's chief medical examiner bowed to pressure from Hasidic leaders and released Kahane's body for burial without the usual postmortem.[10] Since autopsies in homicides are virtually mandatory, the defense seized on the break from routine to create doubt in the jury's mind. Also, the prosecution was unable to prove that Nosair had actually fired the .357 magnum. His prints weren't on the gun, and there was no evidence that paraffin tests tying him to the revolver had been performed. There was even conflicting testimony on how many shots were fired, and evidence suggesting that JDL members at the death scene were also armed.

"Even though there was a smoking gun, it was not positively identifiable," said an alternate juror after the verdict.[11]

Soon after the start of the trial, Salem worked his way into the crowd of Egyptians outside the court. Like most successful undercover assets, his greatest liability was also his strength—in this case, Salem's ability to lie convincingly about his background.

As an Egyptian army veteran he didn't have to veer very far from the truth, incorporating the real elements of his personal life into his new undercover persona.

On his second day among the protesters, Salem introduced himself to Nosair's cousin Ibrahim El-Gabrowny. "I told him I was a jeweler," Salem recalled later. "I told him that I lived in Manhattan and I can manage my time by myself. I am here to support Mr. Sayyid Nosair."[12] There was some truth to the story: Salem's new girlfriend, Karen Goodlive, ran a growing jewelry business out of the apartment they shared on Broadway and Eighty-sixth Street.

Meanwhile, Salem presented himself as earnest, and willing to do whatever it took to free "brother Nosair." He quickly offered to print labels and stuff envelopes for the accused assassin's defense fund. On that second day, El-Gabrowny embraced Salem and told him, "It's good to have a brother like you to help El Sayyid."

Almost before he got started, though, Salem's cover was nearly blown after a chance meeting outside court with Anticev and Napoli. The Egyptians regularly chatted up the Feds as they passed in and out of the building; it was their way of keeping tabs on "the enemy." Now, during one of the breaks between court sessions, unaware of Salem's relationship with the Bureau, Nosair's cousin El-Gabrowny introduced him to the FBI agent and the cop.

"Brother Emad, he is one of the good brothers," El-Gabrowny told them. Then he joked, "Why don't you find me a job with you guys?" Anticev and Napoli traded looks. There was a moment of awkwardness, until Salem made a joke to cut the tension.

"I am ex-Army," he said. "Explosives expert. Why don't you find *me* a job as well?"

Suddenly, El-Gabrowny squeezed Salem's shoulder. He excused himself and pushed the informant far enough away so that the agent and the cop couldn't hear him. Glaring at Salem, El-Gabrowny said, "Are you crazy? Telling the FBI that you are an *explosives* expert?"

"What's wrong with that?" asked Salem. "I am U.S. citizen. It's a free country."

"But now they're going to monitor you," growled El-Gabrowny. "They are going to spot you, and if something happens they will come to pick you up first."

At this point Abouhalima, the Red, jumped in. The man whose apartment Anticev and Napoli had searched, posing as Con Ed workers, had been followed by the Feds for some time. "You watch them," he said. "They are always on us. If you are not careful, they will try and recruit you as a spy." Looming over the smaller Salem, he boasted, "Anticev and the cop used to surveil me. I used to drive my car all the way to Connecticut, go to a coffee shop, [then] drive back—drive them crazy behind me all the way home." Abouhalima stabbed at Salem's chest with his big index finger. "Do you *understand*? They are watching me. They will watch you. They will try and get you to turn." He stabbed at him again.

Emad swallowed hard, but kept a smile on his face.

"*Never*," said the FBI informant. "Never could they get me to inform on my brothers." He eyed El-Gabrowny and Abouhalima to see if they'd bought his explanation. There was a moment's hesitation, then the Red gave him a bear hug.

Emad Salem said a private prayer of thanks to Allah that he hadn't been wired.

"Pretty soon El-Gabrowny had invited Emad home for dinner," recalled an FBI source. "He was in like Flynn. After that, he was acting almost like the Sheikh's personal bodyguard. Louie and John had been trying to get a line on this guy for so long, and now they had somebody in the inner circle. To them this was the mother lode."

A few weeks later, when the stunning verdict was announced, Salem became the FBI's last best hope.

8

BLOOD IN THE CITY

On December 7, 1991, though found guilty of lesser charges, El Sayyid Nosair was acquitted of Rabbi Meir Kahane's murder. Even the estimable William Kunstler, his lead defense attorney, was caught off guard. When the Saturday night verdict was announced, Kunstler rushed down to the courthouse to find JDL demonstrators holding a mock electric chair and screaming, "Jewish blood isn't cheap." A miniriot broke out on Center Street. "You pig," yelled one of the Hasidim. Another exhorted, "Kahane chai"—Kahane lives—shaking a placard demanding a federal trial. On the other side of the police barricades, Mahmud Abouhalima hoisted Kunstler up on his shoulders, while Nosair's cousin El-Gabrowny and his newfound friend Emad Salem chanted, "Allah-u-Akhbar! Allah-u-Akhbar!"

The next day the exuberant supporters slaughtered three lambs and held a celebration party on the second floor of the Abu Bakr Mosque in Brooklyn. Dressed in jeans, a plaid shirt, and a red ascot, Emad Salem sat among them. Noticing that one of the followers had a video camera, he offered to take over while the man ate. Zooming in on the faces, Salem shot Abouhalima and his brother Mohammed, another big redhead. He shot footage of El-Gabrowny, Siddig Ali, and Mohammed Salameh, captured against a wall in a green sweater picking his nose.[1] That night Salem offered to make copies of the tape for the congregation. He quickly handed it off to Nancy Floyd, and the FBI made the duplicates.[2] If Napoli and Anticev needed any reassurance that Abouhalima and Salameh were card-carrying members of the Nosair cell, here was proof in living color. Salem had taken a risk by volunteering to shoot at the mosque, and a greater risk in spiriting the tape out for duplication by the FBI. But the postverdict video was a major intelligence coup for the Bureau, and another vindication of Nancy Floyd's asset.

In the meantime, while Nosair's acquittal on the murder charge was a tactical victory for the cell, the celebration at Abu Bakr obscured the fact that "brother Sayyid" had been found guilty of gun possession and charges of assault on postal inspector Carlos Acosta, the elderly Irving Franklin, and cabdriver Franklin Garcia. At trial the cabbie admitted on the stand that when Nosair pressed "something cold and hard" to the back of his head, he got so scared he "make wet" in his pants.[3]

Now, at sentencing, Judge Alvin Schlesinger declared that the "not guilty" homicide verdict "defied reason." He socked Nosair with the maximum for the lesser charges: seven and a third to twenty-two years. The Egyptian would be sent to Attica, one of the starkest prisons in the New York system. But Nosair—a radical who'd kept cyanide in his locker in the basement of the court building where he'd worked—would be eligible for parole in six years.

By early 1992, Rudolph Giuliani, who had made his reputation busting organized crime families as U.S. attorney, was gearing up to run for mayor. But as history would prove, Nosair's cell posed a much greater threat to the city than the Colombos, the Genoveses, or the Gambinos at the height of their power. The stunning "lone gunman" miscalculation by the NYPD and the screwups over the evidence seized from Nosair's house had left the Feds reeling. The FBI retrieved the forty-odd boxes from the 17th Precinct, and the current U.S. attorney, Otto Obermaier, pledged to review requests by Jewish leaders that the Justice Department bring a civil rights charge against Nosair in the rabbi's murder.[4] Given the evidence problems, though, any prosecution would be problematic.

At this point, in February 1992, Napoli and Anticev had identified Nosair as a member of al Gamma'a Islamiya (IG),[5] the radical Egyptian hate group led by the blind Sheikh.[6] The IG was Egypt's largest Islamic militant organization.[7] After assassinating the speaker of Egypt's parliament in 1990, the group tried to kill President Hosni Mubarak in a 1995 limousine ambush and went on to slaughter fifty-eight European tourists in 1997.[8] The fact that the FBI had linked Kahane's killer to such a violent terror group five years earlier is evidence of how deep his roots went in the dangerous new jihad that was directed at America.

Jamal al-Fadl, the Sudanese informant, would later testify that al Gamma'a Islamiya was directly tied to Osama bin Laden's terror network. But at the time, Nosair's association with the group was another unconnected dot on the line of evidence heading toward 9/11.*

"There was a cell structure here, and the other individuals [Abouhalima and Salameh] were part of the cell structure," said Napoli. "It was obvious that there were a lot more people involved with the Kahane bullshit than the PD said. We felt there was a lot more, and we started to investigate that."9

But the linchpin of their probe was Nancy Floyd's recruited asset Emad Salem. With no other sources who came close to his level of access, Anticev and Napoli had to wait on the sidelines to see if he could deliver. Fortunately for them, Salem was getting deeper into the cell—so deep that soon the Sheikh himself would ask him to commit murder.

Within days of penetrating the inner circle around the Nosair defense, Salem was acting as Abdel Rahman's chauffeur. Having quit his job at the hotel to work full-time for the Bureau, he got wind that the Sheik was planning to attend an Islamic conference in Detroit. Salem offered to supply his five-passenger Pontiac for the trip.

"It is small," said the Sheikh. "You said you are a jeweler. Can you get us something bigger? We are going to be six. Can you get us a van?"10 Salem smiled. "I can get you a van, sir." The FBI gladly provided one.

On the way to Detroit, Salem turned on the radio. Suddenly, music erupted from a pop station. The Sheikh quickly pronounced it "satanic" and ordered that they play tapes of the Koran instead. Salem, who rarely attended mosque, faked a smile.

"Not a problem." The tapes played for the next sixteen hours.

At one point Salem took a break from driving. He was about to move to the shotgun seat when the Sheikh asked that he sit beside him. Rahman inquired about Salem's military service, and wondered aloud if he had any experience with explosives. Salem mentioned that he had fought in the Egyptian army against Israel in the 1973 war. That would make

---

*Timeline #17. p. 4.

him "a good *mujahad*," or holy warrior. "I did my part in jihad," said Salem proudly.

But the Sheikh snapped back. "No. You are not a mujahadeen, because fighting for an infidel government is not jihad. To do a jihad means you should do work without getting paid. You do it for God's sake."

"How can I make up with God?" asked Salem, playing the role.

"By turning your rifle's barrel to President Mubarak's chest, and kill him," said Rahman.

Salem almost couldn't believe it. He'd only been undercover a short time, and now here was the central target of his investigation giving him a *fatwa* (permission) to murder a head of state. In the Sheikh's view, Mubarak was little more than "a loyal dog to the Americans." The bitter cleric described the United States as a snake with two tails: Egypt and Israel.

Salem was beginning to understand what a "nest of vipers" he'd walked into. When they arrived at the hotel in Detroit, one of the Sheikh's followers, Hamdi Moussa, questioned Salem suspiciously about why he'd brought along a camera. Emad quickly responded, "I know it's a lecture. I should take pictures with the Sheikh."

But the wily Moussa snapped, "Nobody will take pictures of the Sheikh."

That night at the hotel the Sheikh laid out the sleeping arrangements. Salem slept on the floor, with the suspicious Moussa close by. The next morning, Emad felt his heart pound when he discovered that somebody had gone through his wallet during the night.

Later, Salem came to understand the Sheikh's power to raise money. At just one of the mosques, Salem and the other followers were directed to stand outside the door. After the blind cleric had held forth, they collected seven to eight thousand dollars.

The Detroit trip proved to be an eye-opener for Salem. The Sheikh's *fatwa* on Mubarak, and the volume of cash raised along the way, gave him an extraordinary inside view of a cell that had violent plans for New York and the rest of the world.

"Emad lived this life," said a Bureau source. "He knew what to say to these people. He knew how to dress. How to present himself. There's no question. He was in."

Calls to Battle

Now, in media coverage of Sheikh Rahman, news organizations like the *New York Times* and ABC News photographed a man thought to be the Sheikh's new bodyguard. He was everywhere—on Rahman's arm, protecting him from crowds, helping him in and out of his van, even arranging press briefings. It was Emad Salem.

The FBI asset couldn't wait to tell the agents about the Sheikh's assassination *fatwa* and the other intel he was getting from his regular visits to Rahman's mosques in Brooklyn and Jersey City.

But according to a source deep inside the investigation, there was a problem.

"John and Louie were supposed to be meeting him," said the source. "Salem wasn't wearing a wire, and he needed to get rid of this information quicker. It was all in his head. But he could never get hold of Anticev or Napoli. Their idea was to meet him every week or ten days."

So, faced with the need to download the intelligence, Salem turned to Nancy Floyd. She ended up working in the Bureau's Foreign Counter Intelligence GRU squad by day and then meeting Salem at night. They usually had dinner at a TGI Friday's on Broadway near 26 Federal Plaza. Nancy would debrief him over dinner, then go back upstairs and write up her notes in the form of FBI serials to Salem's asset file.[11] Each report began with his designated New York office number and the code number 134, indicating that he was an intelligence asset. At the top of each serial Floyd assessed Salem's reliability based on the evidence he was continuing to furnish.

"Nancy was working double duty," said Len Predtechenskis, the senior agent who was her mentor in FCI. "Working all hours, debriefing Salem, driving home to Stamford [Connecticut] where she lived, then back in the morning where she'd put in a full day in GRU. But the longer it got, the more pissed off her supervisor was becoming, because Nancy was spending too much time working something that had nothing to do with Russians."

Floyd finally complained to Napoli. "You have got to start writing this stuff up. Emad is telling me he couldn't get with you."

Napoli denies that he was inaccessible. "During the time Emad was working [undercover] I had a cell phone," the detective contended. "The reason why he was calling her was that at times he felt he wasn't getting anywhere with us. Salem wanted to do things his way."[12]

Still, a source close to the investigation said that Napoli was often unavailable on the nights Salem needed debriefing. "Louie would complain that his kid had a play or something like that," said the source. "He'd make excuses. But when somebody is undercover you have to be answerable; especially with something like this. Given the violence surrounding the Sheikh, Salem was in danger every minute he stayed inside."[13]

At one point a lawyer asked Salem if he was paranoid. The undercover informant nodded and tasted the acid in his throat. "Sir, since I got involved in this . . . I'm always paranoid."[14]

Almost every night Salem would listen to the Sheikh's lectures after the evening call to prayer. Though Rahman's primary venue was the dingy al-Salaam Mosque in Jersey City, Salem began to frequent the Abu Bakr and Al Farooq Mosques in Brooklyn where the cleric also lectured. After each prayer session a dozen of the faithful would surround the Sheikh as he sat in a white *gallabiyah*[15] under the red-and-white-velvet hat that was the sign of his rank as an imam from Al Azhar University.

"The jihad is our only path," said the Sheikh, his disfigured eyes turned upward. Around him sat Mahmud Abouhalima, Mohammed Salameh, and Nosair's cousin El-Gabrowny, the contractor. Salem, the FBI's asset, sat at the Sheikh's right arm. Also present on many such occasions was Ahmed Abdel Sattar, a U.S. postal worker, and Ahmed Amin Refai, the accountant who worked for the New York Fire Department. Refai and Sattar were among the many middle-class Egyptian immigrants who had gravitated to the Sheikh's inner circle. Refai himself sometimes walked arm in arm with the Sheikh. During the cleric's sermons, Salem and the others would close their eyes and listen as the Sheikh lashed out. His sermons sounded more like calls to battle than prayers.

"The laws of God are usurped by Crusaders' laws," warned the Sheikh. "The hand of a thief is not cut off, the drinker of liquor, not whipped. The adulterer is not stoned. Islamic holy law should be followed to the letter. Against them make ready your strength. Fight to the utmost of your power." Salem nodded piously as the Sheikh admonished them: "Mount steeds of war. Strike terror into the enemies of Islam."[16]

Concerned about what might be in the works, Salem slipped out early on one of these evenings. He took the Holland Tunnel into Manhattan from Jersey City and drove south toward the FBI office at 26 Federal Plaza.

Glancing behind him to make sure he hadn't been followed, Salem turned east on Chambers Street. He pulled his car to the curb near Broadway and got out. Looking left, then right, he stood in the shadows for a moment, making sure he was completely alone. This late, the street was deserted. Finally, he went to a pay phone.

Three blocks north, the phone on the desk of Detective Lou Napoli rang and rang. By now, Emad had almost given up trying to reach the detective in a hurry. He would leave messages, and Napoli would eventually get back to him. But tonight Salem had left the mosque with a sense of urgency, so when Napoli failed to pick up he dialed Nancy Floyd.

As on most nights, the agent was at her desk catching up on GRU paperwork.

"Nancy used to joke that she would work past the hour when the rats came out," said a source who knew her well. "She wasn't kidding. Twenty-six Federal Plaza had been built on landfill in Lower Manhattan, and there were sewer rats in the walls. At night, when everybody left, they would come out and scurry across the floor."

Now, when Nancy's phone rang, she picked up right away. Emad sounded worried. "I just got out of there. The man is rabid."

"Wait a second," said Nancy, grabbing a pen to take notes. "What's going on?"

"The ones at the mosque are planning something," said Salem, sounding concerned. "They want me to go to Attica to see Nosair."

"What do you think it is?" asked Nancy, writing it all down.

"I don't know, but tonight the Sheikh talked like he was ready to go to war. . . . I want you to hear this—I have one of his tapes." Salem slipped a cassette of one of the Sheikh's packaged sermons into a small recorder and held the speaker up to the phone. As Nancy Floyd leaned forward with the receiver, she heard a strained high-pitched voice in Arabic. Then Salem began to translate.

"Hit hard and kill the enemies of God in every spot, to rid it of the descendants of apes and pigs fed at the tables of Zionism, communism, and imperialism."

He stopped the tape. On the other end of the phone, Nancy Floyd sucked in hard. "*Jesus.* What do you think they're going to do?"

"I don't know," said Salem. "Ibrahim [El-Gabrowny] had me to his house for dinner. He turned up the TV thinking maybe FBI is bugging him. Then he asked me if I can build bombs. I mention Molotov cocktails, and he said, 'No, we need high-powered explosives.'"

Nancy took furious notes. "Is there anything specific in the works?" she asked. Salem told her no. "Maybe I will know more when I meet El Sayyid up at the prison. But I will tell you this right now—the death of the rabbi was just the beginning for them. They are bold now. And if we don't stop them . . . there will be blood in this city."

9

TRUTH FROM
THE ASHES

The drums were beginning to pound, and though he was a firefighter by profession, Ronnie Bucca was starting to hear them. On the weekends when most other reservists attended routine drills, Bucca was getting high-level briefings at the Army's 242nd Military Intelligence Battalion. With his Top Secret security clearance, he was beginning to see intel suggesting that the cell surrounding the blind Sheikh was worthy of the Defense Intelligence Agency's attention.

Manuals on the Army's M2/M3 Bradley Fighting Vehicle had turned up in the home of El Sayyid Nosair, along with other secret Special Forces files from Fort Bragg. Few DIA analysts at this point where aware of the connection between Nosair, Mahmud Abouhalima, and Ali Mohammed, the mysterious ex–Egyptian army officer who'd become a U.S. Army sergeant and served both the Green Berets and al Qaeda. The FBI was notorious for hoarding intel, and if anybody had passed the Calverton training photos on to DIA, Ronnie Bucca's unit had not been briefed. But at his monthly reserve sessions he kept picking up snippets of intelligence about this Sheikh Rahman, who was increasingly in the press denying any connection to the Kahane murder and seeking to distance himself from his follower Nosair. Like many law enforcement officers, Nancy Floyd made it a practice to keep business out of the house. When her mother, Joan, came to live with her in Stamford, Nancy never even hinted at her work with Salem—or the GRU for that matter. But

Ronnie Bucca had a different approach. He involved his family in his work as much as possible.

"I think it came after the fall," said Eve. "He knew how worried we were, so he started including us more and more."

Ronnie kept his work with military intelligence strictly confidential, but when it came to firefighting and rescue he gave Eve and the kids every detail. "If we were out riding and Ronnie heard sirens," said Eve, "he would pull over, roll down the windows, and if the kids smelled smoke he would ask them what it was. What kind of volatile? Was it gasoline or kerosene? Sometimes he asked them to look at the color of the smoke and tell him if it was a wood fire or chemicals. He did this because he loved his job. He wanted us to respect and understand fire rather than fear it."[1]

So on a regular basis, Ronnie took both eleven-year-old Ronnie Jr. and thirteen-year-old Jessica to work with him. By 1992 he'd been a fire-fighter for fifteen years. He loved the job, and gave it everything he had. In fact, he'd won medals for bravery in 1989 and 1990. But he was becoming increasingly restless.

"Maybe it was because he sensed something else going on in the background," said Eve. "But Ronnie was feeling more and more like he wanted to get at the *cause* of fires, as opposed to the outcome. He'd been thinking about moving into fire investigation." The final push in that direction, she remembered, came on a cold day in March when he took little Ronnie to work with him.

They drove down to the city and parked across from the firehouse on West Forty-third between Ninth and Tenth. Rescue One was the grand-father of every heavy rescue company in the country, and the house had a lot of history. Over the years the men of One responded to every second-alarm fire south of Fifty-ninth Street and every third-alarm below Harlem—among them the legendary 1942 blaze aboard the French cruise ship *Normandie* at Pier 88, and the crash in dense fog of an Army B-25 bomber into the Empire State Building in 1945.

Every high-rise scaffold or bridge rescue in Manhattan—every tunnel entrapment and river helicopter crash—was handled by the men of Rescue One.

In 1960 the company moved into a new house at 33 West Forty-third Street, but as fate and irony would have it, a fire in an eight-story warehouse next door burned the beloved quarters to the ground twenty-five years later. All that was left was the red rolling door and the brown granite front piece, so in 1989, when a new house rose on the same spot, they were preserved and built into the house's back wall. This was the company that Bucca had fought so hard to get back into, and he would take his children there so that they could appreciate it in the same way he did.

Now, on that March day, Ronnie headed toward the back of the house with his son. They stopped at the midsection of the Mack R rig. Behind the huge cab was a long walkway down the middle of the truck where the firefighters would stand holding on to straps like subway riders as the Mack R screamed through Manhattan. On either side of the walkway, floor to ceiling, and along the exterior sides of the truck, were compartments for the tools and gear.

"Quiz time," said Ronnie, opening one. He gestured to the array of equipment stored in the compartment. "What can you name?"

Little Ronnie hesitated for a moment. His dad was known for his practice of quietly entering a room and assessing a situation before leaping into action. Now the bright-eyed eleven-year-old took a moment.

"Let's see . . . Haligan tools. Cobra hammer. The Hurst—'jaws of life,' right?"[2]

Ronnie nodded and smiled as his son ticked off each one. "You're just warmin' up. Keep going." He closed the first compartment and opened two more.

"All right, that's the oxyacetylene," said little Ronnie, pointing to a torch. "All your Stanley tools . . . Rabbit tool . . . The high angle rope stuff . . . Griphoist . . ."

Just then, Lt. Steve Casani came up behind them. He shook the boy's hand and gestured toward the locker room. There was still a joke poster stuck on the door of Ronnie's locker from the days after his fall. It showed Bucca falling upside down from the tenement. He was attached to a parachute with the letters FDNY on top. The balloon coming out of his mouth said, "This can't be right!" But the poster also read "Get well soon," and it was signed on the bottom by veteran firefighter Joe Angelini and the other men of the house. Now, as Casani popped open his own locker, he pulled out one of those leashes that mothers use to keep track of wandering children.

"Your mom gave me this to make sure he wouldn't take any more dives." He eyed little Ronnie. "You want it?"

The boy smiled. "Nah. The way my dad takes chances, you might still need it."

Casani laughed. The kid was a chip off the block.

All of a sudden the house bell sounded for a run. Out of nowhere, four men rushed to the back of the truck and jumped into their boots. The bunker pants were inside them already, so all they had to do was pull up the suspenders. They climbed onto the back of the rig and donned their turnout coats and Cairns helmets, which were hanging along the walkway ready to go. As the chauffeur jumped in the cab and hit the ignition, little Ronnie turned to his father.

"Can I, Dad?" Ronnie moved toward Casani, who was also in motion. "What do you think, Lieu? Okay if he rolls?" Casani didn't hesitate. "Absolutely." He grabbed a short chauffeur's coat and threw it around Ronnie Jr. He found an off-duty firefighter's helmet. The brim went down to little Ronnie's eyes when Casani put it on his head.

Then, while Ronnie grabbed his own gear, Casani gestured for the boy to run to the front so he could ride between him and the chauffeur in the cab.

As they sped west on Forty-third and shot left down Eleventh Avenue, Lieutenant Casani yelled to Little Ronnie over the sound of the siren, "If you're lucky, it'll be a good fire."

The translation for anyone outside the FDNY would be a "bad fire," but these men seemed to live for the challenge of beating back the flames. Until 9/11, when the reality of just how dangerous the job was struck not just the men but their wives, most firefighters would look forward to "an all-dayer," a multiple-alarm blaze. The danger was always there for fire suppression units, but you could multiply it by ten for rescue companies.

In *Report From Engine Company #82,* perhaps the greatest book ever written on firefighting, Dennis Smith described conditions at his company in the South Bronx at the height of one of the worst fire epidemics in New York history. In the kitchen, wrote Smith, there was a handwritten sign. Every man saw it when he reported for his tour. The sign said, "This could be the night."

Very few American workers live with that kind of risk. Ninety-nine point nine percent of the population leave for work in the morning expecting to be home that night for supper. But firefighting is a dangerous trade—rescue work exponentially *more* dangerous, and Ronnie wanted to prepare his children for what someday might happen.

Now, by the time the truck turned left onto Little West Twelfth Street, the fire in the warehouse had been knocked down. Ronnie got off the rig and motioned for his son to wait. He went inside and surveyed the scene to make sure it was safe, then came back, found little Ronnie an oversized pair of boots, and cocked his head for them to go in.[3]

Inside, Ronnie Jr. spotted two men in red jackets sifting through the debris. They were collecting evidence samples in paint cans with orange labels.

His father led him across the charred warehouse floor, and introduced him to Fire Marshals Lou Garcia and Jimmy Kelty. The boy shook hands with them both and eyed their jackets. On the back of each one in big white letters it said MARSHAL. An insignia on their sleeves read Bureau of Fire Investigation. But what he noticed first was their guns. Each of them was wearing a Smith and Wesson snub-nose .38.

"So what are you—like, cops?" asked Little Ronnie.

Garcia winked. "Better than that. We figure out who sets these things." He looked around the fire-ravaged warehouse.[4] Ronnie explained that both men had started out as firefighters: Garcia in Rescue One, Kelty with 258 Engine. Between the two of them, they'd battled thousands of fires.

"The way we look at it," said Garcia, "you can come in after it's started and put it out, or you can catch it before they light the match."

Little Ronnie thought it over. That made sense. He eyed the two men, then their guns, then the evidence sample cans with the orange labels. Finally he turned to his father.

"So how come you're not a marshal, Dad?"

Kelty winked at Ronnie. "Yeah, *Daaaad*. How come?"

Back to the Rock

Two weeks later, Ronnie passed the exam for the Bureau of Fire Investigation. On the morning of April 4, he found himself back at The Rock, the FDNY Fire Academy on Randall's Island. He was one in a class of fifty, beginning a thirteen-week course that would transform him from a firefighter into a law enforcement officer.

The office of New York City Fire Marshal dates back to 1854, making it one of the oldest investigative agencies in the world.[5] Following the lead of famed detective branches like the Sureté in Paris (1813) and London's legendary Scotland Yard (1842), uniformed investigators began probing the cause and origin of fires in New York City long before the formation of the NYPD's Detectives Bureau, the Secret Service, or the FBI.

The Bureau of Fire Investigation (BFI) was born officially after the tragic Triangle Shirtwaist Factory fire in 1911. One hundred and forty-six female garment workers perished in that blaze—mostly Jewish and Italian girls between the ages of thirteen and twenty-three. Until September 11, the Triangle Shirtwaist disaster represented the largest land-based loss of life from a single New York City fire in this century.[6] Dozens of terrified young women, trapped in the smoke and flames, jumped to their deaths from ninth-floor windows.[7]

In his first day of class at the Fire Academy, Ronnie Bucca listened as his instructor told the story of the blaze that broke out in the cutting room on the eighth floor of the Asch Building on the afternoon of March 25, 1911. The nearest company (72) was only six blocks away, and they arrived within minutes.[8] But their ladders rose only to six floors back then, preventing them from effectively fighting what amounted to a high-rise fire. Life nets held by firefighters broke when the terrified women jumped in groups of three and four. Veteran firefighters stood by, unable to get water to the upper stories as bodies piled up on the sidewalk.

"I remember Ronnie talking about it that night when he got home," said his wife, Eve. "The images of those firefighters watching helplessly as those poor girls jumped. The ladders not high enough to save them. It really had an impact on him."

Ronnie Bucca, the ex–Green Beret paratrooper, had made dozens of rescues in his twenty years on the job. He had rappelled down the sides of skyscrapers to pluck dangling victims to safety. He had jumped into the frigid waters of the East River to save people from drowning, and pulled half a dozen bodies out of smoke-choked infernos. But in every case he'd been dealing with the *consequences* of fire and other life-threatening events. He had spent his career *reacting*; now he was determined to act, to interdict the threat before the damage was done.

Over the next thirteen weeks, Ronnie and the other ex-firefighters in his class learned from architects, chemists, and cops. They studied building construction, the chemistry of incendiaries, and the properties of flammable liquids. They studied the pathology of pyromaniacs, who were driven to set fires. The instructors taught them how to trace a line of volatiles from the point of origin, and how to take samples for analysis at the NYPD lab.[9] They were walked through arson fire scenes, and shown how torches tried to fool investigators by starting fires with oil-soaked mattresses leaned against walls over candles. They learned how to look for "plants," the melted bottoms of plastic milk jugs filled with accelerants.[10]

As the days went by, Ronnie and the other prospective marshals also learned how to "follow the money." They got a fast education in the kind of white-collar crime that leads to fire. One instructor taught them how landmark building status often doomed a city building to arson because the laws made them too expensive to renovate. He showed them the link between wrecking companies and arson fires, where building owners, realizing they had an uninhabitable structure on their hands, would pay to have it knocked down. Then, days after the demolition contract was signed, the building would burn to the ground.

"It's a helluva lot easier for some demo crew to push the debris aside with a bulldozer," the instructor told them, "than to take a building down piece by piece."

Ronnie took furious notes, paying closest attention when instructors came to the point in the course where they talked about arson in the first degree. He had seen his share of death over the years, and he was fascinated when the BFI instructors talked about the relationship of homicide to fire. A 10-45 Code One was the FDNY response call to a fire with death at the scene.

"A lot of times when you walk into a 10-45(1)" said an instructor, "if it's arson, the fire was set to cover the murder. So if you see a body and you're ready to call it accidental—maybe it looks like they've been smoking in bed—look further." In the Bureau of Fire Investigation, arson was known as "the poor man's gun."

By July it was time for the marshal candidates to move up to Camp Smith, the shooting range in Peekskill used by the police department, the fire department, and all the federal agencies, including the DEA and the FBI. In 1992, fire marshals were authorized to carry a .38-caliber revolver as their primary weapon. Ronnie, an expert marksman from his years in Special Forces, chose a Dan Wesson Model 15 .357 magnum, with a Seecamp .32 ACP semiautomatic as his backup gun. Most of the other men had never held a gun before, so while they studied the fundamentals of shooting,[11] Ronnie practiced off to the side, putting tight little two-inch patterns into perp targets.

On July 4, 1992, forty-nine of the fifty original candidates completed the BFI course.

A few weeks later his entire family watched proudly at graduation as the chief fire marshal handed Ronnie a red shield with the number 317 under an eagle holding a flaming torch. He was now a duly sworn law enforcement officer, charged with carrying out the mission of the Bureau of Fire Investigation: to uncover "truth from the ashes."[12]

10

ICE WATER
AND BOMBS

While Ronnie Bucca began his first weeks on the job as an FDNY fire marshal, Ramzi Yousef was halfway around the world plotting to use his skills as a bomb maker to wreak havoc for the jihad. By 1991, after graduating from bomb school, Yousef returned to Baluchistan province in Pakistan. In Turbat, where his family was from, he courted and married a pretty Baluchistani girl who was the sister of Abu Hashim, a Pakistani militant. Yousef is said to have bought a house in Quetta, the Baluchistan capital, and settled down for a time with his young wife. They had two daughters, one born in 1992, the other during Yousef's years on the run.

But though his father was a Baluchistani and his roots were there, Yousef considered himself a Palestinian by way of his mother's family. He spoke Arabic with a Palestinian accent, and more than any other motivation, he was driven by an antipathy for Israel. While other jihadis called for a "perfect Islamic state" that would return them to the seventh-century caliphate,[1] Yousef's hatred was born in the *intifada*, the decades-long struggle of Palestinians for an independent homeland. In his logic, the Israeli suppression of the Palestinians, backed by U.S. support, qualified American civilians as targets.

"I have numerous relatives in Palestine," Yousef said in an interview after his capture. "If terrorist means to regain my land and fight whoever attacks me and my kinsmen, then I have no objection to being called a terrorist. . . . I believe Palestinians [are] entitled to strike U.S. targets because the United States [finances] crimes committed in Palestine. . . . This money is taken from taxes paid by Americans. This makes the American people responsible for all the . . . crimes to which the Palestinian people are subjected. It is no excuse that the American people do not know where their federal tax money goes."[2]

Yousef later compared his World Trade Center bombing to America's use of atomic bombs at Hiroshima and Nagasaki.[3] If these weapons of mass destruction forced the Japanese to surrender, argued Yousef, why not employ the same tactics to get the United States to change its policy toward Israel? What made the bomb maker such a chilling adversary was that he made this argument in a calm, lawyerlike manner. "He's extremely polished and cosmopolitan," said Steve Legon, who represented Yousef in the second World Trade Center bombing trial.[4] He never seemed to resort to the volatile rhetoric of the blind Sheikh, or the fist-pounding theatrics of coconspirators like Abouhalima and Salameh.

"Ramzi was cool," said Frank Gonzalez, the ex–federal agent hired to assist the Yousef defense team. "The man had ice water in his veins—and when you consider some of the things he had planned—the staggering power of the devices he designed, he had to."[5]

Though his personal grudge was with Israel, by 1991, Yousef was ready to enlist in the broader "holy war" that had begun against the Soviets and was now turned toward the West. Despite suspicions that his direction and funding came from Baghdad, the evidence is now overwhelming that from the moment he arrived in America, Yousef's four-year terror campaign was largely financed by Osama bin Laden and endorsed by Sheikh Omar Abdel Rahman.

The effective starting and ending point of Yousef's terror spree was the Philippines, where the first direct Yousef–bin Laden link was forged. In 1988, bin Laden sent his brother-in-law Mohammed Jamal Khalifa to Manila to make contact with Abdurajak Janjalani, the Libyan-trained Filipino jihadi who had fought in Afghanistan against the Soviets.[6] Janjalani's Abu Sayyaf Group (ASG) was ultimately responsible for the kidnap and murder of a number of U.S. tourists and missionaries. Now it was among the first beneficiaries of bin Laden's funding.

According to Edwin Angeles, a onetime Abu Sayyaf leader, Ramzi Yousef met with Janjalani in the summer of 1991 on Basilan Island off the southern Philippines province of Mindanao.[7] At the time, he introduced himself as an emissary of bin Laden and offered to train ASG operatives in the use of explosives. Angeles, who later became an informer for the Philippines National Police, remembered Yousef as "a very humble man, a good man, but a dangerous man." He said Yousef wanted to use the Philippines as a "launching pad" for a worldwide terrorist campaign.[8]

Bin Laden saw the Philippines as ripe for conversion. An English-speaking country with a large Islamic population exploited for decades by Christian leaders like Ferdinand Marcos, the island nation was centrally located in East Asia. Yousef and his coconspirators could operate there under Abu Sayyaf's protection and spread terror in a series of strikes worldwide. The most significant piece of intelligence to come from Angeles was the fact that Yousef (whom he called "the Chemist") had come to the Philippines on behalf of bin Laden *and* Sheikh Omar Abdel Rahman. Later, it was the blind Sheikh who made the phone call to Pakistan that summoned Yousef to New York.[9]

But for now, in the spring of 1992, the Sheikh didn't need him. Rahman's cohorts were counting on another "brother" in their midst who'd boasted of his explosives training: Nancy Floyd's undercover asset, Emad Salem. The Egyptian's identity as an FBI informant had gone undetected by the members of the blind Sheikh's cell. But as with the Mob, snitches paid a heavy price for ratting out al Qaeda. Edwin Angeles, who gave the Philippines police so much information about Yousef, was later shot to death with a bullet to the head by a member of ASG, the very group he had once led.[10]

12 Jewish Locations

By early May of 1992, Salem had burrowed so deeply inside the Sheikh's trusted cell that he was invited to accompany Nosair's cousin El-Gabrowny and another follower on a trip to Attica to visit the rabbi's killer. The gas for the ten-hour car ride was paid for by the FBI. Salem and El-Gabrowny spoke to Nosair in a large visitor's room, where seventy to eighty other people were meeting inmates. The stay lasted five hours, but right away the impatient Nosair spit bile.

"You are doing *nothing* to get me out," said the Egyptian. "I did my part. What are *you* doing?" El-Gabrowny urged patience while they worked on Nosair's appeal. But Kahane's killer eyed the guards and motioned his visitors closer.

"Target the Jews," he said, mentioning specifically Brooklyn assemblyman Dov Hikand and Alvin Schlesinger, the judge who sentenced him. "He was not merciful with me," said Nosair, "and we should have no mercy with him."[11]

"But what do you want us to—"

El-Gabrowny didn't even have the words out when Nosair shot back, "Kidnap them. Hold them until they release me."

Even Salem couldn't hide his skepticism over this plan. "Kidnapping a judge?" he said. "Where are we going to hide him? I mean . . . The FBI is all over."

"You've got to realize these people do not have twenty-four-hour security," said Nosair. "By the weekend, if you surveil him, you can maybe even shoot him. . . ."

"But for this I would need a motorcycle and a sharpshooter," argued Salem.

Nosair leaned forward, boasting, "I was not a sharpshooter, and there were the three hundred in the room. Nobody saw who killed Kahane." Nosair moved his hand to belt level and fired off a mock shot.

"Bingo," as John Anticev would say. Nosair had confessed to the rabbi's slaying. The FBI didn't need permission to bug conversations in the prison visitors' room, and if they'd had audio and video on Nosair, they could have introduced it in court even if Salem hadn't testified to authenticate it. But nobody in the New York office took any serious steps to tape Nosair's Attica rantings until six months later.*

By now, Nosair was amped up. He turned to Salem. "You need to build bombs, set up safe houses. I am rotting in here."

"What kind of bombs?" asked Salem.

"Simple, with a beeper for a detonator," said Nosair. He described an improvised remote detonator in which the bulb would be removed from a pager and replaced with "a Christmas tree bulb." The bulb filament

---

*Timeline #20. p. 5.

would be broken and the device placed near high explosives. When a caller dialed the beeper it would send a charge through the filament, causing a spark that would, in turn, detonate the bomb. "You were in Sadat's army," said Nosair. "Can you do this?"

Salem, the FBI informant, swallowed hard. "Let me think about it, broth—"

But Nosair cut him off. "GET ME OUT!"

As soon as he was back to the city and away from the other Egyptians, Salem phoned Nancy Floyd. She'd been working late again, waiting for his call. When she picked up, Salem almost couldn't contain himself.

"They want me to help them build bombs."

A month later, on June 14, Salem was summoned to Attica again for a progress report. The Egyptian undercover asset brought a fuse he'd bought in Chinatown, but Nosair couldn't be placated. He excitedly told Salem that he'd heard the United States had entered into a deal with Iran to exchange political prisoners. Nosair admonished Salem and another mosque member to contact the Alkifah Center in Brooklyn to see if they could arrange a swap.

It was another signal to the FBI of the importance of the center as a base for the Sheikh's cell. Later, Nosair talked about his plan for bombing a series of targets in the Jewish community. He demanded that Salem get a *fatwa,* from the blind Sheikh.[12]

Within days, the plot began to thicken. Salem learned that the cell planned to set off bombs at a dozen "Jewish locations" in Manhattan and Brooklyn, including banks and synagogues. Salem tried to slow things down by telling Nosair's cousin El-Gabrowny that he would have to get detonators from overseas. El-Gabrowny suggested Afghanistan. But a member of the cell referred Salem to a "Dr. Rashid." He might provide the detonators.

When Salem met the Black Muslim at the Abu Bakr Mosque, "Rashid" told him that he could provide all the weapons he needed, including Uzis and M-16s. Salem briefed Napoli about the meeting— but once again the JTTF missed an important link that would have helped them understand the full dimensions of the Sheikh's cell. As Napoli later found out, "Rashid" was none other than Clement Rodney Hampton-El, one of the shooters photographed at Calverton in 1989.

Apparently, no one at the Bureau thought to show their key informant, Salem, the surveillance photos.*

The failure to tie Hampton-El to the Sheikh's cell was a double miss for the Bureau.

In the surveillance photos of the Calverton shooting sessions, Hampton-El's gray T-shirt had a map of Afghanistan bearing the words *Services Office*. This was the same network that had been transformed by Osama bin Laden into al Qaeda—and by 1991 the Alkifah Center, which Hampton-El frequented and which Nosair hoped would help arrange a swap with Iran, was its Brooklyn hub.

On June 27, 1992, El-Gabrowny met with Salem after another trip to see his cousin Nosair. The rabbi's killer was getting more and more impatient. Having stalled on Dr. Rashid's offer to provide weapons and fully assembled devices, Salem was under increased pressure from the Sheikh's cell to help carry out the citywide bombing plot. After only seven months undercover, he had achieved a position of extraordinary trust among Rahman's followers. If the FBI ever had a chance to understand the links between the blind Sheikh, Osama bin Laden, and the Alkifah Refugee Center—now an al Qaeda front—this was it.

"The plans had been formulated," said an FBI agent inside the investigation. "How many bombs they wanted Salem to build with the help of the other people, who they wanted to target. The thing had been firmed up from the bad guy's side. That's when the ball really got dropped."[13]

"Get That Bitch Off This Case"

From the moment Salem had gone undercover back in the fall of 1991, the Terrorism branch of the FBI's New York office had been operating without a direct supervisor or an assistant special agent in charge. That changed in April 1992, when Special Agent John Crouthamel became branch supervisor and Carson Dunbar, who had been the administrative special agent in charge of the entire New York office, took over as ASAC.

Dunbar, a former New Jersey State Trooper, hadn't worked in the

---

*Timeline #23. p. 6.

field for years. He'd been promoted up the ranks in the FBI's New York office working primarily as an administrator.

"Carson was a paper guy," said an FBI source close to the investigation. "No agents answered to him. But then they moved Terrorism underneath him. Back then the branch was a dumping ground. No one thought it was a plum assignment."

Dunbar was the product of a little-known aspect of the FBI: the two-tiered system that separates brick agents like Floyd and Anticev, who are investigators, from the hierarchy of supervisors, ASACS, and SACs known collectively as "management."

In other law enforcement agencies, like the NYPD, uniformed officers can advance to plainclothes but must then return to uniform at the precinct level in order to move up the ranks. This forces the brass to maintain their street ties, and reminds them of what it takes to make cases.

But the FBI system forces agents who wish to go beyond the top pay grade of GS-13 to volunteer for management. Once that happens, they leave "the street" and the ranks of investigators for the remainder of their Bureau careers.

"All it takes to go management is raising your hand," said retired special agent Len Predtechenskis. "You do a couple of years as a supervisor at headquarters, then you go to a field office as a supervisory GS-14, and you return to headquarters as you move on. But all this time you're a desk jockey. You've stopped being an investigator. So what you have is a system in which managers, many of whom haven't been in the field for years, are signing off on and second-guessing the work of agents who are down in the streets dealing with the real world."[14]

The worst part about the system, says Predtechenskis, is that it forces agents who have developed a specialty in an area like terrorism to leave their field of expertise. "So you have bosses like Carson Dunbar, who had zero terrorism experience, judging them," he said.

Now, in the late spring of 1992, Dunbar's appointment came at the very moment Salem was starting to get results. But when Dunbar and his supervisor, Crouthamel, took charge, they radically altered the game plan for Nancy Floyd and her asset.

"You have to remember that Nancy is meeting with Salem almost every night," said Predtechenskis. "She's holding his hand, debriefing him, supporting him at a time when he can't get through to Anticev and Napoli. He calls her at home. She stays till midnight. Sometimes he meets her at one or two o'clock in the morning. He's come to trust her. The guy is in an extremely dangerous situation, risking his life. He has to have somebody he can count on."

At this point John Crouthamel, the new Terrorism supervisor, called a meeting with Salem, Anticev, and Napoli without Nancy's knowledge. The meeting took place at a midtown hotel. One source remembers Crouthamel trying to convince Salem to work directly with Anticev and Napoli. "We want to remove Nancy from the situation," he reportedly said.[15]

But Len Predtechenskis recalled that the tone was much nastier. According to the decorated ex-agent, Crouthamel told Salem, "We're gonna get that bitch off this case."[16]

Soon after that meeting, the situation was complicated further when John Anticev collapsed on the street with a brain embolism. Though Anticev wasn't permanently disabled, the incident incapacitated him at a critical juncture. "He was completely out of it," said the source. "He couldn't drive. He had to have an agent pick him up."

Anticev would be out of work for the next three months. This meant that if Nancy was removed from the operation, the entire burden of working Salem would fall on NYPD detective Lou Napoli, whom the informant had found elusive in the first place.

The operation began to fall apart when Dunbar learned of a polygraph Salem had taken earlier in the year. The lie detector test had been done behind Nancy's back, while she was on vacation, and the results had come back "inconclusive." But as Lou Napoli later acknowledged, "inconclusive to the Bureau means you failed."[17]

"When she found out about the polygraph, Nancy was upset," said an FBI source. "The way she saw it, they had polygraphed an asset of hers who'd been vindicated many times over."[18]

Floyd felt that the polygraph, routinely given to new informants, was unnecessary for Salem. It created a false cloud of doubt in the Bureau about the ex–Egyptian army major's credibility. Now it was coming back to haunt them, as Dunbar attempted to assert control over the ongoing undercover operation that had preceded him—an investigation launched not on the criminal side of the Bureau that Dunbar knew best, but the counterintelligence side.

In the absence of a Terrorism supervisor and SAC, Nancy Floyd's bosses Jim Sherman and Jack Lowe had hired Salem as an asset months before. Now, rather than embrace him and the extraordinary intelligence he was delivering, Dunbar insisted that Salem reaudition for the part.

The Egyptian was shaken, said the FBI source. "Here he was deep inside the Sheikh's cell, risking his ass, and now the Bureau was changing the play."

With Anticev out of the picture, the only other Bureau agent who could speak directly to Salem's bona fides was Nancy Floyd. She had already been called a "bitch" by Crouthamel, who was trying to get her removed as Salem's control agent, and she soon learned that Carson Dunbar didn't trust her.[19] All of this was going on while Sheikh Rahman's cell continued to plan a deadly wave of bombings intended to rock New York City.

Flying Blind

On July 6, 1992, events went from bad to worse when Dunbar demanded to meet Salem face to face and alone, without Nancy Floyd. Despite the obvious risks in having a clandestine asset appear at the FBI, Dunbar insisted that the meeting take place in his office at 26 Federal Plaza.[20] It would prove to be a defining moment that would have an impact not only on the World Trade Center bombing but on the FBI's capacity to understand Osama bin Laden and his al Qaeda network for years to come.

According to a confidential source, this is how it went:

"First, Salem came in. Carson had his shoes off, and sat across from him cross-legged on the couch, which Salem found to be very insulting. Second of all, Salem felt that Carson had not read the case file. He wasn't familiar with how much crucial information Salem had learned from these guys. Next, Carson talked to Salem like he was a towel-head. That's the exact word Salem used. Carson was talking down to him like he was some dumb, uneducated, stupid person. And he basically told Salem, 'Either you wear a wire and agree to testify, or I don't want to see you anymore.' "[21]

Salem reportedly shot out of that meeting and went straight to see Nancy Floyd and her immediate supervisor in Foreign Counter Intelligence, Jim Sherman.

Months earlier, when Sherman and his ASAC Jack Lowe had brokered the deal with Salem, they'd assured him that as a pure intelligence asset he would never be required to testify as long as he didn't wear a wire in his clandestine meetings. Now, Dunbar's threat to make him testify brought back all his fears. If his identity were exposed, the Sheikh and his cell would surely seek revenge upon him. Salem reportedly paced around Sherman's office, wide-eyed and furious that the tables were being turned on him.

"If I go to court on these men, I am dead," he said. "Please tell me, is it true? If I wear a wire, will I have to testify?"

Nancy looked over at Jim Sherman, who looked back at her. Both of them nodded. Salem later exited, feeling betrayed. The undercover operation was now in jeopardy.

In an interview for this book, Carson Dunbar described the meeting in a much different way. While acknowledging that he may have greeted the Egyptian with his shoes off, Dunbar insisted that he wanted to keep Salem in the game.

"The whole purpose of the meeting was to try and get him to cooperate," said Dunbar.[22] "I told him that there were a whole bunch of things we could do that would prevent him from testifying if he didn't wear a wire."

But Dunbar admitted that one of the options he presented to Salem was that "he could walk away from the case."

"What you can't do," said Dunbar, "is give a one hundred percent guarantee that the person would never be found out as an informant. But that's what he [Salem] was demanding."

In his decision to require Salem to wear a wire, Dunbar was supported by Jim Roth, the principal legal officer in the FBI's New York office.

Speaking publicly for the first time in an interview for this book, Roth made it clear that he had little respect for the Egyptian asset or his recruitment agent, Nancy Floyd.

"Salem is telling Carson and his supervisor all this fantastic information about pipe bombs, but he doesn't want to do anything to help corroborate it, and he's resisting," said Roth. "That was because that dipshit

Floyd would tell him everything they [the supervisors] were thinking about, and how to deal with them."[23]

Roth contends that Nancy had become too possessive of Salem. "She suffered what many agents suffer from in dealing with sources," said Roth. "I call it 'my-guyism.' Only he's not *your* guy. He's the government's guy. You have a business relationship. But with her [and Salem] there were questions in my mind as to who was working for who."

Len Predtechenskis, who was close to the investigation, disagrees.

"Nancy believed, as I did, that we could have kept Salem under," he says. "There were various options we could have pursued. We could have recruited another agent to go in to corroborate what was going on and later testify. We could have done surveillance. But there was no effort by management to find anybody else or get wiretap warrants. Management had already made up its mind. Salem had to testify or he was out. People like Dunbar and Roth, who were sitting behind their desks, had no idea how close a brick agent gets to an informant. You have their life in your hands, and when you fight to protect them, inevitably you're going to have disagreements with management. That's what happened with Nancy."[24]

"The fact that Dunbar still refers to Salem as an 'informant' gives some clue to his state of mind back in 1992," said Kris Kolesnik, the former director of investigations for the Senate Judiciary Subcommittee that investigated the FBI's handling of the incidents at Waco and Ruby Ridge. "Rather than viewing Salem's role as *preemptive,* Dunbar continues to see him in the context of a criminal case."[25]

But Dunbar counters: "You call the public information office at FBI headquarters in Washington. Ask them, asset or informant, if a case goes to court, if there's anybody that can guarantee a person's anonymity. Go ahead. Call them. Don't take my word."[26]

However Salem's role was defined, Dunbar made his distrust for the Egyptian very clear. In late July 2002, during the first public interview he's given about this investigation, the retired ASAC called Salem "a prolific liar."

"We couldn't control him," said Dunbar.[27]

Further, despite the fact that Salem had already gone deep into the Sheikh's cell at the time Dunbar met with him in July of 1992, the ASAC claimed, "We didn't even know if [Salem] had the ability to infiltrate the group. . . . If *we* couldn't trust him, we didn't know if *they* would trust him. He was not believable to us."

An FBI agent at the heart of the investigation, interviewed in early 2003, reacted with shock at that remark. "Saying that Salem couldn't have infiltrated them, when he'd been undercover for months, just tells you that Dunbar hadn't read the file," said the agent. "To take that position, especially now, years later, is remarkable."[28]

But back in July of 1992, the larger question was *Why?* Why, at that point in the investigation, had Carson Dunbar forced Emad Salem into a fish-or-cut-bait position? Dunbar later admitted that, while Salem had given the FBI information about "possible" bombings and kidnappings, there was no case yet to be "taken down."[29]

Under the asset rules of the FBI's Foreign Counter Intelligence branch (FCI), Salem could have continued undercover and unexposed. But Dunbar backed him into a corner, forcing him to either tape his undercover conversations or prove himself with another lie detector test. "I tried to encourage him to wear a wire," Dunbar later testified.[30] "When he decided that he did not want to do that, then I asked him if he would submit to a polygraph."

Following the contentious July 6 meeting with Salem, Dunbar told Nancy Floyd to set up the second test. She felt it was unnecessary, given Salem's track record, but Floyd followed orders. Salem came away from it unhinged.

"For some reason the [polygraph] examiner made the room where the test was conducted really cold," remembered a source close to the test. Extremes in temperature are not conducive to reliable test results. Furthermore, said the source, the examiner and Salem got into a full-blown shouting match. "They were screaming at each other. One of the agents asked the examiner, 'How do you expect this man to pass a polygraph when he's so upset?' "[31] The results of this test and a third poly ordered by Dunbar in September are subject to debate. The source referenced above said the tests were "inconclusive." Jim Roth insisted that they indicated Salem was being "deceptive."

"You have to ask whether this was an exercise in CYA," said FBI oversight expert Kolesnik, "whether the management in the New York office was looking for a way to justify their loss of this potentially valuable asset, once he'd been shut down."[32]

In any case, Dunbar held to his demand that Salem wear a wire if he was to continue undercover. He also required that Nancy Floyd step down as Salem's contact agent.

"They tried to get Nancy out of it," said Len Predtechenskis. "They should have been kissing her ass, because she got [Salem] totally on her own, but Dunbar wasn't believing that Nancy could get something. Before he was an FBI agent, he was a Jersey State Trooper. . . . His background was all criminal. So he was immediately applying the [standard of] wiretaps, [and] testifying. And Nancy's saying, 'No. No. We're not there. Let me find out. Let me work him.' "

Nancy was certain, based on the Bureau's tradition of maintaining pure intelligence agents, that Salem could continue undercover without having to wear a wire. At that point Dunbar had no way of knowing if Nosair's bombing plot would lead to indictments, and he acknowledged later that there were other ways that he could have confirmed information from a confidential informant like Salem, including surveillance.[33]

"It would just take a little more work" on the Bureau's part, an FBI source confirmed. "We'd have to take his leads and do surveillance. Follow these guys and contain the threat. This is what the FBI does."

Predtechenskis was more specific: "I'd have gotten all the information that Emad provided: on this day, at this point, they're gonna do *boom, boom, boom*. Then we would have set up a very discrete, loose surveillance—multiple vehicles—and we'd neutralize them. But you don't give up the source. There was no need to cut this man loose."[34]

Jim Roth, the FBI's lead New York attorney, insisted that without another agent to go undercover and corroborate Salem, the FBI had no choice but to demand that he testify. "Maybe if somebody had searched further around the Bureau and tried harder we would have found somebody," said Roth. "But the bottom line was, we didn't have anybody else. So at that point, for Floyd, there was a duty of loyalty. Dunbar had made a decision, and she should've gotten on board or gotten out of it. Instead, she actively tried to frustrate what Carson was trying to do."

Predtechenskis said that Nancy simply disagreed with Dunbar and sought to lobby others in management to find a way of keeping Salem. She went to her own boss, Jack Lowe, the ASAC in charge of the GRU branch, and reminded him of the Bureau's long-standing practice of running pure intelligence assets who never had to testify. But Lowe, who had approved Salem's undercover role in the first place, was reportedly reluctant to buck another ASAC, and Dunbar prevailed.*

Days later, faced with Dunbar's insistence that he testify, Emad Salem, the FBI's secret weapon inside the bombing conspiracy, decided to withdraw.

"We did not cut him loose," Dunbar insisted in the July 2002 interview. "He walked away from us."

Still, Lou Napoli admitted that Dunbar was the immediate cause of Salem's withdrawal. "Carson pushed it and caused it to end," he said. "Carson pushed it to a point that Emad was fearful that the Bureau would fuck him and he would have to testify."

At that point, Floyd's supervisor told her, 'That's it—let's close him up.'"[35]

To protect his Foreign Counter Intelligence branch, which had initiated Salem's recruitment, supervisor Jim Sherman asked Nancy to give him a memo laying out all the details of Salem's recruitment and the level of intel he'd furnished. The memo was to include the specifics of Dunbar's demand that Salem be worked as a criminal informant, and how the entire operation had unraveled.

Floyd got together with Len Predtechenskis, her mentor, and Bob Burkes and John Sapanara, two other agents from FCI. "We helped her put it down on paper," said Len. "She wrote it up on a twelve-page yellow legal pad. The story of how it happened. Every step. What she did. What Salem did."

The memo was addressed to Jim Fox, the assistant director in charge of the New York office, but it was handed to Nancy's supervisor, Jim Sherman, to be typed and circulated. According to Len Predtechenskis, Sherman read it and put it into his outbox. Nancy was confident that the truth of what happened with Salem would reach the upper management in the New York office.

Now the question remained how the Bureau could best separate from Salem. The ex-Army major, who had quit his job and risked his life for five hundred dollars a week, was told that he would be paid for the next three months while he found other work. But he was no longer an official

---

*Timeline #24. p. 6.

FBI asset. Salem, who had achieved the trust of the blind Sheikh's closest followers, was now faced with his own withdrawal problem: how to get out of the cell without arousing suspicion. The members of the cell were calling him, demanding to know when he would produce the detonators and start building bombs. Finally, Salem told El-Gabrowny that he *had* to withdraw from the plot. He used the excuse that he suspected the FBI was tailing him. Given the earlier encounter with Anticev and Napoli outside Nosair's trial, El-Gabrowny bought the story.

What had developed as perhaps the most important undercover operation in the history of the FBI's war on terrorism was over.

Now, when it came to Nosair, the bombing plot, and Sheikh Omar Abdel Rahman—the Federal Bureau of Investigation was essentially flying blind.

11

A VERY
DANGEROUS JOB

A few weeks later, Ronnie Bucca was on the range at Camp Smith practicing with a new semiautomatic he'd just purchased. Now that he'd gone on the job in plainclothes, he wanted a weapon that was easier to conceal than the bulky .357 revolver. He'd chosen the Sig Sauer P 228, and already his accuracy had improved. He was now getting the two-inch patterns into targets thirty feet away.[1] Since serving as a door gunner on a helicopter in Vietnam, Ronnie had never fired a weapon at another human being, and he hoped he'd never have to. But he'd been worried of late over some intelligence he'd picked up through DIA, so he wanted to stay sharp.

He'd kept his discussions about terrorism to a minimum, especially around his kids. But on this day in early August of 1992, when Eve picked him up, Ronnie seemed uneasy. In the car on the way home, she asked him what was wrong.

"Something's going down in the city," he said.[2]

"Like what?" asked Eve, knowing he could only tell her so much of what he'd learned from his work in Army intel.

"The Bureau had a source who infiltrated the cell of this blind Sheikh in Jersey," said Ronnie. "Word is they're making a move on some major targets."

Eve kept her eyes on the road.

"So that's good, right? They know ahead of time."

"Yeah," said Ronnie. "Except now the guy's out."

"How come?"

"We don't know."

There was a pause between them; then Eve smiled. "Whatever it is, they'll stop it, right? I mean they're the FBI."

Ronnie thought it about, then nodded. "Yeah. Maybe."

At this point he changed the subject. He'd just received his orders after putting in his application for an assignment in the Bureau of Fire Investigation. Manhattan was the borough most marshals wanted to work in, but it was reserved for the more senior men. Ronnie had requested Bronx Base because he thought he'd see more action there. The Buccas lived north of the city, so it was also closer to home.

He pulled out his BFI assignment letter and handed it to Eve. She was thrilled. Her husband was a fire marshal now. For the first time in years, he'd be going into buildings *after* the fires were out.

Little did she know just how life-threatening the job could be.

In his first few months in the BFI, Ronnie Bucca began to distinguish himself as an investigator. "I got word about Ronnie even before he came into the BFI academy," said his instructor Bill Manahan. "He was a special guy. In the Bureau we attract a lot of guys who can't get along in the firehouse. Ronnie was the opposite. He was a top-notch firefighter, and when he came through training he was one of the best I ever had."[3]

Years after his fall on the Upper West Side, Ronnie's close friends in Rescue One still called him "the flying firefighter." But when he became a marshal, he never traded on his rep. Even his partners had no idea how extensive Bucca's background was in the Special Forces or rescue. His first partner and mentor in the marshals was also stunned by his humility. Leroy Haynes had spent twenty-eight years with the FDNY. He became a marshal after almost losing his life while fighting a fire in the Bronx with 92 Engine.

"It was back in '78," said Haynes. "We were doing six thousand runs a year at 92 and 88 Engine alone."[4] An African American, Haynes came on the job at a time when many people in the inner city saw all uniforms—even firefighters—as hostile representatives of "the man."

"Back then they would set a diesel fuel fire on an upper floor," said

Haynes. "It would take longer to put out, and then they'd come in behind you and set a gasoline fire and you'd be trapped."

Having come so close to being an arson victim himself, Haynes decided to put in for the BFI. He'd been a marshal for fourteen years and was one of the most experienced investigators in the Bronx when he was assigned to break in a rookie named Ronnie Bucca.

"I see this white boy, and I'm thinking I'm going to have to watch his back," said Haynes. "To protect him from the ways of the street. But it was just the opposite. Ronnie *was* street. He'd come out of the Queens projects, and he'd been in Rescue. He carried himself real low-key. He wasn't confrontational. And that was important, 'cause we used to roll up into some neighborhoods that the cops wouldn't even go to without backup. This can be a very dangerous job."

Haynes remembered one incident, when he and Bucca were checking a crack house in a derelict building. "We got out of the car. I said to Ronnie, 'I've got your back,' and he just smiled. So we went up in there and the place was full of hard-core users. You could see burn marks on the floors and walls from where they'd used those butane torches to light the pipes."

The two fire marshals got separated in the hallway and Haynes went in first. "All of a sudden, I feel this guy right behind me," said Haynes. "On my back. One of the users. He's like, 'Hey, man, who the hell are you?' And before I could put my hand on my weapon, Ronnie came up and had the guy. Slam-bam. That fast."

Haynes looked at Ronnie and said, "What part of Queens did you say you were from?"

As he learned the craft of fire investigation, Bucca found himself bringing all his skills to bear: his Special Forces operational training as well as his knowledge of "the red devil," the term FDNY veterans use to describe fire.

"He was also a great interrogator," said Haynes. "Ronnie knew how to talk to people. How not to be confrontational. To get down on the level of a suspect and relate. He was never judgmental. I think humility is maybe the most important quality in an investigator. Humility and tenacity, and Ronnie had both."

Now, as the summer of 1992 ended, Ronnie would need all those qualities. Across the city, a plot was being set in motion that would soon result in the greatest arson fire in New York history.

The Evil Genius

It's still unknown precisely how El Sayyid Nosair's "twelve Jewish locations" bombing plot escalated to the next deadly stage. The evidence seized at Nosair's home after his arrest shows that the World Trade Center had been considered a possible target by the blind Sheikh's cell as early as 1990. Now, two years later, as his trusted bodyguard and explosives expert Salem withdrew from the bombing conspiracy, Sheikh Rahman decided that his "army" should take the jihad to another level. The time had come to take down "the edifices of capitalism," and that required a bomb maker with technical skill and great vision.

Sometime in August, the Sheikh placed a call to a number in Pakistan: 810604.[5] Later that month, Ramzi Yousef bought a first-class ticket on a Pakistan International Airlines flight to JFK. The "evil genius" was coming to New York.

When PIA Flight 703 from Karachi touched down at Kennedy on the evening of September 1, 1992, the two men who emerged from first class couldn't have looked more different. Ahmad Mohammed Ajaj, twenty-five, was dressed in jeans and a T-shirt. He had lived for a time in Houston, and worked as a Domino's Pizza delivery man.[6] To look at him, you would never think that inside his luggage were four passports, videos of suicide car bombings, documents on fabricating fake IDs, and plans for constructing bombs.

His partner in first class had a passport and airline ticket in the name of Azan Mohammed. Dressed in a three-piece Afghan suit with enormous puffed sleeves over shalwar pants, he looked like he'd just escaped from a Mideast detention cell. The two men quickly parted and went to separate INS stalls in JFK's international arrivals terminal.

When the swarthy, bearded Ajaj pulled out a Swedish passport in the name of Khurram Khan, INS Agent Cathy Bethom's eyes narrowed. It was clear that the picture of Ajaj had been crudely pasted over the face of a Swedish national. Bethom peeled the picture away and signaled for armed INS agents to grab Ajaj. Suddenly he erupted, screaming.

"No! My mother was Swedish. My father was Pakistani. If you don't believe me, check your computer!"

During all this commotion, the man in shalwar pants had worked his way up to the counter of the next stall. He politely eyed INS Agent Martha Morales. She looked up at him, then down at the Iraqi passport and ticket in the name of Azan Mohammed.

"You have no U.S. visa," said the agent. "Do you have any other ID?" The man smiled and pulled out an identity card from the Al Bunyan Islamic Center in Tucson, Arizona. It contained his picture, but the name on the card said Khurram Khan.

Agent Morales nodded to Cathy Bethom in the next stall. "Didn't that last guy say his name was Khan? Khurram Khan?" Bethom nodded. Agent Morales turned back to the man in the puffed sleeves standing over her. In contrast to Ajaj, he was very calm.

"What is your full true name?" she asked. Without even blinking, he shot back, "Ramzi Ahmed Yousef." He eyed her for a second and then said, "I want political asylum."

Moments later, in an interrogation room, Ajaj's luggage was being examined by other INS agents. Inside, under a false bottom, they found the videos and bomb books, along with fake passports from Jordan, England, and Saudi Arabia. Ajaj's picture was on each one.

The young Palestinian was read his rights and placed under arrest. He would soon be transported to the INS detention center on Varick Street in Lower Manhattan.

But by now, in a nearby room, Agent Morales was pressing Yousef. She took him through the form for refugees requesting asylum. Yousef raised his right hand and swore that if he were not allowed to remain in the States he would be persecuted on his return. He told her that he had been locked up in one of Saddam Hussein's prisons. He'd been subject to brutal torture. Yousef showed her his scars, which he said he'd received at the hands of Iraqi interrogators.

Despite his low-key demeanor, Agent Morales didn't like the way all this looked—the fact that this Yousef had presented an ID card with the name of another Middle Eastern passenger who'd been found with multiple fake passports and bomb-making manuals; the fact that the two of them had been seated next to each other on the plane; the fact that they'd flown in first class, far from the norm for most political refugees.

So she followed her gut and went to her supervisor. Reviewing the evidence, Morales suggested that Yousef be detained. But the supervisor disagreed. Ajaj had just gotten the last bed in the Varick Street detention facility. There was no more room for another detainee.

"Give him a walk-in 240," said the supervisor, ordering Agent Morales to give Yousef the form he would have to fill out to get an asylum hearing date.

"But sir, I think this guy's dirty."

"Give him the form."

Agent Morales bit her tongue and returned to the room where Yousef was sitting. She told him that he would be granted an asylum hearing on December 8. Yousef quickly filled out the form 240 and nodded.

Agent Morales stared at him. Yousef eyed her back.

"What will happen to me now?" he asked in the tone of a grateful refugee. Agent Morales rolled her eyes.

"You're free to go," she said. The words tasted bad as they came out.

Yousef looked stunned. He had just watched his accomplice Ajaj get arrested. "What are you telling me?"

"You can leave, Mr. Yousef. Welcome to the United States."

Yousef smiled. He got up and left the terminal as fast as he could without running. He couldn't believe it had been so easy. Ajaj had been his intended smoke screen, but he never expected that his path into New York would be so clear.

Despite the first-class ticket, Yousef had arrived with next to no money in his pocket. So he walked along the line of cabs outside the terminal until he found one with a Pakistani driver. Dressed in the Afghan suit, Yousef tapped on the driver's window.

"Brother, I've just arrived from Karachi," he said. "I have friends who will pay. Would you please perform an act of kindness and take me to this place?"

He handed the cabbie a piece of paper that said "552 Atlantic Avenue," the address of the Al Farooq Mosque where the Alkifah Refugee Center was located.

This was the place that the murdered Mustafa Shalabi had founded on behalf of the murdered Abdullah Azzam; the center for propaganda and fund-raising that had become a front for Osama bin Laden's al Qaeda network. It was from this address that the FBI Special Operations

Group surveillance team had followed Mahmud Abouhalima, Moham-med Salameh, and Nidal Ayyad to their Calverton shooting sessions three years earlier. Now, as the taxi headed west on the Belt Parkway, Yousef was on his way to meet them.

If anyone could design a device that would strike terror into the hearts of the infidels, it was the man with the milky-gray eyes from Baluchistan. Yousef's own personal fight was with the state of Israel, but like thousands of other "Afghan Arabs," the radical young jihadis in Yousef's province had never forgotten the Crusades. They had never forgiven the Christian hordes that had poured down out of Europe to wipe out Islamic princes like Saladin. These new soldiers in the holy war had waited a thousand years for revenge, and it was up to Yousef to give it to them.

The FBI didn't make the mistake of allowing Yousef into the country. That was the responsibility of the INS.* But once he'd arrived, they would miss a dozen chances to capture him.

Follow "The Red"

By early October, Ramzi Yousef was well on his way to designing and building a huge explosive device. He had moved into an apartment with Mohammed Salameh at 251 Virginia Avenue in Jersey City, across the river in New Jersey.

This was the site of his early planning meetings with Mahmud Abouhalima and an Iraqi student named Abdel Rahman Yasin. Soon they were joined by Nidal Ayyad, a naturalized Kuwaiti. Tall and lanky, Ayyad had a degree from Rutgers in chemical engineering. Solidly middle class, he lived with his mother and younger brothers in the Jersey suburbs. He made thirty-five thousand dollars a year working at Allied Signal, and had just become engaged. Like many of the 9/11 hijackers years later, he didn't fit *any* known profile of a terrorist plotting to com-mit mass murder. But it was Ayyad who opened the first in a series of bank accounts with Salameh to fund the plot. Some were individual accounts and others were jointly held. Over the next few months, more than a hundred thousand dollars would be wired into the accounts, transferred from banks in Germany and the Mideast.

---

*Timeline #26. p. 6.

By late November, Yousef began acquiring the chemicals that would feed the bomb. The other members of the cell called him "Rashed,"[7] but Yousef, as always, was a man of many names. Using the alias Kamal Ibraham,[8] he paid $3,615 in cash for a thousand pounds of urea from City Chemical in Jersey City. On the same day, using the same name, Mohammed Salameh rented a ten-by-ten-foot storage locker at the Space Station, a facility on Mallory Avenue. He paid the ninety-dollar monthly rent in cash. The chemicals were delivered to Kamal and Company at the storage locker, along with 105 gallons of nitric acid and 60 gallons of sulfuric acid. Yousef/Kamal specified that the nitrogen content of the urea crystals be high (46.65 percent); the sulfuric acid had to be 93 percent pure.

"Ramzi was a genius when it came to bomb building," said ex–U.S. postal inspector Frank Gonzalez, who met with Yousef years later as part of his defense team. In more than seventy thousand bombs that had been examined over the years by the FBI lab, they had never encountered such a urea-nitrate–fuel oil device.

As the weeks passed, Yousef and Salameh moved to another apartment, at 40 Pamrapo Avenue in Jersey City. This became the bomb factory. Given the size of the device, it took them days to generate enough of the lethal mixture. Yousef would soak the urea in a water solution inside a blue trash can, then add the nitric acid, spreading out the mixture to dry. Salameh would then drive each new batch to the storage locker.[9]

Meanwhile, though he'd ended his formal relationship with the FBI in July, Emad Salem was still receiving his weekly salary of five hundred dollars a week to tide him over until he found another job. During the summer of 1992, Nancy Floyd would meet with him at the Subway sandwich shop near the FBI's New York office to give him the remaining cash payments.

She'd had less and less contact with her asset since Dunbar had forced him out. Now, at their final meeting in the fall, Salem looked worried. He'd warned Nancy previously that things were going on in the Sheikh's cell, and that the Bureau should be following Ibrahim El-Gabrowny. They should be taping his visits to his cousin Nosair in Attica. More important, they should be watching El-Gabrowny's other cousin,

Mohammed Salameh, and his partner in crime, Mahmud Abouhalima—the two men seized at Nosair's house the night of Kahane's slaying.

Unbeknownst to the Feds, Salameh had become Yousef's right arm in the bomb construction. He was with him literally around the clock, driving his 1978 Chevy Nova to and from the storage locker and the various banks they were using. Abouhalima was helping to move the chemicals back and forth and acting as overall facilitator. In recent weeks Emad Salem had kept his distance from the principal players, like Nosair's cousin El-Gabrowny, so he didn't know many details. But by early fall he'd picked up rumors that another bombing plot was afoot. As Salem met with Nancy, he implored her to talk to Napoli and Anticev.

"Get them to follow the Red," he said, referring to Abouhalima. "This is what the FBI does, right? They follow people?"

Having recovered from his brain embolism, Special Agent John Anticev had since returned to work. But without their key informant inside, his investigation with Detective Napoli had hit a wall. By mid-September, two weeks after Yousef's arrival, the two of them had grown so desperate that they issued subpoenas to Abouhalima, El-Gabrowny, and twenty-six members of the Abu Bakr and al-Salaam Mosques. They ordered them down to the FBI's New York office in the faint hope that maybe they could shake one or two of them into confessing.

As usual, the Egyptians were way ahead of them. Meeting at the Abu Bakr Mosque the night before, they ran through a game plan that would confound the Feds. The next day, September 15, about twenty of them assembled at the Warren Street Mosque in Lower Manhattan and walked to 26 Federal Plaza. Ahmed Sattar, the mailman, even used his federal ID at the door to help get them into the lobby.[10] The agents came down and brought them upstairs, where they were immediately confronted by the Calverton surveillance photos. The men were fingerprinted and interrogated about the Kahane and Shalabi murders and a rumored plot to kill Egyptian president Mubarak. In order to preserve his cover, the FBI included Salem in the group.

In separate interrogation rooms they pressed the Egyptians. "Do you know Nosair?" they demanded. "What about Sheikh Omar?" It was a ham-handed attempt to shake them. At one point Anticev issued a warning to Sattar: "We're going to get them," he said. "Abdel Rahman and

Nosair. Sooner or later we will. John Gotti was put on trial two times and we got him."[11]

But if the Feds thought they could rattle the Egyptians into admitting they were terrorists, they were dead wrong. Nobody confessed to anything. Everyone who was questioned left. Not a single charge was filed, and the FBI was back to square one.

Now, in early October 1992, as Yousef worked away on his bomb in Jersey City, Emad Salem was about to leave Nancy Floyd with a chilling warning. She'd come to this last meeting at the Subway shop with Ray Palmowski, a fellow agent. As she handed Salem his final envelope of cash, the ex-asset reminded her about Abouhalima and Salameh. The Bureau should be following them.

Nancy said she'd pass the message along, but she was no longer involved in the investigation. She had transferred to an undercover detail with the Special Operations Group. Salem just shook his head.

Nancy thanked him for all he'd done, for putting himself at risk by going under. Loyal to Nancy, but bitter that Dunbar had forced him to withdraw, Salem got up to leave. He was almost to the door when he stopped and turned to face her. The last thing he said was, "Don't call me when the bombs go off."

12

DOT AFTER DOT
AFTER DOT

As Yousef and the Sheikh's cohorts built the device, the blind cleric himself was becoming an embarrassment to another federal agency—the Immigration and Naturalization Service.

In April of 1991, the INS had approved the Sheikh's application for permanent residence—this despite the fact that he'd slipped into the country with his name on a State Department Watch List and had since been linked in the media to Kahane's killer and the death of Mustafa Shalabi. But now the fifty-five-year-old cleric, who feigned helplessness, was becoming a liability for the Clinton administration, which was counting on Egypt as a key ally in the Mideast peace process. A firebrand when he got behind the pulpit, Abdel Rahman openly called for the murder of Egyptian president Mubarak, advising his followers that "assassination for the sake of rendering Islam triumphant is legitimate."[1] The blind Sheikh was pushing his luck.

In June of 1992, with his welcome back in Egypt unlikely, and happy to use metropolitan New York as a staging ground for terror, the Sheikh boldly made an application for political asylum. In a true measure of his audacity, the application was filed at the very moment his disciple Nosair was exhorting Emad Salem to bomb a series of "Jewish locations" across the city.

The application backfired. By August, the Sheikh was stripped of the green card the INS had given him the year before. But deportation proceedings were protracted. The first INS hearing on his application for asylum was recessed in October and rescheduled for January 20, 1993. Now, after the first of the year, even as Yousef and his followers built their bomb, the Sheikh was waiting for the United States to grant him a permanent safe haven.

Despite the plot that was being carried out in secret by his cell members, the Sheikh's own public profile was very high. On January 7, 1993, the *New York Times* ran a major profile on the cleric entitled "A Cry of Islamic Fury, Taped in Brooklyn for Cairo."

Noting that the Sheikh's sermons were regularly taped for distribution worldwide, the piece by Chris Hedges quoted an Egyptian official as wondering "why the U.S. authorities allowed [Sheikh Rahman] to enter the country" in the first place. At that point, according to the story, the FBI was "investigating the Sheikh for possible involvement in the slaying of Mustafa Shalabi . . . as well as the slaying of Rabbi Kahane." As late as February 13, less than two weeks before the World Trade Center bombing, the FBI obtained a warrant under the Foreign Intelligence Surveillance Act (FISA)[2] and began tapping the blind Sheikh's phone calls. The very granting of a FISA warrant suggested that the FBI had evidence Abdel Rahman and his associates were "a group engaged in international terrorism or activities in preparation thereof."

Over the coming months the FBI recorded hours of Rahman's conversations—sixty-three tapes in all before the surveillance was ended. But even though the Sheikh was in regular contact with Abouhalima and had met for dinner with Ramzi Yousef, the FBI later claimed to have no prior knowledge of the enormous bomb being built at 40 Pamrapo Avenue.

Again, the question is *Why?* Without its inside mole, Emad Salem, the FBI had lost a key asset. But given the intelligence he'd already generated and the depth of the file on the Sheikh's cell going back to Calverton in 1989, the Bureau had ample opportunity to pick up on Salem's warning and follow Abouhalima and Salameh. The big redheaded Egyptian and the diminutive Palestinian were interacting with Yousef daily. Properly surveilled, they could have led the FBI straight to the bomb.

There's little question that by now the Bureau had probable cause for warrants to search their homes and wiretap their phones. Anticev and Napoli had the paramilitary training photos from Calverton showing Abouhalima and Salameh firing semiautomatic weapons. They had the boxes of evidence from Nosair's house full of Top Secret manuals, bomb recipes, and maps of New York targets, including the Trade Center.

Abouhalima and Salameh had been seized in Nosair's home at the very moment that evidence was collected. Beyond that, Anticev and Napoli had linked Abouhalima to Nosair via the killer's multiple phone calls to Weber (the Red's wife). They'd heard a neighbor describe the big Egyptian as a terrorist. They'd even obtained a warrant to search his apartment as far back as 1991. At that point Anticev and Napoli had probable cause; now they had even more compelling evidence that the two were tied into a bombing conspiracy.

Mohammed Salameh was Ibrahim El-Gabrowny's cousin. El-Gabrowny had brought Salem into the plot to bomb "twelve Jewish locations." He'd asked Salem to obtain detonators to set off "high-powered explosives." Salameh was a disciple of the blind Sheikh. On the trip to Detroit, Abdel Rahman had asked Salem if he was capable of setting off explosives and killing the Egyptian president.

By February 1993 the Feds had enough probable cause to suspect the Sheikh that they began tapping his phone,[3] but somehow they couldn't pull it together to follow Abouhalima and Salameh. Salem had proven himself to be a reliable informant who would have certainly generated probable cause under the *Rosario* rules.

The reports to the asset file that Nancy Floyd had dutifully typed after each of Salem's sessions with the Sheikh's cohorts laid all this out. After being cut loose, he virtually begged the agents to follow Salameh and the Red.

"Could they have followed these guys? Absolutely," said Frank Gonzalez, the agent who spent twenty-one years with the U.S. Postal Inspection Service.[4] "The FBI unit in charge of domestic terrorism could have proceeded the same way they conduct an organized crime investigation. You ID the main players, find out through surveillance who their associates are, and you go out and find them. On the basis of Emad Salem's word alone, they could have gotten Title III warrants for pen registers and traps to trace their phone calls.[5] They could have then verified their addresses and sat on them, then followed people like Abouhalima to see where he went."

Eluding the Group That "Got Gotti"

As 1992 turned into 1993, the New York FBI couldn't seem to find either Mahmud Abouhalima or Mohammed Salameh.

Why not? In the days after the bombing, Anticev would say simply, "You can't monitor somebody twenty-four hours a day."[6] But of course the Bureau could do just that. In fact, if there was ever an FBI office equipped for round-the-clock surveillance, it was New York. By 1993 it was being run by James Kallstrom, the special agent in charge who had built his legendary reputation in the Bureau by setting up the FBI's Special Operations Group.[7]

The New York SOG was the elite black bag unit that "got Gotti." After three failed attempts to convict the mob boss, the SOG installed listening devices in the apartment of a woman who lived above the Teflon Don's social club. The tapes of Gotti's clandestine conversations with his capos helped put him away.

As journalist Ron Kessler noted in the first of two extraordinary FBI studies,[8] Kallstrom's agents would "conduct surveillance in criminal cases, install wiretapping devices, break into homes and offices to install bugs, bypass alarm systems, place tracking devices on cars, break into computers, wire undercover agents for sound, command suspects' answering machines to play back messages, and pilot surveillance planes."[9] It was the kind of cloak-and-dagger capability that had cemented the Bureau's crime-fighting reputation.

Back in 1989, suspecting "international terrorism," it was this same New York SOG that had committed a half dozen agents and five vehicles on four Sundays in a row to follow Abouhalima, Salameh, Nosair, and Ayyad as they trained with automatic weapons at Calverton. Now it was three and a half years later, and the evidence of an international conspiracy to bomb New York was mounting. The question is, why couldn't the FBI use a similar detail to track down Abouhalima and Salameh once more? Either of those cell members would have led the FBI straight to Ramzi Yousef, a man who made John Gotti look like a Disney character.

Now, at that very moment, he was across the river in Jersey City building a device designed to killed thousands. Given the go-ahead by FBI supervisors in New York, why couldn't the SOG locate him? It wasn't as if Yousef were invisible. In fact, in the months before the bombing, he'd had multiple contacts with police.*

In November 1992, Yousef actually paid a visit to a Jersey City police station. Using the named Abdul Basit, he filed a report of a lost passport. He later showed up at the Pakistani consulate in Manhattan and applied for a new passport under the Basit name.

Yousef also made regular trips to locker 4334 at the Space Station, where the chemicals were stored, and the telephonic trail he left was riddled with clues. He was repeatedly seen by witnesses using a pay phone outside the Pamrapo Avenue apartment.[10] He made more than eighteen thousand dollars worth of phone calls from the bomb factory to contacts in the Middle East, Pakistan, Turkey, and Yugoslavia.[11] Further, if the Feds had installed a trap to monitor Abouhalima's calls, they would have discovered at least eight from Pamrapo Avenue[12] and four on February 3, 1993, from the Trade Center itself.

Ramzi Yousef was so bold during this period that he even allowed himself to be captured by an ATM camera withdrawing funds while he made a phone call using another person's phone card.[13] In one of the comic ironies of this story, after Yousef's flight to Pakistan following the bombing, his parents were reportedly harassed by phone company representatives seeking to collect on the exorbitant phone bills that he owed. Once the name Yousef surfaced in the press alongside his original name, Abdul Basit, the dunning notices went out. The *phone company* managed to locate Yousef's parents. Why couldn't the FBI?[14]

In December, Yousef went so far as to contact his first-class JFK travel mate Ajaj, who was serving an eight-month sentence at Otisville federal prison in upstate New York. Using his phone privileges from lockup, Ajaj called a phone number registered to Big Five Hamburgers in Mesquite, Texas. A coconspirator there used Southwestern Bell's three-way calling feature to patch Ajaj through to the man he called "Rashed"

---

*Timeline #29. p. 7.

at the Pamrapo Avenue apartment. In a series of conversations Yousef openly discussed a way to retrieve the bomb-making manuals seized when Ajaj was arrested.

The two of them used code words, calling the bomb plot "the study" and the bombing manuals "the university papers." But the secrecy was hardly necessary. The calls were taped by the prison, but apparently not reviewed until much later.

"I don't think they ever listened in on Ajaj until it was too late," said Frank Gonzalez. "Here's this guy calling interstate to a burger joint in Texas from jail and getting through to Ramzi while he's building the bomb and the Bureau never knew. Amazing."[15] It was another key lead that was missed.

But the next lead the Feds blew was even more astounding. On December 22, 1992, a judge in the U.S. District Court for the Eastern District of New York ruled that the government had to return all of Ajaj's belongings seized at JFK—including his bomb manuals. That victory resulted in a three-way call from Ajaj to Yousef via Texas on December 29. Yousef asked that the manuals be sent to him at Pamrapo Avenue.

After initially agreeing, Ajaj began to worry that the shipment might threaten Yousef's "business . . . which would be a pity." So the documents remained with the government.[16] Among the materials being held by the Feds was a letter of introduction to the Khalden al Qaeda training camp in Afghanistan, where Ajaj had reportedly met Yousef.[17] But even more important, one of the bomb manuals contained words written in Arabic, which the government had mistakenly translated as "The Basic Rule." Later, terrorism expert Stephen Emerson concluded that the translation should have been "The Base," a literal translation of "al Qaeda."[18] Here was evidence, seized by the INS and held by the Feds in 1992, that the man Ramzi Yousef had entered the United States with was linked directly to Osama bin Laden's terror network.

"Had the Government correctly translated the material," Emerson said, "it might have understood that the men who blew up the World Trade Center and Mr. Bin Laden's group were linked."

"One would think," said a lawyer with knowledge of the investigation, "that the FBI's Terrorist Task Force, which had been warned by its own informant of a bombing conspiracy, might monitor a federal proceeding where bomb manuals were at issue."[19] This was another enormous dot missed—and as the days passed in January and Yousef constructed the bomb, there would be more.

Escape to New Jersey

On January 21, a traffic accident gave the Feds yet another chance to interdict the plot. Driving Yousef in his Chevy Nova on the way to a meeting with Abouhalima, Salameh lost control of the car and hit the curb with such force that he was thrown to the pavement. The car was totaled, and Yousef, pinned inside, was given a neck brace. He was taken to Rahway Hospital in New Jersey where he was strapped down on a board for ten hours.[20] The bomb maker actually gave his name as Ramzi Yousef, the same name he'd used at JFK when he was granted an asylum hearing.

Yousef had been given a hearing date of December 8, 1992. It was now seven weeks later. Having failed to show up for the proceeding, he was technically now in the country illegally. The bomb maker could have been arrested on the spot by INS agents. But he was so confident the Feds wouldn't find him that he actually used his bogus phone card to order chemicals via the hospital phone.

In mid-February, Nidal Ayyad took a day off from work, rented an Oldsmobile, and made a reconnaissance trip to the World Trade Center with Mohammed Salameh.[21]

He left the car in the Twin Towers' garage and sketched the floor plan, noticing that the Port Authority vans that serviced the Trade Center were yellow.

Then, incredibly, as Salameh drove back to Jersey, he was sideswiped by another car and questioned by police for forty-five minutes.* The Palestinian, who had failed his driving test four times, was ultimately released, but the accident was the last straw for Yousef. Concerned about Salameh's driving skills, the bomb maker reached out for a new wheelman. He put in a call in to Eyad Ismoil, a lifelong friend now living in Dallas. Ismoil, a Jordanian who had studied in Kansas, showed up twelve days later. He later gave interrogators the preposterous story that he

---

*Timeline #29. p. 7.

believed the van he'd been called to New York to drive was to be loaded with shampoo.[22]

On February 24, with the bomb in the final stages of construction, Ayyad rented a red Chevy Corsica and drove Salameh to DIB Leasing, a Ryder rental dealership on Kennedy Boulevard in Jersey City. Salameh put down a four-hundred-dollar cash deposit and rented a ten-foot yellow panel van for fifty-nine dollars a day. The address he gave the Ryder clerk was 57 Prospect Park Southwest, Apt. 4C, Brooklyn, New York. It was the former residence of convicted shooter El Sayyid Nosair, currently occupied by his cousin Ibrahim El-Gabrowny.*

El-Gabrowny was the same man who had coaxed Salem into the first bombing conspiracy; the man who had personally obtained a reported twenty thousand dollars from Osama bin Laden for Nosair's defense. He was also one of the Egyptians the FBI had subpoenaed and released on September 15. How much of a stretch would it have been for Anticev and Napoli to make those connections and find Salameh—especially if they'd been monitoring El-Gabrowny's visits to Attica?

As it turned out, Mohammed Salameh had accompanied his cousin El-Gabrowny to see Nosair less than two weeks before he picked up the Ryder van.[23]

Afterward, Abdel Rahman Yasin, the Iraqi who earlier shared an apartment with Salameh at Kensington Avenue—gave the Palestinian driving lessons. With Yousef's plot nearing completion, you couldn't be too careful. Yasin, a City College student, was the only native-born U.S. citizen in the bombing plot.

Now, in the final stages of bomb construction, Yousef decided that he needed compressed hydrogen to increase the bomb's blast radius. But the chemical, considered a signature of Mideast terror bombers, couldn't be located. Then, on the morning of February 25, Ayyad called from his company, Allied Signal, to tell Yousef that he'd found a company that would sell them four tanks. They were delivered to the Space Station storage facility and loaded into the yellow Ryder van, which had an Alabama license plate: XA70668. Present for the delivery was Mahmud Abouhalima, who was driving his blue Lincoln.

---

*Timeline #33. p. 8.

For weeks now, the big cabdriver had acted as Yousef's chief expeditor in the plot. He'd ferried chemicals back and forth from the Pamrapo Avenue bomb factory in the trunk of his Lincoln and purchased the black powder Yousef used to wrap into slow-burning fuses. It's difficult to see how the redheaded Egyptian could have slipped off the FBI's radar screen. In fact, as late as December 1992, Emad Salem called Anticev to tell them that Abouhalima had left a message on his phone machine.* So the FBI knew he was around. Still, for all its high-tech surveillance capabilities, the New York office couldn't find him.

Until now, the reason was a mystery. Then, in an interview for this book, Detective Lou Napoli offered an unsettling explanation: The FBI couldn't locate Abouhalima, he said, *because he'd gone to New Jersey.*

"Abouhalima beat feet on us," said Napoli. "We were trying to locate him, but he went to Jersey. Salameh was in Jersey. You've got to remember there are boundaries. The Hudson River separates New York and New Jersey. To work on Abouhalima and Salameh I would have had to work through [the FBI office in] Newark. The Task Force is a New York terror task force. Our boundaries are New York."[24]

But a veteran FBI agent who worked in the New York office disagreed. "What Napoli said would be totally false," said the source. "I worked numerous cases [out of the New York office] where the subjects lived in New Jersey. The idea that they couldn't have followed Abouhalima across state lines or needed to get permission is ridiculous."[25]

So if it wasn't a question of jurisdiction, and the FBI had the technical know-how to mount surveillance, how did they blow it?

"There were supervisors in the New York office who came from this arrogant point of view that nobody was ever going to attack the United States," said the FBI source.[26] "To them these Muslims were not a threat. They were a Bedouin people running around the desert with no education. We were the big bad USA, smart and intelligent, and they weren't."

Julian Stackhouse, an agent in the New York office at the time, suggested that some share of responsibility must rest with Carson Dunbar.

---

*Timeline #31. p. 7.

As the ASAC who approved the deployment of surveillance resources for the Special Operations Group, it was Dunbar's job to sanction the monitoring of suspects like Abouhalima and Salameh.[27]

It's unclear whether the ASAC formally rejected any requests to track the two men, but a Bureau source said it was unlikely that Dunbar would have approved such a surveillance. "Mr. Dunbar didn't believe anything Salem said, so why would he give his approval to go after these two on his [Salem's] recommendation?"[28]

Carson Dunbar himself openly rejected that assertion. "In all the areas in which we could use technical surveillance, we did," he said in an interview for this book. "There was never a time that I disapproved any type of surveillance that was in question."[29]

But according to *The Cell*, the book by John Miller, Michael Stone, and Chris Mitchell, Dunbar was also responsible for terminating another key FBI probe that had sprung from the Calverton shooting sessions.[30] This second investigation, also ongoing during the fall of 1992, would have put agents within striking distance of other blind Sheikh cohorts who were engaged in paramilitary training sessions and gunrunning. One of the trainees under surveillance was Mohammed Abouhalima, brother of the Red. Another was Siddig Siddig Ali, a Sudanese national.[31]

Ali, who later became a government witness, admitted that he and Abouhalima's brother had gone to Harrisburg, Pennsylvania, for a series of clandestine sessions designed to teach them assassination techniques. At one such meeting they had even exploded a test bomb on behalf of the Yousef cell. A parallel team of FBI agents from the New York JTTF had been tracking these cell members prior to the Harrisburg sessions, but in January of 1993, just weeks before the Trade Center blast—reportedly out of a concern that this second probe was sapping FBI manpower—Carson Dunbar shut it down as well.

It was another dot lost on the chart.

At 10:00 P.M. on the night of February 25, Mohammed Salameh called the Jersey City police from a phone near a Pathmark supermarket on Route 440 and told them the Ryder van had been stolen. In his third direct encounter with police in a month, Salameh was taken by the cops to the local station, where he filled out a stolen vehicle report to serve as a cover story when the van was blown.

Now, just before midnight, having eluded the FBI, Ismoil, Salameh, and Abouhalima loaded the elements of the bomb into the van for the trip into Manhattan. Yousef's first date with Ground Zero was just hours away.*

---

*Timeline #35. p. 8.

13

THE BLACK
BOTTOMLESS PIT

The convoy of three vehicles left Jersey City in the early morning hours of February 26. Mohammed Salameh was behind the wheel of the rented red Corsica, the Ryder van was in the middle, and Mahmud Abouhalima followed in his blue Lincoln. Eyad Ismoil, Yousef's Jordanian friend, was driving the van, with Yousef in the shotgun seat. But this was no truck full of shampoo. Behind them rested the most deadly improvised explosive device ever constructed on U.S. soil.[1] The Ryder Ford Econoline was three years old. It had 295 cubic yards of cargo space. Ismoil and Yousef sat on a single cushioned bench that ran across the front of the van. On his lap Yousef balanced a precarious cargo: four containers of highly volatile nitroglycerine in a box with newspaper wadding.

The bomb itself consisted of four cardboard boxes filled with a slurry of urea-nitrate and fuel oil (UNFO), with waste paper as a binder. The boxes were surrounded by four-foot red tanks of compressed hydrogen. They were connected by four twenty-foot-long slow-burning fuses of smokeless power wrapped in fabric. To keep the smoke level down, Yousef had run the fuses through surgical tubing. When the time came, he would insert a nitro container in each of the boxes as an initiator. Once lit, the fuses would set off the nitroglycerine, which in turn would detonate the hydrogen gas and the UNFO slurry. Typical high explosives have a velocity of three thousand feet per second. But Yousef had designed this device to explode at a velocity five times that. At fifteen thousand feet per second, a projectile on the river side of the Trade Center Towers in Lower Manhattan would be blown into New Jersey in less than a second.

The convoy passed through the Holland Tunnel. Once in Manhattan, it turned down West Street and took the Battery Tunnel to the Harbor Motor Inn in Brooklyn. The original target time for the bombing was to be just after 9:00 A.M., as the Twin Towers were filling up with workers. But that night, incredibly, Yousef overslept, and the hapless Salameh failed to wake him. When he got up that morning, Yousef looked across New York Harbor at the Trade Center. The day was cloudy, and snow had been predicted. It would be noon by the time they reached Manhattan, but Yousef wasn't worried. Even at lunchtime the Trade Center complex held enough people to populate a city the size of Dearborn, Michigan.

The population belowground was much smaller. The enormous towers sat in a vast concrete "bathtub" imbedded in the ancient colonial landfill of lower Manhattan. The size of eight city blocks, it had walls seventy feet high and three feet thick to keep out the Hudson River. Three hundred men worked in the seven-story basement area, along with a handful of women.

One of them was Monica Smith, a pretty thirty-five-year-old immigrant from Ecuador who worked as a secretary in Room 107 on the B-2 basement level. It was Monica's job to check the time sheets submitted to the Port Authority by outside contractors hired to clean the Trade Center. She had met her husband, Eddie, a machine salesman, at the Twin Towers. They had bought their first house in the Long Island suburbs, and now Monica was seven months pregnant with their son, a little boy they planned to name Eddie Jr.[2]

At a few minutes before noon on that Friday, she was sitting at her desk eating a lunch of homemade eggplant parmigiana when the yellow Port Authority van on the ramp outside pulled away. Moments later, Monica barely noticed when another yellow van rolled in. When Ismoil shut off the ignition, Yousef carefully handed him the box of nitro. The bomb maker then went into the back and painstakingly inserted a nitroglycerine container into each of the four boxes. He put a Rockmaster blasting cap in each container, then inserted the surgical tubing surrounding the fuses. When that was done, Yousef set them on fire with a cheap cigarette lighter.

He nodded calmly to Ismoil and they exited the van as the fuses started to burn. The Ryder van was parked along the load-bearing south wall of the North Tower. It was Yousef's hope that when the fifteen-hundred-pound device detonated, the force would blow laterally, cracking the supports at the skyscraper's base.

Now, as they climbed into the Corsica and sped to the exit, the high-strung Mohammed Salameh's heart almost stopped. There, at the mouth of the garage ahead of them, another van was blocking the exit. The fuses would ignite the huge bomb in less than twelve minutes. Yousef checked his watch. Eleven minutes and thirty seconds to go. Salameh slammed on the Corsica's horn. The van driver waved him off, so Salameh got out, almost frantic, and began screaming at him.

Two minutes went by as the fuses burned down, and Ramzi Yousef wondered to himself if Allah had willed him to be a casualty of his own device. By now, Ismoil was pushing the horn over and over.

Worried that Port Authority cops might respond, Yousef grabbed the Jordanian's wrist, but Ismoil jumped out and began bellowing at the van driver with Salameh. The two of them were almost apoplectic. Ismoil checked his watch: eight minutes to go.

But Yousef, the man with ice water in his veins, stayed calm.

Finally the van pulled out, and Salameh jumped back into the driver's seat. Ismoil was barely inside when Salameh gunned it and screeched out into the cold February chill of lower Manhattan.

At that moment Mahmud Abouhalima, the big Egyptian whom the FBI had lost track of, was standing at the window inside J&R Music World on Park Row. He was worried. According to the schedule, they should have been out by now. He began pacing back and forth along the window, cursing under his breath in Arabic. A few people flashed looks at the big redhead but he didn't care. Something must be going wrong.

A few blocks away, Nancy Floyd was having lunch with a girlfriend visiting from California. Since her last contact with Salem in the fall, Nancy had buried herself in work with the Special Operations Group. In her off hours she was getting her home in Stamford ready for the arrival of her mother, who was coming to Connecticut to live with her.

Nancy hadn't heard from her asset Salem in months. At this point in late February, the last thing on her mind was the aborted investigation into the bomb plot. She glanced at her watch as they headed up Church Street. It was 12:17 P.M.

A few moments later, at 12:17:37, the flames hit the blasting caps. The shock wave detonated the nitroglycerin, causing it to vaporize into a gas with the force of 150,000 pounds per square inch. The other containers exploded and obliterated the van, which tore through the office wall into Room 107. In the millisecond it would take a human being to read the word *bomb,* the shock wave seared the imprint of Monica Smith's sweater into her shoulder. The fragments of concrete block from the imploding outer wall blew her across the office. Her lungs, arteries, and internal organs were ripped open by the blunt impact trauma. Her shoulders, ribs, and pelvis were shattered. The fetus she was carrying was instantly crushed.[3]

Monica's husband, Eddie, was in a meeting at work when a coworker came in to announce that there had been a "fire" at the Trade Center. Eddie was worried, but concern moved to panic a few minutes later when the man came back and said that it had been an explosion. Eddie immediately began calling Monica's number in what was now the shattered Room 107 at ground zero. When he got no answer, he raced to his car and headed downtown.

Fifty-five thousand people worked in the Trade Center complex. Another ninety thousand traveled through every day. Now, as tens of thousands of workers rushed down the smoke-clogged stairwells, hundreds of fire, police, and EMS workers surrounded the sixteen-acre site. A total of 775 uniformed firefighters from 135 companies responded from the FDNY alone.[4] Lower Manhattan was thrown into a state of gridlock.

It wasn't until eleven o'clock that night that Eddie Smith, keeping the vigil at Monica's brother's house, got word through a friend that his wife's body was at the city morgue. Eddie's knees buckled when he heard the news. He dialed the medical examiner's office, but the person who answered refused to tell him anything other than that he ought to come down. Eddie was getting ready to make the drive in to the morgue on First Avenue, when he called his father on Long Island. A Nassau County police officer who was there referred him to an NYPD detective. Heart pounding now, Eddie dialed the cop, who confirmed that his wife was dead. Eddie almost collapsed, but he recovered enough to ask about his son. After all, there was still hope. "What about the baby?" he said. There was a pause; then the detective said, "Sir, do you have any *idea* how bad it was?"[5]

A Four-Story Drop

The first call into the FDNY's Manhattan Fire Communications office after the blast came at 12:18 P.M. Dispatcher Herb Eysser in the Alarm Response Dispatch position picked up. A woman, her voice trembling with fear, said, ". . . an explosion in the garage of the Vista Hotel."[6]

In less than a minute the firefighters from "Ten and Ten" (10 Engine and 10 Truck) roared around the corner from their house on Liberty Street and ran into the lobby of the twenty-two-story luxury hotel at the base of the South Tower.[7] Panicked people were rushing outside to West Street. Initial reports to the FDNY indicated a "transformer fire," so the first responders from Ten and Ten had no idea of the devastation that lay beneath them.

Ramzi Yousef's urea-nitrate bomb had blown through three floors of eleven-inch-thick rebarred concrete. The crater was 200 feet long, 125 feet wide, and four stories deep. The fractured pieces of cinder block that had killed Monica Smith rocketed across the hall from Room 107 to a lunchroom where three Port Authority workers had just finished eating. Bob Kirkpatrick, sixty-one, the Trade Center's chief locksmith, was blown across the room and crushed. Concrete pellets drove like bullets into the face of fifty-seven-year-old Bill Macko, a heating specialist. Particles of concrete moving at a thousand miles per second shot into the eyes of forty-eight-year-old Steven Knapp.[8]

Outside in the garage, John DiGiovanni, a forty-five-year-old dental equipment salesman, had just parked his car when the sparks from Yousef's fuses hit the Atlas Rockmaster blasting caps. His body was blown thirty feet up a ramp near the exit to West Street. In the chaos that followed, DeGiovanni lay wounded for almost an hour before an EMS rescue team found him and rushed him to St. Vincent's Hospital. He was pronounced dead at 2:20 P.M.

The body of the sixth victim, thirty-seven-year-old Willie Mercado,

NEW LOWER PRICE

More doing.

PROVIDES 30% WATER SAVINGS

 $58 WAS $68

**EXCLUSIVE AMERICAN STANDARD®
SYMPHONY BATH FAUCET**
- Chrome finish, 4" centerset
- Includes mounting hardware
- Lifetime warranty (153656)

More doing.℠

wasn't located for days. A receiving agent for Windows on the World, the restaurant atop the North Tower, Mercado was sitting in a chair, taking a break on the B-2 level, when the nitro ignited the UNFO slurry. The hurricane force of the explosion picked him up and hurled his body down into the enormous four-story pit below. Crushed under twelve feet of concrete, he was still in the chair when they found him.

The blast shorted out five of the eight high-voltage feeder lines from Manhattan's electrical grid. Elevators stopped between floors, loaded with terrified people. One of them, with seventy schoolchildren inside, dangled hundreds of feet above street level for five hours.[9] Thousands of terrified office workers rushed in the dark down the emergency stairwells, now thick with black smoke.[10] They spilled onto the plaza below, choking, covered in soot, bleeding, and crying. A pregnant woman went into labor on the ninety-second floor. But in the initial minutes after the blast, few people had any sense of what had caused the Towers to quake.

Ronnie Bucca had been investigating an incendiary fire in the Bronx when word came over his BFI radio that there'd been an incident at the Trade Center. He went to his Chevy, switched to the FDNY Dispatch frequency, and heard the transmission of a 10-76—the code for a major high-rise "working fire." The response called for four engines, four ladders, and four battalion chiefs, along with Rescue One. Ronnie's first thought was to call his old company and find out how bad it was, but they were probably out the door, so he turned on WCBS Radio. By now the anchor was reporting "an explosion" on the B-2 level. Ronnie hit the ignition and slammed the red "Kojak" bubble on his roof, racing back to Bronx Base to await orders.

Soon the Trade Center bomb would produce the largest movement of apparatus in FDNY history. Fire and EMS units rushed 228 people to area hospitals. Another 474 of the injured were treated on the scene for smoke inhalation, including 155 firefighters. But one of them came close to death that day—and, as fate would have it, he was one of Ronnie Bucca's closest friends.

Kevin Shea had been on the job for nine years. He'd made it through 227 Engine in Brownsville and 108 Truck in Williamsburg, two of the roughest companies in Brooklyn, before qualifying into the coveted Rescue One house on West Forty-third Street.

Seconds after the 10-76 came in, Shea jumped into his boots and onto the back of the Mack R. The truck roared off the apparatus floor and down Eleventh Avenue to West Street.

"On the way downtown, as one alarm came in and then another," said Shea, "the word we got was 'transformer explosion.' "[11] As they screeched up in front of the Vista Hotel, Shea, his partner, Gary Geidel, their lieutenant, and three other men from the company headed into the lobby. People were running out screaming. Frightened Port Authority workers said others were trapped downstairs. The firefighters headed into a service stairwell and formed a single line searching for survivors. At that point the smoke was black and acrid; it had a smell consistent with transformer fluid, but the men from Rescue One had no idea what they were walking into. Suddenly, the lieutenant at the head of the line heard a man calling for help. Firefighters Shea and Geidel opened a door onto what they thought was a stairwell in the direction of the voice.

"The smoke was pitch, pitch black," Shea recalled. "We were calling out. Gary had his arm along the wall as we moved down what we realized now was a ramp to the parking garage. I kept my arm on Gary, so we had a wider search area. We got the callback, 'Help! Help!' The smoke condition was so dense, visibility was just a few inches. As we moved along, we didn't realize it, but we were approaching the edge of the crater. We couldn't see our feet in front of us."

By now they had their masks on; breathing from the Scott packs on their backs. Then, as they inched their way forward, a part of the floor gave way. Pieces of concrete began to break off. Geidel slipped into a knee-deep hole, and Shea went over the edge.

Unknowingly, they had come to a point where the floor to B-1 had sheared off. Shea quickly grabbed onto two pieces of rebar protruding from the concrete, but his gloves caused him to slip. Geidel's eyes went wide as he leaned forward and saw orange flames from the inferno below. "Gary said, 'There's fire beneath you, Kev. If you drop, just roll.' "

Shea looked down and saw the orange glow. "I figured I was going into the transformer pit," said Shea. "I couldn't hold on anymore, and I fell."

But instead of dropping ten feet to the floor below, he kept going, down toward the ruptured concrete garage floor on B-4. As he fell, Shea saw flashes of orange flames on the fractured floors at each level of the parking garage. He remembered Ronnie talking about that day when he'd dropped the five floors into the alley. Now he was heading feet first into what seemed like a black bottomless pit, ringed with thousand-degree flames.

PART II

14

THE FIFTH
BATTALION

Kevin Shea didn't realize it at the time, but burning cars were hanging like Christmas tree ornaments, dangling from the edge of each level as he fell. He dropped past the B-2 level, then B-3, and continued to fall until he landed feet first on the fire-covered floor of the B-4 level, forty feet down.[1]

Just as they had for Ronnie back in 1986, Kevin's mask and helmet had saved his life. "I broke my nose," said Shea. "I fractured my skull. I broke my right ankle, my left knee, and the back of my leg got impaled on the rebar." The muscles were torn off Shea's left knee, and the rebar severed his quad tendons. Now he was at the bottom of the black hole, with flames licking at his back. Shea's Handie-Talkie radio crackled, and the first thing he heard was "The guy's dead." But he was able to transmit a response back. His partner, Gary Geidel, yelled down, "Get into a safe spot. We're coming."

Still, Shea's evacuation by the best rescue company in the world would be a problem. "The rebar was hanging off the B-1 floor like the prongs of a rake," said Shea. "If they lowered a man down, they wouldn't be able to pull us up." The edge of the B-1 floor was still breaking off like ice on a frozen pond.

As the minutes went by, the danger increased. Shea kept hearing a series of windlike noises followed by crashes. He soon realized what it was: the sound of burning cars dropping off the fractured parking ramps from above and exploding on the floor around him. If he didn't get out of there soon, he would bleed to death—or be crushed.

Finally, Lt. John Fox of Squad Company went over on a rope and dropped to Shea's position. Moments later, Firefighter Jack Teague from Rescue Five got down to the B-4 floor, along with Gary Geidel and two ESU cops who had cut their way through a wall.

They loaded Shea into a meshed stokes basket and snapped down the cover, locking him in. If Ronnie Bucca's roaring Fifth Avenue evacuation had been dramatic, this was another one for the annals of Rescue One.

"They formed a human chain," said a grateful Shea, "passing the basket hand to hand. Guys from different companies passed me along horizontally, vertically. At one point they ran me straight up along the rails of a portable ladder. I was so close to the debris I could feel the concrete scratching my face." He was taken in an FDNY ambulance to Beekman Downtown Hospital.

In the chaos that followed the blast at noon, Ronnie Bucca had worked a double tour. But by 10:00 P.M. he'd heard the news about Kevin, and was able to go down and see him.

"Ronnie and I had the same perspective on things," said Shea. "We were both quiet, a little cynical about the system, and we clicked." Ronnie's nickname for Shea was "Round Peg," because Kevin used to joke that he felt like he was always trying to fit into a square hole.

"It was pretty late on the night of the bombing when he came," said Shea. "By then, we knew there had been a massive explosion. We just didn't know who did it. Ronnie came in, looked at me, and said, 'So what? You had to try and outdo me with the fall?'" Shea laughed. "I told him it was only four floors."

Ronnie grinned. He moved a table next to the bed and sat down with a bag from McDonald's. "He told me, 'You can't be eating hospital food,'" said Shea. "So he pulled out a couple of shakes." Ronnie and Shea reminisced for a while about their time in Rescue One. Kevin promised that, like Bucca, he would be back on the job. Ronnie nodded.

"Then he asked me if I wanted to talk about it," said Shea. "I was pretty medicated at the time, but I said 'Yeah,' and he started asking me about the damage."

Bucca stayed for an hour, took notes, then told Shea he was going to meet up with a couple of other marshals. They would visit the subbasement to look at the crater firsthand.

"It was still pretty hairy at that point," said Shea. "Nobody was really sure about the extent of the damage. They weren't sure if more floors were going to collapse." So Shea asked Ronnie why he was going in so soon. Bucca drained his chocolate shake and smiled. "Hey, Round," he said, "I'm a marshal now. This thing was twenty-three alarms. The biggest arson fire in history."

Later, in the early hours of Saturday morning, Ronnie and two other marshals from Bronx Base were crawling through the debris on the B-1 level.[2] Willie Mercado was still unaccounted for, and search and rescue teams were combing the fractured floors. By now the smoke had cleared and Ronnie stood at the edge of the broken ramp where Kevin had fallen. He thought back to that afternoon in 1986 when he'd gone off the fire escape back first in broad daylight. But that was different from what Kevin must have experienced—to fall into a pit of fire through dense black, not knowing how far you were dropping. Bucca had made a number of night jumps off the ramps of C-130s in his time, but he'd never gone into a drop zone that was on fire.

Photo of B-1 level by Ronnie Bucca

Ronnie had brought along a small disposable camera. He moved to the edge of the B-1 ramp from where Kevin had fallen and snapped a picture of the broken concrete and protruding rods of rebar.

Ronnie Bucca was a professional, but as he made his way across the rubble that morning, anger began to well up inside him. In the hours after the blast, the press had reported that nineteen separate groups had claimed credit for the bomb.[3] But it didn't matter who they were. Not only had they almost killed his friend and injured 155 of his brothers, they had blown a hole into the borough he was born in, with the intent of killing tens of thousands of innocent human beings.

To Bucca this was an audacious attack on his city and his country.

He'd only been a fire investigator for nine months, but that morning at the foot of the crater, he made a vow: he was going to work this case and do whatever he could to help bring these men down.

150 Suicidal Soldiers

By now the men in question had long since dispersed. Five minutes after screeching out of the Trade Center garage, the red Corsica sped to a mailbox in lower Manhattan.[4] One of Yousef's coconspirators jumped out and dropped in five letters addressed to various newspapers. The letters had been drafted on Nidal Ayyad's computer in New Jersey. The copy published in the *New York Times* a month later was eerily prescient of things to come. Yousef called his cell the "fifth battalion in the Liberation Army."

> The following letter from the Liberation Army regarding the operation conducted against the WTC. We . . . the fifth battalion in the Liberation Army, declare our responsibility for the explosion on the mentioned building. This action was done in response for the American political, economical, and military support to Israel, the state of terrorism, and to the rest of the dictator countries in the region.
>
> Our demands are:
> 1. Stop all military, economical and political aids to Israel.
> 2. All diplomatic relations with Israel must stop.
> 3. Not to interfere with any of the Middle East countries' interior affairs.
>
> If our demands are not met, all of our functional groups in the army will continue to execute our missions against military and civilian targets in and out of the United States. This will also include some potential nuclear targets. For your own information, our army has more than hundred and fifty suicidal soldiers ready to go ahead. The terrorism that Israel practices (which is supported by America) must be faced with a similar one. The dictatorship and terrorism (also supported by America) that some countries are practicing against their own people must also be faced with terrorism.

The American people must know that the civilians who got killed are not better than those who are getting killed by the American weapons and Supports.

The American people are responsible for the actions of their government and they must question all of the crimes that their government is committing against other people or they, Americans will be the targets of our operations that could diminish them. We invite all of the people from all countries and all of the revolutionaries in the world to participate in this action with us to accomplish our just goals. If then anyone transgresses the prohibition against you, transgress ye likewise against him.

Liberation Army, fifth battalion.

Al-Ferrek Al Rokn, Abu Bakr Al Makee.[5]

After the letters were mailed, the Corsica sped to the Jersey waterfront, where Yousef got out to witness the results of his villainy. When he saw the two Towers still standing, he flashed anger. He had intended to send Tower One crashing like a 110-story domino into Tower Two. At one point Yousef had even considered a chemical mixture that would have produced cyanide gas. It would have risen through the smoke up the elevator shafts and stairwells, possibly killing thousands. Now he regretted abandoning that plan.

Yousef returned to the Pamrapo Avenue bomb factory, showered, shaved, and put on a brand-new designer suit. The man of many aliases was transforming himself once again, from the bomb maker Rashed into Abdul Basit, a prosperous Pakistani businessman—the very opposite of the decrepit Iraqi refugee in shalwar pants who had arrived at JFK on September 1. Yousef zipped his Basit passport and a first-class ticket on Pakistan International Airlines into his carry-on bag. Mohammed Salameh was waiting outside in the Corsica to take him and his wheelman, Eyyad Ismoil, to the airport.[6]

On their way to Kennedy, Yousef heard radio news reports indicating only a single death. For a moment he wondered whether only the blasting caps had ignited. But by evening, as he waited in PIA's first-class lounge and watched Channel 2's coverage of the explosion, he knew he'd inflicted extraordinary damage. At one point the local TV anchor reported that at 1:35 P.M. a group calling itself the Serbian Liberation Army had taken credit for the blast. Suddenly, Yousef felt a pang of jealousy. Who were these fools claiming credit for his work? Did the media cretins have any *comprehension* that such a blast had been conjured from urea fertilizer pellets and fuel oil?

When the television death toll had climbed to five, Yousef got up and went to a pay phone. Unwilling to wait until his letters reached the print press, he dialed an NYPD 800 tip line that had run at the bottom of the television screen and claimed credit for the Trade Center bombing in the name of the Liberation Army, fifth battalion. He was sure his declaration was recorded, because he heard a "beep" in the background.

Now the bomb maker sat back down and waited. He took out the first-class ticket he'd purchased three days before at Pakam Travel in Jersey City. He'd paid $1,006 in cash for a one-way flight to Karachi, connecting on to Quetta in West Pakistan.[7]

But now the departure of Flight 714 had been pushed back for unexplained reasons. He got up and politely asked the lounge attendant if it was mechanical trouble. She said she didn't know, but would make an inquiry. Yousef sat back down and closed his eyes, willing himself to stay calm. Long ago he had learned to control his pulse rate as he built more and more intricate killing devices. As midnight approached, though, his mind began to race. Had his ego become his undoing? Could the police have traced his call back to the pay phone? No—he hadn't been on long enough. Or had he?

He went outside to the hallway and walked to a window that looked out toward the tarmac, straining to see the PIA 747, searching for signs of the Feds.

Yousef wasn't religious man. Years later, his lawyer Bernie Kleinman would compare him to "a High Holy Day Jew."[8] He was driven by politics, not theology; he called on Allah only when he needed Him. But as the clock ticked past midnight, Yousef began to feel that he needed Him now.

The terrorist closed his eyes and silently recited the six Islamic articles of faith: "I believe in Allah. I believe in the angels of Allah. I believe in the revealed holy books of Allah. I believe in the messengers of Allah. I believe in life after death. I believe in the power of Allah and the Day of Judgment."

When he finished, Yousef learned that the flight had been pushed back further.

From his first days as a student of bomb building at the Jalozai Camp near Peshawar, Yousef had moved through life like a fighting gamecock. He'd aligned himself early on with Osama bin Laden's terror network. He'd had the audacity to make a move on the second tallest buildings in the world, and but for a miscalculation over the load-bearing walls, he'd almost brought them down. He had gotten away safely—but now this.

In the men's room he checked to see if he had enough cash in his money belt for another ticket. He went to the lounge desk to ask about other departing flights, but at this hour there were few takeoffs to any countries that wouldn't demand a visa. Now, as he sat down and checked his watch again, the cold throb of panic began to form at the base of Yousef's skull. He bit his own tongue and tasted the blood. No. He would not die here. He would not be captured. He closed his eyes and willed it.

"I believe in Allah. I believe in the angels of Allah. I believe in the revealed holy books of Allah. I believe in the messengers. . . ."

Vindication

Ramzi Yousef didn't know it, but he had little to fear. As the FBI set up a command center in the ballroom of the Vista Hotel, and agents from the Bureau and ATF began to crawl through the crater to assess the massive damage, the authorities gave no order to hold or delay any flights departing for the Middle East. In the hours after the explosion, FBI supervisors scrambled to run down false leads like the Serbian Liberation claim of credit. But at least two investigators inside the Joint Terrorist Task Force knew that there were other much more promising suspects.

John Anticev and Lou Napoli were worried. Was it possible that Abouhalima and Salameh, men they'd been concerned about since Calverton in 1989, were somehow involved in this? The thought sent a chill into the investigators, especially since they had followed the terrorists and lost them. If these two were involved, it would be the equivalent of the blunder back in 1963 when Lee Harvey Oswald had walked into the FBI's Dallas field office just weeks before the Kennedy assassination and threatened to blow it up.[9] Bureau agents back then hadn't followed up, even though they knew Oswald was working at the Texas School Book Depository. They also failed to inform the Secret Service, which would have put Oswald on its threat list. Until then, that had been perhaps the biggest oversight in FBI history: now, as the post-bombing minutes ticked by, it was beginning to look as if the New York office might have committed the second.

Two floors above them in the FCI section, Nancy Floyd didn't even have to guess. Back in the fall, when she'd passed the last five hundred dollars to Emad Salem, he'd warned her flat out: "Don't call me when the bombs go off." He'd risked his life and gained the confidence of the blind Sheikh. He'd been asked to build bombs. He'd advised the FBI to follow Abouhalima and Salameh. The Bureau had failed to do that, and now his prediction had come true.

Not long after she rushed back from lunch, Nancy got a call from Ray Palmowski, the agent who'd been with her in the Subway shop when Salem had issued that final warning.[10]

"He was right, wasn't he?" said Palmowski.

At 3:10 P.M. that afternoon, Salem checked into St. Claire's Hospital, complaining of an inner-ear infection.[11] As soon as he got to a room with a phone, he called Nancy Floyd.

"Did you hear what happened?" Salem asked, his voice trembling.

"Yes," Nancy said. Her ex-asset had been vindicated, but right now she felt nothing but sadness—for the victims, and for the opportunity lost.

"I am very nervous about it," said Salem. "Nobody listened, and I am very concerned that the FBI will involve me in this."[12]

"Don't worry about it," said Nancy.

"But you *know* it was them," said Salem. "You know that it had to be. I don't understand, Nancy. Why didn't they take the information? Why didn't they do anything?"

"They have an arrogant attitude," said Floyd. "They don't think these people are smart enough to do this stuff, and this has taken them for a shock."

"I feel bad," said Salem. "I feel here is people who don't listen."

"Hey, it wasn't like *you* didn't try," she said. "You can't force people to do the right thing. This thing was handled completely wrong from the very beginning."[13]

"Uh-huh," said Salem.

"You know, Emad, you've done the best you can. I've done the best I can. You're just a citizen. I'm just a street agent, and I don't have the power to override management."

"But we have to do someth—"

Of course they did. Nancy stopped him before he could finish. "All right," she said. "I'll talk to my supervisor. If something happens, just page me."

Moments later, Agent Floyd called Jim Sherman, her boss in the Foreign Counter Intelligence Division. Sherman was the FBI supervisor who had first approved Salem's undercover assignment.

"Emad says he's got some information," Nancy told him.

According to an FBI source, Sherman told her to call the Terrorism section. "We're not gonna be in the middle of it anymore," Sherman said. "If they want to get this guy, let them do it." Nancy felt shock, but not surprise.

"Her supervisor had made it clear [months before] when they closed Salem out," said the FBI source, "that if it came back to bite somebody in the butt, it wasn't going to be Foreign Counter Intelligence. So [after the bombing] he told her to give it to Terrorism."[14]

Nancy was chafing to get back into the investigation. But she'd been warned months earlier to distance herself from Salem.

She was also feeling heat from inside the New York office—pressure from management that she would later describe under oath as "harassment." She had heard whispering in the corridors. Over the cubicles separating the desks in her section, people had begun hinting that her relationship with Salem had been more than agent-asset—that there was something sexual between them.

"All of a sudden she was starting to get, 'Hey, are you Mata Hari?'" said Len Predtechenskis. "Somebody was putting this word out that the only way she got this information was by having sex with Salem. And they were just flat-out wrong."

To some close to the investigation, the motives behind the gossip seemed clear: since Salem had been cut loose, he needed to be diminished as a source by FBI supervisors. It was the same reasoning that explained Carson Dunbar's demand that Salem undergo additional polygraphs in July and September 1992, after he'd withdrawn from the investigation—the tests that suggested Salem had been "deceptive."

Now, as FDNY fire units were still knocking down flames from

Yousef's bomb, Nancy called Salem back. "Here's the deal," she said. "My supervisor says that if you've got information, you're gonna have to deal with Louie." She told her ex-asset to sit tight, then called Napoli and reported that Salem was willing to talk.

That night after work, Nancy had drinks with the few agents she could trust. One in the group recalled that Nancy was really down. "She was upset because people had died and were injured, and if anybody had just listened back when, it could have been prevented."[15]

Now, at 1:00 A.M. on the night of the biggest terrorist attack in U.S. history, Napoli and Anticev were in the office of Jim Fox, the FBI's New York assistant director in charge.

Mary Jo White was running the meeting. The chief assistant in the U.S. Attorney's Office for the Eastern District of New York (Brooklyn), she had recently been tapped to be the top federal prosecutor in Manhattan. Now, twelve hours after the bombing, she was pushing the assembled agents for ideas, leads—anything that might help break the case. At some point Napoli mentioned that they had an asset "that was very close to these people."

Asset? *What* asset, demanded White, a prosecutor with the short-haired look of a nun and the grit of a pit bull.

"He's feeling really remorseful . . . broken up," said Napoli. "He didn't want to wear a wire, and he was—" "*What?*" snapped White, demanding to hear the full story. Napoli gave her a short version of the conflict between Dunbar and Floyd: how the ASAC had questioned Salem's honesty, his ability even to get inside a cell he'd long since infiltrated. How Dunbar had forced him to take two additional polys and demanded that he testify or quit.[16]

The U.S. attorney was impressed enough to want to meet the Egyptian herself. "Let's get him in here," she said.

Napoli and his partner traded looks. Anticev, a Justice Department employee far below White in the pecking order, deferred to the New York cop.

"Well," said Lou, "we were paying him like five hundred a week. This time, you know, considering what's happened, he's probably gonna want—a million dollars."

White shot back without hesitating. "I don't give a damn *what* he wants. If he can deliver, give it to him."

Mary Jo White had made a shrewd call. A devastating act of terror had taken place just over a month into Bill Clinton's presidency. The White House was demanding immediate answers.

While the hapless SACs down at the Vista were chasing Serbians, Napoli and Anticev had a source who already knew all the players. A decision had to be made to restore confidence in the Bureau. If Carson Dunbar had made a mistake, it had to be rectified. They needed to get Salem back inside the Sheikh's cell.

The man whose polygraph tests had read "deceptive" and "inconclusive"—the man Dunbar called a "prolific liar"—was about to become the fair-haired boy once again.

"All of a sudden, after the bombing, everybody has pie on their face that Nancy was right all along," Len Predtechenskis recalled.

Floyd and her asset had been vindicated by a fifteen-hundred-pound bomb that had carved out a crater four stories deep and killed six. Now the Feds wanted Salem back, and it didn't matter how much it cost. One can only wonder what might have happened if the penny had dropped a few hours earlier and the FBI had begun scouring the airports for Middle Eastern nationals exiting toward suspect countries. But that meeting in Fox's office didn't happen until after midnight.

By the early morning hours of Saturday, Ramzi Yousef was buckling his seat belt in the first-class section aboard PIA Flight 714 as the 747 lifted off from JFK. He would be in Karachi later that day, then take a connecting flight to Quetta, the frontierlike town in the heart of his home province of Baluchistan. From there he would disappear into the dark underbelly of radical Islam, safe to plot even more deadly acts of terror. The FBI's decision to bring back Emad Salem, the one man who might have found him, had come too late.

The Mozart of Terror was gone.

15

THE RYDER
SIDESHOW

In the historical mythology surrounding the FBI's investigation into
the World Trade Center bombing, the conventional wisdom has
always been that the case was broken by great sleuthing. Just hours after
Yousef's flight had cleared Kennedy airspace on Saturday morning, ATF
Agent Joe Hanlin and Donald Sadowi, a detective with the NYPD's
bomb squad, came across a piece of twisted metal on the B-2 level below
the Towers.

"Hey, look at this," said Hanlin.[1] It was a section of differential housing from some kind of van. When they turned the piece over they saw
that it contained a C-VIN, the confidential vehicle identification number
stamped on parts of motor vehicles so that cars and trucks that are stolen
or broken apart by chop shops can be traced. The partial VIN led back
to the E-50 yellow Ford Econoline Ryder van that Mohammed Salameh
had rented at DIB Leasing in Jersey City. The twenty-five-year-old Palestinian with questionable driving skills had gone back to the Ryder agency
just hours after the bombing to confirm his earlier report to Jersey City
police that the van had been stolen.

Salameh had purchased an eighty-dollar infant's ticket on Royal Jordanian Airlines. Now he was demanding that DIB refund his four-
hundred-dollar rental deposit, hoping to use the money to upgrade to an
adult fare and escape. But the Ryder rental clerk told Salameh that he'd
have to produce a police report on the stolen van, so he rushed back to

the Jersey City Police Department that night. He returned to DIB twice more before the FBI got the hit on the C-VIN. But by Thursday, March 4, the link had been traced, and the Feds were ready for him. This time they had the place surrounded with agents waiting to pounce. Dozens of them were hiding on rooftops, in unmarked cars—even behind trees.

But the arrest was almost aborted when *Newsday* got word of the C-VIN–Ryder van link. An enterprising reporter called the FBI for confirmation that the Trade Center bomb had been traced to DIB. Incredibly, no one in the Bureau asked the paper to hold off on the story and it ran in the morning edition on March 4. Hours later, two local TV news vans were circling the Ryder lot at 1558 Kennedy Boulevard in Jersey City.

The Feds quickly went into damage control mode. Patrick Galasso, the Ryder agent who'd rented the van to Salameh, came out and convinced the video crews that they had the wrong address, so they moved on. But this forced a change in plans for the Feds. They had been hoping to follow the Palestinian to see if he led them to the other coconspirators. But now, with the media hovering, that was out of the question. They would have to nail him on-site.

Meanwhile, inside the office, FBI agent Bill Atkinson was posing as a Ryder "loss prevention analyst," checking the hidden camera and tape recorder as his team prepared for the sting.[2] When everything was set, Galasso called Salameh to come in for his refund. What happened next was a scene out of a Joe Pesci movie.

When he showed up at the DIB office, Salameh began negotiating with Atkinson. For more than half an hour, as the agents waited outside, the five-foot-six-inch terrorist haggled with Galasso and Atkinson to up his payback. Technically, Salameh owed $271.69 for the three-day rental, leaving him with a refund balance of $138.32. But Salameh, claiming the van was stolen, wanted his entire four-hundred-dollar deposit back. The problem was that instead of giving him the money and letting him leave, Atkinson seemed to relish his caught-on-tape role. So he offered to settle for two hundred.

"Is not justice," Salameh exclaimed. "This is not justice."[3]

"But it's business," Atkinson responded.

"I give him four hundred dollars," said Salameh, pointing to Patrick Galasso, the DIB rental agent who'd leased him the doomed van.

"But you've *lost* our van," argued Atkinson, as if he were a *real* Ryder flak. Hemming, hawing, and acting like the money was his own, Atkinson finally agreed to go up to two hundred and fifty.

"Would that get you out of here?" said Atkinson. "We're taking the burden."

"Now listen to me—" said Salameh.

Just then, the phone rang. Galasso, the real Ryder agent, picked up. He said, "Yes. Be right out." The cadre of FBI agents outside was getting restless. What the hell was taking so long? At one point, Atkinson started asking Salameh why he'd rented the van in the first place. The terrorist claimed he was using it to help a friend move to an address on Kensington Avenue in Jersey City. The FBI agent was really milking his part, and the SACs on scene were worried. If they didn't wrap this up soon, the TV crews would be back and they'd all end up on Eyewitness News.

But inside, the haggling went on. Salameh was now asking for a fifteen-dollar rebate for the gas he'd bought. Galasso, wanting to get it over, agreed. But the FBI agent kept on going, asking Salameh to "bring the key and we'll give you twenty dollars . . . because really, how do we know the van isn't out there? You got the key and the van and two hundred dollars. . . ."

This provoked an indignant reply: "I'm a Muslim," said Salameh. "I'm, ah, honest."

Finally the deal was concluded, but Salameh dragged it out further, insisting he couldn't possibly return that day with the key, since it was Ramadan.

Now, as the sitcom inside continued, agents in the lot outside were getting angry. This was the biggest lead on the biggest case to hit the New York FBI office in years, and it was starting to feel like a bad episode of *COPS*.

Finally, just after 10:30 A.M., with two hundred dollars in hand, Salameh walked out the door. In a matter of yards, he was surrounded by FBI agents in blue windbreakers. After they cuffed him and read him his rights, they searched his pockets and found a copy of a passport photo of El Sayyid Nosair.

Hours later, the Feds descended on the address at 34 Kensington Avenue that Salameh had claimed he was moving the friend to. There they seized Salameh's briefcase, which contained bank records of the accounts he'd set up for Ramzi Yousef. That address led to a phone record search, which, in turn linked Salameh to Mahmud Abouhalima. The next day the Feds hit the apartment on Prospect Park in Brooklyn that Salameh had used as his address on the Ryder rental contract. There they found Ibrahim El-Gabrowny, Salameh's cousin, the Egyptian contractor who was also cousin to Kahane's killer, Nosair.

The Justice Department claimed an enormous victory. "It's a remarkable day in the history of the FBI," said Acting Attorney General Stuart M. Gerson.[4] But few people outside the Bureau knew the real story: that a year earlier the FBI had had an asset named Emad Salem sitting in a Brooklyn mosque eating slaughtered lamb across from Mohammed Salameh and Mahmud Abouhalima—an asset who also dined regularly at El-Gabrowny's apartment in Prospect Park and made multiple trips to visit El-Gabrowny's murderous cousin Nosair—the same man found standing next to Salameh in a photograph recovered from the Kensington Avenue apartment.

Gerson was right. It *was* a remarkable day in FBI history, but not for the reasons the public thought. Just hours after the Salameh "victory," some agents from New Jersey were about to make a titanic error in judgment that would haunt the Bureau for years to come.

When they raided the Kensington Avenue apartment, the agents from the FBI's Newark office also found Abdul Rahman Yasin, the American-born Iraqi City College student who had taught Salameh to drive the fatal van. Yasin immediately feigned innocence, proclaiming that he had no knowledge of the bombing plot. He even offered to take the Feds to Yousef's Pamrapo Avenue bomb factory. Thanking him for being so helpful, the gullible agents listed Yasin as a "cooperating witness." In a sworn affidavit, FBI agent Eric Pilker described Yasin as a confidential informant with "no training or experience in explosives or the production of explosive devices."[5] The agents asked the Iraqi to stay in touch, then let him go.

The supervisory special agent who led the bombing investigation later said that Yasin "was not a major player." "I don't want to use the word gopher," he said, "but I think he was more of a helper."[6]

Even though they were working the biggest bombing in U.S. history, nobody in the Bureau thought to hold Yasin's passport, or even jail him as a material witness. But at the time he was questioned, unbeknownst to the Feds, Yasin had in his possession an airline ticket to Jordan. The very next day he fled to Amman, and then on to Baghdad. The FBI made a naive attempt to get his older brother to coax him back to the U.S., but Yasin laughed at the gesture. In August 1993 he was indicted on charges of plotting the bombing with Yousef and helping him construct the deadly UNFO device. In retrospect, the Bureau decided that Yasin was a "major player" after all. He's currently on the FBI's list of the twenty-two Most Wanted Terrorists. The price on his head is twenty-five million dollars.[7]

In the summer of 2002, Carson Dunbar, the ASAC leading the Joint Terrorist Task Force at the time, was asked why the FBI had let Yasin go. His response: "We had to have probable cause to hold him."[8]

Abdul Rahman Yasin had been the roommate of Mohammed Salameh, the man just arrested for his link to the van carrying the bomb to the Twin Towers. The Iraqi admitted to training Salameh as the van driver, and he had enough knowledge of Yousef's whereabouts to lead the Feds to the factory on Pamrapo Avenue where the bomb was built. If ever there was probable cause to hold a bombing suspect, this was the case. But the Bureau let him go, adding a dot to the chart the size of a basketball.*

The Bureau's Spin

No one in the media had any sense of the FBI's negligence at the time. Given that the New York office had blown the investigation up front, it was in the Bureau's interest to diminish the importance of Yousef's cell. So from the earliest hours of the bombing investigation, Jim Fox, the head of the FBI's New York office, put a spin on the case that for years affected the public perception of the bombers.[9]

On Saturday, February 27, just hours after the postmidnight meeting where Anticev and Napoli suggested that the bomb was the work of the Sheikh's cell, Fox was quoted as being reluctant to even label the blast the work of terrorists.[10] After traces of nitrate had been found the next day, the New York Times was told that the bomb was made of "conventional dynamite."

"It definitely was just dynamite," an official was quoted as saying,

---

*Timeline #42. p. 9.

"which leads you to the conclusion that it was unsophisticated people." It was an allegation that Fox did nothing to dispute.[11] Downplaying the complexity of the bomb and casting Yousef's cell as a disorganized crew of rank amateurs helped take the sting out of the FBI's failure to uncover the plot earlier.

On March 9, a headline in the *New York Times* read: "Trade Center Bombing Suspect Not a Patsy, Officials Conclude."[12]

But in truth Salameh was just that. He'd been set up by Yousef to take the fall. Left destitute and in need of money to make his escape, Salameh's role was to distract the Feds while Yousef escaped. Wittingly or otherwise, the Palestinian was meant to draw the heat from the master bomb maker—just as Ajaj, who'd carried a suitcase full of bomb books, was sacrificed to the INS when Yousef slipped in.

That same *Times* story quoted federal and local investigators as saying that Salameh "played a significant role, if not a central one" in the conspiracy. But the crash-prone Salameh, whom Yousef later described as "stupid,"[13] was never more than a minor expeditor who helped Yousef ferry chemicals back and forth to the storage locker and lay out the bomb slurry to dry.

In the weeks to come, Ralph Blumenthal and Alison Mitchell of the *Times* did some groundbreaking stories that got to the truth. But in the days after the bombing, the *Times,* like most of the media, largely reported the Bureau's spin. It was the nature of daily deadline reporting, complicated by the fact that this was a story involving national security. The major news organizations simply had to rely on law enforcement agencies like the Bureau for details of the ongoing investigation, and the FBI wasn't even hinting at the truth.

The *Time* magazine cover story on the Monday after the bombing contained a three-quarter-page sidebar entitled "Who Could Have Done It?"[14] Most of the piece was devoted to the theory that "Balkan factions" were responsible. The piece went on to list "Palestinian factions," Iranians, Iraqis, Libyans, and even Russian nationalists as possible suspects, but there was no mention of radical Egyptians or Sheikh Omar Abdel Rahman.

Time contributed further to the FBI's disparagement of the bomb cell. "The black comedy of errors that followed the explosion," wrote the *Time*'s Jill Smolowe, "suggests either a costly mistake—or the work of rank amateurs."[15]

The night of his arrest on March 4, Salameh, who worshiped at the al-Salaam Mosque, was immediately linked to the blind Sheikh.[16] But Rahman went on a media offensive. Two weeks later he appeared on CNN and ABC's *Prime Time Live,* where he denied any involvement in the plot. He even denied knowing Mahmud Abouhalima, who'd been his driver and personal assistant for years. The cleric told ABC's Chris Wallace, "I did not encourage, I did not know, and I had no relation to this."[17]

Meanwhile, even after Rutgers grad Nidal Ayyad was arrested and his joint bank accounts with Salameh were uncovered, showing wire transfers of eight thousand dollars in cash from Europe and the Mideast, investigators were still using the word *inept* to describe the bombing cell. "I wish I knew if I had amateurs, wannabe terrorists, or terrorists here," one senior law enforcement official told the *New York Times.* "It's illogical, that's for certain," said another high-ranking official, referring to Salameh's Ryder sideshow. "Maybe it was their first time out of the box."[18]

Another *Times* story quoted experts in the chemical industry describing Yousef's sophisticated bomb as "cheap and easily made."

"It's very easy to make one of these things," said Edward M. Roy, an explosives expert at the New Mexico Institute of Mining and Technology. "I tell my students, a lot of explosives I can make in my waste basket."[19]

The FBI would later admit that Yousef's device was unique among all the bombs it had studied, but the article quoted other "experts" who said that "such a bomb could have been made by almost anyone with the help of one of scores of manuals obtainable in bookstores and libraries."

For many reporters, a key FBI background source was Neal Herman, the supervisory special agent in charge who ran the Joint Terrorist Task Force. In several previous accounts of the Trade Center bombing, Herman is portrayed as a figure of almost mythic proportions. In the John Miller, Michael Stone, Chris Mitchell book *The Cell,* Herman is lionized: "Beginning in 1990," they write, "Neal Herman's domestic terrorism unit at the JTTF represented the best hope America had of preventing a new international form of Islamic militantism from metastasizing into a potentially implacable threat."[20]

In *The New Jackals,* Simon Reeve's exhaustively researched biography of Yousef and bin Laden, Herman is quoted more than two dozen times.

He's described as "A veteran anti-terrorist specialist with the appearance and demeanor of a seasoned poker player."[21]

As boss of the task force since 1990, Herman was below Carson Dunbar in the hierarchy of the FBI's New York office. Although it's unclear what role, if any, he played in Salem's departure, it was on Herman's watch that the debacle over the Egyptian asset went down. Now, in what was being dubbed the TRADEBOM investigation, Neal Herman assumed the position of behind-the-scenes FBI spinmaster. He would later imply that the FBI got its next major break in the case through old-fashioned investigative work: "By the middle of the first week we were beginning to fan out with names on ticket manifests of people who had fled."[22]

At that point Mahmud Abouhalima, the next major player in the plot, had been seized in his native Egypt; Herman claimed that "we traced him through a series of investigative leads and tickets and people he had worked with at his car service."

What Herman didn't say was that the Bureau found out that the Red was in Egypt from Nancy Floyd's asset, Emad Salem.[23] In fact, since the meeting in Jim Fox's office late on the night of the bombing, the FBI had been frantic to coax Salem back undercover. There's little doubt that they needed him. The best minds the government had at its disposal couldn't compare with the forty-three-year-old Egyptian when it came to unraveling the bombing plot.

Salem Locates the Red

On March 28, the *New York Times* published the letter from Yousef's "fifth battalion" warning of future attacks by "more than 150 suicidal soldiers."[24] When the paper received the threat letter days after the bombing, it was turned over to NYPD Chief of Detectives Joseph Borelli, the man who had foolishly declared El Sayyid Nosair a "lone gunman." Borelli passed the letter on to the FBI, who deemed it "authentic."

But the next day, the *Times* quoted a "top investigator" as saying that there was "no reason to believe that the threat is real."[25] Government officials in Washington said that they'd never heard of the Liberation Army Fifth Battalion. Dr. Ayyad Abu Khalid, scholar in residence at the Middle East Institute in Washington, said that the signature on the letter, "Al-Farrek Al Rokn, Abu Bakr Al Makee," translated as "Lt. General Abu Bakr of Mecca."[26] In antiquity, Abu Bakr was a close friend of the Prophet Mohammed, and the first Caliph after his death. There were Abu Bakr Mosques all over the world. But it would be just like Yousef to boldly slip a hint into his Liberation Army letter that tied the plot to the mosque in Brooklyn where the blind Sheikh preached. William Kunstler, now representing Ibrahim El-Gabrowny, denied any link between his suspect and the bombing, but El-Gabrowny, Nosair's cousin, was a board member at the mosque.

Emad Salem knew the truth. He knew that the bombing cell was dominated by the Egyptians surrounding the Sheikh—men who used the Abu Bakr, Al Farooq, and Al Salaam mosques as their base. In fact, Salem had been visited by Salameh's cousin El-Gabrowny immediately after the bombing, while he was still in the hospital.

Now, soon after checking out of St. Claire's, Salem was watching TV coverage of the almost-aborted bust of Salameh when the phone rang. It was Special Agent John Anticev.

"I feel terrible," said Salem. "I sit here and watch TV and I'm pulling my hair. If we was continuing what we was doing, this bomb would never go off."[27]

"I know," said Anticev, admitting culpability. "But don't repeat that."[28]

Salem agreed to meet with Anticev and Napoli the next day. They needed him badly now, and he knew it. But after his dealings with Dunbar, the ex-asset was wary that the Bureau would try and somehow implicate him in the bombing plot. He was prepared to protect himself, even if it meant blowing the whistle on the FBI.

Anticev and Napoli picked Salem up from his apartment at Eighty-sixth and Broadway and headed down toward the bombing crime scene in Lower Manhattan. The NYPD detective was driving. Salem was in the shotgun seat and Anticev was behind him. As they passed the Towers, Salem exclaimed, "I told you that this is one of their targets. You forgot. You have your papers. Go back to it. World Trade Center, Empire State Building. Grand Central. Times Square."[29]

Napoli eyed Anticev in the rearview mirror and shook his head. *Uh-uh.* Anticev leaned forward in his seat. "I looked over my notes," he said. "I didn't see anything about a target."

"I was there also," said Napoli. "I don't remember you saying 'target.'"

But Salem continued to chastise the two investigators. "All of these things, you didn't think it was serious."

"We knew it was serious," said Napoli. "It wasn't that we didn't believe you. It was just that the only way you could have stay[ed] was that you had to testify."

Later, Salem pressed them further. "You get paid, guys, to prevent problems like this from happening." But Anticev and Napoli wouldn't back down. They agreed that Salem had warned of a broad bombing plot first conceived by El Sayyid Nosair, but they insisted the Trade Center hadn't been a part of it.

In any case, Salem was quick to zero in on the person he felt was most responsible for the Bureau's screwup.

"Do you deny your supervisor is the main reason of bombing the World Trade Center? We was handling the case perfectly well until the supervisor came and messed it upside down," said Salem.

This time Anticev didn't deny it.

Salem felt so strongly about the Bureau's failure to stop the bombing that he told Anticev that he wanted to complain "to FBI headquarters in Washington." But Anticev dissuaded him.

"I don't think the New York people would like the things out of the New York office to go to D.C.," he said.[30]

After the car ride past what was now being referred to as "ground zero," Anticev and Napoli invited Salem up to the JTTF office at 26 Federal Plaza. But this resulted in another gaffe that almost sent Salem packing again.

As he walked into the task force area, Salem noticed a board with a series of pictures and mug shots of the suspected bombing conspirators. His picture was among them.

"Why [are] you putting my picture here?" demanded Salem angrily. "Why am I on the board? Do you think I bombed the World Trade Center?"[31]

Anticev quickly tried to placate Salem. "Our assistant put this up for the people who get mug shots," he said. "It was an accident. Don't you remember when we brought you in with the others in September on the subpoenas? We wanted to maintain your cover. You're not a suspect, Emad. Believe me."

The conversation soon turned to Mahmud Abouhalima, Mohammed Salameh's cohort. Given Salameh's arrest, it was a sure bet that the Red had been a player in the bombing, so they asked Salem if he could help the Bureau find him.

The next day Emad appeared at the Abu Bakr Mosque in Brooklyn. He was worried at first that the "brothers" might suspect something, but instead they made fun of him.

"Oh, you don't show up your face unless there is a crisis or something," they said, ribbing him.[32] Salem breathed a sigh of relief and told them he'd been in the hospital, mentioning that Ibrahim El-Gabrowny had visited him just before he was arrested.

Salem asked about Abouhalima, who was now missing, and learned through El-Gabrowny's brother that he had escaped with his German wife and four children to Saudi Arabia. The next day Salem went to visit Abouhalima's brother, Mohammed, and discovered that the Red had moved on to Egypt. Salem immediately told the Bureau, and the information was passed to the Egyptian government, which quickly arrested him.[33]

When Neal Herman described Abouhalima's arrest as the result of "a series of investigative leads," he failed to mention that it was Emad Salem who had done the heavy lifting.

On March 20, Alison Mitchell reported in the *New York Times* that the Feds had waited almost three weeks to search Abouhalima's one-bedroom apartment in Woodbridge, New Jersey. Calling the delay a "tactical decision," the Feds also claimed that it had taken that long to get probable cause. But what was the real story? Why had the FBI waited so long to comb the last known residence of Yousef's key "facilitator"? Anticev and Napoli had generated sufficient probable cause for a search warrant of Abouhalima's Brooklyn apartment in 1991. Was it simply, as Napoli indicated, that they couldn't find him?

As it turned out, the big Egyptian had been living with his wife and four children openly at that address in the Colonial Apartments since September 1, 1992. His younger brother, Mohammed, had lived upstairs from him. Salem wanted to know why Anticev and Napoli had lost the trail when Abouhalima crossed the Hudson.

"It takes a bomb with you guys to wake up and start to move," Salem told them. He insisted that he'd been telling them all along "these guys [are] building bombs. These guys [are] going to bomb the city."

In an interview for this book, Detective Lou Napoli denied that he and his partner had any prior knowledge that the Trade Center was targeted.

"On the first meeting we had with Emad after we took him back, he said, 'I told you about the World Trade Center,'" Napoli remembered. "And I said, 'Emad, you know me. My mind's like a steel trap, and if you had told me I would have remembered it. I'm telling you right now—back off.'"[34] But even though Napoli sparred with Salem, he respected him. He called him "the Colonel," in deference to Salem's retirement pay grade—one cut above the rank of major—and the detective had real admiration for how far Salem had burrowed into the Sheikh's cell.

"When Emad left, there was a big void" in the investigation, said Napoli. "The other individuals we had were peripheral at best. He was an incredibly valuable asset."

Speaking almost a decade after the bombing, Napoli admitted that if Salem had remained with the investigation and been permitted to link to people like Abouhalima, the Trade Center blast would never have happened.

"If Emad would have stayed with us, yeah, he would have prevented it," said Napoli. "But he was afraid of testifying. He was afraid of the repercussions."[35]

As a gesture of good faith, Salem had located Abouhalima in Egypt for the Bureau. He told Napoli and Anticev that he would risk his life again, and *this* time he'd be willing to testify if the Bureau put him in Witness Protection. He would help them make their case—to do what they should have done in the fall of 1992.

In the weeks to come, Emad Salem would burrow deep into the Sheikh's deadly cell. He would uncover a plot one federal prosecutor called "a scheme and a plan so horrible, so monstrous, so vicious that if it had been successful the lives of every person in this city and in this nation would be changed forever."

But this time he wouldn't come cheap. Instead of the five hundred dollars a week he'd earned before, the government would end up paying him more than $1.5 million.

16

THE $1.5 MILLION MAN

E ight months earlier, Emad Salem had been terminated as an FBI asset on the word of a single ASAC. Now the process of getting him back involved half a dozen lawyers and senior agents from the Bureau's New York office and Washington headquarters. The negotiations went on for weeks. "The Bureau came up with the sum of one million," said one agent inside the investigation. "He didn't say, 'Here's what I want.' They came up with a proposal and gave it to Emad."[1]

Napoli, who admitted that he was the first to bring up the million-dollar figure, now began acting as an unofficial consigliere for "the Colonel," coaching him on how to bargain for the best deal. His motivation seemed to be both a genuine appreciation of what Salem could do, and a need to quickly bring him into the fold so that he could start working the Sheikh again.

"We were driving him home," Napoli recalled. "And he says to us, 'I don't know how to do this.' It was me and John at the time. And we said, 'Look, just put down what it's gonna cost. How much a house is gonna cost you. You've got two kids. You've got life insurance. Your wife has a business. And you gotta figure a house. You may lose it 'cause you might get seen [in Witness Protection]. So go two times that.' And we added it all up."[2]

Napoli said that they came up with a figure of six hundred thousand dollars for the houses. They figured another hundred thousand to get his two kids through college. "And I said to him, 'Here. This is what your expenses are gonna be.' And he said, 'Okay.' So that's what he asked for."

But at first the government balked, and Salem started getting angry. Did they want him to do this or *not*? The way he saw it, he was risking his life. Once he went back under, his world and that of his family would be turned upside down. They'd have to live in hiding forever.

Worse, Salem remained terrified that somehow the Bureau would try to implicate him in the WTC bombing. At one point in the negotiations, he was so upset that he threatened to go to CNN and tell them that the FBI had blown the investigation the first time around.[3]

"He did it because he thought we were gonna leave him out in the cold," said Napoli. "It was the attitude he'd gotten from management. He just thought that they were gonna fuck him over. That we were just using him to do all this and then he was gonna go [to prison] with the rest of them."

"I don't want to negotiate," said Salem angrily at one point. So Napoli assumed the role of his agent, asking, "Do you want me to go to a million five—then, if there's negotiation, you can bring it down to what you're happy with?"[4]

Salem was fed up, but the financial talks dragged on and on. For weeks after he'd gone back into the Sheikh's cell, Salem had no formal deal and no guarantee of Witness Protection.

"The FBI kept putting him off and putting him off," Napoli recalled. "The deeper he got into this investigation, the more he got stressed and was worried about his family's safety. He felt that we were pushing him off."[5] When this second investigation began, Anticev and Napoli were assigned as his contact agents; but once again Salem relied on Nancy Floyd.

"Salem kept reaching out to her," said an FBI source. "He'd get so pissed that he'd call Nancy and say, 'I've had it. I'm on a plane and getting out of here.'"[6]

Agent Floyd was working undercover herself in New Jersey at this point, but almost every night during the months of this new investigation, she would get a call from Salem.

"She was constantly talking to him at night," said the source, "trying to smooth his feathers, keep him happy, keep him working. But Salem was really pissed at the supervisors."

Finally, after months, the negotiations were concluded. Salem signed a contract in which the government agreed to pay him $1,056,200.[7] He would get an advance of $116,000. During the period of the undercover investigation, and in preparation for any trial, he would get $7,000 a month, plus another $2,700 a month from the U.S. Marshals during his time in Witness Protection. The government also agreed to pay $2,628.22 in hospital bills, $553.61 for Salem's cell phone, $200 for his parking tickets, and the $400 attorney's fee he'd paid the lawyer who reviewed his contract. The Feds even pledged to buy him a $200 shotgun for personal protection. In total, the package amounted to roughly $1.5 million.[8]

Considering what the FBI got in return, it was a bargain.

In less than two months from the time he officially went under, Emad Salem uncovered a plot by Sheikh Rahman and eleven other coconspirators to strike at New York's landmarks with a series of ammonium-nitrate–fuel oil (ANFO) bombs. In what the Feds later dubbed the Day of Terror plot, the devices were intended to explode simultaneously at a dozen locations around Manhattan including the George Washington Bridge, United Nations headquarters, the two tunnels connecting the city with New Jersey—even the building that housed the FBI's New York office.

A federal prosecutor later told a jury just how valuable an asset Emad Salem was: "Faced with those threats, the Government had to do something," he said. "They needed someone on the inside of this terrorist ring to stop what they had already promised was going to happen. But you can't just click your heels and get in the inside of a terrorist ring. You need someone who speaks their language; not the language of Arabic but the language of hate that fuels them. It can be impossible to infiltrate such a group."[9]

The Angry Cleric on Tape

Now, as he went back undercover, the FBI finally got its chance to wire Emad Salem. The Bureau's elite Special Operations Group gave the Egyptian an array of surreptitious devices. He had a Nagra SN recorder in a briefcase. There were two recorders planted in the trunk of his car. He even wore a specially designed pair of pants with an electronic "chip" in the groin area that recorded voices. Between May 7 and June 23, 1993, Salem made sixty-three separate recordings for the federal government.

Early on, he reconnected with Siddig Siddig Ali, the Sudanese who had run the assassination drills at a training camp near Harrisburg, Pennsylvania. Ali had even tested a sample of Yousef's bomb for Mahmud Abouhalima, and he'd driven the Red and his family to Newark airport as they made their escape. This was a crucial revelation because it tied this second Day of Terror plot to the World Trade Center bombing.

The link to the Sheikh's cell was cemented further by Salem when Siddig Ali named Clement Rodney Hampton-El as a source for explosives. The American Black Muslim, also known as "Dr. Rashid," had met Salem in the spring of 1992, while he was still working the original bombing plot inspired by Nosair. Back then, Hampton-El had offered to supply Salem with weapons and ready-made bombs. Now Salem learned that Hampton-El had been a senior member of the Sheikh's cell all along. He even confessed that he was the original backup man for the Kahane murder.[10]

This was an irony made more bitter when Anticev and Napoli looked over the 1989 Calverton shooting surveillance photos and saw Hampton-El's face. He'd been on their radar at least twice before, and they'd missed him each time.*

It was another dot on the chart of negligence.

Now, after years of underestimating the enemy, the FBI was finally beginning to see the Sheikh's followers as soldiers in a "jihad army," and Siddig Ali was emerging as one of its generals. It was Ali's plan to drive a bomb-laden vehicle into the parking garage beneath the UN. He later expanded the plot to include 26 Federal Plaza, the bridge and tunnels.

Salem got it all on tape. His role was to act as facilitator in the same way Abouhalima had helped Yousef. Salem provided the group with a van, courtesy of the FBI, and a warehouse in Jamaica, Queens, that the Bureau wired for video and sound. Salem also supplied the expertise to build what Ali and the conspirators thought was a series of ANFO devices similar to Yousef's UNFO bomb. The Egyptian even furnished his own video camera for the surveillance when he and Ali inspected the Lincoln and Holland Tunnels, conspiring to plant the devices at the midpoints of each tunnel under the Hudson River for maximum damage. Finally, Salem taped Ali and a rogues' gallery of other plotters as they mixed the chemicals.[11] Since the FBI had the bomb factory under

---

*Timeline #47. p. 10.

twenty-four-hour video surveillance, the actual danger to the public was minimal.

In his undercover role, however, Salem himself was in constant danger of exposure. At one point he had to put chewing gum on his briefcase to hide a flashing red light the FBI had installed to indicate when the tapes were running.[12] Another time, late one night when he was with the blind Sheikh in the cleric's kitchen, Salem held the briefcase right up to the blind cleric's mouth as he requested the Sheik's *fatwa,* or blessing, to bomb the FBI office. But the Sheikh told him, "Slow down. Slow down a little bit. The one who killed Kennedy was trained for three years. We don't want to do anything in haste."

Undaunted, Salem asked about Siddig's plot to blow up the UN.

SALEM: We are preparing for something big. Something big that will bring it upside down. So is this considered licit or illicit?

RAHMAN: It is not illicit; however, will be bad for Muslims. Find a plan . . .

SALEM: Yes.

RAHMAN: . . . to inflict damage on the American Army itself.[13]

Bingo! Salem had captured the Sheikh threatening the U.S. military. His *fatwa* was consistent with Yousef's "fifth battalion" letter, which warned of attacks on "military targets." At last, Rahman had been caught red-handed issuing advice for a terror plot. This was crucial to the government's case because the Sheikh's earlier suggestion that Salem turn his rifle on President Mubarak had occurred when Salem was unwired. Now the Feds had the angry cleric on tape.

Emad Salem was earning every dollar of that $1.5 million.

"There Is Somebody Following Me"

By late June of 1993, the FBI was preparing to round up the entire crew. Then, as the investigation closed in on the Sheikh, Carson Dunbar and his supervisors made another judgment call that came close to derailing the entire operation. It was an exercise in second-guessing that so angered Emad Salem he almost walked.

Siddig Ali and his coconspirators were working late into the night at the warehouse Salem had rented at 139-01 Ninetieth Avenue in Jamaica, Queens.

They had stolen trash barrels off the street and were using them as cauldrons to mix the potentially deadly combination of fertilizer and fuel oil. One of the cell members was due to supply diesel from a gas station he owned in Yonkers.[14]

"At that point, Emad purchased a timer, which we adapted," Lou Napoli recalled. "He brought it into the safe house."[15] The timer, which Salem bought for eighteen dollars in Chinatown, was identical to one he'd purchased for the original Nosair bombing plot in the summer of 1992. But when they learned that an operational timer had gone into the bomb factory, Dunbar and his supervisors got cold feet.

"They said [to Salem]. 'We want you to take that out of the safe house and bring that back to us,'" Napoli remembered. "They didn't want it popping up in somebody else's hands in an explosion down the road. I understood their point, but the safe house was totally covered. Totally wired. CCTV. Covered. We had agents around the block monitoring it. You couldn't have gotten in or out of that fucking place without us knowing."

But Dunbar and his supervisors wanted the timer removed so that it could be neutralized, then put back in place.

"This was crazy," said Napoli. "Emad yelled and screamed. He called me and said, 'How am I gonna do that? What happens if one of the bad guys comes and he says, 'Let's go to the safe house' and the thing is not there?"

Later, Salem told Agent Anticev that if Siddig Ali "feels I'm playing games behind his back, I'm the one who will be killed."[16] After Salem refused to make the swap, an FBI agent slipped into the warehouse and stole the timer—but he failed to replace it with a dummy. When Salem found out about the error he erupted, threatening to drop out of the plot and expose the FBI if the device was not replaced.

Dunbar later testified about the incident. "I remember there was some controversy about we had to make sure that the timer was still there so everything looked like it was in place, but I don't specifically remember."[17]

The incident caused Salem to recall his original run-in with Dunbar, whom he seemed to hold accountable for the Trade Center bomb: "We came to the same point from the first bomb," said Salem in a May 29 phone call to Anticev. "When I was discussing things, Mr. Carson he said, 'That's *my* way.' I said, 'I cannot do that.' He said, 'No.' I said, 'Fine.' He closed the whole case and then oops [the WTC bomb] went off. . . . I think we came to the same point again."[18]

At that moment the Bureau had yet to close its deal with Salem, even though they'd promised him the $1.5 million. Irate that the supervisors would risk his exposure over the timer, he called Nancy Floyd.

"Emad told her, 'I'm [getting] on a plane,'" said a source close to the investigation. "He was taking his family and getting out of there." But as she always did, Nancy calmed him down and got him in touch with Napoli. The detective agreed with Salem.

"It's the Bureau mentality," he told him. "CYA. Everybody wants to cover themselves."

The difference was, the supervisors were sitting behind desks: Salem was in the middle of a bomb cell.

Now, as the cell members began to construct the bombs, Salem was becoming increasingly worried that his cover might be blown. He told Anticev, "I have felt that there is somebody following me. I don't want to jeopardize my life."[19]

Salem's paranoia intensified after he learned that there were a number of Egyptian and Arab followers of the Sheikh who worked for the government and the phone company—worshipers partial to the blind cleric who might tumble to Salem's real identity.

"I was worried," Salem said later. "People told me they have people in New York Telephone. They have people in the Motor Vehicles Department and they will check me out if I'm informant or not. They even told me they know how they can check me out."[20]

Salem's fear reached a fever pitch when Ahmed Sattar, the mailman who frequented the Abu Bakr Mosque, learned of Special Agent John Anticev's home address on Staten Island. Sattar, one of the Egyptians grilled by Anticev in September 1992, had seen the FBI agent while he was working on his special-delivery postal route. Salem later warned Anticev that Sattar had shared the address with another member of the Shiekh's cell who walked off with him into a corner of the mosque.[21]

If the cell members could get the home address of *an FBI agent,* Salem felt it wouldn't be long before they found the Upper West Side apartment he shared with his common-law wife and the two children he'd brought to the United States from Egypt.

But the FBI didn't take Salem's worries seriously. No attempt was made to follow up on his suggestion that informants partial to the blind Sheikh's cell were in sensitive positions with the government or the utilities. Later, the Feds alleged, mailman Ahmed Sattar would act as a mole for the Sheikh and the Egyptian terror group al Gamma'a Islamiya. But years would pass before the FBI finally caught him.[22]

A Time Bomb Waiting to Happen

By late June, the Feds were ready to take down the Day of Terror bombing cell. Emad Salem had taped dozens of incriminating conversations with the cell members and organized the safe house where the Bureau got it all on tape. If the FBI's New York office had doubted Salem's reliability, now he had finally proven them wrong.

In the early morning hours of June 24, 1993, as five members of the bombing cell mixed the chemicals, the FBI swooped down on the safe house on Ninetieth Avenue. Three other cell members were picked up as agents fanned out across the city. Jim Fox, the ADIC who ran the New York office, announced the bust triumphantly. "The subjects were actually mixing the witches brew," said Fox, who'd been on the defensive for months amid rumors that his office had failed to stop the Trade Center bombing. "We entered so fast some of the subjects didn't know we were in the bomb factory until they were in handcuffs."[23]

The Sheikh himself was stunned to learn that his trusted bodyguard was a double agent. Asked later what he thought of Salem, Rahman replied, "He is Satan."[24]

Many informants about to go into Witness Protection after a takedown are alerted ahead of time, to give them a chance to get their affairs in order. But Salem was never warned. Right up to the moment of the bust, Carson Dunbar refused to trust him.

"They didn't tell him they were gonna take him down when they did," said an agent inside the investigation. "When they arrested him they handcuffed him and harassed him and used force with him.[25]

"The Bureau treated him like he was Sammy 'the Bull' Gravano," said

Lou Napoli, "which he was not. He lied. Every source does. Every source embellishes. Fine. But the moral of the story was that he brought it home. The reason Salem got to the blind Sheikh was that he really wanted it. He wanted to accomplish something. He knew the group was evil. So the guy worked eighteen hours a day. You never had to tell him, 'Go look at this.' He was self-motivated. A dream asset. He threw everything to the wind and just went after them."[26]

Few people were happier about the bust than U.S. Attorney Mary Jo White, who had wisely endorsed Salem's return to the Bureau in the hours after the Trade Center blast. At an afternoon press conference she quoted Siddig Ali, whom Salem had recorded boasting that the Twin Towers bombing was a message to America that "We can get you any time."[27]

"Law enforcement's answer is 'No you cannot,'" Ms. White declared. "The message sent is 'We will not be driven from our community. We will not live in fear. We will not permit the likes of these defendants to live in our city.'"

What went unsaid, of course, was that since 1989 the FBI and the Justice Department had permitted these men to live in New York while they hatched three other conspiracies: the Kahane murder, Nosair's "Twelve Jewish locations" plot, and Yousef's Trade Center bombing. Even Supervisory Special Agent Neal Herman admitted finally that they had dropped the ball:

"I've always thought that the 26-month period between the Kahane assassination and the first World Trade Center bombing was a key period," Herman was quoted as saying years later. "A time when we could have really made a statement. But that time was just lost. I'm not saying we could have prevented everything that followed, but it would have given us a fighting chance."[28]

Part of the problem was that FBI officials at headquarters felt the New York office had kept them out of the loop. Oliver "Buck" Revell, the former FBI associate deputy director for investigations, later told a congressional committee:

"I was in charge of Bureau operations at the time and I *never* received any information that the assassin of Meir Kahane was connected with any sort of organization that might have a terrorist agenda. As it turned out later there was substantial information available that, if it had been properly translated, processed, authenticated, and analyzed, would have led to a direct association between the assassin of Kahane and the group that bomb[ed] the Trade Center and was conspiring to carry out other heinous acts of terror."[29]

An agent inside the New York office at the time was more specific: "Those of us who worked this knew it was just a time bomb waiting to happen."

Until Emad Salem helped break the Day of Terror plot, damning admissions like that had stayed inside the Bureau. Soon, however, people on the outside would begin to catch on.

17

THE BOOTLEG TAPES

The indictments announced on June 25, the day after the bust, referred to an unnamed "informant" who was a key to the unraveling of the plot; Emad Salem was never mentioned by name. Now, a rumor began to circulate that the FBI might have had knowledge of the Sheikh's murderous cell long before the takedown in the Queens warehouse.

New York Times reporter Ralph Blumenthal was the first to raise questions. He quoted Mike Guzofsky, international chairman of the pro-Kahane movement Kahane-Chai, suggesting that "a proper FBI investigation into Mr. Nosair's connections after the shooting of the rabbi 'would have clearly led to Mr. Salameh and prevented the loss of life at the Trade Center.'"[1]

Congressman Charles Schumer (D-NY)—today New York's senior senator—asked, "Why didn't they look at it further?"[2] He agreed that the Nosair killing "should have sent out more signals." The chairman of the House Subcommittee on Crime and Criminal Justice, Schumer ordered FBI director Louis Freeh to testify at a hearing into how the Bureau had handled the Trade Center bombing.[3]

By late September 1993, after Salem's name had become public, his ex-wife said that on the day of the WTC explosion, Emad told her that if the FBI had only *listened* to him the bombing could have been stopped. The FBI's New York office denied the claim, and Salem's credibility was attacked.

"Authorities say that Mr. Salem was a difficult personality," reported the *New York Times,* "and not deemed credible until after the blast."[4]

This stance put Carson Dunbar and those attacking Salem in the uncomfortable position of impeaching the U.S. attorney's star witness in the upcoming Day of Terror case. It was a difficult position to defend. Why would Salem be credible *after* the blast but not before? And if he wasn't credible, why had the Feds agreed to pay him $1.5 million as their linchpin witness?

In late October, pouring gasoline on an internal FBI fire, officials from the New York office went on record alleging that Salem "had *not* warned them that the Trade Center was to be attacked nor, they said, could he have done that by the time his relationship to the Bureau was interrupted, half a year before the attack."[5]

The truth was that Salem's last meeting with Nancy Floyd had been in the fall of 1992. He'd also stayed in touch with the central players: Abouhalima had called him in December, and Salem had made a trip to Attica to visit Nosair less than two months before the February 1993 bombing. But officials in the FBI's New York office insisted that he'd been out of the loop and unable to predict or stop the blast.

The fallout soon spread to Washington. FBI headquarters announced that it was beginning an immediate internal probe into the way Salem had been handled. At a news conference to discuss television violence, Attorney General Reno was hammered with questions about Salem. Taking no pleasure in the controversy, Nancy Floyd told Salem that "heads would roll."

The first victim was Jim Fox, the assistant director in charge of the New York office. Fox was an FBI veteran who knew how to work the press. The man credited with "getting Gotti," Fox made a celebrated quote to the press after the Justice Department's fourth and ultimately successful attempt to put the mob boss away. "The Teflon is gone," Fox told reporters. "The Don is covered with Velcro and all the charges stuck."[6] Now the Velcro seemed to be covering Fox's own shop and he became fiercely defensive.

When Yousef's fifth battalion letter had surfaced the month after the bombing, warning of a "hundred and fifty suicidal solders" ready to attack U.S. "military and civilian targets," Fox dismissed the allegation. This put him at odds with evidence Salem uncovered weeks later, when Siddig Ali revealed to him on tape that he had people "very well trained" for "suicidal missions."[7]

Now, in late October, New York *Newsday* and the *New York Times* quoted Salem in page-one stories criticizing Agent John Anticev:

"I told you the World Trade Center [was a target] but nobody listened."[8]

On December 4, appearing on Channel 11's *News Closeup*, Fox had had enough. Asked about the allegations, he denigrated Salem: "He gave us nothing. No one gave us anything. If we had information, we would have prevented the bombing."

But investigators at FBI headquarters, now probing Salem's charges, knew better. Worse yet, Fox was openly attacking Mary Jo White's central witness. For the head of the New York office, it turned out to be the interview that all upper-level federal bureaucrats fear—the dreaded CTM, or career-terminating moment. Almost immediately, with Fox just weeks away from retirement, FBI director Louis Freeh sent him packing.

"Director Freeh made the decision to place Assistant Director Fox on administrative leave with pay until his retirement in January," said John Collingwood, a Bureau spokesman. "He did so after carefully reviewing inappropriate public comments Fox made about a pending prosecution."

Now an internal conflict was splitting the New York office. On one side were the street agents who knew the truth about Salem. On the other, supervisors who allegedly wanted a cover-up.

One active-duty FBI agent with direct knowledge of the situation put it bluntly: "The supervisors were saying they didn't know anything; that we didn't have any information ahead of time. No sources. No nothing. But the street agents were going, 'Yes we did.' "[9]

What Did They Know and When Did They Know It?

As with many internal disputes in the FBI, none of the details of this struggle would have come to light except for the very device that Carson Dunbar insisted Emad Salem use in the first place: a tape recorder. The Egyptian informant was so distrustful of Dunbar and the other supervisors that when we went undercover a second time, he didn't just tape the bad guys, he also taped the Feds.

Days after the Day of Terror bust, Salem told an assistant U.S. attorney that for months he'd been making his *own* bootleg tapes: dozens of recordings on his home phone, and with a hidden microcassette recorder he carried when he met with agents. Who knew what Salem had said on those tapes about the way he'd been handled by the Bureau? Was it possible that he'd warned the FBI about the Trade Center bomb, and they'd ignored him? Senior supervisors had visions of Nixon and Watergate: what did the FBI know about the bomb, and when did they know it? Fear shot through the upper floors at 26 Federal Plaza.

Carson Dunbar was determined to find those tapes. Almost from the moment he first met Emad Salem, Dunbar had seen him as an informant who was beyond Bureau supervision. Now the bootleg tapes seemed to confirm his suspicions.

"He was an informant that was out of control," Dunbar said in 2002, "the ultimate opportunist."[10] Jim Roth, the FBI's top New York lawyer, agreed, and he extended his criticism to Salem's control agent Nancy Floyd.

"Salem was a shaky character [and] she was a shaky character," Roth said in an interview for this book.[11]

"Jim Roth didn't trust Floyd," a source close to the investigation confirmed. "He saw her as an agent who had crossed the line and become too loyal to her asset [Salem]. There was a sense between Roth and Dunbar that the tapes would confirm this."[12]

The federal prosecutors wanted the bootleg tapes for other reasons. Salem had first mentioned the taping as he was being debriefed at a nearby location by Assistant U.S. Attorney Andrew McCarthy. A street-smart thirty-four-year-old, AUSA McCarthy had put himself through Columbia College by working as a deputy U.S. marshal.[13] Having worked Witness Protection in the Southern District of New York (SDNY), he understood the pressure Salem must have been under. The Egyptian was terrified now that his cover had been blown. He had dozens of questions: Where would he go with his family? How would they live? Most important, how could he trust the Feds to protect them?

The news about the tapes caused McCarthy some concern, but he kept a poker face. He would need Salem's trust in the months ahead as they prepared for trial. McCarthy carefully explained to Salem that he needed to hear the bootleg tapes for practical reasons. Under the Brady rules, all exculpatory material had to be turned over to the defense.[14] In the upcoming trial, the principal defense would surely be entrapment—

the argument that if not for Salem's inducement, the other plotters would never have built the bombs.

If, somewhere in those bootleg tapes, there was evidence that Salem had coerced the defendants beyond what they were predisposed to do without him, the case could fall. McCarthy *had* to hear them.

But Salem was adamant. "No. I give you tapes of bad guys—the CMs, but not the rest. . . . It is not a crime to record somebody in New York. I have checked."

Salem was right on the law. The CMs were the tapes of Salem's "consensual monitoring," done under strict FBI guidelines. As far as his *own* recordings went, he couldn't be held liable. New York was a "one party consent state," meaning that as long as the person *doing* the recording agreed to be taped, the bugging wouldn't violate privacy laws. So McCarthy didn't press the point: Salem still had some of the official CM tapes at his apartment, and the prosecutor needed his cooperation to get them.

Besides, pressure was the worst tactic to use on the Egyptian at this point. Salem was emotionally drained. The Feds hadn't trusted him enough to give him notice of the safe house bust. They'd even roughed him up a bit in the takedown. Salem complained of having a "panic attack," and was hospitalized for a time. Now he'd been discharged and was waiting with McCarthy at the debriefing location. There were some personal items in his apartment that he needed. But the only one he would trust to retrieve them was Nancy Floyd.

In the months since the Trade Center bombing, Nancy had left Foreign Counter Intelligence and was working with the FBI's Special Operations Group—the black bag unit. But virtually every night, as she had during Salem's first trip under, she would talk to him by phone or in person.

"They'd formed a real bond," said Floyd's mentor, Len Predtechenskis. "Salem felt that Nancy was the only person in the Bureau who would tell him the truth. So she was working double duty again, just to calm him down and keep him working."

On June 29, McCarthy called Carson Dunbar and told him that if he wanted the tapes, he would have to involve Nancy Floyd. On the other end of the line, Dunbar must have winced. He not only disliked Floyd, he didn't trust her. He'd told another agent as much right in front of her.

"Somebody has to answer for the agents who run amok," said Dunbar years later, and to him Salem's bootleg tapes were proof positive that the ex-Egyptian was way out of line. But now he was stuck: if he wanted to hear those bootleg tapes, Dunbar would have to suck it up and reach out to Nancy Floyd. So she was contacted at her SOG off-site location and ordered to report to 26 Federal Plaza immediately.

When she got there, Nancy found Dunbar sitting with Jim Roth, the head lawyer in the FBI's New York office. According to an FBI source, they asked her about the bootleg tapes, implying that Salem had hinted she knew about them in advance.

Floyd denied any knowledge of the unauthorized recordings and said she couldn't believe her trusted asset would say such a thing about her. As she eyed Dunbar and Roth, Nancy, the Texan, felt as if she was being fitted for a noose. There was only one way to stop the hanging.

"Let's call him," said Nancy. "Let's get Emad on the phone."

"I've Gotta Take the Hit"

They called Salem at the debriefing site and put the call on the speaker-phone. Nancy had to know from her asset what he'd said about the tapes. "Emad, did you tell them that I knew where some tapes were in your office?" she asked.[15]

"Absolutely not," shot back Salem. Furious that the one agent he trusted was taking the heat for all this, Salem told them that he would allow Nancy, and Nancy *alone,* to go to his apartment and pick up the consensual tapes, plus some personal things he had in his closet. At that point Floyd looked over at Dunbar. According to a source with knowledge of the meeting, she thought to herself, "You lying sack of shit. You were trying to set me up."[16]

"Nancy wasn't feeling real comfortable," said the source. "She began to suspect that something was going on—and it wasn't just Dunbar. Now Jim Roth was in on it. He was sitting right there and he knew what was going on."

What Floyd *didn't* know at the time was that the management of the New York office was getting called down to Washington to answer questions about whether they had any prior warning of the Trade Center bombing.[17] Since Salem was at the heart of those allegations, and he'd made all these tapes, Dunbar and Roth wanted to hear them. Finally,

Andrew McCarthy jumped on the line. Nancy asked him if he was sure there was nobody else who could retrieve them.

"No. Absolutely," said the AUSA. "He won't let anybody else, and I need those tapes, Nancy. I need to know what's on them. He's agreed to let you go in. He's signed a consent."

At the time, Nancy hadn't seen the consent form or read the wording. It was her understanding that Salem was granting her limited access to his apartment to obtain *only* the CMs, or "bad guy tapes." Salem told her exactly where they were hidden: under the cushions of a green chair in his bedroom and the living room sofa.

The document that he signed stated: "I, Emad Salem, give Special Agent Nancy Floyd, FBI, permission to enter my residence, number 525, 2350 Broadway, New York, New York, to retrieve tape recordings currently located there."

At this point the versions differ. A source close to Floyd said that it was her understanding that Roth would remain outside in the hall while she entered Salem's apartment, and that Lynn Harris, a female FBI agent from the New York office, would wait at the doorway as an observer. According to the source, Floyd's belief was based on Salem's word that she and she alone had permission to enter the apartment.

But Roth saw it differently. "The consent was broad," he said later. "It said 'tapes.'"[18] As far as he was concerned that meant that any tapes could be seized—CMs or otherwise.

For his part, Dunbar remains adamant: "I had nothing to do with [Floyd] or what the strategy was to go and get the tapes," he said in a recent interview for this book. The former ASAC even denied calling Floyd to the FBI office to discuss the tapes in the first place. "I know there was a meeting with Nancy before she went to the apartment. I don't remember specifically if I was there. I could have been there, but [the allegation] that I had her brought in—that's totally incorrect."[19]

In any case, a major conflict was about to erupt.

When they arrived at Salem's building, Nancy entered the apartment and immediately found fifteen to twenty of the consensual monitoring tapes under the cushions, exactly where Salem had said they would be. She was in his closet picking up some of the personal items he'd asked for, when suddenly Roth entered the apartment.

"The next thing Nancy knows, she comes out of the closet and Roth is going through the desk," said a source. "She [was] freaking out."

Nancy confronted the lawyer. "What the hell are you *doing*?" she demanded. Nancy looked down on the desk and saw that Roth had discovered another cache of cassettes: the bootleg tapes.

"We weren't supposed to take those," said Nancy. "We only have permission to do this." She showed him the CMs she'd retrieved. "I'm the one that got Emad into doing this. You've got to stop right now." By that point, Roth had discovered thirty to forty tapes.

"There was a desk that was directly where this green chair was," said Roth, "and there were two tape recorders there. They were hooked up. There were two tapes in the tape recorders. So we took them. We looked through a couple of the desk drawers and got more tapes there, and also there were some pictures he had taken for a book he was writing that showed how he had concealed the tape recorders in his vehicle. We had a trial coming up, and who knew at that point if it was going to be evidentiary?" So Roth took the pictures as well.

But Nancy wouldn't give in. "You can't do that," she said, lecturing the lawyer. "This is illegal. You had no right to open those drawers in the first place." She was so worried that she'd been set up to participate in an illegal search that she asked Roth if she should retain her own lawyer.[20]

Roth got on the phone with Dunbar, and the two of them agreed that all the material seized would be taken to the debriefing location where Salem was being held.

At that point Nancy was in shock. "I'm out of here," she said. "I don't want anything to do with this. I'm not losing my job. I'm not getting sued. What you people are doing is wrong, wrong, wrong."[21]

The atmosphere in the car on the way to the base was like ice. Roth drove, with Agent Harris in the front passenger seat and Nancy fuming in back. Nobody said a thing.

When they got to the debriefing location, Roth underscored how little trust Dunbar had in Floyd or Salem at this point. "The instruction that we had from executive management was that she was not to be left alone with him," Roth said later. "She was not to be placed in a position where she could have a conversation with him. Unfortunately, something got screwed up and as he was coming into the room where we were, she had an opportunity to say some things to him. My recollection is that she said, 'I told them not to do this.' "

Salem erupted. "He was livid," said a source. "He started screaming at Nancy. For the first time in their relationship, he felt she'd betrayed him."

Roth reportedly told Salem to sit down and shut up.[22]

AUSA McCarthy intervened and asked Salem to calm down. He assured him that Nancy Floyd had no idea additional tapes would be taken. She hadn't even seen his consent to search. Salem almost broke down crying. He pulled Nancy away into a room the size of a closet, where Roth couldn't hear them, and began apologizing.

"I'm sorry, sorry, sorry," he said.

Finally McCarthy, the level-headed ex-U.S. marshal, spoke to Salem and Nancy alone. He explained that all Salem's dangerous undercover work would be for naught if he didn't turn over the bootleg tapes. McCarthy had to listen to the recordings so that they could be shared, if necessary, with the defense. That was the law, the American system of justice. If they didn't follow the rules, they had no case.

Salem, who'd been mistreated so many times by the Bureau, nodded. He looked at Nancy. "Some of those tapes have you and John [Anticev] and Louie," he said. He reminded her that she'd made some comments about her bosses in the Bureau that might prove embarrassing.

Now Nancy understood why Salem had been trying to hold on to the tapes—to protect her and his other two control agents. She smiled. "Emad, I can't imagine anything I said on there that wasn't true. Even if I cussed, what I said was true, and whatever I said, I've gotta take the hit because Andrew needs them and you've gotta give 'em over." She nodded toward McCarthy. There was a long pause as Salem looked into her eyes. He couldn't trust anybody else. Finally, he nodded and they went into the next room where Roth was sitting.

"Now she had *two* top managers in the New York office pissed at her," said Len Predtechenskis. "Carson Dunbar, the administrative special agent in charge, and Jim Roth, the head lawyer."

Dunbar characterized his feelings years later. "When something happens," he said, "we look to somebody to blame."[23] As far as he was concerned, that person was Nancy Floyd.

But Len couldn't disagree more. For years one of the New York office's top Soviet counterintelligence agents, Predtechenskis was appalled by the way Agent Floyd was treated; it was one of the reasons he agreed to be interviewed for this book.

"Nancy Floyd was a straight, honest, incredibly hardworking street agent," he said. "If Emad Salem had been the key to bringing down the blind Sheikh's cell, she was the FBI agent most responsible. She not only recruited him, but she stuck with him day and night, for months, for years, until he delivered."

Now Nancy was being cast as the scapegoat. From early on, as an agent from another branch of the New York office—and a straight-talking woman from Texas at that—Floyd had rubbed the management of the Terrorism branch the wrong way. Supervisor John Crouthamel had called her a "bitch" and tried to separate her from Salem; Dunbar said openly that he didn't trust her. There had been the unproven allegations of sexual impropriety floated about the office. But none of that prepared Nancy for what was to come.

Nailing the Coffin Lid Down

Within a few days of going head-to-head with Jim Roth over the tape seizure, Nancy Floyd got word that she was now the subject of an investigation by the FBI's Office of Professional Responsibility. "She was in shock," said a source close to Nancy.

The FBI's OPR is the Bureau equivalent of a police department's Internal Affairs Division.[24] The office was designed as a well-intentioned internal watchdog unit, set up to root out corruption in the Bureau's ranks. But by the late 1990s, it had developed into a two-tiered entity, with street or brick agents like Nancy Floyd subject to discipline much harsher than agents above the rank of SAC (special agent in charge). At least that was the perception.[25]

Worse, an OPR investigation could be opened on a street agent on the basis of little more than a whisper or an anonymous phone call, casting a cloud over the agent's career that could linger for years.[26] Now such a case had been opened against Nancy Floyd, and it not only threatened her status as an agent, it could have resulted in jail time.

"A recommendation went down to headquarters," said Roth, "to open up a criminal investigation [on Floyd] for leaking information to this guy [Salem]."

Roth was actually recommending to the Justice Department that Floyd be prosecuted. "But something happened over at Justice," he continued.[27] "They declined to prosecute, and the matter was dialed back to an OPR Administrative Inquiry." That meant that while Nancy was no longer subject to a potential prison sentence, she might still lose her job.

"All of a sudden in '93, Nancy gets a call from Allen Kroft," said Len Predtechenskis. "He's the head of the voucher section. He calls and asks her, 'Is something going on with you?'" Nancy felt a chill and asked him why. "'Cause management's over here,'" Len said, quoting Kroft. "'They're asking about all your financial records. All your vouchers.'"

The implication was that, in her many dealings with Salem, perhaps Nancy hadn't fully accounted for the five hundred dollars in cash he was getting each week in increments. Salem had been paid an additional thousand dollars a month to cover his expenses. Now the voucher section chief was letting Nancy know that management couldn't find all the receipts she was supposed to have submitted.

Floyd kept meticulous records, though, and soon she was able to establish that any financial discrepancies were the Bureau's fault, not hers. The Feds had been transitioning to a computerized expense-reporting system, and some of her paperwork hadn't been logged in. The incomplete computer files had made it look as if she was holding something back. Floyd called the voucher people and offered to furnish them with a copy of every receipt Salem had signed. "Later they called her back," said a source, "and dropped [that part of] the case."

Still, the overall OPR investigation continued. "Nancy Floyd got treated the way people get treated when they cross their supervisor in the FBI," said Richard Swick, a partner in the D.C. law firm of Swick and Shapiro, which handled Nancy's case.

Swick represented dozens of FBI agents as counsel to the FBI Agent's Association, and over the years he remembered a number of OPR cases involving Carson Dunbar.

"I'm not saying he did stuff in bad faith," said Swick, "but if [Dunbar] decides somebody needs to get hammered, he sets out to do it."[28]

Again, Dunbar adamantly disagreed. "As far as the OPR goes," he said, "I had nothing to do with that. I was interviewed by OPR and I gave a deposition [regarding Floyd] that I believe was correct. I had nothing to do with her OPR."

Like most agents who become subject to an OPR investigation, Floyd had very little sense of the specific charge in the beginning. "Whenever they start an investigation," said Swick, "they just give a two- or three-word blurb, like 'the subject agent was insubordinate.'" Then agents assigned to OPR conduct a series of interviews to see if the charge or charges have merit.

While an OPR is ongoing, agents are typically prevented from advancing in Bureau ranks, or getting transferred to their OP (office of preference).

As such, the system is subject to abuse.

"Once an agent has an OPR opened against him, he is really knocked out of competition for any promotions," said Diane Bodner Duhig, a former attorney with Swick and Shapiro who worked on Nancy's case.[29] The system can get downright draconian. In his 1993 book, *The FBI*, Ron Kessler interviewed Gary Penrith, a special agent in the FBI's Newark office who described the impact of an OPR: "As soon as OPR is called in, you are stigmatized," said Penrith. "It's all secret stuff. As soon as they get to the office and do their first interview we have a rumor. No matter what the outcome is, everyone remembers that OPR came out and interviewed Gary Penrith."[30]

In Nancy's case, besides the unfounded sexual rumors, her situation was inflamed by Salem's bootleg tapes. In a number of secret recordings made by the Egyptian without her knowledge, Nancy referred to the FBI management as "gutless" and "chickenshits" who "got caught with their pants down after the World Trade Center explosion."

On another tape, she related a conversation she'd had with her supervisor. Not realizing she was being recorded, she expressed the fear that telling the truth about what she knew of the Trade Center bombing could have repercussions for her down the line.

"I may be nailing my coffin lid down," said Nancy, "but this thing was handled completely wrong from the very beginning. . . . Emad had the information about the bombs and where they wanted to have them placed. If we had done what we were supposed to have done, we would have known about it. We would have used our heads and come up with a solution of trying to neutralize the situation."[31]

The implication was clear: there was blood on the hands of the management in the FBI's New York office.

Suddenly, as word of the tapes got around in the office, Nancy began to feel isolated and frozen out. "I was told, 'Don't talk to Nancy,'" recalled Len Predtechenskis, the closest thing to a father figure Floyd had in the office.

The Twelve-Page Memo Disappears

Matters went from bad to worse when Floyd tried to retrieve that twelve-page memo she'd written with Predtechenskis and the other two agents back in the summer of 1992, recounting the history of her dealings with Salem. Now Nancy wanted to give it to Assistant U.S. Attorney McCarthy, but she found that it had mysteriously vanished.

"It disappeared," said Predtechenskis. "The last time anybody saw it was in the outgoing basket of Nancy's supervisor [Jim Sherman]. Now it was gone."

So agents began to shy away from her. "They hid in their cubby-holes," Predtechenskis recalled. "She was under this cloud, which was totally and completely unfair. As I said, they should have been kissing her ass, and now they were trying to make her out to be the scapegoat."

Predtechenskis was one of the few agents who went to bat for Nancy. As the lead counter-Soviet intelligence agent in the office, his history of service to the Bureau was impeccable. "They couldn't get to me," he noted. "I had a track record."

At that point in 1993, Predtechenskis had already put in enough time to qualify for his FBI pension. He'd reached the point in the Bureau where he was considered KMA. "It stands for Kiss My Ass," said Predtechenskis candidly. "It's a big thing in the FBI. It means that I have twenty years in as an agent and I've reached the age of fifty. I could retire at the end of the day if I wanted to. It's a comforting feeling, 'cause if they're going to zero in on you and OPR wants to start investigating, you can retire before they can open up the paperwork."

To hear that from a decorated Bureau veteran is an indication of the atmosphere of fear that exists among FBI street agents today—the fear that expressing even modest disagreement with a supervisor, or staying loyal to an asset the way Nancy Floyd had, might result in an investigation with career-ending implications.

Special Agent Floyd had done little more than disagree with Carson Dunbar over a matter of tactics. The ASAC had wanted Salem to wear a wire and become a criminal informant, risking exposure. Floyd believed Salem could safely continue on as an intelligence asset without having to testify. Now, in the summer of 1993, she was being punished for some tough but honest street language captured on Salem's bootleg tapes long after the fact.

A central charge of Nancy's OPR was that she had been "insubordinate." But had she openly *disobeyed* management or had she merely done her job, then refused to fall on her sword when the bootleg tapes surfaced? Because of the secret nature of the OPR process, the answer to that question remains locked in FBI files. But the evidence does seem clear on one matter—whether Floyd was singled out. In 1993, the average OPR lasted three to four months.[32] The investigation of Nancy Floyd would cast a shadow over her career for the next five and a half years.

18

INTO THE ABYSS

On the day after the Trade Center bombing, as he moved across the fractured B-1 level below the Towers, Fire Marshal Ronnie Bucca had no idea that the area would soon be off-limits to the Bureau of Fire Investigation. Except for a token presence, the FBI was about to exclude the BFI from the bombing investigation. The Feds' decision was ironic, considering that it was a pair of FDNY marshals who first discovered the epicenter of the blast.

Less than fifteen minutes after the explosion on February 26, Fire Marshals Phil Meagher and Bob Putney were heading east on the Belt Parkway in Brooklyn, responding to a report of a dead body in a rubbish fire on King's Highway.[1] A few minutes after 12:30 P.M., the radio crackled with a call from their supervisor, Jimmy Bannon: "Forget the dead body in Flatbush," he said. "Respond forthwith to the World Trade Center. There's been a major explosion."[2]

Meagher had spent thirteen years with 60 Engine in the South Bronx and 332 Engine in East New York. For the past twelve he'd been a senior fire marshal assigned to Brooklyn Base. Putney was a rookie.

Meagher hit the siren of their unmarked Chevy Caprice, and Putney switched the department radio to Manhattan. They did a 180 on the parkway and headed west.

"As soon as we made that turn around Owl's Head Park, where you could see Lower Manhattan," said Meagher, "we caught sight of heavy gray smoke pushing out of the Twin Towers at about the fiftieth floor. I looked at Bobby. He looked at me. We didn't say a word. As we got into the Brooklyn Battery Tunnel, all you could see were the flashing lights of the police, fire, and EMS vehicles. It was surreal. We knew we were heading into a major, major disaster."

As the fire marshals drove past the Vista Hotel, they saw that the huge metal parking garage doors leading down into the Trade Center garage had been blown out. Hundreds of people were racing out of the hotel lobby. "Their faces were smoke-stained," said Meagher. "They were bleeding, coughing, in shock."

When Meagher and Putney entered the lobby, Chief Fire Marshal John Stickevers had already set up a field headquarters. Over the next fifteen minutes, twenty-five fire marshals, four supervisors, and two deputy chiefs had assembled. Stickevers broke them down into teams. Most were designated to interview victims. Others were sent to locate plans of the Trade Center complex. Stickevers gave Meagher and Putney the "cause and origin," making them the lead team to determine the source of the blast. They headed down into the crater, accompanied by their supervisor, Jimmy Bannon, and John Strandberg, a firefighter assigned to the FDNY Forensic Unit.

"We started making our way down into the abyss," said Meagher. "It was a sight to behold. The area was filled with smoke. There were car alarms and horns going off. There were ruptured water pipes all over with water shooting out, electrical conduits hanging, gigantic pieces of concrete dangling held in place by half-inch rebar. It looked like a Brazilian rain forest on fire."

The danger faced by the marshals at this point was acute. There was the real possibility of secondary explosions or an additional collapse. But as ex-firefighters, Marshals Meagher, Putney, and Bannon knew the risks. If they were ever going to find the men who had done this, it was crucial in those early postblast minutes to locate the area of origin before key forensic evidence was obliterated by fire or buried under debris.

Over the next three hours, using handheld flashlights, the fire marshals worked their way through the treacherous bombed-out subbasements. They tracked their way back to the ramp outside Room 107 by checking for signs of brisance, the path of the bomb's explosive force as the Ryder van shattered outward.

Firefighter Strandberg snapped the first, most important photographs of the pristine epicenter. In order to get some angles, he had to lean out over the four-story crater, with Meagher and Putney holding him by his belt. Along the way the marshals encountered a bizarre, almost miraculous site amid the debris. There was a car teetering on the edge of the B-2 level with its trunk blown open. Atop the trunk lid, held in place by a twisted piece of metal, was a single porcelain angel, completely intact. Meagher later determined that the car belonged to a Dominican Roman Catholic nun who had intended to give the angel as a gift. She'd parked on the B-2 level just before the explosion. "She was lucky to be alive," said Meagher.

But if the marshals thought for a moment that God had intervened in all this, their minds changed when they encountered the shattered remains of the lunchroom adjacent to Room 107 where Monica Smith and the other three WTC workers had died.

"There was a fifteen-inch steel I-beam that had been bent like a pretzel and hurled into the room," said the veteran fire marshal. "The force of that blast had to be tremendous."

Then Meagher looked up and spotted a pair of columns fifty to sixty feet away. The numbers on them had once designated parking areas on the B-2 level. He drew a small diagram of the blast scene and related the lunchroom to the columns.[3]

By 4:00 P.M. the marshals were back in the lobby reporting to Chief Stickevers. A Port Authority engineer arrived with blueprints, and using the column numbers he'd copied, Meagher was able to virtually pinpoint the position of the Ryder truck. The area of the blast had been immediately south of the southernmost bearing wall of the North Tower. It was in between the two structural support columns Meagher had marked.[4]

Considering that the "cause and origin" had been done in the midst of a raging fire suppression and rescue operation, it was a good day's work. But the BFI's role as lead agency in the bombing investigation wouldn't last long.

"Later that night we were told that NYPD had command of the scene," said Meagher. "And by Monday morning, after they'd tied the C-VIN to the van, it belonged to the FBI."

As the lead investigators who had gone down into the crater first, Meagher and Putney were allowed into the probe. Over the next three months, dozens of agents from the FBI, the ATF, and the NYPD's Arson and Explosions unit would work the investigation. But Meagher and

Putney were the only two fire marshals given official search team IDs by the Bureau.

Many marshals were bitter over the exclusion. "You have to understand that this was the most significant arson event in city history," said Robert McLoughlin, a retired marshal who's now a vice president at Citibank.[5] "But we were treated like second-class citizens."

The slight became even more ironic when the Feds on Meagher's search team, afraid their plastic safety helmets wouldn't be sturdy enough to protect them, asked the marshals for help.

"They wanted to know if the fire department could supply them with some of our Cairn's helmets," said Meagher. "So I called Chief Stickevers. He went right to the commissioner's office and we provided them with eight helmets immediately."

The thought of federal agents crawling around the blast site under fire helmets was a bit much for some marshals, especially since all but two of them were officially excluded from the probe. "We were basically told by the FBI, 'You can go in,'" said McLoughlin, "'but you will enter the scene under the auspices and guidance of an FBI agent. You will not determine anything. The Bureau of Fire Investigation is shut down.'" McLoughlin said that the word had come down to the marshals from FDNY headquarters.

Law enforcement agencies are notorious for petty rivalries, and the FBI is an easy target because of the Bureau's reputation for being a one-way street when it comes to sharing information. Clearly a terrorist incident like the Trade Center bombing had to be an FBI show from start to finish. But the degree to which the Bureau seemed to shun the input of experienced investigators is key to this story. One of the major findings in the Senate-House Joint Inquiry into the intelligence failures that led to 9/11 was that agencies like the FBI failed to communicate with "local and state authorities," depriving the intelligence community of "access to potentially valuable information in the 'war' against Bin Laden."[6]

In the years when terrorism was primarily a tactic of radical groups abroad, local U.S. law enforcement agencies had little to worry about. But on February 26, 1993, Osama bin Laden and Ramzi Yousef carried their violent jihad to the streets of Manhattan. Now, except for a token presence, the marshals who had been responsible for fire investigation in New York for decades were removed from the fight.

Few members of service understood that better, or felt stung by the exclusion more, than Ronnie Bucca. On March 1, the FBI officially commenced the TRADEBOM investigation. But two days before they shut down the crime scene, Ronnie had gone down to look at the crater for himself. In the early morning hours on Saturday he'd driven down to the site with fellow marshals Jimmy Reilly and Jim Mallon. They'd parked on Vesey Street by the North Tower and entered the parking garage at street level.

"There were a few NYPD squad cars there," said Reilly, "but I couldn't believe there was no other security."[7]

The marshals in their red jackets just walked right in and made their way down to the B-1 level, passing along a corridor where a cinder-block wall had buckled from the force of Yousef's blast. Ronnie had brought along that disposable camera, and he banged off a picture.

"We got to this point where Ronnie figured Kevin had gone in," said Reilly. Bucca got close to the edge and took a shot of the broken concrete floor of the B-1 ramp.[8] The rebar was protruding, just as Shea had said. Later, when they got to the B-4 level, Ronnie took a picture of a blue van flipped like a Matchbox toy. "All of us knew that the Feds had to run this," said Reilly, "but we figured, as experienced fire investigators, we'd have some kind of place in it. That didn't happen."

In the days ahead, as he worked his tours at Bronx Base, Ronnie couldn't get the images out of his mind: the shattered concrete and pieces of twisted rebar that had impaled Kevin's leg, and the blood-stained debris in Room 107 where Monica Smith had died. He began to keep a file in his locker marked "The Towers."

He poured over the daily press accounts and picked up every piece of intel he could from his buddies in the military.

By mid-March, Ronnie had begun to form his own "mosaic" of the event. Bucca never believed the Bureau spin that the bombing had been the work of amateurs. The device was too sophisticated—so powerful that a piece of the van's bumper was blown up the B-1 ramp hundreds of yards and out onto West Street, where it shattered the rear window of a passerby's car, demolished an empty child seat, and embedded itself as a molten ball in the dash.[9]

Ronnie talked to structural engineers who told him that if the Ryder van had been placed near the seawall side of the "bathtub" that enclosed the sixteen-acre site, it could have ruptured, inundating Lower Manhattan as the Hudson River poured in. The terrorists' mistake had been one of architecture, not bomb design. Ronnie couldn't wait to get down to D.C. and discuss the bombing with his fellow reservists at DIAC, the Defense Intelligence Analysis Center.

Then, at the end of March, during a long reserve weekend, Bucca made a startling discovery. He came across some intelligence about the bombing that stopped him in his tracks—evidence suggesting that the threat to New York and the Trade Center wasn't over.

Eve Bucca said she'll never forget the night Ronnie came home from that weekend away. He was still in uniform when he rushed into the kitchen. It was late, and the two kids, Jessica and little Ronnie, were asleep.[10]

"You've gotta see this," said Ronnie. He opened up a DIA file and started pulling out mug shots.

"Wait. If you show me these are you gonna have to kill me?" Eve joked.

"It's declassified," said Ronnie. He pointed to a picture of Emad Salem. "This is the snitch the Bureau had working the Sheikh's cell. They cut him loose. Now they're about to pay him like a million and a half to make a case he could've made before."

"What?" said Eve. "The bombing?" Ronnie nodded. "You're telling me they *knew*?"

"They knew some kind of bombing was going down," said Ronnie. "The Bureau's been following these mutts for years." He pointed at the mug shots of Abouhalima and Salameh.

"Are you saying they could have stopped it?"

Ronnie nodded. "All they had to do was follow this guy." He pointed to Abouhalima. "He would've led them straight to the guy who built the bomb."

"Where's *his* picture?" asked Eve.

"He's an unsub," said Ronnie. "Unknown subject. The intel says they called him 'Rashed.' He got away the night of the bombing and guess what? He's coming back."

Eve reacted with shock.

"What? Here, to New York? Why would he? Why risk it?"

"Unfinished business," said Ronnie. He pulled out a clip from the *New York Times*. "This is the letter he sent to the *Times* claiming credit. Whoever this guy is, he calls his group the Liberation Army. Says he's got a hundred and fifty suicide soldiers ready to hit us again."

"Maybe he's just talking big," said Eve.

"Maybe," said Ronnie, "except for one thing. They pulled the letter off the computer of the guy in Jersey who typed it—Ayyad, an engineer. But when they went into his hard drive they found something else."

Ronnie handed Eve a copy of a printout: ". . . our calculations were not very accurate this time. However we promise you that next time it will be very precise and the Trade Center will be one of our targets."

"Jesus." She looked at Ronnie.

"Yeah. I know. The guy who did this expected the damage to be a helluva lot bigger. To me, this says he's coming back to finish it."

Eve was stunned. "But what can you do? You're a—"

"Fire marshal," said Ronnie. "With access to intelligence."

"I know who you are," said Eve. "But you told me the BFI was out of it. What are you going to do?" There was a long pause as Ronnie looked at her.

Finally he said, "My homework."

"The Bureau Doesn't Get It. This City Is Vulnerable"

Over the next few days Ronnie Bucca took a crash course in the recent history of Islamic terror. He pulled double tours, known as "mutuals," working back-to-back twenty-four-hour shifts so he could take some time off and hit the New York public libraries.

"He went into the stacks and just read," said Eve. "He used the microfilm machines and copied dozens of articles."

Bucca had amazing stamina. Sometimes he'd get caught up in the research and stay in the city. He'd sleep at a firehouse, wake up, and go back to the library. "Ronnie could go for twenty-four hours," said Eve, "then take a two-hour 'power nap' and work straight through another tour."[11]

As he pored over the articles, Ronnie eyed a picture of the hooded Black September terrorists who seized eleven Israeli athletes in the

Munich Olympic Village back in 1972. After the West Germans bungled a rescue attempt, nine of the hostages and five terrorists lay dead. Ronnie studied the more successful 1976 raid on the Entebbe airport, when members of the German Baader-Meinhof gang and the PFLP (Population Front for the Liberation of Palestine) had hijacked an Air France jet with 258 people aboard. After the forced landing in Uganda, Israeli commandos stormed the hostage site and rescued them all.

He read about the Iran hostage crisis in depth: How President Carter had underestimated the power of Ayatollah Khoumeini when he allowed the ailing Shah of Iran to seek treatment in the United States. Ronnie learned how the former head of the Defense Intelligence Agency had visited Iran just before the embassy was seized. At the time, the CIA's station chief had been begging for more Farsi-speaking agents, but he'd been turned down. They seemed so clueless in the embassy to the revolution about to hit that the DIA boss literally slipped out a back window and moved through the streets of Teheran where he got a sense of the crisis that was coming.[12] The embassy seizure and failed rescue mission would help cost Jimmy Carter a second term.

But no president seemed immune. On April 18, 1983, sixty-three people, including the CIA's Middle East director, were killed and 120 were injured when a 400-pound suicide truck bomb destroyed the U.S. embassy in Beirut. That was on the watch of Ronald Reagan—a president Ronnie Bucca had voted for. Then, only five months later, an almost identical suicide truck bomb destroyed the Marine barracks a few miles away at the Beirut airport; 242 Marines died in their bunks that Sunday morning. Another 58 French troops were killed almost simultaneously when another suicide truck bomb detonated at the French base. In both cases, the Islamic Jihad claimed responsibility.

As he read the accounts, Bucca, the Special Forces veteran, was stunned. Three almost identical truck bombs in the same city in less than half a year. Why hadn't the Marine barracks been fortified? Why hadn't they hardened the site? What other warnings did they need? When would they stop dismissing these terror cells as disorganized and ignorant?

By the mid-1980s it was clear that U.S. civilians abroad were being targeted by Islamic extremists. In June of 1985, TWA Flight 847 was hijacked. American TV screens were filled with the cockpit pictures of the pilot with a terrorist's gun to his head. After a Navy sailor was murdered,[13] the White House and Tel Aviv capitulated. The plane was flown to Algiers, and 435 Lebanese and Palestinian prisoners were released. Later that year, the Abu Nidal Group hijacked an Egyptian airliner with several Americans aboard. And the decade ended with the greatest act of air terror in history until then: the bombing of Pan Am Flight 103 over Lockerbie, Scotland, killing all 259 passengers and crew on board plus another eleven people on the ground.

All of this reinforced Ronnie's sense that New York was vulnerable. Islamic extremists had been successful time and time again. In most cases the Israeli-Palestinian crisis was central to their demands. The Trade Center bombing letter, promising reprisals by a "hundred and fifty suicidal soldiers," was directed at Israel. New York was the Jewish capital of the world. The radical imams, in their hatred of Western excess, saw the financial center in Lower Manhattan as the home of "the Great Satan."

The hidden warning found on Nidal Ayyad's computer proved that the Trade Center bombers had intended to inflict much greater damage. The Beirut bombings showed that these men were capable of repetitive tactics and simultaneous strikes. They hit military targets, but civilians were no longer immune. Yet in one of the *New York Times* stories Ronnie copied at the end of March, FBI officials were quoted as saying, "There's no reason to believe these threats are real."[14]

To Ronnie Bucca, a street-smart product of the Woodside Projects in Queens, the FBI seemed to be making a gross miscalculation. Like the embassy flaks in Iran back in 1979, they were underestimating the threat.

The intel he was seeing told Ronnie that members of blind Sheikh Rahman's cell had been operating almost openly in New York for years. They had succeeded in eluding the FBI's Special Operations Group, the best surveillance unit in the country. Several of them had slipped easily into the country. The cell had used a sophisticated system of international monetary transfers to fund the operation. The bomb builder had constructed a device of massive killing power using chemicals and fertilizers that were freely available. More troubling, his support group was made up of middle-class members of the community. None, except perhaps the bomb maker himself, fit any traditional terrorist profile. These were men with full-time jobs, men devoted to their families, who worshiped regularly.

They had burrowed into the infrastructure of this city and planned the operation for months. Most astounding of all, as they watched the device being built, each of these coconspirators was willing to become an accomplice to mass murder.

Ronnie was sure that the support group went way beyond the immediate cell. "It might not have been as large as a hundred and fifty people," said Eve, "but Ronnie felt there were others still out there who were dangerous. He kept saying over and over, 'The Bureau doesn't get it. They don't have the street sense. The agencies aren't talking to each other. This city is vulnerable.'"

The Egyptian Inside

Bucca himself had no way of knowing it, but one of the blind Sheikh's trusted cohorts was working inside his own department.

The mild-mannered Egyptian accountant Ahmed Amin Refai, who worked in the department's Capital Budget Unit, had been acting strangely ever since the attack. "He called in sick the day of the bombing," says Kay Woods, Refai's former boss, now an FDNY assistant commissioner.

"When he came back the next day [after the Trade Center blast] he was very shaken up," she remembered. "He was usually an amiable kind of guy. But he came back and he was extremely agitated. I remember asking him, 'What happened?' and he said that the FBI had his house bugged. That he found a bug in his garage and they were watching his house."[15]

At the time, Woods told her boss about Refai's edgy demeanor. "This is very bizarre," she said.

"The FBI was pulling in friends of his for interviews," said Woods. "[Refai] said, 'They probably have the phones at work bugged.' As a matter of fact, I think he looked. He checked the phones in the office, and I said, 'Ahmed, you're being paranoid.'"

But later, she returned from lunch and found the door to her office locked.

"I'm knocking on the door," she said. "No answer. I said, 'Who's in my office?' It was a good four minutes I'm standing there, and then Ahmed opened the door bashfully and said that he was saying his prayers. I'm like, 'You lock my door and you're saying *prayers*?' I was very concerned at the time."

Woods said she was so troubled by Refai's behavior that she spoke to her cousin, who was with the NYPD.

"I flagged him down on the street one day and said, 'You've got to tell somebody this. Who do you tell this to?' And he was like, '*Okaaaay*.'" He seemed to find the story preposterous.

Still, Woods reported Refai to her bosses, confident that if he constituted a real danger, the FBI would stop him. "I thought, if the FBI has his house bugged they'll find whatever it is," she said in an interview for this book. "They'll know that this is weird."

According to an FDNY report, Refai was interviewed by federal agents twice after the Trade Center bombing. But he was never arrested or questioned further, and he continued to hold his job with the fire department—even after FDNY employees saw him in TV news stories walking arm in arm with Sheikh Rahman.

Refai wasn't the only intimate member of the Sheikh's cell who worked for the government. Ahmed Sattar, the Egyptian mail carrier who had learned the home address of John Anticev, would later be indicted for allegedly plotting violent acts of international terror on behalf of the Sheikh from his home on Staten Island. But as with Refai, the FBI ignored his activities for years.[16]

"'When's the Bureau gonna put this together?'" said Eve. "That's what Ronnie said me to all the time. 'When are they gonna get it?'"

A Bit of a Mystery

Within weeks after the bombing, three principals of Yousef's cell had been arrested: Salameh, who'd rented the Ryder truck; Nidal Ayyad, who'd helped Yousef purchase compressed hydrogen; and Mahmud Abouhalima, who'd been extradited from Egypt. Nosair's cousin Ibrahim El-Gabrowny, who had been so close to Emad Salem, was seized at his home.

By mid-March of 1993, though, the Bureau realized that the four men arrested were just supporting players. The real lead was the shadowy figure that fugitive Iraqi Abdul Yasin had told them lived at the Pamrapo Avenue bomb factory.

Having lost Abouhalima in the months before the bombing, Detective Lou Napoli redeemed himself as he accompanied Abouhalima on a military flight from Cairo to Stewart Airport in Newburgh, New York. Along the way, the detective got the big Egyptian to admit that he knew about Pamrapo Avenue. Then Abouhalima blurted out the name of the master bomber, giving Ramzi Yousef's alias, "Rashed."[17]

Soon, through his reserve contacts at DIA, Ronnie Bucca was hearing rumblings that the Feds had finally put a face to the name.

"He came home really pumped," said Eve. "Some kind of indictment was going to come down, and one of Ronnie's buddies was going to call him when he got the news."

Bucca was tired of being on the outside of the Trade Center bombing hunt. He told Eve that he was thinking about applying to the NYPD-FBI Joint Terrorist Task Force.

"Ronnie got together his résumé and his record with the Green Berets," said Eve. "He felt that if anybody from the fire department had a shot, he did. After all, he had Top Secret clearance and a lot of operations experience in the Special Forces." Besides, the FDNY had taken the biggest hit in terms of injuries the day of the blast. As first responders, they were the most likely to feel the brunt of any terrorism to hit the city again—and by now Ronnie Bucca was sure that there would be more.

Late that night the phone rang. Ronnie picked up quickly so as not to wake Eve. His buddy on the other end said, "It's in the *Times*. Metro section." Ronnie thanked him and hung up. Trained for quick exits during his years in Rescue, Ronnie threw on his shirt and pants, grabbed a jacket and the keys to his Chevy. He drove a few miles to a nearby shopping center where they had a vending machine for the *New York Times*. It was empty, so he waited for the morning delivery.

Sitting there in his car, Ronnie thought back to that night after the blast when he and the other marshals had gone down into the Trade Center garage. The device that had blown a hole down to level B-4 had been the creation of a brilliant engineer, somebody imported for the job. Another rumor floating around DIA was that the Bureau's informant, Salem, had been enlisted originally by the Sheikh to build some kind of device, but that when he'd dropped out, calls went out for this mysterious "Rashed."

It was just after four-thirty when the *Times* truck turned into the lot. The driver jumped out and cut open a bundle of early editions. Ronnie was out of the car with a buck in his hand before the guy had even gotten them into the machine. He paid the driver and grabbed the top paper on the pile, thumbing though the Metro section until he came to page B3. There he saw a picture of a bearded young man with heavy eyebrows and protruding ears. He was almost smiling. It was the mysterious "unsub" known as "Rashed"—Ramzi Yousef.

The headline said "Missing Suspect Charged in Trade Center Bombing." Seeming to confuse Abouhalima and Yasin with Yousef, the article mistakenly identified him as "a 25-year-old taxi driver born in Iraq or the United Arab Emirates." The story talked about how Yousef had shared an apartment with Salameh. By now the FBI had learned of the traffic accident when Yousef was hospitalized before the bombing. They had seized Salameh's damaged Nova. But perhaps the most memorable line in the story was the understatement made by Leonard Wineglass, the attorney representing Nidal Ayyad. He described the master bomber as "a bit of a mystery."

It was April Fool's Day, 1993. As Ronnie stood there reading the story, he promised himself that he would meet this guy. Whether the Feds let him into the hunt or not. Ramzi Yousef, he sensed, was the one who would come back to haunt New York City. Now he was staring out from that picture in the *Times,* almost smirking. Someday they would be in the same room together. Ronnie thought back to Kevin Shea, the deep black crater, and the blood in Room 107, and he wondered what he would do when that day came.

19

THE HUNT
FOR RASHED

I n the wake of the Trade Center bombing, Ramzi Yousef became a
celebrity in the circles of radical Islam. "The Che Guevera of fundamentalist Muslims," one ex–U.S. intel officer called him; "a killer
afforded rock star status."[1]

Yousef's reputation was only enhanced on April 2, when the FBI
expanded its Ten Most Wanted list to include his name. The bounty was
two million dollars. Interpol issued a "Red Notice" signaling Yousef's
importance as a fugitive.

Few law enforcement agencies in the world had the FBI's capacity to
process and analyze forensic evidence after the fact, and while it missed
Yousef up front and failed to prevent the bombing, the Bureau was now
in a frenzied race to apprehend him. The evidence pile that Yousef had
left behind was extraordinary—but it did more to remind the FBI of
how much it had overlooked than it did to lead Neal Herman and his
team to Yousef now.

The first key to his identity came from the stub for his plane ticket,
which he'd left behind at the Kensington Avenue apartment in Jersey
City. Yousef's prints on the ticket matched those found at the Space Station storage locker and the Pamrapo Avenue bomb factory. For the outgoing flight Yousef had used his birth name, Abdul Basit Karim. Then,
when the storage locker connected him back to his JFK entry in September, the Feds tumbled to Mohammed Ajaj.

Ironically, Yousef's Palestinian travel companion and "cover" had just been sprung from six months in federal lockup, so the FBI promptly rearrested Ajaj and charged him as a coconspirator.

Meanwhile the Feds examined the traffic from the phones used by the bombing cell. They did computer cross-checks on the hundreds of international and local calls "Rashed" had made as he racked up eighteen thousand dollars in phone bills before the bombing.

Herman chose three top federal agents for the Yousef hunt: Frank Pellegrino and Chuck Stern from the FBI, and Secret Service Agent Brian Parr. Along with a cadre of detectives from INS and the State Department's Office of Diplomatic Security, Herman also included two NYPD JTTF veterans: Lou Napoli and Detective Tommy Corrigan. Both of them had a personal stake in the hunt because they'd been working parallel investigations prior to the bombing, and both of them had been shut down by Neal Herman's boss, Carson Dunbar.[2]

It was a full-court press by the Bureau, but Ramzi Yousef, the ex–engineering student, would show the same genius for avoiding capture that he demonstrated as a bomb maker. The rumors were rampant. Yousef was sighted everywhere from the U.K. and Canada to the West Bank and Colombia.[3] Ironically, in the first few weeks after the bombing, he was exactly where his PIA escape ticket said he would be: Quetta, the capital of his home province of Baluchistan, 375 miles from Karachi. But finding him there was another matter.

A lawless border town of unpaved and unmarked roads, Quetta had been a prime staging area for the CIA's covert mujahadeen supply operation during the Afghan War. By 1993 it remained a wide-open third-world outpost for heroin smugglers, gunrunners, and wild-eyed jihadi killers. Yousef's wife and baby daughter lived there, along with his brothers and a support group of friends who would die before giving him up.

The rabbit warren of single-story sand-colored buildings on the edge of Quetta's slums offered the perfect opportunity for Yousef to disappear. This was a town beyond the day-to-day control of Pakistan's two primary law enforcement agencies: the Federal Investigation Agency (FIA), Islamabad's equivalent of the Bureau, and the Inter-Services Intelligence Agency, a CIA counterpart known as the ISI. At one point in the spring of 1993, FIA officers flew into Quetta on a C-130, accompanied by agents of the State Department's Diplomatic Security Service. They raided Yousef's home, but they were reportedly two hours late. The phantom bomber had slipped away.[4]

What the Feds didn't know at this point was that Yousef was being sheltered by his maternal uncle Zahid Al-Shaikh, a principal with Mercy International, a Saudi nongovernmental organization (NGO) akin to the Alkifah Center in Brooklyn, that had raised a fortune for Afghan War veterans.[5] During this period Yousef was moving between Quetta and Peshawar, another frontier town in West Pakistan, where he stayed at the Bait-Ashuda House of Martyrs guest house. Evidence recovered later by the FIA showed that both Mercy International and the guest house were controlled by Osama bin Laden. In fact, when Zahid Al-Shaikh's home was raided by Pakistani FIA agents, they found a stack of pictures of bin Laden taken during the Afghan War.

Now, in the summer of 1993, as he moved toward the top of the Bureau's Most Wanted List, Yousef demonstrated his audacity again. With the full force of the FBI scouring Pakistan for him, Yousef accepted a contract to assassinate Benazir Bhutto, the forty-year-old Harvard and Oxford graduate who was a reform candidate for prime minister of Pakistan.

The murder-for-hire deal was initiated by members of the Sipah-e-Sahaba (Army of the Companions of the Prophet), a sect of Sunni Muslim extremists at war with Shiite landowners in the Punjab province of Pakistan. The conspirators reportedly offered Yousef three million Pakistani rupees, or $68,000 U.S., for the hit.

Coming off his triumph in New York, Yousef agreed. But some Pakistani investigators felt that the mission was personal. Not only was Bhutto an attractive, educated, pro-Western woman seeking to run a Muslim nation, her father, Zulfiqar Ali Bhutto, had suppressed a major tribal uprising in Baluchistan during his own tenure as prime minister. The incursion had reportedly led to the deaths of ten thousand people in Yousef's home province. Perhaps in retaliation, Yousef now accepted the mission to detonate a bomb outside the younger Bhutto's residence in the wealthy Clifton district of Karachi.[6] According to a Pakistani agent who interrogated Abdul Shakur, one of Yousef's coconspirators in the plot, it went like this:[7]

A small car rolled passed Bhutto's residence, Bilawal House, just after dawn on a September day. A pair of guards patrolled outside the two-story white villa. The car parked half a block away. Yousef's old friend from Kuwait Abdul Hakim Murad was driving. Ramzi was in the front seat. He looked through the windshield of the tiny car and spotted a storm drain in the street near the exit to Bhutto's driveway.

In English, Yousef told Murad to pull close to the house. As they drove forward, Yousef retrieved a small shoe box from the seat behind him. He lifted the lid. Inside was an old Soviet-made detonator wired to a quantity of Semtex, a Czech form of C-4 plastic explosive.

As the car idled, Yousef carefully wired a receiver from a remote control device to the detonator. It was a crude setup. The remote had been fashioned from a garage door opener.

When the device was set, Yousef nodded and Murad pulled forward, next to the storm drain. Yousef opened the passenger door, removed the drain cover, and leaned down, placing the bomb at the base of the drain. Then he replaced the cover. The plan was for Yousef and Murad to lie in wait at a distance and set off the device as Bhutto exited her estate.

They were about to roll off to a surveillance point when a police car cut across their path. A uniformed cop called out to them in Urdu from the shotgun window: "What are you doing there?"

Thinking quickly, Yousef told the policeman he'd dropped his keys. The stench from the drain was overwhelming. He wondered if the policeman might help him find them. The cop eyed Yousef and Murad, both dressed like a couple of poor kafirs. Finally he turned to his partner and motioned for him to drive on. Murad sighed, relieved, and threw the car into gear. But Yousef stopped him. In case the cops returned, he wanted to retrieve the device.

He opened his door and leaned down to reach for the box. But then, as he lifted out the bomb, the old Soviet blasting cap exploded in his face.

Yousef was blown back into the car. Murad shot a look across at the startled guards by Bhutto's residence. Yousef was bleeding heavily from a cut above his eyes. So Murad quickly reached across him, slammed the car door shut, and roared off.

Minutes later, the small car screeched up to the emergency entrance at Aga Khan Hospital in Karachi. Yousef was semiconscious. Two of his fingers were badly damaged and his face was covered in blood. A pair of emergency room orderlies rushed out.

"Quick," said Murad. "My friend. He was changing a butane canister when it exploded."

The orderlies put Yousef onto a gurney and rushed him inside with Murad running behind them. "What's his name?" yelled one of the orderlies. Grasping for an alias, Murad chose the name of Yousef's home province. "Adam Baluch," he said.

The brush with death only hardened Yousef's will. He was determined to finish his deadly work. By October he'd recovered enough to make another run at Bhutto.

This time he conceived a *Manchurian Candidate*–style hit, planning to murder Bhutto with a sniper rifle while she was addressing a campaign rally in Karachi.

On the day of her speech Bhutto heard that her life was in danger, but she pressed ahead, appearing on a stage ringed by armed gunmen. Only after she had become prime minister did Bhutto learn the reason the plot was foiled: the rifle Yousef planned to use had not arrived in time.[8] Still, the plan itself demonstrated that Yousef was willing to strike non-Western targets, and to forgo high explosives in favor of the traditional weapon of a trained assassin. He was thinking outside the box.

The following June, Yousef was linked to an attack on the Imam Reza Shrine in the city of Mashad, Iran's most sacred Shiite place of worship. Crossing the border with a small group of radical Sunnis that included his father and brother, Yousef is said to have placed a bomb in the women's section of the shrine's mausoleum.

Reportedly fashioned with U.S.-made C-4 explosive, the bomb exploded, toppling a wall and caving in the dome of the prayer hall. A total of twenty-six pilgrims died, and another two hundred were injured.

But the mosque bombing was far from Yousef's most audacious encore to New York. He also plotted to take down the Israeli embassy in Bangkok with a device similar in design to the Trade Center payload.

If that bomb had gone off, the death toll would have been in the thousands. Once again Yousef used a rented truck to deliver the device. It weighed literally a ton, five hundred pounds more than his Trade Center bomb. In this instance, Yousef reportedly used ammonium nitrate mixed with diesel fuel.[9] The slurry was contained in a water tank in the back of the six-wheeled truck. The detonator was made up of six sticks of C-4.

Just as the ANFO bomb was an improvement on his earlier urea nitrate–fuel oil device, Yousef had learned from the Salameh–Ryder van incident. This time he ordered his coconspirators to steal the truck rather than rent it and leave a paper trail.

Of course, hijacking a truck meant that the driver had to be dealt with—a forty-three-year-old Thai named Chom Pila. The bombers snapped his neck and tossed his body into the ANFO mixture. There was enough high explosive in the back of the truck to take down a city block.[10]

But then, as the bombers headed down Bangkok's Chitlom Road toward the Israeli embassy, a motorcycle-taxi swerved into the truck. The taxi driver, twenty-one-year-old Boonserm Saendee, jumped off and started screaming. Suddenly, an Arab man leaped from the truck and handed him money to shut up.[11]

A crowd began to gather and the Arab heard sirens, so he took off. It's unknown whether this was Yousef or one of his coconspirators. By the time the police arrived, he was gone.

Incredibly, the cops never bothered to search the truck. They simply drove the bomb-laden vehicle with the dead driver in back to the Lumpini police station. A week later, when the truck's owner came to claim his vehicle, he noticed a strange stench. He went in back, pulled the cover off the water tank, and stood aghast to find the partially decomposed body of his driver Chom Pila. After a massive manhunt, seventeen Iranians were arrested in the plot, but later all but one were released.[12] A man named Hossein Shahriarfar was later found guilty in the attempted bombing and sentenced to death, but most of the evidence used to convict him was circumstantial, and he was later freed on appeal. Yousef was never charged, and the bomb plot remains unsolved, but he would later return to Bangkok in a plot to blow up a series of U.S. airliners. That operation would be a precursor to his most ambitious and catastrophic act of terror to date.

The Dog Day Siege

Sheikh Omar Abdel Rahman understood well the concept of coup d'état: the toppling of an adversary for one's advantage. He was still a young man in 1952 when Gamal Abdel Nasser, the man he called "the wicked pharaoh," deposed King Farouk in Egypt. In 1989 the blind cleric stood in the shadows as Osama bin Laden effected a de facto coup against

Abdullah Azzam, taking over the Services Office (MAK) network that had raised millions for the mujahadeen.

The Sheikh had staged his own coup at the Alkifah Refugee Center in Brooklyn, wresting power from Azzam's appointee, Mustafa Shalabi, who was later found murdered. Centers like Alkifah and its sister in Tucson soon developed into brick-and-mortar al Qaeda outposts.

Days after the Trade Center bombing, with the heat focused on his shabby third-floor mosque, the al-Salaam in Jersey City, Sheikh Rahman decided he needed a new base of operations. He set his sights on the more upscale Abu Bakr Mosque on Forrest Avenue in Brooklyn. The Sheikh had preached there a number of times in the past, but the board of directors, composed mostly of Islamic moderates, had refused to grant him official "imam in residence" status. Since the previous October, though, the Sheikh's militant followers had led a campaign to dominate the mosque's board. Ibrahim El-Gabrowny had been elected president, and Mahmud Abouhalima had pushed to install four other cohorts on the seven-member board.

Now, little more than a week after the Trade Center bombing, Abouhalima was a fugitive suspect and El-Gabrowny had been arrested. The mosque's members met on March 6, hoping that the negative publicity surrounding the Sheikh might cause the majority to defy the board and restore the milder Sheikh Maged Sobh as full-time imam. But Rahman's followers were defiant. The meeting dragged on for hours and ended in a series of fistfights. The militants prevailed, and the blind cleric was installed.

Over the next three months, the congregation lost three-quarters of its membership as responsible Islamics left its ranks. The hard core of militants backed programs that taught the youth of the mosque martial arts and other paramilitary techniques. When one of the few remaining moderates questioned those programs, an associate of Abouhalima issued a chilling warning: "Be quiet, or you'll end up like Shalabi."[13]

On the day of that March 6 coup, the U.S. State Department finally took some responsibility for allowing Rahman into the country in the first place. In a *New York Times* story, officials admitted that the U.S. embassy in Khartoum had overlooked the Sheikh's presence on the Watch List when granting him a visa.[14] Worse, after the visa was revoked, the INS office in Newark mistakenly gave him a green card, granting Rahman permanent resident status. Even after the Sheikh went overseas in 1991 and was detained at Newark airport on his return, the government allowed him to reenter.

But by the spring of 1993, with the rerecruited Emad Salem back at Rahman's side, the Feds had new firsthand intelligence about just how dangerous the Sheikh could be. Even as he was publicly proclaiming his innocence, the cleric had privately issued his *fatwa* to Salem, authorizing him to make strikes against the U.S. military. The Sheikh had already put a hit on Egypt's president Mubarak, and now he was acting as the spiritual guardian of Siddig Ali's bridge and tunnel plot.

Sheikh Rahman was also becoming a major embarrassment to President Clinton's newly appointed attorney general, Janet Reno. Even after the Feds' takedown of the Queens warehouse on June 24, the Sheikh had not been charged. Despite the evidence Salem had unearthed, Reno seemed troubled about jailing a religious figure. The Sheikh's supporters called the evidence against him "fuzzy." Some Feds even suggested it would be good to leave Rahman free as a "surveillance tool" so that those around him could be followed.[15]

This left the Clinton administration open to blistering attacks from politicians like New York Republican senator Alfonse D'Amato, who couldn't resist a chance to blame the state's Democratic governor for the indecision. "The terrorists are laughing at us," D'Amato said. "While New York sends jobs to New Jersey, they send us their terrorists. We need the death penalty. Mario Cuomo just doesn't get it."

Now, in the heat of early July 1993, a kind of *Dog Day Afternoon* scenario was brewing, with the Sheikh and his followers holed up in the Abu Bakr Mosque as the Feds wrung their hands and tried to figure out what to do with him. As the hours passed, hundreds of demonstrators surrounded the mosque. It was becoming a replay of the Nosair trial, with Islamic militants on one side of police barricades yelling "Allah-u-Akhbar! God is great! God is merciful!" while Hasidic and JDL supporters on the other side screamed back, "Drop dead! Drop dead!"

Six weeks earlier, the attorney general had waffled over the standoff at the Branch Davidian complex in Waco, Texas. That siege ended in a fiery conflagration that left eighty dead, including twenty-five children.[16] So Reno needed to prove herself here.

The situation got worse after two recent bomb threats disrupted traffic in the city still reeling over the bridge and tunnel plot. The NYPD retrieved a suspicious object in the Brooklyn Battery Tunnel and inspected an abandoned car at JFK.[17] The tunnel "bomb" turned out to be a length of rope wrapped in a garbage bag. But as more and more followers on both sides arrived outside the mosque, the standoff grew tense.

Then, in the early morning hours of Saturday, July 2, a man wearing the Sheikh's trademark white robe, velvet hat, and sunglasses was whisked outside by supporters and into a maroon van.

FBI and INS agents jumped into Suburbans and gave chase, followed by local TV crews in their remote broadcast trucks. After a short pursuit they stopped the van. The Feds jumped out with guns drawn, yelling, "Get out! Get out!" only to find that the "Sheikh" inside was an imposter. If anyone in the Justice Department had studied Abdel Rahman's file, they would have seen that he'd used the same decoy ploy to escape house arrest in Egypt back in 1990. But the comic incident did little to diffuse the heat that was building outside the mosque.

The Feds had set up a command post at 250 Engine, a firehouse across from the Abu Bakr on Forrest Avenue. Here they negotiated with the Sheikh's lawyers. Ironically, the standoff was taking place just a five-minute walk from the Brooklyn block where Meier Kahane had lived at the height of the Jewish Defense League two decades earlier. Many of the men screaming at each other across the barricades were the same ones who had skirmished outside the trial of Kahane's slayer, Nosair.

As the hours passed on Saturday, the scene became even more volatile when Rahman's supporters mounted a siren on the rooftop of the mosque calling worshipers to prayer. Arabic music and the sermons of the Sheikh blared from speakers. By late afternoon, the tension outside the mosque was palpable.

Concerned about the potential for a riot near the firehouse, the FDNY sent a team of armed marshals to keep watch. One of them was Ronnie Bucca.[18] Even if he hadn't been assigned to the job, Ronnie would have volunteered. In the months since the Trade Center bombing, as he'd educated himself on Islamic fundamentalism and read the intel from his reserve unit, Ronnie had become convinced that Sheikh Rahman was key to the continuing threat faced by New York City.

On his own, Bucca had begun to connect the dots. He'd learned through military sources about the Calverton surveillance photos. He'd been shocked to discover that a fellow Army sergeant from Fort Bragg (the traitorous Ali Mohammed) had actually instructed these men in firearms training. He was stunned to learn that Top Secret manuals from Bragg had been unearthed in the boxes of evidence seized by the Feds at Nosair's house in 1990. Now, two and a half years later, with the Trade Center bombing fresh in everyone's mind and Rahman still in the city without a valid green card, Bucca thought, *Why wait? Why give him another media op? Why not just go in and grab him?*

Ronnie listened quietly in the background as the negotiations continued. Finally, around 6:00 P.M., lawyers for the Justice Department reached an agreement with the Sheikh's attorneys. Rahman would not be charged. He would be put into "protective detention" at the federal prison in Otisville, New York, and held until his residency status was resolved. Bucca felt anger as he listened to the lawyers negotiate over the Sheikh's due process rights. This man wasn't even a *citizen*. He was a world-class terrorist who had defrauded America on entry, then plotted seditiously as he courted the media.

Ronnie believed in the Fourth, Fifth, and Sixth Amendments. He'd joined the Army to protect them. But to him, splitting hairs over Abdel Rahman's status was absurd. The Sheikh was exploiting his position as a holy man. The attorney general had hesitated at Waco over concerns about the Branch Davidians' religious status, and innocent people had died. When were the Feds going to wise up? If the public knew what *he* knew about how the FBI had underestimated the Sheikh and blown the original bombing investigation, they'd be terrified.

Bucca nodded to fellow fire marshal Bobby McLoughlin, who had come in to relieve him at the six o'clock tour change. Just then, they heard screams outside as a dozen of the Sheikh's closest followers led him through the phalanx of cops into federal custody.

Bucca and McLoughlin moved outside as several local news reporters recorded "standup" commentaries to go with their reports. The Sheikh's seizure had been a media victory for Janet Reno, the Justice Department, and the New York office of the FBI. Coming on the heels of Emad Salem's sting operation, it appeared, at least to these reporters, that the Sheikh's people were on the run.

But knowing what he did, Ronnie Bucca felt sure they were wrong.

Later, on the way home, Ronnie took the Brooklyn-Battery Tunnel into Manhattan and headed up West Street, past the Towers, toward the West Side Highway. A few blocks to the east was Foley Square and the FBI office at 26 Federal Plaza.

Bucca had been thinking about approaching the Joint Terrorist Task Force, but he'd held off when the Feds had announced the Day of Terror arrests. Now, after this day at the mosque—after experiencing first-hand the level of hatred among the Sheikh's followers—Ronnie was sure that this wasn't over. These men were hardened and determined. Besides, Yousef, the master bomber, was still out there. The Feds were still searching for him, and Ronnie wanted to be able to contribute what he knew to the hunt. The first thing Monday morning he would call the Task Force to see what it would take to make an application.

20

PREPPING FOR THE "BIG NOISE"

To begin planning the most horrific act of terror ever contemplated, Ramzi Yousef called on the two men who were closest to him: his uncle Khalid Shaikh Mohammed and his lifelong friend from Kuwait Abdul Hakim Murad. With plans still in the early stages, intelligence sources say they met in Khalid Shaikh's house in Karachi in July 1993.[1] But evidence now suggests that the seeds of the plot were planted even earlier.

Murad, the handsome twenty-five-year-old son of an oil worker, was a native Baluchistani transplanted, like Yousef, to Kuwait. He first met Ramzi in the early 1980s at a mosque in Fuhayhil, the Persian Gulf town where they grew up. They'd lost touch for a time when Yousef went to study in England, but reunited in Pakistan after Yousef finished his bomb training in 1991.[2] That same year, Murad got his single-engine private pilot's license at the Emirates Flying School in Dubai. He was anxious to learn how to fly a multiengine commercial aircraft, and the best training in the world was in the United States. So on November 19, 1991, during Nosair's trial in New York, he flew to Heathrow and on to Dulles Airport outside Washington, D.C. After staying with his brother in Virginia, Murad traveled to Bern Stages, Texas, near San Antonio, where he enrolled in the Alpha Tango Flying School. One of the instructors was Sudanese; the chief pilot was a Pakistani named Hamed Afzel.[3]

Murad trained at the school for three weeks with Saudi Nasir Al

Mubarek, a fellow student from the Emirates, but the Texas school had a narrow runway and lacked approach aids at the time, so Murad and Mubarek bought a brown Hyundai and drove three days to the Richmore Flying School in Schenectady, New York.

The training didn't come cheap.

By January of 1992, Murad had run through the eleven thousand dollars he'd brought with him for flight lessons, so he went to an upstate bank and got a wire transfer for another nine thousand.[4] But he couldn't take the frigid cold near Albany, so after two months at Richmore he flew back to Alpha Tango, where he trained during March and April of 1992.

In the late spring of 1992, Murad went back to Richmore for more lessons. By May he'd switched to a third school, Coastal Aviation in New Bern, North Carolina, where he trained on a simulator and finally got his multiengine pilot's certification on June 6. On another return trip to Richmore, Murad passed through Manhattan, where he did a visual inspection of the Trade Center. At Richmore he and Mubarak met another alumnus of the Emirates School. The three of them then drove cross-country to Red Bluff, California, three hours north of San Francisco, where Murad enrolled in the California Aeronautical Institute. Then, after paying thirteen hundred dollars for classes to get his inspection rating, the peripatetic Murad left without finishing the course.

On July 27 he flew to Bahrain in the Persian Gulf, then went back to stay with his uncle in Dubai. A month later he got a call from his old friend Ramzi, who told him that he'd just finished "chocolate training."[5] When Murad feigned that he didn't understand, Yousef simply said, "Boom." He told Murad he was going to New York to find "employment," but by now both men knew what this meant.

A few weeks later, Yousef arrived at JFK to knock down the very Towers that Murad had surveilled for him earlier in the year. The terrorist pilot later boasted that he personally chose the Trade Center as Yousef's target.

In the trail of evidence that leads to 9/11, there's no indication that Murad began his flight training with the Trade Center in mind. The idea of taking down the 110-story buildings with fuel-laden airliners came to Yousef later, after the bomb he planted on the B-2 level failed to deliver the catastrophic results he intended.

But after fleeing New York, as he conceived the plan that would culminate on September 11, there's little doubt that Yousef was inspired by his old friend's American flight-school training. The flying schools were plentiful and full of innocent, well-intentioned Middle Eastern men that Osama bin Laden's jihadis could hide among. All it took to qualify was an entry visa and enough cash to finance the tuition. While the FAA regulated the schools, no one screened the students. Once the plan was set in motion, Yousef's "brothers" could train openly with little fear of detection.

The funding for the plot would come directly from bin Laden, via his brother-in-law Mohammed Jamal Khalifa, who would set up a front company in Malaysia to channel the financing. Yousef's uncle Khalid Shaikh Mohammed would be the conduit for the money; Murad would supply the operational expertise and help arrange flight school training for other jihadis. Bin Laden's close friend Wali Khan Amin Shah would handle logistics. But it would take months, perhaps years, to field pilots in sufficient numbers who were willing to commandeer the cockpits of commercial jets and undertake suicide missions for Allah. At this point in 1993, as Yousef met with Murad and Khalid Shaikh Mohammed in Karachi, al Qaeda didn't yet have the bench strength to mount such a plan. So in the interim, Yousef conceived a plan to commit mass murder aboard commercial aircraft that would be easier to implement.

From his days spent training with the "brothers" from Bosnia, he chose a name for the operation: Bojinka. It was Serbo-Croatian for "big noise."

Pushing for Sammy the Bull's Deal

On August 25, 1993, the other shoe dropped. After holding him for weeks on the immigration charges, U.S. Attorney Mary Jo White indicted Sheikh Rahman and eleven others, including Siddig Siddig Ali and El Sayyid Nosair, alleging that they were engaged in a plot to wage "a war of urban terrorism against the United States."[6]

For the first time since 1989, the Feds seemed to get it. The indictment reached back to the Calverton training sessions, up through Nosair's murder of Kahane and the Trade Center bombing itself, tying the Sheikh and his cell to a "seditious conspiracy" that had been in the making for years.

With the help of Nancy Floyd's recruit Emad Salem, the Feds had redeemed themselves. By including murder charges against Nosair for the rabbi's death, they even made up for the NYPD's misguided conclusion that he'd acted alone. The twenty-count indictment was based on a Civil War–era statute aimed at stopping plots to overthrow the government. Yousef was still at large, but four of his cohorts were in custody, and White wasted little time bringing them to trial.

The lead-off case in the government's war on terror would be the first World Trade Center bombing trial. In early October, little more than seven months after the blast, proceedings got under way in U.S. District Court against Mohammed Salameh and Mahmud Abouhalima, along with Rutgers grad Nidal Ayyad, who had helped obtain the chemicals, and Mohammed Ajaj, the Palestinian who'd arrived at JFK with Yousef and a suitcase full of bomb manuals.

In his opening statement, Assistant U.S. Attorney J. Gilmore Childers painted a chilling portrait of the workaday life inside the Towers that was shattered at the moment of the blast.

"It was lunchtime," he said, describing how visitors filled the elevators, secretaries cleaned up their desks, and maintenance workers sat down to eat. "All of these people [were] unaware that one minute later at 12:18 P.M. their lives would change forever. . . . February 26, 1993, would become a day that would mark, for all time, the single most destructive act of terrorism ever committed here in the United States. From that point forward, Americans knew that 'this can happen to me, here in the United States.' "[7]

Later, Abouhalima's lawyer Hassen Ibn Abdellah ridiculed the prosecutor.

"He plays on your patriotism," he told the jury. "He plays on your emotions, but the Government's case is based on cosmetics." Standing behind his big red-haired client, Hassen said, "Mahmud Abouhalima is asking you for nothing but fairness."

What the jury didn't know was that, months earlier, the Red had asked the Feds for much more. In May, while between attorneys, the mercurial Abouhalima, who had spilled his guts to the Egyptians under torture, put out a feeler to prosecutors from his cell in the Metropolitan Correctional Center (MCC), the federal jail in Lower Manhattan. He was willing to talk plea.[8]

Childers had visited him, along with his cocounsel, Assistant U.S. Attorney Henry DePippo. Abouhalima demanded a deal like the one the Feds had brokered with Sammy "the Bull" Gravano, the Gambino capo who served up his boss, John Gotti. In return for his testimony, Gravano was rewarded with hundreds of thousands of dollars and a drastically reduced sentence.

Abouhalima, who had been Yousef's chief facilitator in the bombing, now wanted an even bigger deal—not just a fortune in cash, but his sentence cut to time served, plus U.S. citizenship for his German wife and their four kids, who were facing deportation.

Next to Yousef, the Red took the prize for audacity.

But Childers didn't blink. Despite the forensic evidence tying the C-VIN to Salameh and the Ryder rental, his case was largely circumstantial. He'd never be able to introduce Abouhalima's tortured confession from Egypt, and the brains behind the bombing conspiracy was not in the courtroom: Ramzi Yousef was still a fugitive.

Reportedly, the Feds considered some kind of deal. But when Judge Kevin Duffy, a salty twenty-one-year veteran of the bench, got word that the prosecutors were considering a "proffer" from Abouhalima without defense counsel present, he shut the negotiations down.

Now at trial, jury members covered their eyes as autopsy photos of Monica Smith and the other blast victims were introduced. One female juror wept.[9] But Childers and DePippo were dogged by the fact that they were trying only the second string. Yousef's name didn't even come up until more than a month into the trial, when an INS inspector identified the bomb manuals found in Ajaj's luggage.[10]

As the weeks passed, the media began to question how the full truth behind the bombings could ever come out. After all, the chief architect, Yousef, was missing—not to mention one of his main coconspirators, Abdel Rahman Yasin, the Iraqi who had talked the FBI into letting him walk. At this point the press was still referring to Yousef mistakenly as "an Iraqi," based on his request for political asylum on entry.[11]

The argument that the Yousef cell had gotten its marching orders from Baghdad was later espoused by Laurie Mylroie, a scholar at the

Washington Institute for the Near East, whose main supporter in the theory was the dismissed head of the FBI's New York office, James Fox.[12] But JTTF investigators like Special Agent John Anticev and Detective Lou Napoli knew better. Except for Yasin's involvement, virtually all the evidence pointed to a conspiracy crafted largely by Egyptian immigrants in the circle around Sheikh Omar Abdel Rahman. In fact, the U.S. attorney had said as much in the indictment of the blind Sheikh and his crew.

U.S. v. Mohammed Salameh et al. was the first step in establishing the line of terror that commenced with the Calverton shooting sessions in 1989. But by early December, in the second month of the trial, the government was dealt an extraordinary setback.

The Conspirators' Calling Card

Willie Hernandez Moosh, an attendant at a Shell station in Jersey City, was key to Childers's strategy of proving that Abouhalima and Salameh were part of the convoy of vehicles accompanying the Ryder van in the early morning hours before the bombing.

Reportedly, Yousef had pulled up to a pump in the yellow Ford Econoline van, with Abouhalima behind him driving his dark blue Lincoln. Salameh was said to have parked the red Corsica at another pump. Because New Jersey had a law forbidding gas station self-service, Willie Moosh came out of his Plexiglas cubicle and was reportedly told by Yousef to "fill it up."[13]

After his arrest, the bomb maker would tell his interrogators that the gas station incident never occurred—that the Ryder van had been driven directly to Brooklyn late in the night before the bombing.[14] But now at trial the Feds were expecting a big payday.

The testimony of the attendant who worked the midnight-to-eight shift would tie the defendants to the master bomber still at large. As Childers took him through the events of February 26, Hernandez described the three-car convoy in great detail. According to his testimony, two of the men he saw near the gas pumps could easily have been Salameh or Abouhalima.

Then it came time for the crucial courtroom ID—the dramatic moment that becomes the climax of so many movie trials. Zeroing in on Abouhalima, Childers asked, "Do you see that man now in this courtroom?" Moosh came down from the stand and glanced briefly at the defense table, where the big, redheaded terrorist sat. But then, apparently disoriented, he turned toward the jury. Moosh walked toward the press section and eyeballed the reporters covering the trial. Then he came back and gestured toward one of the *jurors,* a man with reddish hair.[15]

"It was a person like that one," Moosh said, amid gasps from the gallery.

"The record should reflect that the witness is pointing to Juror No. 6," said Judge Duffy. Childers eyed the jury and smiled, but rather than cutting his losses he decided to brass it out. He asked Moosh to identify Salameh, who had become infamous for his Ryder van rental dispute.

Now, despite all the publicity Salameh had enjoyed as the hapless accomplice, Moosh pointed toward a *second* jury member, this one a man with dark hair and a close-cropped beard.

"It was a person like this," Moosh said, speaking Spanish through an interpreter. "Indicating Juror No. 5," said Judge Duffy, and the Feds' star witness was excused.

Ajaj's lawyer called the testimony "devastating," but Childers, known as a lawyer who was cool under pressure, quipped, "I don't think it's devastating unless I plan to indict Juror No. 6."[16]

Still, as the trial entered the first weeks of 1994, the case against Abouhalima, in particular, looked thin. No witness (beyond Moosh) could put him with the other conspirators, and there was seemingly no other direct evidence connecting him to the bomb factory. The Feds were paying the price for their failure to follow Emad Salem's advice and tail the Red.

The best forensic evidence they had was a pair of Abouhalima's work boots, with a quarter-sized sulfuric acid stain on the big toe.[17]

Ironically, it would be an analysis of phone records—which the FBI had failed to do up front—that tied the Red to the plot. Records showed that eight calls from the phone registered in the name of Mahmud's German wife had been made to the Pamrapo Avenue apartment as Yousef built the device. Then there were those four calls in February charged to Abouhalima's phone and made from the Trade Center itself.[18]

In his summation to the jury, AUSA Henry DePippo called the Red's phone record "the conspirators' calling card." "That card links them to the conspiracy," said the prosecutor, shouting now: "*He's caught.*"[19]

What went unsaid was that the investigators in the FBI's Joint Terrorist Task Force could easily have traced the same calls in the weeks before the bombing. Even if, as Napoli said, Abouhalima had "beat feet" to New Jersey, the phone records would have given the FBI a road map of the conspiracy.

By March 4, though, none of that mattered. As the clerk read off the verdicts, the jury foreman pronounced the word *Guilty* thirty-eight times.

Suddenly the four defendants, who'd sat like choirboys for five months, erupted with hate. "*Allah is great,*" Salameh cried out. Ajaj's brother screamed obscenities at the jury from the back of the courtroom. "You are fucking liars! *Liars!*" Judge Duffy gaveled down and ordered them ejected, but as he was dragged off Salameh pounded on the table, yelling, "*Cheap people. Cheap government!*" He lunged toward the bench as the U.S. marshals pulled him away. Then Ajaj began a chilling chant that echoed through the courtroom: "*Il-ya! Il-ya Islam!*" *Islam will be victorious.* It seemed more a threat than a prediction.

Once again, U.S. Attorney Mary Jo White had a victory. "This verdict," she said, "should send a clear and unmistakable message that we will not tolerate terrorism in this country."[20]

In preparation for the sentencing, Judge Duffy finally gave Eddie Smith a chance to find his own justice. In heart-rending testimony, he described the moment he knew that his wife, Monica, was gone.

"I had lost my wife, my best friend, my idol and my son," said Smith. "We would never get the opportunity to hold baby Eddie in our arms. We would never get to hear Eddie say his first word."[21]

The four defendants, wearing headsets for the translation, listened indifferently. At one point, Salameh reportedly stuck his finger in his nose and wiped it on his pants. But Eddie pressed on, looking up at the bench.

"Judge Duffy, we ask that you remember [that] the crimes committed just a few blocks away from this courtroom were not abstractions. We who have buried our dead, without a chance to lay a comforting hand on their heads, ask that you remember [that] this bombing was an act of multiple murder."

Finally he turned to the four bombers, who refused to look at him, and recited the names of those dead. As they echoed through the courtroom like tiny bomb blasts, he ended with: "Monica Rodriquez Smith, daughter, wife, expectant mother, best friend, born 1958, died February 26, 1993. Our son, Edward, died February 26, 1993, never born, except in our hearts."

For a moment the courtroom was still. Then the defendants had their turn. Mohammed Ajaj stood up and went on for three hours about the history of Zionism. The others voiced petty complaints. Only Ajaj called the bombing a "horrible" crime.

In the end, Judge Duffy, a tough Irishman from the Bronx who had presided over the Pizza Connection Mafia trial, delivered a series of sentences that dwarfed those in any proceeding against the mob. Calculating the number of years the victims might have lived, he sentenced each of Yousef's cell members to 240 years behind bars.

Just the Beginning

For a short time, there was a sense of peace and satisfaction in Lower Manhattan. But the verdicts left many more questions unanswered. Who was truly behind the Trade Center bombing and who funded it? In his summation, DePippo had finally acknowledged that fugitive Ramzi Yousef was the "evil genius" who built the bomb. But were these men part of a ragtag crew, as the FBI suggested early on, or something much bigger?

"You don't have answers to all those questions," admitted U.S. Attorney White, whose Southern District office was now gearing up for round two: the Day of Terror trial against the Sheikh and company.

Special Agent Nancy Floyd was never called as a witness at the first proceeding; nor was Emad Salem, the man who had infiltrated the cell, interacting with Salameh and Abouhalima way back in 1991. The FBI's handling of that initial investigation was something the Justice Department would just as soon forget.

By October, news stories had begun to break about Salem's bootleg tapes. Questions were being asked about how much warning the Feds might have had about the blast. And the larger question persisted: Just how broad and deep was this conspiracy? The phone records introduced at trial proved that Yousef had help with Ajaj from a third party in Texas. The bank records showed transfers of tens of thousand of dollars from banks in Germany and the Middle East. Ajaj alone raised questions with his itinerary. He had traveled from Houston to Pakistan to the United Arab Emirates and back to Pakistan before arriving on that first-class flight with Yousef. Among his possessions seized at JFK, Ajaj had a letter of introduction to a mysterious training camp near the Pakistan-Afghan border and that book with the words that—if properly translated—might have been recognized as *al Qaeda*.

Despite the progress they'd made in convicting the four conspirators, at this point there's little evidence that the Feds grasped the bigger picture—that New York had become the flashpoint for a new global jihad, driven by radical Egyptians aligned with Osama bin Laden; that the blind Sheikh himself was their pope, and that the Trade Center bombing wasn't the *end* of their campaign but the *beginning*. All of this would be established in years to come, but for now the real power behind Ramzi Yousef remained a mystery.

Just hours after the verdict, Muslim militants in Cairo warned that the trial outcome would ignite a wave of bloody revenge attacks against Americans.

"The Islamic Group (IG) will find any American here in Egypt that it can get its hands on to hunt in retaliation," said a leader of the group.[22]

Detective Lou Napoli had known for years that El Sayyid Nosair was an IG member. By now the Feds knew that Sheikh Rahman was the group's leader. But he was in custody, and investigators seemed convinced that the terror cell was being contained.

The Yousef hunt was priority number one in the Bureau's New York office, but few investigators seemed to pay much attention to the warning letter typed on Ayyad's computer—the promise that "next time . . . the Trade Center will be one of our targets," or the threat that hordes of "suicidal soldiers" were ready to do the cell's bidding.

Also overlooked was a conversation that Abouhalima had with his cell mate, Theodore Williams, while he was awaiting trial in the MCC. Williams, a onetime henchman of the late heroin czar Leroy Nicky Barnes, was convicted of beating a man to death with a bat. Yet he was shocked at Abouhalima's apparent lack of remorse for helping to set a bomb that potentially could have killed thousands. In an idle moment, he asked the Red, "How did you and five guys expect to blow up the whole thing?"[23]

Abouhalima eyed him, then replied: "It's not us. It's three hundred men across the country who would do anything to hurt the United States." Now, if there were hundreds of committed jihadi in America, how many thousands were there worldwide? As they spoke, Ramzi Yousef would soon be on his way to the Philippines to make good on that hidden warning the Feds had found on Nidal Ayyad's computer.

". . . our calculations were not very accurate this time," the warning said. "However we promise you that next time it will be very precise."

21

THE WESTERN FRONT

The New York Joint Terrorist Task Force was driving the Yousef hunt, but at this point in 1994, apparently unknown to the JTTF agents, the next front in bin Laden's jihad was opening in the American Southwest. Arizona was the state where al Qaeda had the most resources outside of greater New York, and within days of the Sheikh's indictment some of his supporters showed up there.

James Hauswirth, a retired twenty-seven-year FBI veteran, said that as early as 1994 the FBI's Phoenix office got word that followers of Sheikh Rahman had come to the region for bomb training. "Individuals associated with this blind Sheikh had recruited someone who was being trained as a suicide bomber," Hauswirth said.[1]

Hauswirth, who worked the Special Operations Group in the Phoenix office, said that he had been tasked to do a surveillance of the bomb training by the International Terrorism Squad known as Squad Five. "We were able to select a location where this testing was to take place," he said. "We had a camera up on top of a mountain and we videotaped them."

The ex-agent said that the tape showed individuals throwing a "hand-held device" at a car, but it failed to detonate. "We were told by Squad Five that these were heavy-duty associates of the blind Sheikh who had fled New York after the '93 [bombing]."

The Squad Five agent who had requested the surveillance was Ken Williams, a former San Diego police officer who had trained as an FBI sniper and SWAT member before becoming a counterterrorism specialist with the Bureau. A twelve-year veteran of the FBI, William's eight- to ten-member squad didn't get much attention in the office.

"The drug war was the big thing back then," said Hauswirth, "and terrorism was way on the back burner."

In an interview for this book, Hauswirth said that sixty of the two hundred and thirty agents in Phoenix were working drug cases at the time. "Why is that," he asked, "if we have an agency called DEA?"

By 1994 the Drug Enforcement Administration had more than seven thousand agents and support staff assigned full-time to the "war on drugs." But nationwide, and in offices like Phoenix, the FBI was committing up to a quarter of its resources to the same fight. Hauswirth believed that this focus came at the expense of counterterrorism. Further, he charged that the drug busts being made in Arizona were relatively minor. "These were not drug barons," he said. "They were street-level dealers at best . . . even if you caught them with the goods, it wasn't going to make any difference."

Hauswirth specifically blamed the lack of support for Squad Five on Bruce Gebhart, the former special agent in charge of the Phoenix office; Ray Churay, the administrative special agent in charge; and Lupe Gonzalez, the ex-Marine who succeeded Gebhart as the Phoenix SAC. (After 9/11, in an interview with the *Los Angeles Times,* Gonzalez admitted that in the mid-1990s international terrorism was "job four" in the Phoenix office behind "organized crime and drugs, white collar crime and crime on Indian reservations."[2]

Three months after the September 11 attacks, Hauswirth put his complaints in a letter to FBI director Robert Mueller. "The director had made a statement, that one of these days we're gonna have suicide bombers in this country," said the retired agent. "And my God, here seven years ago we were watching one being trained."

In contrast to the FBI leadership in Phoenix, Hauswirth described Special Agent Williams as "very proactive." "Kenny wasn't going to sit back and wait for something to happen," said Hauswirth. "He was gonna make it happen."

But Williams was not without his critics.

In 1994, at the same time as the suicide bombing surveillance, Williams had developed an asset with access to top-shelf intelligence in the Mideast. Based in Phoenix, Harry Josef Ellen was an American businessman who had converted to Islam in 1990. Using the name Abu Yusef, Ellen made four trips to Gaza during the 1990s, offering humanitarian aid to the beleaguered West Bank. His contacts with the PLO were so good that at one point Ellen brought together all five of the major Palestinian resistance factions and convinced them to give safe passage to a group of U.S. doctors treating children in Gaza.[3]

Over the course of four years, the FBI funneled more than one hundred thousand dollars through a charitable foundation Ellen had set up to aid Palestinian refugees. In addition to providing invaluable insights into the PLO, the evidence indicates that Ellen/Abu Yusef may have helped the peace process and saved lives. His story of aid, espionage, and betrayal reads like a plot from Le Carré.

Ellen becomes an important player in this story because he had direct dealings with a man who came to Arizona from New Jersey in 1993 and bragged about being close to both Sheikh Rahman and Ramzi Yousef. Ellen, who called the man Abu Sief, said that he was active in the Phoenix-Tucson Islamic community.

Shortly after Sief's arrival, Ellen said he was asked by Agent Ken Williams to monitor the Palestinian's activities.

"The FBI asked me to keep an eye on him," said Ellen in an interview for this book.[4] "I know he was involved with Ramzi Yousef. He had a key chain with a soccer ball and the name of the al-Salaam Mosque in Jersey City that he used to flash to impress people."

Tucson's Al Bunyan Information Center had already become an adjunct of the Services Office network that was eventually subsumed by al Qaeda. When Ramzi Yousef arrived at JFK in 1992, he had an ID card from Al Bunyan, marked with the post office box of one of Tucson's most notorious jihadis: Wadih El-Hage.

El-Hage was the enigmatic figure who had once bought automatic weapons for Mahmud Abouhalima.[5] He'd shown up in New York at the time of the Shalabi murder and visited El Sayyid Nosair in jail. A naturalized U.S. citizen, El-Hage had lived in Tucson from the late 1980s to 1992. In 1989 he'd been connected to the murder of Rashid Khalifa, a liberal imam who was killed by associates of al Fuqra, a Black Muslim splinter group.[6] A close New York associate of al Fuqra was Clement Rodney Hampton-El,* a.k.a. Dr. Rashid, who'd been spotted in the FBI's 1989 Calverton surveillance photos and was recently indicted with the blind Sheikh in the Day of Terror plot. But El-Hage's real importance in the line of evidence leading up to 9/11 was the link he formed between the blind Sheikh's New York cell, Ramzi Yousef, and Osama bin Laden.

After the Afghan War, bin Laden had returned to his native Saudi Arabia, but he'd angered the Saudi royal family after writing a series of treatises denouncing them for harboring U.S. troops during the Gulf War. In 1991 the Saudis expelled bin Laden, and he moved his entourage to the African nation of Sudan.

Eventually, El-Hage moved to the Sudanese capital of Khartoum and became bin Laden's personal secretary. Later he would become one of the key coconspirators in al Qaeda's bombings of the U.S. embassies in East Africa.

El-Hage was a major al Qaeda operative, with ties in both New York and Arizona. If properly surveilled by the Bureau, he could have led the Feds directly to bin Laden as early as 1991, but the Feds didn't catch up with him until the late 1990s.

The FBI's failure to connect him earlier was another lost dot on the chart.†

Now, like Emad Salem in New York, Harry Ellen (a.k.a. Abu Yusef) was developing extraordinary intelligence on the inner movements of Islamic radicals in Arizona. By the mid-1990s he would pass information to FBI agent Ken Williams that would put the Bureau in perhaps the best position yet to stop the 9/11 attacks.

But just as the FBI blew its initial relationship with Salem, they would squander this opportunity as well. Ellen, too, would have a major falling-out with the Bureau, and key intelligence would be lost.

The events in Arizona become important because of what was going on at the time in another part of the world. At the same time Special Agent Hauswirth learned that an associate of the blind Sheikh was training suicide bombers in Phoenix, Ramzi Yousef was formulating a plan

---

*Timeline #03. p. 1; #47. p. 10.
†Timeline #05. p. 2; #11. p. 3.

for U.S.-trained Islamic suicide pilots to hijack airliners and fly them into buildings like the World Trade Center and the Pentagon. Evidence uncovered in this investigation now shows that Yousef began designing the plot in the early fall of 1994. With elements of the jihad now ongoing in New York and Arizona, Ramzi Yousef was about to open a new front in the Philippines.

$2 Million Reasons to Stop Terror

On July 4, 1994, *Newsweek* called him "America's Most Wanted."[7] But by then the FBI was so desperate to nail Yousef, and their leads were so thin, that the last best hope for his capture seemed to be a program at the State Department to circulate his wanted poster throughout the Mideast.

The Rewards for Justice program offered cash to people willing to blow the whistle on terrorists. The program had enjoyed some success, including the apprehension of an Iraqi cell that had targeted a series of U.S. airlines in East Asia in 1991.[8] But the program kicked into high gear under the direction of Bradley Smith, an agent with the State Department's Diplomatic Security Service.[9]

Smith, an ex–Air Force pilot, was another outside-the-box thinker. Coining the slogan "We Can Give You $2 Million Reasons to Stop Terrorism," Smith printed posters depicting suitcases full of cash and had them distributed throughout the Mideast and Asia. He also produced a series of TV spots with movie stars like Charlie Sheen, Charlton Heston, and Charles Bronson, recorded in a dozen languages from Arabic to Farsi to Serbo-Croatian. He set up an international tip hot line (1-800-Heroes-1), and was among the first to use the Internet, promoting the rewards with a website: www.heroes.net.

"The act of terrorism is designed to cause human suffering," said Smith.[10] "It's designed to inflict pain and I think the people responsible have to be brought to justice."

Ramzi Yousef became the program's first two-million-dollar poster boy, quickly followed by Amir Aimal Kansi, another Baluchistani, who had gunned down two CIA employees outside the agency's headquarters in Langley, Virginia, a month before the Trade Center bombing.[11]

A tenacious investigator and counterterrorist, Smith had made the hunt for Ramzi Yousef his personal mission after being diagnosed with

Lou Gehrig's disease. Given only months to live, he stayed alive with the hope of bringing Yousef to ground via the program. But as his health deteriorated, Smith was forced to fight another battle with the State Department for wheelchair access to SA-10, the building in Foggy Bottom where the DSS agents were based.

Ironically, like Nancy Floyd, Smith found himself spending as much time battling his own agency and enduring the stress of office politics as he did chasing the bad guys. Smith worked in a secure area in SA-10 called the SCIF (Sensitive Compilation of Intelligence Facility). At one point, after breaking his leg, he returned to work to discover that his office on the fifth floor had been given away. Tormented by supervisors who had little belief in the Rewards program, Smith was relocated to a room off the garage.

For weeks he was forced to urinate in a jar because he couldn't reach a nearby lavatory without help.[12] At one point, on his way to the bathroom, a steel door slammed back knocking him out of his wheelchair and breaking his leg again. A decorated DSS agent, Smith finally sued the State Department and won the right to continue the Yousef hunt from his home.[13]

Now, as time passed without any hard results in the FBI's Yousef investigation, Smith got the idea of putting the wanted posters on matchbook covers.

It was a low-tech plan, but Smith, who had been posted in Istanbul, was concerned that too many of the Rewards posters were hanging on embassy bulletin boards. Word wasn't getting out on the streets of the Mideast, where it could do the most good.

"So many people smoke in that part of the world," said Smith. "We wanted to get those want posters into the hands of the people who might be the most likely to furnish intelligence—people who may not have seen the TV spots or the posters."[14]

The matchbook idea was ridiculed by Smith's bosses at State who were afraid of offending political leaders in the host countries.[15] One of them was a career diplomat named Barbara Bodine, who would resurface at several other points in this story.

"Bodine and some of the others at State were concerned that the matchbooks would send the wrong message," said Rob Born, Smith's former partner. "Their reasoning was that it would make the United States appear to be encouraging smoking overseas."[16]

But by the summer of 1994, as Yousef continued to strike terror across the globe, it became clear that the FBI was no closer to grabbing him than on the night he fled New York.

When it came to fighting terrorism, Brad Smith embraced the age-old military dictum "It's easier to beg forgiveness than to ask permission." So he amped up the Rewards program and ordered thirty-seven thousand matchbooks to be air-dropped throughout Pakistan, with the heaviest concentration in Yousef's backyard of Baluchistan.

"If traditional investigative work wasn't cutting it," said Smith. "We were going to take the fight to them. We needed to hunt the bad guys just as lawmen did in the old west."[17]

In August of 1994, as Yousef flew from Quetta to Karachi, he flipped through the July 4 *Newsweek*, which featured his picture staring out from a matchbook cover. Like Smith's superiors at State, the master bomber scoffed that the American Feds must be desperate. He eyed his matchbook with a combination of pride and disdain. After all, he was the world's most hunted man. Was this the best the Americans could do to bring him down?

The bomb maker had studied the great terrorists of the postwar era, men like Carlos the Jackal and Abu Nidal. From Munich to the *Achille Lauro,* terror had been a tool, a device they wielded for political change. Terror was the poor man's weapon, and Yousef was determined to carry the jihad to exponentially higher levels of mayhem. From now on each of his targets would have global importance. Where previous al Qaeda operatives had blown up a single plane, he would take down a dozen. Where he had once been sent to move on a regional leader like Bhutto, now he would take out the pope. Yousef would soon send the American apostates a message: they would never be safe, even within their own borders.

His old friend Abdul Hakim Murad had trained in four U.S. flight schools. While he was in America, Murad had visited New York to study the Trade Center. He had examined the news coverage and the postblast engineering reports, helping Yousef determine what had gone wrong with the bomb placement. The mistake, he now saw, was in hitting the towers from below. The next time it would be different.[18]

By the summer of 1994, Yousef had begun sketching in the rough draft of three plots that would culminate in his return to the United States.

The attack on the Trade Center would necessarily be a suicide mission. So he concentrated first on Bojinka, his plan to take down a series of U.S. airliners in rapid succession. The key to the plot would be devising a set of bombs that could be planted onboard the aircraft and detonated *after* the planes had landed and his jihadi cohorts had disembarked safely. This would save them for the ultimate suicide mission.

Following the crash of Pan Am Flight 103, which went down after a bomb in a Toshiba boom box was smuggled aboard in luggage from Malta in 1988, most international carriers either X-rayed luggage, or warned travelers that checked bags would be subject to rigorous inspection.[19] The beefed-up security had been a deterrent, and there hadn't been an onboard explosion since.

Now Yousef began thinking about how to build an undetectable device.

After watching a CNN report about sophisticated new equipment set up at international airports to sniff out explosives, Yousef came upon the design. The bomb would be composed of apparently innocuous elements that could pass airport security. The conspirator would then assemble the bomb on the first leg of a two-leg flight, plant it, and exit the plane. Hours later, on the next leg, the aircraft and its passengers would be blown out of the sky. Such a plan would demand an explosive that was light and innocuous to airport screeners. To find it, Yousef reread the eleventh edition of *Hawley's Condensed Chemical Dictionary* cover to cover, for the tenth time.[20] He finally settled on a diluted form of nitroglycerin, with nitrocellulose, or "gun cotton," as the initiator. The nitro would project as a clear liquid in X-ray machines. The cotton would seem benign to airport security personnel.

The uncertainty of flight departures, and his desire to ensure maximum casualties, would also require a timer that could be set hours, even days, in advance. When he came across a Casio DBC-61 databank watch, Yousef was in business: the watch had an alarm that could be set 23 hours, 59 minutes, and 59 seconds ahead, and a "schedule mode" that allowed it to go off up to a year after being programmed.[21]

By the summer of 1994, Yousef had all the elements in place to execute his plan. All he needed was a haven where his bombing cell would have little chance of detection. It had to be a country with a well-financed al Qaeda support group; a third-world nation where the impoverished citizens might even serve as unwitting accomplices; preferably an English-speaking country where airport security would be lax.

As Yousef scanned the atlas on his Toshiba laptop, he didn't have to look far. In 1991 he'd responded to a call from Abdurajak Janjalani, a veteran of the Afghan campaign, and ventured to the Philippines to train the jihadis of the group named after Janjalani's nom de guerre, Abu Sayyaf. The former U.S. colony of islands in East Asia would now be Yousef's base for Bojinka.

He would travel first to Karachi, where he would link with Abdul Hakim Murad and give him a course in explosives before carrying the operation to the next level. On the flight from Quetta, Yousef closed his eyes and dreamed of the next set of bombs he would build. He refused to admit to himself that his tactics were different from those of other terrorists. Never before had one man targeted so many civilians. Never before had the intended body count been so high. But the distinction was lost on Yousef. As far as he was concerned, any taxpayer of a nation that fostered violence on Islam was culpable. Ramzi Yousef was the self-appointed general of his own Liberation Army, and he was already in an advanced state of battle.

Lounge Lizards of Terror

For finance and support, Yousef turned to his maternal uncle, thirty-year-old Khalid Shaikh Mohammed. A pudgy figure at five-foot-four with large, piercing eyes, Mohammed seemed to be a man of two lives. Born to devout Pakistani parents, he joined the local chapter of the radical Muslim Brotherhood, which was headed by his brother Zahid Al-Shaikh in Fuhayhil, south of Kuwait City where he was raised.[22] The Egypt-based Brotherhood, whose leading theoretician, Sayyid Qutb, had also influenced Osama bin Laden, espoused a militant return to the strict principles of Islam.[23]

Enrolling at Chowan College in Murfreesboro, North Carolina, in 1983, Mohammed was dubbed "the Brain" by al Qaeda operatives. "Khalid was so smart," remembered fellow student Mohammed al-Bulooshi. "He came to college with virtually no English. But he entered directly in advanced classes." Attending all-night bull sessions and jawing with fellow students at the local Burger King, the mysterious Mohammed showed that he had a lighter side.[24] "He was a funny guy, telling jokes twenty-four hours straight," remembered al-Bulooshi.

But Mohammed was becoming radicalized during his time in the States. After transferring to and graduating from North Carolina A&T in Greensboro, he followed his brother Zahid Al-Shaikh to Afghanistan, where they trained with the swarming ranks of "Afghan Arabs" arriving to battle the Soviets.

With the road to 9/11 leading directly back to the Afghan war, it was here that Khalid Shaikh Mohammed met up with Osama bin Laden. To help fund al Qaeda's Asian campaign, bin Laden dispatched his brother-in-law Mohammed Jamal Khalifa to underwrite Abdurajak Janjalani's Abu Sayyaf Group (ASG) in the Philippines. Through a series of ostensibly charitable NGOs, Khalifa dispersed hundreds of thousands of dollars to the ASG. Part of Khalid Shaikh's role in Manila would be to act as a conduit to Khalifa in setting up clandestine accounts to bankroll his nephew Ramzi's plots.[25]

Like Yousef, Mohammed was a chameleon, one day wearing a kaffiyah and posing as a billionaire sheikh from Qatar, another passing himself off as an ex-priest.[26] Over the years he accumulated up to sixty aliases, including Asraf Refaat Nabith Henan, Khalid Abdul Wadood, and Fahd bin Abdellah bin Khalid. But when he rented a posh condo in Manila and started flashing cash, he was Salem Ali, a wealthy plywood exporter who liked to party.

Secret documents obtained from the Intelligence Command of the Philippine National Police now show that Yousef's uncle stepped far outside the rigid confines of the puritanical Islam he espoused. In fact, during the fall of 1994 he behaved more like a lounge lizard than a devoted believer. Still, the sly Mohammed never forgot the mission, using the local B-girls he ran with as fronts to insulate himself and the members of Yousef's cell from the police.

In August, Mohammed checked into the Sir William Hotel on Timog Avenue in Quezon City.[27] He needed someone he could control to open a bank account—and when he walked into the Sir William Karaoke Bar, he found her.

Rose Mosquera y Tabalos was a sexy twenty-two-year-old hostess. Though married to one Bobby Malila, she worked nights at the bar and made her tips feeding drinks to the customers. Rose was sitting in a booth when Mohammed introduced himself. He said he was staying at the hotel in the same building, but that first night he was discreet.

Sizing up the young hostess to determine how much he could trust her, Mohammed showed up the next night, and the night after that. Each time he requested Rose as a companion. As colored lights flashed and mirrored balls spun above their heads, he joked and bought drinks for the hostess and her friends Helen and Jovy. Finally, on the third night, Khalid invited Rose to his room. She had told him that she wanted to visit Davao City in the south with her husband. Khalid promised that he'd buy her the ticket if she did him a favor.[28]

The next day they met at a local Wendy's for lunch, and then rode a bus to the SM Megamall. With cash from the man she knew as Salem Ali, Rose opened an account at the Far East Bank and Trust Company. As soon as she emerged from the bank, Mohammed grabbed the bank book. Minutes later, he paid the Philippine equivalent of $806 for a cell phone, which he impounded after Rose registered it in her name. If the pretty young bar girl thought she'd locked into a sugar daddy, she was wrong. All she got for that first day's work, besides a burger and fries, was twenty dollars in cab fare.

That night, Rose called and demanded to know about her ticket. Not wanting to cause a stir this early in the operation, Mohammed met her the next day at Wendy's and bought her a boat ticket to Davao City for $56.15. He took her to a clothing store in the mall and spent twenty dollars on a blouse and skirt, giving her another twenty for cab fare and sixty dollars for pocket money. He promised to stay in touch, but she never saw him again.

By then, the coldhearted Khalid had his phone and bank account—
and he'd moved on to Jane Ramos, another stunner he'd met on the
karaoke circuit. He'd also left the Sir William in favor of an upscale
apartment at the Tiffany Condos, where he waited for his murderous
nephew to arrive.

22

THE TEMPTRESS
AND THE SPY

The year 1994 turned out to be a brutal one for Special Agent Nancy Floyd. As word of her comments on Emad Salem's bootleg tapes leaked out, she found herself more and more isolated in the Bureau. Her supervisors had heard the recordings of her telling Salem how the FBI might have prevented the bombing if they'd just let him do his job. The evidence now shows that she was correct, but truth was no defense in the media-conscious FBI. By the fall of 1993, transcripts of the tapes were being passed by defense lawyers to the press.

That past August, Floyd had been ordered by ASAC Carson Dunbar to terminate any further contact with Salem.[1] Now in Witness Protection, the Egyptian was gearing up to be the government's star witness in the case against the blind Sheikh.[2] There were rumors that Nancy might be called to testify—not by the Feds, but by the defense team anxious to prove that the Sheikh's cell had been victims of entrapment.

For that defense to succeed, the lawyers would have to prove that, apart from Salem's inducement, their clients would not otherwise have been predisposed to build the bombs. But they were on shaky ground, since the FBI had videotape from the Queens warehouse showing multiple acts of predisposition by the defendants as they built their devices.

So without an effective entrapment defense, the Sheikh's lawyers looked for another potential weakness in the Feds' case. The word soon came that Dunbar himself might be called to the stand. Depending on how tough the questioning got, his testimony about how he'd handled Salem the first time out could prove embarrassing to the Bureau.

By 1993, Nancy Floyd had transferred out of Foreign Counter Intelligence and into a slot with the New York Special Operations Group. After months of working her day shift on the GRU unit and meeting at night to debrief Salem, the workload had taken its toll. She now spent her days doing routine surveillance work: sitting on wiretaps, staking out buildings, and following suspects at the center of other agents' cases.

It was a significant letdown for Nancy, an experienced counterintelligence agent who had not only brought Salem in but worked double time to hold his hand through the first bombing probe, the blowup with Dunbar, and his critical work rounding up the Sheikh's cell in the Day of Terror sting. But by the end of 1993, after Jim Fox was fired as head of the New York office, the supervisors at 26 Federal Plaza were gunning for a scapegoat, and Nancy was the junior agent in the case.

"Carson Dunbar—any FBI management guy can be vindictive if they think they've been crossed," said Richard Swick, whose law firm represented Nancy on behalf of the FBI Agent's Association.[3]

"Mistakes were made the first time, so they decided to hang it on Nancy," says her mentor, Len Predtechenskis.

As the subject of an ongoing investigation by the FBI's Office of Professional Responsibility, Floyd was technically unable to advance in the Bureau or qualify for a promotion until the proceedings had ended. "Once an OPR is opened, many agents tend to steer clear of you," said Diane Bodner Duhig, the attorney who handled Nancy's OPR case for Swick's firm.[4] "The most she could do for herself now was keep her head down and ride things out until her OPR was over."

And something else was hanging over Nancy's head. For a while now, she had been hearing the whispers at 26 Federal Plaza that she was somehow romantically involved with Salem. This was disproven by Salem's own bootleg tapes: the ex–army major had taped hours of conversations with Nancy, and there wasn't even a hint that the relationship was more than professional. Still, rather than endure the rumors and isolation of day-to-day work at the New York office, Agent Floyd moved into the Special Operations Group.

The change of pace seemed to be doing her some good.

"Nancy would report to whatever offsite location SOG was working on a given shift," Predtechenskis recalled. "There she was with a team of agents she felt she could trust. She was just beginning to find some peace for the first time in a while, when all hell broke loose."

On the night of Friday, March 11, 1994, Nancy was on an SOG stakeout in the Bronx when one of her team members came up to her carrying a *New York Post*. "Oh my God, Nancy," he said. "Have you seen this?" The agent handed her the paper and showed her a story with a banner headline across the top:

NEW YORK POST, SATURDAY, MARCH 22, 1994

TEMPTRESS & THE SPY

"Nancy reacted with shock," one source remembered. "She couldn't believe what she was reading."

An FBI agent is under investigation to see if she had an affair with a key confidential informant, The Post has learned. The agent, Nancy Floyd, was assigned to be the government contact for Emad Salem, the former Egyptian army colonel who blew the whistle on the terror plot to blow up New York landmarks and assassinate political figures.

Justice Department and law enforcement sources said the FBI decided to do an internal investigation after:

- Rumors of an affair became a hot topic among the agent's colleagues in the New York offices.

- Salem secretly recorded conversations between the two of them. When her superiors heard the tapes they became alarmed at "the degree of familiarity and comfort they displayed with each other," a Justice Dept. official told the Post.[5]

The article went on to admit that "the tapes contain no conversations that are specifically about sex. But the agent is heard several times suggesting to Salem that the two meet alone, without John Anticev, a male agent who also worked the case."

What the story *didn't* say was that Floyd had been forced to meet with Salem night after night when Anticev was out for three months with the brain embolism and the Egyptian couldn't get through to Detective Napoli.

Farther down, the story admitted that "the rumors" may have been "planted by a lawyer for one of the defendants in the terror case." But the clear implication of the piece was that Nancy and Salem had engaged in private love trysts: "In addition to reviewing tapes," the story continued, "the FBI is examining financial records—including hotel receipts—that were kept in connection with Salem's case."

"When they'd asked Nancy about her vouchers," said Len Predtechenskis, "she had furnished all of them. That issue had been put to rest months before that. At one point, in the course of working Salem, a meeting was held with him at a hotel, but John Crouthamel, the supervisor, had been present with Salem along with Nancy, Anticev, and Lou Napoli. So the suggestion that she'd been running off with Salem was unreal."

The *Post* story ended by citing four excerpts from Salem's bootleg tapes. Each of them involved Nancy's comments about how the New York office may have dropped the ball on the original Trade Center investigation. But not a single quote contained a whiff of the sexual innuendo expressed in the banner headline.

"This story was the ultimate cheap shot," said Len. "An attempt by people in the New York office to smear a great young agent."

Even Jim Roth, the FBI's New York lawyer who was one of Nancy's most vociferous critics, didn't believe the rumors. "I don't think she had any kind of sexual relationship with this guy," Roth said. "I honestly don't think that she did."[6]

Nancy finished out her tour that night, but she couldn't believe that things had gone this far. Two days later she got a call from her brother Tom, an Army first lieutenant stationed in Germany. The story had run worldwide on UPI, he said, and members of his company were wondering if this agent in the story who was sleeping with her asset could be Nancy.

Then fate struck even closer to home, in the form of a personal loss. Nancy had managed to get through the summer by looking forward to September, when she would travel to Pennsylvania to be in the wedding party of Martha Dixon, a fellow agent who'd been one of her best friends since Quantico. Nancy and Martha were roughly the same age. On their first postings, each of them had qualified for their local office SWAT team. While Nancy was working Savannah, Martha was six hours north in Knoxville, Tennessee. Once they earned their badges as FBI brick agents, both women became married to the job.

Then, in 1992, Martha began dating Special Agent George Martinez. Two years later he proposed, and in early September they were married at St. Anne's Church in Castle Shannon, Pennsylvania, Martha's hometown, near Pittsburgh. Nancy stood on the bride's side of the aisle along with Icey Jenkins, another classmate from Quantico.

After returning from their honeymoon, Martha was detailed to the Cold Case Squad at the Washington, D.C., police headquarters. On the afternoon of November 22, George tried paging his wife, but she never paged back. That very morning Martha had told him that she thought she might be pregnant. When another urgent page went unanswered, George became worried.

He didn't know it at the time, but tragedy had already struck.

At 3:30 P.M., Benny Lee Lawson, a gangbanger in his mid-twenties, had walked into the Cold Case Squad, pulled out a Tec-9 semiautomatic, and started spraying the bull pen. One of the 9mm rounds instantly killed a D.C. police sergeant and wounded an FBI special agent. Martha was in an adjoining office when she heard the gunfire. As she drew her weapon and rushed in, she noticed another of her partners, Special Agent Michael John Miller, sprawled dead on the floor. She quickly turned and fired toward Lawson, wounding him. But on his way down, the murder suspect fired another shot, killing Dixon.

Nancy Floyd was on another SOG stakeout when her pager went off. The return number had a D.C. area code. It was from Icey Jenkins, her classmate with Martha at Quantico. At the end of the number it said 9-1-1. Nancy called back from a cell phone at the stakeout. As Icey related what she knew of the murders, Nancy almost collapsed.

Half-numb, she walked back to her car. She got in the driver's seat, took a deep breath, then laid her head down on the steering wheel and started to weep.

Days later, in the same church where she and Icey had celebrated

Martha's wedding a few months before, they helped to carry her coffin. Not since she was twenty, when her father had died from a sudden heart attack, had Nancy Floyd felt such a loss.

In the three years since she'd first met Emad Salem, Nancy Floyd had suffered considerably. She'd run afoul of Dunbar and Jim Roth, the head lawyer in the New York office. She'd been called everything from a liar to a bitch by her own supervisors. She'd been vilified in the tabloid press, and she was the subject of an ongoing internal affairs investigation that could cost her her badge. There were times when she'd thought of giving up and quitting the Bureau.

But the death of Martha Dixon was a jolt that reminded her who she was. "I buried somebody who put her life on the line to protect this country," said Nancy. "That's what we were sworn to do. That's the job. My love for the Bureau was deep and I realized that no matter what happened to me, my situation was insignificant compared to the price Martha paid."

As 1994 ended—perhaps the toughest year in Nancy Floyd's life— she promised herself that she was going to dig in for the long haul, give one hundred percent to the Special Operations Group, and do whatever she could to make sure that the blind Sheikh, and the other men Emad Salem had risked his life to stop, came to justice.

Battle of the Badges

Whatever isolation Nancy Floyd was feeling on the inside of the Bureau, Ronnie Bucca was feeling doubly frustrated on the outside. At this point Bucca held the rank of a top sergeant in the 3413 Military Intelligence Detachment of the 800th MPs.

He'd been through the Second U.S. Army Intelligence School at Fort Bragg, and had extensive operational training with the 11th Special Forces. On his monthly reserve tours at the Defense Intelligence Analysis Center, Bucca had seen the intel suggesting that the FBI had severely underestimated the strength and intent of the cell surrounding Sheikh Omar Abdel Rahman.

Determined now to get more directly involved in the ongoing investigation and hunt for Yousef, Bucca reached out to the Joint Terrorist Task Force through a contact in the police department. At this point the

JTTF had grown to more than forty members, including agents from the Secret Service, Treasury, INS, DEA, and the New York State Police, along with NYPD detectives like Lou Napoli. The very purpose of the Task Force was to allow input from local law enforcement officers. But the JTTF had never admitted a fire marshal.

"Ronnie wasn't surprised," said Fire Marshal Henry Raven, who worked with Bucca on the BFI's Social Club Task Force. "We'd been getting the short end of the stick from the PD for years."

In a city of tribes, the rivalry between the "reds" and the "blues" in New York went back decades. Historically both departments were manned from the Irish enclaves, filled with the sons and grandsons of immigrants from Kerry, Mayo, and Cork. As in all tribes there was a pecking order, and over the decades, in the eyes of the city fathers, the cops always seemed to come first. Headquarters for the PD was a sky-scraper called One Police Plaza. Until 1998, when they moved into Metrotech (the new headquarters in Brooklyn), the fire department made do in a broken-down commercial building on Livingston Street.

Even though the Bureau of Fire Investigation was the city's lead agency when it came to determining the cause and origin of arson, they didn't even have their own lab. When they filled their paint cans with volatile samples, the marshals had to bring them to the police lab on Twentieth Street, which was under the control of A&E, the NYPD's Arson and Explosions unit. Worse yet, the marshals were routinely stymied when, just as they were about to make an important arson collar, case after case was grabbed by the detectives from A&E.

"It was incredibly frustrating," said Phil Meagher, the veteran marshal who was the first to "call" the epicenter of the Trade Center blast. "A&E could take control of any fire investigation they wanted and it usually happened after the fire marshal had done the legwork and developed the leads."[7]

It got so bad that, in the early 1990s, detectives from A&E had begun calling the Bureau of Fire Investigation each morning for a full report on the cases the ex-firefighters had developed the night before. " 'What do you have?' they'd demand from the supervisor on duty," said retired marshal Bobby McLoughlin. "And the supervising fire marshal had to report to the PD any fires or incidents of importance so that the cops could decide whether or not they were worthy of their investigation."[8]

By 1995 the resentment between the two departments had boiled over, giving rise to an incident captured with a front-page headline in the New York *Daily News:* "BATTLE OF THE BADGES." Rumors had been rampant that the NYPD's Emergency Services Unit was about to take over all emergency rescue work, a large part of which was traditionally handled by the FDNY. On this occasion, a motorist had been pinned in his car after a crash on the Grand Central Parkway in Queens.

The FDNY's 105 Truck responded and immediately deployed a Hurst tool (also known as the "jaws of life") to cut out the driver before he bled to death. Suddenly a police ESU unit pulled up and an argument broke out over who was going to save the man first. One thing led to another, and one of the firefighters knocked a uniformed cop to the ground. The blues radioed their precinct, and were ordered to withdraw. The motorist was freed, and removed to a hospital by an FDNY ambulance. Finally, 105 Truck "took up," as firefighters call it when they leave a scene. Then, on the way back to the firehouse, a pair of police radio patrol units literally cut the truck off and forced the chauffeur to pull to the side of the parkway. Two sets of uniforms jumped out and grabbed the firefighter who'd thrown the punch. They took him off the rig, and "back-cuffed" him with his turnout coat and boots on.

There was simply no love lost between these men.

Still, Ronnie Bucca was an optimist. His younger brother Bobby was a cop, and as an ex–Green Beret, Ronnie resented the infighting that often plagued the armed services. "He hated turf wars and territoriality," said fellow marshal Henry Raven, who knew Bucca well. "As far as Ronnie was concerned the enemy was the bad guys, not the members of service, who were all on the same side of the line."

A case like the unsolved Mustafa Shalabi murder was just the kind of local crime with international implications that an investigator like Ronnie would have sunk his teeth into. "He brought so much to the party," said Raven. "Ronnie was thinking macro, not micro. How did the pieces fit in the grand scheme of terrorism? This guy was above and beyond your average investigator."[9]

Bucca had been waiting for weeks to hear back from that JTTF contact in the PD when he got the call. In a polite but short conversation, the detective told him that the Task Force wasn't taking on any more members.

Ronnie said he'd heard that they were expanding to fifty from local law enforcement agencies. He was an arson investigator. He felt he could contribute.

The detective countered that they already had arson covered by A&E.

But how many of those cops had his security clearance? Ronnie asked.

The detective acknowledged that Bucca's résumé was impressive, but at that point the JTTF just wasn't going to involve the FD—simple as that. *If you get any real leads,* the cop said, *call me.* With that he hung up.

Ronnie just stared at the receiver.

"He was heartbroken," said his wife, Eve. "Ronnie had really been up for this. He'd educated himself about the Islamic radicals. He had access to some amazing intelligence. But it was 'Thanks, no thanks.'" It did Bucca little good to appeal to the fire department. "Except for a handful of men," Eve said, "no one in the department seemed to realize how dangerous it was to be out of the interagency loop. Ronnie felt that if a terrorist incident happened, Fire would be first on the scene—and without a broader picture they'd have unnecessary casualties."

Not long after that, Ronnie told his brother Alfred what had happened. Driving back from a family event in Brooklyn, they passed Foley Square in Manhattan. Alfred gestured over to One Police Plaza, the NYPD's impressive high-rise headquarters.

"What'd you expect?" he said. "Guess which department marches first on Saint Paddy's Day and which one brings up the rear?"

"Look," said Ronnie, "it's just wrong for the FD to be out of this."

He told Alfred he wanted to show him something and drove up to his office. The Bronx Base of the BFI was located on the second floor of a rundown firehouse in the borough's Melrose section. When they entered the bull pen it was quiet, just a single supervising fire marshal on watch. The other men were out in the field. Ronnie went to his locker, pulled out his "Towers" file, and spread the contents out on his desk.

When Alfred saw the evidence that Ronnie had gathered, he was stunned it. His brother was a driven man.

Ronnie unrolled a two-by-three-foot chart. In the lower right corner it said "Declassified." The chart had a picture of Yousef and the original Trade Center cell: Abouhalima, Salameh, Ayyad, and Ajaj. Next to that was a mug shot of the blind Shaikh and the Day of Terror plotters. It was a system for connecting the terrorists that was being developed by the Defense Intelligence Agency (DIA). They called it link chart analysis.

Alfred, a major in the Army Reserve, studied the chart and read off some of the names. "Mohammed, Muhamed, Mahmud . . ." He wondered how Ronnie could keep track of them.

"That's one of the problems," said Ronnie. He opened a file and showed his brother a picture of the Al Farooq Mosque in Brooklyn.

"There's a center on the first floor," he said. "Sometimes they spelled the name Alkifah; sometimes Al-Kifa." The cell members used multiple aliases and Social Security numbers, and they operated out of three different mosques—the Al Farooq, the Abu Bakr on Forrest Avenue, and al-Salaam in Jersey City.

"It makes tracking the mob look like cake," said Ronnie.

Alfred eyed him. "And you're telling me this because . . ."

"It's almost as bad on our end," said Ronnie. "Nobody talks to anybody else. DIA barely talks to Langley, and neither of *them* talk to the Bureau. They call it 'the black hole.' Intel goes in, but it never comes out. And nobody talks to the locals. That's what the Task Force was supposed to be, a clearinghouse. But the Bureau, Christ—they got the four yahoos convicted for the Trade Center, now they're teeing up for the Sheikh. But they still don't have him . . . ."

Ronnie nodded at Yousef's want poster, the big green-and-white $2 million reward notice from Brad Smith at the State Department. Yousef's black-and-white passport picture stared out from the bottom right corner.

"What happens when he does it again?"

Alfred pointed to Yousef's picture. "Who? This guy? Come on. Those people shot their wad. Look at the little guy who went back to Ryder for the refund. They're done. They'll try that blind bastard and the rest of 'em, and it'll be finished."

"That's just what the Bureau thinks," said Ronnie.

"Maybe they're right," said Alfred.

But Ronnie wasn't buying. He was convinced that Ramzi Yousef was an enormous continuing threat. He gestured to the bomb maker's picture.

"I'm telling you, bro. He's out there, and he's planning something. This thing isn't over."

23

DELIVERING THE "CHOCOLATES"

In August of 1994, as Khalid Shaikh Mohammed trolled the karaoke bars of Manila, Ramzi Yousef flew to Karachi and checked into the Embassy Hotel.[1] He summoned his old friend Murad, who'd rescued him after the Bhutto bombing, and described his ambitious plan to take down American airliners. This would be no simple attack on a single plane, said Ramzi. He wanted to destroy a dozen U.S. jumbo jets. The plot would bring worldwide air travel to a halt.

To build the intricate devices, however, Yousef would need help. So he traveled with Murad to Lahore, Pakistan, for eighteen days of "chocolate training." Yousef found an abandoned warehouse near the Lahore slums, and the two of them camped out. The bomb maker tested his ignition theory, hoping to detonate the nitrogen-soaked cotton by using the spark from a broken bulb initiator. For an electronic switch to send low-voltage current from the Casio watch through a pair of nine-volt batteries, Yousef discovered the C106D, a tiny silicone-controlled rectifier (SCR). Once the cover was removed from the back of the Casio there was just enough room inside to solder the SCR with a tiny connector plug.[2]

It was work that called for steady eyes and hands, and since Yousef had never fully recovered from his blast wounds, he counted on Murad to do the soldering. The two of them worked night and day in the derelict warehouse, which was roofless in some sections. They built a couple of test timers and exploded a few charges in the poor neighborhood that police rarely patrolled. By early September they were done; Yousef traveled to Quetta to stay with his brother, and Murad went back to Dubai to await instructions.

For the fourth member of the immediate Bojinka cell, Yousef selected a jihadi who outranked even him when it came to operational experience and scars. Wali Khan Amin Shah was an ethnic Uzbeki from the border town of Miram Shah, located on the western Pakistani frontier between Quetta and Peshawar. He'd fought alongside bin Laden against the Russians. The backs of his legs were deformed from the shrapnel of Soviet mines, and three fingers were missing from one of his hands. The thirty-eight-year-old Shah was macho, audacious, and athletic. Each day he did elaborate calisthenics to stay in shape, including painful leg scissors that he performed while balanced on his head. Later, in custody, he would make two daring jailbreaks.[3]

Like Yousef and his uncle Khalid Shaikh Mohammed, Shah was a man of multiple identities. He had passports under his own name from Pakistan and Afghanistan, even Norway.[4] He roared around Manila on a red Honda scrambler dirt bike, and seduced a gorgeous young bar girl named Catherine Brioso whom he'd met at the Manila Bay Club. But unlike Mohammed, who used Rose Mosquera and then dumped her, Shah moved in with the sexy Filipina, who dressed in tight clothes and went by the name Carol Santiago. He gave her cash for a pager, and the two of them went off to find suitable quarters for Yousef's bomb factory.

By mid-November the streets of Manila were filled with posters advertising the arrival of Pope John Paul II, who was scheduled to visit the Philippines in mid-January 1995 to celebrate mass before thousands. When Shah passed on the news that the most revered figure in Christendom would be in town, it was a target Yousef couldn't resist. He decided to plot the pontiff's murder as a precursor to Bojinka, and told Shah to find a place along the pope's parade route.

So, on November 8, Shah and Carol walked into the rental office of the Dona Josefa Apartments at 711 President Quirino Boulevard. Not only would John Paul II's motorcade pass in front of the six-story, twenty-eight-unit building, but the pope would be staying a block and a half away.

Carol filled out the rental application for Mina Senario, the Dona

Josefa's receptionist. Listing her address as 22 M Natividad in Santa Cruz, she paid the cash equivalent of five hundred dollars in rent and was handed the keys to Room 404, a furnished one-bedroom.

A month to the day later, Ramzi Yousef arrived, this time presenting the fake passport of one Naji Owaidah Haddad, a mechanical engineer from Morocco. Yousef opted for the apartment with the best view of the pope's parade route: Room 603 on the top left corner.[5]

Despite a wife and two young daughters back in Baluchistan, Yousef soon began dating a pretty twenty-one-year-old named Aminda Custodio. By day she worked as a waitress at Kentucky Ranch, a fast-food outlet, but after dark she doubled as a "receptionist" in the karaoke bar of the Manor Hotel. Posing as his uncle's cousin "Adam Ali," a chemical engineer, Yousef induced the aspiring dancer to rent a cell phone. He would use it to direct the Bojinka and pope plots.

Now, with their bank account, communications, and safe houses established, Yousef needed funding. So Wali Khan Amin Shah traveled to Malaysia to set up Konsonjaya, a "cutout" or front company, ostensibly created to export palm oil.

On the board of Konsonjaya along with Shah was Riduan Ismuddin, an Indonesian cleric known as Hambali who would later be linked to both the 9/11 attacks and the Bali nightclub bombing in November 2002 that left 180 dead.[6]

But the real money man behind the scenes was bin Laden's brother-in-law Mohammed Jamal Khalifa. A thirty-eight-year-old Saudi who had earlier bankrolled Janjalani's Abu Sayyaf wing of al Qaeda, Khalifa was married to a Filipina.

Lately he'd been convicted in Jordan of funding a terror group that had staged a series of deadly cinema bombings in Amman.[7] The conviction (in absentia) carried a death sentence.

Documents obtained from the Philippine National Police show direct links from Khalifa through Konsonjaya to Wali Khan Amin Shah and Yousef's Manila cell dating back to 1994. They show a relationship between Yousef and bin Laden much more direct than ever previously disclosed (see chart page 304).

Yet just as the bomb maker was finalizing his plans, Khalifa was arrested in San Francisco by the INS for visa fraud and other violations. Literature had been found in his luggage advocating Islamic military training in "assassination, explosives, weapons" and the "wisdom of bombing churches and murdering Catholic priests."[8]

At that point, in late 1994, the FBI's file on Osama bin Laden was beginning to grow. As far back as 1991 the Bureau knew that the Saudi billionaire had kicked in for Nosair's defense. Supervising Special Agent Neal Herman admitted that bin Laden's name had surfaced in 1993, when the New York office sifted through phone records following Yousef's escape.

As the Feds prepped for the blind Sheikh's trial and began to recognize the Kahane murder and the Trade Center bombing as part of one big conspiracy, bin Laden loomed in the background. Now his own brother-in-law was in U.S. custody. It was an extraordinary intelligence opportunity—especially given the death sentence hanging over Khalifa's head in Jordan, which might have induced him to talk.

This time, the FBI quickly translated Khalifa's violent literature and lobbied with the INS and the Justice Department to hold him. But there was a problem. The U.S. State Department was pushing for his deportation. According to PNP documents, Secretary of State Warren Christopher wrote to Attorney General Reno on January 5, 1995, arguing that "to permit Mr. Khalifah to remain at large in the United States in light of his alleged activities and criminal conviction in Jordan . . . would have potentially serious adverse foreign policy consequences."[9]

Of course, the U.S. attorney in San Francisco wasn't asking for Khalifa to be *released,* merely held for questioning. Khalifa had traveled the world as Osama bin Laden's "banker." He was a potential intelligence gold mine. At the moment of his arrest he was in the process of funding Yousef's Bojinka and Pope John Paul II assassination plots—even as Yousef was laying the groundwork for what became the 9/11 attacks.

During his "chocolate" (bomb) training in Lahore back in September, Yousef had talked with Murad about the viability of suicide attacks to promote the jihad.[10] As he and Murad tinkered with the Casio timers in the derelict warehouse, Yousef told Murad that martyrs would be needed to promote their cause. When they finished the bomb training in September 1994, Yousef and Murad began implementing a plan to send additional jihadis to America for flight training.

Now, by late December, the evidence uncovered in this investigation shows that flight training for some students was well under way. The extent of Yousef's planning, and the details of how much the FBI knew about it, are the subject of Chapter 29. But it's clear that Yousef's immediate funding came from Khalifa, who was then being held by the Feds in San Francisco.

How much would an interrogation of Khalifa have revealed in late 1994? We'll never know. In January the State Department prevailed. Khalifa was deported to Jordan, where, at a later trial, a witness recanted and he was set free.

In light of what we now know was going on in Manila at the time, Khalifa's release has to be considered one of the most grievous instances of negligence in the years leading up to 9/11.* Even given the need to appease Jordan, a key U.S. ally in the Mideast, the release of Khalifa represents disturbing evidence of just how badly the FBI and State, two of the nation's top antiterrorism agencies, were at odds.

"I remember people at CIA who were ripshit at the time," said Jacob L. Boesen, who worked as an analyst tasked from the Department of Energy to the CIA's Counter Terrorism Center. "Not even speaking in retrospect, but contemporaneous with what the intelligence community knew about bin Laden, Khalifa's deportation was unreal."[11]

At the time of Khalifa's arrest in San Francisco, the Philippine National Police were closely monitoring his status. They'd observed the young Saudi for years. As regional director of the International Islamic Relief Organization (IIRO), a Manila-based charity, Khalifa had funded both the Abu Sayyaf and the Moro National Liberation Front (MNLF), a radical paramilitary group with links to the deadly Egyptian al Gamma'a Islamiya (IG).

A month after Khalifa was released by the Feds, Sheikh Rahman, the IG's leader, went on trial in New York for "seditious conspiracy" against the United States. Clearly the Justice Department and the State Department, two of the nation's Big Five intelligence agencies, were out of sync.

The Wet Test

Meanwhile, the Philippine National Police had no idea that Ramzi Yousef, the world's most wanted man, had arrived in Manila and was

---

*Timeline #64. p. 14.

planning to use their country as a stage to assassinate the pope. Nor did they have a whiff of his Bojinka plot. Since the previous summer, though, the PNP had noticed an unusual number of Middle Eastern men entering Zamboanga Airport in the southern Philippines, an area rife with Abu Sayyaf and MNLF activity. PNP intelligence officers, like Col. Rodolfo Mendoza, began to sense that something was afoot.

"We had our suspicions," said the colonel, looking back. "But at the time we had no idea what was about to come down on us."[12]

Not long after moving into the Dona Josefa, Yousef conceived of yet another plot that would have put the Benazir Bhutto strikes to shame. Through press accounts he learned that President Clinton would transit Manila on November 12 on his way to the Asian Economic Summit. Yousef's first thought was to attack Air Force One with an improvised ground-to-air missile similar to the RPG-7s he'd trained on near Afghanistan. Barring that, he thought of setting bombs that would disrupt Clinton's motorcade in time for Yousef to unleash an attack with phosgene gas.[13]

Yousef certainly had the ability to manufacture the deadly chemical; he highlighted a section on it in his dog-eared copy of *Hawley's Condensed Chemical Dictionary*. But after surveying the various sites the U.S. president would visit in Manila, Yousef decided that security would be too tight and scrapped the plan. Given the enormity of the other operations he was plotting, though, the fact that Yousef even *considered* adding Clinton to his target list was another startling measure of his ambition and audacity.

Now, toward the end of November 1994, Yousef decided it was time for the first "wet test" of his new liquid-based device. At around 9:30 P.M. on the night of December 1, he paged Wali Khan Amin Shah on Carol Santiago's beeper. Half an hour later, Shah arrived on the Honda scrambler he kept parked in front of the Dona Josefa Apartments. Yousef gave him a small package and instructed him to plant it in the ninth seat of the fourth row in Cinema "C" at the Greenbelt Theater on Taft Avenue in Manila. Yousef had set the Casio timer to detonate minutes after Shah placed it. Given the time of the late-night screening, he wasn't sure how many casualties there would be.

Now, as the Uzbeki terrorist entered the theater, he looked around. The place was virtually empty, but he waited for the screen to change to a night scene, then moved up and placed the bomb under the fourth-row seat.

Shah left the theater and mounted the Honda, kick-starting it and revving the motor as he checked his watch and counted down the seconds. Yousef had synched Shah's Casio to the bomb timer, and at precisely 10:35:00 Shah heard the blast inside. Suddenly people began running out, coughing, bleeding, and covered with tiny particles of plastic debris. Shah popped the clutch on the dirt bike and took off.

When Mario Ignacio, a bomb tech from the PNP's Makati station, arrived, he had to cover his nose from the stench. Yousef had laced the nitrocellulose with sulfur. Ignacio looked around. The walls were pockmarked with particles from the plastic container. He moved up toward the front of the theater. The ninth seat in the fourth row was obliterated.[14]

Twenty minutes later, Shah dialed Yousef and smiled. His "chocolates" had been delivered. That night, Yousef partied with Shah, Khalid Shaikh Mohammed, and their Filipina dates at the XO Karaoke Bar. They spoke Urdu, the native language of Pakistan, so that the women would not understand. There was some disappointment that the Greenbelt device hadn't caused more damage, but Yousef told his "brothers" that he would conduct the next test himself. This time, they would surely draw blood.

The Undetectable Bomb

Ten days later, on December 11, Yousef got up just after 3:00 A.M. He went to the window and peered down at President Quirino Avenue. The broad boulevard, divided by a concrete center barrier, was deserted. After showering, Yousef shoved a container of what looked like contact lens cleaner into a small shaving kit. He stuffed in a small bag of cotton balls, a toothbrush, some Signal 2 toothpaste, a plastic razor, and a tube of Brut lather shave. He eyed himself in the mirror and decided to leave the stubble on his chin, then slicked his hair back with an application of L'Oreal styling cream.[15]

Yousef pulled on a pair of Orlando brand underwear from the dresser and stepped into a pair of slacks. He put on a blue dress shirt, open at the collar, and shoved a blue-gray tie in the pocket of a blue sports coat.

Then he moved past the divider that separated the bedroom from the dingy living room. There were a series of wires and snap connectors on the kitchen table.

He zipped them into the side pocket of the carrying case for his gray Toshiba laptop. From another pocket of the case he pulled out a one-way ticket on Philippines Airline Flight 434 from Manila to Cebu City in the southern Philippines. It was scheduled to depart at 5:30 A.M. The name on the ticket, Amaldo Forlani, was a slight variation on the name of an Italian politician (Arnaldo Forlani) that Yousef had found mentioned in the atlas bundled with the Toshiba's Windows software.[16]

The bomb maker had already prepared a fake ID with his own picture and the fake name, which he shoved in his wallet. He wouldn't need any of his bogus passports. This was a domestic flight.*

Next Yousef bent down and picked up a pair of black wing-tip shoes. He twisted back the heel on the right shoe and placed a nine-volt battery in a hollowed-out section; after doing the same with the left shoe, he twisted the heels back and pressed a small nail into each one to hold them in place.

Finally, he opened a drawer and pulled out a Casio Model 676 data-bank watch. He took off his own gold timepiece, wrapped it in a sock, and stuck it into a dresser drawer. There was a small female connector protruding from the back of the Casio, but as he strapped it onto his wrist Yousef shoved the plug under the watchband.

At the airport counter, Yousef presented his ticket and the Forlani ID. Flight 434 was a two-leg hop, from Manila to Cebu City and then on to Narita Airport in Japan. Yousef was handed a boarding pass with 35F as his seat assignment. He politely asked the counter attendant if the flight would be crowded.

No, she said; only about fifty passengers on this leg. He'd have plenty of room to stretch out. She asked if Yousef had any luggage. He smiled; just some carry-on. He gestured to the shaving kit and his laptop. Then he headed toward the gate.

Now, as he approached the security checkpoint, Yousef looked down at the plastic arch of the metal detector. Just as he suspected, there was a

_____

*Timeline #61. p. 13.

one-inch platform at the bottom on each side of the arch. The actual mechanism for sensing metal objects started just above heel level.

He wasn't worried about the security agents inspecting the contents of his laptop; all the sensitive files had been encrypted. Yousef placed the shaving kit and the Toshiba onto the conveyer. As they passed through, one security agent eyed the X-ray picture of the toiletries, including the cotton balls and plastic bottle of contact lens cleaner. He looked at the side pocket of the computer containing the power cable and a phone jack cord along with some other wires. Nothing seemed out of the ordinary. Then suddenly, as Yousef entered the metal detector, the alarm went off. A second security agent motioned for him to stop and go through it again. Sure enough, it went off a second time.

The agent asked Yousef to step forward and scanned him with a hand wand. When it passed across Yousef's wrist, it went off. The Casio.

Yousef took a chance.

"Do you want me to take off my watch?" he said. If the agent had said yes, he would have seen the small female connector protruding from the back. But before he could respond, the wand passed over Yousef's chest and went off. The master bomber smiled and opened his collar. It wasn't the watch: there was a Saint Christopher medal around Yousef's neck.

The guard eyed him, then looked at Yousef's ticket. *Forlani*. Of course—an Italian Catholic. There was a moment's hesitation as Yousef pressed down on the heels of his shoes with the two hidden nine-volt batteries. Finally, the guard smiled and waved him through.

The 747 lifted off at just past 5:35 A.M. On board, PAL flight attendant Maria de la Cruz glanced quickly at the man in the blue jacket with the beard stubble in seat 35F. She would later remember his hawklike nose. By 5:43 the plane had reached its cruising altitude of 33,000 feet. Capt. Edwardo Reyes came over the PA to announce that the three-hundred-mile flight to Cebu would take just over forty minutes.[17] He was turning the seat belt sign off.

Yousef moved quickly. The preparation for landing on PAL domestic flights generally came fifteen minutes before arrival. That would give him less than twenty-three minutes to build the bomb and place it in a position where it would blow Flight 434 out of the sky.

Yousef had studied the layout of the 747. The center fuel tank was located in the floor just below row 26. He moved up to the row and sat down in seat 26K. He looked around—left, then right—and noticed that, for a second, the stewardess was eyeing him.

Yousef smiled, then picked up an inflight magazine from the pouch in the chair back in front of him and flipped through it. When the stewardess began to busy herself in the galley, Yousef reached down and felt underneath the seat. He pulled out a small packet containing a life jacket. It was about the size of his shaving kit. There would be just enough space below the seat to stow the bomb. Now all he needed was a place to build it. Yousef put the life jacket back in its place below the seat and looked around.

He thought first about the lavatory, then reasoned that if he was in there too long, a complaining passenger might summon the flight attendants. Looking behind him, he spotted an area by the window a few rows back that was isolated from the prying eyes of other passengers. Yousef got up and moved to the seat.

He put his laptop in the empty seat next to him, unzipped the side pocket, and pulled out the wires he'd prepared in advance. The fusing system consisted of a circuit interspersed with two snap connectors for the nine-volt batteries. Yousef slipped off his shoes and retrieved the two black Eveready Energizers. He snapped them in place on the circuit. He took off the Casio, then snapped the male end of the circuit onto the female connector he'd previously wired into the SCR soldered into the watch. Now he had everything: timer, switch, and power source. On the other end of the fuse circuit, Yousef connected a small section of wire tipped with a tiny incandescent E72332 nine-volt flashlight bulb. He broke the glass on the bulb and exposed the filament.

Working quickly now, using rehearsed moves, and constantly eyeing the cabin to see if anyone was coming, Yousef unzipped his shaving kit and took out the bottle of contact lens cleaner. It was filled with diluted nitroglycerine. He opened the plastic bag of cotton balls, which he'd already soaked in nitric acid to create nitrocellulose or gun cotton— the same explosive used in dynamite. He shoved the cotton balls into the nitro solution, filling up the container, then pushed the wire with the broken bulb initiator inside it. He screwed on the cap, making sure not to bend or snap the wire. Finally he put the entire contents of the impro-

TIMELINE
PART I

01 • September 16, 1986 (page 16)

FDNY firefighter **Ronnie Bucca** falls five stories during a rescue attempt at a burning West Side tenement. He breaks his back and is not expected to live, but Bucca, an ex–Green Beret paratrooper, vows to return to Rescue One. A year later, he qualifies back into the company.

Bucca

02 • Late 1970s–late 1980s (page 40)

In Afghanistan, the Islamic mujahadeen have been battling the Soviets since 1979. CIA Director Bill Casey backs more than $3 billion in U.S. aid to the rebels, who are called "freedom fighters." One of the principal supporters of the struggle is young Saudi billionaire **Osama bin Laden**, who has been in Afghanistan since 1979. To further the war effort, **Abdullah Azzam**, a Palestinian scholar, sets up a worldwide network of centers called the Services Office (or MAK) to raise money and recruit for the mujahadeen. The New York City MAK outpost is based at the Alkifah Center in the Al Farooq Mosque on Atlantic Avenue in Brooklyn.

bin Laden

Azzam

03 • July 1989 (page 33, 374)

Over four weekends FBI surveillance teams follow **Mahmud Abouhalima, Mohammed Salameh, El Sayyid Nosair, Nidal Ayyad,** and **Clement Rodney Hampton-El** from the Al Farooq Mosque to a shooting range in **Calverton, L.I.** There they train with **Ali Mohammed**, an ex–Egyptian Army officer now working with the U.S. Special Forces at Fort Bragg. Abouhalima, aka "the Red," and Hampton-El are both Afghan war veterans.

FBI Calverton surveillance photo

Abouhalima

Salameh

Nosair

Ayyad

Hampton-El

Mohammed

04 • **1989** (page 41)

Azzam's hand-picked representative, an Egyptian named Mustafa Shalabi, runs the Alkifah Center on the first floor of the **Al Farooq Mosque**. Millions of dollars are raised there each year for the mujahadeen cause.

Al Farooq Mosque

05 • **1989** (page 51)

At an Islamic conference in Oklahoma City, **Mahmud Abouhalima** meets **Wadih El-Hage**, a Lebanese Christian convert associated with the Al Bunyan Islamic Center in Tucson, another Services Office outpost. El-Hage agrees to supply AK-47s to Abouhalima.

Abouhalima   **El-Hage**

06 • **November 1989** (page 41)

As the Soviets leave Afghanistan, a dispute breaks out among the "Afghan Arabs" over the best use of the fortune that continues to pour in. **Azzam** wants to use the money to set up an Islamic regime in Kabul. **Osama bin Laden** wants to use it for a worldwide jihad against the West. Mysteriously, Azzam and his two sons are murdered in a car bombing. Though bin Laden professes grief, intelligence analysts believe he was responsible. Within months, with the support of his Egyptian allies **Dr. Ayman al-Zawahiri**, **Mohammed Atef**, and **Sheikh Omar Abdel Rahman**, bin Laden takes over Azzam's Services Office network, using it as a grid for his new terror network, al Qaeda.

Azzam

bin Laden   **al-Zawahiri**   **Atef**   **Rahman**

07 • **1990** (page 24)

Abdul Basit, a Baluchistani who grew up in Kuwait, graduates from a U.K. engineering school. He enrolls at the University of Dawa and Jihad, an al Qaeda training camp in Pakistan. Adopting the name **Ramzi Yousef**, he begins studying bomb making.

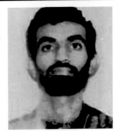

Yousef

08 • July 1990 (page 42)

The CIA helps **Sheikh Rahman** enter the United States by approving his visa in Sudan even though he is on a U.S. Watch List. When he arrives at JFK airport he's picked up by Mustafa Shalabi and **Mahmud Abouhalima**, who becomes his chauffeur and aide.

Rahman

Abouhalima

09 • November 5, 1990 (page 33)

At the Eastside Marriott, **Rabbi Meir Kahane** is murdered by **El Sayyid Nosair**, one of the Calverton trainees. **Abouhalima**, who has a NYC hack license, was to be Nosair's getaway driver.

Kahane

Nosair

Abouhalima

10 • November 6, 1990 (page 37, 374)

Later, at Nosair's New Jersey house, **Abouhalima** and **Salameh** are taken into custody by the NYPD, who seize boxes of evidence including Arabic tapes of the Sheikh threatening the WTC, Top Secret Special Forces manuals from Fort Bragg, and bomb formulas. But the NYPD treats the case as a "lone gunman" shooting. They conclude there was no conspiracy; Abouhalima and Salameh are set free.

Abouhalima

Salameh

11 • March 1991 (page 50)

A power struggle breaks out between **Sheikh Rahman** and Mustafa Shalabi over control of the Alkifah's money. Shalabi is later found murdered in his Brooklyn home, holding two red hairs in his lifeless hand. **Abouhalima**, who

Rahman

Abouhalima

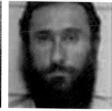
El-Hage

IDs the body for the NYPD, is never charged, and the crime remains unsolved. **Wadih El-Hage** has just arrived from the Tucson Islamic Center to watch over the Alkifah's finances. Even though he has been tied to a murder in Arizona in 1989, El-Hage isn't questioned by the NYPD. Now Shalabi's death gives Osama bin Laden control of Alkifah, which becomes an al Qaeda outpost in NYC.

12 • 1991 (page 42)

After returning to Saudi Arabia following the Afghan conflict, **bin Laden** becomes enraged when U.S. troops are stationed in his country during the Gulf War. He begins writing treatises against the Saudi regime, but gets ousted and moves to Sudan.

3

bin Laden

13 • 1991 (page 45)

Nosair's cousin **Ibrahim El-Gabrowny** gets $20,000 from **bin Laden** for Nosair's defense. The FBI later admits that this is the first time bin Laden's name comes up in association with the New York cell members around the blind Sheikh.

El-Gabrowny

bin Laden

14 • Fall 1991 (page 59)

FBI Special Agent **Nancy Floyd** recruits **Emad Salem**, an ex–Egyptian Army major, to infiltrate the blind Sheikh's cell. He's paid $500 a week by the Bureau. The agreement with the FBI is that Salem will act as a pure intelligence "asset." He will not have to wear a wire or testify.

Floyd

Salem

15 • July 1991 (page 82)

Yousef goes to the Philippines and begins training members of the Abu Sayyaf Group (ASG), part of **bin Laden**'s al Qaeda network. The group is financed by **Mohammed Jamal Khalifa**, OBL's brother-in-law. ASG leader **Edwin Angeles** calls Yousef "a dangerous man."

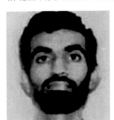

Yousef

bin Laden

Khalifa

Angeles

16 • 1991–1992 (page 198)

From November 1991 to July 1992, Yousef's oldest friend, fellow Baluchistani **Abdul Hakim Murad**, trains at U.S. flight schools in Texas, New York, North Carolina, and California. He obtains his commercial pilot's license and surveys the World Trade Center as a possible target.

Murad

17 • 1992 (page 66)

Nosair is convicted in the Kahane shooting and sent to Attica. Meanwhile, Nancy Floyd's asset **Salem** has burrowed deep into the cell and is getting close to **Sheikh Rahman**. On a trip to Detroit, the cleric asks Salem to murder

Nosair

Salem, Rahman

Egyptian president Hosni Mubarak. Salem learns that Rahman is the leader of al Gamma'a Islimaya (IG), an Egyptian terror group that tried to assassinate Mubarak in 1990. Soon the FBI discovers that Nosair is also an IG member.

18 • 1992 (page 44)

During renovations in the old inspection section of the FDNY, **Ahmed Amin Refai**, an Egyptian who works as an FDNY accountant, obtains the blue-prints for the **World Trade Center**. Refai worships at the Al Farooq and Al Salaam mosques, where Rahman preaches.

Refai

WTC

19 • 1992 (page 36)

Amid the forty-seven boxes of evidence seized from Nosair's house are Arabic writings in which Rahman's followers are exhorted to attack New York's "civilized pillars" and "high world buildings." But because of an alleged shortage of **FBI** transla-tors, the threat to the WTC isn't recognized by FBI investigators until after the building is bombed in 1993.

20 • 1992 (page 83)

El-Gabrowny visits his cousin **Nosair** in Attica with **Emad Salem**. Plotting his release, Nosair demands that Salem help build a series of bombs to be detonated at "twelve Jewish locations." He wants the undercover FBI asset to help kidnap the judge who sentenced him.

El-Gabrowny

Nosair

Salem

21 • 1992 (page 68)

Operating undercover without a wire, Salem complains to **Nancy Floyd** that he can't reach Special Agent **John Anticev** or his partner on the Joint Terrorist Task Force NYPD, Detective **Lou Napoli**. So Floyd, an agent in the Russian (GRU) branch of the FBI's NY office, works double time to debrief the Egyptian.

Floyd

Anticev

Napoli

22 • May–July 1992 (page 85)

As Salem gets deeper into the bombing plot, **Carson Dunbar**, an ex–NJ State Trooper—and now FBI Asst. Special Agent in Charge of the NY office—takes over the Terrorism branch. In a meeting with Anticev, Napoli, and Salem, Dunbar's subordinate, Supervisor John Crouthamel, calls Nancy Floyd "a bitch" and says he wants her off the Salem investigation.

Dunbar

23 • June 1992 (page 85)

Clement Rodney Hampton-El offers to supply **Salem** with ready-made bombs, but Napoli and Anticev don't show Salem the Calverton photos in which Hampton-El wears a T-shirt from the Services Office network, now part of al Qaeda. The FBI fails to link the 1989 training to the current bombing conspiracy, and a chance to connect the Nosair cell to bin Laden is lost.

Hampton-El

Salem

24 • July 1992 (page 88)

As **Salem** gets deeper into the bombing plot, Carson Dunbar demands that he wear a wire and testify in open court. Angry that the FBI is changing the terms of his undercover agreement, Salem withdraws. The FBI agrees to pay him $500 for the next three months, and Nancy Floyd continues to meet with him. But by late July, Salem withdraws from the Sheikh's cell. The FBI now has no asset inside the bomb conspiracy.

Salem

25 • July 1992 (page 79)

Ronnie Bucca is sworn in as a fire marshal with the FDNY's Bureau of Fire Investigation. From his military intelligence detachment in the Army Reserves, he hears that the FBI had a mole inside a bombing plot, but cut him loose.

Bucca

26 • September 1, 1992 (page 98)

After Salem leaves the bomb plot, **Sheikh Rahman** calls Pakistan, and **Ramzi Yousef** arrives at JFK. With him is **Mohammed Ajaj**, carrying multiple passports and bomb books. He's arrested and gets the last INS cell. But Yousef is given an asylum hearing and set free.

Rahman

Yousef

Ajaj

27 • Fall 1992 (page 101)

Yousef builds the bomb in Jersey City, helped by three of the Calverton crew: **Ayyad**, who supplies chemicals; **Salameh**, who helps build the device; and **Abouhalima**, the overall facilitator. Ayyad and Salameh set up bank accounts, and thousands of dollars to fund the plot are wired from the Mideast and Europe.

Yousef

Ayyad

Salameh

Abouhalima

28 • Fall 1992 (page 104)

In his last meeting with **Nancy Floyd**, Salem pleads with her to make sure Anticev and Napoli follow Abouhalima and Salameh. But Floyd has effectively been removed from any terrorism investigative work by Dunbar. Salem's parting words: "Don't call me when the bombs go off."

Floyd

Salem

29 • Fall 1992 (page 109)

From November 1992 up until the bombing in February 1993, **Yousef** and his cell are highly visible. **Salameh** is in three car accidents. Yousef is hospitalized and uses a stolen phone card to order chemicals. He runs up $18,000 in phone charges and is recorded by an ATM camera. He talks regularly to **Ajaj** in federal prison, using three-way calling via a Texas burger restaurant, but the Feds fail to monitor the calls in time. Yousef reports his passport stolen to police and obtains a new one from the Pakistani Embassy in New York. Though he missed his asylum hearing, neither the INS nor the FBI discovers his presence as he builds the 1,500-pound bomb in an apartment on Pamrapo Avenue in Jersey City.

Yousef

Salameh

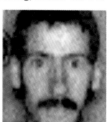
Ajaj

30 • November 1992–February 1993 (page 111)

After Salameh's many accidents, Yousef calls on **Eyad Ismoil**, another old friend, who flies to New York to be the wheelman.

Ismoil

Abouhalima

Salameh

31 • February 1993 (page 113)

During this period Anticev and Napoli lose track of **Abouhalima** and **Salameh**. Napoli later says they weren't able to follow them because they fled to New Jersey. But the redheaded Egyptian is living openly with his German wife and four kids. The Feds know her name (Weber). In fact, they searched Abouhalima's house in 1991 after tracing calls to Weber from Nosair. But as Yousef builds the bomb, they fail to obtain wiretap or search warrants; nor do they use the FBI's Special Operations Group to follow the Red effectively. If the FBI had sat on Abouhalima, he would have led them straight to Yousef and the bomb.

32 • February 1993 (page 106)

In mid-February, alleging that **Sheikh Rahman** is involved in "international terrorism," the FBI has sufficient probable cause to get a FISA wiretap on his phone. The Sheikh suspects the wiretap and says nothing of the bombing conspiracy.

Rahman

33 • February 1993 (page 112)

In late February, **Salameh** pays $400 in cash to rent a yellow Ryder van. His former roommate **Abdul Yasin**, an Iraqi City College student, teaches Salameh how to drive it.

Salameh   **Yasin**

34 • February 25, 1993 (page 112)

On his office computer, **Nidal Ayyad** types up a letter composed by Yousef claiming credit for the bombing in the name of the the fifth battalion of the Liberation Army. He orders compressed hydrogen to increase the bomb's blasting radius; **Abouhalima** is present for the delivery of four canisters at the Space Station storage locker in Jersey City.

Ayyad   **Abouhalima**

35 • February 26, 1993 (page 115)

In the early morning hours of February 26, **Yousef, Abouhalima, Salameh,** and **Ismoil** load the bomb into the Ryder truck. A three-car convoy heads to Brooklyn, where Yousef spends the night with Salameh.

Yousef   **Abouhalima**   **Salameh**   **Ismoil**

36 • 12:17 P.M. (page 119)

Just after noon, Yousef parks the Ryder van outside Room 107 on the B-2 level between the **Twin Towers.** At 12:17:37 the bomb detonates, blowing a four-story crater down to the B-4 level. Monica Smith, a pregnant secretary in Room 107, is instantly killed along with her unborn child. The blast kills 5 others, injures 1,000, and causes half a billion dollars in damage.

Bomb damage at the WTC

37 • (page 123)

Kevin Shea, a close friend of Ronnie Bucca's from Rescue One, is almost killed after falling into the four-story crater. Early the next morning, after visiting Shea in the hospital, Ronnie goes down to the B-2 level to photograph the edge of the ramp from which Kevin had fallen.

Shea

PART II

38 • February 27, 1993 (page 130)

Ronnie Bucca is determined to investigate the bombing, but the FDNY is effectively shut out of the probe by the FBI. So Bucca begins his own investigation, which leads him to the discovery of an unpublished warning from the bombers: They know what they did wrong in failing to topple the WTC, they say, and they pledge to return and finish the job.

Bucca

39 • February 27, 1993 (page 137)

The morning after the blast, **Yousef** escapes to Pakistan. He is disappointed that the North Tower didn't snap at its base and crash into the South Tower; he had expected 250,000 deaths. A fragment of the unpublished threat letter later discovered by Bucca reads: "Our calculations were not very accurate this time. However we promise you that next time it will be very precise and the Trade Center will be one of our targets."

Yousef

40 • February 28, 1993 (page 146)

Immediately after the bombing, **Emad Salem** contacts **Nancy Floyd**. He tells her the FBI could have prevented the blast if they had just listened to him and followed Abouhalima and Salameh. He soon tips the Feds that Abouhalima has fled to Egypt, and the Red is captured.

Salem

Floyd

41 • March 4, 1993 (page 138)

A VIN number discovered in the rubble leads the FBI to the Ryder agency, where **Salameh** is arrested after demanding a refund of his $400 deposit. He and **Abouhalima**, whom the FBI had under surveillance as far back as 1989, are now charged as coconspirators in the bombing.

Salameh

Abouhalima

42 • March 5, 1993 (page 142)

Salameh's arrest leads the FBI to **Yasin**, but he convinces the agents that he knows nothing about the plot, even though he was Salameh's roommate. The Feds let Yasin go—and he immediately flees to Iraq, where the price on his head is now $25 million.

Yasin

43 • March 1993 (page 151)

Realizing their catastrophic mistake in cutting Nancy Floyd's asset loose, the FBI rehires Emad Salem to go back undercover. Within months he learns of a bombing plot in the Sheikh's cell, targeting the bridges and tunnels into Manhattan as well as the UN. The Feds, who paid Salem $500 a week before the first bombing, now agree to pay him $1.5 million.

44 • Spring 1993 (page 152)

Vindicated after the WTC bombing, Nancy Floyd helps the Bureau bring Emad Salem back undercover and keeps him in the fold during the subsequent Day of Terror investigation.

9

45 • 1993 (page 180)

FDNY Fire Marshal **Ronnie Bucca** educates himself on the recent history of Islamic terror. With a Top Secret security clearance and operational experience as a Green Beret and decorated firefighter, Bucca wants to contribute to the Yousef hunt, but his application to the NYPD-FBI Joint Terrorist Task Force is rejected. The JTTF effectively excludes the FDNY.

Bucca

46 • June 1993 (page 157)

The FBI raids a safe house set up by Salem, exposing the plot to blow up a series of NYC landmarks including the **UN, George Washington Bridge,** and two **tunnels into the city.**

GWB

Lincoln Tunnel

UN

47 • June 1993 (page 153)

In the course of the sting **Salem** nets **Siddig Siddig Ali** (a Sudanese), **Clement Rodney Hampton-El**, and **Rahman** himself, plus nine others. Salem becomes the linchpin witness in the Feds' case.

Salem

Ali

Hampton-El

Rahman

48 • June 1993 (page 166)

But after the safe house takedown, **Salem,** now in Witness Protection, admits that in addition to the "bad guy tapes" he recorded his own "bootleg tapes" because he didn't trust FBI superiors. Carson Dunbar and the FBI's top NY lawyer order **Nancy Floyd** to go to Salem's apartment to retrieve the tapes. Knowing nothing about the unauthorized tapes, which include her own criticism of FBI superiors, Floyd visits the apartment and gets into an argument with FBI attorney

Salem

Floyd

Jim Roth over which tapes Salem has consented to release. The attorney takes them all, and Floyd is later heard discussing with Salem how FBI supervisors might have prevented the original WTC bombing if they had let him do his job the first time. She's also heard on tape calling her FBI bosses "gutless" and "chickenshits." In apparent retribution for her candor, the FBI opens up an OPR internal affairs investigation of Floyd. Rather than being rewarded as the heroine who recruited the FBI's key Day of Terror asset, Agent Floyd is isolated and chastised.

49 • July 3, 1993 (page 196)

After a siege outside a Brooklyn mosque the Feds take Sheikh Rahman into custody. Two of his loyal followers are Egyptian naturalized citizens and government employees: **Ahmed Amin Refai**, the FDNY accountant, and **Ahmed Abdel Sattar**, a U.S. postal worker.

Refai

Sattar

50 • 1994 (page 192)

As the FBI hunts him, **Yousef** goes on a killing spree. In March 1994 he reportedly builds an ammonium nitrate–fuel oil bomb targeting the Israeli Embassy in **Bangkok**, but the truck carrying the device gets into an accident in heavy traffic and the plot is aborted. The driver is found with his body floating in the bomb mix.

Yousef

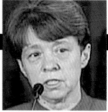

Bangkok

51 • March 4, 1994 (page 205)

Abouhalima, **Salameh**, **Ayyad**, and **Ajaj** are convicted in the World Trade Center bombing. But Yousef and Ismoil are still at large. The U.S. Attorney for the Southern District of New York, **Mary Jo White**, declares that the verdict should send "an unmistakable message that we will not tolerate terrorism in this country."

White

Abouhalima

Salameh

Ayyad

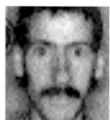

Ajaj

Floyd

52 • March 11, 1994 (page 223)

Agent **Nancy Floyd** becomes the object of a story leaked to the *New York Post* suggesting that she is being investigated by the FBI for an alleged affair with Emad Salem. Later, under oath, Floyd vehemently denies the charge, and the bootleg tapes exonerate her. An ongoing OPR investigation finds no evidence to support the charge.

53 • June–September 1994 (page 189)

In June, Yousef, a Sunni Muslim, explodes a bomb at the sacred **Mashad Reza** Shiite mosque in Iran, killing 26. In September, he makes the first of two attempts on the life of Pakistani prime-minister-to-be **Benazir Bhutto**—first with a bomb, then with a rifle.

Mashad Reza Mosque

Bhutto

54 • 1994 (page 210)

FBI Agent **Ken Williams** of Squad Five—the counterterrorism unit of the Bureau's Phoenix office—orders a surveillance of an associate of **Sheikh Rahman** who is training other Middle Eastern men in Arizona as suicide bombers.

Williams

Rahman

55 • July 1994 (page 213)

By July 1994, **Ramzi Yousef** is the world's most wanted terrorist. **Brad Smith**, a Diplomatic Security Service Agent at the U.S. State Department, runs Rewards for Justice, a program that offers $2 million for Yousef's capture. Diagnosed with Lou Gehrig's disease, Smith is given just months to live, but he vows to stay alive until Yousef is arrested.

RAMZI AHMED YOUSEF
DESCRIPTION

DATE OF BIRTH:	May 20, 1967 and/or April 27, 1968
PLACE OF BIRTH:	Iraq, Kuwait, or United Arab Emirates
HEIGHT:	6'
WEIGHT:	180 pounds
BUILD:	medium
HAIR:	brown
EYES:	brown
COMPLEXION:	olive
SEX:	male
RACE:	white
CHARACTERISTICS:	sometimes is clean shaven
ALIASES:	Ramzi A. Yousef, Ramzi Ahmad Yousef, Ramzi Yousef, Ramzi Yousef Ahmad, Ramzi Yousef Ahmed, Rasheed Yousef, Rashid Rashid, Rashad, Kamal Ibrahim

Smith

56 • September 1994 (page 216)

Recovering from his wounds after the aborted Bhutto bombing attempt, **Yousef** conceives three plots. (1) He will kill **Pope John Paul II** on a visit to Manila in January 1995. (2) He will create an undetectable bomb to be smuggled on board eleven U.S. jumbo jets entering the United States from Asia. Yousef names this plot Bojinka, after the Serbo-Croatian term for "big noise." (3) With **Abdul Hakim Murad**, the pilot trained at four U.S. flight schools, Yousef will coordinate the training of Islamic pilots at U.S. schools who will then commandeer airliners and fly them into buildings in America. This third plot becomes the blueprint for the 9/11 attacks.

Yousef

Pope John Paul II

Murad

57 • November 1994 (page 236)

Yousef plans a fourth plot to assassinate **President Clinton** during a stopover in Manila en route to an Asian summit. After contemplating hitting Air Force One with a ground-to-air missile and exploding bombs along the president's motorcade route, Yousef rejects the plan and concentrates on the other three plots (the pope, Bojinka, and the precursor to 9/11).

Clinton

58 • December 1994 (page 257)

On Christmas Eve, in what may have been a dress rehearsal for Yousef's "third plot," Algerian Islamic terrorists with ties to Osama bin Laden hijack an Air France jumbo jet laden with fuel. According to witnesses, the suicidal hijackers intended to fly the plane to Paris to take down the **Eiffel Tower**.

Eiffel Tower

Murad

Yousef

59 • 1994 (page 232)

To help execute his three plots, which he and **Murad** will stage from Manila, **Yousef** calls on his uncle **Khalid Shaikh Mohammed**. The fourth conspirator is **Wali Khan Amin Shah**, an Uzbeki veteran of the Afghan war whom Osama bin Laden calls "the lion." Wali sets up a front company in Malaysia called Konsonjaya to fund the three plots. On the board is an Indonesian cleric named **Riduan Ismuddin** (aka **Hambali**), who will later be linked to the U.S.S. *Cole* and Bali bombings. The money for the three plots will come from bin Laden's brother-in-law **Mohammed Jamal Khalifa**.

Mohammed

Shah

Hambali

Khalifa

60 • November 1994 (page 232)

Using his Filipina girlfriend as a front, Shah rents a safe house at the **Dona Josefa Apartments** along the pope's parade route in Manila. Yousef later checks in to Room 603.

61 • December 11, 1994 (page 238)

Creating a series of false IDs, **Yousef** mimics the identity of **Arnaldo Forlani**, an Italian government official. He buys a ticket from Manila to Cebu on PAL Flight 434, with ongoing service to Japan.

Yousef

As Forlani

Using apparently innocuous parts consisting of a Casio DBC-61 watch as a timer and diluted nitroglycerine in a contact lens cleanser bottle, Yousef boards PAL Flight 434 and builds the bomb on the first leg of the two-leg flight. He puts the assembled device in the life jacket pouch under seat 26K by the center fuel tank of the 747, then deplanes in Cebu.

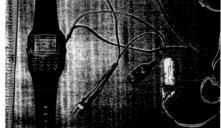

Exclusive photo of Yousef's undetectable bomb trigger

Cabin damage

When PAL Flight 434, bound for Japan, reaches cruising altitude, the Casio alarm ignites the filament of a broken bulb Yousef has embedded in the nitrocellulose explosive. The bomb detonates—killing the passenger in seat 26K and narrowly missing the center fuel tank. The 747 is forced to make an emergency landing on Okinawa.

62 • December 11, 1994 (page 237)

That night in a Manila karaoke bar, Yousef celebrates his successful "wet test" of the undetectable Casio bomb with **Wali Khan Amin Shah** and his uncle **Khalid Shaikh Mohammed**.

Shah

Mohammed

63 • December 1994 (page 248)

Since the 1993 WTC bombing, **Ronnie Bucca** has developed a database of Islamic terror groups. One of them is the Abu Sayyaf Group (ASG), which operates out of the Philippines. When they take credit for the PAL bombing, Bucca becomes convinced Yousef is involved.

Bucca

64 • January 1995 (page 235)

Yousef's chief financier, **Mohammed Jamal Khalifa**, is in U.S. custody in San Francisco. The FBI wants to hold him for questioning; but Secretary of State Warren Christopher prevails on Attorney General Janet Reno to extradite Khalifa to Jordan, where he's been convicted of murder. Once out of U.S. hands, Khalifa gets a new trial and is set free. The decision by State represents a massive loss for U.S. intelligence officials and allows Khalifa to continue financing Yousef's plots.

Khalifa

65 • January 6, 1995 (page 263)

On the night of January 6, while mixing chemicals in his Dona Josefa bomb factory, Yousef accidentally ignites a small fire that fills the room with smoke. The Manila police are called. Yousef and Murad tell a rookie cop that they are just playing with firecrackers. He buys the story and leaves.

66 • January 6, 1995 (page 265)

But when the cop reports the firecracker story, veteran PNP Captain **Aida Fariscal** becomes suspicious and orders the young cop and a sergeant back to the Dona Josefa. There they confront Abdul Hakim Murad.

67 • January 7, 1995 (page 267)

As the police escort Murad out of the Dona Josefa lobby, he takes off running. The patrolman pulls his gun and fires a shot that zings past the terrorist's ear. Murad suddenly trips and goes down, whereupon the cops arrest him. He tries to bribe **Fariscal** with $2,000 in American Express checks,

Fariscal

but she demands to see Room 603, where he's been staying. When she enters the room, Fariscal is shocked to find a picture of the pope, priest's cassocks, a map of the pontiff's parade route, and a laboratory of chemicals and bombs in various stages of construction. She also finds Yousef's Toshiba laptop, which lays out the entire Bojinka plot to blow up 11 U.S. jumbo jets. By playing a hunch, this local Filipina police captain has found the lair of Ramzi Yousef, the world's most wanted man.

68 • January 7, 1995 (page 268)

But as Murad is led away by the police, **Ramzi Yousef** watches from across the street. Early the next morning he takes a flight to Pakistan, where he is joined by his uncle **Khalid Shaikh Mohammed**. The Mozart of Terror escapes. Both men will go on to plan the 9/11 attacks.

Yousef

Mohammed

PART III

69 • January 7, 1995 (page 276)

Telling PNP officials his name is Saeed Ahmed, **Murad** is taken to Camp Crame in Manila for questioning. Allegedly tortured, he refuses to talk until he is turned over to Col. **Rodolfo Mendoza**, an expert on Islamic terror groups. Murad soon confesses details of the WTC bombing. He also admits his role in the pope and Bojinka plots.

Murad

Mendoza

70 • January 20, 1995 (page 277)

Two weeks after his capture, Murad confesses to a plan to fly a small single-engine plane into CIA headquarters in Langley, Virginia, but says the plot is just in the early planning stages.

71 • February 1995 (page 282)

Finally, after Mendoza threatens to turn him over to the Israeli Mossad, Murad admits to Yousef's third plot, which is well into the planning stages. He tells Mendoza that ten Islamic terrorists are currently training in U.S. flight schools. The ultimate targets will be the **CIA,** the **Pentagon,** the **World Trade Center,** the **Sears Tower** in Chicago, the **Transamerica Tower** in San Francisco, and a U.S. nuclear facility.

CIA Headquarters

Pentagon

World Trade Center

Sears Tower

Transamerica Tower

72 • February 1995 (page 286)

Meanwhile, as the hunt for Ramzi Yousef intensifies, DSS agent Brad Smith amps up the Rewards program with **posters** and matchbooks with Yousef's image promising a $2 million reward.

73 • February 1995 (page 286, 329)

But the master bomber remains undaunted. From hiding in Pakistan, Yousef recruits a young Islamic South African, Istaique Parker, and induces him to plant **nitrocellulose bombs** hidden in toy cars inside luggage to be checked onto United and Delta flights in Bangkok. Yousef's laptop seized at the Dona Josefa contains details of the Bojinka plot. Within hours after the Room 603 search, Delta and United Airlines are put on high alert. A number of flights are aborted, and some are forced to land.

But at the last minute, Parker gets cold feet. He returns to Islamabad and calls the U.S. Embassy. DSS agents debriefing him learn that Yousef will be returning to Islamabad in a few days. When Yousef calls Parker from the Su Casa, a guest house controlled by Osama bin Laden, DSS agents raid it with Pakistani authorities. The bomb maker is arrested. But his uncle Khalid Shaikh Mohammed, staying downstairs, escapes. Astonishingly, Mohammed gives an innocent-bystander press interview and is later quoted in *Time* magazine.

Exclusive photo of toy cars and nitrocellulose seized in a raid on Yousef's Islamabad lair

74 • February 1995 (page 298)

On a 707 bound for the United States, **Yousef** confesses to FBI agents his role in the pope and Bojinka plots. He also gives minute details of the **WTC** bombing. But on his arrival back in New York, as he's being flown by helicopter past the WTC, Yousef delivers a chilling warning. An FBI agent eyes the Twin Towers and says, "You didn't get them after all." Yousef replies, "Not yet!"

Yousef

WTC

75 • February 1995 (page 299)

A week before Yousef's capture, the Day of Terror trial begins. The Feds accuse **Sheikh Rahman** of leading a "jihad army" dating back to the first firing range sessions at Calverton, L.I. in 1989. Included in the ongoing plot are the slaying of Rabbi Kahane by **Nosair** (whose defense was funded by **Ibrahim El-Gabrowny**) and the WTC bombing. **Siddig Ali** admits to being the operational leader who chose the UN and the Lincoln and Holland tunnels as targets. He admits that he and **Clement Rodney Hampton-El** attended training sessions in Pennsylvania where Yousef's bomb was tested with the help of

Mohammed Abouhalima. This demonstrates further that the FBI could have stopped Yousef if they had followed Mohammed's brother **Mahmud**, "the Red," who was working directly with Yousef as he built the WTC device.

Rahman

Nosair

El-Gabrowny

Ali

Hampton-El

Mohammed Abouhalima

Mahmud Abouhalima

76 • 1995 (page 324)

Emad Salem, **Nancy Floyd**'s recruit, is the Fed's linchpin witness. At one point in testimony he admits that the Day of Terror plot was almost foiled when Carson Dunbar ordered him to remove a timer from the safe house. Called as a defense witness, Floyd is heard on Salem's bootleg tapes pointedly criticizing FBI supervisors for undermining the first WTC bombing investigation.

Salem

Floyd

Meanwhile her OPR investigation continues. A fellow agent speculates that Floyd is being punished by her FBI superiors for telling the truth about the failure of the New York office to stop the first bombing.

77 • April 1995 (page 280)

Col. **Rodolfo Mendoza** turns over the details of Murad's confession to the U.S. Embassy in Manila, including the names of ten Islamic pilots then training in U.S. flight schools and a list of Yousef's six targets in the airline hijack plot including the WTC and the Pentagon.

Mendoza

The FBI acknowledges Mendoza's evidence in a memo classified as **SECRET/NOFORN**. The memo warns of potential "future attacks" by Yousef against the CIA and a nuclear facility. Later the FBI investigates two of **Murad**'s U.S. flight schools. But the Bureau makes no other mention of **Yousef**'s third plot, and, for unknown reasons, further investigation of the airliner hijacking scenario is dropped.

Even more surprising, while the FBI memo's author suspects Yousef of having links to Osama bin Laden, it describes his WTC bombing cell and the Day of Terror bombers as "a loose group of politically committed Muslims." The memo con-

SECRET/NOFORN REL TO T

RAMZI AHMED YOUSEF: A NEW GENERATION
                  TERRORISTS

INTRODUCTION:

RAMZI AHMED YOUSEF FIRST CAME TO
BOMBING OF THE WORLD TRADE CENTER (WTC
1993.   AFTER THE ATTACK, HE DISAPPEARE
REAPPEARED IN THE PHILIPPINES IN JANUA
SUCCESSFULLY UNCOVERED HIS PLOT TO ATT
POPE.   THE 7 FEBRUARY ARREST OF YOUSEF
JANUARY ARREST OF ABDUL HAKIM MURAD. A

Excerpt from SECRET/NOFORN FBI memo

cludes that they do "not belong to a single cohesive organization." This finding conflicts with the U.S. attorney's allegation in the ongoing Day of Terror trial that Yousef and Sheikh Rahman are part of a "jihad army" wreaking a war of urban terror in New York.

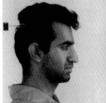

Bureau of Prisons booking mug shots of Abdul Hakim Murad and Ramzi Yousef

Perhaps most incredible is an admission made by Murad to FBI agents during their flight to New York. As Special Agents Frank Pellegino and Thomas Donlon later record in an **FBI 302 form**, Murad advises them that "Yousef wanted to return to the United States . . . to bomb the World Trade Center a second time."

FEDERAL BUREAU OF INVESTIGATIC

On 4/13/95, SA's Francis J. Pellegrin
conducted an interview of ABDUL HAKIM A
[HASHEM MURAD. MURAD was interviewed a
ted from Manila, Philippines to New Yor
ndictment issued by the United Stated
r the Southern District of New York.

I wanted to return to the United State
World Trade Center a second time.

Investigation on   4/12-13/95   at Aircraft in Fl;

SA FRANCIS J. PELLEGRINO, FBI
y SA THOMAS G. DONLON. FBI

FBI 302 Abdul Hakim Murad confession

At 9:00 A.M. on April 19, a 5,600-pound bomb made of ammonium nitrate and nitromethane detonates in a yellow Ryder truck parked outside the **Murrah Federal Building** in Oklahoma City, killing 168 people, including 19 children. Eyewitnesses describe several suspects exiting the area, including a Middle Eastern man.

Murrah Federal Building

81 • April 19, 1995 (page 309)

Police sketches are released for a **Robert Kling**, described as a 180-pound, 5'10" white man, and **John Doe No. 2**, described as 5'9" with olive skin, a thick neck, and slicked-back hair.

Kling

John Doe No. 2

82 • April 19, 1995 (page 310)

Within hours of the blast, **Timothy McVeigh** is in police custody; **Terry Nichols** later surrenders. While McVeigh bears a striking resemblance to the eyewitness sketch, Nichols looks nothing like the swarthy John Doe No. 2. Yet within months the FBI drops its worldwide manhunt for the third suspect.

McVeigh

Nichols

83 • April 19, 1995 (page 313)

Hours after the Oklahoma City bombing, Abdul Hakim Murad (now in federal jail in New York) takes credit for the blast in the name of Ramzi Yousef's Liberation Army. FBI agent Frank Pellegrino, who interrogated Murad on his trip from Manila, reports the terrorist's declaration in an **FBI 302** later admitted at trial.

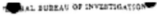

84 • April 1995 (page 313–14)

A growing body of circumstantial evidence suggests that Ramzi Yousef may have designed the Oklahoma City device for Terry Nichols when he was in Cebu, Philippines, in 1994–95. **Nichols's passport** shows four trips to the Philippines since 1990; **Edwin**

Nichols's passport

Angeles

Angeles, a former leader of the Abu Sayyaf terror group, swears to police that Nichols, aka "The Farmer," met Yousef in the Philippines in the early 1990s.

85 • 1995 (page 313)

Passport records show that on November 3, 1994, Wali Khan Amin Shah and Ramzi Yousef applied for Philippines visas while in Singapore. On November 4, Terry Nichols applied for his Philippines visa in Chicago.

86 • 1995 (page 316)

The most curious circumstantial evidence comes from Michael Fortier, the government's star witness in *U.S. v. Timothy McVeigh*. Fortier swears under oath that the only ammonium nitrate–fuel oil device McVeigh ever built was a dud. Then, after Nichols was in Cebu City at the same time as **Ramzi Yousef**, Nichols and McVeigh built the 5,600-pound ammonium nitrate–nitromethane bomb that destroyed the Murrah Building.

Yousef

87 • January 17, 1996 (page 327)

Sheikh Rahman is sentenced to life in prison for his role in the Day of Terror plot. But in a precursor of things to come, Egyptian U.S. postal worker **Ahmed Abdel Sattar** vows that "the man will never be silenced," and the al Gamma'a Islamiya (IG)—the Egyptian terrorist group that the Sheikh heads—threatens to attack U.S. civilian targets.

Rahman

Sattar

88 • 1996 (page 332)

Meanwhile, **Jamal Ahmad al-Fadl**, a young Sudanese who worked as an aide to the murdered Mustafa Shalabi at the **Alkifah Center**, walks into a U.S. Embassy and becomes CS-1, a secret informant for the Feds. In extraordinary testimony he confirms the existence of al Qaeda, describes how **Osama bin Laden** runs training camps for the worldwide jihad, and tells the FBI that one of bin Laden's closest associates is Assad, aka "the lion," the nom de guerre of Ramzi Yousef's Manila coconspirator **Wali Khan Amin Shah**.

al-Fadl

Alkhifah Center

bin Laden

Shah

89 • 1996 (page 332)

For the New York office of the FBI, this intelligence completes a circle of evidence dating back to the surveillance photos of the Calverton shooting sessions in 1989—proving a direct link between al Qaeda, bin Laden, and WTC coconspirators **Abouhalima**, **Salameh**, **Nosair**, and **Ayyad** as well as Day of Terror defendant **Hampton-El**. The revelation comes six years before 9/11, but the public doesn't get a hint of the link until February 2001, and the FBI itself doesn't understand the connection between Special Forces Sgt. **Ali Mohammed** and bin Laden until 1998, following two more al Qaeda bombings.

Abouhalima

Salameh

Nosair

Ayyad

Hampton-El

Mohammed

90 • 1996 (page 329)

Yousef's uncle **Khalid Shaikh Mohammed** is secretly indicted by the Feds, who missed him at the Su Casa guest house when his nephew was arrested. In 1997 the FBI learns that Mohammed is in the Persian Gulf nation of Qatar, but when a team of FBI agents rushes to seize him, he escapes with the help of a wealthy Qatari named Abdullah bin Khalid al-Thani. Mohammed flees to the Czech Republic, where he continues to lay the groundwork for Yousef's 9/11 plot.

Mohammed

91 • May 29, 1996 (page 333)

In the first of two prosecutions, **Yousef** goes on trial in U.S. Federal Court in Manhattan for the Bojinka plot and the murder of the passenger on PAL Flight 434. Judge **Kevin T. Duffy** allows Yousef to represent himself, with the assistance of attorney Roy Kulcsar. In his opening statement the bomb maker claims he was imprisoned in Pakistan at the time the Bojinka and pope plots were set in motion in Manila. There isn't a word, from federal prosecutors or Yousef, however, about his third plot—the plan to hijack airliners.

Yousef at trial

92 • June 1996 (page 350)

Although eleven Philippine National Police officials testify, Rodolfo Mendoza, who elicited the 9/11 plot confession from **Murad,** is never mentioned. His own assistant, Maj. Alberto Ferro, testifies that he "cannot really recall" who questioned Murad. Though Murad's training in four U.S. flight schools is mentioned, there isn't a word in the nearly 6,000-page transcript of **Yousef**'s plan to fly airliners into the WTC, the Pentagon, and other U.S. buildings. But the forensic evidence against Yousef is overwhelming. On July 18, 1996, the Feds are about to introduce part of Murad's confession giving details of the Bojinka plot, but then . . .

The defendants

93 • July 17, 1996 (page 341)

On the night of July 17, **TWA Flight 800** bound from JFK to Paris crashes near Long Island, killing 230 people. The explosion takes place near row 26, adjacent to the center fuel tank—an area identical to the detonation point aboard PAL Flight 434. When the wreckage is assembled in a hangar, the high explosives RDX, PETN, and nitroglycerine are found near row 26. The explosion mimics the Bojinka plot; Yousef's attorney, Kulcsar, argues that the news event will prejudice the jury.

TWA 800 wreckage

94 • 1996 (page 346)

James Kallstrom, head of the FBI's New York office, immediately suspects terrorism, with Yousef's cell at the top of the list. But the National Transportation Safety Board believes the cause of the center fuel tank explosion was mechanical error. The presence of high explosives is explained as residue from a test on the plane with a bomb-sniffing dog a month before the crash. But despite the lack of definitive proof that a spark of fuel vapors caused the explosion, the presence of RDX in the aft cargo hold (where the dog never visited), and other evidence of an explosion, Kallstrom bows to pressure from the NTSB and other senior Bureau officials, and after 16 months the investigation is ordered "shut down."

Kallstrom

95 • September 5, 1996 (page 347)

The question of whether **Yousef**'s cell had a hand in the downing of TWA 800 becomes moot by Sept. 5, however, when he's convicted with Murad and Shah for the Bojinka plot. FBI Agent Frank Pellegrino, who interrogated Murad, calls his FBI supervisor to say, "It's over. We won." But even from federal lockup, Yousef continues to plot further terrorist acts.

Yousef

96 • October 1996 (page 355)

Meanwhile, in Phoenix, FBI intelligence asset **Harry Ellen**, who has close ties to **Yasser Arafat** and the PLO, tells his FBI control agent, Ken Williams, about an Algerian flight school instructor he's seen talking to a reputed associate of Sheikh Rahman. Ellen advises Williams to monitor the instructor, but Ellen is reportedly told to "leave it alone." Soon after that, 9/11 hijacker **Hani Hanjour** begins pilot training at CRM Airline Training Center in Arizona.

Ellen with Arafat   **Hanjour**

97 • 1996–1997 (page 338)

Now, in a desperate effort to trap Yousef, the Feds enlist the help of **Gregory Scarpa Jr.**, a Colombo crime family member and an inmate in the cell adjoining Yousef's in the Manhattan federal jail. With a female FBI agent posing as a paralegal, Scarpa is given a camera to photograph Yousef's bomb formulas and allowed to use a telephone "patch-through" whereby calls can be made outside the jail (monitored by the FBI). But the plan backfires: Yousef is reportedly able to use the connection to make a number of al Qaeda–related calls to Afghanistan and to sources procuring passports for jihadis entering the United States.

Scarpa

98 • August 1997 (page 358)

In August, FBI agents raid the home of **Wadih El-Hage** in Kenya and discover evidence of an East African cell plotting terrorism with ties to the "Haj"—aka Osama bin Laden. Under the mistaken belief that they can turn El-Hage, who was bin Laden's personal secretary, they allow him to flee Kenya for New York. There he stonewalls in front of a federal grand jury and is set free. A walk-in to the U.S. Embassy in Kenya warns of a possible bombing, but he's ignored.

El-Hage

99 • August 31, 1997 (page 361)

Ghasoub Ghalyoun, a Syrian with links to al Qaeda, takes what Spanish officials later describe as possible **surveillance video** for the 9/11 attacks. The WTC is taped along with other U.S. landmarks, including the Sears Tower. The Syrian even has himself taped next to a sculpture in the WTC Plaza—one of the few pieces to survive 9/11.

Ghalyoun   **WTC video**

100 • August 1997 (page 364)

Meanwhile, back in New York, **Ramzi Yousef** comes to trial again, this time with Eyad Ismoil for the 1993 WTC bombing. Described by Asst. U.S. Attorney David Kelly as a "cold blooded killer," Yousef allows **Roy Kulcsar** (left) to represent him this time. But after months of trial and three days of jury deliberations, the pair is found guilty on all counts. It's another victory for the Feds, who seem assured that the threat from Yousef, the blind Sheikh, and their associates is now over. But within days there's a chilling reminder of the ongoing threat.

Kulcsar *(l.)* **and Yousef**

101 • 1997 (page 366)

Six terrorists from the IG, the Egyptian Islamic Group tied to Sheikh Rahman, slaughter 62 people at **Luxor** in Egypt including three generations of the Turners, a British family. The terrorists slit open the bodies and insert leaflets demanding the release of the blind Sheikh from U.S. prison.

Luxor ruins

102 • 1997 (page 367)

In the wake of their victory over Yousef, the Luxor massacre represents another missed series of dots for the New York Feds. As far back as 1991 Det. Lou Napoli had linked El-Sayyid Nossair to the IG, which **Sheikh Rahman** was directing. Now, unknown to the FBI, **Ahmed Abdel Satta**r, the U.S. postman, is allegedly conducting the IG's business out of his home on Staten Island while receiving Rahman's directions from federal prison in Minnesota. His reported activities are later set forth in an April 2002 federal indictment.

Rahman   **Sattar**

103 • January 8, 1998 (page 330, 367)

Calling **Yousef** "an apostle of evil," **Judge Duffy** sentences him to 240 years in solitary—one year for the combined ages of his WTC victims. Defiant to the end, the bomb maker says, "I am a terrorist and I am proud of it." The same day, the Feds unseal a secret indictment of Khalid Shaikh Mohammed dating back to 1996. For unknown reasons, the Justice Department has kept the hunt for Mohammed quiet for almost two years—in contrast to the well-publicized Yousef hunt, which helped trigger his capture.

Yousef at his sentencing

104 • January 8, 1998 (page 369)

Now, as with his nephew, the announced reward is $2 million. But by 1998 **Mohammed** is in the advanced stages of executing Yousef's third plot. As Islamic pilots train in U.S. flight schools, Mohammed prepares to establish a cell in Hamburg, Germany. **Mohammed Atta**, an Egyptian, will take the place of Murad as chief hijacker-pilot in what Mohammed will later call "Holy Tuesday."

Mohammed   **Atta**

105 • **January 1998** (page 362–363)

Despite Yousef's imprisonment, **Ronnie Bucca** believes the threat from the bomb maker's al Qaeda associates is ongoing. Now serving with the Army Reserve's 3413th Military Intelligence

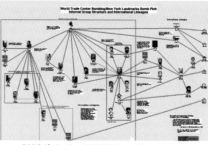

Detachment of the 800th MPs at the Defense Intelligence Analysis Center in Washington, Bucca studies **declassified DIAC**

DIAC link chart/WTC/Day of Terror plots

Bucca

link charts that show a direct connection between Ramzi Yousef and Osama bin Laden. He warns his colleagues and superiors in the FDNY of an ongoing threat to New York in general, and the WTC in particular.

106 • **February 5, 1998** (page 371)

Testifying before Congress, **Dale Watson**, the FBI's assistant director for counterterrorism, says, "Although we should not allow ourselves to be lulled into a false sense of security, I believe it is important to note that in the five years since the Trade Center bombing, no significant act of foreign-directed terrorism has occurred on American soil." Watson later tells Congress that he knows of only three al Qaeda suspects in the United States prior to August 1998. But this testimony directly conflicts with evidence in FBI files linking the Yousef-Rahman cells to Osama bin Laden as early as 1991.

Watson

107 • **February 1998** (page 372)

Within days, **bin Laden** issues a *fatwa* under the banner of the "International Islamic Front for Jihad on the Jews and Crusaders." In it he encourages Muslims to kill Americans—including civilians—anywhere in the world where they are found. From this point on, the warnings increase exponentially . . .

bin Laden

108 • **1998** (page 372)

Steve Gale, a terrorism specialist at the University of Pennsylvania, warns the FAA of two possible scenarios for U.S. attacks. One calls for crashing planes into nuclear plants. The second warns that terrorists might crash a FedEx cargo plane into the WTC, Pentagon, White House, Sears Tower, or Golden Gate Bridge.

109 • **1998** (page 372)

The FBI's chief pilot in Oklahoma City reports that he had seen Middle Eastern men "who appeared to be either using planes or obtaining flight training . . . that could be used for terrorist purposes." But the information never leaves the Bureau field office.

110 • **August 1998** (page 372)

The most shocking dot comes in August 1998, when the FAA and the Bureau pick up intelligence that unidentified Arabs are planning to fly "an explosive-laden plane" from an unnamed country into the World Trade Center. The FAA reportedly finds the plot "highly unlikely, given the state of the foreign country's aviation program." The FBI's New York office files the intel away without taking action.

111 • August 7, 1998 (page 372)

During a search of the apartment of Khalid al-Fawwaz, who headed al Qaeda's London office, investigators discover bomb-making manuals virtually *identical* to the ones that **Mohammed Ajaj** brought into JFK with Ramzi Yousef in September 1992. But that discovery is eclipsed by events that take place in Africa the same day—events the FBI had been warned about a year earlier, when it penetrated the al Qaeda cell in Kenya.

Ajaj

112 • August 7, 1998 (page 359)

Nearly twelve months after the FBI found evidence of a potential al Qaeda bombing plot at Wadih El-Hage's Kenya residence, the U.S. Embassies in **Nairobi** and **Dar es Salaam, Tanzania**, are struck almost simultaneously by truck bombs. The combined death toll is 234, with more than 5,000 injured.

Nairobi

Tanzania

113 • September 1998 (page 374)

A month later the FBI arrests **Ali Mohammed**, the traitorous Egyptian who had worked as a U.S Special Forces Army sergeant while training **Nosair**'s cell. But Bureau agents are stunned to learn how many missed signals he'd given them over the years.

Not only had Mohammed trained **Abouhalima** and **Salameh** at **Calverton** in 1989, but he'd supplied the Top Secret manuals from Fort Bragg that were seized in **Nosair**'s apartment and overlooked by the NYPD and the FBI.

Mohammed

Calverton

Abouhalima

Salameh

Nosair

Even worse, Mohammed used his knowledge of Green Beret operations to train al Qaeda's top commanders in al Khost, Afghanistan, as well as **bin Laden**'s personal bodyguards in Sudan. He even took reconnaissance photos prior to the **African embassy bombings**.

bin Laden

African embassy bombing victims

24

114 • October 1998 (page 374)

In October, playing catch-up, the Feds finally indict **Wadih El-Hage**, a key link between Yousef, the Sheikh, and Osama bin Laden. But over the years he's left a trail of dots that the FBI repeatedly missed. He supplied guns to Mahmud Abouhalima in 1989. He came to Brooklyn from Tucson at the time of Mustafa Shalabi's murder, and visited El-Sayyid Nosair in jail. He frequented the Al Bunyan center in Tucson, and the same al Qaeda–linked center was cited on the fake IDs used by Yousef and Ajaj when they flew into JFK in 1992. El-Hage became bin Laden's personal secretary in Sudan in the mid-1990s and was part of the Nairobi bombing cell.

El-Hage

115 • October 1998 (page 376)

By now, **Mohammed Atta** and **Ramzi Binalshibh** have set up a safe house at 54 Marienstrasse in Hamburg. Over the months to come it will serve as a combination crash pad and flight training center for the suicidal jihadis who will perfect Ramzi Yousef's third plot.

Atta   **Binalshibh**

116 • October 1998 (page 377)

After five and a half years, Special Agent **Nancy Floyd** is given a thirty-day suspension for "insubordination" in her dealings with ASAC Carson Dunbar over the matter of whether Emad Salem should have worn a wire back in 1992. The FBI internal affairs investigation, which typically involves dozens of interviews and lasts a few months, reportedly comes down to statements by Agent John Anticev, Det. Lou Napoli, and Dunbar. Floyd appeals, but is ultimately given a "two-week hit." The agent who had recruited arguably the most important intelligence asset in the recent history of the New York office is forced to surrender her badge and gun and is put on the street for fourteen days.

Floyd

117• August 1999 (page 385)

Assigned to work on terrorism issues full-time for the FDNY, **Ronnie Bucca** learns that **Ahmed Amin Refai**, the Egyptian-American accountant with the FDNY, has submitted a false report for a lost ID. The second ID would have allowed access to fire department headquarters. After learning that Refai has told multiple lies to law enforcement officers relating to the "lost" ID, Bucca begins

Bucca   **Refai**

investigating. He learns that Refai has made frequent trips to Egypt (on a $35,000 salary) and had obtained the blueprints of the WTC prior to the bombing in 1993.

118 • August 1999 (page 390)

Bucca, who believes **Refai** is a potential al Qaeda mole inside the FDNY, later discovers TV news footage showing Refai *(left)* acting as **Sheikh Rahman**'s personal bodyguard. Bucca turns over the file on the accountant to the FBI's Joint Terrorist Task Force, but the Bureau takes no action.

Refai *(l.)* with Rahman

The CIA gets advance notice of a meeting in Kuala Lumpur attended by two young Saudi veterans of the Chechen campaign: **Khalid al-Midhar** and **Nawaf al-Hazmi**. They had met previously in Hamburg with Mohammed Atta. Malaysian authorities take surveillance photos.

The meeting, which turns out to be a key planning session for the 9/11 attacks, is also attended by **Khalid Shaikh Mohammed** and his No. 2, **Ramzi Binalshibh**. Also present is **Riduan Ismuddin** (aka **Hambali**), a board member of the Konsonjaya front company in Malaysia that

al-Midhar   al-Hazmi

bankrolled Yousef's Bojinka and pope plots as well as this third plot. The meeting is held at the same condo that will later play host to **Zacarias Moussaoui**, the French national later dubbed "the twentieth hijacker."

Mohammed   Binalshibh   Hambali   Moussaoui

If there was ever a time for the U.S. intelligence agencies to share the intel, it was now. But it takes the CIA more than a year and a half to inform the FBI that al-Midhar has multiple U.S. entry visas. Al-Midhar and al-Hazmi aren't put on a Watch List until the late summer of 2001, when they are already in the United States and finalizing plans for their roles as hijackers aboard American Airlines Flight 77, which hits the Pentagon on September 11. This staggering misstep was the result of the same "need-to-know" mentality that caused the FBI to exclude capable local law enforcement officers like Ronnie Bucca from the Joint Terrorist Task Force.

On the 20th anniversary of the JTTF, U.S. Attorney **Mary Jo White** celebrates with Task Force members at Windows on the World, the restaurant atop the WTC's North Tower. Citing "the close to absolutely perfect record of successful investigations and convictions," White notes that in her seven years in the Southern District of New York she has put away twenty-five Islamic terrorists, including Ramzi Yousef and Sheikh Rahman. But in treating Osama bin Laden's jihad

Kallstrom (l.); White (c.)

as a series of legal cases rather than a global threat to U.S. security, the Feds have made a serious miscalculation. Now, as they party, Ramzi Yousef's extended family of Islamic radicals begins finalizing a plot to take down the very building where the JTTF members are celebrating.

If the Feds ever needed a reminder of al Qaeda's ongoing threat and the importance of **Sheikh Rahman** to **Osama bin Laden**, they get it a few days later, when the Saudi billionaire issues another video *fatwa*.

Wearing a dagger, surrounded by al Qaeda's Egyptian leaders **Mohammed Atef** and **Dr. Aymen al-Zawahiri** as well as **Refa'i Taha Musa**, the head of the IG, bin Laden sits next to Rahman's son, who calls on jihadis to "avenge your Sheikh" and "go to the spilling of blood." Bin Laden also tells his followers to remember **El Sayyid Nosair**, the man who spilled al Qaeda's first blood in New York in 1990 with the murder of Rabbi Kahane.

While many intelligence analysts continue to link Iraq with the WTC bombing, it is clear by now that al Qaeda's leadership under bin Laden is dominated by Egyptian radicals. Expelled from Sudan since 1996, the Saudi billionaire now operates from Afghanistan. As is often the case, his *fatwa* is a precursor of violence to come.

Rahman

bin Laden

Atef

al-Zawahiri

Taha Musa

Nosair

On the morning of October 12, two al Qaeda suicide bombers load a device made of C-4 explosive into a small skiff and take off across the harbor in Aden, Yemen. **The U.S.S. *Cole***, an advanced guided missile destroyer, is at the refueling dock. As the skiff approaches the ship, the jihadis smile and wave at *Cole* crew members, who wave back. Then, when the white fiberglass boat pulls alongside, the bomb detonates, blowing a four-story hole in the side of the ship. The two bombers and seventeen U.S. sailors are killed.

The U.S.S. *Cole*

Tawfig bin-Atash, a coconspirator in the bombing, had attended the January 5, 2000, Kuala Lumpur meeting where the 9/11 attacks were planned.

John O'Neill, the FBI's chief bin Laden specialist, arrives in Yemen with three hundred agents determined to break the case, but he runs afoul of U.S. Ambassador **Barbara Bodine**, who demands a much lower Bureau profile. The career diplomat goes so far as to block O'Neill's return visa to Yemen after he flies to the United States.

O'Neill

Bodine

Assistant FBI Director **Dale Watson**, the man who downplayed the U.S. al Qaeda presence before Congress, later tells the *Washington Post* that "sustained cooperation" with the Yemeni government "has enabled the FBI to further reduce its in-country presence." The same day, Yemen's prime minister tells the *Post* that no link has been established between the *Cole* bombers and al Qaeda.

Watson

123 • January 2001 (page 400)

The FAA issues the first of fifteen advisories warning that terrorists might try to hijack or destroy American aircraft. On January 24, Italian authorities record an Islamic imam discussing fake IDs for "the brothers going to America."

124 • January 30, 2001 (page 401)

Ziad Samir Jarrah, a Lebanese national, is stopped for questioning in the United Arab Emirates. The CIA reportedly requests that he be interrogated, but the Agency later denies that. Like Yasin, the Iraqi who was let go by the FBI after the WTC bombing, and Wadih El-Hage, released by the Bureau prior to the African embassy bombings, Jarrah is set free. The FBI later concludes that he was the hijacker-pilot aboard United Flight 93, which crashed in Pennsylvania on 9/11.

Jarrah

125 • February 2001 (page 401)

Hani Hanjour, studying at Arizona flight schools since 1996, begins training on flight simulators. FBI agent **Ken Williams**, who has transferred out of counterterrorism, apparently misses Hanjour's presence. But the FAA is informed of "concerns" of Pan Am International Flight Academy instructors that Hanjour lacks the English skills to fly multiengine jets. The FAA reportedly responds by offering to provide an interpreter for Hanjour, who goes on to fly American Flight 77 into the Pentagon on 9/11.

Hanjour   Williams

126 • February 23, 2001 (page 402)

Zacarias Moussaoui arrives at Chicago's O'Hare Airport using a French passport with a ninety-day visa. The previous fall he had enrolled at Airman Flight School in Norman, Oklahoma, but proved such a disastrous pilot candidate that he was later grounded. The Feds might have been alerted to Moussaoui if they'd picked up on testimony at the ongoing New York trial (in absentia) of Osama bin Laden, in which the billionaire's ex-pilot discusses his former co-pilot's training at Airman Flight School.

Moussaoui

127 • April 2001 (page 403)

In April, the U.S. intelligence community learns from a source with terrorist connections that **Osama bin Laden** is interested in using commercial pilots in future attacks. The source says that law enforcement investigators should consider the possibility of "spectacular and traumatic" attacks akin to the first WTC bombing. No time frame for an upcoming attack is mentioned, and because the source is determined to be speculating, the information is not disseminated to U.S. intelligence agencies.

bin Laden

128 • April 2001 (page 403)

Al Qaeda cells are raided in Milan, Frankfurt, and London. The FBI's **John O'Neill** is quoted as saying, "al Qaeda cells are everywhere." By April 18, the FAA warns that Middle Eastern terrorists might try and hijack or blow up a U.S. plane. Air carriers are told to "demonstrate a high degree of alertness."

O'Neill

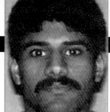

129 • May 2001 (page 403)

In early May, the Visa Express program begins in Saudi Arabia, making it easier for Saudi nationals to get U.S. travel permits. Five of the 9/11 hijackers take advantage of the program, including **Khalid al-Midhar**, who attended the January 2000 Malaysian meeting. Meanwhile, on May 1, al-Midhar's partner

al-Midhar   al-Hazmi

Nawaf al-Hazmi, already in the United States, reports an attempted street robbery to Fairfax, VA, police. He declines to press charges, and since his name is not yet on the Watch List, he escapes scrutiny.

130 • May 2001 (page 402)

In May, apparently in urgent need of additional flight training, **Zacarias Moussaoui** travels to Minnesota, where Ramzi Binalshibh, Khalid Shaikh Mohammed's No. 2 in the 9/11 plot, wires him $14,000 for simulator training.

Moussaoui

Hanjour   Raissi

131 • June 2001 (page 404)

By June the FBI, citing security threats, pulls its agents out of Yemen, severely curtailing the probe into the *Cole* bombing. At the same time, **Hani Hanjour** signs up for a month of flight simulator training at Sawyer School of Aviation in Phoenix. He will soon train almost side by side with **Lotfi Raissi**, the Algerian pilot whom ex-FBI intelligence asset **Harry Ellen** said he warned his control agent (Ken Williams) about in the fall of 1996.

Ellen

132 • June 22, 2001 (page 405)

The U.S. Central and European Command imposes "Force Protection Condition Delta" out of concern that a terrorist attack is being mounted. The same day, "chatter" regarding potential attacks causes the Pentagon to pull U.S. Navy ships out of Bahrain. Four days later, the State Department issues a worldwide caution warning American citizens of possible attacks. National Security Adviser **Condoleezza Rice** later reports that there was a "threat spike" at the time focusing on Americans or U.S. targets overseas.

Rice

133 • July 5, 2001 (page 405)

Terrorism czar Richard Clarke calls a White House meeting with officials from the FBI, FAA, Coast Guard, Secret Service, and INS warning that "something really spectacular is going to happen here, and it's going to happen soon." The next day, Clarke chairs a meeting of the National Security Council's Counterterrorism Security Group (CSG) and orders a suspension of all nonessential travel by the staff.

134 • July 10, 2001 (page 406)

FBI agent **Ken Williams** sends a memo to FBI Headquarters. He reportedly identifies eight Middle Eastern men studying at Arizona flight schools and urges the Bureau to do background checks. The communiqué, which will go down in history as the "Phoenix memo," is also sent to agents in the FBI's New York office, the Bureau's office of origin for all bin Laden–related terrorism cases. At least three people in the office see the memo, but no action is taken.

Williams

135 • August 2001 (page 408)

By now, Ronnie Bucca is so concerned about the threat intelligence he's picking up through his reserve unit that he's putting his family through alert drills. For years, as Ronnie left for work, his wife, Eve, had slipped little notes in his pocket for him to discover later in the day—notes that read "I love you" or "Stay safe." Now Eve's notes read "Watch yourself."

136 • August 6, 2001 (page 412)

In his daily briefing, **President George W. Bush**, at his ranch in Crawford, Texas, gets a top-secret report warning of potential hijackings reportedly entitled "Bin Laden Determined to Strike in U.S." More alarming, the briefing reportedly contains a reference to a British intelligence report that hijackers might grab an airliner in an effort to free Sheikh Rahman.

Bush

137 • August 15, 2001 (page 396, 411)

Few lapses in the days before 9/11 equal the FBI's blunder when alert agents in the Minneapolis field office make an application for a FISA search warrant on Zacarias Moussaoui after the French would-be pilot is arrested on visa violations. Questions were raised after he tried to rush his flight training and asked instructors how much damage a hijacker could do with a fully loaded 747.

138 • August 23, 2001 (page 410)

John O'Neill, just retired from the FBI, starts work as head of WTC security. That same day, the CIA finally warns the FBI that al-Midhar and al-Hazmi, photographed in Malaysia in 2000, are now in the country. If the FAA had been alerted, they might have picked up the two hijackers in the reservations system: the Saudis were so audacious they'd bought their 9/11 tickets in their own names. But nobody at the FBI in Washington seems to connect al-Midhar and al-Hazmi to the escalating hijack threat, even though the same unit got the Phoenix memo.

O'Neill

139 • August 2001 (page 411)

When FBI Headquarters refuses the FISA request, a Minneapolis agent E-mails headquarters warning that Moussaoui might be "involved in a larger plot to target airlines." But a headquarters agent complains that the Minneapolis office is getting people "spun up" over Moussaoui. The office replies that they are trying to make sure Moussaoui "did not take control of a plane and fly it into the World Trade Center." An amazingly prescient warning, coming just a month before 9/11.

140 • August 29, 2001 (page 412)

Khalid Shaikh Mohammed gives the final "go" for the attacks, but **Mohammed Atta** chooses the date. In a coded phone call to Ramzi Binalshibh he describes "two sticks, a dash and a cake with a stick down" the right side: 11-9, or September 11.

Mohammed   Atta

141 • September 10, 2001 (page 413)

The final fatal irony underscoring the Justice Department's approach to terrorism comes on September 10. Despite all the warnings throughout the year, when the FBI asks Attorney General **John Ashcroft** for an increase of $58 million in its counterterrorism budget, he turns them down. Acting FBI Director Tom Picard is later quoted as saying, "Before September 11, I couldn't get half an hour on terrorism with Ashcroft. He was only interested in three things: guns, drugs and civil rights."

Ashcroft

8:43 A.M. Mohammed Atta and the hijackers aboard American Flight 11 hit WTC Tower 1

9:03 A.M. As if he's been waiting for the attacks for eight years, Ronnie Bucca responds immediately with Supervising Fire Marshal Jimmy Devery. They arrive on Liberty Street at the base of the South Tower when suddenly . . .

Marwan al-Shehhi and the hijackers aboard United Flight 175 slam into WTC Tower 2

Bucca, who knows the Towers like the house he grew up in, leads Devery up a stairwell in the South Tower. When they get to the 51st floor, Devery runs into Ling Young, a badly burned victim. As he takes her down to safety, Bucca races up to the fire floor, 78. There, with Battalion Chief Orio Palmer, he finds water pressure and begins fighting the blaze with a standpipe hose. Meanwhile . . .

 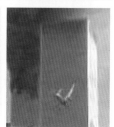

Hani Hanjour and the hijackers aboard American Flight 77 crash into the Pentagon.

10:05 A.M. As **Devery** tries to return to **Bucca** in Tower Two, he becomes disoriented and enters the North Tower. He is crossing over to West Street when suddenly the South Tower collapses. Ronnie Bucca, the one man who saw it all coming years before, dies as a firefighter beating back the flames. Ironically, John O'Neill, another prophet who warned of future al Qaeda attacks, also perishes in the collapse.

Devery and Bucca

10:10 A.M. One hijacker short after Moussaoui's arrest, United Flight 93 is the only one of the four flights to miss its target.

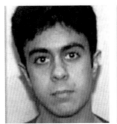

Ziad Jarrah and the hijackers aboard United Flight 93 crash in Pennsylvania.

10:28 A.M. Devery, who escaped the first collapse, is now engulfed in a dark black cloud. Around him he begins to hear the PASS alarms of fallen firefighters. Somehow making it through the debris, he finds a group of fire marshals. Half in shock and not realizing the extent of the devastation, Devery exhorts them to go back for Ronnie. But one of the marshals pulls him aside and tells him that Ronnie Bucca is gone.

Special Agent **Nancy Floyd**, who watched the 9/11 attacks from the George Washington Bridge, transfers to a small FBI regional office in the far west. A month before September 11, Emad Salem, her old asset, tries to contact her, but she has long since been forbidden from communicating with him.

Floyd

A month later, **Ronnie Bucca**'s body is recovered from the "pile" where the Tower once stood. When his widow, Eve, is able to bring herself to clean out his Manhattan Base locker, she finds a file that Ronnie kept of his ongoing investigation of Ramzi Yousef and Islamic terrorists. Inside she finds the report on the Egyptian accountant Ahmed Refai, who Ronnie believed had compromised FDNY security.

Bucca

April 4, 2003 (page 9)

On 9/11, **Ramzi Yousef** watches the execution of his 1994 third plot from a 10- by 13-foot cell in the Supermax prison in Colorado. Within hours of the attacks FBI agents try to question him, but Yousef refuses to talk. He's then moved to another cell without a radio or TV. On April 4, 2003, he loses the appeal of his 240-year sentence.

Yousef and his Supermax cell

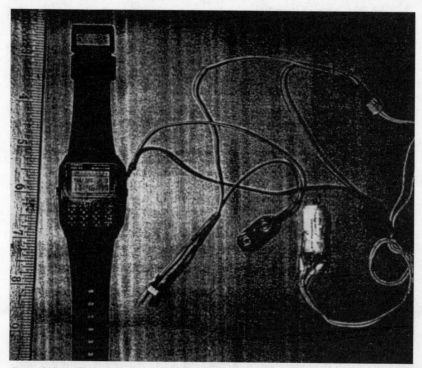

One of Yousef's Casio timers later seized by the Philippine National Police during a search of Room 603 at the Dona Josefa Apartments.

vised bomb into his shaving kit. Yousef checked the Casio. It was almost 6:00 A.M. He set the timer on the watch ahead four and a half hours. By then he would have landed back in Manila, and Flight 434 would be on its way to Japan.

Once the timer was set, Yousef got up and went back to seat 26K. When he was sure nobody was watching, he took the shaving kit bomb and shoved it into the pouch below the seat next to the life jacket.

The 747 touched down at the airport in Cebu City at 6:25 A.M.

Yousef had already prepared his alibi. With luck he'd be on his way back to Manila by the time the bomb went off. He exited the plane and quickly went to a ticket counter, paying cash for the next outbound flight. He would arrive back before noon, rush to the Dona Josefa, sneak up the back fire stairs to Room 603, and then casually emerge for the day around 1:00 P.M.

The downstairs guard, Roman Mariano, kept a logbook of the tenants' comings and goings. Naji Haddad, the Moroccan engineer in Room 603, had come in the night before around 9:40 P.M., and as far as the guard knew, he hadn't left since.[18]

But back in Cebu, as Yousef rushed across the airport terminal to make the next flight out, Haruki Ikegami, a soft-spoken twenty-four-year-old Japanese engineer, had just made it through the metal detector. The gate attendant checked his ticket. He would be sitting in seat 26K when the second leg of Flight 434 took off for Narita. The gate attendant smiled and wished him a good flight. Ikegami bowed politely, anxious to get home.

Mayday! Mayday!

Ramzi Yousef was already in the air when the continuation of PAL Flight 434 took off for Japan. This time the plane was three-quarters full, with 273 passengers and a crew of 20. When the seat belt sign went off, Haruki Ikegami dropped his seat back and closed his eyes.

It was just after 10:44 A.M. PAL Flight 434 was back at 33,000 feet, heading north over the Philippine Sea. The 747 was approaching reporting point "Mike Delta," the tiny island of Minamidaito, forty nautical miles south of Okinawa.[19] Captain Reyes was about to contact the controller at Naha Airport on the southern tip of the island to give him his bearings.

Now, in the life jacket pouch below Haruki Ikegami's seat, the seconds counted down. At precisely 10:45 A.M. the alarm went off, sending a low-voltage surge through the SCR. In a millisecond, power coursed across the fusing circuit through the batteries, creating a charge designed to light up the nine-volt bulb. But the broken glass caused the filament to short out and spark, setting off the gun cotton and detonating the container of nitroglycerine.

The blast blew a hole in the 747's floor. In the cockpit, the crew members were jolted from their seats. The enormous aircraft suddenly banked to the right.

Captain Reyes jumped on the radio: "Mayday! Mayday! This is PAL four-three-four—explosion on board—request emergency landing." The Naha controller asked Reyes if he had control of the aircraft, Reyes told him they were on autopilot. The 747 had pulled right and was back on

course. At that point he disengaged and attempted to fly the plane man-
ually. Pushing forward on the controls, he was able to get the nose
dipped slightly, but was unable to turn the plane.

"Cannot turn," said Reyes, staying calm. "The hydraulics may have
been severed."

He instructed his copilot to use the heading selector, but the plane
still wouldn't change course, so he switched back to autopilot. Just then,
the purser came into the cockpit and reported that a passenger had been
killed—the Japanese man in seat 26K. In the smoke-filled cabin, the
wall, ceiling, and seats around row 26 were covered in blood. Fernando
Bayot, a flight steward, had rushed toward the blast point moments after
the bomb detonated. He found the upper half of Haruki Ikegami's body
protruding from a hole below the twenty-sixth row. In the smoke, Bayot
couldn't tell whether the passenger was alive or dead, so he tried to pull
him up. When the torso wouldn't budge, he called for another attendant
to help them. When they tugged again they realized the young Japanese
man was dead; his body had been severed by the blast.

Back in the cockpit, Reyes thought quickly about his next move.

Given the position of the bomb, he wasn't sure if he was leaking fuel
or if a spark from the controls could set off a secondary explosion. But he
had to get the plane down. So he held his breath, counted "one, two,
three," then disengaged the autopilot again. This time he was able to
turn the aircraft.

It took the captain forty-five minutes to ease the jumbo jet onto a
proper approach to Naha Airport in Okinawa.

"That was the longest forty-five minutes in my life," steward Bayot
later recalled.[20]

Finally, as PAL Flight 434 made its approach to Naha, a convoy of
fire trucks and emergency vehicles raced onto the runway.

Still airborne, Reyes's next worry was whether or not the hydraulic
damage would allow him to lock the landing gear. As he approached the
Naha tower for a fly-by, the controllers did a visual inspection, but they
couldn't be sure if the gear was down, so a nearby private Lear jet made
two passes below the 747 and confirmed by radio: "A.O.K. Gear down
and locked."

Moments later, as the 747's tires kissed the tarmac, a cheer went up
from the surviving passengers in the cabin.

That night, a different kind of celebration took place in the shadows of the Firehouse Karaoke Bar along Roxas Boulevard in the Manila suburb of Pasay City. As a CNN report on the PAL explosion flashed across a TV over the bar, Yousef and his uncle Khalid Shaikh Mohammed clicked glasses. His calculation for the bomb placement had been just inches short. The explosion had miraculously missed the 747's center fuel tank, which was located just below the twenty-fifth and twenty-sixth rows.

If he'd planted the device slightly forward, under a seat in row 25, the tank, with its jet fuel and vapors, might have ruptured, blowing the 747 out of the sky.

The experiment had failed to bring down Flight 434, but to Yousef it was cause for celebration. By designing and wet-testing the first undetectable airline bomb, he'd achieved a giant leap forward in the history of modern terrorism. The foot soldiers of al Qaeda now had a device that, if properly placed, could bring down a jumbo jet anyplace in the world. It was just a matter of assembling the pieces on board and setting the timer.

As they eyed the CNN footage of the wreckage inside the cabin of PAL Flight 434, Yousef smiled. "Imagine this times twelve," he said, clicking glasses with his uncle again. "To Bojinka."

"Bojinka," said Mohammed. "As Allah wills it, so it will be done."

24

HOW MANY
MORE FIRES?

B ack in New York, Nancy Floyd took a day off from her surveillance work to come into Manhattan and have lunch with her mentor, Len Predtechenskis. The Bureau's lead counter-Soviet agent in New York was concerned about Nancy. By mid-December 1994, Agent Floyd's OPR investigation had dragged on for more than sixteen months.[1]

Sensing that she might be the victim of politics in the New York office, the judge handling the Day of Terror case had reportedly ordered that agents from *outside* New York investigate. But as far as Nancy knew, none of the agents she worked with in the Salem investigation had been interviewed. Worse, given the secretive nature of the OPR process, she still wasn't sure what the charges were against her.

"At first, Agent Floyd heard there were three things," said a source in the New York office. "One, whether or not she was having sex with Salem, which they threw out right away; second, whether she'd misused the vouchers, which they also got rid of when she produced all the records. But now they were trying to say she had divulged classified information."[2]

That third charge purportedly stemmed from an anecdote one of Nancy's supervisors told her during the Nosair "twelve Jewish locations" investigation as a way of illustrating how the Bureau protected its intelligence assets. The story was related to her at the time Carson Dunbar was pressuring Emad Salem to testify.

"Floyd went to her ASAC, Jack Lowe," said the source. "She said to him, 'Listen. They're trying to get this guy [Salem] to wear a wire. He doesn't want to. Whatever happened to our policy of using assets for pure intelligence? Keeping them under where they supply us with information that's important but we don't force them to testify?'"

According to the source, Lowe told Nancy the story of a sitting U.S. senator who had been under investigation by the Bureau for taking a bribe. As it turned out, the only way the Justice Department could bring charges against the lawmaker was to blow the cover of the informant who'd given them the information. Just as they'd done with Salem, the Bureau had promised the source that he'd never have to testify. "So we just walked away," Lowe told Nancy, "knowing this guy was still sitting in the Senate and he was corrupt."[3]

It was just a war story told by an ASAC to one of his agents to help her understand Bureau policy. Nancy had merely related the story to Salem. She'd never named the senator or the state he represented. She'd used the story just as her boss had, as a simple example. Now, according to the rumors, she was being investigated for telling that story and allegedly divulging "classified" information.

Jim Roth thought Nancy's disclosure of the anecdote was serious. "At the time, that was rather singular information from a fairly valuable asset," said Roth. "You can't be sitting down giving information like that to a source. There are a lot of ways to stroke sources without doing that."

But Predtechenskis, a twenty-five-year Bureau veteran, couldn't believe the pettiness of it, or the fact that the investigation had gone on for so long when most OPR's were wrapped up in a few months.

Now, after their lunch, Nancy stood next to him at a restaurant pay phone as he called a supervisor he was close to at FBI headquarters in Washington. Predtechenskis had phoned him earlier to get a sense of when the investigation might come to an end.

Now he was calling back.

Predtechenskis listened intently and nodded. "When is she going to know the specific charges?" he asked.

There was a pause as Len repeated the answer. "At the hearing. Okay, so when's that?"

He looked at Nancy, who couldn't wait to know.

"None's been scheduled," said Len, repeating the answer.

He could see Nancy was disappointed.

"It sounds like catch-22," Predtechenskis told the supervisor. "She's got a cloud over her head. She can't fight the charges 'cause she doesn't know what they are, and until she gets a hearing and it's resolved, she can't get a promotion or transfer. Does that seem fair?"

Nancy nodded, encouraging Len. Finally he hung up.

"What'd he say?" asked Nancy anxiously. Predtechenskis eyed her and shook his head.

"He said, 'That's the FBI.' "

The OPR on Nancy Floyd had effectively ended any involvement she had with Emad Salem or the investigations into the blind Sheikh, the World Trade Center bombing, and the Yousef hunt. But at least she was *inside* the Bureau.

On the outside, Ronnie Bucca had accepted the fact that the JTTF was closed to any formal representation from the FDNY. But by December 1994 he was as committed as ever to finding Ramzi Yousef. He stayed current on the hunt for the bomb maker through his intelligence work with the Army Reserve.[4] As the months went by, Yousef sightings were reported from Colombia to the U.K.

Meanwhile Ronnie followed the first Trade Center trial closely and read everything he could about the case. He pored over the U.S. State Department's annual reports that outlined patterns of global terrorism. Bucca studied each region, focusing specifically on Islamic radical cells. He memorized the names of fundamentalist groups, writing them down on index cards that he kept on a key ring in the glove compartment of his FDNY Chevy Caprice. Each new name or link he found in connection with Yousef or the blind Sheikh went onto a card.

Still, as Christmas 1994 approached, Ronnie began to focus more and more on his work with the BFI's Social Club Task Force. It had been set up after a flash fire in 1990 killed eighty-seven Honduran immigrants packed into a place called Happy Land. The blaze had rushed through the premises with such intensity that some of the bodies were found still upright, charred where they stood. Dozens of patrons were crushed to death in their panicked attempt to escape. The social clubs were to bars what gypsy cabs were to taxis—unlicensed venues that serviced immigrant neighborhoods. Hidden in basements and the dark corners of abandoned buildings, they were dangerous places, often unventilated and devoid of safe egress in the event of a fire. In many neighborhoods the cops wouldn't go near them. So it was up to the fire marshals to find them and shut them down.

Task Force work required a lot of overtime on nights and weekends. Ronnie had gone back to school and was working on an associate's degree, so he'd been forced to put the hunt for Ramzi Yousef on the back burner.

"That's when he heard the news on the radio," said Eve. "About the bomb on the plane."

It was Monday morning, December 12. Ronnie was on his way to work, listening to WINS, one of New York's all-news radio stations. He was heading down the Major Deegan Expressway when he heard that the Abu Sayyaf Group had claimed credit for the blast. Ronnie hit the brakes and took the next exit.

He pulled over and popped open the glove compartment. Rifling through the index cards, he found a reference he'd made from a State Department report. "November '93, the radical Islamic Abu Sayaf Group (ASG) . . . threatened to attack foreign missionaries and tourists. . . . December 13 . . . stopped a bus, executed nine Christians."[5]

That night, Eve was making dinner when Ronnie came in. He kissed her and smiled. "I think I know where he is."[6]

Eve looked at him. "Who?"

"Yousef," said Ronnie. He pulled out his "Towers" file and Yousef's wanted poster. "I think he's moving east." Ronnie explained how after the Trade Center bombing Yousef turned up in Pakistan, where he tried to kill the prime minister. In March they found an ammonium nitrate bomb in Bangkok. Now yesterday, this rebel group in Manila had taken credit for a bomb on a 747.

Eve looked at Ronnie and smiled. She loved her husband, but this was pretty thin. "Kind of a stretch, don't you think?"

"Maybe," said Ronnie, "but this Abu Sayyaf Group . . . the guy who founded it was in Afghanistan at the same time as Yousef and the blind Sheikh."

Eve walked across the kitchen and put her arm on his shoulder.

In the months after Kevin Shea fell into the crater, Ronnie had been obsessed with the Trade Center bomb; then the pressures of work and school had forced him to back off. Now this.

"Maybe if he's in the Philippines it means he won't be—"

"Back?" said Ronnie. "Don't bet on it." Ronnie had read everything he could find on the bomb maker. The guy was cocky. He was making moves on political leaders. He had gone after some of his own people in Iran. Ronnie didn't see him stopping.

"There hasn't been an airplane bombing in years," he said. "Then Yousef shows up in Asia, and *boom*. . . ."

"All right," said Eve. "But you've got your tests coming up."

"I know. I just hate being out of it."

Eve nodded and pulled him close. "You know, some smart guy I once knew told me, 'You can only do what you can do.'"

"Yeah," said Ronnie. "We'll see."

He went into the bathroom to wash up for dinner. The kids would be home soon. Eve shook her head and stared at the face of Ramzi Yousef, the man with the milky-gray eyes. She wondered just how many more fires he would start and how many more people would die.

The Maltese Cross

A few weeks later Ronnie Bucca walked into Suspenders, a firefighter's watering hole on Second Avenue and Thirty-eighth Street in Manhattan.[7] He was due to meet his father-in-law, Bart, the retired battalion chief. As usual, Ronnie got there early. Right away he ran into Fire Marshals Lou Garcia and Jimmy Kelty, sitting on stools near the window trading shots. Louie and Jimmy were the fire marshals who'd first encouraged him to join the Bureau of Fire Investigation. Louie had recently been appointed supervising fire marshal of Manhattan Base, the BFI's flagship office.[8]

Ronnie had known Louie since his days in Rescue One. He was a larger-than-life character, as much at home in nightspots like Elaine's as he was working a fire scene. He'd had the keen political sense to back Giuliani and offer him off-duty marshals for security in the early days of Rudy's first mayoral campaign. In those days many cops, still stung by Giuliani's prosecution of police corruption, shied away from him. Now Louie was on the fast track to becoming chief fire marshal.

As soon as Ronnie walked in, Garcia pointed at him and asked for his drink order. "What are you having? And don't tell me iced tea." Ronnie grinned; Louie knew that he rarely drank. Ronnie nodded to Wanda, the owner, who was behind the bar. "Okay," he said. "Make it *hot* tea." Garcia started laughing and broke into a smoker's cough.

Ronnie walked over to Kelty, the supervising fire marshal who was Garcia's closest friend. A tough, outspoken Irishman, Kelty, like many marshals, had started out in blue before joining the FDNY. Whenever he was asked why he'd left the NYPD to become a firefighter, he didn't skip a beat. "Simple," said Kelty. "My first day in uniform as a cop I walked into a precinct and everybody wanted to pat me down for a wire. It was during the Knapp Commission, after Serpico blew the whistle on police corruption and the average station house was under siege. My first commanding officer didn't talk to me alone for a year. It was scary. But my first day on the job in a firehouse, the lieutenant came up and threw his arms around me. He said, 'Kid, I'm gonna teach you everything I know, 'cause one day you're gonna pull me out of a burning building.'

"That's the difference between the cops and firefighters. When you're a cop everybody's suspicious of you. But when you put out a fire or save somebody's kid, you're the man. The pay and benefits are the same, but you tell me where you'd rather spend your twenty—in an armed camp or a family?"[9]

Now, at the bar, Ronnie asked Kelty about a case Kelty'd been working for months. It involved a suspected arson fire at Today's Styles, a boutique on Grand Avenue in Maspeth, Queens, that had claimed the life of FDNY Lt. Thomas Williams, a man who'd spent thirty of his fifty-one years on the job.

The fire had broken out in the ground-floor storefront. Williams died trying to rescue tenants who were trapped upstairs, and Kelty, tenacious pit bull that he was, didn't rest until he'd tracked the conspirators, who had set the blaze for the insurance.[10]

Ronnie congratulated Jimmy for hanging tough and pursuing the investigation. Kelty nodded and asked about "that bombing thing" he'd been working on. Ronnie said that after he'd heard the radio report about Abu Sayyaf, he'd called his contact on the Terrorist Task Force to ask him about the Philippines device. The detective blew him off again.

"Typical Bureau," said Garcia.

"BOHICA," Kelty jibed. "Bend over. Here it comes again."

"They don't give a damn that you're a marshal," said Garcia. "Or the fact that you've got clearance in the reserves to be a spook. As far as they're concerned, you're a fuckin' fireman."

"Damn right," said, Jimmy, toasting Garcia with a shooter of Jameson's.

By now, most of the marshals Ronnie worked with had heard his theory that the Trade Center bombing was just the beginning. As Henry Raven, the marshal who worked with Bucca on the Social Club Task Force, reflected later, "With Ronnie it wasn't a matter of *if*, it was a matter of *when* they'd be back."[11]

George Kreuscher, who spent sixteen years in Rescue One, remembered Ronnie making an uncanny prediction. "One night we talked about what could happen in New York if they ever came back," Kreuscher said after 9/11. "This was very early after the first Trade Center incident. Ronnie said that they would probably take down one building and wait until we brought in emergency services. And then, when we had them in place, they'd hit us with another one. As God is my judge, Ronnie said that."[12]

"Still," said Kelty, "you really think that prick's comin' back? I mean, Manila's a long way from New York."

"You too?" said Ronnie. "You don't buy it?"

Kelty was skeptical. His brother Gene was captain at 10 Engine and 10 Truck on Liberty Street behind the Trade Center. Nobody wanted to see the Towers hit, he said. But they'd been locked down and reinforced for years.

"Janet fuckin' Reno couldn't get into that underground garage," Kelty said.

Garcia agreed. It seemed like a long shot.

But Ronnie knew the history. "Call it payback for an old score," said Bucca.

"I don't follow," said Kelty.

Ronnie pointed to the Maltese cross on the navy blue Ten-and-Ten T-shirt Jimmy was wearing, a gift from his brother. "You know where that came from?"

"Knights of Malta? The Crusades, right?" said Garcia.

"Yeah," said Ronnie. "The eleventh century. When the knights came down from Europe and hit the castles of the Saracens, they poured burn-

ing naphtha down on them. So the knights organized the first fire
brigades. We've worn that cross ever since."

Kelty eyed him.

"Sooooo. You're saying this thing with the Arabs started when?"

"A thousand years ago," said Ronnie. He walked over to the window,
looked out on First Avenue, and pointed downtown toward the Trade
Center.

"We took *their* castles, and now they're gonna come back and take
ours."

Kelty looked at Garcia. *Jesus Christ.*

25

THE THIRD PLOT

After the success of his Casio bomb on PAL Flight 434, Ramzi Yousef allowed himself to relax for a time. He'd spend his days working with Khalid Shaikh Mohammed procuring chemicals, then party late into the night at the XO and Firehouse Karaoke Bars. Yousef's accommodations at the Dona Josefa may have been low-rent, but he and his uncle had money to burn.

At one point Yousef used his Toshiba laptop to draft a request that $75,000 be transferred to account #4789-03411-2 that Mohammed had set up with Rose Mosquera at the Far East Bank and Trust. Yousef addressed the request to "Salem Ali," one of Mohammed's aliases, and signed it with one of his own: "Dr. Adel Sabah."[1]

Plotting mass murder by day, Ramzi and his uncle behaved like a pair of frat boys at night. At one point, despite his association with bar girl Jane Ramos, Mohammed became smitten with a female dentist who worked at the Sheafa Dental Clinic on M. Adriatico Street in the Ermita district, where Mohammed was staying. One day in December, he and Yousef showed up at the Airline International Aviation School and plunked down $650 to rent a helicopter for half an hour. Mohammed had boasted to the comely dentist that he regularly chartered private aircraft, and she teased that she didn't believe him. So once the chopper was airborne, Yousef's uncle directed the pilot to fly over the Sheafa Clinic.

Then he called the woman on his cell phone and waved to her as they flew by.[2]

Even at the height of the bomb building, Yousef and his uncle took time for recreation. They made plans to spend New Year's scuba diving at a resort in the southern Philippines. When they were on the town, both men favored gold watches and Italian designer suits. They always flew first class and paid for everything in cash.

The Toshiba laptop revealed yet another side of Ramzi Yousef. He used its Windows desktop publishing capabilities to create fake IDs. In addition to pulling the Amaldo Forlani persona from the Windows atlas, Yousef designed multiple IDs for himself and Abdul Hakim Murad. In one, Yousef was mustachioed Dr. Paul Vijay, a "chemical specialist" from the International Trading Corporation at 93 Sloane Gardens, London WC4N 2BW. In another, using the same address, he was Dr. Adel Sabah, the beardless "chemical specialist" from Cairo who'd requested the wire transfer. Demonstrating a sick sense of humor, Yousef listed the ID's date of issue as February 26, 1993, the date of the World Trade Center bombing.

He created two more IDs with the same address for a pair of fictitious Brits: Dr. Alex Hume, an "industrial engineer," and Dr. Richard Smith, whose position was "nuclear engineer."[3] In another moment of levity, Yousef even designed a joke wanted poster for his coconspirator Murad. Purportedly issued by the Persian Gulf state of Qatar, the poster featured a picture of Murad, identified as "Allah Baskhsh Balouch Khan," with a phony pirate's patch over his left eye. "WANTED DEAD OR ALIVE," read the poster. The bounty listed was "$100,000,000,000.00" Murad's date of birth was listed as April 1, 1910, his occupation cited as "Int. Terrorist and Fugitive."[4]

"The fact that Ramzi could play around like this while he was plotting mass murder is one of the most chilling things about him," said Frank Gonzalez, who worked on Yousef's defense team months later. "The guy could be ice-cold one minute, then spend his night in a bar singing karaoke songs and wake up to plant a bomb on a plane."[5]

With Bojinka, of course, Yousef wasn't planning to plant just one bomb but a dozen. And as the December days passed and he began accumulating the chemicals and timers he needed for the plot, he became more secretive.

Joseph Cruz, who ran the cleaning crew at the Dona Josefa, remembered Yousef as a "mysterious" figure who wore sunglasses day and night. "One of his eyes is hollow," he said, "deeper and smaller than the other."[6] Beginning on December 20, Cruz said, Yousef told him to stay out of Room 603.[7]

Now, as the Christian holiday approached, he turned Room 603 into a bomb factory, with enough volatiles and explosives to blow the top two floors off the Dona Josefa. In addition to the nitric acid and glycerin Yousef mixed into nitro, he imported sodium azide, the primary explosive used to detonate airbags, along with mercury fulminate, another explosive.[8] In the small kitchen area of Room 603 Yousef had boxes and jars full of sodium chlorate, nitrobenzene, sulfur, picric acid, acetate, sodium carbonate, perhydrol, hydrogen peroxide, and methenane, used in the manufacture of the high explosive RDX. Along with bags of cotton ready to be turned into nitrocellulose, and multiple Casio watches, wires, connectors, lightbulbs, and fuses, Yousef purchased a series of small portable 60-Hz Tecnogas model Tec-6 heating stoves.[9]

Of all the bomb-making tools in the Dona Josefa factory, these were perhaps the most disturbing.

Yousef would later tell Murad that he intended to bring the brand-new stoves along with the Casios to their radical brothers in Egypt, France, and Algeria.[10] There he would share his new design for the undetectable bombs with fellow jihadis who were ripe to spill blood in the name of Islam.

Like many geniuses, Yousef was dynamic and capable of adapting his game plan if the circumstances changed. He had spent the first phase of his career designing enormous payloads built to be moved to a fixed site by vehicle. But the Trade Center bombing had taught him that the damage such bombs could inflict was often a function of *placement*, no matter how powerful the devices. So now he began to move from macro to micro in his thinking. His new creations weren't so much *bombs* as detonators.

These new Casio-timed "blasting caps" could be smuggled in pieces inside carry-on luggage. They were designed to be assembled by men with little technical experience and placed near the fuel tanks or flight controls so that each airliner would *itself* become an enormous bomb. Once detonated aboard a plane the size of a jumbo jet, the devices would guarantee hundreds of casualties. And the low cost and flexibility of the Casio timers would allow their placement aboard multiple aircraft, set to explode days, weeks, even months in advance.

Once the first Bojinka device went off, Yousef was certain that he would paralyze worldwide commercial air traffic. When the plot was later discovered, an assistant U.S. attorney in New York labeled Bojinka "48 Hours of Terror." He estimated the potential death toll at four thousand. But the AUSA had underestimated. Yousef's plan could kill thousands more over days and even weeks, as the hidden bombs ruptured the fuel tanks or cockpit controls of the huge 747s and DC-10s in series.

The damage could occur almost anywhere—over oceans, on runways, outside terminals jammed with travelers, or worse, in the air over highly populated areas.

By the end of 1994, as Yousef awaited the arrival of his chief accomplice, Abdul Hakim Murad, he was setting in motion a plot that the world would never forget.

The 9/11 Rehearsal?

Egypt, Algeria, and France were the three countries Yousef would visit to bring his deadly new technology to local Islamic radicals. Given the dominance of Egyptians in al Qaeda, Egypt was understandable. But why France and Algeria, its former Islamic colony on the north coast of Africa? The answer to that question may lie in a bloody airline hijacking plot that was about to unfold at 11:15 A.M. on the morning of Christmas Eve 1994 at Hourari-Boumiediene Airport in Algiers.

The ordeal began when four members of Algeria's Armed Islamic Group (GIA) slipped on board Air France Flight 8969 posing as Air Algiers employees. They quickly commandeered the cockpit and overpowered the crew of the A-300 Airbus.[11] Before their three-day siege was over, seven people were dead and another sixteen wounded. But that murderous mission, aborted by members of France's elite GIGN "super gendarmes," offered the first hint that the concept of a 9/11-like attack had been considered by Islamic radicals as far back as 1994.

The group was made up largely of "Afghan Arabs" who had fought with Osama bin Laden against the Soviets. Earlier in the year bin Laden had given seed money to the GIA,[12] and operatives of the group had trained at several al Qaeda camps.[13]

After publishing plans to eliminate Algeria's "Jews, Christians, and Polytheists," the GIA had commenced attacks on non-Islamic foreigners. Two priests and five nuns were killed between October 1994 and December 1995. Six months later, the group beheaded seven monks.

Now, on Saturday, Christmas Eve, having taken the cockpit and sealed the doors of the Air France Airbus with 239 passengers and crew on board, the group began killing hostages.[14] Wielding miniature AK-47s and screaming "Allah-u-Akhbar," the hijackers lined up an Algerian policeman and a Vietnamese diplomat. The cop pleaded, "Don't kill me—I have a wife and child." But each man was quickly shot in the back of the head.

The hijackers dumped their bodies on the tarmac.

As the hours ticked by and the siege waged on, the leader of the group demanded to be flown to France. He threatened that the plane had been loaded with dynamite, rigged to blow up with everybody on board. In a chilling precursor to 9/11, witnesses recalled fanatical talk among the terrorists, who spoke repeatedly about "flying to the eternal paradise" and "Allah's perpetual white light," an Islamic vision of holy death.[15]

By early Sunday morning, the Algerian government allowed the Airbus to take off for Marseilles in the south of France. There, as it sat on the tarmac surrounded by GIGN snipers and French paratroopers, the hijackers gave a signal of their ultimate plan. Announcing that they were heading for Paris, they demanded twenty-seven tons of jet fuel. But the normal load for such a flight was only ten tons. Hostages rescued later reported hearing the GIA radicals talk about exploding the jumbo jet in the center of Paris.

French investigators eventually learned that the Eiffel Tower was the target.*

The plot was broken after the hijackers shattered the window of the Marseilles Airport control tower at 5:17 P.M. on Monday, December 26. GIGN commandos stormed the plane. Automatic weapons fire criss-

---

*Timeline #58. p. 12.

crossed the aircraft. Inside the main passenger cabin, the air became thick with the smell of cordite and blood.

By 5:35 P.M. it was over. But the assaulting gendarmes were chilled to find twenty sticks of dynamite on board. With a full payload of fuel and suicidal hijackers in the cockpit, the Airbus could have turned into an enormous flying bomb, capable of taking down France's most beloved landmark.

A week later, Philippine investigators found among Yousef's belongings the January 5 issue of *Time*. Its cover story, "Anatomy of a Hijack," detailed every moment of the Marseilles siege.[16]

It would be years before investigators began asking whether that Christmas hijacking by Yousef's Algerian "brothers" was a dress rehearsal for his own plans, or merely an inspiration.[17] There's no definitive proof that he was directly involved with the plot, but Yousef's admitted ties to Algerian terrorists, and the evidence that he followed the incident closely, demonstrate that he was thinking about the concept of flying an airliner into a national landmark as early as 1994.

The widely known Air France hijacking is also significant for what it says about the potential prior knowledge of U.S. intelligence officials in the years before 9/11. Nine months after 9/11, in May 2002, National Security Adviser Condoleeza Rice claimed that the scenario of hijacked planes flying into buildings was never envisioned: "I don't think anybody could have predicted that these people would take an airplane and slam it into the World Trade Center, take another one and slam it into the Pentagon; that they would try and use an airplane as a missile," she said.[18]

It's unclear whether the failure of the Air France hijacking spurred Yousef to move up the deadline for the Bojinka plot. But it's certain that he wanted his U.S.-trained pilot friend, Murad, with him right away. He'd sent his fellow Baluchistani $1,200 earlier in the month, and on the day after Christmas, as the French GIGN stormed flight 8969, Murad arrived in Manila from Dubai on a Singapore Airlines flight.

A New Definition for Terror

Per Yousef's instructions, Murad had purchased a quantity of Casio DBC-61s at the airport duty-free shop along the way. He'd also bought five different colors of L'Oreal hair dye, and when he linked with Ramzi at Manila's Las Palmas Hotel Yousef turned hairdresser and helped Murad change his appearance to look more European. Murad had also bought blue contact lenses and dye that would help them both lighten their skin color.

The next night, Yousef and Murad went to visit Khalid Shaikh Mohammed at his apartment on Mabini Street in the Ermita district. He treated them to chocolate, potato chips, and nonalcoholic beer.[19] No one besides those three men knows for sure what was said, but based on the subsequent interrogations of Yousef and Murad, and secret documents obtained from the Philippine National Police, we now have a good idea of the conversation that took place.

By that point Ramzi Yousef was well into the planning of his three successive plots. In two weeks, he intended to assassinate the pope during the pontiff's visit to Manila.

Within weeks after that, Yousef, Mohammed, Murad, and Wali Khan Amin Shah would execute Bojinka, planting the improvised Casio bombs on a series of U.S.-bound flights. Then, sometime down the line—far enough ahead so that worldwide air travel would have recovered—Murad would lead their "brothers," then training in U.S. flight schools, in the execution of the third plot. On a single day they would seize the cockpits of a half dozen U.S. airliners and fly them into a series of skyscrapers and government buildings.[20] This was the "suicide" plan that Murad and Yousef had discussed in the warehouse in Lahore back in September. Murad boasted that he himself would be ready to give his life for Allah and steer one of the big planes into the World Trade Center—a target he had chosen for Yousef back in 1992.[21]

As he listened to the details of this last plot, though, Yousef's uncle Mohammed urged caution. Mindful of the failure of the hijacking at Marseilles, he suggested that they take more time to plan Yousef's return to New York. Just as Sheikh Rahman had urged Emad Salem to "slow down," the wily Mohammed, perhaps al Qaeda's best strategic planner, reminded them that the most successful operations sometimes took years to execute. Instead, he urged, they should focus on more immediate targets: the apostolate pope would be in Manila on January 12. It was now December 26. The press was predicting that crowds totaling in the millions would line his parade route.

Yousef said that he and Murad would purchase clerical robes and crosses so that they could get close to Manila stadium, where the pope was scheduled to say mass. Mohammed advised that the stadium was too hard a target; they should think about planting devices along the route, which would be packed ten, twenty, perhaps thirty people deep. Yousef agreed and said he planned to use pipe bombs with remote detonators for the assassination.[22]

Now the talk turned to Bojinka, Yousef's most elaborate plan. He had used the *Overseas Airline Guide,* a monthly schedule of airlines carried by businessmen, to work out the scenario on his laptop.[23] The bomb parts would be smuggled on board in small carry-on bags. Once assembled, the devices would be hidden in lavatories near the cockpits or in life-jacket pouches along the 25th row of the Boeing 747s. Yousef had learned from his mistake on board PAL 434. Placement in row 26 had been too far back. Now the Casio-nitro devices would be hidden right over the center fuel tanks.[24]

Two days after the pope's assassination, Murad would take an Air France flight to Singapore, where he would board the first leg of United Flight 806 bound for Hong Kong, San Francisco, and Chicago.[25] He would get through security by filling his bag with Bibles and wearing Catholic medals to foil the metal detector.

On the first leg, Murad would carry a Casio device similar to the one Yousef had wet-tested on PAL Flight 434—only this time there would be two larger bottles of "contact lens cleaner," with a capacity of 320 and 350 milliliters.[26] On the Singapore–Hong Kong leg, brother Murad would enter the cockpit area lavatory and plant the bomb in a pull-out section below the sink. He would then depart in Hong Kong as the plane carried the ticking bomb toward America.

The next morning, Murad would get on United Flight 805 in Hong Kong and place a bomb on the leg to Singapore before the 747 turned around and headed back to California and Illinois.[27] Over the next two days, the rest of them would plant devices on Northwest and Delta flights bound for Bangkok, Taipei, and Japan connecting to L.A., San Francisco, Chicago, and New York. There would be eleven flights in all. When it was done, they would all link back in Pakistan.

Mohammed marveled at the brilliance of the plan, but he cautioned that they should set the alarms well in advance. If they set them to blow over the Pacific, air travel would be grounded after the first or second flight went down.[28] Airports would get locked down, and they would be prevented from planting the others. All the devices should be hidden onboard before the first fireball fell from the sky. Like Ronnie Bucca, Mohammed had read Sun Tzu's *The Art of War,* and he knew that the battle had to be won before the first bomb went off.

If the alarm on each Casio was set to go off days in advance, the agony and uncertainty of when the next device might explode would strike fear into the heart of every infidel who might contemplate boarding a plane. Not knowing which planes were targeted, searches would have to be done by virtually every international carrier, worldwide. The process could interrupt air travel for months. Murad nodded as Mohammed embraced his nephew. The three of them toasted to the prophet with their nonalcoholic beer.

That night Yousef stayed in Murad's room at the Las Palmas. He watched CNN before going to sleep.[29] If all went according to his plan, in the days ahead the American news networks would be filled with images that would redefine the word *terror.*

26

MIRACLES FROM GOD

Ramzi Yousef, his uncle, and Wali Khan Amin Shah spent New Year's at Puerto Galera, a resort across from Batangas on the southern Philippine island of Luzon. Shah was a certified PADI scuba diver, but there was a more sinister purpose to their trip. Over the New Year's holiday, tourists at the nearby Coral Beach Resort in Matabungkay noticed a series of Pakistanis and other Arabs involved in what looked like some kind of regimented training.[1] The group, which also included Palestinians and Egyptians, was called into formation early each morning and afternoon.

Their leader, described as "slightly built" with "hollow cheekbones," had introduced himself to the tourists as a Pakistani. He used a whistle to control the other trainees, who interspersed physical training sessions with prayers. The group identified themselves to other tourists as "students." They passed out Islamic literature from the International Relations and Information Center, an NGO tied to Osama bin Laden's brother-in-law Mohammed Jamal Khalifa, who was being held by the Feds in San Francisco at that very moment.

The Philippine National Police had been monitoring Islamic cells on the southern island for months. In a January 6 memo, the PNP made the link between the group in Matabungkay and Khalifa, who was al Qaeda's key Asian financier.

"The group's real intention and objective in Matabungkay is a cause for concern," said the memo, "especially considering the coming visit of the Pope."[2] When the group left, PNP investigators found a burned

Gideon Bible in their cottage. But at this point in the first week of 1995, neither the PNP nor the FBI had any idea that Ramzi Yousef was back in Manila.

The break in the case didn't come from the investigative work of the Bureau or America's other four premier intelligence agencies. It came as the result of a simple mistake by Ramzi Yousef and the instinct of a local Manila policewoman who followed up on it.

On the night of Friday, January 6, Yousef and Murad were hard at work in Room 603 of the Dona Josefa Apartments. Stripped to their underwear, they had several Casio timers finished and more under construction. Strewn about the kitchen area were fuse wires, snap connectors, incandescent bulbs, and SCRs. There was a tool kit containing jeweler's screwdrivers, wire cutters, and a small drill. Nearby there were books on detonators, explosives, and booby traps.

The apartment was a makeshift laboratory of chemicals in bottles and boxes and the equipment to mix them with: thermometers, beakers, graduated cylinders, and a mortar and pestle. Amid the chemicals were two mysterious juice bottles (Mott's and Welch's) filled with volatile liquids. Off to the side was Yousef's Toshiba laptop, which contained fake IDs, threat letters, requests for wire transfers, and the entire blueprint of the Bojinka plot.

In the kitchen–living room, Yousef had stored the components of the pipe bombs he would plant along the path of the pope's motorcade. He'd marked the parade route on a map. At one point the "Popemobile" would pass right beneath his sixth-floor window. With a powerful enough remote, he might be able to blow the bombs from inside the Dona Josefa without even risking exposure. That would allow him to view the carnage firsthand—a luxury he'd been denied in New York.

Since Yousef had declared the room off limits to the Dona Josefa cleaning crew, no one outside the bomber's cell would have seen any of this—but for a mixing error made by the master bomber himself. At approximately 10:30 P.M. on Friday, January 6, Yousef stood at the kitchen sink showing Murad how to burn a mixture of potassium chlorate and sodium chlorate.[3] Then, as soon as he added sugar to the mixture, the compound ignited, erupting in clouds of dense gray smoke. The two bombers gasped for breath. Yousef yelled for Murad to open the windows. Choking, Murad rushed across the room, but the smoke continued to billow up from the sink.

Now, in Room 601, tenant Ray Mandaluyo smelled smoke. He opened his door and saw the two Pakistanis rush out of Room 603, pulling on their pants and carrying their shoes. Mandaluyo called the front desk, and security guard Roman Mariano ran outside the building with receptionist Mina Senario. They looked up and saw "dirty white" smoke pouring out of the windows of Room 603. Mariano yelled to Senario in their native Tagalog: "Call the fire department." He then raced upstairs and accosted Murad and Yousef.

"What is going on?" demanded the guard. "Is there a fire or something?"

Yousef laughed and quickly placated him. "We're very sorry. No fire. We were just mixing salt and powder for firecrackers. Just celebrating the late New Year. It's nothing."[4]

Fifteen minutes later a fire truck pulled up down below on President Quirino Boulevard. Firefighters ran upstairs, but by the time they got to Room 603 the smoke had dissipated. One of them got a call on a fire department radio and responded, "Negative. Negative. No fire." So they took up and withdrew. But by now Mina Senario, the receptionist, had already called the police.

Although the Malate station was minutes away by car, it wasn't until 11:30 P.M., almost an hour later, that rookie PNP patrol officer Aerial Fernandez arrived. Right away, Yousef hit him with the firecracker story. The gullible young cop eyed the two smiling Pakistanis and decided to believe them. "I'm just doing my job," he said.

"We understand," said Yousef, grinning. Fernandez never bothered to look in the room. He stared at them for another moment, then took off.

Yousef and Murad couldn't believe their luck. The crisis was over. Murad went in to Room 603 to clean up, and Yousef walked down to smoke a pipe by the front door of the building. In a few minutes he would go back upstairs. They would finish building the devices, and when the plot was executed they would produce a death toll a thousand times greater than what he'd accomplished in New York.

And that's the way it might have gone. But as midnight approached, Yousef was about to be undone by a middle-aged female police captain.

"Too Big for Just Firecrackers"

Aida Bantay Fariscal had spent her career bucking the odds. More than two decades before, her husband, policeman Gregorio Fariscal, had been killed in the line of duty. Jobless and a thirty-year-old mother of four, Aida, who had once worked as a fingerprint aide for the Philippine National Bureau of Investigation, put in her application to the PNP.[5] After struggling through the police academy as a full-time mother, she was sworn in as an officer in 1972. For the next ten years she broke a number of cases involving carjackings, robberies, and assaults. In 1982 she was instrumental in helping to crack an organized crime syndicate, and by 1990 Aida Fariscal was named one of the "Ten Outstanding Policemen" in Manila.

At 12:40 A.M. on the morning of January 7, Fariscal was working as night duty officer in the Western District's Malate station when Patrolman Fernandez walked back in. Fariscal, who'd sent him earlier to investigate smoke at the Dona Josefa, wanted to know why he'd taken so long. "More than an hour," she said. "What happened?"[6]

The young cop gave his simple report. "There's no fire, Mom," replied Fernandez, using the maternal term of respect reserved for older women in the Philippines. "Just these guys from Pakistan playing with firecrackers."

Pakistanis. Fariscal's eyes narrowed. She got up from the front desk and walked to a bulletin board, where a memo had been posted that day. Titled "Operation Holiness," the memo warned all PNP officers to be alert during the pope's upcoming visit. The day before, Fariscal's commanding officer had met with high-level PNP brass worried about the pontiff's security.

It was now the middle of the night. Fariscal had spent all day in a series of meetings at the PNP's National Capital Regional Command. She was tired. The smoke was gone. There'd been no other complaints. Another dozen middle-aged cops might have let it go. But like all accomplished police officers, Aida was driven by instinct. That very day at Camp Crame she'd heard some "background noise" about Middle Eastern men drawing attention down in Batangas over New Year's, something about burning a Bible. She eyed a picture of the pontiff on a poster announcing his January 12 visit. Then she looked over at Patrolman Fernandez.

"Round up Sergeant Tizon," she said. "We are going back to take a look."

In the hour between Fernandez's first visit and Fariscal's return, Murad had called Yousef on his cell phone. After the near-miss with the cop, Yousef wanted to regroup. He told his coconspirator to meet him at the 7-Eleven on nearby M. Adriatico Street. Then he paged Wali Khan Amin Shah. The three of them linked there and moved to a location where they could talk in private, a karaoke bar around the corner on Mabini Street.[7]

At the bar Yousef told Murad to give Shah his passports. He ordered Shah to give Murad $2,000 in cash in case he needed traveling money. Shah counted out twenty $100 American Express checks. Yousef then told Murad to go back to Room 603 and retrieve his Toshiba laptop. The hard drive was encrypted, but it contained all the details of the Bojinka plan: plane schedules, bomb recipes, bank account numbers, their IDs—everything. Once Murad got it back, they'd lay low for a day to make sure the heat was off, then get back on track.

The three men parted as they always did, by invoking the name of Allah.

Back at the Dona Josefa, the three cops pulled up in Fernandez's small car. Aida Fariscal asked Mariano for the keys to Room 603. When she went upstairs and opened the door, the smell inside was still acrid. She looked around and saw the jars of chemicals, the timers, and the colored wires, but as she moved into the bedroom Aida saw something that literally caused the hair to stand up on her head.[8]

"My heart started pulsating very hard," said Aida. "I felt feverish." There, on the bureau, she found Bibles, rosaries, hair dye, and contact lenses. The bed was covered with cotton that had been treated with some kind of chemical. Slipped into the frame of a mirror was a picture of John Paul II.

Suddenly, the phone rang.

Aida remembered the recent Sylvester Stallone movie *The Specialist*, where a bomb was set off by remote control via telephone. The phone rang again but she wouldn't answer. She told Sergeant Tizon and Patrolman Fernandez to go to the lobby. They would wait for the room's mysterious occupants to come back.

Downstairs, moments later, she phoned the PNP's Bomb Disposal Unit. Then, as soon as she'd hung up, Mariano, the security guard, ran in with news: Murad had just pulled up in a taxi.

Instead of having her men surround him, Fariscal, dressed in plain-clothes, walked up to the terrorist nonchalantly.

"Good evening, sir," she said. "I am the superior of the young officer you had met." She flashed her shield and nodded to Fernandez. "We are just waiting for you so that you'll drop by our police station to explain what happened inside your room."

Murad swallowed hard and forced a smile.[9] "Oh, yes, ma'am," he said. "That is why I came back, because I am going to your station." It was an obvious lie. Murad had no expectation that the cops would return; he was merely trying to ingratiate himself with them, playing for time until he could make his escape.

"Are you willing to go with us now?" asked Fariscal.

"Yes," said Murad. "To explain what happened."

At that point, Fariscal read Murad the PNP version of the Miranda warning. "Sir, you have the right to remain silent. . . ."

He was effectively being placed under arrest, but Aida wanted to keep things as low-key as possible. The patrolman and the sergeant got on either side of him and they started walking him out of the building, when, suddenly, Murad bolted. He took off down the sidewalk running.

Fernandez drew his gun, dropped into a double-handed Weaver stance, and fired a shot. The bullet zinged past the terrorist's ear, but Murad kept on going. Then, about ten yards down the sidewalk, he tripped over the root of a coconut tree that had recently been exposed by a typhoon.

"It was a miracle," said Aida. "First the fire, then the root of this tree, as if God had put it right in the man's path."

Murad went sprawling, and the three cops surrounded him. Tizon, the sergeant, grabbed him by the scruff of the neck and pulled him up, forcing him against the side of the building.

"We'll shoot you if you move," said Fernandez. Murad, who now seemed genuinely worried, turned to the officer in charge.

"Please," he said to Aida, "if you help me get out from this mess, I will pay you. I have two thousand dollars U.S. in travelers checks in my sock. American Express."

He started to bend down toward his ankle, but Sergeant Tizon held him firm.

"Hmmmm," Fariscal said to the terrorist. "Two thousand dollars is two years' pay for most in this country. I think maybe it is too big a bribe for just firecrackers." She nodded to the other cops. "Put the cuffs on him."

But Tizon and Fernandez had left the station quickly, forgetting to bring handcuffs. So Mariano, the security guard, pulled the drawstring from his windbreaker, and they tied Murad's hands behind his back.[10]

Across the street, Ramzi Yousef was watching all this from the shadows. When Murad hadn't called him back to tell him he had the Toshiba, Ramzi became concerned. He'd taken a cab back, only to find his friend in the hands of the police.

Yousef wanted to leap across the concrete barrier dividing Quirino Boulevard and free Murad. But there were too many cops. How many, he didn't know. He looked up at Room 603 on the top left corner of the Dona Josefa. The light was on. Could there be more cops inside? He had to go back for the laptop. Maybe he could slip up the fire stairs, as he'd done the day of the PAL bombing. Yousef started to cross the street. He walked west toward Adriatico Street, thinking he'd double back around the building. But just then, he heard a siren. The PNP bomb squad was pulling up out front. When they went through the apartment, they would find his prints everywhere.

He'd left them in the storage locker in Jersey City and the Pamrapo Avenue apartment. He wondered how long it would take for the Philippine dogs to realize that Naji Haddad, the Moroccan in Room 603, was really Rashed, the fugitive with $2 million on his head.

As the bomb techs left their truck, Yousef ducked back in the shadows. He walked west to Roxas Boulevard and hailed a cab.

"The airport," he told the driver, and sank down in the backseat, crestfallen. He would have to call his uncle and tell him. It had been a stupid accident. Now the pope plot was blown, and so was Bojinka.

But there would be other chances to place his Casio bombs, other opportunities to hunt down the apostolate pope. What troubled Yousef the most at that moment was the effect this would have on his third plot. Murad had been ready to take an airliner and fly it into the Trade Center. Others were training to hit other U.S. targets, but Yousef couldn't be certain how long it would take them to get proficient in the cockpits of big commercial jets.

Besides, he didn't know these men the way he knew his old friend Abdul Hakim. Now, with Murad arrested, Yousef would have to postpone his revenge.

The fire, and the loss of his laptop, would set him back months, and it made him angry. As soon as he was in a safe location, he would send a letter from the Liberation Army. He would warn the Philippine dogs that if they didn't release Murad he would kill their president and poison the water in Manila. After that he would gas them. This was war, and as far as he was concerned Abdul Hakim Murad was a hostage.

Yousef prayed that no matter what the cops did to Murad, he wouldn't give up the third mission—that he would die like a martyr, as he'd pledged, before revealing the details of their intended return to New York.

Hours later, using a passport in the name of Adam Qasim, Yousef paid $848 in cash for a first-class ticket on a Cathay Pacific flight from Manila to Hong Kong and on to Singapore.[11] He was so desperate to get out of town that he agreed to be wait listed.

The tension was even greater now than it had been that night in the PIA first-class lounge at Kennedy. After all, the pope was coming to this heavily Catholic country, and the cops had just stumbled onto a bomb factory created in part to kill him. It was a good thing this had broken so early on a Saturday morning. Soon the dogs would fan out across Manila and lock down the airports. He had to get out or they would be on him.

Yousef tried to stay calm as the passengers with boarding passes made their way onto the plane. He looked around to see how many others might be competing for the standby seats. When they finally announced, "Mr. Qasim," Yousef almost didn't hear it, he was so tired. He'd used so many names and lived so many lives for the jihad. The gate attendant called out the name one more time. "IS THERE A MR. QASIM HERE?" Suddenly, Yousef snapped to. "Yes. I'm here." He rushed up to the gate attendant and grabbed his boarding pass. Then he caught himself, exhaled, and walked slowly but deliberately onto the plane.

Back at the Dona Josefa, Room 603 filled up with PNP generals backslapping and congratulating themselves on breaking this plot. The holy pope would be safe.

Soon, like Nancy Floyd, Aida Fariscal would be pushed into the background as her superiors took credit for the success. But as they eyed the chemicals and the cassocks and the picture of the pontiff, none of them knew at that moment what this meant. They had no idea that this was the bomb factory of Ramzi Yousef, the most wanted man on earth—and that now, once again, he had vanished.

PART III

27

TRUTH FROM A
VALUE MEAL

The search inside Room 603 at the Dona Josefa went on until 10:30 P.M. the night after the fire. Forty-nine separate pieces of evidence were recovered, including the chemicals, Casios, Bibles, and the map of the pope's parade route.[1] At the moment of his capture, Murad had repeated the firecracker story to Capt. Aida Fariscal and insisted that his name was Saeed Ahmed.[2] But the discovery of the lab full of explosives and the ingenious collection of wires and timers told the PNP intelligence operatives that they had stumbled onto a much broader conspiracy. The pontiff was due to arrive in five days, so whatever it took to open up this Pakistani, they would do it.

Back-cuffed and blindfolded, Murad was led downstairs and into the car of Col. Avelino "Sonny" Razon, deputy commander of the Presidential Security Group (PSG).[3] In the backseat he was wedged in between two PNP generals and driven three miles across the Pasig River to PSG headquarters at Malacanang Park, adjacent to the palace of President Fidel Ramos, a former general, who had come to power in 1992. Given the potential of this threat to the pope, the PNP wasn't taking any chances on the debriefing being botched in some local police precinct.

Later, at trial in the U.S., Murad's lawyers would allege that after his arrest he was tortured. He was forced to drink urine, they claimed, and electrodes were placed on his genitals.[4] Though transcripts of Murad's interrogation suggest that he was denied water and force-fed liquids, the allegations of outright torture were never proven. Still, there's little doubt that early on his interrogation was harsh. Murad was held a total of sixty-seven days without being charged or brought before a magistrate.

PNP officials testified at his subsequent U.S. trial that on the morning of January 7, he was brought to Camp Crame, the headquarters of the Philippines Intelligence Group.[5] There he was held in an empty office inside a one-story bungalow. During most of his questioning Murad was cuffed and blindfolded. But whatever the severity of treatment may have been in those first few days, the suspect said nothing that would have led the PNP to Ramzi Yousef.

The transcript of his questioning on January 7 reveals that Murad first denied that there had been a plot against the pope, but soon relented and described the plan to put pipe bombs in the road along the pontiff's motorcade and detonate them by remote control.[6] He discussed the chemistry of making nitrocellulose, and the use of Casio watches as timers. At one point he even boasted, "Nobody in the world can make this timer except us."

He also described the structure of the Bojinka plot, saying that the goal had been "killing Americans." He disclosed an affiliation with a "Liberation Army," but never mentioned Yousef by name. In fact, Murad falsely identified his bomb-making partner as one "Nasser Ali." Whatever his interrogators may have done to him, he said nothing about the third plot to hijack airliners and fly them into buildings.

Still, the PNP officials sensed that he knew much more. It was clear from his fingerprints on the bomb-making material in Room 603 that Murad was a member of the conspiracy, but they couldn't get any more out of him with the methods they were using. So they decided to change interrogators.

Col. Rodolfo "Boogie" Mendoza was group commander of the Special Investigations Group for the PNP. A former intelligence specialist, he'd made his bones pursuing guerillas in the Communist New People's Army. Mendoza had been running Blue Marlin, a PNP operation designed to penetrate Islamic terror cells operating in the Philippines.[7]

At that point in early 1995 the colonel was years ahead of the FBI in identifying Osama bin Laden and his brother-in-law Mohammed Jamal Khalifa as the money men behind Muslim groups like the Abu Sayyaf and the MNLF.[8] He also had a unique approach to interrogation, preferring trickery and guile to the cattle prod.

The other PNP interrogators had pretty much given up on Murad by the time Colonel Mendoza took over. Before he was done, Yousef's lifelong friend would not only give him up, but would spill the details of the terrifying plot that would culminate on September 11 six years later. In retrospect, the only thing more shocking than the revelation of the plot itself is the fact that the critical intelligence Mendoza gathered was provided to the U.S. government years before 9/11.

Now, for the first time, in an interview for this book, Colonel Mendoza reveals in depth the startling details of that interrogation. It was a line of questioning, he said, that began with a Big Mac, fries, and a Coke.

A Virtual Blueprint for 9/11

Before he got into a room with Murad, Colonel Mendoza wanted to make sure his prisoner was hungry, so the PNP handlers at Camp Crame kept the terrorist from eating. Murad was lying on a cot in the bungalow room where he'd been questioned earlier. Mendoza came into the room and placed a burger and fries from McDonalds on a table near the bed. Though he was blindfolded, Murad could smell the food and began to salivate. He got up and sat at the table, though he was still cuffed and chained to the bed. The colonel introduced himself.

"My name is Mendoza," he said. "People call me Boogie." He nodded to the Philippine equivalent of a Value Meal and said, "Are you going to eat that?" Murad was wary. Some of the harshest interrogators had started out friendly.

"What is it?" he answered in English.

"It is a Big Mac, my friend," said the colonel. "One hundred percent all beef. There is no pork, I assure you."[9] Mendoza nodded for his assistant, Maj. Alberto Ferro, to lift Murad's blindfold. The terrorist's eyes went wide as soon as they adjusted to the light.

He started to lunge for the burger, but Mendoza stopped him. "No. If you want it, you have to give me something first."

"Like what?" asked Murad wearily. "I have told the others everything."

Mendoza, who had a baby face and a soft disposition, smiled.

"You don't understand, sir. That is why I am here. I am your last, best hope. If you have nothing else to say, then the only decision I have is whether or not to turn you over to the Americans or the Mossad."

Suddenly, Murad pulled back. The prospect of going to Israel terrified him. "What do you want me to say?"

"Just what you know," said the colonel. "We captured your brother Wali on Singalong Street. He almost escaped. He had your passport. He had several of them, in fact. I see that you have been to America. You were in Washington in 1991 and you stayed seven months. You left out of New York. You are a bomber. Tell me something now or I will call Tel Aviv."

Murad eyed him defiantly. Then Mendoza nodded to Major Ferro, who grabbed the burger and fries. Both of them started to leave the room, when Murad blurted out. "The Trade Center . . . I—"

"What?" said the colonel, turning on his heel.

"I'm involved in it," said Murad. "The ones who did it—Salameh, Abouhalima—I know them."

"Those names you could have read in the paper," said Mendoza. He was about to take off again.

"I am *telling* you," Murad exclaimed, "they are using fuel oil and nitric acid. It is ignited with an improvised det cord—gunpowder rolled in cloth. They cover it in plastic to keep down the smoke."

Mendoza was intrigued, but cautious. He moved up and leaned over the table.

"The *name* of the one who lit the fuses!"

Murad hesitated. Mendoza slammed the table and turned to Major Ferro.

"Call Israel."

"No. Wait!" said Murad. "I will tell you. I know him. . . . It was— Abdul Basit."

"That name means nothing to me," said Mendoza.

"That is his real name, I swear by Allah."

"What name does he go by?" demanded the colonel.

Murad hesitated again, then spoke the name in a muffled voice.

"What?"

"Ramzi Yousef."

"Yousef?" said Mendoza, wide-eyed. "The terrorist the Americans are after?" Murad nodded sadly and turned away.

Col. Rodolfo Mendoza had just made the investigative break of the decade. Ramzi Yousef was the suspected mastermind of the World Trade Center bombing, the person *Newsweek* had called the most wanted man on earth. The colonel leaned forward and nodded to Ferro, who handed Murad the burger, Coke, and fries.

"We were really shocked," Mendoza reflected later. "Remember, at this time Yousef [was] one of the biggest fugitives in the world. After some time Murad told me that he would cooperate, provided that he not be brought to Israel, and we untied his handcuffs and blindfold."

Over the days that followed, as he loosened up with Mendoza, Murad revealed the intimate details of the Bojinka and pope plots: how he had gone to America to study flying, how he'd been to schools in Texas, North Carolina, California, and upstate New York, and how he'd even come up with a plan to fly a small plane into CIA headquarters. Throughout the questioning—as in the following exchange, from one of the few transcripts made public—he continued to refer to Yousef as "Basit."

MURAD: I told Basit that there is a planning what about we dive to CIA building.

MENDOZA: CIA building?

MURAD: Yes. He told me O.K.

MENDOZA: And you are willing to die for Allah or for Islamic—

MURAD: Yes.

MENDOZA: Really?

MURAD: Yes.

When Mendoza first wrote the debriefing memo for that session on January 20, he didn't take the CIA plot very seriously. "With regards to their plan to dive-crash a commercial aircraft at the CIA Headquarters," he wrote, "subject alleged that the idea of doing same came out during his casual conversation with ABDUL BASIT and there is no specific plan yet for its execution."[10]

For months after 9/11, U.S. intelligence officials pointed to the almost casual uncertainty of that memo to suggest that Murad had said very little that would be a precursor to September 11. "It's a big leap from stealing a Cessna to commandeering a 767," one former senior CIA official told the *Washington Post*.[11]

In his book *Breakdown,* an analysis of the prior intelligence warnings leading up to 9/11, *Washington Times* reporter Bill Gertz quoted Bob Blitzer, assistant section chief for the Counterterrorism and Middle East Section of the FBI from 1991 to 1995: "Murad, during debriefings, indicated that he had it in his head to personally fly a small plane loaded with fuel or explosives into CIA headquarters in Langley. I remember that. I don't ever remember seeing anything about Yousef talking about that or any other members of the cell saying, 'We're working on trying to put plans together to use passenger aircraft as bombs.' I remember this one guy talking about the small plane attack, but that was it."[12]

The reference to Murad's plan of flying a small plane into the CIA has been widely reported.[13] But what happened in the days that followed has not.

As Murad became more relaxed with Mendoza, he got considerably more specific. *In fact, he disclosed a virtual blueprint of the 9/11 attacks—* a more elaborate description than ever previously revealed.

"One day he is kind of cocky," Mendoza recalled in an interview for this book.[14] "Murad is saying, 'You don't know something that I do.' And I asked him what it was, and he started discussing the plan to hijack commercial airliners. He told me *airliners,* not airplanes. So I asked him, 'What is the specific plan?' And he hesitated, so I turned to Major Ferro and said, 'Call the Mossad.' And he picked up a phone. We had one of our people in the other room on the line and he is making an Israeli accent. And this got Murad worried."

Finally the terrorist blurted it out.

"Okay. The plan is to hijack commercial airliners."

"And you are the guy who will execute the hijacking?" responded Mendoza.

"Yes," said Murad. "Yousef asked me if I can do that and I told him that, offering a supreme sacrifice, I can do that."

The colonel then asked him if other pilots were involved.

"Who are these people?"

Murad eyed him coyly. "You have to find out," he said. "You have to work for it."[15]

This cat and mouse game went on for days, with Murad holding back and Colonel Mendoza threatening to send him to Israel. At one point Mendoza even resorted to the good cop–bad cop ploy, allowing one of his cohorts to rush into the room claiming to be a local police official threatening to kill Murad. Suddenly, Mendoza became protective of his witness and forced the "cop" out of the room.

"I said, 'Goddamn you, get out,' to the guy," recalled Mendoza. "I then told the subject [Murad] that we would have the Red Cross there soon to guarantee his human rights and safety. Of course, these are our people. But over time the subject came to trust us more and more."

And little by little, Yousef's oldest confidant coughed up the details of this third plot.

"He discussed with me," said Mendoza, "even without me mentioning, that there is really formal training [going on] of suicide bombers. He said that there were other Middle Eastern pilots training and he discussed with me the names and flight training schools they went to. This is in February of 1995."

Finally, Murad revealed some of the targets.

"CIA headquarters," Mendoza recalled, "the Pentagon, and an unidentified nuclear facility." Mendoza asked Murad where he had discussed the targets with Yousef and he said, "Quetta, Pakistan," Yousef's hometown.

"Murad is talking about a plan that is separate from Bojinka," Mendoza said. "Murad is talking about pilot training in the U.S. and Murad is talking about the expertise of Yousef. Not only was this a parallel plot to Bojinka, but what is the motive of Murad to have flight training in the U.S., and who are the other pilots met by Murad in the U.S.? That is an enormous question."[16]

Further evidence collected since 9/11 suggests that the intent of Yousef's original scheme with Murad was even deadlier than what took place that day. One of the first reporters to talk to Colonel Mendoza about this third plot was Maria Ressa, the Manila bureau chief for CNN. On September 18, 2001, she conducted a related interview with Philippines Secretary Rigoberto Bobby Tiglao, the spokesman for President Fidel Ramos.

In addition to the CIA, the Pentagon, and the nuclear facility, Tiglao said, Murad confessed that other targets of the airliner hijacking scheme would include the Transamerica Tower in San Francisco, the Sears Tower in Chicago, and—as Ronnie Bucca had suspected—the World Trade Center.[17]

Murad was handed over to the FBI on April 13, more than two months after his arrival at Camp Crame. Agents Frank Pellegrino and Thomas Donlon were there to receive him at Ninoy Aquino International Airport along with members of the FBI's Hostage Rescue Team. During the flight home, with Murad's consent, the two agents questioned him for more than five hours. On May 11, 1995, they put the details of that debriefing into a seventeen-page single-spaced FBI 302, an official Bureau memo prepared by agents in anticipation of trial.[18]

Prior to publication in this book, the full contents of the Murad 302 have never been made public. According to the document, Murad revealed minute specifics of the aborted Bojinka and pope plots. He discussed his longtime relationship with Ramzi Yousef and gave up extraordinary details about the bomb maker's background, including the fact, unknown to the Feds at the time, that Yousef was married and had two daughters.

The memo also documented Murad's detailed description of Yousef's PAL Flight 434 bomb and revealed that Yousef intended to allow the Abu Sayyaf (ASG) Philippine terror group to take credit for the pope's murder so that it might "enhance their stature."

This was an important admission by Murad that gave the FBI another hint of the link between Yousef and Osama bin Laden, since PNP documents handed over to the U.S. by Colonel Mendoza showed that bin Laden's brother-in-law Khalifa had been a financial backer of the ASG.[19]

But the most remarkable line in the 302 came on pp. 12–13. In response to a question from the agents about Yousef's intent, the 302 said, "MURAD advised that RAMZI wanted to return to the United States in the future to bomb the World Trade Center a second time." A composite portion of the 302 is reproduced opposite. A copy of the entire memo can be found on pp. 499–517.

- 1 -

FEDERAL BUREAU OF INVESTIGATION

—

Date of transcription _____ 5/11/95

FD-302 (Rev. 3-10-82)

On 4/13/95, SA's Francis J. Pellegrino and Thomas G.
Donlon, conducted an interview of ABDUL HAKIM ALI, AKA ABDUL
HAKIM ALI HASHEM MURAD. MURAD was interviewed as he was being
transported from Manila, Philippines to New York as a result of a
sealed indictment issued by the United States Federal District
Court for the Southern District of New York.

MURAD advised
that RAMZI wanted to return to the United States in the future to
bomb the World Trade Center a second time.

Investigation on __4/12-13/95__ at _Aircraft in Flight_ File #

SA FRANCIS J. PELLEGRINO, FBI
by _SA THOMAS G. DONLON, FBI_____ Date dictated _4/19/95_

Murad's extraordinary revelation, now confirmed in black and white
and documented by the FBI, was a vindication of what Ronnie Bucca
had suggested for years—that Yousef was coming back to finish off the
Trade Center.

Still, even though the memo discussed Murad's U.S. flight training in
detail, it contained not a word about Ramzi's third plot, in which commercial jets would be used as flying missiles to destroy the Twin Towers,
the Pentagon, and/or other U.S. buildings. This despite the fact that,
only days before his rendition back to the States, Murad had told Colonel Mendoza that "there were pilot trainings going on in the U.S."

In his interview for this book, Mendoza said he believed that Yousef
and Murad came up with the airliner hijacking–flying missile plot after
failing to topple the Twin Towers the first time.

"Murad is a dedicated man," said Mendoza. "He provided the structural analysis of the World Trade Center. This may be speculation. But
when the truck-bombing scheme did not work [in 1993] they decided
that the only way to take down a symbolic target like the World Trade
Center would be to steal a plane. He went to the United States and
trained in flight training schools, and he told us about taking a plane and
hitting the CIA, a nuclear facility, and the Pentagon."

Colonel Mendoza insists that he turned over all his briefing tapes, transcripts, and reports on the Murad interrogation to the U.S. Embassy in Manila. When asked which U.S. officials specifically received the files he declined to name names to avoid embarrassing them.

However, when asked whether the U.S. government got the intelligence on the "third plot," Mendoza said, "I am very sure of it."[20]

Capt. Aida Fariscal, the woman who foiled the Bojinka and pope plots, said that she was certain the FBI got the information. In fact, the events of 9/11 have embittered her on the subject.

"It's so chilling," she told a reporter for the *Washington Post.* "Those kamikaze pilots trained in America just like Murad. The FBI knew all about Yousef's plans. They'd seen the files; been inside [Room] 603. This [9/11] should never ever been allowed to happen. All those poor people dead."[21]

Sonny Razon, the former colonel who transported Murad from the Dona Josefa Apartments, was later promoted to general in the PNP after he supervised the Bojinka investigation. In the aftermath of 9/11, he was equally shocked at the failure of the FBI to heed the warnings from Murad's interrogation.

"We told the Americans about the plans to turn planes into flying bombs as far back as 1995," he said. "Why didn't they pay attention?"[22]

Of all the dots on the chart of negligence leading up to September 11, the FBI's failure to understand the significance of Yousef's "third plot" was the most glaring misstep to date.*

There would be others.

---

*Timeline #71. p. 15.

28

BRAD SMITH'S
BIGGEST "GET"

By January 8, two days after the Friday night fire at the Dona Josefa, Ramzi Yousef had slipped back into the dark safety of his home province of Baluchistan. At this point, few Americans had any idea what a significant break in the World Trade Center bombing investigation Capt. Aida Fariscal's collar had been. That weekend, fingerprint evidence gathered in Room 603 by the PNP was just being analyzed. Yousef's Toshiba laptop was confiscated by the PNP and locked up at Camp Crame.[1] Murad had not yet confessed Yousef's true identity to Colonel Mendoza. But even though the bomb maker was in hiding, word of his aborted Bojinka plot was beginning to raise alarms in the security offices of the U.S. airlines that serviced Asia.

Glen Winn, then manager of corporate security for United Airlines, was awakened at 6:00 A.M. Chicago time on Saturday, January 7. An immediate analysis of Yousef's Toshiba laptop had revealed some sort of plan to place bombs on United flights exiting Asia, and the FAA's Watch Center in Washington was calling to alert him.

Speaking for the first time publicly in an interview with the author, Winn remembered: "They called basically to tell me that *we* were it. Intelligence had been obtained indicating that suspects involved with the bombing of airplanes had targeted us among other carriers."[2]

The Philippine National Police had already alerted the FBI to the Bojinka plot, and agents in the Bureau's Strategic Incident Operations

Center (SIOC) had warned the FAA of the possible "bombs on board" scenario. The intelligence was considered so urgent that the FAA contacted security officials like Winn on unsecured "open" lines.

Winn immediately notified United's Operations and Control Center at UA headquarters in Chicago, and word was flashed to all United flights inbound and outbound from Asia. At least three fully loaded UA flights were stopped on runways as they taxied for takeoff.

Dick Doubrava, Winn's counterpart at Delta, remembered the FAA reporting a "credible and very substantial threat to the operations of U.S. air carriers serving Asia."[3] Doubrava said that Delta stopped traffic on the ground in Bangkok and other Asian cities it serviced. Each plane was subjected to a rigorous inspection. "We were required to pull all the seat backs and seat bottoms up and check all the life vest bags underneath," he said.

Clearly, the Feds had made the connection between the PAL Flight 434 bomb and the Casio-timer liquid bomb plot laid out on Yousef's laptop. "We were looking for small amounts of liquid that could be easily concealed," said Doubrava. For weeks to come, airline passengers throughout Asia were prevented from boarding commercial jets carrying any kind of liquid.

"If you talk to anybody in the business who traveled the Pacific right after this," said Winn, "everything went. I don't care if you had aftershave, expensive perfume, or a five-hundred-dollar bottle of wine, it went into a bucket at the gate."

The travelers on the ground were lucky. In the days immediately following the discovery of Bojinka, a number of airborne flights were forced to land. A United flight bound for Honolulu from Japan was forced back to Narita,[4] and two Hong Kong–bound United flights were ordered to land before reaching their destinations.[5]

As it turned out, the FAA's fears were well founded. As soon as Ramzi Yousef returned to Pakistan, he began planning to fulfill at least part of the Bojinka plot. He decided to build a series of prewired Casio nitroglycerine devices and plant them on United and Northwest flights out of Bangkok. The bombs would be hidden inside a series of toy cars.[6] To help him execute the audacious plan, Yousef recruited another young jihadi from the seemingly endless reserve of Islamic militants in Pakistan.

In May 1994, Yousef's sister-in-law had introduced him to Istaique Parker, a South African Muslim student at the militant Islamabad University. Back then, Yousef had reportedly asked Parker how he might go about marrying a South African girl so that he could obtain yet another passport.[7] The twenty-five-year-old Parker would later claim he didn't know Yousef's true identity until months later. Now, in January of 1995, two weeks after his Manila escape, Yousef contacted Parker again.

According to Simon Reeve in his expansive Yousef biography, *The New Jackals,* the bomb maker summoned Parker to a meeting at the Pearl Guest House in Islamabad's Section F-7/4. Yousef told Parker he wanted him to travel to Bangkok and plant the toy car bombs inside suitcases to be checked aboard two outbound U.S. flights.[8] The master bomber, who learned constantly from other terrorists' mistakes, had studied the 1988 downing of Pan Am Flight 103. Investigators eventually broke that plot and traced it back to two Libyan nationals because they'd packed the Toshiba boom box bomb in a cheap suitcase stuffed with scattered, unmatched clothing from a shop in Malta.[9]

This time, Yousef showed Parker "many new suits" worth "hundreds of dollars." He gave him $7,000 to buy two first-class airline tickets and a pair of expensive suitcases that wouldn't alert airport screeners to the presence of a terrorist bomb. Parker reportedly balked, but Yousef warned him that his name was on the laptop seized in Manila. The Feds would soon be on him if he didn't make this sacrifice for the jihad. The young South African had a wife, Fehmida, and a two-year-old son.[10] Yousef made it clear that if Parker didn't cooperate, they too could be in danger.

So Parker flew to Bangkok. Along the way he picked up a *Newsweek* with a piece on Yousef that mentioned Brad Smith's $2 million Rewards for Justice program.

By this time, Smith was in the late stages of Lou Gehrig's disease. In fact on the day after Parker flew to Bangkok, Smith underwent a vent-trach operation that effectively prevented him from breathing without a portable volume ventilator.[11] Once Yousef was linked to the Manila bomb factory, Smith rallied and decided it was time to amp up publicity about the Rewards program. He asked his partner, DSS agent Rob Born, to fly to Pakistan to arrange for a broader distribution of the matchbooks and posters bearing Smith's slogan "We Can Give You $2 Million Reasons to Stop Terrorism."[12]*

Born made sure a heavy concentration of matchbooks was spread around Yousef's home province of Baluchistan, especially the capital of Quetta. He had no idea at the time that Parker, one of the DSS's most valuable informants, would read about the reward in *Newsweek* on a flight bound for Thailand.

Yousef caught a later plane and met Parker at Bangkok's Grace Hotel. He flashed anger when he saw the soft-shell suitcases Parker had bought. He'd given him enough money for expensive hard-shell luggage, and the young Muslim had come back with cloth.

Yousef sent the terrified student shopping again, then went to work on two new bombs identical to the device that killed Haruki Ikegami on

One of the toy cars with nitrocellulose (gun cotton) seized in a raid on Yousef's lair.

---

*Timeline #72. p. 15.

PAL Flight 434. Only this time he wrapped them in gun cotton and hid them inside a pair of miniature police cars.[13]

The next day, shaking with fear, Parker hung around Bangkok International Airport, unable to muster the nerve to check in the bomb-laden luggage. He had two separate first-class tickets that would have permitted him to check the bags aboard the United and Delta flights. But the young student got cold feet.

"I couldn't go through with it," Parker later told DSS agents. "I thought about all the people who would die on board the aircraft."[14]

Parker called Yousef later to confess, but rather than losing his temper the bomb maker was cool with him. He told Parker to meet him back at the hotel, where he dismantled the toy car bombs and poured the nitro down the hotel drain. Even in a diluted state, the unstable liquid had enough blasting power to blow a hole in the Bangkok sewer system. Yousef told Parker to take the nitrocellulose with him back to Pakistan and meet him in five days. He could make up for his failure by undertaking another mission for the jihad.

On the flight back to Islamabad, Istaique Parker realized that he was a moth who'd come too close to a very explosive flame. That night, when he came home to his wife and son, Parker decided he had only three choices. He could do Yousef's bidding and become an accomplice to mass murder; he could try to run; or he could become an informer. Parker's wife, Fehmida, helped him make the decision. Murder wasn't an option: It was not Allah's way. The Parkers had limited resources. They could never survive as fugitives with Yousef hunting them.

So Istaique decided to drop a dime and run the risk of turning in the world's most wanted man. If he was lucky, he would qualify for the $2 million reward. With that money he and his young family could start a new life, away from the jihadis who seemed driven by their hatred of the West. Bradley Smith's Rewards for Justice program was about to yield its biggest "get."

The Su Casa Takedown

The next day, a panic-stricken call came into the Marine post at the U.S. Embassy in Islamabad.[15] "A crazy Pakistani man pounded on my door and forced his way in here," said a female embassy employee who was calling from her home. "Get someone here right away." The "crazy Pakistani" was Istaique Parker.

Jeff Riner, an agent with Brad Smith's Diplomatic Security Service, got the call forwarded to him in the Regional Security Office (RSO) at the embassy.

For *Relentless Pursuit,* his riveting account of Yousef's takedown, author Samuel Katz interviewed Riner and his partner Bill Miller, an ex-Marine from Georgia. Parker knew the embassy employee's home address, it turned out, and had shown up on her doorstep seeking sanctuary rather than risk being seen at the embassy gates.

While Parker paced nervously in the woman's yard, she pleaded with the DSS agents. "You got to get this guy out of here. He is so scared, He's scaring me to death. He says he knows something about someone you are looking for."

Within hours, Riner and Miller had Parker in an empty embassy office, where he brandished the *Newsweek* with Yousef's picture.[16]

"I know him," he said.

Riner and Miller eyed each other. *Damn it.* If this guy was right, they had a shot at nailing the most notorious terrorist since Abu Nidal.[17] Word quickly reached Neal Herman and the JTTF agents in New York who were keeping the Yousef watch. Special Agent Ralph Horton, the Bureau's legal attaché in Bangkok, flew in. Over the next few days, the three agents debriefed Parker, who said that Yousef was due to call him when he arrived back in town. He showed them the nitrocellulose he was keeping for the bomb maker, and confirmed that he'd been moments away from planting two bombs on board United and Delta flights. The new intelligence, coupled with the Bojinka plot discovery in Manila, raised concerns at the FAA even higher.

As they awaited word from the master bomber, the agents spirited Parker around under a blanket in the back of an embassy Chevy Suburban. Over the next few days Parker gave them extraordinary insights into Yousef—a terrorist with a personal style unknown in the annals of radical Islam.[18]

Incredibly deadly, he was also fastidious and something of a clotheshorse. He wore expensive suits and designer sunglasses. According to Parker, he seemed as concerned about his personal appearance as he was with the worldwide jihad.

During one debriefing, Parker revealed that Yousef, in his endless quest to take down a jumbo jet, had exhorted him to smuggle a bomb aboard a plane as cargo, hidden in a package containing a cutlery set. But Parker convinced him that Thai officials would demand an export license (requiring his photograph and fingerprints) before they'd let him ship anything in the cargo hold of an international flight. So Yousef backed off again.

The agents gave Parker one of those old book-size Motorola cell phones and let him go, admonishing him to call the second he heard from Yousef. Finally, on the night of February 6, the terrorist slipped back into town. He called Parker and told him that he wanted to fly with him the next day to Quetta in Baluchistan.

Right away, Parker contacted the agents. If Yousef escaped back to Quetta, it would be like the proverbial rabbit going back to the briar patch. They might never get him out. It's unclear whether the bomb maker gave Parker his whereabouts. But in any case, the agents made arrangements to meet him at the airport the next morning and grab Yousef then. As it happened, FBI Special Agent Brad Garrett was due to fly in at the same time in his quest to find CIA shooter Mir Aimal Kansi. The agencies were friendly rivals overseas, and DSS agent Riner decided that handing Yousef to the FBI agent would be a nice welcoming present.

But Yousef pulled a change-up. As the agents waited the next morning at the terminal, Parker called to say that Yousef had decided to take a bus to Afghanistan.

This sent DSS agent Bill Miller in a Suburban to wait near the depot, as a Pakistani foreign service national, who would be less conspicuous, scoured the passengers for signs of the bomb maker.

But Ramzi Yousef hadn't eluded detection for two years without extraordinary survival skills. Something told him to change the game plan again. Just before 9:00 A.M., he called Parker and said he wanted to meet him. In fact, he was staying in Room 16 at the Su Casa guest house across the street from Parker's apartment.

The Su Casa was a two-story white split-level B&B that had been frequented by Afghan "freedom fighters" during the war against the Soviets. Later, the FBI would discover that the guest house was owned by an NGO controlled by Osama bin Laden. For the time being, though, that remained another dot the Bureau failed to connect.*

*Timeline #73. p. 15.

Telling Parker he was at the Su Casa was Yousef's way of letting the young South African know he was within striking distance of his wife and child. Parker was petrified. Yousef summoned him to the second-floor room and told him to get ready for a trip: they were heading to Baluchistan. He was to meet Yousef back there later.

Events now moved quickly. Informed of this third change of plans, the Feds quickly contacted the Pakistani authorities. They were taking a big chance. Yousef had sources within the government: a raid of his brother's house just after the Trade Center bombing had reportedly been spoiled after a tip to Yousef by a Pakistani official. But the Feds had no choice. Politically, they couldn't seize Yousef, a Pakistani national, without the government's approval. They would also need official clearance to extradite him for trial in the U.S.

Once again, Yousef's fate turned on the decision of a woman. When a motorcade of DSS and ISI agents sped to the prime minister's compound, the head of state whose approval they needed for Yousef's takedown was none other than Benazir Bhutto, the female PM Yousef had tried twice to kill in 1994. She soon gave the okay for his rendition to the U.S.

Now, just before 9:00 A.M. on February 7, a series of Pakistani and embassy vehicles surrounded the Su Casa. ISI agents dressed in tan and gray shalwar Kameez robes and carrying AK-47s took positions outside.

Miller, Riner, and two DEA agents, Cliff Best and Greg Lee, waited nearby. The plan was for Parker to go into Room 16, make sure Yousef was there, and then come out to the street and run his hand through his hair.

As soon as the signal came, Riner radioed: "We have to do this now." Fifteen ISI agents stormed into the Su Casa lobby. The leader pointed a Kalashnikov at the manager, demanding to know if anyone was in Room 16. The trembling man nodded and the agents rushed upstairs.

Kicking the door in, they found Yousef lying on his bed. A *Newsweek* with his picture was open beside him. Around the room the agents noticed gun cotton, wires, the toy cars, and some baby dolls about to be turned into bombs.

One of the ISI agents grabbed Yousef and pressed his face against a window while another flex-tied his wrists behind him. When Yousef turned to look at the ISI agents ransacking the room, he was slapped and told he'd be throttled if he looked their way again. But the terrorist remained calm, speaking to the agents in Urdu. He uttered something about his papers, assuming that perhaps this was just a local immigration roust.

His back was to the two DSS agents who had now slipped into the room. They stayed quiet until the Pakistanis had finished the search. Then Riner moved forward and banged off a Polaroid. The flash startled Yousef, who was then confronted by Miller. In a Georgia drawl, the agent said, "What's up, Ramzi?"

Suddenly Yousef began trembling. His eyes went wide and his knees buckled. After almost twenty-four months on the run, he realized now that the Americans had him.

The Bureau Claims Credit

A man later identified by *Time* magazine as a Karachi businessman staying on the ground floor was quoted as saying: "It was like a hurricane. A big panic. They were dragging him downstairs. He was blindfolded, barefoot, and had his hands and legs bound." According to the eyewitness, Yousef was shouting, "I am innocent. Why are you taking me? Show me your arrest warrant!"[19]

Back in D.C., a cheer went up in the FBI SIOC, where agents had been monitoring the takedown via satphone.[20] Agents Garrett and Horton (the Bangkok LEGAT) soon showed up at the guest house, but by the time they got there Yousef had been removed.[21]

This had been a DSS operation from start to finish, and word soon got back to Brad Smith as he lay recovering from the vent-trach at his home in Virginia. His much-maligned Rewards program had prompted Parker to cooperate. Two fellow DSS agents had turned the South African and effected the bust. But once again, in another example of the interagency fighting that paved the way for 9/11, something happened that altered the public record of this story.

Days earlier, when DSS agents had first heard from Parker, they'd cabled their State Department superiors in D.C. on the best way to proceed.

A decision had to be made quickly about which agency would assume the lead in Yousef's takedown: the Diplomatic Security Service, which Parker had first contacted, the FBI, or the CIA. The cable came on the Friday of a weekend that saw one of the worst snowstorms in Washington memory. If the three agencies were permitted to jockey for position over which one should make the bust, valuable time might be lost. So when Special Agent Fred Burton, a DSS deputy director, got word that Parker had turned himself in, he made a judgment call. Parker would be handled in-house. DSS agents would take the lead in debriefing him and attempting to capture Yousef.

It turned out to be the right decision. DSS agents in country typically had the best feel for handling foreign nationals. Besides, nobody in the DSS had hidden anything from the Bureau. FBI LEGAT Horton had been summoned from the Bangkok embassy to share in Parker's debriefing, and FBI Agent Garrett was informed of the possible Yousef arrest as soon as he hit town.

Still, for whatever reasons, Horton and Garrett had found themselves playing catch-up on the morning of the bust. Neither of them was present at the Su Casa at the time of Yousef's arrest.

Then, just as the State Department was getting ready to publicize its role in the historic arrest, a Justice Department official put in a call to Secretary of State Warren Christopher. DSS agent Fred Burton, who'd decided to let his own agents effect the arrest, reportedly learned he was about to become the object of an Inspector General's investigation. The reason: his alleged "failure to communicate the events through the proper channels."

In effect, Burton's decision to give his own agency the lead in Yousef's arrest was being second-guessed. A jurisdictional battle over which agency should have gone in first in the takedown was about to erupt. It was just another petty inside-the-Beltway skirmish, but it was a fight that might be exploited by the bomb maker's defense attorneys down the line.

Because of the potential impact on Yousef's prosecution, Secretary Christopher was reportedly asked by Justice to minimize the involvement of his own DSS agents. Despite Brad Smith's reward, which Parker was about to receive in full, despite the yeoman work of Riner and Miller (not to mention the DEA agents), official credit for the Yousef arrest would go to the FBI.

Later, at the Bojinka trial, DSS agent Riner testified under oath that FBI agent Bill Horton arrived at the Su Casa fifteen minutes after the Yousef seizure. Garret showed up, he said, five minutes after that.[22] But the reputation of the Bureau—the agency that always got its man—

remained intact. In a *60 Minutes II* piece that aired after 9/11, Garrett was featured as the man who got Yousef. In fact, in an interview for that story, Garrett—who had arrived in Islamabad on a completely different case—made it sound like he ran the operation:

"I got a call from headquarters and they said Ramzi Yousef might be located, and we're not really sure at this point, at a location in Islamabad. We drive to the guesthouse and in short order the Pak military go in the house. I go in behind them with a couple of State Department agents and a DEA agent, walk up the stairs and they're probably ten seconds, fifteen seconds in front of me. . . ."[23]

The broadcast later noted that "Garrett took [Yousef] to a secure location, fingerprinted him, and began the first interrogation of one of America's most wanted terrorists."

That was true, but the first interrogation of Yousef was also conducted in the presence of DSS agent Bill Miller.

The FBI had first failed to capture Yousef as he built the bomb in New York. The Bureau had lost him and haplessly chased him for two years until he was undone by another agency. Now they were getting credit after the fact for the takedown.

Author Samuel Katz, who's written a number of books on intelligence and special operations, called the Bureau's action with regard to Yousef typical.

"They take credit for everything," he said.[24] "If you speak to anyone who works in law enforcement—state, local, or even federal—on any case that does well, the FBI immediately takes credit. It wouldn't matter, except it builds resentment with other agencies, and in this ongoing war on terror, that can be dangerous."

Agents like Riner and Miller and Brad Smith, who'd stayed alive for Yousef's capture, had to settle for the satisfaction of knowing that it was the DSS that brought the master bomber to ground.

And what became of the investigation of DSS Special Agent Fred Burton? Ironically, it was called off only after Burton threatened to contact Mike Wallace and expose the FBI's dubious claim—on the *original 60 Minutes.*[25]

29

A CHILLING
WARNING

Less than an hour after his capture, Ramzi Yousef was seated across a table from FBI Agents Garrett and Horton and DSS Agent Bill Miller. He'd been taken to an ISI military station, where he was fingerprinted and read his rights. Even though he would soon face charges for the murder of Haruki Ikegami and the Bojinka plot, not to mention the original Trade Center bombing, Yousef seemed compelled to regale the agents with his accomplishments. When asked his name, he gave his latest persona, "Ali Baloch," then added: "I have many."[1]

It was a relatively brief interview. Secret Service Agent Brian Parr and FBI Agent Chuck Stern were on their way to Islamabad aboard a government 707 to effect Yousef's transfer back to New York.[2] Airborne, they would question him for hours.

But at this point, the bomb maker, dressed in a mustard-colored jumpsuit, seemed to be as preoccupied with his appearance as his custody status. He asked the agents if he could get a suit coat, dress shirt, tie, trousers, socks, and dress shoes on the off chance that he might be exposed to the press.

Ramzi Yousef was one terrorist who kept his own clippings.

He had been a fugitive for almost two years. As al Qaeda's chief bomb maker and operational point man, he was in possession of an extraordinary number of secrets. It had taken days for determined PNP interrogators just to get his *name* out of Abdul Hakim Murad. Yet now, in the course of this first interrogation, Yousef seemed almost casual in his willingness to talk.

"I masterminded the explosion [at the Trade Center]," he boasted, alleging that the bomb cost him $20,000 to build. He admitted he'd been wired money by some "friends" in Pakistan, but said nothing more about his sponsors.

As to his motivation, Yousef insisted that he was primarily driven to attack America because of U.S. support for Israel.[3] At one point he told the agents that he was "most affected" by a BBC report that showed Israeli soldiers breaking the hand of a Palestinian who was throwing rocks. More than any single element, the treatment of the Palestinians seemed to factor into Yousef's scheme for terror.

That issue becomes important when determining who was truly behind him—Iraq, as many analysts alleged, or Osama bin Laden.

It's quite possible that Yousef gave up the details of the Trade Center bomb to divert the Feds' attention from his more ambitious "third plot," to hijack airliners and use them as missiles. But without realizing it, Yousef was giving the agents clues about his true patron. In repeated public announcements and *fatwas* over the next five years, Osama bin Laden denounced what he called the "Zionist-Crusaders." His closest Egyptian cohorts had suffered humiliating defeats by the Israelis in 1973 and 1967. Yousef's own mother was Palestinian; he later told a reporter that his grandmother had a home in Haifa that was denied him.[4]

Still, in a *New York Times* story the day after Yousef's arraignment in Manhattan,[5] the FBI's former associate deputy director was quoted as saying that Yousef may have been sponsored by Iraq.

That was a pet theory of Jim Fox, the prematurely terminated head of the FBI's New York office.[6] Those who believed that Saddam Hussein had sent Yousef to America pointed to the fact that the bombing happened on February 26, 1993, the second anniversary of the Kuwait liberation, and that Yousef had entered JFK six months earlier on an Iraqi passport.

The issue of Yousef's sponsorship wasn't a major focus of the interrogation. Bits and pieces of the story surfaced at different points as the bomb maker responded to the agents' questions. Without even intending to, though, Yousef revealed evidence that should have signaled the FBI to his true backers: Osama bin Laden and Sheikh Omar Abdel Rahman.

For example, Yousef revealed that the date of the WTC bombing was capricious. He struck when he did, he insisted, because the rent was coming due on the Pamrapo Avenue bomb factory in Jersey City and the cell had run out of money.[7] The Iraqi passport, he explained, was a cheap hundred-dollar item he'd picked up in Peshawar, where they were plentiful because of the number of Iraqi rebels who had raided passport offices in northern Iraq.[8] As to the theory that he'd hijacked a Kuwaiti's identity with the help of Saddam's intelligence agents, Yousef said that he'd actually worked in the Kuwait Ministry of Planning, but was forced to flee the country when Iraqi troops invaded in August of 1990.

He also confessed to the agents that he was "interested" in Sheikh Omar Abdel Rahman, who had just gone on trial in New York for the Day of Terror plot. Yousef said he'd requested an audience with the cleric through Mohammed Salameh, and he'd had dinner with the blind Sheikh at his Jersey City apartment.

But potential ties between Abdel Rahman and Saddam Hussein were unlikely: In 1991 the Sheikh had been booed off the pulpit of the Al-Farooq Mosque for a blistering speech attacking the Iraqi invasion of Kuwait. Saddam was just the sort of Arab leader fundamentalists like Rahman and bin Laden abhorred. Their mutual mentor, Sayyid Qutb, had railed against pan-Arabists. Secular Islamists like Saddam Hussein ranked third on their enemies list behind Jews and Christians. As the Sheikh and bin Laden saw it, rulers like Saddam who permitted Western dress and the consumption of alcohol had created what Qutb called a "schizophrenia" among Muslims.[9]

Still, the myth that Yousef and al Qaeda got their marching orders from Iraq would persist right up through the capture of Baghdad in April 2003.

When the plane for Yousef's extradition touched down in Islamabad, the first interrogation ended and he was delivered to agents Parr and Stern on the tarmac. They read him his rights again, and he was marched aboard the plane by members of the Hostage Rescue Team, which specialized in fugitive renditions. At the back of the 707, Yousef was examined by a doctor and given an orange Bureau of Prisons–style jumpsuit.

The agents created a makeshift room in the middle of the aircraft by hanging blankets around a series of seats. Now it was their turn to take a crack at the great "Rashed." Although he was reminded that anything he said could be used against him, Yousef agreed to talk. But he demanded that the Feds take no notes or record him. He may have believed that preventing a record of his confession would allow him to deny it later on. But what Yousef didn't realize, as he began to open up, was that the entire conversation was being monitored via satellite at SIOC inside FBI headquarters in Washington.[10]

Once airborne, Yousef signed a "waiver of rights" and proceeded to talk for hours about his childhood in Fahayhil, his engineering studies at the West Glamorgan Institute, and his education as a bomb maker in the Afghan training camps—one more hint of his al Qaeda ties.

The bomb maker then gave the agents another dot that would have tied him directly to bin Laden, if it had ever been connected to other intelligence. He admitted that on his entry into JFK he'd carried with him a card from Al Bunyan, a newspaper and Arizona cultural center controlled by the Saudi billionaire.

Yousef also told the agents that Mahmud Abouhalima was present at the Pamrapo Avenue apartment as he built the bomb—confirming Emad Salem's charge that if the Feds had followed Abouhalima in the fall of 1992, they would have tumbled to Yousef himself. But the federal prosecutors were wrong, he said, when they tried to put Abouhalima at the Jersey City gas station the night before the bombing. In fact, claimed Yousef, the Ryder van, which had already been reported stolen, had been driven directly to Brooklyn that night. (If true, of course, this would explain why attendant Willie Moosh couldn't possibly have identified Salameh or Abouhalima at trial.) Right or wrong, the allegation revealed how closely Yousef had followed the WTC trial while on the run.[11]

Later, Yousef admitted that Wali Khan Amin Shah was a member of his Manila cell. He said that Shah had given him the business card of Mohammed Jamal Khalifa, the Saudi whose release from detention in San Francisco the State Department had forced earlier that year. Here Yousef was giving the agents two more links to Osama bin Laden: Shah had fought alongside Osama in Afghanistan, and Khalifa was bin Laden's brother-in-law.*

---

*Timeline #15. p. 4; #59. p. 13.

But Yousef stopped short of giving up his true sponsor: he acknowledged that he was "familiar" with the name bin Laden, and knew him to be a relative of Khalifa's, but refused to elaborate.[12]

As the plane closed in on the U.S. mainland, Yousef talked in depth about the Bojinka plot, but according to the FBI 302, he never once mentioned the extensive U.S. flight training of his best friend, Abdul Hakim Murad.

Yousef was also questioned about his plot to kill the pope and his abortive plan to assassinate President Clinton. But the 302 didn't say a word about the airline hijacking–suicide plot Murad had described to Colonel Mendoza.

It was after dark Eastern time when the 707 touched down at Stewart Airport in Orange County, New York. Yousef was transferred to a Sikorsky helicopter for the trip south to the Metropolitan Correctional Center in Lower Manhattan. Later, while the chopper approached the heliport near the Battery, Yousef gave FBI agents a chilling warning of what was to come. As the Sikorsky descended past the gleaming 110-story skyscrapers, one of the agents lifted Yousef's blindfold and gestured toward the Towers. "See," he said. "You didn't get them after all." Yousef eyed him, then fidgeted in his heavy cuffs and snapped back: "Not yet."[13]

At 8:15 A.M. on the morning of February 9, 1995, Ramzi Yousef, dressed in a dark blue suit with a silver-gray tie, was led before federal judge John F. Keenan.[14] With his hands cuffed behind his back, Yousef smiled and chatted with his court-appointed defense lawyer, a young man named Avraham C. Moskowitz.

The fact that his attorney was Jewish didn't seem to affect the bomb maker, who addressed the judge in English with a high-pitched voice. Moskowitz later commented that Yousef seemed "remarkably calm considering what he's facing."

After Yousef entered a plea of not guilty, a date was set for a pretrial hearing before Judge Kevin Duffy, the no-nonsense jurist who'd presided over the original WTC bombing trial. At this point Yousef was being charged with eleven counts in connection with the 1993 bombing. The Feds would later indict him for the PAL Flight 434 bombing, the murder of Haruki Ikegami, and the Bojinka plot.

Secret/Noforn

Yousef's capture, rendition, and arraignment was a stunning victory for the Feds, who suddenly seemed to be on a roll. Only ten days earlier, on January 30, they had begun the Day of Terror conspiracy trial against Sheikh Rahman and eleven others. Now, during a morning session, Judge Michael B. Mukasey interviewed the jurors in chambers to make sure they hadn't been prejudiced by the publicity about Yousef's arrest. He ruled they hadn't, and the epic trial went on.

In his opening statement, Assistant U.S. Attorney Robert Khuzami signaled that the Feds had come to understand the long trail of evidence that connected the Calverton shooting sessions in 1989, the 1990 Kahane murder, and Yousef's Trade Center bombing in 1993. It was a trail, he said, that led all the way to June of that year, when FBI agents descended on the Queens safe house and busted cohorts of the blind Sheikh mixing the "witches brew" meant to blow up twelve New York landmarks.

"This is a case about war," Khuzami told the jury in his opening statement. "The enemy in this war was the United States of America. The battlefield in this war was the streets and the buildings and the tunnels of New York City. The weapons in this war were car bombs and terrorism and homemade explosives. The soldiers who fought this war are seated before you in this courtroom. They called their war jihad."[15]

The Feds had finally come to see the blind Sheikh as the leader of a "jihad army"—a "criminal organization" that included two more Egyptians; the Kahane assassin, El Sayyid Nosair, and his cousin Ibrahim El-Gabrowny. Another coconspirator was Clement Rodney Hampton-El, who had trained at Calverton back in 1989 with Nosair and two of the convicted Trade Center bombers, Abouhalima and Salemeh. One of the masterminds of the current conspiracy was Siddig Siddig Ali, the Sudanese who had helped Abouhalima escape after the Trade Center bombing.

Borrowing the military metaphor from Yousef's own "fifth battalion" threat letter, Khuzami said that the Sheikh's "jihad army . . . spoke of war, they had weapons and committed . . . the kind of destruction and death any Army would be proud of."

The question is, given Yousef's arrest and the intelligence gathered by the Philippine National Police, how much sense did the FBI have of the bigger picture?

Yousef had worked directly with members of the Sheikh's cell who had ties to the Alkifah Center in Brooklyn. With Mustafa Shalabi's death in 1992, the center had turned into an al Qaeda outpost. Hampton-El and Abouhalima had both fought in Afghanistan with "Afghan Arabs" tied to bin Laden. The Sheikh had come to New York, in part, to take over the center's operation.

In effect, both the Sheikh and Ramzi Yousef were agents of the Saudi billionaire. But did the FBI realize that as they analyzed the treasure trove of evidence from the Philippines? The Bureau was now beginning to connect the dots on the threat that the Yousef-Rahman cell had posed to New York. But did they have any sense in 1995 that the "jihad army" was part of bin Laden's global network? Al Qaeda had grown into a terror grid that stretched from the Philippines to Brooklyn to Arizona, but how much did federal investigators know about it back then?

In examining the evidence on the road to 9/11, the answer lies in a once-secret FBI analysis from 1995. The memo, obtained by the author from sources in the Philippines, was designated "SECRET/NOFORN REL TO THE PHILIPPINES."[16] The source is unknown, but its pedigree as an FBI document has been confirmed.[17] The memo was distributed to intelligence officials in the Philippine National Police.

It began with an admission by the FBI that after the WTC bombing in 1993, Yousef had "disappeared" from FBI scrutiny.

SECRET/NOFORN REL TO THE PHILIPPINES 151

RAMZI AHMED YOUSEF: A NEW GENERATION OF SUNNI ISLAMIC
                     TERRORISTS

INTRODUCTION:

     RAMZI AHMED YOUSEF FIRST CAME TO OUR ATTENTION WITH THE
BOMBING OF THE WORLD TRADE CENTER (WTC) BUILDING ON 26 FEBRUARY
1993. AFTER THE ATTACK, HE DISAPPEARED FROM OUR SCREENS. YOUSEF
REAPPEARED IN THE PHILIPPINES IN JANUARY 1995 WHEN YOU
SUCCESSFULLY UNCOVERED HIS PLOT TO ATTACK U.S. AIRLINES AND THE
POPE. THE 7 FEBRUARY ARREST OF YOUSEF IN PAKISTAN, AND YOUR
JANUARY ARREST OF ABDUL HAKIM MURAD, ARE MAJOR COUNTERTERRORISM
VICTORIES. WE BELIEVE THE INFORMATION WE HAVE LEARNED TO DATE
ABOUT YOUSEF AND HIS PLANS TO LAUNCH ATTACKS, HOWEVER,
UNDERSCORES A LARGER THREAT FROM ISLAMIC TERRORISTS. WE CONTINUE
TO TRACK DOWN LEADS FROM THE INVESTIGATION AND ARE STILL
ATTEMPTING TO IDENTIFY AND LOCATE OTHER ASSOCIATES OF YOUSEF.

The memo confirmed that the Bureau had received Colonel Mendoza's intelligence from his briefings of Murad. It acknowledged that "Yousef and Murad . . . discussed future attacks in the U.S. including possibly flying a plane filled with explosives into the CIA building" and possibly attacking "a U.S. nuclear facility."

```
     A.  NORTH AMERICA

          1) THE WTC BOMBING IN 1993 CLEARLY DEMONSTRATES
YOUSEF'S ABILITY TO ENTER THE UNITED STATES, ESTABLISH A SUPPORT
STRUCTURE, RECRUIT A TERRORIST TEAM, AND SUCCESSFULLY CARRY OUT
AN ATTACK.

          2) YOUSEF IS ABLE TO USE HIS FRIENDS AND ASSOCIATES IN
FOREIGN COUNTRIES TO IDENTIFY POSSIBLE TARGETS.  AN EXAMPLE OF
THIS IS YOUSEF'S REQUEST TO MURAD, WHILE HE (MURAD) WAS IN THE
U.S. FOR PILOT TRAINING, TO CHOOSE AN APPROPRIATE SITE FOR AN
ATTACK.  MURAD CHOSE THE WTC BUILDING.

          3) YOUSEF AND MURAD ALSO DISCUSSED FUTURE ATTACKS IN
THE U.S. INCLUDING POSSIBLY FLYING A PLANE FILLED WITH EXPLOSIVES
INTO THE CIA BUILDING.  MURAD ALSO MENTIONED THAT IN JUNE OF THIS
YEAR HE WAS TO TRAVEL TO THE U.S. AND POSSIBLY ATTACK A U.S.
NUCLEAR FACILITY.
```

Concluding that Yousef was part of "a new generation of terrorists" with "access to a worldwide network of support for funding, training and safe haven," the memo linked Yousef with the Day of Terror plotters then on trial in New York. At first glance, then, the memo appeared to be a cogent analysis of the combined intel from New York and Manila. It recognized bin Laden and the presence of a "worldwide network." But then the memo reached an astonishing conclusion:

```
     --THOSE INVOLVED IN THE WTC BOMBING AND A SECOND GROUP OF
EXTREMISTS WHO PLOTTED TO BOMB OTHER LANDMARKS IN NEW YORK CITY,
INCLUDING THE UNITED NATIONS BUILDING, DID NOT BELONG TO A
SINGLE, COHESIVE ORGANIZATION, BUT RATHER WERE PART OF A LOOSE
GROUP OF POLITICALLY COMMITTED MUSLIMS LIVING IN THE AREA.  THEY
WERE OF VARYING NATIONALITIES INCLUDING EGYPTIAN, SUDANESE,
PAKISTANI, PALESTINIAN, AND IRAQI.
```

While recognizing a "larger threat from Islamic terrorists," the memo denied the existence of a "cohesive organization" that could follow through on the threat. Within the very same document, FBI analysts seemed unable to connect the dots.* Further, while the memo noted Murad's early confessed plan to hit the CIA with a plane, it said nothing about the broader third plot, which called for the hijacking of commercial jetliners—or about his intended targets, which included the Pentagon and the Trade Center. There was no mention of Murad's extensive U.S. flight school training, or the fact that jihadis were training at American aviation schools *at that very moment.*

All of this had been revealed by Murad and reported to the FBI by Mendoza. But none of it seems to have been factored into the Bureau's analysis.

Jim Gomez and John Solomon of the Associated Press later reported that the PNP had given the U.S. authorities a list with the names of ten men Murad had met with, who were then engaged in U.S. flight training.[18] The *Washington Post* confirmed that in 1996 FBI agents questioned officials at two of Murad's flight schools, Coastal Aviation in New Bern, North Carolina, and Richmore Aviation in Schenectady, New York.[19]

But apparently the investigation went no further.

On the weekend of Yousef's capture, John P. O'Neill had just taken over as head of the FBI's counterterrorism section. A brash, high-profile FBI veteran, the forty-two-year-old O'Neill had been assistant special agent in charge of the Bureau's Chicago office. He was later celebrated in the media as "the Bureau's most committed tracker of Osama bin Laden and his Al Qaeda network."[20] He went on two years later to become agent in charge of the National Security Division in New York.

"The first time I ever heard the name Osama bin Laden, was from John O'Neill," said Robert "Bear" Bryant, the Bureau's former deputy director.[21]

O'Neill was the best and the brightest the FBI had on matters of counterterrorism. If there was anyone in the Bureau who recognized the threat from bin Laden, it was John O'Neill. He was widely credited with predicting the 9/11 attacks. In fact, a 2002 PBS *Frontline* documentary on O'Neill was entitled "The Man Who Knew."

---

*Timeline #78. p. 17.

But when it came to the FBI's follow-up on Murad's startling revelations from the Philippines, the documentary acknowledged that "agents were dispatched and withdrawn. The investigation languished."

What went wrong? Why didn't the Bureau catch on to the connections between Yousef and bin Laden back in 1995? A trail of heretofore secret documents suggests that the Philippine National Police had given them more than enough evidence to connect the dots.

In the spring of 1995, Colonel Mendoza of the PNP sent the Feds a flow chart that spelled it all out. Entitled "Liberation Army Connection," the chart drew a straight line between bin Laden, through Khalifa, to the deadly Abu Sayyaf terror group. It showed that funding for Yousef's cell came via the front company Konsonjaya, set up by bin Laden's brother-in-law Khalifa. From Konsonjaya, the money flowed through Wali Khan Amin Shah ("Usama Asmorai") to Yousef ("Adam Ali") and his uncle Khalid Shaikh Mohammed ("Salem Ali"). Their partner in crime was Abdul Hakim Murad. The chart (see p. 304) even showed how Shah, Yousef, and Mohammed had used the Philippines B-girls as fronts.

Another 1995 FBI secret/noforn memo on the evidence seized in Room 603 at the Dona Josefa acknowledged a "Konsonjaya connection." It speculated that documents found relating to "International Trading Corporation may be identifiable with . . . Laden International Company for Trading Ltd, headquartered in the Sudan." The memo noted that this "may be an umbrella company for other enterprises fully or partially owned by Saudi investor and al Gamma'a Islamiya supporter Usama bin Laden."[22]

The al Gamma'a Islamiya, or IG, of course, was the Egyptian radical group dominated by blind Sheikh Rahman. As early as 1991, Lou Napoli in the New York JTTF had tied the IG to El Sayyid Nosair, Kahane's shooter. Now the FBI, in a secret memo, was drawing a link between the group and Osama bin Laden himself.

The question is obvious: if the FBI had so much evidence tying Ramzi Yousef and his uncle Khalid Shaikh Mohammed to al Qaeda and bin Laden in 1995, why didn't they pull out the stops to investigate Murad's revelations about the airline hijacking plot? The answer harkens back to a division inside the Bureau that haunted the first WTC investi-

NETWORK DIAGRAM OF THE INTERNATIONAL TERRORISTS' ("LIBERATION ARMY") CONNECTIONS*

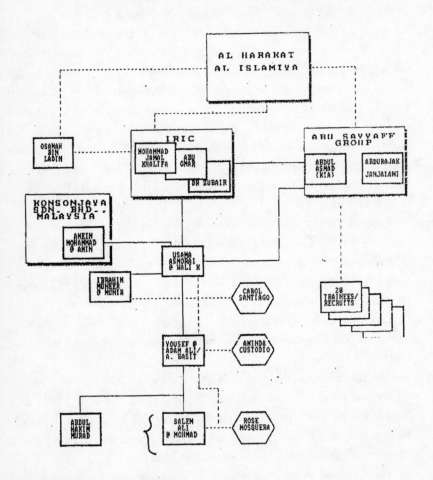

* BASED ON DATA OBTAINED FROM THE OPERATION

gation: the distinction between intelligence gathering and criminal prosecution. Identifying this as a key reason for the FBI's failures leading up
to 9/11, in 2002 the Joint Congressional Inquiry would dub this bureau-
cratic chasm "the wall."[23]

Actually, there were multiple walls. The first was the barrier that separated the FBI's intelligence branches from those that investigated and
prosecuted criminal cases. Nancy Floyd's Foreign Counter Intelligence
unit was able to run "assets" to gather information on threats to national
security—moles who could burrow into threat groups and never be
expected to testify.

Emad Salem was recruited under the rules on that side of the wall;
then, after Salem developed evidence of Nosair's potential bombing
conspiracy, Carson Dunbar pushed him over the wall to the criminal
side.

The investigation of terrorism is a "hybrid," FBI agent John Anticev
told Salem at the time.

"It's half counter intelligence rules, half criminal. And how to apply
one from the other is still a gray area. Things can happen when you're
doing an intelligence case. All of a sudden it turns immediately into a
criminal case."[24]

The matter was complicated by Rule 6E of the Federal Rules of
Criminal Procedure, which prevented the disclosure of grand jury material,[25] and another administrative rule adopted in 1994 that prohibited
the FBI or CIA from contacting prosecutors in the Internal Security Section of the Justice Department.[26] The principle of grand jury secrecy has
its origins in seventeenth-century British practice. Rule 6E was fashioned
to service a multitude of interests: prevention of jury tampering, protection of the innocent who might later be exonerated, prevention of flight
by the accused, and the hope that secret proceedings might make witnesses more candid.[27]

FBI agent Michael Rolince later testified before the Joint Inquiry that
the rules separating criminal and investigative cases in the FBI "became
so complex and convoluted that in some FBI field offices agents perceived 'walls' where none actually existed. In fact, one New York supervisor commented that 'so many walls had created a maze.' "[28]

In her book *The War Against America,* scholar Laurie Mylroie observed that "once an arrest is made, the Justice Department declares the matter subjudice and denies information to the national security bureaucracies."

By 1995, the primary focus in the incipient war on terror was moving from the street to the courtroom. This, according to Mylroie, created "an organizational firewall"[29] between intelligence gatherers and prosecutors.

At this point, Abouhalima, Salameh, Ajaj, and Ayyad had been convicted in the 1993 bombing; Yousef had been indicted; the blind Sheikh et al. were on trial for the Day of Terror conspiracy; and Justice Department lawyers were preparing indictments against Yousef, Murad, and Wali Khan Amin Shah for the Bojinka plot.

The government was becoming a victim of its own success. Despite prosecutor Khuzami's reference to the jihad "war," the Justice Department was breaking up the conspiracy into a series of prosecutions rather than viewing Ramzi Yousef and Sheikh Rahman as part of a much broader threat to American security.

In a Justice Department where the career paths of assistant U.S. attorneys and FBI agents were tied to conviction rates, not the prevention of future crimes, the Feds couldn't see the forest for the trees. Now that they had Ramzi Yousef, the last big "get" in the "jihad army" conspiracy, there was a sense in the Southern District that this would all soon be over. The office that "got Gotti" was going to mop up the last remnants of what the noforn memo had called "a loose group of committed Muslims."

Bob Blitzer, assistant section chief for the FBI's Counterterrorism and Middle East section, seemed to speak for the Bureau's failure to grasp the intelligence it possessed after the TRADEBOM and Day of Terror investigations. "In the aftermath of the [1993] bombing, we were seeing people that we had never seen before. Much of it made sense during these criminal investigations. Many, many new people came on our radar screen. However, nothing we had then, indicated either an imminent attack or defined the long term threat picture."[30]

But there was one man in New York who believed the threat was still ongoing. On the morning of Yousef's arraignment, Ronnie Bucca was sitting in the back of the courtroom. He'd finally gotten into a room with the mysterious Rashed, but Yousef was quickly whisked from court immediately after his plea. Ronnie's reserve unit, attached to the Defense Intelligence Agency, was just beginning to get a sense of the multilayered terror plots Yousef had spun in the Philippines. Now the master bomber was caught.

That night, back at home, Eve asked Ronnie if he was happy. Yousef, the mastermind behind the WTC bombing, was out of commission at last. He could relax now.

But Ronnie eyed her. "I don't know. I'm not sure."

"What do you mean?" said Eve. "They've got the guy."[31]

"That's what they said when they arrested Nosair back in '90," said Ronnie. "There's a lot more intel coming in from the Philippines. I want to look at that and see what it says."

"So you still think there's some kind of danger from these people?"

Ronnie looked away, then he turned to her.

"Remember the letter he sent to the *Times*? He was talking about a hundred and fifty suicide soldiers. The DIA figures there are thousands of these guys who fought the Russians running around the world. Are you asking me if there could still be a problem?"

Eve nodded—as anxious as the next person to finally put all of this to rest.

"My gut tells me, yeah," said Ronnie. "There is."

30

JOHN DOE NO. 2

Nine weeks later terror struck America again, in the form of a bomb delivered in another yellow Ryder truck. At 9:00 A.M. on April 19, 1995, a twenty-foot GMC twin-axle model parked outside the America's Kids Day Care Center at the Alfred P. Murrah Federal Building in Oklahoma City.[1] Inside was a 5,600-pound device made of ammonium nitrate and nitromethane, a racing fuel. At 9:02:13 A.M. it detonated. In an instant, 168 people, including nineteen children, were dead.

An hour and a half after the blast, on Interstate 35, an Oklahoma highway patrolman stopped a yellow Mercury Marquis that had been driving without a plate. Behind the wheel, carrying a loaded .45 caliber Glock pistol, was Timothy McVeigh, a former Army sergeant. He was immediately arrested and locked up in the courthouse in nearby Perry, Oklahoma.

Soon, in a remarkable replay of the WTC investigation, the FBI traced a VIN number on the axle of the Ryder to a rental agency in Junc-

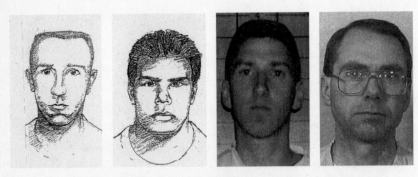

Left to right: Artist's sketches of Robert Kling and John Doe No. 2; photographs of Tim McVeigh and Terry Nichols.

tion City, Kansas. There, witnesses gave police a description of the two men who rented the truck. An artist's sketch was prepared. One suspect, who gave his name as Robert Kling, was described as five-foot-ten and 180 pounds, with light hair and a medium build.[2]

The second man, who would become known as "John Doe No. 2," was variously described as five-foot-nine to -ten, with a dark complexion, brown hair combed straight, and a tattoo on his left arm.[3] Using the sketch in a door-to-door canvass, police traced "Kling" to a motel in Junction City, where he'd rented a room under his real name: Tim McVeigh. As his place of residence he'd given the address of a farm in Decker, Michigan, that was occupied by James Nichols. When an FBI SWAT team swooped down on the farm, they learned that Nichols's younger brother Terry lived in Kansas.

The next morning, in a routine phone check, the police discovered that McVeigh was already in custody. When Terry Nichols learned that the Feds were after him, he promptly surrendered.[4]

But there was a problem. While the suspect sketch for John Doe No. 1 was a dead ringer for McVeigh, Nichols was a pale-skinned Anglo with a thin neck and glasses. He looked nothing like the dark, swarthy John Doe No. 2 in the sketch. Furthermore, in the hours immediately after the bombing, an APB had gone out for suspects seen near a brown Chevy pickup. They were described as being of Middle Eastern extraction. Acting on what he'd heard in those early hours, David McCurdy, former U.S. congressman from Oklahoma and chairman of the House Intelligence Committee, announced that the bombing was the work of Middle Eastern terrorists.[5]

The evidence linking Nichols and McVeigh to the bomb was convincing. The pair had first met in 1988 during Army basic training in Georgia. Nichols later served with McVeigh at Fort Riley, Kansas. The previous September, Nichols had bought two thousand pounds of ammonium nitrate fertilizer; two weeks later he bought another ton.

An associate, Michael Fortier, who became a government witness, described how McVeigh had experimented with pipe bombs and other explosives. McVeigh and Nichols had rented storage lockers together where materials were kept.

On April 17, a Ryder truck like the one that carried the bomb was seen behind Nichols's house in Kansas. The next day, a Ryder truck and a pickup resembling Nichols's GMC Sierra were seen near a lake where investigators soon found a substance believed to be fuel oil. Investigators later identified this as the point where the delicate mixture of racing fuel and fertilizer was combined.

But the FBI said it was pressing ahead in the hunt for "John Doe No. 2." In fact, the federal indictment named Nichols, McVeigh, and "others unknown," suggesting, at that point in early May, that the Feds still believed the two angry ex–Army buddies were involved in a broader conspiracy.[6]

The Bureau then embarked on the biggest manhunt in American history.[7] Ten thousand phone tips were processed, and dozens of John Doe No. 2 lookalikes were interviewed. The suspect was further described by witnesses at McVeigh's motel as being five-foot-nine with dark brown hair brushed back and olive skin.

On the morning of the bombing, a witness at a tire store said that McVeigh had stopped to ask directions to the Murrah Building. The man with him was "dark skinned." Daina Bradley, who lost a leg in the explosion, remembered seeing the yellow Ryder truck pull up minutes before the blast; a man got out, she said, wearing a dark blue jacket and baseball cap.[8] Bradley, who also lost her mother and two children in the bombing, testified that the man was not McVeigh. Nor, apparently, was it Nichols. According to his wife, Marife, Terry was at home in Herington, Kansas, at the time.

Perhaps the most probative description of John Doe No. 2 came from FBI Special Agent Henry C. Gibbons, a twenty-six-year FBI veteran. In a sworn affidavit, Gibbons reported that on April 19 "a witness near the scene of the explosion saw two individuals running from the area of the Federal Building toward a brown Chevrolet truck. The individuals were described as males, of possible Middle Eastern descent."[9]

But once Nichols and McVeigh were charged, and federal prosecutors began gearing up for trial, the Justice Department quietly dialed back on the hunt for a third suspect. By 1997 federal officials were asserting that the original sketch of the dark, olive-skinned man was based on a mistake by a witness.[10]

Nichols and McVeigh were eventually convicted and McVeigh executed, insisting to the end that there had been no outside help.

Both Bomb Makers in Cebu

The case for a Mideast connection to the blast is circumstantial but worthy of review, given what we now know about Ramzi Yousef's capabilities, and about a curious series of events and connections leading up to the blast. None of them, in isolation, is conclusive, but as pieces of the larger "mosaic" they raise questions.

On the morning of April 19, while sitting in his cell in New York federal jail, Abdul Hakim Murad made a startling claim. After listening to a radio report on the Oklahoma City bombing, a Bureau of Prisons guard went to Murad's cell. When the guard asked what Murad thought about the bombing, the prisoner shot back, "That was us."

"What are you talking about?" asked the startled guard.

"Oklahoma City. The bomb," said Murad. "We did that."

The guard eyed him. How could he possibly be connected with a bombing in another state when he was in federal jail?

Murad had just arrived in New York six days earlier after leaving the Philippines, where he'd been held in detention for more than two months. But the terrorist asked for a paper and pen. He wrote down some words and passed the note back to the guard.

It said "We claim credit in the name of the Liberation Army."[11]

If a boast like that had come from just any prisoner, it might have been dismissed out of hand. But the claim of credit was now coming from the oldest friend of the world's most notorious bomber.

Yousef was down the hall in the ultrasecure Special Housing Unit of the MCC, where he'd been held since his rendition on February 8. But two other coconspirators from his Manila cell were still on the loose. Wali Khan Amin Shah had escaped from the PNP at Camp Crame after his arrest on January 12, and Yousef's uncle Khalid Shaikh Mohammed was virtually unknown to the Feds at this point.

Was it possible that Ramzi Yousef could somehow have been tied to this second strike on America? Murad's claim seemed preposterous, but the FBI wasn't taking any chances.

The day after the bombing, Special Agent Frank Pellegrino and Secret Service Agent Brian Parr were dispatched to the MCC. They interviewed the guard's boss, Lt. Philip Rojas, who confirmed that Murad had made the statement. The agents then summarized their findings in an FBI 302.* In the trial of Yousef, Murad, and Shah for the Bojinka plot a year later, the Feds would point to that 302 as evidence that as late as April 19, 1995, Murad was still involved in a conspiracy.[12]

That fact alone doesn't necessarily tie Yousef to the Murrah Building bomb, but there's a pattern of other circumstantial evidence connecting him to the device. All of it relates to McVeigh's bombing partner, Terry Nichols.

Yousef and Shah applied for their final visas to the Philippines in Singapore on November 3, 1994.[13] The very next day, at the Philippines consulate in Chicago, Nichols got his visa.[14] Trial records and documents from the Philippine National Police show that Nichols was in Cebu City at the same time as Yousef in December 1994—staying in a section of the Visayas island group that was a hotbed of Islamic fundamentalism.

Nichols had extensive Philippine connections. In 1989, after divorcing his first wife, a Las Vegas real estate broker named Lana Padilla, he married Marife Torres, a nineteen-year-old Filapina from Cebu City.[15] Nichols was a disaffected ne'er-do-well who had railed against the government for years. An out-of-work farmer, he seemed to have been virtually destitute from the early 1990s to the moment of his arrest. In 1992 Nichols was sued by Chase Manhattan Bank for $17,860 in unpaid credit card debt.[16] In March 1994, in an effort to avoid paying taxes, he filed an affidavit declaring himself a "non resident alien."[17] That same month he moved Marife to Marion, Kansas, where he answered a help-wanted ad in a farm journal and took a job as a ranch hand.[18]

Yet Nichols seemed to have unknown sources of funding. From 1990 to 1994 he made at least four trips to the Philippines and lived with Marife for a time in Cebu City, not far from where the Abu Sayyaf terror group was active.†

Before departing on his last trip to Cebu on November 22, 1994, Nichols gave his ex-wife, Padilla, a series of letters and instructions to be implemented if he didn't return within sixty days.

One handwritten note told McVeigh to clean out a pair of storage lock-

---

*Timeline #83. p. 18.
†Timeline #84. p. 18.

ers and "Go for it." The postcript said, "This letter would be for purposes of my death." Fearing her ex-husband might be suicidal, Padilla opened her letter immediately. It directed her to a bag hidden in her kitchen containing $20,000 in cash.[19]

There were keys to a storage locker, which contained a bizarre cache of wigs, ski masks, panty hose, and gold coins, along with gold bars and bullion estimated to be worth $60,000. The Feds later claimed that this was the swag from a robbery Nichols had committed in Arkansas, but evidence presented at Nichols's and McVeigh's separate trials later challenged that theory.[20]

Whatever the source of the income, the notes Nichols left with Padilla suggested that he believed his last trip to the Philippines would be dangerous. Nichols stayed in Cebu City from late November until January 16, 1995—the same period when Yousef was in Manila planning the plot against the pope, the Bojinka airline bombings, and the suicide hijackings.

That might be dismissed as coincidental—except for a sworn affidavit from Edwin Angeles, the former leader of the Abu Sayyaf Group, who later cooperated with the PNP.

During a police interrogation in 1996, Angeles swore that he had met Yousef, Shah, and Murad in Davao City in the southern Philippines as early as 1991. Present at the meeting, he said, was a man named Terry Nichols, who was introduced to Angeles as "a farmer."[21] Angeles said that they discussed "training on bomb making and handling." In a summary of the police report on the interrogation, Angeles identified the site of the meeting as the Del Monte labeling factory in Davao City.[22] He later drew a sketch of the so-called "farmer" that bore a striking resemblance to Nichols.*

PNP intelligence documents show that Murad was training at a Philippines flight school from December 1990 to January 1991.[23] Yousef was on the southern Philippines island of Basilan training Abu Sayyaf terrorists in the summer of 1991.[24]

There was other official evidence of a possible Yousef-Nichols connection.

In 1996 Oscar P. Coronel, chief of the Intelligence Division of the

*Timeline #84. p. 18.

Philippines Bureau of Immigration, issued a report to his commissioner regarding interviews he conducted in reference to Marife Nichols. His handwritten notes in an attachment entitled "Summary Information Sheet" indicate that a "group of aliens of [the] Nichols group" included "Pakistanis, Abu Sayaf [sic], Arab Nationals," and "other middle east terrorist[s]."[25]

Meanwhile, after Nichols left Manila, a phone card used by him and McVeigh in the name of Darryl Bridges showed a total of seventy-eight calls to a guest house in Cebu where Marife had been staying. The guest house was owned by her uncle, who had once lived in Saudi Arabia. It was reportedly frequented by Muslim fundamentalist students from a nearby college. There were twenty-two attempts to get through to the guest house on February 14 alone.[26]

Was Nichols simply desperate to connect with Marife's family, or was he calling for follow-up advice on how to build an ammonium nitrate–nitromethane bomb?

Yousef had fled Manila by the time Nichols left in mid-January 1995, and there's no hard evidence that the two ever met in December 1994. The only time that Yousef was known for certain to be in Cebu during this period was for a few hours as he fled back to Manila following his "wet test" on the PAL flight December 11. But the logbook of the Dona Josefa Apartments shows visits to Room 603 by a man named "Nick" while Yousef was in residence.[27]

It's impossible to say whether that "Nick" was Terry Nichols, but the idea that two men connected to the two most notorious bombings on U.S. soil would be in the same remote town in the Philippines seems more than coincidental, especially considering that each of them was connected to a fertilizer-fuel device of enormous destructive power, delivered to its target in a yellow Ryder truck.

At McVeigh's trial, his lawyer Stephen Jones tried to introduce evidence of "others unknown," referencing a Philippine connection to the bombing, but the evidence was excluded.[28] Jones had developed information that as early as August 1990 Nichols had asked a Philippines tour guide named Daisy Legaspi if she "knew someone who knows how to make bombs."[29] Further, a number of calls on the Darryl Bridges card were made to Starglad Lumber in Cebu. The manager of Starglad was one Serafin Uy, whose brother was slain after being suspected in a series of kidnappings in Mindanao. When a U.S. consulate representative interviewed Uy, he said that Marife Nichols's father—a former policeman he knew—had found a book on the making of explosives in Nichols's personal effects left in Cebu.[30]

Jones was convinced that Nichols had gone to Cebu on that last trip to study bomb making from the master himself: Ramzi Yousef.

"Tim couldn't blow up a rock," Jones told *Insight* magazine.[31]

But right after that trip Nichols and McVeigh reportedly began building a device of enormous destructive power—despite the fact that they were relatively inexperienced as bomb makers. That point was underscored at trial by Michael Fortier, the government's star witness.

He testified that while the pair experimented with small pipe and bottle bombs, McVeigh's one attempt at exploding an ammonium nitrate–fuel oil device in a milk jug "didn't work."[32]

"The one time that we know of when McVeigh experiments with an ANFO bomb it's a dud," Oklahoma attorney Mike Johnston said in an interview for this book.[33] "Then Nichols goes to the Philippines while Ramzi is there, and after that these guys build an even more sophisticated ammonium nitrate–nitromethane device that takes down the federal building. What are the odds?"

Also interviewed for the book, Jones said that his own explosives experts, hired for McVeigh's defense, doubted whether he or Nichols had the expertise to build the Murrah Building device. McVeigh made a crude sketch of the bomb for the experts, but when pressed on where he got the knowledge to build such a complicated device, McVeigh came up with a vague story.

"He said, 'Well I found this book at the Kingman Library,'" said Jones, recalling McVeigh's explanation. "And I said, 'You found a book in the Kingman, Arizona, Public Library that tells you how to build a *bomb* that will blow up a building and kill a hundred and sixty-eight people?' And he said, 'Yes.'"[34]

Jones said he asked McVeigh for the book's title, but the self-confessed bomb builder couldn't remember. So Jones's investigators searched the Kingman library.

"Of course, they couldn't find anything like it," he said.

McVeigh insisted to the end that he and Nichols had acted alone. But his own lawyer remains unconvinced.

"There simply is no evidence," said Jones, "that Terry Nichols or Tim McVeigh or anybody known to have been associated with them had the expertise, knowledge, skill, [and] patience to construct an improvised device that would bring down a modern nine-story office building."

In the absence of any other explanation, Jones believes today that Nichols and McVeigh got their bomb-building knowledge from Ramzi Yousef.

"The Philippines connection is the most credible, most consistent, and frankly most complete explanation of how they built the bomb," he said. "It's not perfectly complete, but there's no other explanation. There's nobody else that's been identified. No other organization that's been identified. There simply is a lack of evidence of anybody else."

Attorney Mike Johnston agrees, but he believes that Yousef had a different paymaster than Osama bin Laden. On March 14, 2002, he filed suit in U.S. District Court against the Republic of Iraq.[35] Suggesting that Yousef was an Iraqi agent, the complaint alleged "dramatic similarities" between the 1993 World Trade Center bomb and the Oklahoma City device.

In a motion for Summary Judgment filed March 3, 2003, Johnston added a tantalizing new piece of evidence to his theory that Yousef designed the bomb for Nichols and McVeigh. He claimed that a cell phone rented in Manila for Abdul Hakim Murad "showed continued usage until March 1995"—that is, after Murad's arrest, suggesting that someone else involved with the Yousef cell was using it.

Four calls on the phone were reportedly made from the Philippines to area code 918, which is in eastern Oklahoma. According to Johnston, the Daryl Bridges phone card used by Nichols and McVeigh showed calls to Starglad Lumber in Cebu "during this exact time."[36]

"You had the most notorious bomb-building terrorist on earth in the same Philippines city as one of the Oklahoma City conspirators," said Johnston. "Both Nichols and McVeigh were lightweights when it came to explosives. Terry goes to Cebu, and when he comes back he helps build a device with the same kind of design and explosive power as the Trade Center bomb. That's a fact pattern that simply defies probability."[37]

O.K. City Bomb Threatens Day of Terror Mistrial

Is it conceivable that Ramzi Yousef, in the midst of planning three ambitious acts of terror, found the time to teach Terry Nichols how to build a weapon of mass destruction?

Yousef was clearly a teacher. Testimony in the Bojinka case would show that he made diagrams of his Casio-nitroglycerine bomb for both Murad and Wali Khan Amin Shah.[38] He'd given bomb-making lessons to the Abu Sayyaf Group, and had planned to visit Egypt, France, and Algeria to teach al Qaeda terror cells how to build his undetectable bomb. The Oklahoma City device reportedly bore similarities to both the UNFO bomb Yousef used at the Trade Center and the ANFO bomb he was suspected of designing to destroy the Israeli Embassy in Bangkok.

But Yousef's own attorney scoffs at any hint of an Oklahoma City bombing tie.

"The allegations of a connection between my client and the Murrah Building bomb are completely specious," said Bernie Kleinman, who has represented Yousef since after the Bojinka trial.[39] "It was Stephen Jones's ridiculous attempt to find some other basis for representing his client. There's zero in that. There were a lot of guys in the Philippines looking for wives, and Nichols happened to be there when Yousef was there. I also thought it was funny that the one purported witness [Edwin Angeles] turned out to be an incredibly good sketch artist. What a coincidence. It was like the people who see UFOs."

Nevertheless, Kleinman said, he suspects that Nichols and McVeigh may have had outside help—from right-wing militia groups.[40]

At one point after sentencing, McVeigh was actually on the same cell block as Yousef in the Supermax prison. Incredibly, the two convicted bombers were able to converse. A source close to Yousef in the prison said that the bomb maker had expressed the opinion that McVeigh was incapable of building the Oklahoma City device on his own.[41]

As to Yousef's connection to Nichols, Kleinman said he asked his client about the issue only once. "He didn't say no," said Kleinman. "But there was an expression on his face like 'What a stupid thing to say.'"

Still, conspiracy Web sites and journalists on the political right and left alike have continued to support the theory, and in October 2002 it was given further credence by an article and editorial in the *Wall Street Journal*.[42]

Whether Yousef was involved or not, the timing of the OKC bombing threatened to cause a mistrial in the case against his supporter in the Trade Center bombing, Sheikh Omar Abdel Rahman. The day after the Murrah Building devastation, lawyers for the defendants in the Day of Terror case alleged that the graphic news from Oklahoma City prevented their clients from getting a fair trial. Their motion came three months into the epic proceeding, after 7,500 pages of testimony had been heard. A mistrial at that point would have been incredibly costly for the government, and in the absence of any hard evidence that the jury had been prejudiced by the Oklahoma bombing publicity, Judge Mukasey denied the motion. Also, just as he'd done earlier in the days following Yousef's arrest, he refused defense requests to sequester the jury.

When word of the Murrah Building disaster spread, the blind Sheikh's reaction was true to form. He had earlier denied any connection to Abouhalima or Salameh after the Trade Center bombing, even though the two terrorists had interacted with him closely for months. Now, on the day after Judge Mukasey's decision to continue his trial, Rahman's lawyer Lynn Stewart stood on the courthouse steps and told the media that her client had "expressed shock" at the news from Oklahoma City.[43]

31

THE DEVIL HIMSELF

R amzi Yousef had spent the past two years criss-crossing the globe in first class as he plotted mass murder. Now he was kept in twenty-three-hour-a-day solitary lockdown on the ninth floor of the Metropolitan Correctional Center. During the single hour he was permitted to exercise, his only option was to submit to a strip cavity search. Following that he would be shackled, cuffed to a belly belt, and led through six steel doors before arriving at the twelfth-floor recreation cage on the roof of the federal jail. An inch-thick wire mesh canopy covered the cage, and before Yousef was allowed out onto the roof it was given a shakedown by Bureau of Prisons guards.[1]

More often than not, though, Yousef chose to exercise in a small gallery area near his cell. The man whose taste ran to fine clothes and karaoke bars now lived in an orange jumpsuit, with an olive-drab fatigue jacket to shield him from the cold. The enigma with two dozen names was now a number: 03911-000. Yet despite his confinement, Ramzi Yousef maintained the same level of bravado he'd exhibited when detonating his first gasoline can bomb in the Jalozai training camp five years earlier.

Just days after his arrival, Yousef boldly agreed to talk openly with FBI agents and prosecutors. It was a move that few defendants facing life in prison would consent to unless they were expecting a deal. But given the political pressure surrounding his terror spree, there was zero chance the Feds would ever allow Yousef to cop a plea.

Nonetheless, on February 13, 1995, in a room at the U.S. Courthouse across from 26 Federal Plaza, Yousef met with Gil Childers, who'd prosecuted the first Trade Center bombing case, and the two assistant U.S. attorneys who had worked with him: Lev Dassin and Michael J. Garcia.[2]

Also present were FBI agents Pellegrino and Stern and Brian Parr of the Secret Service. The prisoner was accompanied by his court-appointed lawyer, Avraham Moskowitz. The meeting began with the signature of a written proffer by Childers and Moskowitz. Proffers open the door for a defendant to become a possible cooperating witness. In the early stages of talks, to ensure that the accused doesn't make an incriminating statement that can be used against him, the proffer defines the scope of the material to be discussed. In this case Yousef's attorney agreed that the meeting would be limited to the role of Yousef and the other four defendants in the Trade Center bombing.[3] Bojinka and PAL Flight 434 were off the table.

Right away, Ramzi launched into a lecture on the design of the 1,500-pound Trade Center device, noting that it was constructed using a booster with a 20-kilogram mix of ammonium nitrate, nitromethane, and analite. (A similar lethal mixture would be used less than three months later in the main body of the Oklahoma City bomb.)[4]

Yousef then confirmed the participation of Salameh and Abouhalima in the WTC bombing plot, reinforcing Emad Salem's contention that if the FBI had followed them closely they could have nailed the bomber known as "Rashed" in the fall of 1992. Yousef also admitted that Ayyad had typed the "Liberation Army" letter on his computer after Salameh had given him Ramzi's draft, and acknowledged that he'd met Ajaj at a camp in Afghanistan—another hint of Yousef's al Qaeda links.

But the bomb maker said little more about his true sponsor until two months later.

On April 10, Yousef consented to an interview with Raghida Dirgham, New York bureau chief for the Arab-language daily newspaper *Al Hayat*. The interview was published in Arabic two days later, and though a few lines were quoted in U.S. dailies,[5] the full details of Yousef's long talk with Dirgham have never been published in English until now.

Dirgham had earlier interviewed El Sayyid Nosair, and apparently

Yousef knew her work. The bomb maker insisted that she bring only a pad and pen to the session; he refused to allow a tape recorder. He met her in what the reporter described as "a cold room" at the MCC, containing only a table and two chairs. There was no lawyer present, and though a pair of guards waited outside, the terrorist wore no handcuffs as he sat across the table from Dirgham, a slender, attractive Lebanese woman.

In what would be the only on-the-record public interview he gave after his arrest, Yousef admitted to being "an explosives expert" and "an electronics engineer." He said his real name was Abdul Al-Basit al Baluchi and told Dirgham that he didn't care if he was characterized as a "terrorist." When asked if he thought of himself as a genius, Yousef smiled shyly and said "Yes."[6]

The prisoner had come to the interview armed with a yellow legal pad covered with notes in both English and Arabic. "He wanted to express his agenda," said Dirgham. "So I let him talk without being judgmental. As a result, he opened up to me even more."[7]

As he had before in his interrogations with the FBI agents, Yousef said that although he was a Kuwaiti by birth, his main "affiliation" was with the Palestinians.

"I believe that this [Liberation] movement, and Palestinians generally, are entitled to strike U.S. targets because the United States is a partner in the crimes committed in Palestine," said Yousef, "considering that it finances these crimes and supports them with weapons."

Dirgham asked if Yousef's agenda included U.S. "civilian targets."

The bomb maker nodded. "They [Israel] are the ones who started with civilian targets in Palestine . . . so they practice the collective punishment system against us, such as curfews, demolition of homes, and the sealing off of buildings. These are the means to which Israeli authorities resort. If any individual carries out an operation in a city, they punish everybody. The United States is applying the system of collective punishment against Iraq and Libya. When either government makes any mistake, the United States punishes the people in their entirety for the government's mistake. We are reciprocating the treatment."

For months now, media speculation that Yousef was an agent of Iraq had been growing.[8] But to Dirgham he denied the idea flatly.

"I have no connection with Iraq or with other governmental circles," he said. "I only support the Liberation Army." When Dirgham asked who headed it, Yousef said, "This is confidential." But he went on to say that "one of the Liberation Army's goals has been to aid members of Egypt's Islamic Group (IG) and Jihad Group, Palestine's Hamas . . . Islamic Jihad, and Algeria's FIS (Islamic Salvation Front) and armed Islamic movements."

In that one sentence, Yousef was handing the Feds a series of dots that connected him directly to al Qaeda and Osama bin Laden. First, the IG (al Gamm'a Islamiya), was the radical group led by Sheikh Rahman.*

The Philippine National Police reports turned over to the FBI after Murad's extradition linked bin Laden directly to the IG. The other Egyptian group mentioned, the Egyptian Islamic Jihad (EIJ), was directed by Dr. Ayman al-Zawahiri, al Qaeda's chief theoretician and bin Laden's right-hand man.† The traitorous Ali Mohammed, seen training Abouhalima, Salameh, and Nosair in the 1989 Calverton photos, was a card-carrying member of the EIJ, and at that point he was training bin Laden's bodyguards in Sudan. Furthermore, bin Laden had funded both the Algerian FIS and the GIA,[9] the group that had hijacked the Air France jet in December with the reported intention of flying it into the Eiffel Tower.†

"I didn't realize it at the time," said Dirgham in an interview for this book, "but Yousef was telling me then about his affiliation with al Qaeda. We hadn't heard the name al Qaeda at this point, but as soon as September eleventh happened and people began talking about al Qaeda, I said to myself, 'Oh my God, he was telling me about that back then.' "[10]

Yousef then gave Dirgham even more hints about his affiliation. When asked about Sheikh Rahman, currently on trial, Yousef said, "I know him and I admire him."

He insisted that the Liberation Army was "an international movement" with military divisions, "each of which takes care of Islamic

---

*Timeline #6. p. 2.
†Timeline #58. p. 12. Yousef's mention of the Algerian FIS might have tipped the Bureau to the December 1994 Air France hijacking, which witnesses said targeted the Eiffel Tower.

movements' affairs in various countries." Asked if he was "the brains behind it," Yousef said no.

As the interview drew to a close, Dirgham asked, "Who do you admire greatly?"

"The apostle, God's prayers and peace be upon him," said Yousef, referring to the prophet Mohammed.

"And who [is] the figure that you hate most?" she asked.

At that point, the prison guards came in and ended the interview. But as Yousef was being led off, he looked back and said, "Satan."

He didn't say whether he was referring to "The Great Satan," as many fundamentalists called America, or the devil himself.

The COO of al Qaeda

On June 27, 1995, after five months of trial and 120 witnesses, the Feds rested in the Day of Terror case against Sheikh Abdel Omar Rahman.[11] Having introduced more than one hundred hours of Emad Salem's secretly recorded CM or "bad guy tapes," the government had painted a case involving a sprawling jihad conspiracy that ran from the Kahane murder through Yousef's Trade Center bombing up through the bridge and tunnels plot.

Now it was the defense's turn, and they came out swinging. They argued that the Sheikh and his followers had been entrapped by Salem, whom they called a "vicious liar" and an agent of the Egyptian government.[12]

But their entrapment defense went south just days into trial, when Siddig Siddig Ali, the operational commander of the bombing plot, cut a deal. Pleading guilty on the day before Yousef was grabbed in Pakistan, Siddig admitted that he not only *knew* Yousef, but had helped test explosives for the Trade Center device. As to the Day of Terror plot, he was hardly entrapped by Salem; indeed, Siddig said, it was *his* idea to blow up the United Nations and a string of other targets including the George Washington Bridge, the Lincoln and Holland tunnels, and 26 Federal Plaza.[13]

The defense's only hope now was to impeach Salem. And the way they proposed to do that was by calling Nancy Floyd.

She took the witness stand on July 26, 1995. Hoping to capitalize on the innuendo of the "Temptress & the Spy" headline, the Sheikh's attorney, Lynn Stewart, tried to suggest that Nancy's relationship with Salem was more than "purely professional." But the straight-talking agent from Texas made it clear that she and Emad "didn't associate outside the realm" of the job.[14]

Later, when asked by another female lawyer if she had considered "leaving the Bureau to begin a personal relationship" with Salem—then in his mid-fifties—Floyd, an attractive redhead two decades his junior, looked shocked. "Absolutely not," she said.[15]

Now, the best the defense could do to shake Agent Floyd was to replay some of her conversations with Salem. In a number of Salem's bootleg tapes, her description of her FBI supervisors was far from complimentary.

"Emad, it's me and you against everybody," Floyd said on one tape, "with them trying to make it look like . . . we were doing something wrong." Noting how she and Salem had tried to warn FBI supervisors to further investigate the 1992 bombing plot, Nancy said, "They're just trying to cover their butts."

Later, under direct examination by the defense, Floyd gave a hint at the "harassment" she was enduring as a result of her candid comments. Jim Roth, the FBI's top New York lawyer, "didn't like" her "at all," she said, and Carson Dunbar, the ASAC she'd run afoul of over Salem, told another agent that he didn't trust her.

But none of this came easy. The defense lawyers had to pull it out of Floyd, who remained loyal to the Bureau itself. At one point she even denied that she was being made a "scapegoat," though the evidence clearly suggested that she was.

"Salem was the key to the government's case and Nancy was his control agent," said retired agent Len Predtechenskis. "Now, to get at *him* the defense was trying to attack *her*—trying to get at the Bureau and the government through her. It was a cheap shot, and all Nancy could hope for was that the jury would see through it."

Eight weeks later, the defense rested. For seven days, the jury of six African Americans, two Hispanics, and four whites deliberated.

Finally, on October 1, the biggest terrorism trial in U.S. history ended when the Sheikh and the remaining nine defendants were found guilty on forty-eight of the fifty charges. The government had even succeeded in convicting El Sayyid Nosair for the murder of Rabbi Meir Kahane.[16]

Hailed as "a sweeping victory" for the Feds, the verdict was also a total vindication for Nancy Floyd, who'd believed in Salem from the start and suffered along with him as her supervisors cut him out and then raced to bring him back in.

But it also raised a series of what-ifs.

What would have happened back in July of 1992 if Carson Dunbar had allowed Emad Salem to continue undercover? The ASAC who had judged Salem a "prolific liar" and subjected him to multiple polygraphs now had to accept the fact that victory had come almost entirely on the basis of the Egyptian's testimony and undercover work.

What would have happened if Detective Napoli and Agent Anticev had had Dunbar's full backing in the fall of 1992 and used the FBI's Special Operations Group to follow Abouhalima and Salameh as Yousef built the bomb? The warehouse where the Day of Terror plot had unfolded was now being cited as a triumph for the SOG: it had been fully wired for video and sound and provided startling pictures of the conspirators mixing the "witches brew." In honor of James Kallstrom, who had championed the development of the Bureau's black bag capabilities, the Feds were calling it "The House that Jimmy Built."[17]

But the summer and fall of 1992, when the FBI had Salem for $500 a week, had been lost to the Bureau. Now, their decision to make up for that loss would cost the government $1.5 million. The ex–Egyptian Army major wasn't the only one who got rewarded: Later, several FBI agents connected to the Day of Terror investigation got cash bonuses for their work. FBI agent Chuck Stern, who interrogated Yousef on his way back to America, was promoted to supervisory special agent.[18] Frank Pellegrino, who'd grilled Murad, received the Attorney General's Award, and Neal Herman, who ran the JTTF, got the FBI Director's Award for excellence in managing the World Trade Center bombing investigation. There was an awards ceremony, but Special Agent Nancy Floyd didn't even get invited.

"The only thing Nancy got," said Len Predtechenskis, "was an ongoing OPR investigation. None of her supervisors came to bat for her. They weren't even interviewed. She's the one agent who pretty much *made* this entire thing happen, but when it was over she got hung out to dry."[19]

At sentencing on January 17, the angry Sheikh delivered a 100-minute diatribe chastising the U.S. as an "enemy of Islam" and portraying himself as a victim of an "unlawful trial."[20] But Judge Mukasey was unmoved.

"You were convicted of directing others to perform acts, which, if accomplished, would have resulted in the murder of hundreds, if not thousand of people," he told the Sheikh before sentencing him to life in prison.

Rahman retorted that "the United States is trying to kill me" with "a slow death." Then he delivered a warning: "God is great and he will be revengeful."

As a troubling signal of things to come, Ahmed Abdel Sattar, the mailman who had found Special Agent Anticev's home address, warned that the blind Sheikh "will never be silenced." And in Cairo, the Islamic Group issued a pledge: "The Gamma'a al'Islamiya vow[s] to God that it will respond blow for blow. American interests and people will be a legitimate target."[21]*

It was a credible threat from the IG, which had killed a number of policeman, civilians, and foreign tourists in Egypt. Ramzi Yousef had linked the IG to his Liberation Army in the April *Al Hayat* interview, and the group was directly tied to Osama bin Laden, who, in years to come, would make repeated demands for the Sheikh's release. But at this point, in January 1996, John O'Neill was just setting up Station Alex, a dedicated FBI-CIA unit to track bin Laden, and few in the Bureau's New York office took the IG's threat seriously.

They were buoyed by another victory. A month earlier, in midDecember, the FBI had apprehended the third missing coconspirator from Yousef's Bojinka plot. Wali Khan Amin Shah was arrested in Malaysia after reportedly leading the Bureau on a manhunt through half a dozen countries.[22]

"Once they had Wali, there was a sense up at the JTTF that they'd taken all the pictures off the wall," said former U.S. Postal Inspector

---

*Timeline #87. p. 19.

Frank Gonzalez, who worked with Yousef's defense team. "They could put a check mark next to every mug shot. They'd convicted the first four in the Trade Center trial, they'd rounded up the blind Sheikh and the others, they had Ramzi, Murad, and now Wali for Bojinka, and the sense among the Bureau people I knew was that they'd won this big war. Everybody felt safer. But what they didn't realize was that they'd won a series of battles. This thing was far from over."[23]

The Real Man Who Wasn't There

Despite their legal victories in New York, the Feds still had little sense of the enemy. Yousef's Liberation Army may have been contained, but the "suicidal soldiers" of al Qaeda were gearing up for the next onslaught, and one of their main generals was Yousef's own uncle, Khalid Shaikh Mohammed. The pope and Bojinka plots may have been broken, but Mohammed and Yousef had already developed the "third plot" that would take their fight back to Manhattan. As far back as 1994 they had sent young jihadis to train in U.S. flight schools. Plans had been made to target a series of buildings in New York, Washington, Chicago, and San Francisco.

Now, as the FBI geared up to put Yousef away for life, Mohammed would make sure that his nephew's vision was executed. Intelligence officials later labeled him "the chief operating officer of al Qaeda,"[24] the number-three man in bin Laden's terror network, and the man who held the "ignition keys."[25] He was even seen as the successor to Osama himself.[26]

By all accounts his ascendancy within al Qaeda was rapid.

Over the years, after fleeing Manila in 1995, Mohammed emerged as the head of al Qaeda's "military committee."[27] He became director of the terror network's "department of martyrs," the man who later sent the 9/11 "foot soldiers" to their deaths.[28] He was fluent in four languages,[29] comfortably changing his persona as he moved from Karachi to Manila to Islamabad to Qatar.

Mohammed communicated with his jihadi operatives using codes and encrypted E-mails—even short-wave radio. A *wedding*, in his terminology, meant an upcoming event. *Market* was code for Malaysia, *terminal* for Indonesia, and *hotel* for the Philippines, a country he slipped in and out of with ease.

After his nephew Ramzi escaped from Manila following the Dona Josefa fire, Mohammed fled to Pakistan. Incredibly, he was just yards away at the Su Casa guest house in Islamabad when the Feds stormed into Room 16.

As a measure of his audacity and true contempt for the U.S. agents Yousef's uncle actually *gave an interview* to the press at the time.

Earlier, in the discussion of Yousef's takedown, a *Time* magazine article was cited quoting a "Karachi businessman."

"They were dragging [Yousef] downstairs," the witness told reporters. The story, entitled "The Man Who Wasn't There" by *Time*'s Christopher John Farley, attributed the eyewitness account to one "Khalid Sheikh."[30]

It was Mohammed. He was one floor below his nephew, and visible enough to talk to reporters. But with dozens of Pakistani ISI troops and U.S. agents present, somehow Mohammed was able to slide back into the dark.[31]

Given his visibility and the fact that he went on to become the man the FBI later admitted was the "mastermind" of 9/11, the failure of the Feds to capture Mohammed at the Su Casa was a *titanic* dot on the chart.*

On the road to 9/11, after Ramzi Yousef and Osama bin Laden himself, no figure played a more crucial operational role than Khalid Shaikh Mohammed. The FBI had intelligence on Mohammed dating back to 1995, yet he not only eluded the Bureau for eight years, they didn't even *begin* to understand his role in the al Qaeda hierarchy until after the 9/11 attacks. It was only after the capture of Abu Zubaydah, the Palestinian who ran al Qaeda's training camps, that Khalid Shaikh Mohammed came into focus.[32]

Colonel Mendoza of the Philippine National Police had given the FBI the file on Mohammed in April 1995, but "it was not taken seriously," he said.[33] Mendoza found a direct "collaboration" between top al Qaeda operatives like Mohammed and the regional al Qaeda network, from the 1995 Bojinka and pope plots up through the 9/11 attacks. "It [was] a continuing plan," he says.[34] "Khalid was calling the shots."[35]

---

*Timeline #73. p. 15.

THE DEVIL HIMSELF • 329

Yet a senior FBI official admitted that Mohammed "was under everybody's radar. We don't know how he did it," he said. "We wish we knew. He's the guy nobody heard of."[36] In effect, Mohammed was the *real* man who wasn't there.

How did they miss him?

Khalid Shaikh: The FBI's Best Kept Secret

In reviewing the intelligence leading up to 9/11, it's clear now that part of that answer may lie in the way the FBI and the Justice Department chose to conduct the hunt for Mohammed. As far back as 1996, Yousef's uncle was indicted along with Yousef, Abdul Hakim Murad, Wali Kahn Amin Shah, and Abdul Rahman Yasin, the Iraqi who had talked his way out of FBI custody after the Trade Center bombing.

Murad and Yousef were in custody by then, and a worldwide public alert went out for Yasin and Shah. But for some reason the indictment with Khalid Shaikh Mohammed's name was mysteriously sealed.[37]

The indictment noted that Mohammed had stayed with his nephew at the posh Tiffany Mansion Condominium at 21 Eisenhower Street, in the San Juan section of Metro Manila. Yousef had rented the apartment in August 1994. Mohammed had not only financed the Bojinka plot, he was one of the four coconspirators set to carry Yousef's undetectable Casio-nitro devices onto the planes. Yet for unknown reasons the U.S. Justice Department was treating him differently.

The public nature of the Yousef hunt had been the primary factor in his capture. As the main target of Brad Smith's Rewards for Justice program, Yousef's picture was on wanted posters and matchbook covers in every major Islamic country from Pakistan to Abu Dhabi,[38] and he was widely covered in the international press. Yet the indictment of Mohammed wasn't even *unsealed* by the U.S. attorney for the Southern District of New York until January 1998.*

Six months later, Mohammed had advanced the planning of the 9/11 attacks to the point where he was beginning to meet with prospective hijackers in Hamburg, Germany.[39]

---

*Timeline #103. p. 22.

Abdul Yasin, the fast-talking Iraqi the FBI had cut loose, was put on the Bureau's Most Wanted Terrorists list as far back as 1999. Yet Mohammed, Yousef's own uncle and the man FBI Director Robert Mueller now acknowledges was "a key figure" behind 9/11, didn't make the list until October 11, 2001—a month *after* the attacks.

During this period the Bureau was certainly trying to find him. By 1997 the elusive Kuwaiti had found a hiding place in Qatar. He was believed to be staying at the estate of one Abdullah bin Khalid al-Thani, a wealthy al Qaeda sympathizer who had provided support for other Islamic extremists. In December, retired CIA case officer Bob Baer reportedly got word that Mohammed was in Doha, the Qatari capital.[40] The FBI quickly dispatched a counterterrorism team to Doha for the takedown,[41] but according to *Washington Times* reporter Bill Gertz they were told by local authorities to cool their heels in a hotel. The Qataris said they wanted to "put the handcuffs" on Mohammed themselves.

Then, a day later, when the trusting Bureau agents went to the safe house, Mohammed had already fled. Reportedly aided by Qatari officials, he'd run to the Czech Republic, where he began operating under the name Mustaf Nasir. Later Mohammed showed up in South America, and the CIA arranged through a liaison there to apprehend him. But once more the unnamed country's security service was "too late," and the terror master slipped away again.[42]

Again, what went wrong? Why hadn't the Bureau realized the significance of Mohammed as a key al Qaeda player even sooner? The FBI's New York office was the office of origin for all bin Laden–related terror investigations. The intelligence Colonel Mendoza had given the Justice Department in the spring of 1995 confirmed Mohammed's role in the Bojinka and pope plots, as well as Yousef's third plan, for which Islamic pilots were then training at U.S. flight schools. The FBI even had Mendoza's schematic, showing Mohammed (aka "Salem Ali") connected to bin Laden through his brother-in-law Mohammed Jamal Khalifa, who'd been deported by the State Department in early 1995. (See p. 304.)

But the Feds didn't even get around to indicting Mohammed until 1996. Mohammed, as the FBI agent said, was under the radar—an astonishing fact, especially considering that in the spring of 1996 an informant fell into the government's lap who later gave the FBI the virtual keys to al Qaeda.

It was a feast of intelligence that, if properly pursued, would have corroborated Colonel Mendoza's Mohammed file. The informant has already appeared in this story in the context of the Shalabi murder, but his role is worth revisiting because his defection from al Qaeda in 1996 gives new insights into how the Bureau mishandled the hunt for Yousef's uncle.

Jamal Ahmad al-Fadl was the young Sudanese who had worked as assistant to the bludgeoned Shalabi at the Alkifah Center in Brooklyn.[43] In 1989 he went to training camps in Afghanistan and was actually present when Osama bin Laden created al Qaeda as an adjunct to the MAK Services Office network. Al-Fadl traveled to Sudan with bin Laden in 1990 and served as a financial courier, front man, and liaison to Sudanese intelligence.[44]

But he got greedy. After embezzling $110,000 in illicit commissions on the sale of goods from one of bin Laden's companies, al-Fadl walked into a U.S. Embassy and sought Witness Protection. Soon, the Bureau designated him Confidential Source 1 (CS-1).

As he coughed up the names of every key figure in bin Laden's al Qaeda hierarchy, al-Fadl spoke in detail about Osama Asumari, the fierce Afghan jihadi bin Laden had called Assad, "the lion." The Feds already had the same man under indictment under yet another name: Wali Khan Amin Shah, Yousef's Bojinka coconspirator.[45]

Al-Fadl's testimony to the Feds was the icing on a cake that Col. Rodolfo Mendoza had already baked for the Bureau.* By 1997, four years before 9/11, Khalid Shaikh Mohammed should have been a major unchecked mug shot on the wall at the FBI's New York JTTF. He was an indicted coconspirator in the Bojinka plot and the uncle of the recently captured Most Wanted Man on earth.

Given the corroborative intelligence from al-Fadl, why didn't the FBI get the DSS to put Mohammed's smirking face on every matchbook from Doha to Rio to Islamabad? Why didn't they alert the press? Why did they wait until January 1998 to unseal his indictment, and keep him off the Most Wanted List until after he'd executed what he himself called the attacks of "Holy Tuesday"?

These are questions the Feds have never answered.

Months after Mohammed's key role in the 9/11 plot was revealed,

---

*Timeline #88. p. 19.

one Bush administration official called him "the Forrest Gump of al Qaeda."[46] A spokesman for Pakistani President Pervez Musharraf described him as "the kingpin."[47] But where were our intelligence analysts and allies during the years when Mohammed was doing most of his damage?

Khalid Shaikh may well have been the biggest unconnected dot on the chart.

32

THE BOMB MAKER
AND THE MADE GUY

A t this point, in the late spring of 1996, Ronnie Bucca had no spe-cific knowledge of Yousef's third plot to take down the Towers. His belief that the Trade Center was still a target was based on an amal-gam of street sense and the intelligence he picked up in his Army Reserve unit attached to the Defense Intelligence Agency. But on May 29, just as he had for Yousef's arraignment, the fire marshal made sure he had a seat in the courtroom when opening arguments began in the Bojinka trial.

Bucca had studied Ramzi Yousef from a distance ever since he was first identified by federal investigators as the mysterious "Rashed" who'd built the urea nitrate–fuel oil device at the Pamrapo Avenue apartment. Now, as opening arguments began, the bomb maker sat in a dark suit and tie next to his old friend Abdul Hakim Murad, who was also in a suit. Wali Khan Amin Shah wore a blue prison jumpsuit and listened with headphones to a translation of the proceedings.[1]

In his opening statement, Assistant U.S. Attorney Michael Garcia called Yousef's plot "a detailed and synchronized plan," resulting in "forty-eight hours of terror aimed at the U.S. and its citizens."[2] The motive, as Yousef confessed, was "vengeance directed against this coun-try in retaliation for United State support of Israel." There wasn't a hint by the federal prosecutors that Iraq had any involvement in what Garcia called the "plan to murder approximately four thousand civilians in mid-air over the Pacific." Calling Yousef the "mastermind," Garcia told the jurors how "only an accident" in his Manila bomb factory "interrupted that plan."

In the back of the courtroom, Bucca strained for a look at Yousef's face as he listened to the government's case.

The master bomber sat next to his lawyer Roy Kulcsar, a blond, blue-eyed, court-appointed attorney who had replaced Avraham Moskowitz at Yousef's request.

Then, after Garcia had finished, the man who had shocked the world with the Trade Center bomb startled the courtroom with a request. He wanted to address the jury himself.

"Mr. Yousef has indicated that he would like to give the opening statement," said Kulcsar. But Judge Kevin Duffy, the tough Bronx Irishman who had presided over the first WTC trial, shot back, "Mr. Yousef then is going *pro se* throughout the entire trial."

In other words, if Yousef wanted to give his own opening, he'd have to represent himself for the rest of the proceedings. Virtually any defendant, unless incompetent or impaired, has the right to waive counsel, but Duffy warned Yousef about the perils of acting as his own attorney, especially in a case that carried a life sentence.

When Yousef acknowledged the risk, the judge reluctantly allowed him to proceed, providing Kulcsar continued as his legal adviser. Duffy told Yousef that he would have to speak of himself in the third person. He then instructed the jury that nothing Yousef said as his own counsel should be construed as evidence. Finally, the judge nodded and Yousef got up.

Now, the terrorist who had manipulated bar girls into fronting for his bombing plots and convinced young jihadis to die in the name of Allah set about to seduce the jury.

"Ladies and gentlemen, good morning," he said in perfect English as he stood in front of the jury box.[3] "I'm the person named in this indictment as Ramzi Yousef, and I will be referring to myself in the third person or as defendant Yousef."

He quickly launched into his main defense: that "Mr. Yousef" could not have committed the crimes set forth in the indictment, because during the period of the PAL Flight 434 bombing and the Bojinka plot he was, in fact, a prisoner.

From November 1994 until February 1995, Yousef said, "the Pakistani Military Police" had him in custody. During that time, he alleged, he was tortured, deprived of food, and "shackled in a very painful way." Then, after the months he spent "secretly imprisoned," he was "placed" in the Su Casa guest house and "made to appear as if he was just arrested at that time."

To further the conspiracy, he alleged, the Philippine National Police had planted chemicals in Room 603 at the Dona Josefa and "pretended that a fire or an explosion took place," prompting them to raid the apartment. Documents, passports, and other IDs with his picture were fabricated, Yousef said. He declared that "all the evidence in this case without exception," was "found in overseas countries . . . and then . . . handed over to the United States government."

The master bomber concluded by insisting that "defendant Yousef was a victim of two governments which wanted to please the United States . . . by building this case and fabricating most of the evidence."

There was a minor buzz in the gallery as Yousef sat down. Audacious in the practice of terror, he had stayed true to form. But Yousef's argument defied mountains of forensic evidence. The picture it painted was of an epic international conspiracy involving the governments of three countries; the United States, Pakistan, and the Philippines. To have pulled it off, the agents concerned would have had to act with far greater technical competence in *framing* him than they had in attempting to hunt him down.

The truth was, for all the FBI's posturing, Ramzi Yousef had been brought to ground as the result of an accidental chemical fire and media coverage of a State Department reward program. Apart from Capt. Aida Fariscal's actions in Manila, investigative work had little or nothing to do with it.

But now that they had him, the Justice Department was about to present an argument, based on eyewitness testimony and forensic evidence, that was devastating. Over the next ten weeks, Assistant U.S. Attorney Garcia and his cocounsel, Dietrich Snell, built a meticulous case that put Yousef inside PAL Flight 434 as he built the bomb, inside the Dona Josefa as he constructed the Casio timers, and inside Room 16 at the Su Casa as he stuffed nitrocellulose into toy cars in a desperate attempt to perfect the Bojinka plot and blow up U.S. airliners.

The Feds first called PAL flight attendant Maria de la Cruz, who fingered Yousef in court as the "Mideastern" man with "stubbles on his chin" who sat in seat 26K before Haruki Ikegami was blown to death.[4] They called Joseph Cruz, the maintenance man from the Dona Josefa, who identified Yousef as the "mysterious" Naji Haddad—the Moroccan who had asked him to stop cleaning Room 603 after December 20 as the plot ticked closer to B-Day.[5] They called Dona Josefa security guard Roman Mariano, who identified Yousef as the man who ran out of Room 603 as Murad tried to placate him with the firecracker story.[6]

A battery of PNP bomb disposal cops and investigators described the laboratory of chemicals in Manila and the Toshiba laptop covered with Yousef's fingerprints[7]—the same prints found on the *Newsweek* containing Yousef's picture that DSS and DEA agents discovered across the globe in Islamabad at the time of his takedown.[8]

It was the kind of big forensic case that the Justice Department prides itself on presenting. Whatever the Bureau's shortcomings might have been in *preventing* terrorism, the agents were at their best in making a case *after* the fact. And day by day, as the evidence mounted, Yousef looked more and more like a man who would spent the rest of his life behind bars.

Unlike the Sheikh's trial, which moved at a glacier's pace for seven months, Garcia and Snell kept the momentum going for this jury as they laid out a forensic tale of international intrigue that played like a Tom Clancy novel.

Each day, the jurors sat riveted as the Feds introduced evidence of how Ramzi Yousef, the "lawyer" in front of them, had crafted an undetectable bomb. How he'd smuggled the parts onboard the PAL flight, assembled the device, and planted it in the life jacket pouch below seat 26K. How the bomb had ripped open a hole in the floor of the 747 just shy of the center fuel tank. How Haruki Ikegami had been cut in half, sacrificed to what was merely Yousef's "wet test" for the larger plot.

Bojinka, they argued, would have been hundreds of times more deadly, for the bomb maker intended to blow apart eleven jumbo jets— planes from Northwest, United, and Delta, filled with American tourists leaving Asia. The passengers aboard PAL Flight 434 had been lucky: at least their ruptured plane landed safely. If Yousef had had his way, four thousand people would have gone down in fireballs as their planes exploded over the Pacific.

It was a chilling scenario, and the weight of the evidence came down on Yousef with the force of the cinderblocks that had blown out Room 107 beneath the Trade Center. After years of being outsmarted by the brilliant terrorist, the American Feds were about to see justice done.

Al Qaeda and Khobar

Then, at around 10:00 P.M. on the night of June 25, a tanker truck loaded with the equivalent of 20,000 pounds of TNT was driven into the parking lot in front of the Khobar Towers, a residential complex housing U.S. service personnel in Dhahran, Saudi Arabia. Though roof sentries spotted the truck and called for an immediate evacuation, they were too late. The device detonated, shearing off an entire side of the eight-story building. Nineteen Americans were killed and hundreds injured.

The subsequent investigation demonstrated how little cooperation the FBI could expect from foreign governments in the terror war, and reportedly caused a rift between the Bureau's chief bin Laden hunter, John O'Neill, and then FBI director Louis Freeh. On the day of the bombing, O'Neill had invited a group of CIA agents to the FBI's training center at Quantico.

According to a profile of O'Neill in *The New Yorker,* the agents were eating hot dogs and burgers when "everyone's beeper went off."[9] O'Neill immediately assembled a team of almost one hundred agents and law enforcement personnel, and the next day they hit the ground in Dhahran. O'Neill followed a few weeks later with Freeh, who was optimistic that the Saudi government would cooperate in the investigation.

On the way home, though, O'Neill was brutally honest with the director. "You've got to be kidding," he said. "They didn't give us anything. They were just shining sunshine up your ass." Freeh reportedly didn't say another word. For the next twelve hours, as the flight headed stateside, he and O'Neill sat in silence. Freeh later denied the incident, but Joe Cantamessa, an agent in the FBI's New York office, admitted that O'Neill's "aggressive style" put him at odds with Bureau management.[10]

The Justice Department later indicted thirteen members of the pro-Saudi Hizbollah for the blast, but there was evidence that al Qaeda may have played a role and the Feds knew it at the time. The information came in the most unlikely way imaginable—through a "made" Mafia soldier the FBI had recruited to spy on Yousef in his jail cell.

Gregory Scarpa Jr. was the forty-four-year-old son of a capo for the Colombo crime family. Acquitted of five murders, Scarpa was ultimately sentenced to forty years for murder conspiracy, loansharking, bookmaking, and tax fraud.[11] His twenty-three-year-old brother Joey, a drug dealer, was shot dead in 1995 as he sat in a car parked in Sheepshead Bay, Brooklyn. The hit reportedly came from a rival member of the Gambino family. By the spring of 1996, Scarpa was an inmate on the same tier as Ramzi Yousef at the Metropolitan Correctional Center in Lower Manhattan.

Steven Legon, one of Yousef's attorneys, said that his client had grown close to Scarpa, who exercised with him in the gallery area on Nine South. "They would talk to each other," said Legon. "They became friendly."[12]

An unlikely alliance, but the Feds decided to use the mobster to sting the terrorist.

From just before the start of the Bojinka trial until March 1997, Bureau agents used Gregory Scarpa as an undercover informant. They set up a "patch-through" line that allowed Scarpa to make outside phone calls.[13] The plan was for Scarpa to induce the bomb maker to call out to his al Qaeda contacts worldwide. The FBI would then listen in and gather intel. At one point Yousef reportedly trusted Scarpa enough to pass him sketches of his bomb drawings; the Feds furnished the mafioso with a miniature still camera to photograph them.

According to Bernie Kleinman, Yousef's chief counsel, the Feds even used a female FBI agent posing as a paralegal who visited Scarpa to retrieve the film.

In one of the outside calls, detailed by New York *Daily News* reporter Greg Smith, Yousef referenced his own Bojinka plot, suggesting that some form of it might still be executed even though he was behind bars. "The government will never go after bin Laden," he boasted, "because the government knows that within one week of capturing bin Laden, 12 U.S. airplanes would be blown up."

At the time Yousef was using the word *Bojinka*[14] with Scarpa to represent his cell within the al Qaeda network. On June 29, four days after the Khobar Towers bombing, he told Scarpa he was certain that bin Laden's organization was involved in the Dhahran blast.

According to an FBI summary, "Yousef responded that he was sure because Yousef was originally sent on the mission to check out the security measures and that a tanker truck was discussed at that time."[15]

Scarpa made the patch-through available to Yousef in the hope that his cooperation with the Feds would cut short his prison term. But at some point in 1996 the bomb maker was apparently able to turn the tables on the FBI and use the outside call system to his advantage.

"[Yousef] called Afghanistan, his home, his people overseas, his people in New York City," a source told Smith. Most alarmingly, "he was also talking to people who wanted to get passports, to get his people into this country. He had people all over the place. They were plotting to do some crazy stuff."[16]

The scheme had spun out of control, and the question remains whether it may have furthered Yousef's efforts to reach Khalid Shaikh Mohammed, who was then in the process of executing the 9/11 airliner hijacking plot. At one point, the FBI reportedly recorded a "vague discussion" about imminent attacks on U.S. passenger jets.[17]

Sometime in late 1996 the Feds, realizing that they couldn't control Yousef's calls, terminated the program. But somehow Yousef was able to continue using the phone.

"Frankly, Yousef is smarter than most of them," Bernie Kleinman said of the FBI agents. "In the end he was able to make some calls he wasn't supposed to make. Once again, their incompetence is just overwhelming."[18]

The patch-through was acknowledged by Assistant U.S. Attorney Patrick Fitzgerald, the third prosecutor in the Day of Terror trial of the blind Sheikh. After the *Daily News*'s Smith learned of the scheme to use the mobster to monitor Yousef, Fitzgerald called the story a hoax. But a sealed affidavit filed on June 25, 1999, in a follow-up investigation appeared to corroborate the Scarpa story.[19] Confirming that he "provid[ed] an undercover telephone for Yousef to patch through calls to his associates," Fitzgerald asked a federal judge to seal that reference "to avoid public confirmation of the fact that the government has used an undercover patch-through telephone as an investigative technique."

Meanwhile, Legon and Kleinman, who began representing Yousef after the Bojinka trial, were shocked to learn that the Feds had used Scarpa in an attempt to monitor Yousef's calls. Apparently, they weren't the only ones in the dark. "The prosecutors in the SDNY never even informed the prosecutors in the Eastern District of New York," said Legon.[20] "The FBI agents who were handling the terrorist cases never informed the FBI agents who were handling the organized crime case" against Scarpa.

"Frankly, this shows how desperate the FBI must have been to find out how much Yousef knew," said a source close to the original Trade Center investigation. "I can understand an operation to let Yousef make calls so that he might be monitored. But the idea of involving a mob guy—an accused murderer—as a de facto government agent in this? It's ridiculous."[21]

Kleinman and Legon made the alleged Scarpa undercover operation a major factor in Yousef's appeal,[22] but the story is significant for what it says about Yousef's continuing involvement in the airliner-hijacking plot that his uncle was setting in motion. It's also further evidence of Yousef's ingenuity, and the threat he continued to pose even in twenty-three-hour-a-day lockdown.

Finally, in thinking they could use a mobster to trap a terrorist, the story underscores the apparent naïveté of FBI agents and prosecutors in the Southern District.

"Did they actually believe they could trust a guy like Scarpa to help them get the goods on Ramzi?" asked a source familiar with the botched operation. "The fact that Yousef was able to still make calls after they'd shut him down is another indicator of just how much the Bureau underestimated him."[23]

Yousef's prosecution in the Bojinka case continued. But then, on the night of July 17, another incident occurred that almost sent the case into a tailspin.

33

SHUT IT DOWN

At 8:02 P.M. TWA Flight 800 left Gate 27 at JFK bound for Paris, with 230 passengers and crew members aboard. Just after 8:18 P.M., the 747-100 lifted off from Runway 22-R. Heading east along the south shore of Long Island, the plane leveled off at just over 13,000 feet. Then, at 8:31:12 P.M., something in the area of the center fuel tank set off an explosion so catastrophic that a gaping hole was blown in the bottom of the fuselage. The forward section of the jumbo jet was ripped open. The aircraft was torn apart and instantly disappeared from radar screens. Within seconds, everyone aboard was dead.[1]

By midnight, James Kallstrom, the assistant director in charge of the FBI's New York office, had marshaled one hundred agents into action. By week's end, another two hundred had joined them. The immediate suspicion among federal investigators was that TWA 800 had been downed by an act of terror—a bomb or a missile.[2] The missile theory gained ground after eyewitnesses reported seeing an object approaching the plane, followed by a white light and what seemed like a second explosion. Soon conspiracy theorists were alleging that the missile had come from a test being conducted at the time by the U.S. Navy.[3] But six months later, when assembled parts of the aircraft proved that nothing had pierced the fuselage from outside, Kallstrom still couldn't rule out a bomb.[4]

The mystery deepened when FBI analysts, combing the wreckage dredged from the ocean floor, found traces of the high explosives PETN, RDX, and nitroglycerine throughout the 747. Two of the chemicals were detected in the carpeting along the twenty-fifth and twenty-sixth rows, adjacent to the center fuel tank.[5]

Whatever the cause, the tragic crash sent shock waves through the judge's chambers at the Foley Square courthouse where the Bojinka trial was under way.

After six weeks of testimony, the jurors had heard witness after witness describe how Yousef had built a bomb using nitroglycerine and placed it under a seat in the twenty-sixth row of a 747. They listened to prosecutors describe how Yousef, Murad, Shah, and a fourth coconspirator plotted to plant similar devices aboard 747s and other jumbo jets— undetectable bombs with Casio timers designed to blow the planes apart over water. They'd listened as a PAL flight steward described Haruki Ikegami's body after he "fell into the hole" created by the blast, which occurred in the same area on PAL Flight 434 as the point of detonation aboard TWA Flight 800.[6]

To some agents at 26 Federal Plaza, TWA Flight 800 appeared to be Bojinka fulfilled. And in the hours after the crash, Yousef, Sheikh Rahman, and Osama bin Laden became the FBI's three prime suspects.[7] Was it possible that the bomb maker's uncle Khalid Shaikh Mohammed—the fourth Bojinka conspirator, still at large—had somehow arranged for a Casio-nitrocellulose device to be planted onboard the Paris-bound flight?

The circumstantial connection was even more curious given what was going on in federal court. On the very morning after TWA Flight 800 exploded, the Bojinka trial jurors were due to hear the tape of a confession made by Abdul Hakim Murad at Camp Crame on January 7, 1995. During that interrogation, he specifically described how the Casio-nitro bombs would be placed. He even discussed how, after Bojinka, Yousef intended to export his deadly technology to other terrorists in Egypt, Algeria, *and France.*

Now, on the morning after the crash, whether the incident had been an accident or an act of terror, Yousef's lawyer, Roy Kulcsar, appeared in front of Judge Duffy and complained about "the unfortunate confluence of circumstances." He noted that "the transcript" of Murad's interrogation contained "references to Paris."[8]

The jurors had not been sequestered, and Shah's lawyer, David Greenfield, argued that "Whatever [TV] station anybody was watching last night, they know what happened. They know a plane exploded."

"My concern, Your Honor," said Kulcsar, "is that right now whatever general information [the jurors] have . . . we will be faced shortly within the next hour or so with a statement attributed to one of the defendants specifically dealing with the very issue of explosions on airliners."

There was some discussion among Judge Duffy and the other lawyers over whether the word *Paris* should be excised from Murad's interrogation transcript. Clearly Murad had made the reference in 1995 in the context of plans to teach jihadis in other countries; it had no bearing on this specific flight bound for Paris. But Judge Duffy put off making a decision on whether to entertain a mistrial motion. He decided to press on, and began by admonishing the jury.

"Good morning, ladies and gentlemen. Last night near Moriches Inlet out in Long Island an airplane blew up, TWA Flight 800. Now there is going to be . . . all kinds of speculation about what happened. I have no clue what happened, nor do you, nor do any of the people who have been speculating up to this point. All we know is that there was an explosion and the airplane went down. It's a tragedy, there is no two ways about it, but that had nothing to do with this case."

However innocent they may have sounded, Duffy's words amounted to a finding of fact. It was one thing for the judge to minimize the relevance of the Paris reference, but another thing entirely to declare that the TWA crash "had nothing to do" with the Bojinka case. After all, the FBI was just beginning to gather evidence on what caused the explosion; now, just hours after the disaster, the judge was preemptively declaring Yousef and his Bojinka codefendants innocent of any connection.

Later he admonished the jurors to avoid media coverage of the TWA Flight 800 story. Then, after polling each of them, and deciding that none had been prejudiced, he ruled that the Feds could continue the case.

It was the role of the National Transportation Safety Board to determine the cause of the crash. It was the job of the FBI to investigate whether an act of terror had brought down TWA Flight 800. If the Bureau concluded that a bomb had been placed onboard, the NTSB would have had its answer. But as the weeks went by, the FBI was unable to establish definitive proof of a crime.

Eventually, after a sixteen-month investigation, the NTSB reached the conclusion that an electrical short in the area of the center fuel tank had ignited jet fuel vapors. It was a finding that would be debated for years to come.[9] Like the "single bullet theory" proposed to explain Lee Harvey Oswald as the lone gunman in the JFK assassination, the fuel tank ignition spark theory was arrived at by the Safety Board in the absence of any other definitive explanation for the crash—*short* of detonation by an explosive device.[10]

Reluctant for months to embrace the NTSB's mechanical theory, the FBI eventually fell into line with the Safety Board.

Unexplained High Explosive Residue

To explain the presence of RDX, PETN, and nitro aboard the wreckage, Bureau agents pointed to a test done on the aircraft by a bomb-sniffing dog in St. Louis five weeks before the crash. They accepted the theory that residue might have spilled from test explosives that a St. Louis airport cop had used to measure the K-9's ability to locate bombs.

But that test didn't explain the presence of RDX found on the curtain in Flight 800's aft cargo bay, the fact that the door to that cargo area had never been found, or the evidence of spike-tooth tears in the aluminum skin adjacent to the door. Later, jurors in the Bojinka trial would hear testimony from Steven Burmeister of the FBI's lab that chemicals examined from Yousef's bomb factory in Room 603 had included methenane, which is used to make RDX.[11]

Kenneth Maxwell, the retired FBI supervisory special agent in charge who ran the Bureau's TWA investigation on Long Island, said, in an interview for this book, that he was still concerned about a number of unanswered questions.

"The fact that RDX was found on the aft cargo bay curtain is still unexplainable," he said, "and, to be honest, I wasn't entirely satisfied. There are ten doors on a seven-four-seven. We recovered nine of them. You're looking at high-explosive residue. Why do we find *nine* doors? Did that missing door experience more of a force? Was it blown out? There were quite a few of these spike-tooth injuries to the fuselage skin."[12]

What that meant forensically wasn't clear. Maxwell said that, at the time, the government didn't have a comparative database to measure the impact of high explosives on an airplane's skin. But if a blast did occur around the cargo hold, there was evidence suggesting which direction the force might have moved in. As Maxwell recalled, "Most of the spike-tooth tears were pushing *out.*"

Maxwell, who supervised the reconstruction of the aft cargo bay from the recovered debris, said that "there was no evidence of the fuselage being struck by any kind of projectile." But he said that he was still troubled by the possibility that an explosion caused by terrorists might have downed the plane. "The circumstances of the crash," said Maxwell, "the way that it came out of the sky—there was no notification from the crew to the Tower. Certainly the early signs pointed toward an act of terror."

Once a missile was ruled out, Maxwell said, the decision by the FBI to embrace the mechanical theory came as the result of a ruling by William Tobin, the Bureau's chief metallurgist.

"He maintained, based on his field analysis, that there was no indicia of high-explosive damage," said Maxwell. "So that was the ruling authority and that was the way it went." A source close to the investigation acknowledged that Maxwell and metallurgist Tobin were at odds.[13]

Tobin had reached his conclusion in the early weeks of the investigation. In late July, with only 10 percent of the wreckage recovered, the metallurgist declared that the cause was accidental and not a missile or a bomb. This led to an August face-off between Maxwell and Tobin at 26 Federal Plaza. Maxwell wanted more specific lab tests performed to determine definitively if an explosive device was involved. But Tobin reportedly declared, "If there was evidence of a bomb or a missile, we would have found it by now. We're just wasting our time if we keep studying the wreckage."[14]

"The metallurgist made up his mind early on in the case that it had to be an accident because he didn't see any blatant metal evidence [of an explosion]," said Maxwell. "That was a struggle."

But Tobin had thirty-five years with the Bureau and was highly regarded. In the end, his ruling was a definitive factor in the NTSB's conclusion that the cause of the crash was mechanical.

The ruling still troubles Maxwell.

"To this day, as we speak," said Maxwell, "if you read the NTSB report, no one has ever identified the ignition source. It certainly didn't blow itself up. Yet despite all of this scrutiny—studying everything from static electricity to the wiring, to the electrical components of a fuel pump and more—no one could find a specific ignition source."

Maxwell said that a suspicion Yousef's cell might have been involved was "right up there on the board" at the FBI from day one of the investigation. He added that after thirty years in law enforcement he wouldn't be surprised if there was a connection.

"I'm not saying for sure it was a crime or that Ramzi was related," said the former SSAC. "But the thing that gnaws at me is the uncertainty— that we finished all of this investigation with this degree of uncertainty."

Maxwell wasn't the only one. James Kallstrom, the head of the FBI's New York office, had suspected foul play in the crash almost immediately.[15] Over the months of the investigation, as Maxwell supervised the assembly of 95 percent of the recovered aircraft in a hangar—situated, ironically, at Calverton, Long Island—Kallstrom too battled with NTSB investigators who seemed bent on finding a mechanical cause.[16] But by 1997 the investigation had cost the government $20 million. At its height, seven hundred FBI agents were involved.[17] Seven thousand interviews were conducted. More than three thousand leads were processed. All of this without any definitive evidence of a crime.

As the weeks went by, there was growing pressure within the Bureau to bring the probe to an end.

"We were hearing, 'Hey, FBI, when is this over?'" said Maxwell. "You're spending millions of dollars." So finally I got the call [from Kallstrom], 'Shut it down.' It was a very direct order: 'Shut it down.'"

Again, the question is why?

In 1997, after John O'Neill transferred from his post as chief of counterterrorism to special agent in charge of the National Security Division in the New York office, he became concerned that the TWA Flight 800 investigation was sapping crucial resources that might better be directed toward the war on terror. Supervisors at 26 Federal Plaza began to talk of "an exit strategy." The word reportedly came down to Neal Herman, head of the Joint Terrorist Task Force, who had committed a number of his agents to the Flight 800 probe.

According to John Miller in his book *The Cell*, Herman's reply to the request to end the investigation was "My God, what the hell is an exit strategy? We get out of cases when they're over. Since when do we need a strategy to get out of them?"[18]

"O'Neill's discussions with Kallstrom and with Washington and the NTSB were putting on a lot of pressure," said Maxwell. So after sixteen months the FBI's investigation into the downing of TWA Flight 800 came to a close.

In a press conference on November 18, 1997, Kallstrom declared that the FBI had found no evidence of high-explosive damage from either a missile or a bomb. The damage, he said, was "consistent with the over pressurization of the center fuel tank, the breakup of the aircraft, the fire, and the impact of the aircraft into the ocean."

Kenneth Maxwell was one senior Bureau official who felt the decision was premature.

"I said, 'Do you want me to walk away from this thing without covering every base? That's not what we do for a living.' But we closed up shop. Afterward I heard crazy comments, even inside the Bureau, like, 'They wasted too much time on that [Flight 800] case. After all, it was an accident.' "

By early September 1996, the question of whether TWA Flight 800 had been a latent casualty of Bojinka became legally moot. After fourteen weeks of trial, the jury of eight men and four women found Ramzi Yousef guilty of planting the bomb that killed Haruki Ikegami aboard PAL Flight 434. Along with Murad and Shah, he was also convicted in the Bojinka plot to down eleven jumbo jets. As the guilty verdicts echoed through the courtroom, Yousef listened in an open-necked shirt and slacks rather than his customary lawyer's suit.[19] It almost seemed a sign that he was resigned to his fate. But after the verdict, Murad's attorney complained that the crash of Flight 800 "had an impact on the jury" and was a key factor in the convictions.[20]

When JTTF head Neal Herman heard the Bojinka verdict, he was in the hangar at Calverton where the Flight 800 wreckage was still being assembled. FBI agent Frank Pellegrino reportedly called to say, "It's over. We won."

Now, in the light of 9/11, the question is, who really won? Accident or not, the crash was a strategic victory for the forces of al Qaeda. Some intelligence analysts now believe that the combined impact of the Oklahoma City and TWA Flight 800 investigations sapped Bureau resources to such a degree that there was little left for the war on terror.

"From 1995 until early in 1997 there was a lull in work on international terrorism at the FBI, and little interest in looking beyond the immediate actors in the terrorism cases related to Yousef and the blind Sheikh," wrote Daniel Benjamin and Steven Simon, two former terrorism specialists who served on the National Security Council.

In their exceptional post-9/11 book *The Age of Sacred Terror,* Benjamin and Simon concluded that "the Bureau's resources were stretched thin. . . . Within the Bureau there was also an unwillingness to believe that there was more than met the eye. The feeling was that Yousef was a one off, a virtuoso freelancer who wanted to make his mark as the world's greatest terrorist."[21]

Coming on the night before a crucial tape on Bojinka was about to be entered at trial, was the crash of TWA Flight 800 merely a coincidence, or the perfection of Yousef's plan? Was it a coldly calculated attempt to derail his trial at a time when it was turning against him? Was it a strategic ploy by al Qaeda to further distract the FBI from the war on terror? Was it all of the above?

Absent the discovery of that missing tenth cargo door, Kenneth Maxwell and others remain convinced that the true cause of the crash may never be known.

34

INGENIOUS,
DIABOLICAL, AND
RUTHLESS

After the Bojinka verdict, the *New York Times* published what looked like an impressive scorecard for the Feds.[1] Since 1994 the government had now convicted four of the conspirators in the original World Trade Center bombing, the blind Sheikh and nine of his followers including Nosair for the Day of Terror plot, and Ramzi Yousef himself, along with two of his closest cohorts, for Bojinka. Further, since Judge Duffy had split off the Trade Center case from the Bojinka indictment, Ramzi would soon be back in court with Eyyad Ismoil, his WTC wheelman, to face *another* prosecution for the 1993 bombing.

The Bojinka verdict gave U.S. Attorney Mary Jo White another chance to celebrate. "If they'd had their way," she said, Yousef and his coconspirators "would have killed within forty-eight hours, literally thousands of innocent, unsuspecting passengers heading to America."

There was a real sense at that point that the Feds had contained the threat.

"Ramzi Yousef will go down in history as the man who brought massive-scale terrorism to the U.S." said Henry J. DePippo, the former U.S. attorney who had convicted Salameh, Abouhalima, Ajaj, and Ayyad in the first trial.[2]

But like other terrorism specialists at the time, DePippo spoke of Yousef in the past tense, as if contributing to his obituary. By the fall of 1996, Yousef's arrest, conviction, and incarceration caused many Feds to assume that the danger from him was now over. After all, the Baluchistani bomber was in solitary lockdown in federal prison. He'd lost in one trial and was getting teed up for a second in which the same tough federal judge was preparing to add a series of consecutive life sentences to his name. Judge Duffy had warned Yousef, and now, deservedly, the mass murderer would pay.

But was the threat over just because he was now behind bars? In the past, Ramzi Yousef had shown himself to be a terrorist of extraordinary stamina and resolve. He had moved from foiled plot to executed plot with ease. After the Trade Center bombing, he'd planted a bomb that killed twenty-six Iranian Shiites, then made two unsuccessful moves on Benazir Bhutto before getting foiled in the attempted bombing of the Israeli embassy in Bangkok. Undaunted, he'd conceived Bojinka and successfully tested the Casio-nitro bomb, killing one and almost crashing a PAL 747 in the process. Even after the Dona Josefa accident, when he'd finally shot to the top of the FBI's Most Wanted list, Yousef recruited Istaique Parker to strike at two U.S. airliners with the toy car bombs, slightly altering his Bojinka scenario in a tenacious attempt to kill more.

Morris Busby, the former coordinator of counterterrorism at the State Department, described Yousef in 1996 as "ingenious, diabolical, and ruthless."

"While I don't want to glorify him," said Busby, "he is something of a genius bomber."[3]

Now, despite Yousef's conviction, the FBI had evidence from the Philippines that the bomber had conceived another plot to inflict damage on America—the scheme to hijack airliners and fly them into U.S. buildings, including the World Trade Center.

Yet there wasn't a *word* about it in the nearly six-thousand-page transcript of the Bojinka trial. Murad's extensive flight training was discussed. But though the tape and transcript of Murad's first interrogation were introduced, his chief interrogator, Col. Rodolfo Mendoza, who had informed the Feds of this troubling evidence, was never called to testify. Indeed, no less than eleven PNP officers were flown to New York to testify about the Dona Josefa bomb factory and Murad's interrogation, but Mendoza, the man who had opened him up, was never mentioned.

Even when Mendoza's assistant, Maj. Alberto Ferro, took the stand, the colonel's name was not disclosed. In an interview for this book, Colonel Mendoza said that Major Ferro was in the room with him for much of Murad's questioning. He even took over the interrogation after the colonel had finished.[4]

But under oath, Ferro declared, "I cannot really recall who all those people were conducting the [Murad] interview[s]."

Neither Mendoza's identity nor Murad's third-plot disclosures ever became public during the three-month Bojinka trial. The FBI seemed to be going out of its way to avoid even a hint of the plot that was ultimately carried out on 9/11.

When FBI agent Frank Pellegrino took the stand on August 6, 1996, he testified that he had arrived at Camp Crame, the site of Murad's interrogation, on January 17, 1995. At the time, Colonel Mendoza was grilling Murad only a few bungalows away. Yet the FBI agent swore under oath that he didn't even *know* the suspect was being questioned until months later, at the end of March 1995.[5]

In terrorism cases, it's not unheard of for the Feds to let foreign officials get confessions from suspects before they're handed over and read their Miranda rights. But given that Murad was the partner of Ramzi Yousef, it's difficult to believe that the FBI wasn't briefed at every stage of the interrogation by the PNP—especially since Pellegrino and FBI agent Thomas Donlon seemed so well informed during their interrogation of Murad on the flight home. (See FBI 302 of interrogation on pp. 499–517).

We requested an interview with Special Agent Pellegrino for this book, but the New York office of the FBI declined to make him available.

As discussed, the FBI 302 of Pellegrino and Donlon's interrogation contained nothing about the third plot except for Murad's extraordinary admission that Yousef planned to return to the U.S. "to bomb the World Trade Center a second time." Even Murad's early confession about the plan to fly "a small plane" into CIA headquarters was ignored by federal prosecutors.

In a statement before the Joint Congressional Inquiry exploring the intelligence lapses leading up to 9/11, staff director Eleanor Hill said, "The plans to crash a plane into CIA headquarters and to assassinate the

Pope were only at the 'discussion' stage and therefore not included in [the Bojinka] indictment."

Hill went on to testify that "The FBI's criminal investigative file reflects the focus of the prosecution. The Joint Inquiry Staff located almost no references to the plan to crash a plane into CIA HQ in the FBI's . . . files. . . . The other aspects of the plot were not part of the criminal case and therefore not considered relevant."[6]

It seems that even the congressional investigators who spent months researching the road to 9/11 were unaware that in 1995 Murad had disclosed a much bigger hijacking plot to the Philippine investigators.

Now, halfway across the globe from Manila, the plot was beginning to unfold.

The Phoenix Connection

By 1996, Tucson had become a hotbed of radical Islamic activity. In the late fall, FBI asset Harry Ellen saw a man outside an area mosque who was carrying a windbreaker from a local flight school. "He was with two younger guys that looked liked fundamentalists," Ellen said. "It drew my attention."

Engaging the man in conversation, he learned that he was an Algerian pilot who was training other Middle Eastern men to fly. In an interview for this book, Ellen said that he reported the information to his FBI control agent, Ken Williams.

"I told this to Williams. I told him to be very concerned about air schools."[7]

Later, Ellen said that he saw the same Algerian flight instructor talking to Abu Sief, the New Jersey émigré from the al-Salaam Mosque who had claimed to know Ramzi Yousef. Again, Ellen reported the encounter to Agent Williams. "I said, 'This guy is either a good guy or a bad guy,'" recalled Ellen. "'If he's a good guy, he's somebody you should know, and if he's a bad guy he's somebody you should be watching.'"

Ellen subsequently had a falling-out with Williams after a bitter dispute involving Joanna Xie, a Chinese national who Ellen said Williams suspected of being a spy. The fifty-five-year-old businessman had become intimate with the young woman in violation of Bureau protocol, which forbids assets from getting personally involved with subjects they are working. In a sworn affidavit used in an INS deportation hearing targeting Xie, Ellen alleged that Williams ordered him to cut off the affair. When he refused, Ellen said, the FBI agent became so incensed that he threatened to blow Ellen's FBI cover and expose him to the Palestinians.

Ellen claimed that his subsequent termination by the Bureau ruined him financially and torpedoed his efforts to operate a foundation in Gaza that would have distributed humanitarian aid to Palestinian refugees. Earlier, with FBI help and funding, Ellen had set up the Al Sadaqa Foundation to create jobs and deliver medical care to the Gaza Strip. The Bureau saw the foundation as a potential bonanza for intelligence.

In 1998, Ellen brought two Arizona eye doctors to Gaza to treat children. One of them, Dr. Richard Glonek, a Scottsdale optometrist, was concerned at first for his safety, since his wife was Jewish. But once in Gaza he said he felt safe under Ellen's sponsorship. "Everybody knew Harry when he was there," Glonek said. "He seemed to be held in high regard."[8]

"I was able to get safe passage for these doctors," said Ellen, who convinced the five major Palestinian resistance factions to meet. It was the first time they had come together "at one table," according to Soheil Juma al-Gool, a founder of the Gaza branch of Hamas, the Islamic Resistance Movement, who met with Ellen and representatives from the Islamic Jihad, Fathah, the PFLP, and the Democratic Front for the Liberation of Palestine.

"What resulted was historic," wrote al-Gool in a 1999 letter, "the formation of the Jebah Al Salam [Peace Front]."[9] He credited Ellen (aka Abu Yusef) with stopping three "retaliatory bombings" in the interest of making Ellen's Al Sadaqa Foundation work. But Ellen now says all that ended when his control agent, Ken Williams, threatened to blow his cover with the Palestinians. Their falling-out shut down what might have been a crucial U.S. link to Yasser Arafat's organization at a time when the Israeli-Palestinian crisis was spiraling out of control. "Once I split with Williams, my efforts in Gaza came to an end," said the businessman-turned-spy. "I also felt that he'd put my life at risk."

The FBI refused to comment on the allegations, but the controversy became public in a series of articles by Mark Flatten, an investigative reporter for the *East Valley Tribune,* an Arizona newspaper. Ellen's cause was subsequently supported by former U.S. Senator Dennis DeConcini, onetime chairman of the Senate Intelligence Committee. Vouching for Ellen's bona fides as an intelligence asset, DeConcini said, "This guy is for real."[10]

The FBI later refused to meet with Ellen's lawyer or comment on his prior status as an asset. At the request of Arizona Senator John McCain, Ellen's case was reviewed by the Bureau, which found that the complaint against Williams didn't warrant investigation.[11]

Special Agent Ken Williams would eventually go down in history as the man who wrote the infamous "Phoenix Memo," suggesting that the FBI monitor flight schools for suspicious Middle Eastern pilots. He sent the memo to Bureau headquarters and the New York office on July 10, 2001, almost three months to the day before 9/11.

In May 2002, Williams told a congressional committee that if FBI officials had acted on his recommendations, he believed the September 11 attacks might have been thwarted. Later, Senator Arlen Specter (R-PA) called the Phoenix memo "a virtual blueprint" that should have signaled the Bureau to the 9/11 plot.[12]

But in an interview for this book, Ellen insisted that in the mid-1990s, when he told Williams about the Algerian pilot and his meeting with the man tied to Ramzi Yousef, Williams told him to "leave it alone."[13]

"My experience over the years," said Ellen, "is that when somebody tells you to 'leave it alone,' it means 'I don't want you involved in that. I've got it covered.' So I left it alone."

Ellen now believes that Williams sent the July 2001 memo when he did because Flatten's articles were about to appear. "Ken had known about Islamic pilots and flight training in Arizona for years," said Ellen. "But his big memo warning everybody was never sent until he found out that the articles on me and our problems were going to go."

The reporter who wrote the articles agrees. "I started looking into Harry's story about three to four months before they were published," said Mark Flatten.

"My first contact with the FBI was late June, early July of 2001. They knew at that point I was looking into allegations of FBI impropriety with Harry. Then, lo and behold, on July tenth Ken Williams writes this memo saying we ought to start looking at Arab guys. From what we know, the Williams memo dealt with information he'd developed a year and a half to two years earlier, so I don't know why he'd stick it in a memo then."[14]

In an effort to get Williams's side of the story for this book, I contacted the FBI's Phoenix office on April 11, 2003, but the agent reportedly refused to be interviewed, communicating through a Bureau spokesman in Washington that his activities were "classified."[15]

Harry Ellen now believes that one of the young Islamics he saw outside the mosque back in 1996 was an Algerian pilot named Lotfi Raissi. Raissi was arrested by British authorities right after 9/11 and indicted by the U.S. Justice Department on charges of fraud and giving false information on his FAA pilot's application. A British judge set him free months later, declaring there was insufficient evidence to tie him to the 9/11 conspiracy. But the FBI found evidence that Raissi had been in the proximity of one of the key 9/11 hijackers on three occasions.

Hani Hanjour, the Saudi who flew American Airlines Flight 77 into the Pentagon, had been enrolled at CRM Airline Training Center in Scottsdale, Arizona, as far back as 1996.[16] On five dates in 1998 he trained on a flight simulator at the same facility as Raissi, who Ellen says he'd warned FBI agent Williams about years before. Raissi and Hanjour reportedly flew in the identical Piper trainer on the same day or consecutive days in 1999, and the two men enrolled together at Sawyer Aviation School on June 23, 2001, less than three months before 9/11.[17]

Kris Kolesnik, the former Senate investigator and authority on FBI oversight, is now executive director of the National Whistleblowers Center in Washington. In assessing whether or not the FBI could have stopped the attacks of September 11, Kolesnik said the case of Harry Ellen represents a major dot on the chart.*

"What Harry's story shows you," said Kolesnik, "is that if Ken Williams had worked the case the way he should have, as a proper counterterrorism investigation, he himself could have probably prevented 9/11."[18]

After the convictions in the Trade Center and Day of Terror cases, the New York office of the FBI had a mountain of evidence proving that a "jihad army" had done battle in New York City. Why was it so difficult

---

*Timeline #96. p. 21.

for them to understand that the army stretched worldwide—especially when Ramzi Yousef, who was sitting in a Manhattan jail cell, had bragged about it?

The dots on the chart now ran from Jersey City to Karachi to Manila, then back to Tucson and Qatar. In January of 1996 the FBI and the CIA had created Station Alex, dedicated to tracking Osama bin Laden and his operatives. Yet somehow Khalid Shaikh Mohammed, bin Laden's point man and Yousef's uncle, continued to elude them.

In early 1997, as the 9/11 plot began to take shape, Mohammed was busy recruiting the pilots he would later call the "muscle" behind the attacks. In the months ahead he would handpick Mohammed Atta, the severe young Egyptian who would replace Murad as lead hijacker. Later, in Afghanistan, he would reportedly meet Zacarias Moussaoui, the Frenchman dubbed "the twentieth hijacker."

He would even select the coded names for the targets, dubbing the Pentagon the "fine arts" center, and the Trade Center the facility for "town planning."[19]

Mohammed would go on to recruit the other hijackers from al Qaeda's own "department of martyrs." And then, as the clock ticked down, he would give the "go" order to execute the plot, which his nephew had designed with Abdul Hakim Murad in Lahore back in August 1994.

And just as the FBI had missed chance after chance to nail Yousef, Khalid Shaikh Mohammed would slip by them time and time again.

35

RECONNAISSANCE

R onnie Bucca was a fire marshal. By any traditional definition, terrorism wouldn't have been even remotely close to his jurisdiction. But he had seen the 1993 World Trade Center bombing as an act of arson, and one that touched him personally. Now the four main conspirators and the bomb maker himself had been convicted. The blind Sheikh and the other members of his "jihad army" would be locked up for years. Any other investigator might have given up and moved on. But not Bucca. He was the firefighter who had fallen five stories and worked his way back to Rescue One.

As the spring of 1997 arrived, he continued to believe that the Trade Center was still a potential target. "He said, 'They're gonna come back and do it again,'" said Jacob L. Boesen, an analyst who worked with Ronnie at the Defense Intelligence Analysis Center at Bolling Air Force Base in Washington, D.C. "I said to him, 'They did it once.' But he said, 'Some of those people have folded now into al Qaeda.'"[1]

Boesen, who wrote a study on al Qaeda for the National Conference on Homeland Security, said Bucca was a rare combination. "Ronnie's military experience as an intelligence officer gave him an analytical role, and his experience as a Special Ops Green Beret gave him an operational perspective," said Boesen.[2] "[He] was the real deal. But he was frustrated because the Bureau was the lead player in New York when it came to terrorism and he couldn't get anybody on the Task Force to listen."

"Ronnie was tenacious," said his brother Bobby, the NYPD cop. "He would just not let this thing go. Besides, with what he was seeing in the reserves, he knew there was more to this."

By the spring of 1997, the FBI finally seemed to agree. John O'Neill, now running the Bureau's National Security Division in New York, talked publicly about an ongoing Middle Eastern terror threat. "Almost every one of these groups has a presence in the United States today," he told the A.P. "A lot of these groups have the capacity and the support infrastructure in the United States to attack us here if they choose to.[3]

By mid-July, the U.S. attorney for the Southern District seemed to acknowledge that the threat went beyond Ramzi Yousef and the blind Sheikh. A federal grand jury was convened to determine whether Osama bin Laden had been funneling money to them.[4] The secret panel reportedly heard testimony that bin Laden had delivered money to groups in Detroit, Brooklyn, and New Jersey.

The FBI had learned about bin Laden's direct ties to the Alkifah Center in Brooklyn a year earlier, when Jamal Ahmad al-Fadl turned government informer. The FBI had known about bin Laden's links to Yousef's Pamrapo Avenue bomb factory via phone records dating back to 1992, and his contributions to El Sayyid Nosair's defense the year before that.

But the Feds were encouraged by another big "get" in May 1997, when Mandini al-Tayyib, another of bin Laden's brothers-in-law, was seized by the Saudis. Reportedly the chief financial officer for al Qaeda, al-Tayyib agreed to talk in return for asylum.

By August the FBI had hopes of flipping another potential defector— Wadih El-Hage, the Lebanese Christian convert who had purchased weapons for Mahmud Abouhalima, come to New York at the time of Mustafa Shalabi's murder, and visited El Sayyid Nosair at Riker's Island. El-Hage had become personal secretary to bin Laden after his flight to Sudan.

In the late summer of 1997 he was living in Nairobi, Kenya, where a major al Qaeda cell was operating. The FBI confirmed the existence of the cell after a raid on El-Hage's home resulted in the seizure of his computer. A letter was found on the hard drive written by one of Wadih's house guests, Fazul Abdullah Mohammed Haroun. In so many words the letter described the clandestine cell as operating under the direction of "the Haj," an alias for Osama bin Laden.[5]

While one JTTF agent searched his home with Kenyan police, other agents confronted El-Hage at Nairobi Airport. But instead of arresting the bin Laden confidant, the agents suggested he return to the U.S. Since he was a naturalized U.S. citizen, the agents hoped they might be able to turn him like al-Tayyib. But they underestimated Wadih's commitment to his former boss, bin Laden.

In September, El-Hage left Kenya with his wife and seven kids. Stateside, the Feds picked him up and put him in front of the grand jury. Just as Anticev and Napoli had tried to intimidate Abouhalima and Sattar in 1992 by bringing them down to 26 Federal Plaza, the FBI thought putting El-Hage in a grand jury room might induce him to cooperate. But instead of flipping, he just stonewalled, pleading ignorant to any knowledge of bin Laden or a Kenyan cell.

So the Feds let him go.

The Blown Chance in East Africa

El-Hage returned to Arlington, Texas, where he began operating a tire shop in a middle-class neighborhood and bided his time.

Wadih El-Hage was another direct link between bin Laden and the Brooklyn Alkifah Center. In fact, he'd been dispatched from Arizona to run it on the eve of Shalabi's murder. But the Feds would wait another year after his release before charging him.[6]* Despite the computer letter from Fazul, the sense in the U.S. attorney's office in Manhattan was that the Kenyan cell had been broken. El-Hage was mounting tires in Texas, and Abu al-Banshiri, al Qaeda's chief military officer and director of East African ops, had died in a ferry accident on Lake Victoria the year before.

What the New York Feds *didn't* realize was that al-Banshiri's job was soon taken over by Khalid Shaikh Mohammed.[7] In another extraordinary missed opportunity, the Feds failed to follow up on a reference in Fazul's computer letter to a group of "partisans" in Mombassa and the expected arrival of "engineers" in Nairobi. Plans were afoot at that moment for two catastrophic bombings that would devastate the U.S. embassies in Kenya and Tanzania. But the Feds missed the signals.†

Incredibly, once Wadih El-Hage had been chased out of Africa by the JTTF, the CIA pulled its wiretaps out of his home, and the cell's deadly

---

*Timeline #98. p. 21.
†Timeline #112. p. 24.

plans began to move forward. Later the Kenyan embassy got another "walk-in" who warned of a bombing plot. But the informant, Mustafa Mahmud Said Ahmed, had sounded similar warnings at other African embassies in the past, and none had panned out. As far as the Feds were concerned, he was a snitch with a history of crying wolf. Ahmed was given a polygraph, and when he reportedly failed, his warnings were dismissed.

Now, in August of 1997, al Qaeda operatives were back in New York, moving ahead to perfect the plot Ramzi Yousef had designed back in 1994.

On August 31, Ghasoub al-Abrash Ghalyoun, a heavyset Syrian, walked into the lobby of the South Tower of the World Trade Center with a small group of men. One of them was carrying an infant. Ghalyoun pulled out a video camera and began shooting.

"We are at the Twin Towers of Manhattan," one of the men said in Arabic on the tape. "This is the inside of one of the Twins."[8]

The group took an elevator to the observation deck on the South Tower's 110th floor. The camera panned across to the TV and radio antennas on the North Tower and zoomed in and out, focusing on the Tower's outer wall on the south side.

Later Ghalyoun was videotaped sitting in the outdoor plaza at the foot of the Trade Center, with his arm around a life-size sculpture of a businessman that sat at the foot of the Towers. On the same U.S. trip, Ghalyoun and his party took video of the Sears Tower in Chicago and the Golden Gate Bridge in San Francisco.

But this was no ordinary group of foreign tourists. As it turned out, Ghalyoun was a member of the radical al Qaeda–linked Muslim Brotherhood. His videotapes were later seized by Spanish authorities after his arrest in Madrid in April 2002 and described by a judge as possible surveillance tapes for the 9/11 attacks.

"If you wanted to use one word, I would say they were 'target tapes,'" said Gustavo Aristegui, former chief of staff of the Spanish national police.[9] Evidence developed by intelligence officials later discovered that Spain was a staging area used by Mohammed Atta in the months before September 11. In what looked like a chilling reconnaissance for 9/11, the tape showed the camera zooming past the Towers up the Hudson along the flight paths of TWA Flight 11, which Atta later piloted, and United Flight 195, which sliced into the South Tower minutes later.

The sculpture Ghalyoun sat next to, ironically, was one of the few pieces in the Trade Center Plaza that remained undamaged after the Towers collapsed.*

After the tapes were seized in April 2002, the Syrian was released, then rearrested in March 2003 when new evidence against him emerged. According to a statement by Spanish authorities, he taped "installations and monuments . . . which may have been terrorist objectives of al Qaeda."[10] Officials said they suspected that Ghalyoun had passed copies of the tapes to a man believed to be a courier for Osama bin Laden.

The tapes seemed to corroborate what Abdul Hakim Murad had told Colonel Mendoza—that the Trade Center and Sears Tower were among the future targets of the airliner hijacking plot. Jack Cloonan, a former FBI agent working as a consultant to ABC News, described Ghalyoun's tapes as "bone chilling."

Similar surveillance photos had been taken by al Qaeda operatives three to four years before the bombings of the East African embassies in 1998.

"You have a four-year lapse between the surveillance and the actual attack," said Cloonan, who noted that the August 1997 tapes by Ghalyoun followed a similar timetable. Cloonan, who was working in the summer of 1997 on the Bureau's bin Laden squad, didn't see the Trade Center tape until just before ABC aired it in March 2003.

"When I first looked at it, I almost wanted to weep," he said.

Ironically, at the very moment the tape was made, Ramzi Yousef was sitting in a courtroom five blocks away as the second trial began for his *first* attack on the Trade Center. The Feds may have captured him, but preparations for his *second* attack were well under way.

The Apostle of Evil

Ronnie Bucca worked a series of double-shift "mutuals" so he could attend the trial as often as possible. He had made an additional attempt

*Timeline #99. p. 21.

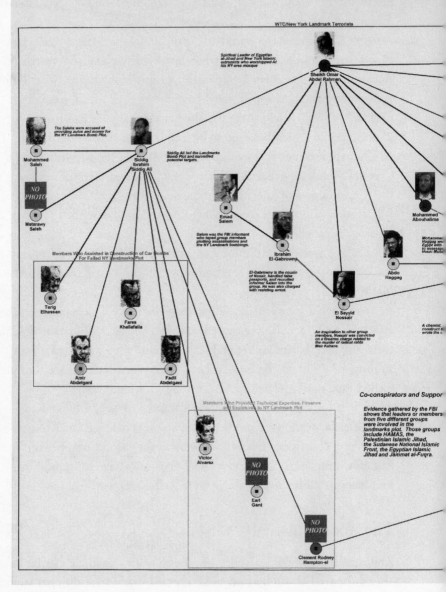

A declassified version of the chart from 8/10/98 shows a direct line from Ramzi Yousef in the lower third of the center box to Osama bin Laden and on to al Qaeda (at right).

ork Landmarks Bomb Plot:
nternational Linkages

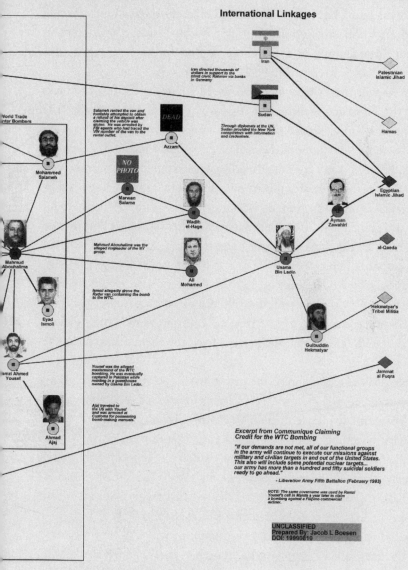

International Linkages

Iran

Iran directed thousands of
dollars in support to the
blind cleric Rahman via banks
in Germany

Palestinian
Islamic Jihad

World Trade
nter Bombers

Salameh rented the van and
foolishly attempted to obtain
a refund of his deposit after
claiming the vehicle was
stolen. He was arrested by
FBI agents who had traced the
VIN number of the van to the
rental outlet.

DEAD

Sudan

Through diplomats at the UN,
Sudan provided the New York
conspirators with information
and credentials.

Hamas

Mohammed
Salameh

NO
PHOTO

Azzam

Egyptian
Islamic Jihad

Marwan
Salama

Wadih
el-Hage

Ayman
Zawahiri

Mahmud Abouhalima was the
alleged ringleader of the NY
group.

al-Qaeda

Mahmud
Abouhalima

Ali
Mohamed

Usama
Bin Ladin

Ismoil allegedly drove the
Ryder van containing the bomb
to the WTC.

Eyad
Ismoil

Hekmatyar's
Tribal Militia

amzi Ahmed
Yousef

Yousef was the alleged
mastermind of the WTC
bombing. He was eventually
captured in Pakistan while
residing in a guesthouse
owned by Usama Bin Ladin.

Gulbuddin
Hekmatyar

Ajaj traveled to
the US with Yousef
and was arrested at
Customs for possessing
bomb-making manuals.

Jammat
al Fuqra

Ahmad
Ajaj

Excerpt from Communique Claiming
Credit for the WTC Bombing

"If our demands are not met, all of our functional groups
in the army will continue to execute our missions against
military and civilian targets in and out of the United States.
This also will include some potential nuclear targets...
our army has more than a hundred and fifty suicidal soldiers
ready to go ahead."

- Liberation Army Fifth Battalion (February 1993)

NOTE: The same covername was used by Ramzi
Yousef's cell in Manila a year later to claim
a bombing against a Filipino commercial
airliner.

UNCLASSIFIED
Prepared By: Jacob L Boesen
DOI: 19950810

to get through to the JTTF detective, but got the cold shoulder again. He hoped that he might pick up some intelligence in the testimony that would help him assemble the pieces of the Yousef puzzle. Lately he had seen classified DIA link charts showing a direct connection between Yousef and Osama bin Laden. The Saudi billionaire was also connected in the chart to Sheikh Rahman through Wadih El-Hage and Egyptian Mahmud Abouhalima, and there was a straight line linking Yousef through bin Laden to something called "al Qaeda."

Since Ronnie didn't have access to the JTTF or any FBI files, he was piecing the "mosaic" together on his own. He still believed that the forces around Yousef would continue to target New York—a suspicion only bolstered at one point in the trial when Yousef's unpublished warning from Nidal Ayyad's computer finally came to light: "We promise you that next time it will be very precise and the Trade Center will be one of our targets." It was an ominous warning. Maybe *now* the Feds would take the threat seriously, Ronnie thought. But there was little coverage of the warning at the time, and its contents didn't surface again in the media until after September 11.[11]

On August 5, 1997, Bucca sat in the back of the courtroom again as Assistant U.S. Attorney Lev Dassin told the jurors that Yousef was part of a "self-proclaimed army of terrorists." Pointing at the bomb maker, Dassin declared, "this man ordered and mixed the chemicals to make the bomb."

But the very composition of the urea nitrate–fuel oil device became a major issue at the trial, following revelations in April of serious problems at the FBI's lab. Evidence in both the World Trade Center and Oklahoma City bombing cases was called into question after the Justice Department's own inspector general issued a report that found "extremely serious and significant problems" at the lab.[12] In the case of Yousef's device, the report concluded that an FBI analyst had identified the explosive "based not on science but on speculation."

This led to some extraordinary testimony in which Yousef—having blown the first trial by representing himself—now deferred to defense attorney Roy Kulcsar. At one point, an executive for the World Trade Center was asked to specify the precise number of toilets and urinals in each tower. When he said there were more than three thousand in each building, the defense argued that the bomb had ruptured sewer lines, spilling thousands of gallons of urine waste into the crater at the B-4 level. Since the Bureau's controversial lab had determined that "urea"— also a component found in human excrement—was an additive in the bomb, Yousef alleged that the building's waste might have skewed the results.[13] It was the kind of desperate argument that Yousef was left with.

An ominous point in the proceedings came when Secret Service Agent Brian Parr described Yousef's confession to him aboard the 707 on the trip back to the States. The bomb maker had related how, just minutes after the 1993 blast, he'd watched the smoldering towers from New Jersey and was disappointed that his original plan to "shear the support beams" hadn't worked.[14]

In his closing argument, Assistant U.S. Attorney David Kelly drew a frightening picture of Yousef. "When you put all the evidence together," he said, "there is only one picture that's painted—that Yousef is a cold-blooded terrorist. He came into this country with a plan to blow people up. He ordered the chemicals from City Chemical. He mixed the chemicals at 40 Pamrapo. He constantly coordinated over the phone with his coconspirators who were renting the van and the Space Station. He was in the van when it was driven into the Trade Center. He detonated the bomb. He ran away. He confessed. He's guilty."

Then he pointed over at Yousef sitting quietly in a dark blue suit next to Ismoil. "The last time that these two people were sitting next to each other, before they came to this courtroom[,] was that day they were sitting next to each other in the van."

"Visualize them driving that van down the subgrades of the Trade Center, driving to their appointed spot next to the Tower. Picture them getting in the back of that van and lighting a fuse, crawling out, hopping in their car and running away, and, moments later, the bomb blew up. The only message that they sent out that day was that these two people are cold-blooded killers."[15]

It took the jury three days to make their decision. In contrast to the outburst at the end of the first Trade Center trial, the formal career of the world's greatest bomb maker ended quietly. With each count of "guilty," Yousef stared straight ahead in silence.

Outside court, Olga Mercado, widow of Wilfredo, the last victim found in the debris of Trade Center blast, said she only wished Yousef and Ismoil had been subject to the death penalty. Speaking in Spanish, translated by her daughter, Mrs. Mercado said she prayed that the two defendants would get life at hard labor. "So they can sweat," she said. "So they can feel some of the pain that the families of the victims feel."[16]

Monica Smith's husband, Eddie, said he felt a sense of great relief at the verdicts, "especially the one guy, Ramzi." Speaking from his new home in California, he promised to come back to New York for the sentencing.

The Bloody IG and the Sheikh

Yousef's second conviction was another triumph for the Feds, but if any investigators in the JTTF thought the war was over, they were wrong. Four days after the verdicts, six assassins surrounded a group of tourists at the famed archaeological site in Luxor, Egypt. They began stabbing and shooting them systematically in one of the bloodiest terror attacks in Mideast memory.

Before it was over, sixty-two people, including four Egyptian policemen, lay dead. The killers wiped out three generations of one British family, including Karina Turner, her mother, and her five-year-old daughter.[17] As they left, the attackers scattered leaflets; one of them was later found stuffed into the slit torso of one of the victims.*

The leaflets called for the release of Sheikh Omar Abdel Rahman.

The attack was the work of al Gamma'a Islamiya, the Islamic Group the Sheikh had run for years. In his *al Hayat* interview, Yousef had declared that the IG was directly affiliated with his "Liberation Army," and documents sent to the Feds by Colonel Mendoza showed a direct link between the IG and Osama bin Laden. By 1997 the IG was being run by another Egyptian named Refa'I Taha Musa.[18]

After the Sheikh was sentenced in 1996, the IG had warned of retaliations. The U.S. State Department later designated it a foreign terrorist organization. Now came the Luxor massacre, four days after the second verdict against Yousef.

The question is, did the FBI recognize the significance of the link?

Detective Lou Napoli and FBI Special Agent John Anticev had been

---

*Timeline #101. p. 22.

aware of El Sayyid Nosair's affiliation with the IG as far back as 1991. In the Day of Terror trial, the New York Feds had tied the blind Sheikh directly to Ramzi Yousef, whose Trade Center bombing was another attack by Abdel Rahman's "jihad army." The bloody Luxor massacre was just the latest signal to the Feds that Islamic radicals associated with this same group were continuing to murder civilians.

But what they *didn't* know at the time, and didn't connect the dots on until years later, was that one of the Egyptians whom they'd missed in the Day of Terror indictment was continuing to operate in New York—allegedly passing information between the blind Sheikh in prison and the murderous IG.

Ahmed Abdel Sattar—the Staten Island postal worker who'd discovered Anticev's home address and feasted on lamb after the Nosair trial—was well known to the Feds. He had been subpoenaed in September 1992. Anticev himself had warned Sattar that the FBI was going to get the terrorists around Nosair as sure as they got Gotti. Emad Salem had alerted the FBI to Sattar in 1993. And on the day of the Sheikh's sentencing in 1996, Sattar had declared to the press that "the man will never be silenced." Yet for reasons unknown, the FBI gave him a pass.*

As Christmas approached, the Feds were savoring their second Yousef victory and looking forward to his sentencing. On January 8, 1998, Judge Kevin Duffy was in rare form as he stared at Yousef for the last time. "Our system of justice has not often seen the type of horrendous crimes for which you stand convicted," said Duffy, who then quoted from the Koran. "Your God is not Allah," he said, bearing down on Yousef, who stood before the bench.

Duffy then hit Yousef with 240 years in prison, matching the sentence he'd given the first four Trade Center defendants. But he made the rare recommendation that the bomb maker serve every day of it in solitary confinement.

"The evil" that Yousef espoused, he said, needed to be "quarantined." Leaning forward on the bench, Duffy confronted the terrorist directly:

"You, Ramzi Yousef[,] came to this country pretending to be an Islamic fundamentalist, but you care little or nothing for Islam or the

*Timeline #102. p. 22.

faith of the Muslims. You adored not Allah, but the evil that you your-self have become. And I must say that as an apostle of evil, you have been most effective."

Still, the Mozart of Terror was defiant to the end.

"The Government in its summations and opening statements said that I was a terrorist," Yousef responded. "Yes I am a terrorist and I am proud of it. And I support terrorism so long as it was against the United States Government and against Israel, because you are more than terror-ists. . . . You are butchers, liars and hypocrites."[19]

Then Yousef, in what he knew to be his last public appearance, went out of his way to spew an additional measure of venom. His target this time wasn't the government in Washington or Tel Aviv but Baghdad.

Noting that Saddam had killed thousands of his own Kurdish citizens with chemical weapons, Yousef went on to declare that he "is killing [innocent Iraqi citizens] because he is a dictator."[20] For a man accused by many of being an agent of Iraq, it was a curious way to bring down the public curtain on his career.

That night, when Ronnie Bucca got home, Eve made a special dinner for him to celebrate. But after they went to bed, Bucca, who usually got along on a few hours' sleep, tossed and turned. Then, late in the night, he woke up suddenly. He was sweating.[21]

"Hey, Ron. Are you okay?" asked Eve, switching on a bedside light.

Ronnie held his hand out. It was trembling. He closed it into a fist and tried to calm himself. After years of rushing into burning buildings he'd had his share of bad dreams, but somehow to Eve this seemed worse.

"Tell me about it," she said. Ronnie looked at her. He shook his head and started to go back to sleep, but she pressed him. "Come on, tell me."

"I saw this fire," he said. "Like I usually see. Only this time, I couldn't knock it down. It wouldn't go out. Then I saw something sparkle. A dag-ger with jewels like from Ali Baba." He shook his head like he was losing the image, so Eve pressed him.

"What else?"

"There was this sound. . . . It started slow, in the background. Then it was like a heartbeat. I could see the heart, and pretty soon it turned into the earth. It was beating like it was alive, and then this knife just stabbed at it." Ronnie winced at the thought. "This beating heart was the world and this dagger just cut right through."

He looked at his wife, who put her arms around him. "Ronnie, you've done everything that you can. You have got to let this go. You're the balanced one, remember?"

"I can't help what I know, Eve."

"But it's over now, right? You said Yousef was the one—the big piece."

Ronnie nodded, then turned toward her. "What if it's bigger than *him*?"

Eve moved closer. "Ronnie, no matter how many fires you put out, there's always another one. All you can do is keep your family close and do your job the best way you can."

Ronnie stared at her, wanting to believe it, but a feeling kept gnawing at him that there was more to this.

The next morning, when he picked up the *New York Times*, he knew he was right. On the inside jump page of the story that covered Yousef's sentencing, there was a reference to something the U.S. attorney had done after the proceedings in court.

Mary Jo White had formally unsealed an indictment naming someone called Khalid Shaikh Mohammed as Yousef's coconspirator. The price on his head was $2 million.[22]

Ronnie thought he knew most of the players around Yousef, but not this guy. And now the Feds had tagged him with the same bounty that had brought Yousef down. That meant he was a heavyweight. The story said he might even be *related* to the bomb maker.

Christ, thought Ronnie, *there's another one out there.*

36

THE DRUMS
GET LOUDER

As 1998 unfolded, the number of dots signaling the FBI's missed opportunities on the road to 9/11 began exploding like bursts from an al Qaeda Kalashnikov. But in an appearance before Congress on February 5, Dale Watson, the FBI's assistant director for counterterrorism, downplayed the threat to the United States.

"Although we should not allow ourselves to be lulled into a false sense of security," said Watson, "I believe it is important to note that in the five years since the Trade Center bombing, no significant act of foreign-directed terrorism has occurred on American soil."[1] Watson later told a congressional committee that he only knew of three al Qaeda suspects in the United States prior to August of 1998.[2]

Watson's assessment suggests that Bureau management perceived the terrorist threat in the late 1990s to be manageable. By 1998 the FBI's New York office, the office of origin for all al Qaeda–related cases, was one hundred agents short of its full staffing level, and 60 percent of the agents who *were* on the job had less than four years' experience.[3]

Yet the very Justice Department that Watson worked for would soon issue an indictment effectively documenting a major al Qaeda presence on U.S. soil dating back nine years. After years of unconnected dots, the U.S. attorney for the Southern District of New York was finally acknowledging that al Qaeda "grew out of the Makhtab al Khidimat (MAK) (Services Office), which maintained outposts in various parts of the world including Afghanistan, Pakistan and the United States, particularly at the Alkifah Refugee Center in Brooklyn."[4]

As John Anticev would say, "Bingo!"

The occasion for that statement was the indictment of Wadih El-Hage, which came in early October. It drew upon the extensive intelligence the New York Feds had in their own files dating back to 1989—evidence showing that:

1. Nosair, Abouhalima, Salemeh, the blind Sheikh, and many of the WTC bombing and Day of Terror plotters were united in a terrorist cell that operated out of the al-Salaam Mosque, the Abu Bakr Mosque, and the Alkifah Center at the Al Farooq Mosque in Brooklyn.

2. From March of 1991 when Mustafa Shalabi was murdered, the Alkifah Center had become a de facto al Qaeda outpost in New York City.

3. Within the United States the al Qaeda network ran from Brooklyn to Arlington, Texas, to Tucson, Arizona.

The Feds were finally acknowledging that what they called the "jihad army" was part of the same enterprise Ramzi Yousef had called the "Liberation Army." In fact, a separate indictment of bin Laden unsealed by the SDNY in November stated that the alternate name for al Qaeda was the "Islamic Army."[5] It was an international Islamic fundamentalist conspiracy, with bin Laden and his Egyptian lieutenants pulling the strings.

All of this was admitted publicly by the Feds in the fall of 1998. Yet before Congress in early February, Watson, a top FBI official, was asserting that al Qaeda had little or no presence in the U.S. homeland. By emphasizing that America had been free for five years of "foreign-directed" terror, Watson *was* effectively lulling Congress into a false sense of security.

Within days of Watson's testimony, bin Laden issued a *fatwa* under the banner of the "International Islamic Front for Jihad on the Jews and Crusaders." In it he encouraged Muslims to kill Americans—including civilians—anywhere in the world they were found.[6]

By this time, members of the academic community were beginning to understand the depth of the threat. Steve Gale, a terrorism specialist at the University of Pennsylvania, warned FAA officials of two possible scenarios for attacks against the United States.[7] One called for crashing planes into nuclear plants along the East Coast; the second, with extraordinary foresight, warned that terrorists might crash Federal Express cargo planes into the World Trade Center, the Pentagon, the White House, the Sears Tower, and the Golden Gate Bridge.*

If a scholar could connect the dots, why couldn't the Bureau?

But within months, the FBI would apparently ignore two new key pieces of information signaling that Yousef's 9/11 plot was in the works.

First, the FBI's chief pilot in Oklahoma City reported that he had seen Middle Eastern men "who appeared to be either using planes or obtaining flight training . . . that could be used for terrorist purposes." But the information never left the Bureau field office.[8]† Later, the FBI received a report that a terrorist organization planned to bring students to the U.S. to study aviation and that a member of the group had frequently discussed his intent to target civil aviation in the United States.[9]

But the most shocking piece of intelligence came in August of 1998, when both the FAA and the Bureau picked up information that unidentified Arabs were planning to fly "an explosive-laden plane" from an unnamed country into *the World Trade Center*.[10] The FAA reportedly found the plot "highly unlikely given the state of the foreign country's aviation program," and the FBI's New York office filed the intelligence away without taking action.**

On August 7, 1998, during a search of the apartment of Khalid al-Fawwaz, who headed al Qaeda's London office, investigators discovered manuals virtually identical to the ones Mohammed Ajaj had brought into JFK with Ramzi Yousef in September 1992.‡ But that discovery was eclipsed by events that took place in Africa the same day—events the FBI had been warned about a year earlier when it penetrated an al Qaeda cell in Kenya.

Back then, during the August 1997 raid on Wadih El-Hage's Nairobi

---

*Timeline #108. p. 23.
†Timeline #109. p. 23.
**Timeline #110. p. 23.
‡Timeline #111. p. 24.

apartment, a New York JTTF agent had found a computer with a letter acknowledging someone called the "Haj," an alias for bin Laden. "We can now state that the security position on the cell is at 100 per cent danger," said the letter. "We, the East African cell members, do not want to know about the operations plans, since we are just implementers."[11]

It was two months later that Mustafa Mahmud Said Ahmed had walked into the embassy to warn that it would be bombed. U.S. Ambassador Prudence Bushnell had written to U.S. Secretary of State Madeline Albright requesting increased security. The Kenyan intelligence service had even warned the CIA about an imminent plot in mid-1998.[12]

Two Embassies; Two Bombs

Then, on August 6, the Egyptian Islamic Jihad, a group tied directly to bin Laden, warned that they would soon deliver a message to the United States. "We hope they read [the message] with care," said the warning, "because we will write it with God's help in a language they will understand."[13]

The next day, the U.S. embassies in Nairobi and Dar es Salaam, Tanzania, were attacked almost simultaneously with truck bombs. The combined death toll was 234, with more than 5,000 injured. Mohammed Al-Owhali, one of the Nairobi plotters, had exploded a stun grenade prior to the first blast, drawing embassy workers to the windows of the twenty-one-story glass tower as glass shards ripped into the building. Ambassador Bushnell herself narrowly escaped death.[14]

If the FBI ever needed a wakeup call, this was it.

A month later the Bureau bounced back by arresting Ali Mohammed, the traitorous ex-Egyptian Army officer who had become a U.S. Army sergeant and served as an instructor in the Special Operations Warfare School at Fort Bragg while working for al Qaeda.

Mohammed soon admitted that he had taken pictures of the Nairobi embassy and passed them to bin Laden prior to the bombing—a surveillance mission that echoed the Trade Center reconnaissance video made by Ghasoub al-Abrash Ghalyoun the year before. Underscoring the kind of detailed planning al Qaeda engaged in before an attack, Mohammed told U.S. interrogators that when he showed bin Laden the embassy pictures, the Saudi billionaire actually pointed to where the bomb truck should go.[15]

Now, as Ali Mohammed confessed, the Feds were stunned to learn how many missed signals he had given them over the years. First, he'd been photographed by the Bureau's SOG team as early as the summer of 1989, training with Abouhalima and Salameh at Calverton, Long Island.* The FBI had found Top Secret training manuals from Fort Bragg that Mohammed had given to El Sayyid Nosair in 1990.† Interviewed by an FBI agent in San Francisco back in 1993, Mohammed had disclosed that bin Laden was "building an army" with the intent of overthrowing the Saudi royal family—but word of the debriefing reportedly never got back to the New York JTTF.[16]** While living in northern California, Mohammed had even served as an FBI snitch on illegal alien smuggling. Officials later admitted that his informant work helped the wily ex-sergeant divert the Bureau's attention from his true terrorist aims.[17]

The sheer audacity of al Qaeda's penetration of the United States became clear as Mohammed kept talking. His FBI interrogators were more and more stunned by each startling detail.

At the same time he was instructing Green Berets at Fort Bragg, Mohammed revealed, he was commuting to New York to train the blind Sheikh's "jihad army." He used his knowledge of Special Forces operational techniques to train the top commanders of al Qaeda in Khost, Afghanistan,[18] along with elite members of bin Laden's own bodyguard in Sudan. In 1996, when bin Laden left Sudan for Afghanistan, it was ex-U.S. Army Sergeant Ali Mohammed who helped move his entourage.

"The fact that Osama was able to put an operative like him into a Special Forces training school should have been a screaming alert to the community," said one intelligence source.[19] "Ali Mohammed was a guy who had intimate knowledge of our military readiness."

By the time of Mohammed's confession, it was debatable which was more of a shock—the fact that bin Laden had succeeded in planting a high-level mole in an elite unit of the U.S. Army, or the fact that the Bureau had failed to read the signals and nail him years before.

The sweeping indictment the SDNY issued against Wadih El-Hage in

---

*Timeline #03. p. 1.
†Timeline #10. p. 3.
**Timeline #113. p. 24.

October also named three other conspirators in the African embassy bombings. It laid bare bin Laden's ties to the Egyptian Islamic Jihad and the murderous IG associated with Sheikh Rahman. Further, it listed each of the countries worldwide where bin Laden's terror network was linked to local jihadi groups. They included Sudan, Egypt, Saudi Arabia, Yemen, Somalia, Eritrea, Djibouti, Afghanistan, Pakistan, Bosnia, Croatia, Albania, Algeria, Tunisia, Lebanon, the Philippines, Tajikistan, Azerbaijan, Indian Kashmir, and Russian Chechnya.

Iraq was not among them.

The following month, Osama bin Laden's own indictment was unsealed. It alleged that al Qaeda had "forged alliances" with the government of Iran and the Hizbollah terror group.

It also asserted that "al Qaeda reached an understanding" that it would not work against Saddam Hussein.[20] Pledging not to attack the Baghdad regime was a far cry from being its puppet, yet scholars with influence in the U.S. intelligence community continued to push the theory that Ramzi Yousef, al Qaeda's most accomplished bomb maker, was an Iraqi agent.[21]

Coming as it did just two months after the embassy bombings, bin Laden's indictment seemed to have been produced with lightning speed. But in truth, much of the al Qaeda intel it contained had been provided by Jamal Ahmad al-Fadl, the Sudanese defector, two years before. Given the warnings the FBI had in 1997 about the Nairobi cell, it was another example of the Justice Department's approach to the war on terror, which was largely reactive.

For more than two decades the FBI had been charged with preempting terror threats on American ground, but when it came to al Qaeda, the Bureau was, in effect, two for four: they had foiled the Day of Terror and Bojinka plots, but they had failed to stop Yousef the first time in 1993, and they missed the intel on the two East African embassy bombings of 1998.

Even the two preemptions could be qualified. Emad Salem had broken the Sheikh's cell *despite* the harassment he'd endured from management in the FBI's New York office. And Yousef would have been well on his way to carrying out Bojinka had it not been for the fire in Room 603 and Capt. Aida Fariscal's follow-through.

Now there was evidence of another horrific Yousef plot festering away

376 · 1000 YEARS FOR REVENGE

in the FBI's files. Colonel Mendoza had passed on Murad's testimony about the third plot. Ken Williams had information about Middle Eastern pilots training in Arizona flight schools. Harry Ellen had warned of a man tied to Sheikh Rahman associating with a Mideast flight instructor. In the Feds' own indictment they had Wadih El-Hage running from Arizona to Brooklyn, to bin Laden's side in Sudan, to Nairobi, and back to New York.

Most amazing of all, Osama himself was issuing what amounted to al Qaeda *press releases,* warning of further attacks on U.S. civilians.

If ever the FBI should have heard the drums pounding, it was in the fall of 1998. They now had proof positive that al Qaeda was capable of audacious simultaneous attacks on U.S. interests in separate cities, using weapons of mass destruction.

But Ramzi Yousef was locked up forever. The Feds had quickly and decisively indicted the embassy bombers. So the Bureau didn't seem to catch a whiff of the plot that was unfolding under the direction of Yousef's uncle Khalid Shaikh Mohammed.

By Halloween 1998, Mohammed Atta, the Egyptian student recruited by Mohammed to replace Abdul Hakim Murad, had leased a four-room apartment at 54 Marienstrasse in Hamburg, Germany. During the months to come, it would serve as a combination crash pad and training center for the suicidal jihadis who would execute Yousef's third plot.

The Two-Week Hit

That same month, Nancy Floyd, the FBI agent who had come closest to derailing Yousef the first time, was about to get the final decision in the investigation into her conduct by the FBI's Office of Professional Responsibility. After a hearing in Washington that summer, her attorney told her things didn't look good.

"In the end, it was going to come down to Nancy's word versus Carson Dunbar's, [and he was] an assistant special agent in charge," said retired agent Len Predtechenskis. "Guess who was going to lose?"

The OPR investigation had been hanging over Nancy's head since the summer of 1993. Given that a typical OPR probe was resolved in a matter of months, Richard Swick, the Washington attorney whose firm represented her, believed the Bureau may have had an agenda in dragging out Nancy's investigation.

"They may have been stringing it out until all of the terrorism cases related to Ramzi Yousef were disposed of," Swick said.[22] The theory seemed to be that by holding the threat of suspension over Nancy's head, the outspoken agent would stay quiet.

Nancy's mentor, Len Predtechenskis, said that the Bureau often used the OPR process to keep agents in line. As noted, during the time an OPR probe was ongoing, agents were ineligible for promotions or requested transfers. But Nancy's situation was even more unusual. Not only were the proceedings more protracted, the file of the case was atypical of the average OPR investigation.

"Even in a short investigation, you can have a file several inches thick," said Diane Bodner Duhig, who handled Nancy's case for Swick's firm. "In this one, without getting into specifics, the file was extremely limited."[23]

According to an FBI source, the file was limited to a heavily redacted statement from Napoli and Anticev describing Nancy's recruitment of Emad Salem, and a statement from Carson Dunbar alleging that Floyd had discouraged Salem from wearing a wire as the ASAC had demanded.

"None of Nancy's immediate supervisors were interviewed," said Predtechenskis. "They didn't talk to me or the other agents who had helped her draft that twelve-page memo that got lost. All Nancy did at the time was obey the directive of her supervisor, Jim Sherman, to tell Salem the truth—that if he wore a wire he'd have to testify. I don't know how you get insubordination to Carson Dunbar out of that."[24]

Jim Roth, the FBI's principal legal officer in New York, contended that the OPR also involved an allegation that Nancy had disobeyed a direct order. "She was told directly by [Deputy Assistant Director] Bill Gavin . . . in June of '93 that she was not to call [Salem] and that if he contacted her she was not to speak to him and she was to report the contact."

Roth said that in the fall of 1993, as Salem was preparing for trial, he told prosecutors that he'd had a number of conversations with Nancy the previous summer. "She never reported it," says Roth, "and that's a problem."

But sources close to Floyd dispute the charge. "The only time Nancy ever met Bill Gavin was in February of 1994, when she went to complain to him about the 'Temptress and the Spy' story," said Predtechenskis. "She wasn't told to stop talking to Salem until August, when Carson gave her the order. Any talks she had with Salem in June or July shouldn't matter."

In an interview for this book, Gavin said that he could not recall the details of the OPR involving Floyd.[25] "I wish I could tell you," he said. "But I can't. I don't know."

Soon, the details wouldn't matter. In the fall of 1998, after a five-and-a-half year investigation, Nancy Floyd received a letter informing her that the allegations of insubordination against her had been *sustained* by the Office of Professional Responsibility. She would be suspended for thirty days.

For Nancy, the news couldn't have come at a more difficult time. Just months before, she had stepped in to help her troubled niece, Shauna Popham, the fifteen-year-old daughter of her sister Kathy, who lived in Texas. After her parents' divorce, Shauna had developed so many personal problems that she had missed her entire first year of high school.

Despite a heavy workload and the fact that her mother, Joan, was living with her, Nancy decided to try and help.[26] "Shauna was going down the wrong path," said Nancy, "and my sister could no longer provide to Shauna what she was going to need to make it into adulthood." Eventually "a decision was made between my sister and me and the court that she would come and live with me and my mother."[27]

So throughout the summer of 1998, Nancy did her best to forget her problems at work, and threw herself into helping Shauna make the transition to life in Stamford, Connecticut.

"I tried to make those first few months as fun as possible," said Nancy. "We went to movies. We took trips. We went up to Newport, Rhode Island. Went to Six Flags. The beach. We shopped for school supplies and clothes."

As a Catholic, Shauna hadn't yet been confirmed, so Nancy enrolled her in classes at the local church. She even took her to an orthodontist, who fitted Shauna for a set of braces.

Then, when school started in September, Nancy and her niece began to feel some growing pains as their relationship evolved. "I had been the fun aunt she had visited in summers prior to that," said Nancy, "and now I had to become the adult, the disciplinarian."

As she met new friends, some of the same temptations that had affected her in the past began to reappear.

"I had to really monitor everyone she was with, and what she was doing," said Nancy. "Eventually she would be driving, and that meant I had to be even more watchful."

Suddenly, the FBI agent with the more-than-full-time job found herself taking a crash course in parenting with a teenager who'd developed some serious problems long before that.

Nancy's care paid off, though, and before long Shauna's grades began to improve. "The bottom line was, Nancy was always there for her," said Len's wife, Carole Predtechenskis, a close friend. "Nancy exerted tough love on Shauna, but the emphasis was on the word *love*."

Shauna Popham completed four years of high school coursework in three, and went on to enlist in the air force, where she finished at the top of her class in basic training. In 2002 she went on to serve in Afghanistan and became a decorated veteran of Operation Enduring Freedom.

"But those first few months of school in the fall were really tough on Nancy," Carole Predtechenskis recalled. "Then, at the worst possible time, she got the news on her OPR."

Nancy had appealed the thirty-day suspension. Then in October she received a letter saying that, pursuant to her appeal, the Office of Professional Responsibility had ruled. She scanned the words of the OPR's final decision, but she couldn't quite believe what she was reading. The allegation that she had been "insubordinate" in her dealings with Carson Dunbar had been sustained. She was to be suspended for fourteen days.

"Nancy should have been *rewarded* for what she'd contributed," said Len Predtechenskis. "Instead she got two weeks on the street." The decision was final. It couldn't be appealed.[28]

Now, with a lump in her throat, Special Agent Nancy Floyd had to go into her supervisor's office and turn over her badge and her gun.

"You have to understand that this was a woman who lived and breathed for the FBI," said Carole Predtechenskis. "To suffer that kind of punishment after she'd done such exemplary work was truly, truly unfair."

After leaving her supervisor, Nancy walked, half-numb, to the cubicle in Foreign Counter Intelligence where Len Predtechenskis had his desk. "As soon as I saw her face, I knew," Len said. "I got up and I told her, 'Look, you'll get past this. You've got to understand that this happened because you told the truth. You protected your asset. You refused to lie to him or put him in jeopardy. You got this hit because you were straight and you did your job. So wear it like what it is—a badge of honor.'"

That night, as she drove home to her mother and Shauna in Stamford, not entirely sure how to tell them, Nancy did her best to keep from crying. She told herself that at least now it was over. She'd endured the worst. She'd lost her dad and then Martha and sat on the stand while lawyers for the Sheikh and his people tried to paint her as a liar and worse. Now it was finished. She'd hit bottom. She was on the street, cut loose by the Bureau she loved. There wasn't any further down she could go than this. At least, that's what she hoped. . . .

37

AN EGYPTIAN MOLE
IN THE FDNY?

Although 1998 had been a rough year for Nancy Floyd, it turned out to be a great one for Ronnie Bucca. Late in the fall, at a fire department function, Ronnie ran into Ed Geraghty, an old friend from Rescue. Geraghty had moved up through the FDNY ranks, eventually becoming a chief at Battalion 9. The two ex-firefighters got to talking about "the white hats"—the chiefs—and how ill prepared the FDNY was for a terrorism event. Geraghty told Ronnie that things might be changing. A bright young captain named Mike Byrne had been working with the city's Office of Emergency Management (OEM), and now he was going to be studying issues of preparedness full-time at Metrotech, the fire department's new headquarters in Brooklyn.

"He's a sharp piece of work," said Geraghty, who told Ronnie to get his résumé together. A few weeks later Geraghty contacted chief fire marshal Mike Vecchi and paved the way for Ronnie to meet Byrne.

"For years Ronnie had been warning us about this threat," said Vecchi. "Then, after the embassy bombings in Africa, the sense was that we really needed somebody here at Metrotech who could focus on the department's response in the event another incident happened in New York—to raise the level of consciousness among the chiefs when it came to terrorism. With Ronnie's intelligence background, he was the only candidate for the job."[1]

Byrne was now working directly for FDNY Commissioner Thomas

von Essen on the ninth floor at Metrotech. When Geraghty introduced him to Ronnie, they hit it off immediately. "After Oklahoma City," said Byrne, "the city became aware of the need for emergency management. A lot of jurisdictions were starting to get funding for terrorism preparedness. When I came back to the FD we were looking for help in strategic planning, and Ronnie turned out to be the perfect guy to help further that effort."[2]

By September, Bucca had been transferred from the Social Club Task Force to Metrotech. "Ron came in and proved to be just relentless in terms of helping us make sense of the terrorism issue and how it impacted the department," said Byrne.

One of the first things Ronnie did was to begin compiling a weekly chronology of terrorism incidents and anniversaries. Mindful that many cells struck on dates that had political significance, Ronnie sent an E-mail copy of the calendar each Monday throughout the FDNY. In the chronology for November 9–15, 1998, he noted the attack by the Abu Sayyaf in the Philippines on November 13, 1995, when U.S. missionary Charles M. Watson was kidnapped. He also noted that November 15 was the tenth anniversary of the date when Palestine declared itself an independent state on the West Bank and Gaza Strip.[3]

By late November, Ronnie was visiting firehouses to discuss terrorism preparedness with the rank and file. In July he'd taken a course in advanced counterterrorism analysis at the Joint Military Intelligence Training Center. In his capacity as an analyst with the 3413th Military Intelligence Detachment, Ronnie and his unit would now meet at least once a month with Jacob Boesen, an analyst with the Defense Intelligence Analysis Center, who would come up from Washington to Fort Dix and deliver chalk talks on the latest terrorism intelligence.

"We were working in asymmetrical threat analysis," said Boesen, "using a program called Analyst's Notebook that helped us produce link charts of the entire al Qaeda organization."[4] The charts, like the one on pages 362–63, allowed DIA analysts to step back and take a broad snapshot of Osama bin Laden's organization and its related cells.

Boesen remembered one session in particular. "After we'd finished," he said, "Ronnie pulled me aside and asked what I thought the chances would be of al Qaeda hitting New York again. At that point the sense in law enforcement had been that Yousef and his cell were finished. But Ronnie seemed to sense there was something else in the works. That's when he asked me about KSM."

Bucca had seen Khalid Shaikh Mohammed's name in the unsealed bin Laden indictment, and he wanted to pick Boesen's brain to see what he knew.

"The truth was, we knew very little about him at that time," said Boesen. "Just what was in the intel from Manila. We knew the FBI had tried to grab him in Qatar. But what we *didn't* know was that he was now in Hamburg meeting with Mohammed Atta and the other members of the 9/11 cell."

By the late fall of 1998, Khalid Shaikh Mohammed was staying well below the radar. He'd made a number of visits to the apartment at 54 Marienstrasse where he met with Atta and Ramzi Binalshibh, a Yemeni, who was also studying on one of several PC-based flight simulators at the safe house. Atta, who had spent fifteen months training in Afghanistan, had returned to Germany.[5] Working with Yousef's uncle to organize the 9/11 attacks, the Egyptian had already made contact with Khalid al-Midhar and Nawaf al-Hamzi, two young Saudi veterans of the Chechen insurrection who were both familiar with the U.S., having lived in California the previous year.

While all of this was going on, Atta was also finishing his dissertation at the Technical University of Hamburg-Harburg. Compared to the murderous plot he was crafting, the paper—which concerned the excavation of the souk (marketplace) in Aleppo, Syria—seemed downright arcane.

As the new year began, Brad Smith finally lost his long battle with Lou Gehrig's disease. Given just months to live when first diagnosed with the illness in 1991, he had survived for eight years—long enough to see not only the capture of Ramzi Yousef but the seizure of CIA killer Mir Aimal Kansi, who was also apprehended as a result of the Rewards for Justice program.

By mid-summer of 1999, Carson Dunbar was ready to retire as ASAC of the FBI's New York office. Governor Christine Todd Whitman had nominated him to be superintendent of the troubled New Jersey

State Police, a department stung by charges of racial profiling. Dunbar, an African American and former State Trooper, seemed like a shoo-in for the job. But his confirmation was clouded by speculation that Democratic senators in Trenton might use public hearings to question him about his role in the World Trade Center investigation.[6]

By late July, the controversy led to a stunning admission by the FBI's former third-highest-ranking official. Oliver "Buck" Revell, the FBI's retired associate deputy director for investigations, suggested to the *New York Times* that Dunbar should be held accountable for the missteps that led up to the Trade Center bombing while he was head of the foreign counterintelligence unit in New York.

"Carson is a good man and a decent person," said Revell, "but he doesn't have tremendous executive skills and I don't think he should have been in that job in the first place. I'm sure he made the decision he thought was best. But in hindsight, it was obviously the wrong move to shut the [Salem] investigation down. If we had continued that investigation, it would have led us to the Sheikh's people, and it's possible we could have prevented the bombing."[7]

There it was: confirmation from a former top Bureau official. Not only had Dunbar mishandled the bombing probe, Revell was saying that if he'd acted differently Yousef might have been stopped. It was precisely the argument Len Predtechenskis had made in defense of Nancy Floyd. But her payoff for disagreeing with Dunbar had been a five-and-a-half-year OPR, capped by a two-week suspension.

In the end, Dunbar's controversial record as New York ASAC didn't seem to matter. He was confirmed as New Jersey's top cop.

In fact, not only did he get the job, but the Justice Department arranged a highly unusual deal for him with the Treasury Department, allowing him to transfer on paper to the Bureau of Alcohol, Tobacco and Firearms and preserve his federal pension benefits while working full-time as the Jersey state police commandant. In addition to paying his $125,000 salary, New Jersey would even reimburse Treasury for his ATF salary.[8]

The Sheikh's Man at Metrotech

By the end of the summer, Ronnie Bucca had been so frustrated in his appeals to the NYPD-FBI Joint Terrorism Task Force that he'd almost given up. Now, in August, he stumbled onto a discovery that sent him back directly to the Feds—the startling revelation that his own department was harboring a man with all the earmarks of an al Qaeda mole.

The discovery came after Ahmed Amin Refai, the Egyptian accountant who'd worked in the Capital Budget Unit, contacted the fire marshals with word that he'd lost his FDNY ID.

When the FDNY had moved its headquarters from the old building at 250 Livingston Street to the new Metrotech complex, Refai had transferred as well. The center of the FDNY's command and control operation, Metrotech housed the plans of virtually every structure in the city. There were blueprints that gave firefighters advance details via CIDS (Critical Incident Dispatch Service) of the entrance, egress, and floor plans of the buildings they were about to enter. Each truck in the Special Operations Command had a computer screen in the cab tied to CIDS; the database was stored at Metrotech.[9]

Metrotech was one of the newest and most secure buildings in the city, with special computer-coded IDs that allowed employees entry to each floor. Access to the building was so tightly controlled that if a fire department employee's ID was lost or stolen, he or she was obliged to report it immediately to the fire marshals.

Now, in mid-August, Ahmed Refai walked up to the ninth-floor office of the BFI's special investigations unit, where the marshals were based, to say he'd apparently misplaced his ID on the PATH train to New Jersey. Fire marshal Mel Hazel asked him if he'd filled out the requisite Lost Access Card Form.

Refai looked evasive. He hesitated, then answered, "Yes."

Hazel asked whom he'd filed it with and when. Refai looked past him, toward the desk of fire marshal Robert Greene, and said, "Greene—I lost it on a Friday the thirteenth. I was out sick Monday. So when I came in on Tuesday the seventeenth, I reported it lost to Mr. Greene."[10]

Hazel accepted Refai's explanation and issued him a temporary ID.

Still, something didn't seem quite right. "He wouldn't make eye contact," Hazel said a few days later, discussing the case with his supervisor, Warren Haring, in the special investigations unit.

"The name sounds Middle Eastern," said Haring. "Where's he from?"

"Egypt," said Hazel.

At that moment Ronnie Bucca was sitting in a nearby cubicle working on his weekly terrorism chronology. As soon as he heard the word "Egypt," he got up and walked over to the two other marshals.

"What'd you say this guy's name is?" asked Bucca.

"Refai," said Hazel. "He's been with the department for twenty-five years. Why?"

Ronnie thought about telling him how deep the Egyptians ran in Sheikh Rahman's cell—how they dominated the Al Farooq Mosque and Abu Bakr where Abdel Rahman had held the Feds at bay back in 1993. How Mohammed Atef and Dr. Ayman Al-Zawahiri, the men on the right and left of Osama bin Laden, were from Egypt. But that would take too long.

Instead he grabbed one of Jake Boesen's declassified link charts on the World Trade Center and Day of Terror investigation.

"You see this?' said Ronnie, counting the mug shots on the chart. "Between the blind Sheikh and bin Laden you've got maybe thirty people. At least a third of them are Egyptians."

Ronnie took the BFI face sheet—the initial report on Refai's "lost ID"—down to his desk in the command and control center on the seventh floor at Metrotech. He eyed the birth date. "DOB 9/21/43 Egypt," it said. "Came to U.S. in 1970. Naturalized citizen in 1976."

Before he went any further, Ronnie picked up a phone and called one of his contacts at DIAC in Washington.

"I need you to run immigration on a subject for me," said Ronnie. "Name—Refai, Ahmed Amin."

When he got the call back the next day, Ronnie Bucca experienced what intelligence investigators call a eureka moment. It was proof of Refai's ties to blind Sheikh Abdel Rahman.

He immediately paged Hazel. When Mel called right back, Ronnie grabbed the phone. "I don't know what you're working right now, but if

I were you I'd get back here ASAP." Hazel asked why. "Your guy Refai," said Ronnie. "I think he's dirty."[11]

Over the next few days, Ronnie Bucca and Mel Hazel treated the Refai investigation like a federal case. They pulled the video of the surveillance cameras from the sixth-floor lobby. The access card readers were on the wall at waist level.

When an employee wanted to get buzzed through the security gate onto the floor, he was required to swipe his card against the reader. Refai had told Hazel that he'd been out sick on Monday, August 16—but a computer log showed that his card had been swiped. Ronnie popped in the tape from that morning and fast-forwarded it.

"Christ, there he is," said Hazel as Ronnie slowed the tape. The two of them watched as the gray-haired accountant brushed his rear against the card reader. Just then, the gate swung open.

"You see that?" Ronnie replayed it again. "He's had the card all the time. It was in his wallet. Back pocket. Check it out."

"Damn," said Hazel. "I asked him for his driver's license when he came up here, and he said he didn't have his wallet on him. He was probably thinking I'd spot the ID."

"It gets better," said Ronnie. "Warren [Haring] came in today and found this on his desk." Ronnie held up a see-through evidence envelope with a copy of a Lost Access Card Form. "It's signed with Bobby Greene's name," said Ronnie. "Only Bobby doesn't *sign* those reports. He uses his *initials,* R.W.E. Besides, it's dated the seventeenth—when Bobby was on vacation."

"I don't get it," said Hazel. "Why would some accountant who's been here twenty-five years lie about his ID and file a false report?"

"Let's get him up here and ask him," said Ronnie.

Half an hour later, Bucca and Hazel were sitting across from the nervous Egyptian at a table in a nearby conference room on the ninth floor.

In a rambling interview, Refai claimed that he'd lied about the ID because he was attached to the card, which had the name of his old unit on it. Now in the Pension Unit, he said that he was nostalgic for his days in Capital Budget; he had wanted to keep his old ID *and* get a new one.

Ronnie and Hazel traded looks. Then Bucca showed Refai another video, in which he slipped past the security gate on another day behind a coworker named Stephen Brown.

Refai looked away, then claimed he was late for work that day and didn't want to get docked any time. So he rushed in behind Brown.

Ronnie asked why he'd lied about calling in sick on August 16, and the accountant didn't have an answer. Ronnie pressed him.

"I don't know," said Refai. "I have apologized. Why are you asking me all of these questions?"

"One more," said Ronnie. "Why did you fake the Lost Card form?"

"What?" Now the Egyptian got indignant. "I did nothing of the kind."

"So you're saying you submitted it to Fire Marshal Greene?" Hazel pressed. Refai nodded. "What's he look like?" Hazel shot back.

"He is a tall man," said Refai, reaching for an answer. Then he changed gears. "I don't have to put up with this." He got up angrily and started to leave when Ronnie hit the intercom. The door opened, and Bobby Greene came in—all five feet, ten inches of him.

For a moment Refai looked startled.

"Do you know this man?" asked Ronnie. Refai hesitated.

"How 'bout you, Bobby?" said Bucca. "Ever seen this guy?"

"Negative," said Greene, coming in to sit down. He picked up the Lost Card form in the envelope and eyed the signature. "I was on vacation. I couldn't have signed this."

Now Refai erupted. "You should *respect* me," he exclaimed. "I've worked here twenty-five years, and you are treating me like a liar."

"But, sir, you *are*," said Hazel. "I mean, you did."

"Well, why *wouldn't* I, the way they treat me in this Pension Unit," said Refai, his anger growing. "I am a good man. U.S. citizen. I have two girls who are doctors. I have rights."

"With all due respect, Mr. Refai," said Ronnie, "whatever you may have accomplished, we have security rules here at headquarters."

At that point, Bobby Greene reminded Refai of the FDNY protocol governing IDs. The Egyptian stood before them with his arms folded, bristling.

Hazel gestured for Ronnie to step outside. In the corridor outside the conference room, Mel lowered his voice. "Man, you're right. This guy's dirty."

Ronnie nodded and whispered back. "Yeah, but right now he's shut down. This is all we're gonna get."

Hazel nodded. The two of them went back into the room. Hazel approached the Egyptian and smiled. "You're free to go, Mr. Refai. Just make sure you keep that ID close, now."

The accountant got up and left.

When he'd gone, Ronnie caucused with Hazel and Greene.

"I think we ought to talk to his boss," he said.

"What more do you think there is?" asked Bobby. Ronnie pulled out a fax he'd received back from DIAC. It was the paperwork he'd requested after his phone call the day before.

"Our guy gave his DOB as 1943," said Ronnie. "Turns out he was born in Alexandria in 1938. He lied about losing the ID, filing the form, and calling in sick. What else is he lying about?"

Refai's old boss in the Capital Budget Unit, Kay Woods, was pregnant at the time. She was due to deliver in a few weeks. Ronnie and Mel promised to keep the interview brief.

"He claims to have some kind of attachment to his old unit," said Ronnie.

Woods rolled her eyes in disbelief.[12] "Really?"

She proceeded to tell them how, during the years they worked together, Refai had acted almost like a ghost employee. How he showed up late, took the maximum sick leave, and did little or nothing when he *was* on the job. She said she thought he had some kind of business on the side in Brooklyn—something related to medicine, because he had no shortage of doctor's notes.

"Maybe with his daughters?" asked Hazel. "He said they were doctors."

Woods cocked her head again. "What? He told you *that*?"

Mel and Ronnie nodded.

"The man has four sons," she said.

Damn, thought Hazel. How many *more* lies was this guy going to tell?

"The truth?" said Woods. "Nothing would surprise me." Just then, she rubbed her stomach. Ronnie sensed that they were keeping her too long.

"If there's anything else, let us know." He and Hazel got up to leave. They were almost to the door when Woods said, "Wait a second. There was that time he got the blueprints."

Ronnie froze, then turned around. "What blueprints?" Woods looked sheepish, almost embarrassed that she'd forgotten.

"It was a long time ago," she said. "Back before the bombing."

"What bombing?" asked Hazel.

"The Trade Center," said Woods. "Ahmed got the plans to the World Trade Center."

Abdel Rahman's Right Arm

Now Ronnie Bucca went into overdrive. After another talk with Woods, he found out that Refai had called in sick the day of the bombing, then told his boss that he was afraid the FBI was watching him. Later Bucca learned that federal agents had questioned Refai twice about the Trade Center blast, in April and June of 1994. But there had been no further action against him by the Feds or the FDNY.

Until then, Kay Woods hadn't really registered just who Sheikh Rahman was. Now she told Ronnie that several FDNY employees had seen news footage of Refai on the arm of the Sheikh, escorting him through a press mob, during one of his many media appearances.

Ronnie was stunned. Hearing that Refai had attended one of Rahman's mosques was one thing, but if he was standing cheek to jowl with the guy—that suggested a far deeper involvement.

That night, Ronnie rode up to the Channel 7 studios on West Sixty-sixth Street and called in a favor from a tape editor he knew at *Eyewitness News*. He asked him to pull some footage on the Sheikh, so the editor put Ronnie in a room by himself with a pile of cassettes. He put in the first one and fast-forwarded through it. Nothing. Same with the next one and the one after that.

Investigative work was tedious. Half the time you went down a road only to find out it was a dead end—and then you had to double back before the scene was compromised or the evidence destroyed. Ronnie figured that this was a long shot. Maybe if he was lucky he'd see Refai's face in the crowd around the Sheikh. But on the sixth cassette he hit gold.

It was a story by Jim Hickey, an ABC network news correspondent, dated March 4, 1993. That was the day Mohammed Salameh was grabbed by the Feds after trying to chisel a $400 refund for the blown Ryder truck.[13] The piece began with shots of the Masjid al-Salaam, the dingy Jersey City mosque where the Sheikh had held forth. There were other shots of a mob of Egyptians crowding him outside an immigration hearing. Ronnie had a copy of Refai's FDNY ID photo with him, and as he fast-forwarded through the piece, his heart jumped.

There he was. As the Sheikh moved through a crowd of reporters, Ahmed Amin Refai was leading him, holding the cleric's right arm and whispering to him as a photographer in front of them banged off some shots. "I *got* it," yelled Ronnie.

Normally soft-spoken, he couldn't contain himself. Just then, the editor came in. "Got what?"

Ronnie nodded toward the tape. He played it again and hit the pause button. "See that guy next to the Sheikh?" said Ronnie. "He's dirty."

"How can you be sure?" asked the editor, whose family, like Ronnie's, came from Sicily.

"Hey, *paisan,*" said Bucca. "Just 'cause you're Sicilian doesn't mean you're mobbed up. But if somebody takes a picture of you walking out of the Ravenite Social Club and you're holding John Gotti by the arm, they can be damn sure you're a made guy."

The video was devastating. There was Refai, not just supporting the Sheikh but whispering in his ear, running interference with the press, huddling with other disciples as they navigated the crowd. Sheikh Rahman was one of the most dangerous Islamic extremists in the world, a man revered by Osama bin Laden, who had adopted two of the Sheikh's sons. Now here on tape was Refai—this ostensibly mild-mannered accountant for the FDNY—behaving like his bodyguard.

As he drove home, Ronnie thought of the pictures he'd seen of the Luxor massacre, where those tourists had been shot and hacked to death by the IG—a group the Sheikh had led for years. Rahman had met directly with Ramzi Yousef before the Trade Center bombing, conspired to murder the Egyptian president, and presided over a cell that had tried to blow up the bridges and tunnels around Manhattan. Now Ronnie Bucca had definitive proof that one of his closest followers was a civilian worker inside the FDNY. A man who had obtained the blueprints of the Trade Center prior to the 1993 bombing, and who had lied repeatedly in an effort to secure a new access card to a high-security building that held all of New York City's architectural secrets. If there was ever probable cause to get a wire on the guy, this was it.

Ronnie couldn't wait to contact the Joint Terrorist Task Force with the news.

"I can't remember Ronnie so pumped," said his wife, Eve. "This was the kind of connection he'd prepared himself for. He understood who the Sheikh was, and he knew what kind of potential security threat this was to the department."

The next morning Bucca phoned his JTTF detective contact and brought a copy of the file down to 26 Federal Plaza. When he called the cop from the lobby, Ronnie assumed he'd get cleared to come upstairs. But the detective told him to wait. He came down and said that whatever Bucca had, he could give it to him there.

Ronnie was disappointed, Eve said. "But he figured maybe it was protocol, so he handed over the file. The detective said he'd get back to him."

A few days passed, and Ronnie heard nothing. He and Mel Hazel had both recommended to their superiors that Refai be terminated, or at least suspended without pay pending a hearing. In any case, they felt, he should be monitored every minute he was in Metrotech.

"We felt he posed a security risk," said Hazel, now retired, in an interview for this book.[14] "The fact that Refai was so close to Rahman, the fact that he wants to get another ID and he's lying about it, the fact that he got the Trade Center plans—I didn't like it and neither did Ronnie. It stunk to high hell."

But soon word came back that the lost ID incident was insufficient grounds for Refai, a civil-service employee, to be terminated. He would continue as a civilian employee of the FDNY.

"And that wasn't the worst part," said Eve. "After he made a call back to the Task Force, Ronnie got word that the FBI wasn't interested in pursuing the case at all."

That night Bucca came home and slumped into a chair in the living room.[15] Eve was in the kitchen. It wasn't like Ronnie to come in and not say a word. When she came in to see him, her husband looked like he'd been kicked in the groin.

"What'd they say at the Task Force?" she asked.

He turned to face her. "That he hasn't broken any federal laws. The Sheikh's a religious figure. This guy's just one of his followers. There's nothing they can do."

"You're kidding," said Eve. "What about the Feds talking to him before? What about the Trade Center plans?"

"They wouldn't say another word," said Ronnie. "They wouldn't even confirm the two interviews that were done in '94. They gave me zip. With the Bureau it's always a one-way street."

Now he got up and started pacing.

"You want to know what kills me? Sometime last year the Feds grabbed this guy named Ali Mohammed. Turns out he was working down at Bragg—a sergeant! And he's like *this* with bin Laden." Ronnie crossed his fingers.

"The guy admits to the Bureau that he was making regular trips up here from Bragg, training the same crew that hung around the Sheikh. The same bunch of Egyptians—Abouhalima and Nosair, the one who killed the rabbi. They're all part of the same cell, and there's a straight pipeline to Osama bin Laden."

"He pleaded guilty, right?" asked Eve.

"Finally," said Ronnie. "Anyway, they already know about this guy Mohammed, a mole who got inside the Special Warfare School at Bragg. Now I'm *handing* them a file on another Egyptian who's this close to the Sheikh. He's *inside* the FDNY, and everyone's blowing it off."

Ronnie stopped pacing. "Eve, I don't know what else I can *do*. I mean, this is the *FBI*. If *they* don't get something like this, who will?"

Bucca didn't think he could get much lower, and then a few days later he did. Word came down about budget cutbacks. The FDNY had to end his detail at headquarters. The BFI needed more marshals on the street. The Refai case was unrelated. It was all about money. So, after nine months on the terrorism watch, Ronnie transferred to Manhattan Base. He was back to investigating fires full-time.

"It was one of the saddest and most frustrating days of his life," said Eve. On the day he cleaned out his desk at Metrotech he went in to see Fire Marshals Mel Hazel and Bobby Greene. He asked them to keep an eye on Refai. They promised they would. On his way out, Ronnie made a copy of the Refai file and tucked it under his arm. There was a picture of Sheikh Rahman attached to the BFI "face sheet." Ronnie studied the blind man's face. His two dead eyes. At that moment a sick feeling came over him. For years he'd had a sense that the Sheikh's followers would come back and hit the Trade Center. Now in the fall of 1999 he was positive.

38

THE LOST CHANCE
IN MALAYSIA

Late in 1999, the CIA picked up word of an upcoming meeting of al
Qaeda operatives in Malaysia. Soon the Agency and the FBI would
have intelligence that could have led the Feds straight to the heart of the
9/11 plot. Word of the meeting came via a CIA intercept from an al
Qaeda logistics center in Yemen.[1] Two of the names mentioned in the
communiqué were Khalid al-Midhar and Nawaf al-Hazmi, the young
Saudi Chechen veterans who had met with Mohammed Atta in Hamburg. The meeting was to take place in early January in Kuala Lumpur,
so the CIA asked Malaysian authorities to photograph it.

Those believed present at the meeting on January 5, 2000, were
Khalid Sheikh Mohammed, the plot leader,[2] Ramzi Binalshibh, Atta's
right-hand man, and Riduan Ismuddin, aka Hambali, a board member
of the Malaysian front company Konsonjaya that had funneled money
to Ramzi Yousef through Wali Khan. Also in attendance was Tawfig bin-
Atash, who would later assume a lead role in the bombing of the U.S.S.
Cole. The meeting took place in the condo of one Yazid Sufaat. He
would later play host to Zacarias Moussaoui, the suspected "twentieth
hijacker" of the 9/11 plot.

There's little doubt that this was a crucial finance and strategy session
for the 9/11 attacks. Given what the FBI had in its files on Hambali and
his relationship to Yousef's Philippine cell, this meeting with three of the
intended hijackers could easily have tipped U.S. intelligence officials to

the upcoming plot. But the opportunity was blown—through a combination of agency infighting and the "need-to-know" bias that continually interrupted the flow of key intelligence between the CIA and the FBI.

Initially, the Agency gave the names of al-Midhar and al-Hazmi to the Bureau but failed to inform the FBI that al-Midhar had a multiple U.S. entry visa.[3]

The prospect that al-Midhar might enter America was important, since he was seen at the meeting associating with men who had been linked to al Qaeda. By that point, Osama bin Laden had been under a U.S. indictment for almost a year and a half. Tawfig bin-Atash, one of the attendees, had even acted as the Saudi billionaire's bodyguard.

Hambali's presence should have indicated to intelligence officials that the operation was being funded by bin Laden. Hambali had been a conduit for money in the Bojinka plot, and his attendance at the meeting should have related the plot back to Ramzi Yousef.* Sufaat would have tied the plot to Moussaoui, whom FBI agents in Minneapolis would find themselves scrambling to investigate in the weeks before September 11.† Moussaoui, apparently a last-minute addition to the hijacking plot, replaced Ramzi Binalshibh, who couldn't get an approved U.S. visa. If Binalshibh's presence at the Malaysian meeting had been passed throughout the intelligence community, he too might have been linked to the plot. Over the next year he made four separate attempts to obtain a U.S. visa.

But even if all those signals had been missed, the meeting should have led the Feds to al-Midhar and al-Hazmi. They already had their U.S. visas, but if the FBI and the CIA had communicated in time, they might have been placed on the Terrorist Watch List, barring them from U.S. entry. As it was, they were able to slip in, flying to California on January 15, just ten days after the meeting. *Newsweek* later reported that the CIA was even aware of al-Hazmi's presence on his flight into the country and the Joint Inquiry found that the FBI actually had an informant interacting with the pair in the summer of 2000, but no alarms were sounded.[4] For months the two Saudis lived in San Diego as they prepped for their

---

*Timeline #119. p. 26.
†Timeline #137. p. 3.

places aboard American Airlines Flight 77, the 9/11 flight that hit the Pentagon.

Months later, after the significance of the Malaysian meeting became known, the CIA and FBI squared off in a finger-pointing exercise on who had known what and when. In the end, their mutual failure to connect the dots on the meeting was another of the catastrophic intelligence blunders that led to 9/11.*

Meanwhile, in New York City, Ronnie Bucca was back investigating fires. The FDNY downsizing had sent him to Manhattan Base on Lafayette Street, five minutes north of the Trade Center. He was off the FDNY's terrorism watch, but he never stopped thinking about the threat to the Towers. He worried about how emergency services would respond to an attack without the proper training and equipment.

"He would go down to the Trade Center on a regular basis," said Jimmy Kelty, now the supervising fire marshal in Manhattan. "Since my brother Gene was at Ten and Ten, Ronnie would drag me down there from time to time. He did this on his own time. He would talk to the guys who worked Trade Center security—see if they had opened up any new means of entrance or egress—how tight the place was—how secure." What he knew about Ahmed Amin Refai put Bucca on an even higher state of alert. "He kept saying to me, 'They're not safe,'" said Kelty. "'Those towers aren't safe.'"⁵

The Feds, however, thought otherwise. In September 2000 they threw a party to mark the twentieth anniversary of the Joint Terrorist Task Force. Agents from the Bureau, the CIA, and fifteen other law enforcement agencies celebrated at Windows on the World, the restaurant atop the Trade Center's North Tower. The group included NYPD detectives like Lou Napoli, along with cops from the Port Authority and the New York State Police. There were no fire marshals present; the JTTF still had not deigned to admit an investigator from the FDNY.

The event was clearly a victory bash. At the party, U.S. Attorney Mary Jo White bragged about "the close to absolutely perfect record of

*Timeline #138. p. 30.

successful investigations and convictions." In her seven and a half years with the Southern District of New York, she had put away twenty-five Islamic terrorists, including Ramzi Yousef and the blind Sheikh.[6]

But while the Feds were downing drinks, Ramzi Yousef's extended al Qaeda cell members were at work finalizing his plot to strike the very building where the Task Force members were celebrating.

Bin Laden's Warning: Free the Blind Sheikh or Else . . .

Abdel Rahman may have been behind bars, but if the FBI needed any reminder of his importance to Osama bin Laden and al Qaeda, it came on September 21, in a videotaped message sent to the Arabic TV network Al Jazeera. In the tape, bin Laden, wearing a dagger, was surrounded by the Egyptian al Qaeda leadership, including Dr. Ayman al-Zawahiri as well as Rifa'i Taha Musa, the new head of the Islamic Group. Seated with them was young Mohammed Abdel Rahman, the blind Sheikh's son.

In a rambling speech, bin Laden issued a warning to the United States. Sheikh Abdel Rahman was to be set free or else. The younger Rahman chanted, exhorting Muslims worldwide to "avenge your Sheikh" and "go to the spilling of blood."[7] Bin Laden himself told his followers to remember El Sayyid Nosair.

If the Feds ever needed a direct tie linking bin Laden and his Egyptian hierarchy to the New York cell, this was it. Nosair was the IG member who had asked Nancy Floyd's asset Emad Salem to build bombs back in 1992. He was the man who killed Meir Kahane in 1990 and trained back in 1989 with Ramzi Yousef's WTC bombing cohort Mahmud Abouhalima, another Egyptian. Beyond bin Laden, al Qaeda was completely dominated by Egyptian fundamentalists.*

Yet a number of intelligence analysts continued to allege that Saddam Hussein was behind Ramzi Yousef and the original World Trade Center bombing. The theory was even endorsed by James R. Woolsey, former director of the CIA.[8]

Now, in September 2000, the bin Laden *fatwa* proved to be a precursor of the danger to come. At 10:45 A.M. on the morning of October 12,

---

*Timeline #121. p. 27.

two al Qaeda suicide bombers loaded a device made of C-4 explosive into a small skiff and took off across the harbor in Aden, Yemen.

The U.S.S. *Cole*, an advanced guided missile destroyer, was at the refueling dock. As the skiff approached the ship, the two jihadis on board smiled and waved at the *Cole*'s crew members, who waved back. Then, when the white fiberglass boat pulled alongside, the bomb detonated, blowing a four-story hole in the side of the ship. Seventeen U.S. sailors were killed.

This time the FBI took no chances. John O'Neill assembled a team of more than three hundred agents and support staff and headed to Yemen. But within days, more agency infighting erupted. Barbara Bodine, the diplomat who had criticized Brad Smith's matchbook Rewards program, was now ambassador to Yemen. She made it clear that she wanted a smaller FBI presence in the *Cole* bombing investigation, reportedly in deference to the Yemeni government.[9] O'Neill, a Justice Department employee, was demanding a balls-out probe.

Bodine reportedly asked the hard-driving FBI counterterrorism boss to consider the fragile diplomatic environment of Yemen. O'Neill responded, "We don't care about the environment. We're just here to investigate a crime."

John O'Neill was one of the few men in an FBI supervisory position who seemed to understand Osama bin Laden and the al Qaeda threat. The *Cole* bombing might have given the Bureau a major lead linking the terror network to the unfolding 9/11 plot. But after O'Neill returned to the United States for Thanksgiving, Bodine refused to approve the visa for his return.

It was an extraordinary move: a U.S. diplomat was preventing a high-ranking FBI supervisor from personally conducting a key terrorism investigation.

O'Neill protested, but he was overruled by the Bureau leadership. Assistant Director Dale Watson, the man who had downplayed the U.S. al Qaeda presence before Congress in 1998, later told the *Washington Post* that "sustained cooperation" with the Yemeni government "has enabled the FBI to further reduce its in-country presence." That same day, Yemen's prime minister told the *Post* that no link had been established between the *Cole* bombers and al Qaeda.[10]

Of course there was a direct link: it was contained in the photos that the CIA had in its files from the January 2000 Malaysian meeting. They showed Hambali, Yousef's 1995 Manila bagman, meeting with Tawfig bin-Atash, the former head of bin Laden's bodyguards, who acted as a direct intermediary in the *Cole* blast. But the CIA didn't fully share the intel on that meeting with the Bureau until July 2001, a year and a half later.[11]

Now, John O'Neill effectively had his wings clipped, and another massive dot on the timeline to 9/11 was lost.

In late October 2000, in an ironic precursor of things to come, the Department of Defense conducted a mass casualty (MASCAL) exercise simulating the impact of a plane hitting the Pentagon.[12] The government was beginning, at last, to realize just how vulnerable we were to a massive terrorist attack.

Earlier that month, the National Commission on Terrorism, led by Ambassador L. Paul Bremer, reached a conclusion that was all too clear: "The U.S. intelligence and law enforcement communities lacked the ability to prioritize, translate and understand in a timely fashion, all of the information to which they have access."[13]

On December 20, White House terrorism czar Richard Clarke presented National Security Adviser Sandy Berger with a strategy paper on how to escalate the fight with al Qaeda following the *Cole* bombing. But the Clinton presidency was ending, so the game plan wasn't presented to Berger's counterpart, Condoleeza Rice, until months later.[14]

Now, in January 2001, as the Bush administration took office, Khalid Shaikh Mohammed and Mohammed Atta were finalizing the details of Ramzi Yousef's deadly plot. Soon there would be so many warnings of the impending al Qaeda attack that the dots would seem like a virtual straight line.

Chatter, Then Spikes

In January, the FAA issued an advisory to airlines and airport personnel warning that terrorists might try to hijack or destroy American aircraft.*

---

*Timeline #123. p. 28.

It was the first of fifteen such warnings issued in the nine months leading up to September 11.

On January 24, Italian authorities recorded an Islamic imam discussing fake IDs for "the brothers going to America."[15]

On January 30, Ziad Samir Jarrah, a Lebanese national who had obtained a U.S. visa in Berlin, was stopped for questioning at Dubai Airport in the United Arab Emirates. The CIA reportedly requested that he be interrogated, but the Agency later denied that.[16] Like Yasin, the Iraqi who was let go by the FBI after the WTC bombing, and Wadih El-Hage, released by the Bureau prior to the African embassy bombings, Jarrah was set free.* The FBI now believes that he was the hijacker-pilot aboard United Airlines Flight 93, which crashed in Pennsylvania on September 11.

In February, Hani Hanjour, who had been studying at Arizona flight schools since 1996, began training on flight simulators.[17] At the time, Special Agent Ken Williams from the Phoenix office had transferred out of counterterrorism Squad Five. At work on an arson case, he apparently missed Hanjour's presence. But during this time frame the FAA was informed of "concerns" by instructors at Pan Am International Flight Academy that Hanjour lacked the necessary English skills to fly multi-engine jets.[18]† The FAA reportedly responded by offering to provide an interpreter for Hanjour, who went on to fly American Airlines Flight 77 into the Pentagon.

None of this activity was known to the American public at the time. The average citizen had only two choices: trust that their government would protect them, or hope that journalists covering intelligence issues would alert them to any warnings. But the reporters who tracked the war on terror were limited to what their sources inside the intelligence community told them—and at times it seemed the Feds were going out of their way to keep the media in the dark.

In early February, testimony was given in a Manhattan federal courtroom that might have led reporters to connect the dots between Ramzi Yousef and the continuing al Qaeda threat. On February 5, the U.S. began prosecuting Osama bin Laden in absentia for his role in planning

---

*Timeline #124. p. 28.
†Timeline #125. p. 28.

the African embassy bombings. On the second day of the trial, Jamal Ahmad al-Fadl, the government's prized CS-1, testified that he had met an associate of bin Laden known as Assad, "the lion."[19] For some reason the Feds never asked Assad's real name. If they had, the public would have learned it was none other than Wali Khan Amin Shah, Ramzi Yousef's Bojinka cohort—who was tied directly to Riduan Ismuddin, the Indonesian cleric known as Hambali. Ismuddin had been present at the 9/11 planning session in Malaysia in January 2000. In October 2000, Zacarias Moussaoui had received fake IDs in Malaysia at Ismuddin's request.

Al-Fadl's testimony might have alerted the media to the intimate connection between Yousef and the ongoing 9/11 plot. But because Shah was referred to only as "Assad," reporters following the case never made the link.

On February 23, Moussaoui arrived at Chicago's O'Hare Airport using a French passport with a ninety-day visa.[20] A week later there was another link to Moussaoui that the Feds themselves should have caught. It came at the same embassy bombing trial, and it proved to be another thundering warning that the FBI should be monitoring flight schools.

Assam al-Ridi was on the stand. Another naturalized Egyptian-born U.S. citizen, al-Ridi was a flight instructor who had met Wadih El-Hage during the Afghan war, when he'd shipped night-vision goggles to the mujahadeen. In 1993 al-Ridi had bought a used jet for bin Laden; the badly maintained plane later crashed in Khartoum while bin Laden was living in Sudan.

Now, as he testified in New York federal court, al-Ridi admitted that his copilot on the ill-fated flight had trained at the Airman Flight School in Norman, Oklahoma.[21]* Four months earlier, Zacarias Moussaoui had arrived in Norman to train at the very same school. Moussaoui proved such a disastrous pilot candidate that the school grounded him in May 2001, but soon he'd made his way to another school in Minnesota, where Ramzi Binalshibh wired him $14,000 for simulator training.

This was a fact pattern with several dots the New York office of the FBI missed. One of their own witnesses had underscored in court that al

---

*Timeline #126. p. 28.

Qaeda operatives were using American flight schools for training. A known bin Laden copilot had trained at the same Oklahoma school as Moussaoui, who in turn had stayed in the same condo where the Malaysian 9/11 planning meeting was held the year before.*

There was a link to an Oklahoma flight school that would be cited later in the summer by FBI agents in Minneapolis as a reason for putting Moussaoui under surveillance. But as the spring of 2001 approached, and the intelligence "chatter" began to point directly at an al Qaeda hijacking plot, the New York Feds seemed clueless to the need for flight-school surveillance.

In April the U.S. intelligence community learned from a source with terrorist connections that Osama bin Laden was interested in using commercial pilots in future attacks. The source said that law enforcement investigators should consider the possibility of "spectacular and traumatic" attacks akin to the first WTC bombing. No time frame for an upcoming attack was mentioned, and because the source was determined to be speculating, the information was not disseminated to U.S. intelligence agencies.[22]†

That same month, al Qaeda cells were raided in Milan, Frankfurt, and London. The FBI's John O'Neill was quoted as saying, "we are getting a lot of intel from each one." But the raids only confirmed the unsettling truth: "al Qaeda cells [were] everywhere."[23]**

On April 18, the FAA warned that Middle Eastern terrorists might try to hijack or blow up a U.S. plane. Air carriers were told to "demonstrate a high degree of alertness."[24] But with every step forward in diligence, the effort to protect U.S. borders seemed to take two steps back.

In early May, a program called Visa Express began in Saudi Arabia, making it easier for Saudi nationals to get U.S. travel permits. Five of the 9/11 hijackers took advantage of the program, including Khalid al-Midhar, who had attended the January 2000 Malaysian meeting.[25] Meanwhile, on May 1, al-Midhar's partner, Nawaf al-Hazmi, already in the U.S., reported an attempted street robbery to Fairfax, Virginia, police. He declined to press charges, and since his name was not yet on

---

*Timeline #119. p. 26.
†Timeline #127. p. 28.
**Timeline #128. p. 28.

the Watch List, which would have alerted Customs and INS agents to his entry, he escaped scrutiny.*

By June, signals had begun to flash from the Middle East to the American Southwest.

Citing security threats, the FBI withdrew its agents from Yemen, severely curtailing the probe into the bombing of the *Cole*. At the same time, in Phoenix, Hani Hanjour signed up for a month of flight simulator training at the Sawyer Aviation Training Center in Scottsdale, Arizona.[26] He would soon be studying almost side by side with Lotfi Raissi, the Algerian pilot whom ex-FBI intelligence asset Harry Ellen had warned Ken Williams about in the fall of 1996.[27]†

On June 11, CIA case officers met with agents of the JTTF in New York who were handling the *Cole* investigation. A year and a half after the infamous Malaysian meeting the CIA was finally showing the FBI photos taken in Kuala Lumpur. The Bureau agents were asked to identify the parties present. Reportedly, they picked out Tawfig bin Atash, the ex-boss of Osama bin Laden's security detail, who was later tied to the *Cole* bombing.[28] But when the Bureau asked for more details, the CIA reportedly refused to cooperate and the meeting turned into a shouting match.[29]

A CIA official later insisted that the FBI was kept in the loop.[30] But that New York meeting was an example of the compartmentalization of intelligence-gathering that had crippled American defenses from the beginning—and shut out motivated investigators like Ronnie Bucca. The FBI had looked down on him because of his status as a fire marshal, and now the JTTF agents were being treated the same way by the case officers of the CIA. In pursuing his own investigation of the WTC bombing, Bucca had to rely on what bits and pieces of intel he could glean from DIA. Now here were America's two premier intelligence agencies squabbling over who had the "need to know" and the right to view the intel.

"It was a stupid, ongoing dogfight among the agencies," said one retired FBI agent.[31] "And the loser was America. While our guys were arguing over who had the proper clearance to see what photos, bin

---

*Timeline #129. p. 29.
†Timeline #131. p. 29.

Laden's people were sleeping on mattresses in rat-shack apartments and staying up all night on flight simulators so they could bring the jihad down on us."

By late June, the drums were pounding more loudly than ever.

On the twenty-second, the U.S. Central and European Command imposed Force Protection Condition Delta, out of concern about an imminent terrorist attack.* That same day, chatter regarding terrorist attacks caused the Pentagon to pull U.S. Navy ships out of Bahrain.[32] Four days later, the State Department issued a worldwide caution warning American citizens of possible attacks. National Security Adviser Rice later reported that there was a "threat spike" at the time, focusing on Americans or U.S. targets overseas.[33] On June 28, CIA Director George Tenet sent a written communiqué to Rice. "It is highly likely," he wrote, "that a significant al Qaeda attack is in the near future—within several weeks."[34]

On July 1, Senators Diane Feinstein (D-CA) and Richard Shelby (R-AL) appeared on CNN's *Late Edition with Wolf Blitzer*, warning of a potential attack by Osama bin Laden. "Intelligence staff have told me," said Feinstein, "that there is a major probability of a terrorist incident within the next three months."[35]

The very next day the FBI warned law enforcement agencies of possible al Qaeda strikes overseas and asserted that domestic strikes couldn't be ruled out.[36]

On July 5, President Bush asked National Security Adviser Condoleezza Rice to assess the al Qaeda threat. Later, after 9/11, Rice admitted that the threat-reporting at the time "had become sufficiently robust—not again very specific, but sufficiently robust. There was a lot of chatter in the system."[37]

That same day, terrorism czar Richard Clarke called a White House meeting with officials from the FBI, FAA, Coast Guard, Secret Service, and INS, warning that "something really spectacular is going to happen here, and it's going to happen soon."[38]†

The next day, Clarke chaired a meeting of the National Security Council's Counterterrorism Security Group (CSG) and ordered a suspension of all nonessential travel by the staff.[39]

---

*Timeline #132. p. 29.
†Timeline #133. p. 29.

The Phoenix Memo

Three days later, Phoenix FBI Agent Ken Williams sent a memo to FBI headquarters. He reportedly identified eight Middle Eastern men studying at Arizona flight schools, and urged that the Bureau do background checks. Williams suggested that the pilots-in-training were associated with a London Islamic group with close ties to Osama bin Laden.[40] The communiqué, which would go down in history as "the Phoenix memo," was also sent to investigators in the FBI's New York office, the FBI's office of origin for all bin Laden–related terrorism cases.

At least three people in the office saw the memo, but no action was taken.*

Some New York agents later admitted that al Qaeda pilots had "previously received flight training in the United States." They acknowledged the connection to Airman Flight School in Norman, Oklahoma, where Zacarias Moussaoui would soon train. But as the Joint Inquiry later found out, "the commonly held view in the Bureau was that bin Laden merely needed pilots to operate aircraft he purchased in the U.S. to move men and material."[41]

Apparently no one in New York—the FBI's flagship bin Laden office—saw anything alarming about the flight school evidence.

Harry Ellen, Ken Williams's former asset in Phoenix, believed that Williams was four and a half years late in sending the memo. He claimed to have told Williams about a potential threat from Middle Eastern flight students as far back as 1996. But even now in July 2001, with all the other warnings of an impending al Qaeda attack, the FBI still took no action and the memo was virtually ignored.

Like the failure to stop Ramzi Yousef in 1992 and the failure to recognize the 9/11 plot in the evidence Colonel Mendoza had turned over in 1995, this was another epic blunder that would haunt the FBI for years to come.

By now, Ronnie Bucca was so concerned about the threat intelligence he was picking up through his reserve unit that he made a point of reviewing disaster scenarios with his family. His daughter, Jessica, now twenty-three,

---

*Timeline #134. p. 29.

had just started working in Manhattan, and within her first few weeks on the job an incident took place that caught her father's attention.

She told him about it at dinner. "During lunch today, they had the HAZMAT vehicles out," she said. "The guys were walking around in chemical suits. Did you hear anything about it?"

Ronnie had been elsewhere, but he'd heard about the incident over the CB in his car. It was nothing serious. The HAZMAT team had been deployed as a precaution. But he frowned just the same.

"Jess, what did I tell you when you see emergency response rigs and big crowds?"

"I know, Dad. Walk in the other direction. I just wanted to see if you were there."

"Sure," said Ronnie. "But if something had happened you would have been in the middle of it. You never know what's going to come down, Jess. I just want you to be ready."

Jessica nodded. Now Ronnie asked to hear the preparedness plan he'd discussed over and over with his family. Jessica, who'd heard it a hundred times, said, *"Daaad . . ."*

"I know you don't like doing this, but let me hear it," said Ronnie.

She sighed. "Go to a firehouse. If we can't make a local call, try and get a call to Aunt Nancy out of state. Let her know we're safe. Keep emergency contact numbers in my wallet. A map of the city. A pocket flashlight. Am I done?"

Ronnie gave his daughter a hug. The little drills were boring, but Bucca was determined that none of his loved ones would get caught unprepared on *his* watch. Finally he smiled. "Anybody for ice cream?"

Ronnie reached into his jacket pocket for his keys. Inside he found a note that Eve had left there that morning. For years, she'd been slipping little notes in his pocket as he left for work that he would find later in the day. They would say things like "Miss you" and "E.B. loves R.B." Now, by mid-July 2001, as he became more and more concerned about the growing terror threat, Eve's notes read like little warnings.

This one said, "Watch yourself."

39

"SOMEDAY SOMEONE WILL DIE"

I n late July, as the G-8 Summit approached in Genoa, Italy, there was another spike in the threat level. The head of Russia's Federal Body-guard Service reported that Osama bin Laden had directly targeted President Bush for assassination at the Summit.[1] CIA Director Tenet expressed concern about the Genoa meeting, and warned again of a "major attack" by al Qaeda.[2] Two days before the summit, the FBI issued another warning to U.S. law enforcement agencies, and the FAA urged airlines to "use the highest level of caution."

Most of this was going on behind the scenes; the American public had little sense of the growing threat. In fact, one pundit who commented frequently on terrorism in the media was actually downplaying the al Qaeda danger.

"To listen to some of the news reports a year or two ago, you would think bin Laden was running a top Fortune 500 multinational company—people everywhere, links everywhere," said Larry C. Johnson, a former CIA officer who was deputy director of the State Department's Office of Counterterrorism during the administrations of President George H. W. Bush and Bill Clinton.[3] "What the evidence at trial has correctly portrayed . . . [is] really a loose amalgam of people with a shared ideology, but a very limited direction."

Johnson was a well-known commentator who regularly offered his analysis on prime-time programs from *Larry King Live* to *Frontline*.

Weeks later he went even further, in an op-ed piece for the *New York Times* titled "The Declining Terrorist Threat."

"Americans are bedeviled by fantasies about terrorism," Johnson wrote.[4] "They seem to believe that terrorism is the greatest threat to the United States and that it is becoming more widespread and lethal. . . . None of these beliefs are based in fact. The overall terrorist trend is down. . . . Nor are the United States and its policies the primary target. . . . Although high-profile incidents have fostered the perception that terrorism is becoming more lethal, the numbers say otherwise, and early signs suggest that the decade beginning in 2000 will continue the downward trend."

Johnson's piece appeared on July 10, the day the FBI's New York office got the Phoenix memo.

Now, while millions of innocent people in New York and Washington went about their work largely unaware of the coming threat, government officials began to take precautions. On July 19, Attorney General John Ashcroft left on a trip to his home state of Missouri aboard a private jet. When asked by reporters why he didn't use a commercial airliner, as was customary, the Justice Department cited what it called a "threat assessment" by the FBI. The attorney general, they said, had been advised to travel only by private jet for the rest of his term.[5]

The next day, as the G-8 leaders met in Genoa, Mohammed Atta was in Spain finalizing the details of the hijacking plot. Egyptian intelligence warned the CIA of a potential suicide attack, in which hijackers might try to crash a plane into one of the host buildings at the summit. Believing the threat credible, the Agency reportedly asked the Italian military to ring the summit site with surface-to-air missiles.[6]

Since fleeing Sudan for Afghanistan in 1992, Osama bin Laden had enjoyed the protection of the Taliban, the radical Islamic fundamentalist regime that came to power in Kabul in 1996 after a protracted civil war following the defeat of the Soviets. Now, at the end of July, an aide to the Taliban foreign minister told an unnamed U.S. official in Peshawar, Pakistan, that bin Laden was planning a massive attack on U.S. soil.

"The guests are going to destroy the guesthouse" was the coded threat. But U.S. officials were already beginning to complain of "warning fatigue."[7]

As July ended and the FAA issued yet another hijacking warning, Zacarias Moussaoui was in Egan, Minnesota, at a branch of the Pan Am

International Flight Academy, the same company that had trained Hani Hanjour in Arizona.

At that point, John O'Neill had made a number of requests for increased funding. The FBI's interim director, Tom Picard, reportedly asked the Justice Department for another $50 million to beef up the terror watch in the New York office, but he was turned down.[8]

Meanwhile, O'Neill, a tough, bigger-than-life executive who'd made his share of enemies, was growing increasingly isolated inside the Bureau.[9] In the summer of 2000 he'd misplaced a briefcase containing classified documents while attending an FBI conference in Florida. The briefcase was found hours later with the papers intact, but as a result of the security breach, O'Neill soon found himself an object of the same kind of OPR investigation that had dogged Nancy Floyd.

Just as someone inside the Bureau had leaked the "Temptress and the Spy" story on Nancy Floyd, now the *New York Times* ran a piece on O'Neill's Bureau troubles. He later told friends he believed the story had been generated by either Acting Director Tom Picard or Dale Watson, the assistant director who'd minimized the al Qaeda threat before Congress in 1998.[10] Both men denied it, but the *Times* story was the final nail in O'Neill's coffin at the Bureau. He soon retired, and, as fate would have it, began working as director of security for the World Trade Center.

On August 23, the day O'Neill started work at the Towers, the CIA finally sent a cable to the FBI warning that Khalid al-Midhar and Nawaf al-Hazmi, photographed at the Malaysian meeting in January 2000, were now in the country.*

Ironically, if the FAA had been copied on the cable, they might have picked up the two hijackers in the reservations system.[11] The young Saudis were so audacious they'd bought tickets for the 9/11 flight under their own names.[12] Nobody at the FBI in Washington seemed to connect al-Midhar and al-Hazmi to the escalating hijack threat—even though the headquarters unit had gotten the Phoenix memo just weeks before.[13]

But few lapses in the final days before 9/11 equaled the FBI's blunder when alert agents in the FBI's Minneapolis field office made an application for a search warrant on Zacarias Moussaoui under the Foreign Intelligence Surveillance Act (FISA).[14] The French would-be pilot had raised

---

*Timeline #138. p. 30.

concerns earlier in the month, after attempting to rush his flight training, calling his desire to fly a jumbo jet an "ego-boosting thing," and asking instructors how much damage a hijacker could do flying a fully loaded 747.[15] Fortunately, an alert manager at the Pan Am International Flight Academy in Egan, Minnesota, contacted the Minneapolis FBI office, and Moussaoui was arrested on visa violations the night of August 15. In his possession FBI agents found a statement showing a deposit of $32,000 at an Oklahoma bank. Moussaoui admitted he'd recently traveled to Morocco, Malaysia, and Pakistan on business, but he couldn't provide any details on his employment.

"Spun Up" Over Moussaoui

On August 17, agents in Minneapolis sent a detailed memo to FBI headquarters describing Moussaoui and his roommate Hussein al-Attas. The memo stated that the office had reason to believe Moussaoui, al-Attas, "and others yet unknown" were conspiring to seize control of an airplane. When Moussaoui refused to let agents search his laptop, they made the FISA request.[16] Then, in what was probably the ultimate act of negligence on the road to September 11, FBI headquarters refused the FISA request, claiming that its street agents in Minnesota lacked probable cause.[17]*

Undaunted, a Minneapolis agent sent an E-mail to a supervisor at FBI headquarters, warning that Moussaoui and al-Attas might be "involved in a larger plot to target airlines." But one agent at headquarters complained to a Minneapolis FBI supervisor that the local office was getting people "spun up" over Moussaoui. The worried supervisor replied that they were *trying* to get the people at headquarters "spun up," in order to make sure that Moussaoui "did not take control of a plane and fly it into the World Trade Center."[18]

Coming less than a month before 9/11, it was a chilling premonition.

In the entire twelve-year history of FBI mistakes leading up to September 11, the fact that FBI headquarters ignored that desperate eleventh-hour plea from its own field agents is perhaps the greatest indictment of the house that Hoover built.

---

*Timeline #139. p. 30.

But the negligence wasn't limited to the Bureau. In his daily intelligence briefing on August 6,[19] President Bush, vacationing at his ranch in Crawford, Texas, got a report that warned of potential hijackings. According to Bob Woodward and Dan Eggen in a *Washington Post* story eight months after 9/11, the top-secret memo was entitled "Bin Laden Determined to Strike in U.S."[20]*

More alarmingly, the briefing reportedly contained a reference to a 1998 British intelligence report that hijackers might grab an airliner in an effort to free blind Sheikh Omar Abdel Rahman.[21]

By August 29, as the intelligence chatter about an impending al Qaeda attack reached a roar, a top official at FBI headquarters reportedly rebuffed a frantic call from a New York agent for an all-out search for al-Midhar and al-Hazmi. In an E-mail that same day, the unnamed agent warned headquarters that if the Bureau didn't put more agents on the search, "some day someone will die—and the public will not understand why we were not more effective at throwing every resource we had" at hunting down the two Saudis.[22]

In the final days of August, Special Agent Nancy Floyd got that call from Emad Salem that still haunts her. After years of being out of touch, the ex–Egyptian Army major she'd recruited was back in New York. Through Lou Napoli he'd asked to speak to Floyd. But Nancy, who had returned to the Special Operations Group, was rigidly bound by the terms of her OPR decision to avoid all contact with her ex-asset. So she was unable to take the call.

"To this day, she still wonders," said an FBI source. "Maybe Salem knew what was brewing and wanted to warn her."

The Deadly Riddle

In the early morning hours of August 29, lead hijacker Mohammed Atta phoned a coconspirator in Hamburg, Germany, to deliver the attack date. It was just after 2:30 A.M. in the darkened safe house at 54 Marienstrasse when Ramzi Binalshibh was awakened by the call. Binalshibh, who had been in line to become the twentieth hijacker until he was unable to get a U.S. visa, became ramrod stiff.

---

*Timeline #136. p. 30.

The voice on the other end said, "A friend of mine has given me a riddle that I am unable to solve and I want you to help me out."

"Is this really the right time for riddles?" said Binalshibh, checking a clock.

"Yes, I know," said Atta, "but you are my friend, and no one else can help me solve it." Binalshibh told him to go ahead.

Atta answered in code: "Two sticks, a dash, and a cake with a stick down. What is it?"

Binalshibh grabbed a pen and drew parallel lines representing the sticks, then a square, like a cake, with a line coming down from the middle.

"Did you really wake me up to tell me this riddle?" he asked.

"What is it?" came Atta's stern reply.

There was a pause as Binalshibh contemplated the drawing. Then he took the pen and rounded the top of the "cake." He moved the stick to the right. That gave him the date: 11-9. September 11.[23]

On September 6, the Taliban foreign minister let it be known that the Afghan government would consider swapping eight Christian Aid workers on trial in Kabul "if Washington allowed the ailing Sheikh Omar Abdel Rahman . . . to go to Afghanistan." Bin Laden and the Egyptian al Qaeda bosses had demanded the Sheikh's release prior to the *Cole* bombing. Clearly this was one of their primary goals.[24]

Ronnie Bucca was back working fire investigation full-time at Manhattan Base. When he saw a Reuters report on the proposed Abdel Rahman–missionary swap, it was just another reminder of how the Bureau blew off his revelations about Ahmed Amin Refai. The accountant who was so close to the Sheikh had retired from the FDNY in the spring; now he was living in suburban New Jersey.

The final fatal irony that underscored the Justice Department's approach to terrorism came on September 10. Despite all the warnings throughout the year—despite the fact that he had retreated to the safety of private jets himself—when the FBI asked Attorney General Ashcroft for an increase of $58 million in its counterterrorism budget, he turned them down. Acting FBI Director Tom Picard was later quoted as saying, "Before September 11th, I couldn't get half an hour on terrorism with Ashcroft. He was only interested in three things: guns, drugs and civil rights."[25]*

---

*Timeline #141. p. 30.

By now, on the evening of September 10, Atta and the other hijackers were writing their final suicide notes. With Zacarias Moussaoui, the twentieth hijacker, now in custody, the plotters would have to carry out their plans for "Holy Tuesday" with nineteen.

In a few hours they would be on their way.

"Just Like Death"

On the last morning of their lives, the nineteen suicide "soldiers" who would fulfill Yousef's plan prepared to board flights in three U.S. cities. Atta, the thirty-three-year-old ringleader, took a connecting flight from Portland, Maine, to Logan Airport in Boston and boarded American Airlines Flight 11 with Abdulaziz Alomari and three other "brothers."[26] Across the terminal at United, Marwan Al-Shehhi, an alumnus of Atta's at the Hamburg Technical University, got his boarding pass for Flight 175, bound for L.A. With him were four other jihadis who had lived for a time in Florida.

In D.C., Hani Hanjour, who'd been studying aviation in the States since 1996, walked aboard American Flight 77 along with the two men who'd attended the Malaysian meeting, al-Midhar and al-Hazmi, his brother Salem, and Majed Moqued, a baby-faced Saudi known to frequent adult bookstores in Maryland.[27] In Newark, Ziad Jarrah, the young Lebanese who'd been stopped in Dubai, boarded United Flight 93 to San Francisco with three more hijackers who'd lived for a time in Delray Beach. Their assault team was one hijacker light, and investigators would later speculate that the last berth on Flight 93 had been reserved for Moussaoui. With one less killer on board, this flight was the only one of the four that missed its deadly mark.

In New York at Manhattan Base, Supervising Fire Marshal Jimmy Devery figured it was going to be a slow day.[28] There had been very little intake from the night before. Two of the men on the eight-to-six tour had already called in to say they'd be a few minutes late. It was election day in the city, and Fire Marshal Keith O'Mara was going to vote. His partner, Andy DiFusco, was celebrating his wedding anniversary. On his way in from Brooklyn, Andy called to say he'd pick up some bagels for the squad room. Devery, who was in charge of the Base's day tour, told the two marshals not to hurry. "There's nothin' doin'," he said.

At around 8:40 A.M., Devery went into the bull pen where Ronnie Bucca was filling out the "job ticket" on his most recent investigation—a small fire in the basement of the Carlysle Hotel on the Upper East Side. As always, Ronnie got to work well ahead of the tour change. That morning when he'd left the house, Eve kissed him and slipped a note into his pocket along with a series of three-by-five cards on a key chain. It was a makeshift study guide she'd made up so Ronnie could prep for an Army Reserve course he was leaving for on Saturday.

The day before, Devery had signed Bucca's request to take thirteen days' leave so that he could report for active duty with the 3413 Military Intelligence Detachment. The advanced course was going to be held in Virginia. Ronnie had already used up his vacation time for the year on other reserve training, and this would cut into his leave for next year. But with the intel he was hearing about the amped-up terror threat, he wanted to stay sharp.

Now, on the morning of the eleventh, he kissed Eve and got into his car. He said he'd try to get home early for dinner. Little Ronnie was now at Tulane, and they were expecting a call from him on whether he could make it home for Thanksgiving.

Later, as he took the Williamsburg Bridge over to Manhattan, Ronnie looked across at the Twin Towers. The sun was hitting them from the east. There wasn't a cloud in the sky. He pulled out the note from Eve and grinned. This time she'd left him with a smiley face.

At 8:46 A.M. Andy DiFusco was on his way up the FDR Drive from the Brooklyn Battery Tunnel when he heard what he later described as "the sound of a dumpster hitting a pot hole."[29] He turned left in the direction of the noise and saw heavy smoke coming out of the North Tower of the World Trade Center. American Airlines Flight 11 had just slammed into the building between the ninety-fourth and ninety-eighth floors.

Eighteen blocks north, at Manhattan Base, Ronnie Bucca heard the noise. He ran to the window in Devery's office and looked out. Down below, firefighters had rushed out of Ladder 20, the house next to Manhattan Base. They were pointing downtown. Ronnie opened the window and asked what it was. One of the firefighters yelled up, "The Trade Center's on fire."

Bucca closed the window and ran into the hall. Fire Marshal Frank

Licausi was just coming out of the bull pen. Ronnie pointed upward, and the two of them headed to the roof.

As soon as they got outside, Ronnie looked south and saw the intense black smoke coming from the North Tower. In the background, somebody mentioned something about a plane.

For years, this was the kind of event he had trained for, not just as a fire marshal but as a Special Forces reservist, so Bucca stayed calm. Licausi had just spoken to his wife and he handed Bucca his cell phone. Ronnie dialed the number of the hospital where Eve was working.

"He said, 'A plane just went into the World Trade Center,'" said Eve, recalling the short conversation. "I could feel all these unspoken words flow between us. But all I could think to say back was 'Be careful. Be careful.' And then he was gone."

Now, as Ronnie took the stairs down to his car, his boss Jimmy Devery came out of the bull pen. An Irishman in his mid-fifties, with gray hair and glasses, Devery jumped into Ronnie's Chevy and switched on the department radio. "Ten and Ten's out already," he said, "Rescue's on its way. This is gonna be an all-dayer."[30]

Without a word, Ronnie slammed the Kojak bubble on the roof and roared south with lights and sirens. Over WINS radio, word came that it might have been a terrorist attack.

"Christ, you called it," said Devery, but Ronnie didn't respond. In one way or another he'd been preparing for this since his buddy Kevin had fallen into the hole back in '93. Now he stayed focused and pushed the pedal to the floor.

By the time the fire marshals got downtown, Broadway was choking with startled onlookers, fire rigs, and emergency response vehicles. Ronnie turned right on Liberty Street and screeched to a stop near Ten and Ten, the firehouse at the base of the South Tower. The two men popped the trunk and pulled on their gear: bunker boots, turnout coats, and helmets. Ronnie grabbed a flashlight on a sling and his own custom first aid kit. They were just about to head to the North Tower when United Airlines Flight 175 sliced into the South Tower's seventy-eighth floor.

"Ronnie, there's stairs here," Devery shouted as they headed toward the downtown tower. But Bucca said, "No. Follow me." He knew those buildings like the house he grew up in.

Inside, they crossed the lobby and Ronnie headed straight for a stairwell in the west corner. Still a five-mile-a-day runner, Ronnie took the stairs two at a time. Soon he was a full floor ahead of Devery, who was racing to catch up. "People were coming down, screaming, crying," said Devery. I asked, 'Where'd the plane hit?' and somebody said 'Seventy-eight.'"

Finally, at the fifty-first floor, Devery almost collapsed from exhaustion. He started to hesitate and called up the stairs to Ronnie. But Bucca was heading toward the fire floor.

"I hear people screaming upstairs," he said.

Devery paused for a moment to catch his breath. Just then, Ling Young, a woman in her mid-forties who'd been badly burned, came down the stairs in a daze. She had her arms out and her eyes closed. She seemed ready to faint. "She practically fell into my arms," said Devery. "So I yelled up to Ronnie, 'I'm gonna take her out.'"

Devery was able to walk the woman down about ten flights, but she didn't think she could go on. Then, miraculously, a firefighter came through a stairwell door on the forty-first floor and said, "You need an elevator?" Devery couldn't believe the luck. He led Mrs. Young onto the car and they headed down.

"When we hit the lobby," said Devery, "some of the cables had been cut [by the plane] and the elevator cars had fallen. People were burned. They were lying dead. But outside was worse."

As he started to pull Mrs. Young out to the plaza between the towers, Devery saw bodies dropping. "We got ten feet out and I saw an arm, then a leg. Somebody else dropped, hit a light pole and just burst, but I kept going with her. Finally we got to an EMS unit."

Back inside the South Tower, Ronnie Bucca had made it up to the seventy-eighth floor. Radio broadcasts recovered later showed that he linked with Oriole Palmer, a battalion chief. Incredibly, Ronnie's wife, Eve, had gone to high school with Palmer, but that wasn't the only irony. The voice on the other end of the chief's radio was that of Ed Geraghty of Battalion 9, the same man who'd gotten Ronnie the terrorism detail at Metrotech back in 1998.

As the radio broadcasts indicate, Palmer and Bucca actually found a standpipe with water pressure and began fighting the blaze. There were bodies strewn across the seventy-eighth-floor lobby. Between fifty and two hundred people lay dead or dying. Burning jet fuel poured down elevator shafts. The Handie-Talkie radio on Palmer's coat crackled with 10-45 Code Ones, the FDNY designation for fires with death resulting.[31] At one point Ronnie took off his flame-retardant turnout coat and used it to cover some crash victims huddled in a corner. He returned to the hose, and did his best with Chief Palmer to advance it.

For Bucca this was a defining moment. He'd made dozens of jumps with the Special Forces, dropped the five stories in 1986 and come back. He'd made thousands of runs with Rescue One, educated himself on the threat from Islamic terrorists, and spent years since Yousef's first bombing trying to warn people that the Towers were still vulnerable to attack.

But now, as he fought the blaze, architecture and science worked against him. At the East African embassy bombing trial earlier that year, testimony in open court had revealed that the Twin Towers were each built to sustain a hit from a fully loaded Boeing 707, the largest airliner flying when the buildings were topped off back in 1971.[32] The Towers' outside walls were supposed to be able to hold up under the force of a raging inferno for four hours. The structural columns were designed to survive for three hours, the floor supports for two.[33]

Now each Tower had been ruptured by much bigger aircraft—185-ton Boeing 767s filled with 24,000 gallons of burning jet fuel.[34] On impact, each plane slid across a series of floors and severed many of the interior steel columns holding the trusses to the center core. The fire temperatures soon reached 1,500 to 2,000 degrees, and the single-bolt connections holding the remaining floor trusses began to fail.[35]

Down below in the Plaza, Jimmy Devery became disoriented. As the bodies dropped around him, and hundreds of firefighters responded to the two buildings now ablaze, he mistakenly ran into the lobby of the North Tower. He headed toward what he thought was the same stairwell that he and Ronnie had climbed, then realized he was in the wrong building. Devery looked out through the three-story glass windows and saw a group of "white hats"—FDNY chiefs—setting up a command post on West Street. So he exited toward them.

"I was halfway into the street when somebody yelled, 'It's coming down,'" Devery recalled. "We looked up, and there's the top of one of the Towers falling. I didn't make the connection at first. I'm thinkin' Ronnie's in the other building. Then it came down."

But it wasn't the North Tower that was starting to collapse. It was the South Tower, where Ronnie was battling the flames. Now, as the trusses failed and each floor pancaked down onto the one below it, Devery started to run. He escaped into a parking garage and waited out the collapse.

Sometime later, when Devery emerged and walked onto West Street, he was aghast at the pile of debris. Multiton pieces of the building's steel facade stuck into the street like giant cross-cut potato chips. All around him there was fire, smoke, and the smell of burning flesh. A dense cloud of gray-white dust held visibility down to just a few yards.

Half in shock, Devery still hadn't grasped which tower had fallen. He looked up at the North Tower, still burning, and thought to himself, "I've got to get up there to Ronnie."

Then, as he started to cross West Street, Devery heard what he later remembered as "that same sickening noise" of debris coming down. Only this time he had no place to hide. So the fire marshal started running. He headed north toward Vesey Street. "But you couldn't outrun it," said Devery. As the cloud began to envelop him, he tripped on some burning debris. Suddenly, he pitched forward in the blackness. His helmet fell off and his glasses went flying. All he could do was hit the ground and cover his head with his hands.

"A minute went by, maybe two," he remembered. "And it was totally, totally quiet. Just like death. And then, all of a sudden, I started hearing the PASS alarms from the other guys." The Personal Alert Safety System alarms, worn on the mask of each firefighter who worked Rescue, were designed to give off a signal if a firefighter went down and didn't move. That way, he could be located. Now, all around Devery, the alarms were going off. He pulled his T-shirt up over his mouth to keep from choking on the dense cloud of asbestos particles and pulverized glass. Finally, he stood up and began walking with one hand in front of him.

Barely able to see more than a few feet, Devery moved slowly through the dust. Every so often he saw a red flashing light and realized it was on one of the surviving fire rigs. He would stop at the fire truck, reorient himself, then move on.

Sometime later he came upon Rich McCahey, the assistant chief fire marshal. McCahey had set up a temporary command post for the BFI, and he was huddling with a small group of marshals.

Almost unable to talk, Devery limped up to them.

"We gotta go back for Ronnie," he said. He looked around, trying to get his bearings, searching for something to remind him where the South Tower was. The dust was too thick to tell which direction he was facing. "Ronnie Bucca," he said. "We gotta go back."

Then one of the marshals pulled him aside. He leaned in and whispered, "Jimmy, you don't understand—Ronnie's gone."

40

THE BLACK HOLE

Ronnie Bucca, one of the few who saw it all coming, died with his boots on. He'd stood his ground with Chief Palmer and they'd gone down attacking the flames. They were attempting to protect the survivors on the seventy-eighth-floor lobby when suddenly, at 10:05 A.M. the outside walls of the enormous tower began to vibrate. The floor trusses beneath them started popping, and it all came apart. When FDNY radio broadcasts from the tragedy were analyzed, it became clear that Ronnie Bucca and Orio Palmer had made it up into the building higher than any other firefighters in either tower that day.[1] They stayed calm and they implemented a plan for attacking the fire. If anyone got off the seventy-eighth floor after Ling Young made it down, there's little doubt that it was due to their heroism.

John O'Neill, the FBI's former counterterrorism boss, also perished. His body was later found under a collapsed stairwell in the same tower Ronnie died in.

Each of these men, in his own way, had predicted the catastrophic attack. O'Neill was on the inside, with access to all the Bureau's intelligence. But Bucca was an outsider pounding on the door to get in. The fact that he'd predicted the destruction of the Trade Center with such precision from his position as a fire marshal makes his foresight all the more remarkable.

That morning, working in a windowless hospital nurse's cubicle with no radio or TV, Eve Bucca had no way of knowing what had happened. When the hospital moved into triage mode, she was quickly recruited to work with a makeshift blood bank. She managed to get in a call to

Jessica, who was safe. As lines formed outside the hospital all day long, she just kept working.

Only when they ran out of blood and closed the bank was Eve able to leave. She stopped for canned goods, bottled water, and batteries. Just before going home to await word from Ronnie, she stopped at her parents' house.

Most of the phones were down in the city, and it took her father, Bart Mitchell, hours to contact headquarters. He finally got through and asked about his son-in-law.

When he got off the phone, the look on his face was grave. "There's a problem," he said. Ronnie had gone into the Towers, and now he was missing. Eve's heart sank. Still, she told herself she wouldn't worry until there was definite news. "I trusted Ronnie's abilities," she said later on. "Even among his friends in Special Forces and Rescue, he had a reputation as a survivor."[2]

Ronnie's son got the word down at Tulane University, where he was a student, but he couldn't get a flight out because the airports were closed. He finally got some friends to give him a ride. It took them three days to drive from New Orleans. For the next few weeks he and Jessica went down to "the pile" as rescue workers and firefighters made their way through the tons of wreckage. A number of marshals volunteered for search duty.

When they found his remains a month later, Ronnie Bucca's helmet was near him. The number on his marshal's faceplate had been 317, but the 3 and 7 were missing, so the helmet simply read "1," the number of Ronnie's beloved Rescue company.

Of the 343 FDNY firefighters who lost their lives on September 11, Ronnie Bucca was the only fire marshal. In fact, he was the first marshal killed in the line of duty in New York City history.

"We survived that day as fire marshals," said Keith O'Mara. "But Ronnie Bucca died as a firefighter."[3]

Many of the FDNY's commands were devastated that day. Rescue One lost eleven of its twenty-five men, among them Gary Geidel, the handsome firefighter who had pulled his partner, Kevin Shea, out of the B-4 level after Yousef's first bomb in 1993.

Also lost in the company was Joe Angelini, the sixty-seven-year-old veteran who had drawn the poster of the "flying fireman" that welcomed

Ronnie back to the job in 1986. In the Bucca household, Joe was such a legend that the successful completion of any outrageous feat was known as an "Angelini." The white-haired firefighter had responded from a light-duty position after the first plane had hit and he heard his son Joe Jr. was missing. Both of them died that day. The company lost nine more of its bravest, including Capt. Terry Hatton, Lt. Dennis Mojica, and Firefighters Gerry Nevins, Bill Henry, Mike Montessi, Kenny Marina, Dave Weiss, Pat O'Keefe, and Brian Sweeney.[4]

"The loss of life was double because of the change of tours," said Jimmy Kelty. "You had guys who had just finished the night tour and guys coming on. They all jumped on those rigs because nobody wanted to miss those fires."[5]

But of all the houses that lost men in the attacks, the Rescue companies were hardest hit. "I heard a captain say something that really came true," said Tony Tedeschi, the chauffeur for Rescue One. "If you worked Rescue on September eleventh, you were dead."[6] Tedeschi, who was off that day, raced to Ground Zero from Long Island, only to find his company decimated. Even the company's big rig was crushed under tons of twisted steel.

Eve Bucca, a remarkably strong woman who never showed grief in public, understood why her husband ran up those seventy-eight stories.

"It's like everything in Ronnie's life got him ready for that day," she said. "The fellas don't wait. They go in. That's their instinct. There's a problem in there, we need to go in and get these people out."[7]

For weeks after Black Tuesday, Eve remained calm. She held her family together as they planned Ronnie's memorial service. Little Ronnie and Jessica made up a booklet of family pictures with copies of all their father's FDNY badges and Army patches. The memorial, packed to capacity, was attended not just by rank-and-file marshals and surviving firefighters, but many of Ronnie's fellow troops from the Special Forces, the 101st Airborne, and military intelligence. Of all the tributes that poured in, Fire Marshal Andy DiFusco may have said it best. He had worked with Ronnie on his last case September 6.

"My brother has this expression," said DiFusco. "When you meet somebody that's like nobody else on the planet, they get a check. People that are rare. People that are unique and make you feel like a better person just 'cause you're around them. You only get to meet a few 'checks' in your life, and Ronnie Bucca was one of them."

Chief Fire Marshal Lou Garcia, who barely survived on 9/11 as he raced in from Queens to link up with his men, said that Ronnie was the embodiment of a fire investigator. "He looked at terrorism the same way we look at fire," said Garcia. "Instead of fighting it *after* the damage is done, you have to be preemptive. Get out in front of it. That's where he was. He was years ahead of the intelligence agencies in predicting what would happen. He specifically, and I mean *repeatedly*, warned that the Towers were vulnerable. The fact that he responded that day and made it up with Chief Palmer higher than anyone else had reached just tells you who the man was."

"The Towers"

Now, as the days passed and Eve faced the fact that Ronnie was gone, she did her best to stay calm—to hide not only her sorrow at his loss, but her deep disappointment that Ronnie's warnings had been ignored for so long. For the sake of her family and children, she kept a game face. A number of weeks went by before she finally got up the strength to go down and clean out Ronnie's locker at Manhattan Base.

When she opened the locker door, her heart sank. There, amid Ronnie's gear, she found the folder he'd marked "The Towers." Inside, among Ronnie's notebooks with lists of al Qaeda suspects and printouts from the link charts, was the BFI face sheet report on Ahmed Amin Refai, the FDNY accountant. Eve sat down, stunned, and read the report.

At Ronnie's memorial and the many funerals she'd attended, Eve had heard the men comment about how the loss of life had been so great because the attack had come between tours. It was almost as if the enemy *knew* the FDNY's protocol for the change in tours and planned the attacks to ensure double the casualties. Was it possible that these terrorists actually had someone inside?

Now, when she saw the notation in the file that Refai had obtained the plans for the World Trade Center before the 1993 blast, Eve got angry. She called Chief Garcia and asked him whatever became of the Refai case. "Ronnie turned it over to the FBI," said Lou. "We never heard back." So Eve asked him to make some calls.

Not long after that, a detective named Bill Ryan from the NYPD's Arson and Explosion squad called the BFI. Ryan said he'd been asked by the Bureau to get a copy of the file on the Egyptian.[8] Garcia thought that was strange, since the FBI had it already—Ronnie had given it to them back in September 1999. Garcia thought it was even stranger that rather than calling *directly,* the FBI had a cop who wasn't even on the JTTF reach out to them. But he told Fire Marshal Bobby Greene to make another copy of the face sheet and give it to the Feds. So in late October, Greene brought it over to 26 Federal Plaza. Now the FBI had two copies of the Refai file.

Months went by, and Eve never heard any more about it. Finally, early in 2002 she reached out to a lieutenant colonel down at Fort Bragg who knew Ronnie well. The officer called FBI headquarters in Washington.

The Bureau had announced it was on the trail of a number of "sleeper cells" in the country. Surely the file on the Egyptian so close to the convicted blind Sheikh could be relevant.

Then, sometime in February of 2002, Fire Marshal Greene got a call from an FBI agent at headquarters in Washington.

"I was told that the Bureau had received everything on Refai and they were happy with what they got," Greene recalled later.[9]

Happy with what they got? thought Eve. What did that mean? Was the FBI looking at the Refai case or not? There were things about this that didn't add up. Right after he referred the Refai file to the FBI, Greene started digging, and learned that for a three-month period around 9/11 Refai's pension checks were being returned to the city uncashed. Refai had retired in the spring of 2001, and presumably those checks would have been a major source of income for him.

"I thought that was very odd," said Greene, "that two or three checks went by and he never even raised the flag." So he investigated and learned that the stoppage was the result of a clerical error. Once Refai had signed the proper papers the checks resumed.[10]

Still, Eve thought it was strange for a retired accountant to miss such a payroll error for three months. "How many people can go that long without a pension check?" she asked.

By September 2002, Eve was growing concerned. The FBI director had announced a series of major reforms in the wake of 9/11—but the evidence her husband had uncovered about this former city employee who'd had direct ties to the blind Sheikh and the WTC plans seemed to be going nowhere within the Bureau. Her anxiety heightened when she learned that the Justice Department had indicted another Egyptian, Ahmed Abdel Sattar, the U.S. postal worker who had attended the same mosque as Refai.[11] The government alleged that he had helped the blind Sheikh run the bloody al Gamma'a Islamiya from his home on Staten Island.

According to the indictment handed down in April 2002, the Shiekh's lawyer had conspired to distract federal prison guards so that Rahman could pass messages to the IG through the mailman. If the accountant Refai had been so close to the Sheikh, Eve wondered if he too could be an ongoing threat.

On September 15, 2002, a copy of the FDNY's Refai file was sent to Mike Byrne, the retired FDNY captain who had been Ronnie's sponsor when he worked on terrorism issues at Metrotech in 1999. Byrne was now a top official in the Department of Homeland Security, which was awaiting full funding from Congress.[12] Given his personal knowledge of Ronnie Bucca, Byrne took the case seriously and called the FBI. A few weeks later, in mid-October, Fire Marshal Bobby Greene was contacted by FBI agent Tom Callaghan, who worked with the JTTF in New York.

"He told me that they had decided to reopen the Refai case," said Greene. But there was something even more significant. Greene said the Bureau had learned that Refai was somehow connected to El Sayyid Nosair, the man who shot Meir Kahane.[13] Kahane was murdered in 1990; Refai had obtained the WTC plans in 1992. Ronnie Bucca had discovered that Refai was close to the blind Sheikh. Was it possible that this retired accountant might be part of the same cell that had planted the bomb beneath the Twin Towers and planned the Day of Terror bombings?

Ronnie Bucca had given the FDNY's Refai file to the FBI in September 1999. He'd learned that Refai had been interviewed twice by federal agents in 1994, but he had no idea if the investigation had gone anywhere. In an interview for this book, Detective Lou Napoli said that he "vaguely recall[ed]" seeing a report on the Egyptian back then, but that he remembered Refai as being "peripheral" to the cell. "Your individual [Refai] was checked out," Napoli said. "Someone else [at the FBI] looked at [the Refai report] and saw nothing there. So we moved on."[14] Now, even though the FDNY's Refai file had been delivered to the Feds twice before, Agent Callaghan asked for it one more time.

So Bobby Greene made a third copy and delivered it to 26 Federal Plaza.

"You have to understand," said Len Predtechenskis, "the Bureau can be a black hole when it comes to information. A cop sends it over, and an FBI supervisor sitting at his desk has to decide, 'Where do I send this piece of paper?' He has to decide based on what kind of investigation it is . . . Criminal or FCI [Foreign Counter Intelligence] or Organized Crime or Terrorism. And information often gets buried in the New York office, unless that supervisor decides that the [file] should go to a head-quarters file and an analytical unit gets hold of it and connects the dots. If that doesn't happen, the file and the information in it can get lost."

On January 8, 2003, in a conversation with the author, Agent Callaghan confirmed that the Refai investigation had been reopened.[15] Around that time Callaghan contacted Kay Woods, Refai's former boss, and asked about the accountant's activities when she supervised him in the Capital Budget Unit.[16]

In February, after learning that Woods had spoken to the Feds, a second female FDNY employee contacted the FBI on her own, out of concern about Refai's possible terrorist ties. In an interview for this book, the woman, who asked not to be identified, said that she remembered talking about the first World Trade Center bombing with Refai. "At the time I said to him, 'Hatred is very destructive,' and I just got the feeling [from him] of this ice wall. When the bombing happened, his picture was all over the TV. He was holding the blind Sheikh's arm. So of course the rumors started flying."[17]

After 9/11, the woman said, she became "really frightened" about Refai. "I waited about a year, but this past February I called the FBI," she said. "I told them, 'I can't prove anything. I just want to make sure that this person [Refai] is on the radar screen.' "

After that, the woman said, FBI Agent Callaghan called her repeatedly and asked to set up a formal interview. But she became worried. "I was losing sleep [and] I just couldn't take it. I was really thinking that [if I said any more] I would have to go into Witness Protection."

In mid-April, the author contacted the Bureau to check on the status of the Refai investigation. At the time, Joseph Valiquette, press spokesman for the FBI's New York office, said, "We can neither confirm nor deny that investigation."[18] But as late as May 25 a confidential FBI source confirmed that the probe of Refai was ongoing.

As to Refai himself, the author made multiple attempts to contact him following the discovery of the allegations regarding the lost ID incident at the FDNY in 1999. After interviewing Refai's former boss, Assistant Deputy Commissioner Kay Woods, in August 2002, the author paid a visit to Refai's home in New Jersey an hour and a half south of New York City. Refai was in Egypt at the time. Now retired, the accountant has an apartment there where he spends up to two months each year.

Refai was in Egypt until early July 2003, but on his return the author again knocked on his door in the company of Joseph F. O'Brien, a retired FBI special agent who is now a private investigator. Refai and his son Khaled, twenty-three, answered and agreed to talk. In an hour-long interview he confirmed that he had been a member of the al-Salaam Mosque in Jersey City, and that he had been photographed by ABC News cameras as he held the Sheikh's arm and moved him through a crowd of reporters outside an immigration office. He claimed that he had "disagreed" with the Sheikh over the issue of whether Rahman was doing too much publicity at the time, but insisted that he had supported him as a member of his mosque.

"He is blind, and anybody in this country would help him," said Refai in the interview. "If he turned out to be a bad guy, I had nothing to do with that. At the time, everybody in the community love him. We see nothing wrong with him."[19]

Refai admitted that he had met El Sayyid Nosair, Mohammed Salameh, and indicted U.S. postal worker Ahmed Abdel Sattar during his visits to the al-Salaam, Abu Bakr, and Al Farooq mosques. He first claimed he didn't know Mahmud Abouhalima, then acknowledged that he did. But though the tiny al-Salaam Mosque accommodated no more than twenty-five to thirty worshipers at any time, Refai claimed he really didn't "know" these men.

With respect to the allegations leveled by Assistant Deputy FDNY Commissioner Kay Woods, contained in the Bureau of Fire Investigation's report, Refai denied almost everything. He said that he had "never" obtained the plans of the World Trade Center prior to the bombing, and that he did not call in sick on the day of the blast, as Woods remembered. At first, he also said that he had not been investigated by the FBI after the WTC bombing. Then he insisted that the FBI's questioning of him in 1994 related to one of his freelance accounting clients.

"Somehow [the FBI] arrested them for money laundering," said Refai, "and because I'm the accountant and I do the operation for them, they asked me, 'Do you know them?' I said, 'Yes, I know them. They are my clients.' They [the FBI] come over here. I give them all the files. That's it."

But during this most recent interview, Refai's story about the current FBI investigation into his activities changed as the conversation went on. First he claimed that FBI agents had come to see him "last fall," but he couldn't remember their names or what they had asked him about. Later he recalled that one of the agents was Tom Callaghan, but still insisted that he, Refai, was not the target of any investigation. Finally he admitted that the agents had contacted several of his clients, and followed one of them, before coming to see him.

"Callaghan and the other guy [agent] came over here," admitted Refai, "and they talked to me about whether I had any investigation with FBI before." But Refai claimed that they never asked about his association with the blind Sheikh.

In the interview Refai did admit that he'd lied to Ronnie Bucca and Fire Marshal Mel Hazel about losing his ID. When pressed about his close association with Sheikh Rahman, who had led the IG terrorist group and been convicted of seditious conspiracy, Refai said, "not everything he's talking about I agree with." And yet, a decade after the Sheikh was publicly vilified as a terrorist conspirator, Refai continued to embrace him.

In four separate instances throughout the hour-long interview, Refai was asked if he would renounce the Sheikh, and every time, he refused, continuing to insist that his closeness to Abdel Rahman, captured on video, had no significance.

"No. No. No. No," said Refai. "What does it mean? I'm holding his arm. He is blind."

But retired FBI agent O'Brien disagreed. "For a man like Abdel Rahman to let somebody get this close to him meant that he trusted Refai with his life," he said following the interview. "Refai had to be an intimate of the Sheikh's."

Ironically, Refai lives in the New Jersey suburb that has the highest concentration of September 11 widows. When asked how he felt about the attacks, he said, "When you talk about the victims that we had [here] I went to the park here holding a candle because of them and nobody asked me to go. I went myself."

But at the end of the interview he seemed to reveal his true feelings about 9/11.

"To be honest with you, a lot of people in my country [and] Arab countries feel that who did 9/11—it's insiders. It's not the Sheikh. It's not bin Laden. It's the U.S. government to help Israel. Do you think the Arabs have the talent to do such a thing?"

As the interview ended, Refai's son asked what this book would be called.

"*A Thousand Years for Revenge*," replied the author. Refai eyed him and then laughed.

"*A Thousand Years for Revenge*. Ha, ha, ha, ha."

41

OPERATION IRAQI
FREEDOM TWO

Just after 11 P.M. on the night of September 11, 2001, in a police office in Pangasinan Province, the Philippines, Col. Rodolfo Mendoza was at work. Now the provincial director of the region for the Philippine National Police, he was finishing a routine report when his cell phone rang, alerting him to a text message. It said "Urgent! Turn on CNN." Mendoza quickly picked up a remote and switched on a TV.

When he saw the pictures of the burning Trade Center towers in New York, the colonel's jaw dropped. Mendoza grabbed the Nokia and dialed back the PNP officer who had alerted him to the attack. As soon as the other cop answered, the colonel exclaimed, "They have done it. They have DONE it!"[1]

Of course, Mendoza had known about Ramzi Yousef's plan to return to the Towers since the spring of 1995, when Abdul Hakim Murad had confessed to him. He had given the entire report to the U.S. Embassy in Manila. He knew the Justice Department had the intelligence because he'd heard that the FBI had made a preliminary investigation of two of Murad's U.S. flight schools.[2] But why had they stopped? Why hadn't the American agents pursued the evidence he'd given them, that Yousef had conceived a plot that went beyond the pope and Bojinka—one that involved the hijacking of airliners by Middle Eastern men training back then in U.S. flight schools?

"After the attacks," said Mendoza, "when I met with several [PNP] police officers who had the knowledge about Murad, they asked me, 'We had great faith in the institutions of the U.S. to prevent it. How did this happen?' "

And so, in the words of Colonel Mendoza, this story ends the way it began, with that question: "How did it happen?"

The evidence uncovered in this eighteen-month investigation suggests a number of reasons, but in the end they boil down to a single word: arrogance. September 11 happened because of the FBI's utter underestimation of Ramzi Yousef and his coconspirators. It happened because of the Bureau's ongoing belief that the threat was the work of disorganized zealots who lacked the competence to deliver weapons of mass destruction. It happened because of the Justice Department's treatment of that threat as a series of legal cases to be prosecuted rather than a worldwide conspiracy to be fought from a global intelligence perspective. It happened because a tradition of interagency biases and "need to know" secrecy prevented the vital sharing of intelligence.

The FBI's repeated inability to recognize, and act upon, the danger from al Qaeda was largely a function of a pathology that existed inside the agency itself. There was a culture in the Bureau that dismissed the work of earnest brick agents like Nancy Floyd and her colleagues in Minneapolis while rewarding the mean-spirited incompetence of supervisors. The evidence uncovered in this investigation suggests that, despite some reforms, that pathology persists today.

Reform comes from the top down. And although some extraordinary mistakes were made by senior FBI officials in the years before 9/11, few, if any, have been held accountable. On the contrary, most of them have been rewarded:

After the 1993 debacle with Salem, Carson Dunbar received that unusual retirement deal, allowing him to transfer to ATF in order to maintain his federal pension while working as superintendent of the New Jersey State Police.[3]

The supervisory special agent who turned down the FISA warrant for Zacarias Moussaoui was promoted in Washington. Pasquale D'Amuro, the ASAC who ran the National Security Division in New York while evidence of the al Qaeda flight school threat was ignored or minimized, was appointed assistant director of the FBI's Counterterrorism Division in Washington.[4]

Lupe Gonzalez, who admitted that terrorism was "job four" on his watch as SAC in Phoenix, was promoted to run the FBI's Dallas office.

Bruce Gebhart, the SAC who ran the Phoenix office while counterterrorism took a backseat to drug investigations, went on to become deputy director—the number two man at headquarters under Director Robert S. Mueller III.

"Not a Single Piece of Paper" in FBI Files

And what of the director himself? Six days after 9/11, he insisted publicly that there were "no warning signs" of the attacks.[5] "The fact that there were a number of individuals that happened to have received training at flight schools here," said Mueller, "is news, quite obviously."

Mueller made that assertion two months after his own agent, Ken Williams, had sent the Phoenix memo, and six years after Colonel Mendoza had warned the Feds of Yousef's third plot.[6]

But Mueller went even further in denying the Bureau's negligence. Speaking at the Commonwealth Club in San Francisco seven months after 9/11, he insisted that "the hijackers left no paper trail. In our investigation, we have not uncovered a single piece of paper—either here in the U.S. or in the treasure trove of information that has turned up in Afghanistan and elsewhere—that mentioned any aspect of the September 11th plot."[7]

Testifying before the Senate Judiciary Committee on May 8, Mueller repeated that assertion, but took an even more defensive stance, suggesting that while the Minneapolis agents had done a "terrific job" in attempting to alert headquarters to the threat from Zacarias Moussaoui, it was doubtful whether any further investigation would have led to the 9/11 plot.

"Did we discern from that there was a plot that could have led us to September 11th?" asked Mueller. "No. Could we have? I rather doubt it."[8]

The agents in Minneapolis didn't take that sitting down. Two weeks later, Coleen Rowley, a courageous lawyer in the Minnesota office, dropped a bombshell. In a thirteen-page letter to Mueller on May 21, she expressed her "deep concern" that the director and other FBI leaders were "shading/skewing" the facts about the Bureau's failures leading up to 9/11.[9]

While acknowledging that "the term 'cover-up' would be too strong a characterization," she nonetheless complained that a supervisory special agent at headquarters had been "consistently, almost deliberately thwarting the Minneapolis FBI agents' efforts" to investigate Zacarias Moussaoui in the weeks prior to the attacks. Accusing the SSAC of "deliberately sabotag[ing]" the Moussaoui case, Rowley wrote that some agents joked at the time that headquarters must have "spies or moles" working for Osama bin Laden to undermine the Bureau's counterterrorism efforts to such a degree. Warning that Mueller himself had not been "completely honest" about "the true reasons for the FBI's pre-September failures," Rowley predicted that "until we come clean and deal with causes, the Department of Justice will continue to experience problems fighting terrorism and fighting crime in general."

Once word of the letter leaked out, Rowley became an overnight heroine. Summoned to Washington, she testified before the Senate Judiciary Committee. She was later named one of *Time*'s 2002 "Persons of the Year" for her courage as a whistleblower.

Mueller, who had initially kept Rowley's letter secret, got lambasted by Congress.

"A cover-up is not going to work," threatened Senator Charles E. Grassley (R-Iowa), a senior member of the Judiciary Committee.

Lewis Schiliro, who'd retired as the FBI's assistant director in charge of the New York office, said that his agents had tried to follow up on flight school intelligence when possible, but while they worried about an al Qaeda airline hijacking, "never once did we really focus on the use of a plane as a weapon." It would have been "very difficult to connect the dots," he said.[10]

Not if they'd examined Rodolfo Mendoza's files, of course. But if ADICs like Schiliro and the New York supervisors didn't know about the planes-as-missiles scenario, who in the Bureau did? Where the buck stopped on Colonel Mendoza's intelligence is one of the great unanswered questions in this story.

Asked if he felt his office bore any responsibility for missing signals leading up to the September 11 attacks, William A. Gavin, who preceded Schiliro as the FBI's New York ADIC, said in an interview for this book, "If wishes were horses, beggars would ride. If we knew at the time what we know now," said Gavin, "of course you could have prevented it, but there wasn't, as far as I could see, a way to know that."[11]

His sentiments were echoed by Jim Roth, the former chief attorney in the New York office, who sided with Carson Dunbar during the Salem controversy. "Hindsight is wonderful," said Roth, "but the dots appear a lot clearer on the chart after the fact than they do when it's going on. I think it's very unfair when they do the hindsighting and they start dragging people up on the Hill and they say, 'Heads will roll.' Then they expect these agents to be risk takers, right? The lesson they learn is, you take a risk and they'll cut your nuts off."[12]

Despite the male metaphor, Roth was describing exactly what happened to Nancy Floyd, who'd taken a number of risks working her asset Emad Salem, only to get suspended in the end. Floyd had been silenced, but now in May of 2002 Coleen Rowley got a national forum for her views.

Eight days after she sent the letter, partly in response to the public outcry, Mueller announced a restructuring of the FBI's approach to fighting terrorism. He pledged to reassign 400 of the Bureau's 11,500 field agents from narcotics investigations to counterterrorism. Mueller also promised that four hundred new analysts would be added at the Bureau's fifty-six field offices and at headquarters, including twenty-five from the CIA. The number of Joint Terrorism Task Forces, he said, would be expanded from thirty-five prior to 9/11 to sixty-six by 2003.

But in a signal that some of Mueller's reforms may have been misguided, the Justice Department announced that it was setting up an entire second tier of task forces in each of the U.S. attorney's offices nationwide. These so-called ATTFs (Anti Terrorist Task Forces) were designed to do what the JTTFs were originally set up to do: coordinate with local and state law enforcement agencies on issues regarding terrorism. Now, in most federal prosecutors' offices, an ATTF operates alongside a JTTF.

"It's an excuse to have more meetings," said one senior special agent in charge from another federal agency who agreed to be interviewed for this book.[13] "If the JTTFs were functioning properly, you wouldn't need ATTFs."

Underscoring evidence of the barrier Ronnie Bucca encountered in trying to interface with the New York JTTF, the Senate-House Joint Inquiry found that "non FBI personnel are prevented in some cases from having access to the FBI's information systems." The congressional inquiry also concluded that "some law enforcement organizations reportedly viewed the JTTF as a way of getting rid of deadwood."[14]

Will the Bureau Be Ready for the Next Attack?

Hundreds of FBI agents have been reassigned and a raft of new task forces have been formed. But would Mueller's changes come fast enough to interdict the next terror threat?

A year after 9/11, the Justice Department's inspector general issued a report declaring that despite the restructuring, the Bureau's failure to create an overall terrorist assessment had actually put the nation at increased risk of future attacks.[15] Worse, in a multipart investigation, the *Los Angeles Times* discovered that despite millions of dollars in appropriations to upgrade the FBI's computer and information-sharing capabilities, the Bureau was still locked in a "paper-driven culture."

The system was so antiquated that immediately after 9/11, frustrated agents in Tampa were unable even to E-mail photos of the nineteen hijackers to the Bureau's regional offices. They had to resort to overnight mail.[16] The Bureau had pledged to upgrade its information systems via a project called Trilogy, but by January 2002 its estimated $485 million price tag had escalated by 30 percent, and the Justice Department's inspector general issued yet another report describing the computer upgrade as a case study in mismanagement.

The FBI did add a few notches to its belt in the eighteen months after 9/11. Ramzi Binalshibh, the 9/11 coconspirator, was arrested in September 2002. Tawfig bin-Atash, a leader in the *Cole* bombing plot, was seized in April 2003. And on March 1, 2003, Khalid Shaikh Mohammed was finally brought to ground.

But there had been limited victories against al Qaeda before. Ramzi Yousef's second attack on the World Trade Center was carried out years after he'd been arrested, convicted, and sent to solitary. The blind Sheikh continued to call the shots—furthering the IG's villainous business from his jail cell—for years before he was stopped.

The question remains: after more than a decade of treating terrorism as a series of legal cases, has the FBI made sufficient reforms in time to prevent the next Black Tuesday?

FBI whistleblower Coleen Rowley suggests that the answer is no. In another letter to Mueller on February 26, 2003, Rowley warned that the course correction inside the Bureau wasn't coming fast enough.

Once Iraq was invaded, she predicted, the Bureau would be ill prepared to contain the increased threat to Americans.[17]

"We should be deluding neither ourselves nor the American people." Rowley told Mueller that "the FBI, despite the various improvements you are implementing, will be unable to stem the flood of terrorism that will likely head our way in the wake of an attack on Iraq. What troubles me most is that I have no assurance that you have made that clear to the President."

Another Case of Blowback?

The White House used the allegation of ties between Osama bin Laden and Saddam Hussein as a justification, in part, for the Iraqi invasion. In *Bush At War, Washington Post* managing editor Bob Woodward quoted Deputy Defense Secretary Paul D. Wolfowitz, chief advocate for the administration's get-tough policy on Iraq, as telling the cabinet, "There was a 10% to 50% chance Saddam was involved" in the 9/11 attacks.[18] A Fox News poll prior to the invasion found that 81 percent of those questioned "believe Saddam has ties to the al Qaeda terrorist group."

In a nationally televised speech last October to rally congressional support for a resolution authorizing war with Iraq, President Bush alleged that Saddam Hussein's government posed an immediate threat to the United States, and that Iraq had trained al Qaeda members "in bomb-making and poisons and deadly gases."[19]

Declaring that "Iraq could decide on any given day to provide a biological or chemical weapon to a terrorist group," Bush insisted that "alliance with terrorists could allow the Iraqi regime to attack America without leaving any fingerprints."

In the weeks leading up to the invasion, as the administration sought consensus from the American people, both the White House and the Department of Homeland Security ratcheted up their public warnings about terrorism. In early February 2003, just days after alleging links between Saddam and al Qaeda, U.S. intelligence officials began warning citizens that bin Laden's network might be in possession of "dirty bombs" encased in radioactive waste.[20]

On February 7, Homeland Security Secretary Tom Ridge raised the terrorism Threat Advisory from yellow to orange, signaling a high risk of terrorist attacks.[21] Later, Ridge advised Americans to put together emergency supply kits that included a three-day supply of water, flashlights, and duct tape to seal doors and windows in the event of a radiological or biological attack.[22]

In a speech at FBI headquarters, President Bush said, "We're trying to protect you. We're doing everything in our power to make sure the homeland is secure." Intelligence officials quoted at the time said they had identified six hundred to one thousand potential al Qaeda terrorists in cells around the U.S.[23]

In answer to reporters' questions linking the al Qaeda threat to the impending Iraq invasion, Defense Secretary Donald Rumsfeld said, "Why now? The answer is that every week that goes by, [Saddam's] weapons of mass destruction programs become more mature [and] he has relationships with terrorist networks."[24]

A Los Angeles Times story quoting supporters and critics of the potential Baghdad attack concluded: "Of all the charges the United States has made, the most hotly debated are those linking Iraq and the Al Qaeda network. Without such a connection, the logic of invading Iraq as a response to September 11th seems weak to many Americans."[25]

Yet in his presentation to the UN Security Council on February 5, Secretary of State Colin Powell failed to produce any compelling proof that Baghdad was even remotely connected to the 9/11 attacks. Powell pointed to a suspected al Qaeda terror camp located near Kurdish-held northern Iraq.[26] Contending that the facility trained al Qaeda operatives to carry out attacks with explosives and poisons, Powell insisted that there was a "sinister nexus between Iraq and the al Qaeda terror network."[27]

The nexus turned out to be a little-known terrorist group called Ansar al-Islam, headed by one Majamuddin Fraraj Ahmad. Speaking in Oslo, Norway, where he fled after Saddam Hussein allegedly tried to kill him, Ahmad, also known as Mullah Krekar, insisted that the Baghdad regime was his enemy.

In the previous five years, the U.S. State Department's own web site had mentioned nothing about a threat to the U.S. homeland from Iraq,[28] and according to the BBC a classified British intelligence report showed no links between al Qaeda and the Iraqi regime.[29] The overwhelming weight of the evidence uncovered in this investigation demonstrates that, apart from Osama bin Laden, al Qaeda remains dominated by Egyptian fundamentalists.

Nevertheless, the first bombs of Operation Iraqi Freedom began to fall on Baghdad on March 19. The next day the ground war began. Though coalition forces got bogged down for a time in Nasirya to the south, U.S. and British troops swept dramatically through the country. By April 9 Baghdad had fallen, and two days later U.S. and Kurdish fighters captured the final stronghold of Mosul to the north. In a campaign that lasted just over three weeks, 300,000 coalition troops had been deployed and only 140 had lost their lives.

With the defeat of Saddam Hussein's regime, there was reason to celebrate: a brutal dictatorship had been crushed. But history seemed poised to repeat itself.

In the late 1980s, the United States had helped the mujahadeen rout the Soviets, but our efforts failed to ensure a lasting peace in Afghanistan. September 11 was the deadly blowback. Now, in the weeks and months after those first pictures of grateful Iraqis and falling statues, there was grave cause for concern. A month and a half after Saddam fled his palaces, power was still out across most of the country. Widespread looting had led to virtual anarchy in many quarters.[30] Because the disabled country was unable to refine gasoline, Iraqis waited up to three days for fuel. This led to a U.S. pledge to import gasoline into a country with the third largest oil reserves on earth.[31]

Meanwhile, without a formal government, Iraq seemed headed toward a political crisis. More than ten thousand angry Shiites took to the streets demanding that U.S. forces withdraw.[32] The Shiites, who make up 60 percent of the country's population, raised the specter that a radical anti-American Islamic regime might be democratically elected, and critics warned that in displacing Saddam, a dictator whose tyranny was directed largely at his own people, we might have paved the way for another Afghanistan or Iran.

The interim government, led by retired Lt. Gen. Jay Garner, only exacerbated the crisis by allowing former officials of Saddam Hussein's Ba'ath Party to occupy positions of power. Iraqi doctors staged an angry protest when an ex-Ba'athist undersecretary was appointed the new head of the Health Ministry.[33] Other Iraqis were enraged when one of Garner's aides reinstated the Ba'ath Party head of Baghdad University.[34]

In a move some critics questioned, Barbara Bodine, the career diplomat and former ambassador to Yemen who had crippled John O'Neill's investigation of the *Cole* bombing, was named regional coordinator of central Iraq, a key position that many described as the "new mayor" of Baghdad. But a month after taking charge, Bodine and Garner were summarily fired by the Bush administration.

In a major shakeup, counterterrorism expert L. Paul Bremer was appointed the new special envoy.[35] The State Department insisted that Bodine's exit was "routine," but she was given only three days to leave the country.[36]

The ongoing lawlessness only amped up the danger to U.S. occupying forces. By mid-July, the number of U.S. deaths from the invasion had surpassed those in the 1991 Gulf War. Nine Americans died in two separate helicopter crashes, another in an accident, but two were killed trying to keep the peace in Baghdad: one GI was shot in the head at close range, another murdered by a sniper. "We're sitting ducks here," said one corporal, and the threat only increased after ground troops were pressed into service to stop the continued looting.[37]

"We won the war, so why are people dying?" asked Fran Stall, whose companion is the father of Troy David Jenkins, a sergeant with the 187th Infantry killed on April 24. "I don't understand why this keeps happening. We have guys getting killed every day."[38]

By early July, as attacks against coalition forces mounted, Pentagon strategists were beginning to face the terrible prospect that the capture of the country in the spring had just been the first phase of a protracted guerilla war. The evidence was increasing that forces loyal to Saddam Hussein were mounting an organized counteroffensive. But Defense Secretary Rumsfeld scoffed at the notion that Iraq might well become another Vietnam.[39]

Another key goal in the U.S. invasion was the removal of Saddam himself. But by late July, even though his two sons were reported killed, the death of the dictator himself had yet to be confirmed.[40] In fact, the U.S. seemed to agree that Saddam had survived, by offering a $25 million reward for his capture.

The concern that "the Butcher of Baghdad" might someday attempt a return to power only increased after a report that Saddam's son Qusay had made off with nearly a billion dollars in cash from the country's Central Bank hours before the invasion.[41]

The dramatic theft, which amounted to the biggest bank robbery in history, gave rise to speculation that the money might be used as a war chest by Saddam and other Ba'ath Party cronies to underwrite anti-U.S. terrorist activities or "finance a comeback."[42]

Perhaps the most unsettling development came when looters ripped apart sections of a nuclear research site, causing acute radiation syndrome among nearby civilians. After a heroic campaign fought by U.S troops with the best of intentions, that one incident raised the specter that the ultimate Pandora's Box might have been opened.[43]

Bechtel and Halliburton

Ironically, apart from the liberated Iraqis, the few immediate postinvasion winners were two giant multinational corporations with close ties to Republican administration leaders past and present. After a secret bid was unsealed, the Bechtel Group was awarded a $680 million contract to oversee the rebuilding of Iraq. "This has never been done before—an American corporation rebuilding an entire foreign country," said Danielle Brian, executive director of the Washington-based Project on Government Oversight.

George Schultz, former treasury secretary for President Richard Nixon, had served as president of Bechtel in the 1970s and later served as Ronald Reagan's secretary of state. Casper W. Weinberger was a Bechtel director, vice president, and general counsel before he became Reagan's secretary of defense in 1981.[44]

But the biggest payoff after the Iraqi invasion went to a subsidiary of the Halliburton Corporation, which was run by Dick Cheney from 1995 to 2000, when he left to become George W. Bush's vice-presidential running mate. In a no-bid contract, Halliburton's Kellogg, Brown & Root (KBR) subsidiary was awarded a $7 billion deal to fight oil-well fires in Iraq over the next two years.

Since the September 11 attacks, KBR has won significant additional business from the federal government and the Pentagon, including the contract to build cells for detainees at Guantanamo Bay in Cuba. KBR is the exclusive logistics supplier for the U.S. Navy and the Army, providing services ranging from construction to fuel transportation.[45]

"A troubling pattern is starting to emerge," said Senator Ron Wyden (D-OR). "We're seeing some of the country's most powerful business interests showing up and getting these contracts. That ought to set off bells." The *Los Angeles Times* editorialized that "the Administration's no-bid contract with a Halliburton subsidiary gives the impression of a grab of Iraqi government resources for American business."[46]

And what of the primary allegations that were used to justify the war—that Saddam's regime had weapons of mass destruction (WMD) and links to Al Qaeda in the 9/11 attacks?

Months after the invasion, little or no evidence had surfaced to support either charge. By May 11, the group directing U.S. search efforts for WMD was beginning to wind down operations without having unearthed any significant proof that Saddam kept hidden caches of such weapons. The 75th Exploitation Task Force, a group made up of scientists and Special Forces troops, had searched nineteen of twenty-one suspected sites and found nothing. Another sixty-eight non-WMD sites were suspected of revealing clues to the more lethal weapons, but by late May forty-five of those surveyed had come up empty.[47]

Defense Secretary Donald Rumsfeld said he now believed that Iraq had destroyed its chemical and biological weapons before the war, which led to the questions: If Saddam had complied with the UN resolution, what was the threat to America? And why mount an invasion in the first place?

Before the war, one of the administration's answers would have been those purported links with al Qaeda. But after months on the ground in Iraq, and virtual control of the country since May, U.S. intelligence agents had yet to find any smoking guns.

An April 28 *Newsweek* cover story called "Saddam's Secret Files" revealed the contents of a small treasure trove of intelligence seized from the Iraqi Intelligence Service, but none of it contained any significant information about al Qaeda, or hidden locations of chemical or biological weapons.[48]

The biggest denials of the Baghdad–al Qaeda links came from two men in the best position to know. In separate debriefings, both Khalid Shaikh Mohammed and Abu Zubaydah, a high-level aide to Osama bin

Laden, said that the Saudi billionaire had vetoed the idea of linking with Iraq because he didn't want to be beholden to Saddam Hussein.[49]

Perhaps most disturbing, allegations by the President himself in his State of the Union address that Saddam had "sought significant quantities of uranium" and White House officials that Iraq "could launch a biological or chemical attack in 45 minutes," were known by the Administration to be false. The firestorm that erupted over the prospect that we may have gone to war under false pretenses caused Democratic Senator Bob Graham to raise the question of impeachment. "If the standard for impeachment is the one the House Republicans used against Bill Clinton," he said, "this clearly comes within that standard."[50]

Americans had supported the Iraqi war largely out of the belief that a victory in Baghdad would make the United States safer in the war on terror. But within weeks after the fall of Saddam there were signs that Coleen Rowley's prediction about an increased terror threat to the United States had come to pass.

On April 11, ten al Qaeda prisoners, including the chief suspect in the *Cole* bombing, escaped from prison in Yemen. A month later, nine al Qaeda suicide bombers mounted synchronized strikes on three housing compounds in the Saudi Arabian capitol of Riyadh; the thirty-four who were killed included eight Americans. Four days later, another series of al Qaeda–linked bombings erupted in Casablanca, Morocco, with a death toll of forty-one.[51] Despite U.S. claims after Khalid Shaikh Mohammed's arrest that the al Qaeda network was in disarray, intelligence officials now admitted that the network was back, and possibly stronger than ever.[52] One senior counterterrorism official estimated that al Qaeda had three thousand active members, including "possible sleepers" in the United States who were awaiting orders.

After lowering the U.S. terror threat level following the conquest of Baghdad, on May 20 the Department of Homeland Security brought the level back up to orange. The move was a response to intelligence suggesting the high risk of a new al Qaeda attack on U.S. soil. Echoing Condoleezza Rice in the summer before 9/11, former White House Press Secretary Ari Fleischer said that "chatter" picked up by U.S. agencies suggested that new attacks were possible.[53]

By late May, the CIA acknowledged that it was reviewing the accuracy of prewar intelligence estimates.[54] After a string of intel failures stretching back twelve years before 9/11, the inability of the CIA and other agencies to predict the actual terrorist threat posed by Iraq is a continuing cause for concern. Apart from the failure to unearth unconventional weapons, the lack of evidence proving al Qaeda links to Baghdad makes the threat to Americans more acute. If al Qaeda is a global network with no borders to attack or command headquarters to bomb, it becomes that much more difficult to stop.

Today, after years of legal victories by the Feds, and more than a decade in which its top operatives have been either killed or arrested, Osama bin Laden's terror network remains an extraordinarily dangerous threat to U.S. interests worldwide. Even the lowest intelligence estimate puts the number of surviving "Afghan Arabs" who fought the Soviets at ten to fourteen thousand. These are hardened men, educated and trained with U.S. weaponry, and devoted to a fanatical view of Islam. If the Arab "street" unites against the United States following the Iraqi occupation, the term *blowback* could take on new meaning.

Further evidence surfaced in late March 2003 that the man who sheltered Yousef's uncle Khalid Shaikh Mohammed was none other than the interior minister of Qatar, the Arab Emirate that played host to CENTOM, the Coalition's Central Command during Operation Iraqi Freedom.

In 1996, when FBI agents closed in on Mohammed in Qatar, he was reportedly given shelter, then helped to escape, by Sheik Abdullah bin Khalid al-Thani, Qatar's interior minister. Quoting former CIA case officer Bob Baer, who described al-Thani as a potential danger to U.S. troops in Qatar, the *Los Angeles Times* revealed al-Thani's cabinet status on March 28, 2003.[55] According to the newspaper, it was unknown whether Defense Secretary Rumsfeld was aware of al-Thani's al Qaeda ties at the time the U.S. signed a cooperation agreement with Qatar to base its command there. But Richard Clarke, former counterterrorism czar in the Clinton and Bush administrations, reacted to the news with surprise.

"I'm shocked to hear [that]," Clarke said. "You're telling me that [al-Thani] is today in charge of security inside Qatar? I hope that's not true." If Clarke—a man who is arguably one of America's best and brightest when it comes to assessing the al Qaeda threat—was surprised, what does that say about the continuing ability of Osama bin Laden's terror network to evade detection?

Who Is Guarding the Guardians?

So we return to the question posed at the outset by the ancient Roman poet Juvenal: "Who *is* guarding the guardians themselves?" If we can't trust our defense and intelligence leaders to act aggressively to protect us from the threat of a widespread international terrorist network like al Qaeda, whom can we trust?

The United States Congress has an oversight function over the intelligence agencies. But our lawmakers have also repeatedly dropped the ball. In December 1995, senior staff members of the Senate Judiciary Committee wrote a detailed memo to Chairman Orrin Hatch (R-UT), urging him to "investigate the FBI's involvement before, during and after a terrorist threat and/or attack."[56]

The memo noted that the issue was "particularly topical in light of the tragic incidents . . . at the federal building in Oklahoma City and at the World Trade Center." (See Appendix II, p. 519.)

The staff members proposed a twofold probe: first, a review of preventive measures then in place to anticipate and "hopefully prevent" such acts; second, an analysis of the existing systems currently available in the event of a terrorist attack. "Using the World Trade Center as an example," they suggested, "we may also want to take a critical view at what has occurred in the past, what could have been done to prevent it and what measures have been taken since that tragedy." In a footnote, the memo suggested, "We have information that some instances like the World Trade Center could have been prevented."

If the Senate had pursued such an investigation, of course, the last decade might have turned out very differently. Perhaps as far back as 1996 the American public would have heard the true story of Nancy Floyd and Emad Salem—how the FBI blew the first investigation and failed to catch Ramzi Yousef before he went on to create the blueprint for so much terror.

But sources familiar with the memo say that Senator Hatch decided not to go forward with the proposal.[57] No investigation was done. Nancy Floyd got sanctioned, the JTTF kept its doors closed to key local investigators like Ronnie Bucca, evidence fell through the cracks, and the deadly al Qaeda juggernaut kept on churning. . . .

* * *

So what lessons have been learned from the twelve-year jihadi "war" that ramped up to September 11? We understand the enemy better, there's no doubt. But is the FBI, the primary agency charged with stopping domestic terrorism, in a better position to do so since 9/11?

Part of the answer is contained in the full report of the congressional Joint Inquiry that held hearings on Capitol Hill in the fall of 2002.

After seven months fighting the release of the 858-page report, the White House relented. But the heavily redacted report left enormous questions unanswered. Claiming that no "smoking guns" were found that would have alerted intelligence agencies to the details of the attacks, the report disclosed that the FBI had an informant in San Diego who was interacting directly with hijackers al-Midhar and al-Hazmi, and the report showed that the Joint Inquiry had focused on the years from 1998, when Yousef's plot was already four years old.

Incredibly, while acknowledging Khalid Shaikh Mohammed as the 9/11 "mastermind," the report repeats the old saw that the extent of Yousef's planning in Manila was limited to "crashing an airplane into CIA headquarters." Even more surprising, the report mistakenly describes this earlier scenario as "one portion" of the Bojinka plot.[58]

The National Commission on Terrorist Attacks on the United States was set up after the families of September 11 victims came to feel that the Joint Inquiry might be too limited. In March 2003 the commission began hearings in New York. But soon there was evidence that even this investigation would not go deep enough.

After resisting creation of the panel for months, the White House failed to include an $11 million funding request for the commission in the supplemental war budget sent to Capital Hill the same month.[59] The *New York Times* pointed out that the $3 million start-up appropriation for the commission could run out in the summer of 2003. At least $14 million was needed for the commission to do its job—a small price to pay when one considers the $40 million earmarked to investigate the cause of the space shuttle Columbia's crash.

Further, in the release of its first report in early July 2003, the Commission alleged that it was being hampered in its investigation by the Pentagon and the Justice Department to the point where witnesses were being intimidated. Commission chairman Thomas Kean, a Republican, alleged that the federal agencies under the control of the Bush administration weren't cooperating quickly or fully enough. By law, the Commission must complete its findings into the negligence of the government leading up to 9/11 by May of 2004.

"The coming weeks will determine whether we will be able to do the job within the time allotted," Commission staffers said. "The task in front of us is monumental."[60]

All together 3,025 people were murdered on September 11, 2001. The body parts of thousands remain in those refrigerated trucks inside Memorial Park. And many more Americans may die at the hands of al Qaeda if the FBI doesn't learn to *prevent* crimes as effectively as it solves them.

The challenge facing the nation was perhaps summed up best by Tim Roemer, a former congressman who's now a Commission member: "Facing the facts" about the truth behind 9/11 "won't kill us. But not getting the truth just might."[61]

EPILOGUE

Eighteen days after the September 11 attacks, Nancy Floyd transferred to an FBI Resident Agency in a small town in the Far West. After eleven years in the New York office, she had done her part in the war on terror—and it had cost her dearly. Now she was determined to do the best job she could in the years she had left with the Bureau. More than any individual in the New York office, Nancy Floyd had put the FBI in the best position to locate and seize Ramzi Yousef before he had set the 9/11 plot in motion. But instead of being rewarded, she was the only agent ever sanctioned for events that took place during that investigation. Now all she could do was follow the advice of her mentor, Len Predtechenskis: keep her head down and get the job done.

By August 2002, Nancy thought she had seen the worst of it. She'd endured the OPR, lost her close friend Martha, and found herself shunned by supervisors who had praised her when she first recruited Emad Salem. The one personal triumph in her life had been the remarkable turnaround of her niece, Shauna Popham. Since moving in with Nancy, she had gone from high school dropout to decorated Air Force enlisted woman. Shauna had distinguished herself in Afghanistan, and had just returned to the States when fate took another tragic turn.

After visiting relatives in Florida in August 2002, Shauna was driving back to her base in Georgia when her SUV left the road and struck a tree. She was killed instantly.

Nancy had been visiting in Washington with Len and Carole Predtechenskis when the call came from her mother. "She just sat down and said, 'Oh my God,'" Carole remembered. "And we hugged her for dear life." Later, after Shauna's funeral, Carole wrote Nancy a letter celebrating the rebound Shauna had achieved before her death. "She got it right," she wrote. "There were 1,600 young people who went into boot camp with Shauna and she finished number three. It's not where you *start* that counts, Nancy. It's where you *finish*."

"That's the way we feel about the FBI," said Carole's husband, Len, who supported Nancy during some of her darkest days in New York. "We love the Bureau and we want to see it make the right course corrections so that it can get the job done in this war on terror. When you think about it, we don't have a choice."

Meanwhile, in the months after her husband's death, Eve Bucca began fighting another war—a battle with the city of New York to keep the Bureau of Fire Investigation from being decimated by proposed budget cuts.

"Four years ago there were 212 marshals and 41 supervisors," wrote Eve in an opinion piece for the New York *Daily News* in September 2002. "Today the numbers are 151 and 35. On any given night there is barely enough manpower to provide three men and a car in each borough."[1] Since she wrote that piece, the department-wide cuts have grown even more severe. After the disastrous losses in the FDNY on 9/11, Mayor Bloomberg's administration proposed reducing the number of firefighters on any given tour from five to four.

In late May, the FDNY was forced to close six firehouses in Brooklyn, Queens, and Manhattan. The city has already shut down the Bureau of Fire Investigation's Bronx Base and reduced the total number of marshals and supervisors to 133. Manhattan Base is now staffed only during daytime hours.

"We are cut to the bone," said Supervising Fire Marshal Jimmy Kelty. "Between February and April 2003, there were two hundred multiple-alarm or suspicious fires citywide that went uninvestigated. Our experience tells us that a third of those are arson fires, but we don't have the manpower to find out. What's happening to this department is insane. We have a heightened terrorist alert in this city, and the law enforcement arm of the FDNY is being broken."[2]

"I don't want Ronnie to have died in vain," said Eve. "He always stood for the fact that you have to be ready—prepared. And in order to do that you have to look at history and learn from your mistakes and then take corrective action. We have no idea what will come from the invasion of Iraq, whether it will make us safer or subject us to more danger. And if it comes, the first responders—the men and women who will jump off those rigs and rush into the next set of buildings—need the best equipment and training we can give them. Speaking as one who lost somebody I dearly loved on September 11, I can tell you that the greatest memorial this city can build is a stronger, better-equipped fire department to deal with the next attack."

When and if that next attack comes, Ronnie's son is determined to be ready. In March 2003, Ronnie Bucca Jr., a cum laude graduate of Tulane, joined the U.S. Army. Three weeks later, his father's military comrades named the first POW camp in south central Iraq Camp Bucca, in Ronnie's honor.[3]

The son of the first FDNY fire marshal to die in the line of duty thinks about his father every day. "I remember he kept this saying near his desk," said Ronnie Jr. "Sometimes it got hidden behind all his books on military history and terrorism. But he would find it, blow the dust off, and put it back in a place where we could see it. The paper was yellow from age and the frame got cracked, but he used to remind us of it all the time. It was a kind of warning: 'Those who forget history are destined to relive it.'"

Much of the history of modern terrorism was written by Ramzi Yousef. But on April 4, 2003, in a sweeping 186-page opinion, the U.S. Court of Appeals for the Second Circuit turned down his appeal of both the Bojinka and World Trade Center bombing convictions. Ruling on forty-three separate issues, the court acknowledged some error at the trial level, but effectively denied all the terrorist's claims.[4]

Yousef's attorney, Bernie Kleinman, has filed a notice of appeal to seek a writ of certiorari from the U.S. Supreme Court. But for now, the Special Administrative Measures that have kept Yousef in restricted solitary confinement remain in place. Every day, the deadliest terrorist in captivity sits in a stark underground concrete cell in the Supermax. Since 9/11 he's been allowed no television, no radio, and no reading material of any kind that would give him a hint of events in the outside world.[5]

Yet Yousef still casts a long shadow over the United States. On May

16, 2003, in a chilling reminder of his "third plot," the *New York Times* reported that his uncle Khalid Shaikh Mohammed had confessed to interrogators that "landmarks in New York and Washington, previously selected by Mr. bin Laden, remain on al Qaeda's target list." Included on that list was the Sears Tower in Chicago,[6] which Yousef had marked for demolition as early as 1994.

Every American who gets subjected to a body search, or has to run his shoes through an X-ray machine, or is required to take a drink from a bottle of liquid before boarding a plane, is paying the price for Ramzi Yousef's villainy. Few individuals have had more influence on the way we live our lives each day. It took seven years for the agents of al Qaeda to execute the bomb maker's 9/11 plot. The Twin Towers are gone, and yet Yousef's curse remains on America's tallest building. Even today, locked down in the Supermax prison, the reed-thin bomber from Baluchistan continues to strike fear in the hearts of Americans.

As far as we've come, and as much as America has learned about the al Qaeda threat, our intelligence agencies continue to underestimate the thousand-year war of revenge being waged by Yousef's "brothers" and the forces of radical Islamic terror.

One of the most chilling signs of that ongoing war was exhibited in Fallouja, Iraq, in a speech at the Great Mosque by Sheikh Jamal Shaker Mahmud, a Sunni cleric, more than two months after U.S. forces helped to liberate him:

"Resist the Americans," he told a throng of his followers. "May God burn the infidel in this house. We must trample the Americans with our bare feet, as they do to us with their boots."

Just as Ronnie Bucca sensed that Yousef would return to New York to take down the Trade Center, there's little doubt that the forces of al Qaeda will one day attempt to mount another spectacular attack inside the United States. We don't know where or when. So we're left with the question raised at the outset of this book: will the FBI be ready?

After an eighteen-month investigation, it's our sense that if history is any judge, and radical changes in the Bureau are not made with lightning speed, our nation will still be at great risk. It's now clear that the FBI has to transform itself from an institution that solves crimes *after* they occur to one that *prevents* them.

The invasions of Afghanistan and Iraq have shown us that simply decapitating a tyrant or replacing a murderous regime is not enough. As the fire marshals of the FDNY believe, we have to stop the fires before they start.

If we don't, Osama bin Laden's next act of revenge against America may be even more devastating than anything we have ever known.

A NOTE ON SOURCES

All reporters stand on the shoulders of the journalists who have pre-ceded them, and while I've disagreed with some of the conclusions reached by others who have covered this story, I owe them all a great debt. This book would not have been possible without the extraordinary reporting done in the years since the World Trade Center bombing. The seminal texts referenced throughout include *Two Seconds Under The World* by Jim Dwyer, David Kocieniewski, Diedre Murphy, and Peg Tyre, the best book on Yousef's first attack on the Towers. The definitive biography of Ramzi Yousef is Simon Reeve's *The New Jackals*, recently published in trade paperback with a post-9/11 update. There is no better telling of Yousef's takedown, or the role of the Diplomatic Security Service in his hunt, than Sam Katz's *Relentless Pursuit*; and Steven Emerson's *American Jihad* offers the best insight into the spread of al Qaeda worldwide.

Through Our Enemies' Eyes, by an anonymous member of the U.S. intelligence community, takes the reader into the dark world of radical Islam as no other book has done, and the three leading post-9/11 inves-tigative books, *Breakdown* by Bill Gertz, *The Age of Sacred Terror* by Daniel Benjamin and Steven Simon, and *The Cell* by John Miller, Michael Stone, and Chris Mitchell, all deliver key elements of the mosaic. To a great degree, my book attempts to pick up where these reporters have left off. I've benefited greatly from the work of the *New York Times,* the *Washington Post,* and the *Los Angeles Times,* in particular the coverage of the original World Trade Center bombing investigation and its aftermath by Ralph Blumenthal and Alison Mitchel of the *New York Times.*

In the months since the 9/11 attacks some of the best investigative reporting on the issue of prior knowledge was done by Maria Ressa, the Manila Bureau chief for CNN, and John Solomon and Jim Gomez of the Associated Press.

As part of an ongoing investigation of the FBI's failures leading up to September 11, Gomez sent Solomon a copy of the very same FBI lab report on the evidence seized at the Dona Josefa and Su Casa Guesthouse that we've reproduced portions of in this book (pp. 241 and 286).[1] The eight-year-old lab report had been discussed openly in two previous federal trials, yet in September 2002, the U.S. Customs Service, acting on a reported request from the FBI, took the extraordinary step of seizing a Federal Express package with the report from a FedEx facility in the Midwest as it was being routed to Solomon in Washington from Gomez in Manila.

"The interception was improper and clandestine," said AP President and CEO Louis D. Boccardi.[2] Sen. Charles Grassley, the lead Judiciary Committee member on FBI oversight, called the seizure "a potential violation of [the] First and Fourth Amendment" and pushed for an FBI OPR inquiry on the matter.

"It's highly unusual for the government to intercept communications of the media," said Grassley, "and I want to make sure we don't have any attempts to censor or stymie the news." An FBI spokesman first alleged that the lab report contained sensitive information that should not be made public, but the Bureau later withdrew their objection and apologized for the interception.

Still, the incident pointed up the potential chilling effect such a seizure could have on journalists seeking to get to the truth behind potential 9/11 negligence inside the nation's most powerful law enforcement agency.

After covering elements of the Justice Department for ABC News, I gained new insights into the FBI through Ron Kessler's two landmark works, *The Bureau* and *The FBI*. Pat Milton's *In the Blink of an Eye* tells the story of the downing of TWA Flight 800 better than any other book on the subject, and Stephen Jones's *Others Unknown* gives an important alternate perspective on the Oklahoma City bombing. While I've taken exception to Laurie Mylroie's theory that Ramzi Yousef was an agent of Iraq, her thoroughly researched *The War Against America* provides material on the 1993 Trade Center bombing story that can be found nowhere else.

A special thanks goes to Col. Rodolfo "Boogie" Mendoza, the remarkable Philippine National Police official who uncovered Yousef's third plot, and Colonel Aida Fariscal, who made the discovery that shut down Yousef's Manila cell and no doubt saved thousands of lives. I also owe a real debt to retired Special Agent Len Predtechenskis, Nancy Floyd's mentor. Men like Len, who risked his life repeatedly to keep this nation safe at the height of the Cold War, represent the best of the old Bureau and hope for the FBI to come.

After tracking the Bureau's failures for eighteen months, I fundamentally believe that the best way to turn the FBI into an effective preemptive force against terror is to give more power to the street agents while providing them with the guidance of veteran agents as mentors. Special Agent Nancy Floyd and Fire Marshal Ronnie Bucca never met, but they shared a number of qualities, including tenacity and heart. Each believed that intelligence comes from the street, not the twenty-fifth floor, and that it never comes without a healthy respect for the enemy. Most important, they believed in the critical need to share intelligence. In August 2002, nine years after the World Trade Center bombing, the NYPD-FBI Joint Terrorist Task Force admitted its first fire marshal. Hopefully, it won't take another al Qaeda attack on America to admit the next one.

NOTES

A NOTE TO READERS

1 Testimony of FBI director Louis Freeh before the Senate Judiciary Committee, September 3, 1998.
2 The FBI, Central Intelligence Agency (CIA), Defense Intelligence Agency (DIA), National Security Agency (NSA), and U.S. State Department's Bureau of Intelligence and Research (INR).
3 Peter Lance, *The Stingray: Lethal Tactics of the Sole Survivor* (Los Angeles: Shadowlawn Press, 2000).
4 After the Florida presidential election crisis and the saga of Elian Gonzalez.
5 Author's interview with chief fire marshal Louis F. Garcia, April 7, 2003.

INTRODUCTION

1 *U.S. v. Ramzi Ahmed Yousef and Eyad Ismoil,* January 8, 1998.
2 See Chapter 41.
3 Tawfig bin-Atash. Josh Meyer, "Suspected Mastermind of Cole Bombing Held," *Los Angeles Times,* May 1, 2003.
4 The 1990 arrest of El Sayyid Nosair, convicted in 1992 in the murder of Rabbi Meir Kahane; the 1995 conviction of Sheikh Omar Abdel Rahman and nine other coconspirators in the Day of Terror plot, and the 1995 seizure of Ramzi Yousef, convicted in 1996 in the Bojinka plot to blow up eleven U.S. airliners and in 1997 for his role in the 1993 World Trade Center bombing.
5 Bill Gertz, *Breakdown: How America's Intelligence Failures Led to September 11* (Washington, D.C.: Regnery, 2002); Daniel Benjamin and Steven Simon, *The Age of Sacred Terror* (New York: Random House, 2002).
6 John Miller, Michael Stone, and Chris Mitchell, *The Cell Inside: The 9/11 Plot and Why the FBI and CIA Failed to Stop It* (New York: Hyperion, 2002).
7 Richard C. Shelby, *September 11th and the Imperative of Reform in the U.S. Intelligence Community: Additional Views of Senator Richard C. Shelby, Vice Chairman, Senate Select Committee on Intelligence,* December 10, 2002.
8 Michael Isikoff, "Censoring the Report About 9–11?" *Newsweek,* June 2, 2003; Josh Meyer, "Graham Alleges a 9/11 'Cover-up,'" *Los Angeles Times,* May 12, 2003; Editorial, "Declassify the 9/11 Report," *Los Angeles Times,* May 21, 2003.

9 Michael Isikoff, "The 9-11 Report: Slamming the FBI," *Newsweek*, July 21, 2003.

10 Greg Miller, "Page After Page, the Mysteries of Sept. 11 Grow," *Los Angeles Times*, July 27, 2003.

11 Greg Miller, "9/11 Probe Frustrates Lawmakers," *Los Angeles Times*, September 18, 2002; Michael Isikoff and Daniel Klaidman, "Why the White House Said Yes to a 9–11 Inquiry," *Newsweek*, September 22, 2002; Press conference, National Press Club, June 20, 2002.

12 Richard Simon, "Push for Terror Panel Gets Boost. Inquiry: White House changes tack, drops opposition to forming commission to probe intelligence failures leading up to 9/11," *Los Angeles Times*, September 21, 2002.

13 Timothy Burger, "9/11 Probe: Aiming High: The Commission investigating the September 11th attacks wants to talk to top Bush Administration officials," *Time*, January 26, 2003; Michael Isikoff and Mark Hosenball, "Kissinger: Probing the Client Controversy," *Newsweek*, December 23, 2002; Editorial, "Step Down, Mr. Kissinger," *Los Angeles Times*, December 13, 2002.

14 Editorial, "Undercutting the 9/11 Inquiry," *New York Times*, March 31, 2002.

15 Phillip Shenon, "9/11 Commission Says U.S. Agencies Slow It's Inquiry," *New York Times*, July 9, 2003.

16 Bob Woodward, *Veil: The Secret Wars of the CIA* (New York: Pocket Books, 1989), pp. 28–33, 194, 234.

17 Associated Press, "Candid FBI Agent Warns on Readiness," March 7, 2003; "Philip Shenon, Agent Who Saw 9/11 Lapses Still Faults F.B.I. on Terror," *New York Times*, March 6, 2003; Reuters, "FBI Whistleblower Says Agency Still Ill-Prepared," March 6, 2003.

18 Associated Press, "FBI Warns of Possible Attacks in U.S.," *New York Times*, May 20, 2003; David Johnston with Don Van Natta Jr., "U.S. Officials See Signs of a Revived Al Qaeda," *New York Times*, May 17, 2003; Mark Hosenball and Michael Isikoff, "Terrorism: Continuing Threats," *Newsweek*, June 9; Josh Meyer, "Al Qaeda May Be Back, and Stronger," *Los Angeles Times*, May 14, 2003.

PART I
1. BLACK TUESDAY

1 Author's interview with confidential source.

2 Author's interview with FBI agent Len Predtechenskis (ret.), August 27, 2002.

3 *U.S. v. Omar Abdel Rahman, et al.*

4 Author's interview with firefighter Tony Tedeschi, Rescue One, July 30, 2002.

5 The 3413th Military Intelligence Detachment of the 800th M.P.s was one of four reserve units in the nation tasked to support the Defense Intelligence Agency's Defense Intelligence Analysis Center (DIAC) at Bolling Air Force Base in Washington.

6 Author's interviews with the Bucca family: June 17 and 24, 2002; author's interview with Jacob L. Boesen, former analyst at DIAC, September 13, 2002.

2. THE FLYING FIREFIGHTER

1 Author's interview with firefighter Paul Hashagen, FDNY (ret.), historian and chauffeur of Rescue One, July 30, 2002.

2 Author's interview with Lt. Steve Casani, FDNY (ret.), September 3, 2002.

3 FDNY report, September 16, 1986.

4 Bob Drury, "Fireman Falls 5 Stories, Lives," *Newsday,* September 17, 1986; Cynthia Fagen, "Hero Fireman's Miracle Land," *New York Post,* September 17, 1986; Vincent Lee and Paul La Rosa, "As He Fell, Firefighter Heard Himself Screaming," New York *Daily News,* September 17, 1986; Vincent Lee and Tony Marcano, "His Fire-escape Is the Greatest," ibid.

5 Author's interview with Eve Bucca, June 17, 2002.

6 Name for the probationary firefighters who go through basic training at the FDNY Academy.

3. BLOWBACK

1 FBI 302 interrogation of Ramzi Yousef, February 7, 1995; Raghida Dirgham, "Ramzi Yousef Discusses WTC Bombing, Other Activities." *Al Hayat,* April 12, 1995.

2 Laurie Mylroie, *The War Against America* (New York: ReganBooks, 2002).

3 *U.S. v. Ramzi Ahmed Yousef et al.,* June 11–12, 1996.

4 His other aliases included: Azan Muhammed, Adam Ali Qasim, Naji Haddad, Dr. Paul Vijay, Dr. Adel Sabah, Amaldo Forlani, Muhammad Ali Baloch, Adam Baloch, Kamal Ibraham, Abraham Kamal, Rashed, Khurram Khan, Adam Ali, Dr. Alex Hume, and Dr. Richard Smith. *U.S. v. Ramzi Ahmed Yousef,* S10 93 Cr. 180 (KTD) indictment and "want" poster, Department of Justice, U.S. State Department Office of Diplomatic Security; Christopher Dickey, "America's Most Wanted," *Newsweek,* July 4, 1994.

5 FBI Lab Report on Dona Josefa seizure; PNP documents on Room 603 search.

6 *U.S. v. Ramzi Ahmed Yousef et al.,* June 11, 1996, and July 17, 1996.

7 "Cold-blooded," Philippine National Police superintendent Samuel Pagdilao, in Simon Reeve, *The New Jackals: Ramzi Yousef, Osama bin Laden, and the Future of Terrorism* (Boston: Northeastern University Press, 1999); "diabolical," FBI assistant director Neal Herman, ibid., p. 249; "evil genius," Mary Ann Weaver, "Children of the Jihad," *The New Yorker,* June 12, 1995.

8 Author's interview with U.S. Postal Inspector Frank Gonzalez (ret.), January 3, 2003.

9 Miller, *The Cell,* p. 120.

10 Weaver, "Children of the Jihad."

11 Dirgham, "Ramzi Yousef Discusses WTC Bombing, Other Activities."

12 Declassified documents from the Philippines National Police obtained by the author.

13 Author's interview with Frank Gonzalez (ret.), January 3, 2003.

14 FBI 302 interrogation of Ramzi Yousef, February 8, 1995.

15 David B. Ottoway and Steve Coll, "Retracing the Steps of a Terror Suspect: Accused Bomb Builder Tied to Many Plots," *Washington Post,* June 5, 1995.

16 See Chapter 30, p. 309.

17 See Chapter 33, p. 341.

18 Somini Sengupta, "Is There Relief in This? Yes. Is it Closed? I Doubt it," *New York Times,* November 13, 1997. Venezuelan terrorist Ilich Ramiriz Sanches was blamed for more than eighty deaths worldwide during his pro-Palestinian terror spree from the 1970s to the 1980s. He is currently serving a life sentence for the 1975 slaying of two French investigators and a Lebanese colleague; "Carlos the Jackal to Appeal Against Life Sentence," BBC News, December 24, 1997.

19 He told FBI agents on the plane flying him back to the U.S. after his capture in 1995 that his birth date was April 27, 1968. FBI 302 interrogation of Ramzi Yousef, February 7, 1995. But his FBI "want" poster also lists his DOB as May 20, 1967.

20 Ibid.

21 Weaver, "Children of the Jihad."

22 FBI 302 interrogation of Ramzi Yousef, February 7 and 8, 1995.

23 "Military Studies in the Jihad Against the Tyrant," p. 141. A 180-page al Qaeda training manual used at a number of al Qaeda terrorist training camps, it was discovered during the search of a bin Laden follower in Manchester, England, and was an exhibit in the East African embassy trial, *U.S. v. Wadih El-Hage et al.*

24 Author's interview with a Filipino intelligence official who had heard the story from a captured member of Abu Sayyaf, the al Qaeda terrorist cell based in the southern Philippines.

25 Weaver, "Children of the Jihad."

26 Literally translated "father of the sword." Janjalani later used "Abu Sayyaf" as the name of the al Qaeda–linked terror group he formed in the Philippines.

27 The blind Sheikh visited Peshawar, Pakistan, during this period raising money for the mujahadeen and aligning himself with Gulbuddin Hekmatyar, an Afghan warlord who later became prime minister once the Soviets were dispatched.

28 Dixon became an instructor at the FBI Academy, and Jenkins later served in Director Louis Freeh's personal detail.

29 Author's interviews with Len and Carole Predtechenskis, December 18, 2002, and January 11, 2003.

4. THE FIRST SHOTS FIRED

1 Patrick E. Tyler, "Explaining Gift, Saudi Envoy Voices Pain for Strained Ties," *New York Times,* November 26, 2002; Greg Krikorian, Greg Miller, and H.G. Reza, "FBI Looks at Saudi's Link to 9/11," *Los Angeles Times,* November 23, 2002.

2 Weaver, "Children of the Jihad"; Steven Emerson, *American Jihad* (New York: Free Press, 2002), pp. 130–131.

3 Yossef Bodansky, *Bin Laden: The Man Who Declared War on America* (Rocklin, Calif.: Forum, 1999).

4 Dr. Ayman al-Zawahiri and the late Mohammed Atef, al Qaeda's former military leader, linked by U.S. investigators to the October 1993 attack on U.S. forces in Somalia, which led to the downing of two Blackhawk helicopters. Atef was reportedly killed in the early days of the U.S. invasion of Afghanistan in November 2001.

5 Al Gamma'a Islamiya (IG) and the Egyptian Islamic Jihad (EIJ). The leader and spiritual adviser of the IG was Sheikh Omar Abdel Rahman, who was also revered by many followers of the EIJ.

6 Jim Dwyer, David Kocieniewski, Diedre Murphy, and Peg Tyre, *Two Seconds Under the World* (New York: Crown, 1994), p. 161.

7 Emerson, *American Jihad,* pp. 55–60. On October 20, 1998, Ali Mohammed pleaded guilty to a series of terrorism charges related to his decade-long work as an al Qaeda agent.

8 *U.S. v. Mohammed A. Salameh et al.,* S5 93 Cr. 180 (KTD).

9 *U.S. v. Omar Abdel Rahman et al.,* S5 93 Cr. 181 (MBM), February 7, 1995.

10 Richard Bernstein, "U.S. Has Kept 2 in Bomb Trial Under Surveillance Since 1989," *New York Times,* February 8, 1995; *U.S. v. Omar Abdel Rahman et. al.,* S5 93 Cr. 181 (MBM), February 7, 1995.

11 Miller, *The Cell*, p. 51.

12 Benjamin, *The Age of Sacred Terror*, p. 236; Reeve, *The New Jackals*, p. 172.

13 Frontline, "The Man Who Knew," www.pbs.org/wgbh/pages/frontline/shows/knew/ etc/cron.html; *U.S. v. Wadih El-Hage et al.*

14 M. A. Farber, "Kahane Trial Sets Off Squabbles by Lawyers," *New York Times*, December 9, 1991.

15 *U.S. v. Omar Abdel Rahman et al.*, S5 93 Cr. 181 (MBM), February 27, 1995.

16 Ralph Blumenthal, "Clues Hinting at Terror Ring Were Ignored," *New York Times*, August 27, 1993; Ronald Sullivan, "In Eye of Storm, Jury Selection Begins in Kahane Killing," *New York Times*, November 5, 1991; John Sullivan and Joseph Neff, "An al Qaeda Operative at Fort Bragg," *Raleigh News & Observer*, November 14, 2001.

17 Dwyer et al., *Two Seconds Under the World*, pp. 138–139.

18 Benjamin, *The Age of Sacred Terror*, p. 6.

19 Miller, *The Cell*, pp. 55–56.

20 Testimony of FBI director Robert S. Mueller II before the Senate Judiciary Committee, March 4, 2003.

21 According to a federal investigator quoted about one of the possibilities surrounding the Kahane slaying. James C. McKinley Jr., "Islamic Leader on U.S. Terrorist List in Brooklyn," *New York Times*, December 16, 1990.

22 Dwyer et al., *Two Seconds Under the World*, pp. 121–123.

23 Karen Freifeld and David Kocieniewski, "The Fateful Hours," *Newsday*, November 8, 1990.

24 McKinley Jr., "Islamic Leader on U.S. Terrorist List in Brooklyn."

25 Miller, *The Cell*, pp. 43–44.

26 Joint Inquiry Report, October 8, 2002, p. 3.

27 Gertz, *Breakdown*, pp. 27–28.

28 Ibid.

29 Benjamin, *The Age of Sacred Terror*, p. 9

30 Joint Inquiry Statement, October 8, 2002, p. 3.

5. AL QAEDA'S NEW YORK CELL

1 James Bruce, "Arab Veterans of the Afghan War," *Jane's Intelligence Review*, April 1, 1995.

2 Stephen Engelberg, "One Man and a Global Web of Violence," *New York Times*, January 14, 2001.

3 Alison Mitchell, "After Blast, New Interest in Holy-War Recruits in Brooklyn," *New York Times*, April 11, 1993.

4 Richard Bernstein, "On Trial: An Islamic Cleric Battles Secularism," *New York Times*, January 8, 1995.

5 Benjamin, *The Age of Sacred Terror*, p. 76.

6 Anonymous, *Through Our Enemies' Eyes* (Washington, D.C.: Brassey's, 2002), p. 270.

7 Ibid., pp. 84–85.

8 This was the same squad associated with Ali Mohammed, the ex–Egyptian Army officer who ran the paramilitary shooting sessions at Calverton in 1989. Mohammed was also a member of the EIJ, and the core of Egyptians he instructed in the use of automatic weapons became devoted followers of the blind Sheikh.

9 Gulbiddin Hekmatyar, who later went on to become prime minister of Afghanistan. Reuters, "Sheikh Offered Refuge," *New York Times*, July 31, 1993.

10 Mary Anne Weaver, "Blowback," *Atlantic Monthly,* May 1996.

11 Peter L. Bergen, *Holy War Inc.: Inside the Secret World of Osama bin Laden* (New York: Free Press, 2001), p. 53.

12 Steven Emerson, "Abdullah Azzam, the Man Before Osama bin Laden," *Journal of Counterterrorism and Security International* 5, no. 3 (Fall 1998).

13 Steven Emerson, *American Jihad: The Terrorists Living Among Us* (New York: Free Press, 2002), pp. 128–130.

14 Ibid., p. 131.

15 *U.S. v. Osama bin Laden,* February 6, 2001.

16 Stephen Engelberg, "One Man and a Global Web of Violence."

17 Ibid.

18 Ibid.

19 This was a technique he would employ years later, when FBI and INS agents tried to smoke him out of the Brooklyn mosque he was holed up in. *New York Times,* July 3, 1993.

20 Questions about the Sheikh's U.S. entry surfaced publicly in early 1993 and continued throughout the year following the bombing of the World Trade Center on February 26, 1993, and the Sheikh's surrender to federal agents on July 3, 1993. Chris Hedges, "A Cry of Islamic Fury, Taped in Brooklyn for Cairo," *New York Times,* January 7, 1993; Timothy Carney and Mansoor Ijaz, "Intelligence Failure? Let's Go Back to Sudan," *Washington Post,* June 30, 2002; James C. McKinley Jr., "Islamic Leader on U.S. Terrorist List in Brooklyn," *New York Times,* December 16, 1990.

21 James Risen, "Case of Spy in Anti-Terrorist Mission Points Up CIA's Perils," *Los Angeles Times,* February 11, 1996.

22 Woodward, *Veil,* p. 355.

23 Gulbiddin Hekmatyar. Alison Mitchell, "After Blast, New Interest in Holy-War Recruits in Brooklyn," *New York Times,* April 11, 1993.

24 Alexander Yonah and Michael S. Swetnam, *Osama bin Laden's al Qaida: Profile of a Terrorist Network* (Ardsley, N.Y.: Transnational Publishers, 2001), p. 38.

25 Author's interview with Kay Woods, July 30, 2002.

26 An FDNY report describing the incident put the date at 1991 based on Woods's earlier recollection, but after checking her records in 2003 she said she believed that Refai obtained the blueprints between July and August 1992. Author's interview with Kay Woods, June 15, 2003.

27 Joint Inquiry Report, October 8, 2002.

28 Weaver, "Children of the Jihad."

29 *U.S. v. Osama bin Laden,* February 6, 2001.

30 Dwyer et al., *Two Seconds Under the World,* p. 151.

31 Mitchell, "After Blast, New Interest in Holy-War Recruits in Brooklyn."

6. OPERATION IRAQI FREEDOM ONE

1 *Army Link News,* March 3, 1999.

2 Rebecca Grant, "Schwarzkopf of Arabia," *Air Force* (Journal of the Air Force Association), January 2001.

3 "Ballad of the Green Berets."

4 Author's interview with Alfred Bucca, July 29, 2002.

5 Mitchell, "After Blast, New Interest in Holy-War Recruits in Brooklyn."

6 Richard Bernstein and Ralph Blumenthal, "Bomb Informer's Tapes Give Rare Glimpse of FBI Dealings," *New York Times,* October 31, 1993.
7 Miller, *The Cell,* p. 65.
8 Mimi Swartz, "The Terrorist Next Door," *Texas Monthly,* April 2002.
9 *U.S. v. Osama bin Laden et al.,* February 6, 2001.

7. A NEST OF VIPERS

1 Author's interview with FBI agent Len Predtechenskis (ret.), August 27, 2002.
2 *U.S. v. Omar Abdel Rahman et al.,* March 7, 1995, p. 4589.
3 Ralph Blumenthal, "Tangled Ties and Tales of FBI Messenger," *New York Times,* January 9, 1994.
4 *U.S. v. Omar Abdel Rahman et al.,* March 7, 1995.
5 Author's interview with confidential FBI source.
6 Author's interview with Detective Lou Napoli, January 10, 2003.
7 *U.S. v. Omar Abdel Rahman et al.,* March 7, 1995, and March 13, 1995.
8 Gertz, *Breakdown,* pp. 88–90.
9 *Rovario v. United States,* 353 U.S. 53 (1957). In protecting the identity of confidential informants in criminal prosecutions, *Rovario* required a "balancing of the public interest in protecting the flow of information respecting criminal activities against the individual's right to prepare his defense." *U.S. v. John Walker Lindh,* Crim. No. 02-37A. Department of Justice Guidelines Regarding the Use of Confidential Informants, January 8, 2001.
10 Dwyer et al., *Two Seconds Under the World,* p. 116.
11 Robert D. McFadden, "For Jurors, Evidence in Kahane Case Was Riddled With Gaps," *New York Times,* December 23, 1991.
12 All dialogue in this section is quoted from transcripts entered in *U.S. v. Omar Abdel Rahman et al.,* March 7, 1995.

8. BLOOD IN THE CITY

1 Video "Brooklyn Mosque Tape." *U.S. v. Omar Abdel Rahman et al.* Copy obtained by author.
2 *U.S. v. Omar Abdel Rahman et al.,* March 13, 1995.
3 M. A. Farber, "Kahane Trial Sets Off Squabbles by Lawyers," *New York Times,* December 9, 1991.
4 M. A. Farber, "Judge Imposes Maximum Sentence in the Kahane Case," *New York Times,* January 30, 1992.
5 Author's interview with Detective Lou Napoli, January 13, 2003.
6 *U.S. v. Osama bin Laden et al.,* February 6, 2001; Michael Grunwald, "Bin Laden Followers Indicted by Grand Jury for Embassy Attacks," *Washington Post,* October 9, 1998; testimony of J. T. Caruso, Acting Assistant Director, Counter Terrorism Division, FBI, before the Subcommittee on International Operations and Terrorism, Committee on Foreign Relations, U.S. Senate, December 18, 2001.
7 "Jamaat al-Islamiyya, Egyptian Islamic Jihad, Terrorism Q&A." Briefing paper. Council on Foreign Relations, September 14, 2002.
8 Barbara Plett, "Bin Laden Behind Luxor Massacre," BBC online, May 13, 1999; Benjamin, *The Age of Sacred Terror,* pp. 119, 131, 150.

9 Author's interview with Detective Lou Napoli, January 10, 2003.
10 *U.S. v. Omar Abdel Rahman et al.,* March 7, 1995.
11 *Serial* is the Bureau term for continuing pages of intelligence to be included in a given asset's file.
12 Author's interview with Detective Lou Napoli, January 10, 2003.
13 Author's interview with confidential FBI source.
14 *U.S. v. Omar Abdel Rahman et al.,* March 8, 1995.
15 The simple white cotton garment known as the djellabh throughout the Islamic world.
16 Richard Bernstein, "On Trial: An Islamic Cleric Battles Secularism," *New York Times,* January 8, 1995.

9. TRUTH FROM THE ASHES

1 Author's interview with Eve Bucca, June 17, 2002.
2 Author's interview with firefighter Tony Tedeschi, Rescue One, July 30, 2002.
3 Author's interview with Ronnie Bucca Jr., June 17, 2002.
4 Author's interview with chief fire marshal Louis F. Garcia, April 9, 2002.
5 Chief Louis F. Garcia and assistant fire commissioner John Mulligan (ret.), "Truth and Justice from the Ashes," Bureau of Fire Investigation WNYF Millennium Article, First quarter, 2000.
6 In terms of sheer numbers, the Triangle Shirtwaist fire was actually dwarfed by a fire aboard the *General Slocum* in the East River, which killed more than one thousand excursioners. Edward T. O'Donnell, "The Fire, and the Forgetting," *New York Times,* June 8, 2003, p. CY3.
7 Marjorie Dorfman, "The Triangle Shirtwaist Factory Fire," www.ct.essortment.com/ thetriangleshi_rkko.htm.
8 Jack Gottschalk, *Firefighting* (New York: D.K. Publishing, 2002), p. 62.
9 Unpainted metal paint cans with lids were the preferred containers for samples because they were less likely than plastic evidence bags to taint debris with conflicting chemicals. *Reference Manual,* Fire Department, City of New York Bureau of Fire Investigation. Revised July 10, 2001.
10 Author's interview with Fire Marshal Bill Manahan (ret.), February 19, 2003.
11 Author's interview with Fire Marshal Henry Raven, February 2, 2003.
12 The motto of the BFI is Veritas Ex Cineribus, literally translated as Truth from the Ashes.

10. ICE WATER AND BOMBS

1 Weaver, "Children of the Jihad."
2 Dirgham, "Ramzi Yousef Discusses WTC Bombing, Other Activities."
3 FBI 302 interrogation of Ramzi Yousef, February 7, 1995.
4 Author's interview with Steve Legon, January 20, 2003.
5 Author's interview with Frank Gonzalez (ret.), January 3, 2003.
6 Reeve, *The New Jackals,* p. 156.
7 Affidavit of Edwin Angeles, Philippines National Police Station, Basilan, the Philippines, November 3, 1996.
8 David B. Ottoway and Steve Coll, "Retracing the Steps of a Terror Suspect: Accused Bomb Builder Tied to Many Plots," *Washington Post,* June 5, 1995.

9 Benjamin, *The Age of Sacred Terror,* pp. 7–8.
10 The hit on Angeles took place in January 1999. Marites Danguilan Vitug and Glenda M. Gloria, *Under the Crescent Moon: Rebellion in Mindanao* (Quezon City: The Philippines Ateneo Center for Social Policy and Public Affairs), p. 205.
11 The dialogue in this section comes from testimony in *U.S. v. Omar Abdel Rahman et al.,* March 8, 1995.
12 Ibid., March 13, 1995.
13 Author's interview with confidential FBI source.
14 Author's interview with FBI agent Len Predtechenskis (ret.), August 27, 2002.
15 Author's interview with confidential FBI source.
16 Author's interview with Len Predtechenskis, August 27, 2002.
17 Author's interview with Detective Lou Napoli, January 13, 2003.
18 Author's interview with confidential FBI source.
19 *U.S. v. Omar Abdel Rahman et al.,* July 27, 1995.
20 Author's interview with confidential FBI source.
21 Ibid.
22 Author's interview with FBI ASAC Carson Dunbar (ret.), June 6, 2003.
23 Author's interview with FBI principal legal officer Jim Roth (ret.), May 30, 2003.
24 Author's interview with Len Predtechenskis, August 27, 2002.
25 Author's interview with Kris Kolesnik, June 15, 2003.
26 Author's interview with Carson Dunbar, June 6, 2003.
27 Author's interview with Carson Dunbar, July 31, 2002.
28 Author's interview with confidential FBI source.
29 *U.S. v. Omar Abdel Rahman et al.,* July 5, 1995, p. 13409.
30 Ibid., p. 13355.
31 Author's interview with confidential source, February 8, 2003.
32 Author's interview with Kris Kolesnik, June 15, 2003.
33 *U.S. v. Omar Abdel Rahman et al.,* July 5, 1995.
34 Author's interview with Len Predtechenskis, December 18, 2002.
35 Author's interview with confidential source, February 8, 2003.

11. A VERY DANGEROUS JOB

1 Author's interview with Fire Marshal Henry Raven, February 3, 2003.
2 Author's interview with Eve Bucca, February 18, 2003.
3 Author's interview with Fire Marshal Bill Manahan (ret.), February 19, 2003.
4 Author's interview with Fire Marshal Leroy Haynes (ret.), August 2, 2002.
5 Benjamin, *The Age of Sacred Terror,* pp. 7–8.
6 All details in this section come from *U.S. v. Mohammed Salameh et al.*
7 *U.S. v. Ramzi Ahmed Yousef and Eyad Ismoil,* September 2, 1997.
8 Curiously, the year before, the body of an Egyptian watchmaker named Ibraham Kamal was found at Kennedy Airport stuffed into the trunk of his car. No connection was ever made to the Yousef-Salameh pseudonym, and that murder, too, remains unsolved. Dwyer et al., *Two Seconds Under the World,* p. 168.
9 At one point Yousef and Salameh tested the explosive at Liberty State Park in New Jersey, overlooking the Statue of Liberty. Yousef wasn't satisfied with the mixture's blasting radius, so he decided to add aluminum powder as an oxidizing agent. *U.S. v. Mohammed Salameh et al.*

10 *U.S. v. Omar Abdel Rahman et al.,* March 13, 1995.
11 Alison Mitchell, "Before Bombing, Inquiry Sought Inroads into Enclave of Suspects," *New York Times,* April 1, 1993.

12. DOT AFTER DOT AFTER DOT

1 Richard Bernstein, "On Trial: An Islamic Cleric Battles Secularism," *New York Times,* January 8, 1995; Alison Mitchell, "Suspect in Bombing Is Linked to Sect with a Violent Voice," *New York Times,* March 5, 1993.
2 Title 50, U.S. Code Chapter 36, Subchapter I, Section 1801.
3 *U.S. v. Omar Abdel Rahman et al.,* February 7, 1995.
4 Author's interview with Frank Gonzalez, January 3, 2003.
5 Pen registers are surveillance devices used by law enforcement agencies to capture the phone numbers dialed on outgoing calls. Trap and trace devices are used to monitor incoming calls. Neither surveillance technique was used by the FBI in the fall of 1992 to monitor Mahmud Abouhalima or Mohammed Salameh.
6 Dwyer et al., *Two Seconds Under the World,* p. 183.
7 timesunion.com, September 11, 2002.
8 Ron Kessler, *The Bureau: The Secret History of the FBI* (New York: St. Martin's Press, 2002) and *The FBI* (New York: Pocket Books, 1993).
9 Ibid., p. 364.
10 Ralph Blumenthal, "Tangled Ties and Tales of FBI Messenger," *New York Times,* January 9, 1994.
11 Reeve, *The New Jackals,* p. 143.
12 Richard Bernstein, "Testimony in Bomb Case Links Loose Ends," *New York Times,* January 19, 1994.
13 Mylroie, *The War Against America,* p. 49.
14 FBI 302 interrogation of Ramzi Yousef, February 7, 1995, p. 21: "[Yousef] said his parents living in Iran part of Baluchistan were aware of his participation in WTC bombing. At one point post bombing, a female who claimed to rep U.S. phone company telephoned his parent's residence and attempted to solicit information pertaining to the whereabouts of RY claiming that Yousef owed the company a significant amount of money. The woman, rebuffed by RY's father, went on to inquire as to the whereabouts of numerous individuals which RY knew to be aliases he had used in past."
15 Author's interview with Frank Gonzalez (ret.), January 3, 2003.
16 *U.S. v. Salameh,* U.S. Court of Appeals for the Second Circuit, August term.
17 Benjamin, *The Age of Sacred Terror,* p. 8.
18 Stephen Engelberg, "One Man and a Global Web of Violence," *New York Times,* January 14, 2001.
19 Author's interview with confidential source.
20 Reeve, *The New Jackels,* p. 149.
21 Dwyer et al., *Two Seconds Under the World,* p. 172.
22 Government Exhibit 221-T, *U.S. v. Ramzi Yousef et al.* In a confession given to federal interrogators entered as an exhibit at the second World Trade Center bombing trial, Ismoil insisted that the phone call had come from a man he knew with "shifty eyes." He claimed that the man had merely asked him to come to New York to help him with his shampoo business and that after his arrival when he drove a "small bus"

(van) he had no idea it contained a bomb. Later, after the bombing, Ismoil said, "I could not believe what took place and I felt that stupidity had overwhelmed me."

23 U.S. v. Omar Abdel Rahman et al., July 26, 1995.

24 Author's interview with Detective Lou Napoli, January 10, 2003.

25 Author's interview with confidential FBI source.

26 Ibid.

27 Author's interview with FBI agent Julian Stackhouse (ret.), June 3, 2003.

28 Author's interview with confidential FBI source.

29 Author's interview with FBI ASAC Carson Dunbar (ret.), June 6, 2003.

30 Miller, The Cell, pp. 57–58, 62–63, 90–91, 96, 103–104.

31 Siddig Siddig Ali would later be the ringleader of the forthcoming Day of Terror plot to blow up the city's bridges and tunnels.

13. THE BLACK BOTTOMLESS PIT

1 The FBI concluded that it was the "largest by weight and by damage of any improvised explosive device that we've seen since the inception of forensic explosion identification—and that's since 1925," Reeve, The New Jackals, p. 154.

2 U.S. v. Mohammed Salameh et al.

3 Testimony of Dr. Jacqueline Lee at U.S. v. Ramzi Yousef, August 7, 1997.

4 Paul Hashagen, The Bravest, Commemorative Edition (Paducah, Ky.: Turner Publishing, 2000), p. 192.

5 U.S. v. Mohammed Salameh et al.

6 Harvey Eisner, "FDNY Rises to the Occasion Following Terrorist Bombing," Firehouse Magazine, August 1993.

7 Paul Hashagen, "World Trade Center FDNY Operations," Firehouse Magazine, August 1993.

8 Dwyer et al., Two Seconds Under the World, pp. 14–29.

9 Tom Robbins, "The Lessons Incident at the Towers," New York Daily News, 1993.

10 Michael Isner and Thomas Klein, "Fire Investigation Report World Trade Center Explosion and Fire," National Fire Protection Association, February 26, 1993, p. 3.

11 Author's interview with firefighter Kevin Shea (ret.), February 18, 2003.

PART II
14. THE FIFTH BATTALION

1 Author's interview with firefighter Kevin Shea (ret.), February 18, 2003.

2 Author's interview with Fire Marshal James Reilly (ret.), February 8, 2003.

3 Robert D. McFadden, "Inquiry into Explosion Widens; Towers Are Shut Indefinitely," New York Times, February 28, 1993; Douglas Jehl, "A Long List of Possible Suspects, as Inquiry into the Bombing Begins," New York Times, February 28, 1993.

4 FBI 302 interrogation of Ramzi Yousef, a.k.a. Abdul Basit Mahmud Abdul Karim, February 7 and 8, 1995.

5 The letter is published here exactly as it appeared in the New York Times. The claim of credit was the first known reference to a "Liberation Army, fifth battalion"; Alison Mitchell, "Letter Explained Motive in Bombing, Officials Now Say," New York Times, March 28, 1993.

6 FBI 302 interrogation of Eyad Ismoil, July 8, 1993.

7 FBI 302 interrogation of Ramzi Yousef, a.k.a. Abdul Basit Mahmud Abdul Karim, February 7 and 8, 1995. In an interview on February 8, during an airborne rendition to the United States following his arrest in Pakistan, Yousef reportedly told FBI agent Bradley S. Garrett that he "operates independently." According to Garrett's FBI 302 summarizing the interrogation, "Muslim leaders/groups may be an inspiration for YOUSEF but YOUSEF stated that no particular individual or group controls or directs him." (FBI 302 2/8/95 by Bradley S. Garrett.) In a subsequent and more lengthy interview during the same flight, Yousef reportedly told FBI agent Charles Stern and Secret Service agent Brian Parr that " 'The Liberation Army-Fifth Battalion' is a genuine organization, responsible for numerous bombings." (FBI 302 Interrogation of Abdul Basit Mahmud Karim, February 7 and 8, 1995, Aircraft in Flight, by Special Agent Charles Stern and Brian C. Parr, File 265A-NY-235983, p. 13.) But testimony in Yousef's two trials later suggested that "the Liberation Army" was Yousef's name for his own cell within al Qaeda. To this day no one has ever determined definitively who called the shots in New York during his preparation of the World Trade Center bomb. Early in the second airborne interview Yousef told the agents that he "became interested" in Sheikh Omar Abdel Rahman and had been introduced to him by Mohammed Salameh. He said that he subsequently visited the Sheikh's Jersey City home and had dinner with him. (Ibid., p. 8.) In 1995, during the opening statement of the Sheikh's trial for a plot to bomb city landmarks, Assistant U.S. Attorney Robert Khuzami referred to Abdel Rahman as "the leader of the Jihad Army" operating in New York. (*U.S. v. Omar Abdel Rahman et al.,* January 30 1995.) In 1996, during the summation for the first of Yousef's two federal trials, Assistant U.S. Attorney Lev Dassin told jurors that Yousef was part of a "self proclaimed army of terrorists" (*U.S. v. Ramzi Ahmed Yousef et al.,* August 5, 1996), and in the indictment of Osama bin Laden handed down secretly in June 1998 and unsealed that November, the U.S. attorney for the Southern District of New York declared that the alternate name for al Qaeda was the "Islamic Army." (Indictment: *U.S. v. Osama bin Laden,* June 1998.) From testimony in the subsequent trial in February 2001 it became clear that bin Laden had directed an al Qaeda cell based at the Alkifah Center in Brooklyn from March 1991, when Mustafa Shalabi was killed. The blind Sheikh was spiritual adviser to the cell, and Yousef was imported to build the World Trade Center bomb. It is unknown where the bomb maker himself ranked in the al Qaeda power structure, but by 1994 he had become al Qaeda's chief operational point man. Not only did bin Laden finance Yousef's Manila-based Bojinka and pope plots, he also underwrote Yousef's design of the 9/11 plot, which was executed by Yousef's uncle Khalid Shaikh Mohammed. Mohammed himself was described by intelligence officials as the "chief operating officer" of al Qaeda following his capture in March 2003.

8 Author's interview with Bernard Kleinman, February 3, 2003.

9 Kessler, *The Bureau: The Secret History of the FBI,* pp. 128–129.

10 Author's interview with confidential FBI source.

11 Later, under oath, Salem testified that he'd been feeling sick the two days prior to the bombing. On the morning of February 26, 1993, he went to a clinic tied to the union he had belonged to during his time employed as a hotel worker. Salem testified that doctors at the clinic examined him and determined that he would have to be hospitalized. He then went to St. Claire's emergency room. There he was examined and admitted to the hospital for the inner ear infection. Salem testified that he stayed three to four days, and during that period he was visited by Ibrahim El-Gabrowny. *U.S. v. Omar Abdel Rahman et al.,* March 13, 1995, p. 4998.

12 Ibid.

13 Richard Bernstein and Ralph Blumenthal, "Bomb Informer's Tapes Give Rare Glimpse of FBI Dealings," *New York Times,* October 31, 1993.

14 Author's interview with confidential FBI source.

15 Ibid.

16 Author's interview with Detective Lou Napoli, January 10, 2003.

15. THE RYDER SIDESHOW

1 Ralph Blumenthal, "Insistence on Refund for a Truck Results in an Arrest in Explosion," *New York Times,* March 5, 1993.

2 Dwyer et al., *Two Seconds Under the World,* p. 89.

3 All quotes in this section are taken directly from FBI transcripts admitted into evidence in *U.S. v. Mohammed Salameh et al.*

4 Robert D. McFadden, "Jersey City Man Is Charged in Bombing of Trade Center After Rented Van Is Traced," *New York Times,* March 5, 1993.

5 Mylroie, *The War Against America,* p. 41; Eric Pilker affidavit, March 5, 1993.

6 Reeve, *The New Jackals,* p. 40.

7 www.fbi.gov/mostwant/terrorists/fugitives.htm.

8 Author's interview with ASAC Carson Dunbar, July 31, 2002.

9 In a September 24, 2001, story, the *Washington Post* reported that "a loosely organized Islamic group planted a bomb under the World Trade Center." This despite evidence revealed in *U.S. v. Omar Abdel Rahman et al.* (the Day of Terror trial), *U.S. v. Ramzi Ahmed Yousef et al.* (the Bojinka trial), and *U.S. v. Osama bin Laden* (the African embassy bombing trial) that Yousef's coconspirators had been part of a tightly organized cell funded by bin Laden that dated back to 1989. Jo Warrick, Joe Stephens, Mary Pat Flaherty, and James V. Grimaldo, "FBI Agents Ill-Equipped to Predict Terror Acts," *Washington Post,* September 24, 2001.

10 Ralph Blumental, "Bomb Is Definite Answer, But All Else Is Mystery," *New York Times,* February 28, 1993.

11 Coming just a few hours after the meeting in his office in which Napoli and Anticev suggested that the bombing might have been the work of men tied to blind Sheikh Rahman (whom asset Emad Salem had infiltrated), it's impossible to say whether Fox was misleading the public or merely distracting the media so that the Salem lead could be followed. But the question became moot by the next day, Sunday, when the C-VIN linked the bomb van to the Ryder truck rented by Mohammed Salameh, a staunch follower of the Sheikh. Robert D. McFadden, "Officials Studying Bomb Clues Seek Several for Questioning. Dynamite Traces," *New York Times,* March 1, 1993.

12 Ralph Blumenthal, "Trade Center Bombing Suspect Not a Patsy, Officials Conclude," *New York Times,* March 9, 1993.

13 FBI 302 interrogation of Abdul Basit Mahmud Karim, February 7 and 8, 1995, Aircraft in Flight, by Special Agent Charles Stern and Brian C. Parr, File 265A-NY-235983, p. 8.

14 Priscilla Painton, "Who Could Have Done It," *Time,* March 8, 1993.

15 Jill Smolowe, "The $400 Bomb," *Time,* March 22, 1993.

16 *ABC News World News Tonight,* report by Jim Hickey, March 4, 1993.

17 Judith Miller, "Sheik Emerges on TV to Deny Link to Bombing," *New York Times,* March 19, 1993.

18 Ralph Blumenthal, "$8,000 in Account of 2 Suspects Traced to Transfer from Europe," *New York Times,* March 11, 1993.

19 Joseph B. Treaster, "Deadly Bomb Was Cheap and Easily Made, Experts Say," *New York Times,* March 11, 1993.

20 Miller, *The Cell,* p. 31.

21 Reeve, *The New Jackals,* p. 16.

22 Ibid., p. 40.

23 *U.S. v. Omar Abdel Rahman et al.,* March 13, 1995.

24 Alison Mitchell, "Letter Explained Motive in Bombing, Officials Now Say."

25 Alison Mitchell, "Investigators and Experts Debate Relevance of Letter Tied to Blast," *New York Times,* March 29, 1993.

26 *U.S. v. Omar Abdel Rahman et al.*

27 The author made a written request on April 10, 2003, to interview Special Agent John Anticev for this book, but five days later Joseph Valliquette, the media representative of the FBI's New York office, denied the request.

28 Richard Bernstein and Ralph Blumenthal, "Bomb Informer's Tapes Give Rare Glimpse of FBI Dealings," *New York Times,* October 31, 1993.

29 Ralph Blumenthal, "Tapes Depict Proposal to Thwart Bomb Used in Trade Center Blast," *New York Times,* October 28, 1993.

30 *U.S. v. Omar Abdel Rahman et al.,* July 5, 1995, and March 13, 1995, p. 13437.

31 Ibid., March 13, 1995, p. 5009.

32 At one point Salem told Anticev that he felt he deserved the $200,000 reward that had been offered for Abouhalima's capture, but the FBI agent laughed at him. The Bureau later took the position that the location of Abouhalima in Egypt had first come from the State Department. *U.S. v. Omar Abdel Rahman et al.,* April, 3, 1995.

33 Author's interview with Detective Lou Napoli, January 10, 2003.

34 Ibid.

16. THE $1.5 MILLION MAN

1 Author's interview with FBI confidential source.

2 Author's interview with Detective Lou Napoli, January 10, 2003.

3 Richard Bernstein and Ralph Blumenthal, "Bomb Informer's Tapes Give Rare Glimpse of FBI Dealings," *New York Times,* October 31, 1993.

4 *U.S. v. Omar Abdel Rahman et al.,* March 29, 1995.

5 Ibid., March 6, 1995.

6 Author's interview with confidential FBI source.

7 *U.S. v. Omar Abdel Rahman et al.,* March 7, 1995.

8 Ibid., March 29, 1995.

9 Ibid., January 30, 1995.

10 Ibid., March 22, 1995.

11 James C. McKinley, "Lawyer Forces Bomb Trial Witness to Admit Trail of Lies," *New York Times,* March 23, 1995.

12 *U.S. v. Omar Abdel Rahman et al.,* March 19, 1995.

13 Ibid., March 16, 1995.

14 Ibid., March 22, 1995.

15 Author's interview with Detective Lou Napoli, January 10, 2003.

16 Ralph Blumenthal, "Tapes Show FBI Agreed to Return Timer for Bomb," *New York Times,* November 8, 1993.

17 *U.S. v. Omar Abdel Rahman et al.,* July 5, 1995.

18 Blumenthal, "Tapes Show FBI Agreed to Return Timer for Bomb."

19 *U.S. v. Omar Abdel Rahman et al.*

20 Ibid., March 30, 1995.

21 Ibid., July 6, 1995.

22 See Chapter 41.

23 Robert D. McFadden, "8 Seized as Suspects in Plot to Bomb New York Targets and Kill Political Figures," *New York Times,* June 25, 1993.

24 William Dowell, "Defending Islam. The Sheik at the Heart of the Conspiracy Speaks," *Time,* October 9, 1995.

25 Author's interview with confidential FBI source.

26 Author's interview with Detective Lou Napoli, January 10, 2003.

27 McFadden, "8 Seized as Suspects in Plot to Bomb New York Targets and Kill Political Figures."

28 Miller, *The Cell,* pp. 55–56.

29 Oliver "Buck" Revell testimony before the House Committee on International Relations, October 3, 2001.

17. THE BOOTLEG TAPES

1 Ralph Blumenthal, "FBI Inquiry Failed to Detect Any Sign of Attack," *New York Times,* March 6, 1993.

2 Ralph Blumenthal, "Clues Hinting at Terror Ring Were Ignored, Officials Say," *New York Times,* August 27, 1993.

3 Dwyer et al., *Two Seconds Under the World,* p. 272.

4 Mary B. W. Tabor, "Informer's Wife Said He Warned of Terrorism," *New York Times,* September 28, 1993.

5 Ralph Blumenthal, "Plot Warning Is Reviewed by the F.B.I.," *New York Times,* October 29, 1993.

6 Reeve, *The New Jackals,* pp. 17–18.

7 *U.S. v. Omar Abdel Rahman et al.,* March 13, 1995.

8 Ralph Blumenthal, "Tapes Depict Proposal to Thwart Bomb Used in Trade Center Blast," *New York Times,* October 29, 1993. The article discussed a conversation Salem taped with Anticev on his own equipment—one of many surreptitious recordings that would soon be known as Salem's "bootleg tapes."

9 Author's interview with confidential FBI source.

10 Author's interview with Carson Dunbar, July 31, 2002.

11 Author's interview with Jim Roth, May 30, 2003.

12 Author's interview with confidential FBI source.

13 Joseph P. Fried, "Sheik and 9 Followers Guilty of a Conspiracy of Terrorism," *New York Times,* October 2, 1995.

14 Prosecutors are required to disclose to the defense evidence favorable to a defendant that is either exculpatory or impeaching and is material to either guilt or punishment. In *Brady v. Maryland,* 373 U.S. at 87, the U.S. Supreme Court held "that the suppression by the prosecution of evidence favorable to an accused upon request violates

due process where the evidence is material either to guilt or to punishment irrespective of the good faith or bad faith of the prosecution."

15 *U.S. v. Omar Abdel Rahman et al.*, March 28, 1995.

16 Author's interview with confidential FBI source.

17 Ibid.

18 Author's interview with Jim Roth, May 30, 2003.

19 Author's interview with Carson Dunbar, June 6, 2003.

20 *U.S. v. Omar Abdel Rahman et al.*, July 26, 1995.

21 Author's interview with confidential FBI source.

22 *U.S. v. Omar Abdel Rahman et al.*, July 25, 1995.

23 Author's interview with Carson Dunbar, July 31, 2002.

24 Kessler, *The FBI*, p. 149.

25 U.S. Department of Justice, Report of the Inspector General, November 15, 2002.

26 Kessler, *The FBI*, p. 157.

27 Author's interview with Jim Roth, May 30, 2003.

28 Author's interview with Richard Swick, December 17, 2002.

29 Author's interview with Diane Bodner Duhig, December 19, 2002.

30 Kessler, *The FBI*, p. 157.

31 Richard Bernstein and Ralph Blumenthal, "Bomb Informer's Tapes Give Rare Glimpse of FBI Dealings."

32 Kessler, *The FBI*, p. 159.

18. INTO THE ABYSS

1 Author's interview with Fire Marshal Philip Meagher (ret.), February 26, 2003.

2 Ibid.

3 Ibid. In an interview conducted with the author ten years to the day after the blast, Meagher recalled that the numbers on the columns were B-22 and B-23, but he couldn't say for sure. However, he was certain that they once marked off parking areas. By synching the columns to blueprints of the B-2 level and relating them to the lunchroom which seemed to have sustained the most damage, Meagher was able to fix the explosion's point of origin.

4 Philip Meagher, "Clues from the Crater," *WNYF* magazine, fourth quarter 1993, pp. 2–9.

5 Author's interview with Fire Marshal Robert McLoughlin (ret.), February 25, 2003.

6 Joint Inquiry Finding #10, December 10, 2002.

7 Author's interview with Fire Marshal James Reilly (ret.), February 8, 2003.

8 See photo p. 129.

9 Author's interview with Fire Marshal Philip Meagher (ret.), February 26, 2003.

10 Author's interview with Eve Bucca, February 18, 2002.

11 Ibid.

12 Woodward, *Veil*, p. 96.

13 U.S. Navy Petty Officer Robert Stetham.

14 Alison Mitchell, "Investigators and Experts Debate Relevance of Letter Tied to Blast," *New York Times*, March 29, 1993.

15 Author's interview with FDNY assistant commissioner Kay Woods, August 30, 2002.

16 *U.S. v. Ahmed Abdel Sattar et al.*, Indictment 02 Crim. 395, April 9, 2002.

17 Reeve, *The New Jackals*, p. 41.

19. THE HUNT FOR RASHED

1 Samuel M. Katz, *Relentless Pursuit: The DSS and the Manhunt for the Al-Qaeda Terrorists* (New York: Forge, 2002).
2 Napoli's original probe of Nosair's bombing plot via Emad Salem and Corrigan's investigation of Black Muslims reportedly tied to the Sheikh's cell.
3 Katz, *Relentless Pursuit*, p. 101.
4 Reeve, *The New Jackals*, p. 49.
5 Weaver, "Children of the Jihad."
6 Ottoway and Coll, "Retracing the Steps of a Terror Suspect: Accused Bomb Builder Tied to Many Plots."
7 Author's interview with confidential Pakistani source.
8 Associated Press, "Bhutto: New York Bombing Suspect Attempted to Assassinate Her," *Chicago Tribune*, March 19, 1995; "Bhutto Seeks U.S. Help," AP Online, March 21, 1995; Reeve, *The New Jackals*, p. 54.
9 "Massive Bomb, Dead Body Found in Truck," *Bangkok Post*, March 18, 1994.
10 "Terrorists Linked to WTC Explosion," *Bangkok Post*, March 19, 1994.
11 "Motorbike Taxi Driver Averts Disaster," *Bangkok Post*, March 18, 1994.
12 "One Iranian Charged in Alleged Bomb Plot," *Bangkok Post*, August 17, 1994.
13 Dwyer et al., *Two Seconds Under the World*, pp. 154–156.
14 Douglas Jehl, "Rahman Errors Admitted," *New York Times*, March 3, 1993, p. 39.
15 Alison Mitchell, "U.S. Detains Cleric Linked to Militants; Sheikh to Be Held While Fighting Deportation," *New York Times*, July 3, 1993.
16 Kessler, *The FBI*, p. 285.
17 Mitchell, "Sheikh to Be Held While Fighting Deportation."
18 Author's interview with Fire Marshal Robert McLoughlin (ret.), February 25, 2003.

20. PREPPING FOR THE "BIG NOISE"

1 Frontline. Timeline: Al Qaeda's Global Context; http://www.pbs.org/wgbh/pages/frontline/shows/knew/etc/cron.html.
2 FBI 302 interrogation of Abdul Hakim Murad, April 12 and 13, 1995. See full 302: Appendix I, pp. 499–517.
3 Philippine National Police transcript of interrogation of Abdul Hakim Murad, January 20, 1995.
4 Ibid. Murad said the money came from his father, who drove heavy equipment for an oil company in Kuwait, but the true source of the financing is unknown.
5 *Chocolate* was an arbitrary code word that Yousef chose to represent explosives.
6 Mary B. W. Tabor, "U.S. Indicts Egyptian Cleric as Head of Group Plotting 'War of Urban Terrorism,'" *New York Times*, August 26, 1993.
7 Ralph Blumenthal, "Prosecutors Describe 'Horror' as Trial in Towers Blast Opens," *New York Times*, October 5, 1993.
8 Dwyer et al., *Two Seconds Under the World*, pp. 252–253.
9 Richard Bernstein, "Jury Sees Photos of Trade Center Blast Victims," *New York Times*, October 8, 1993; Bernstein, "Bombing Trial: Hours of Tedium and Rare Moments of Drama," *New York Times*, October 17, 1993.
10 Bernstein, "Trade Center Witness Tells of Manuals on Bombs," *New York Times*, November 10, 1993.
11 Bernstein, "Trade Center Mysteries Deepen," *New York Times*, November 15, 1993.

12 By her own account Mylroie first met Fox in the summer of 1994. Her first major public espousal of the theory that Yousef was an Iraqi agent appeared in an article entitled "The World Trade Center Bomb: Who Is Ramzi Yousef? Why It Matters," published in the winter 1995–96 issue of *The National Interest*. An expanded version of that piece became a book entitled *Study of Revenge*, published in 2000 by AEI Press, an imprint of the American Enterprise Institute. The Institute is a conservative Washington think tank whose current scholars and fellows include former House Speaker Newt Gingrich, former U.S. Court of Appeals Judge Robert Bork, former U.N. Ambassador Jeane Kirkpatrick, and Irving Kristol, publisher of *The National Interest*. *Study in Revenge* was republished in 2001 as a trade paperback under the title *The War Against America*. In the acknowledgments to *The War Against America*, Mylroie wrote that Clare Wolfowitz "fundamentally shaped this book." Wolfowitz, who taught at the Johns Hopkins School of Advanced International Studies, is the wife of Paul Wolfowitz, the deputy secretary of defense largely considered the architect of the Bush administration's policies that led to the March 2003 invasion of Iraq. In the same acknowledgments Mylroie thanked Mr. Wolfowitz for reading the manuscript prior to publication.

13 *U.S. v. Mohammed Salameh et al.*

14 FBI 302 Interrogation of Abdul Basit Mahmud Karim, February 7 and 8, 1995, Aircraft in Flight, by Special Agent Charles Stern and Brian C. Parr, File 265A-NY-235983, p. 7.

15 Richard Bernstein, "Witness Fails to Identify Two Blast Defendants," *New York Times*, December 8, 1993.

16 No plausible explanation for Moosh's failure to ID the two defendants has ever been given in any of the published accounts of the case. But in the FBI 302 referenced above, FBI agent Charles Stern and Secret Service agent Brian Parr write, "BASIT (Yousef) stated that ABOUHALIMA had never been present with the RYDER van at a Jersey City, New Jersey, gasoline station on the morning of the WTC bombing. He maintained that the government witness who had testified to ABOUHALIMA'S presence at the station had fabricated the story, and opined that the government must have paid him for his testimony."

17 Dwyer et al., *Two Seconds Under the World*, p. 270.

18 Richard Bernstein, "Testimony in Bomb Case Links Loose Ends," *New York Times*, January 19, 1994.

19 *U.S. v. Mohammed Salameh et al.*

20 Richard Bernstein, "4 Are Convicted in Bombing at World Trade Center That Killed 6, Stunned U.S.," *New York Times*, March 5, 1994.

21 *U.S. v. Mohammed Salameh et al.*

22 Michael Georgy, "Egyptian Militants Vow Attacks on Americans," *New York Times*, March 5, 1994.

23 Dwyer et al., *Two Seconds Under The World*, p. 251.

21. THE WESTERN FRONT

1 Author's interview with James H. Hauswirth, November 1, 2002.

2 Greg Kirkorian, "Terrorism Was Job 4 in Phoenix," *Los Angeles Times*, June 10, 2002; Greg Krikorian and Rich Connell, "Response to Terror: FBI Brass Accused of Apathy; Investigation," May 25, 2002.

3 Author's interview with Harry Ellen, February 25, 2003.

4 Ibid.

5 Emerson, *American Jihad,* p. 136.

6 In 1990, El-Hage was reportedly visited by a bearded stranger who questioned him about imam Khalifa, thought by many to be a heretic because of his practice of numerology and polygamy. El-Hage later told a grand jury that he served the man lunch and took him to Khalifa's mosque. The imam was later reportedly murdered by a member of the radical al Fuqra group. "Holy Warriors of Terrorism," Anti-Defamation League, p. 7; Mimi Swartz, "The Terrorist Next Door."

7 Christopher Dickey, "America's Most Wanted," *Newsweek,* July 4, 1994.

8 Steven Emerson, CNN Special Assignment, September 30, 1991.

9 "On the Trail of Killers," *People,* September 20, 1997.

10 *NBC Nightly News,* "American Closeup," July 11, 1997.

11 B. Drummond Ayres Jr., "Gunman Kills 2 Near C.I.A. Entrance," *New York Times,* January 26, 1993; Neil A. Lewis, "Tranquil Campus of C.I.A. Is Shaken by Killings of Two," *New York Times,* January 27, 1993.

12 Affidavit of Bradley Smith, EEOC complaint, August 31, 1998.

13 David E. Kaplan, "Chasing Terrorists One Matchbook at a Time," *U.S. News and World Report,* June 30, 1997.

14 Author's interview with DSS agent Bradley Smith, July 6, 1998.

15 Author's interview with DSS agent Rob Born (ret.), February 18, 2000.

16 Ibid., June 18, 2003.

17 Author's interview with Bradley Smith, July 6, 1998.

18 FBI 302 Interrogation of Abdul Hakim Murad, April 12 and 13, 1995.

19 Placed in a suitcase in Malta, the bomb transited on a flight to Frankfurt, Germany, and was rerouted through London's Heathrow Airport and onto the Pan Am flight; George J. Church, "Solving the Lockerbie Case," *Time,* November 25, 1991.

20 FBI 302 interrogation of Ramzi Yousef, a.k.a. Abdul Basit Mahmud Abdul Karim, February 7 and 8, 1995.

21 *U.S. v. Ramzi Ahmed Yousef et al.,* August 19, 1996.

22 Philippine National Police Debriefing report, Counter Intelligence Group, February 18, 1995.

23 Paul Berman, "Al Qaeda's Philosopher," *New York Times Sunday Magazine,* March 23, 2003.

24 Bill Saporito and Tim McGirk, "Architect of Terror," *Time,* March 1, 2003.

25 PNP Intelligence Command, "Osama bin Laden," April 8, 1994; PNP Intelligence Command, "Summary of Activities Leading Up to Pope's Visit, Dona Josefa Fire and Aftermath," February 27, 1995; PNP Intelligence Command, "Tactical Interrogation Report. Abdul Hakim Murad," February 8, 1995; Rodolfo J. Garcia, Police Superintendent, "Recommendations for Meritorious Promotion," June 8, 1995; PNP Intelligence Command, "Mohammed Jamal Khalifa," August 25, 1996; FBI 302 interrogation of Ramzi Yousef, a.k.a. Abdul Basit Mahmud Abdul Karim, February 7 and 8, 1995; Ottoway and Coll, "Retracing the Steps of a Terror Suspect: Accused Bomb Builder Tied to Many Plots"; Mark Fineman and Richard C. Paddock, "Indonesian Cleric Tied to '95 Anti-U.S. Plot," *Los Angeles Times,* February 7, 2002.

26 PNP profiles of Carol Brioso, a.k.a. Carol Santiago and Rose Mosquera.

27 PNP SECRET briefing entitled "Chronological Activities of Rose Mosquera."

28 Ibid.

22. THE TEMPTRESS AND THE SPY

1 In an interview for this book on June 6, 2003, Carson Dunbar insisted that the order had come from above him, but he wouldn't say from whom. On May 30, 2003, Jim Roth, the head lawyer in the FBI's New York office, told the author that the dictum had come from William A. Gavin, the assistant director in charge who succeeded Jim Fox. In an interview with the author on June 15, 2003, Gavin said that he was sure Agent Floyd "was told to stand down" once the OPR had been opened. But he could not be precise as to "the dates and times and the exact verbiage" regarding any order preventing her from contacting Salem. Sources close to Floyd insist that the order came verbally from Dunbar some time in August 1993. Author's interview with confidential FBI source. Author's interview with FBI agent Len Predtechenskis (ret.), August 27, 2002.

2 At the trial Salem testified that between late June 1993 and early March 1995 he had been relocated by U.S. marshals fourteen times, along with his common-law wife and two children. *U.S. v. Omar Abdel Rahman et al.,* March 7, 1995.

3 Author's interview with Richard Swick, December 17, 2002.

4 Author's interview with Diane Bodner Duhig, December 19, 2002.

5 Colin Miner, "Temptress and the Spy," *New York Post,* March 12, 1994.

6 Author's interview with Jim Roth, May 30, 2003.

7 Letter to author from Fire Marshal Phillip Meagher (ret.), February 26, 2003.

8 Author's interview with Fire Marshal Robert McLoughlin (ret.), February 25, 2003.

9 Author's interview with Fire Marshal Henry Raven, February 2, 2003.

23. DELIVERING THE "CHOCOLATES"

1 FBI 302 Interrogation of Abdul Hakim Murad, April 12 and 13, 1995, p. 16.

2 *U.S. v. Ramzi Ahmed Yousef et al.,* August 26, 1996.

3 In January 1995, shortly after his capture by Philippine National Police in Manila, Shah escaped from a bungalow where he was being housed at Camp Crame, a PNP base. Then on February 7, 1996, after being recaptured and returned to the United States for trial, he broke through a cage covering the rooftop recreation area at the Metropolitan Correctional Center in New York and made his way onto a ledge twelve stories above the city before being apprehended. *U.S. v. Ramzi Ahmed Yousef et al.,* August 7, 1996.

4 Ibid., July 30, 1996.

5 Ibid., June 19, 1996.

6 Maria Ressa, "Investigators Think Sept. 11, 1995 Plot Related," CNN.com, February 25, 2002; Mark Fineman and Richard C. Paddock, "Indonesian Cleric Tied to '95 Anti-U.S. Plot," *Los Angeles Times,* February 7, 2002; Raymond Bonner, "How Qaeda Linked Up with Malaysian Groups," *New York Times,* February 7, 2002.

7 Anonymous, *Through Our Enemies' Eyes,* pp. 138–139. The Jordanian terrorist organization was called Mohammed's Army.

8 PNP: Initial Results re: Investigation on Suspected Islamic Extremists, January 6, 1995.

9 PNP Person Report on Mohammed Jamal Khalifa, August 25, 1996.

10 PNP Debriefing Report, Counter Intelligence Group, March 1, 1995.

11 Author's interview with Jacob L. Boesen, February 16, 2003.

12 Author's interview with PNP colonel Rodolfo B. Mendoza, April 19, 2002.

13 FBI 302 interrogation of Ramzi Yousef, a.k.a. Abdul Basit Mahmud Abdul Karim, February 7 and 8, 1995, pp. 15–16.

14 It's unclear why Yousef ordered the test inside the Greenbelt versus an isolated location. If he wanted to measure the impact of the device on human victims, it was unlikely, at the hour the bomb was planted, that large numbers of people would be in the front rows of the theater.

15 FBI Laboratory inventory: Manila Air Bombing of PAL FLIGHT #434, December 12, 1994, and Subsequent Investigation 265A-IIN-12924, obtained by author.

16 In the atlas Forlani was listed as the general secretary of the Christian Democratic party in Italy. Why Yousef would choose the name of a public figure is unknown, but it's unlikely that Manila airport officials would have made the connection to an existing person for a passenger traveling on a domestic flight. *U.S. v. Ramzi Ahmed Yousef et al.*, July 23, 1996.

17 *U.S. v. Ramzi Ahmed Yousef et al.*, May 30, 1996.

18 Logbook, Dona Josefa Apartments, December 1994–January 9, 1995; obtained by author.

19 *U.S. v. Ramzi Ahmed Yousef et al.*, June 3, 1996.

20 Ibid.

24. HOW MANY MORE FIRES?

1 Author's interview with FBI Agent Len Predtechenskis (ret.), January 11, 2003.

2 Author's interview with confidential FBI source.

3 Ibid.

4 Author's interview with confidential DIA source.

5 The spelling of the ASG's name, "Abu Sayaf," by the State Department was slightly different from the spelling listed in most other sources referencing Abdurajak Janjalani's terror cell, which is "Abu Sayyaf." The difference in the spelling of Islamic names continued to thwart investigators. Though the name Osama bin Laden was used by some intelligence officials and most media outlets, the U.S. Department of Justice spelled it "Usama bin Laden."

6 Author's interview with Eve Bucca, February 18, 2003.

7 The bar at 700 Second Avenue is now called "The Bravest" in honor of the firefighters who died on September 11th.

8 Author's interview with Chief Fire Marshal Louis F. Garcia, April 9, 2002.

9 Author's interview with Supervising Fire Marshal James Kelty, September 4, 1997.

10 On August 15, 1995, Kelty sat in a courtroom as a Manhattan businessman described by *Newsday* as "reputed to be . . . one of the city's worst slumlords" was convicted of conspiring to set the fire. Kelty was quoted as saying, "Maybe now, after three years, Tommy Williams can rest in peace." Patricia Hurtardo, "Landlord Convicted in Deadly Queens Fire," *Newsday*, August 16, 1995.

11 Author's interview with Fire Marshal Henry Raven, June 25, 2002.

12 Author's interview with Firefighter George Kreuscher (ret.), July 30, 2002.

25. THE THIRD PLOT

1 *U.S. v. Ramzi Ahmed Yousef et al.*, July 9, 1996.

2 PNP Debriefing Report, January 20, 1995.

3 Ibid., profile of Abdul Hakim Murad.

4 *U.S. v. Ramzi Ahmed Yousef et al.*, Government Exhibit 355.

5 Author's interview with U.S. Postal Inspector Frank Gonzalez (ret.), January 31, 2003.
6 *U.S. v. Ramzi Ahmed Yousef et al.,* June 11, 1996.
7 Cruz knew Yousef under his alias "Naji Haddad."
8 *U.S. v. Ramzi Ahmed Yousef et al.,* August 15, 1996.
9 FBI Laboratory inventory: Manila Air Bombing of PAL FLIGHT #434, December 12, 1994, and Subsequent Investigation.
10 FBI 302 Interrogation of Abdul Hakim Murad, April 13, 1995.
11 Ibid., FBI Laboratory inventory.
12 Anonymous, *Through Our Enemies' Eyes,* p. 139.
13 Yonah and Swetnam, *Usama bin Laden's al-Qaida: Profile of a Terrorist Network,* p. 40.
14 Sancton, "Anatomy of a Hijack."
15 Specialoperations.com, "GIGN at Marseilles Airport," December 1994.
16 Ibid., Sancton, "Anatomy of a Hijack."
17 In CNN.com's 9/11 timeline, the reported Marseilles hijacking incident with the Eiffel Tower as a possible target is considered the first early-warning sign. CNN.com/interactive/us/0205/intelligence.timeline/content..1..html.
18 CNN.com, "Rice: 'No specific time, place or method mentioned,'" May 17, 2002.
19 FBI 302 interrogation of Abdul Hakim Murad, April 13, 1995.
20 Author's interview with PNP Colonel Rodolfo B. Mendoza, April 19, 2002.
21 PNP Transcript of interrogation of Abdul Hakim Murad, January 7, 1995.
22 FBI 302 Interrogation of Abdul Hakim Murad, p. 11.
23 *U.S. v. Ramzi Ahmed Yousef et al.,* August 26, 1996.
24 FBI 302 interrogation of Abdul Hakim Murad, p. 5.
25 *U.S. v. Ramzi Ahmed Yousef et al.,* July 30, 1996.
26 FBI 302 Interrogation of Abdul Hakim Murad, p. 4.
27 *U.S. v. Ramzi Ahmed Yousef et al.,* Government Exhibit 355.
28 Murad later told FBI agents he planned to set the timer on the first device four days ahead. FBI 302 interrogation of Abdul Hakim Murad, p. 5. During an interrogation after his capture, Murad told the Philippine National Police that the timers could be set even further in advance, raising the prospect that some planes were intended to be detonated as they flew over U.S. cities. This contradicts published reports that all planes were set to explode over the Pacific within hours of being placed.
29 FBI 302 interrogation of Abdul Hakim Murad, p. 3.

26. MIRACLES FROM GOD

1 PNP Memorandum: Initial Results re: Investigation on Suspected Islamic Extremists, January 6, 1995.
2 Ibid., p. 5.
3 FBI 302 interrogation of Ramzi Yousef, February 7 and 8, 1995, p. 17.
4 *U.S. v. Ramzi Ahmed Yousef et al.,* June 18, 1996.
5 1995 President Lingkod Bayan Awardee. Aida Fariscal; autobiography and character.
6 Author's interview with Col. Aida Fariscal, PNP (ret.), April 18, 2002.
7 PNP Debriefing report. Abdul Hakim Murad, Counter Intelligence Group, February 21, 1995.
8 Author's interview with Colonel Aida Fariscal, PNP (ret.), April 18, 2002.

9 Ibid.

10 *U.S. vs. Ramzi Yousef et. al.* June 18, 1996.

11 Ibid., August 26, 1996.

PART III
27. TRUTH FROM A VALUE MEAL

1 Confidential Report of PNP search of Room 603 by Florenio C. Angeles, Chief Inspector, PNP.

2 Memo from Capt. Aida Fariscal, PNP National Capitol Regional Command, to President Fidel Ramos. January 14, 1995.

3 *U.S. v. Ramzi Ahmed Yousef et al.,* July 2, 1996.

4 Ibid., July 18, 1996.

5 Ibid., July 17, 1996.

6 PNP transcript, Interrogation of Abdul Hakim Murad, January 7, 1995. Government's Exhibit 760-T, *U.S. v. Ramzi Yousef et al.*

7 Author's interview with PNP Col. Rodolfo B. Mendoza, April 19, 2002.

8 PNP Memo After Intelligence Operation Report re: Neutralization of International Terrorists, February 27, 1995.

9 Author's interview with Col. Rodolfo B. Mendoza, April 19, 2002.

10 PNP Debriefing Memo Interrogation of Abdul Hakim Murad, January 20, 1995.

11 Matthew Brezinski, "Bust and Boom," *Washington Post,* December 30, 2001. The article reported that the CIA official "dismissed the connection to Bojinka as a 'hindsight is cheap' theory."

12 Gertz, *Breakdown,* p. 27.

13 "The Man Who Knew," *Frontline,* October 3, 2002; http://www.pbs.org/wgbh/pages/frontline/shows/knew/etc/cron.html; Reeve, *The New Jackals,* p. 87. Even the staff statement of the Joint Inquiry concluded that "the plans to crash a plane into CIA headquarters and to assassinate the Pope were only at the 'discussion stage.'" September 18, 2002.

14 Author's interview with Col. Rodolfo B. Mendoza.

15 This exchange was taken from a verbatim recitation of the interrogation by Colonel Mendoza during an interview with the author at Pangasinan police headquarters in the Philippines on April 19, 2002.

16 Ibid.

17 Maria Ressa, "U.S. Warned in 1995 of Plot to Hijack Planes, Attack Buildings," CNN.com, September 18, 2001; transcript of interview with Secretary Rigoberto Bobby Tiglao, by CNN, September 18, 2001.

18 FBI 302 Interrogation of Abdul Hakim Murad by Frank Pellegrino. Thomas Donlon, April 13, 1995.

19 See chapter 29 discussing PNP Intelligence Command "Network Diagram" entitled "Liberation Army Connection" showing the relationship of Yousef's cell, which derived funding from Osama bin Laden through Mohammed Jamal Khalifa, and Khalifa's funding of the Abu Sayyaf Group and Abdurajak Janjalani.

20 The author obtained copies of Colonel Mendoza's debriefing reports and other SECRET files on Yousef, bin Laden, Bojinka, and Operation Blue Marlin.

21 Matthew Brezinski, "Operation Bojinka's Bombshell," *Washington Post,* January 2, 2002.

22 Ed Offley, "First Questions for the Inquests into 9-11," *Defense Watch,* January 9, 2002.

28. BRAD SMITH'S BIGGEST "GET"

1 It's clear from the reaction of various U.S. federal agencies that intelligence about Yousef's Bojinka plot was communicated by the PNP to the Feds almost immediately after the fire at the Dona Josefa on January 6, 1995. But the actual computer (or its hard drive) didn't find its way into U.S. custody until much later. Maj. Alberto Ferro, who conducted the interrogation of Murad with Colonel Mendoza, later testified at the Bojinka trial that on June 7, 1995, he put Yousef's laptop in a locker at Camp Crame, headquarters of the PNP Intelligence Command. *U.S. v. Ramzi Yousef et al.,* July 17, 1996, p. 2387. Mary Horvath, an FBI computer specialist, testified at the same trial that the Toshiba laptop was given to the FBI by the PNP in April 1995. Ibid., July 22, 1996, p. 2552. The computer's hard drive was then sent to Microsoft Corporation for analysis. David Swartzendruber, a Microsoft investigator, examined the drive and concluded that Yousef began entering data into the laptop regarding the Bojinka plot as early as mid-September 1994. Ibid., July 23, 1996, p. 2612.

2 Author's interview with Glen Winn, United Airlines, March 14, 2000.

3 Author's interview with Dick Doubrava, Delta Airlines, March 13, 2000.

4 "United Airlines Honolulu Flight Threat," Reuters, January 14, 1995.

5 "United Airlines Hong Kong Flight Diverted," Associated Press, January 15, 1995.

6 FBI Lab inventory: Manila Air Bombing 4, December 12, 1994, and Subsequent Investigation 265A-IIN-12924. The report begins with evidence seized in the investigation of the bombing PAL #434, which took place on December 12, 1994, and contains a list of evidence seized in Room 603 on January 7, 1995, and the Su Casa Guesthouse in Islamabad, where Ramzi Yousef was arrested on February 7, 1995.

7 Reeve, *The New Jackals,* p. 65.

8 Ibid., p. 97.

9 Roy Roman, "Pan Am #103, Why Did They Die?" *Time,* April 27, 1992; George J. Church, "Solving the Lockerbie Case," *Time,* November 25, 1991; Andrew Rosenthal, "U.S. Accuses Libya As 2 Are Charged in Pan Am Bombing," *New York Times,* November 15, 1991.

10 Richard Bernstein, "Behind Arrest of Bomb Fugitive, Informer's Tip, Then Fast Action," *New York Times,* February 10, 1995; John F. Burns, "Terror Informer Reported to Get U.S. Protection," *New York Times,* February 13, 1995; Bill Keller, "Self-Portrait of Informer: An Innocent," *New York Times,* February 21, 1995.

11 Author's interview with Jeanne Smith, July 10, 1999.

12 Author's interview with DSS Agent Rob Born (ret.), May 5, 2002.

13 Timeline #73. p. 15.

14 Katz, *Relentless Pursuit,* p. 189.

15 Ibid., p. 160.

16 *U.S. v. Ramzi Ahmed Yousef et al.,* August 8, 1996.

17 Born Sabri al-Banna in Jaffa, Nidal split with Yasser Arafat's PLO to form the even more radical Fatah Revolutionary Council. His related groups were blamed over the years for attacks in more than twenty countries that killed hundreds. On August 19, 2002, Nidal was reported to have committed suicide in Iraq, but his body was found with four bullets in the head. Tracy Wilkinson, "Terrorist's Alleged Death as Mysteri-

ous as His Life," *Los Angeles Times,* August 20, 2002; "Abu Nidal Linked to Many Attacks," Associated Press, August 19, 2002.

18 Katz, p. 165.

19 Christopher John Farley, "The Man Who Wasn't There," *Time,* May 20, 1995.

20 Author's interview with confidential DSS source.

21 *U.S. v. Ramzi Ahmed Yousef et al.,* August 8, 1996.

22 Ibid., August 9, 1996.

23 "How the FBI Gets Its Man," *60 Minutes II,* October 10, 2001.

24 Author's interview with Samuel Katz, October 1, 2002.

25 Katz, p. 197.

29. A CHILLING WARNING

1 FBI 302 Interrogation of Ramzi Ahmed Yousef by Bradley J. Garrett, February 7, 1995. Transcribed February 10, 1995.

2 *U.S. v. Ramzi Ahmed Yousef and Eyad Ismoil,* October 22, 1997.

3 Yousef outlined his position on Israel in this first February 7, 1995, interrogation in Pakistan; during the subsequent airborne interrogation the night of February 7 and 8, 1995, and at a meeting with Federal prosecutors on April 23, 1995.

4 Raghida Dirgham, "Conversation with Ramzi Yousef," *Al Hayat,* April 12, 1995.

5 Richard Bernstein, "Behind Arrest of Bomb Fugitive, Informer's Tip, Then Fast Action," *New York Times,* February 10, 1995; David Johnston, "Fugitive in Trade Center Blast Is Caught and Returned to U.S.," *New York Times,* February 9, 1995.

6 Mylroie, *The War Against America,* p. 4.

7 Yousef's World Trade Center bombing cell occupied three different apartments in Jersey City during the fall of 1992 and up until the bombing on February 26, 1993. First, Mohammed Salameh lived with Abdul Yasin (the Iraqi) at 34 Kensington Avenue. Then in October Yousef and Salameh moved into an apartment less than a mile away at 25 Virginia Avenue. Finally, just after the first of the year, Yousef and Salameh moved into the ground floor apartment at 40 Pamrapo Avenue that became the ultimate "bomb factory." *U.S. v. Mohammed Salameh et al.; U.S. v. Ramzi Ahmed Yousef et al.*

8 FBI 302 Interrogation of Ramzi Ahmed Yousef by Chuck Stern and Brian Parr, February 7 and 8, 1995. Transcribed February 28, 1995.

9 Paul Berman, "Al Qaeda's Philosopher," *New York Times Sunday Magazine,* March 23, 2003.

10 Author's interview with confidential DSS source, February 18, 2000.

11 Yousef denied the gas station incident took place, but Assistant U.S. Attorney Henry DePippo made it a key element of his prosecution in the first World Trade Center bombing trial. It's unknown whether the jurors were swayed by Moosh's inability to identify Abouhalima or Salameh in open court. But the defendants were ultimately convicted on all counts.

12 Quoting directly from the FBI 302 with respect to his backers: "BASIT (YOUSEF) would not elaborate on exactly how the WTC bombing was financed, except to say that he had received money from family and friends." FBI 302 Interrogation of Ramzi Ahmed Yousef by Chuck Stern and Brian Parr, p. 14. "When questioned regarding a business card in the name of MOHAMMED KHALIFA, found in BASIT'S apartment in the Philippines BASIT stated that he did not personally know KHALIFA, but

that KHALIFA's business card had been given to him by WALI SHAH, as a contact in the event BASIT needed aid. BASIT also acknowledged that he was familiar with the name USAMA BIN LADEN, and knew him to be a relative of KHALIFA's but would not further elaborate." Ibid., p. 19.

13 Peg Tyre, "An Icon Destroyed," *Newsweek,* September 11, 2001. Note: several books have given different accounts. Lou Michel and Dan Herbeck in *American Terrorist, Timothy McVeigh and the Tragedy at Oklahoma City* (New York: Regan Books, 2001) use the wording attributed to William A. Gavin, the ADIC of the FBI's New York office who was quoted by Simon Reeve in *The New Jackals,* pp. 108–109. In an interview with the author on June 15, 2003, the retired ADIC said that he lifted Yousef's blindfold and gestured to the Towers with the line, "They're still standing." Yousef reportedly said, "They wouldn't be, if I had had enough money and enough explosives." But in *The Cell,* by Miller, Stone, and Mitchell, FBI agent Chuck Stern is cited as the agent who lifted the blindfold and reminded Yousef that the Trade Center was "still standing." In that version Yousef replied, "They wouldn't be, if I'd gotten a little more money," p. 135.

14 Richard Bernstein, "Behind Arrest of Bomb Fugitive, Informer's Tip, Then Fast Action."

15 *U.S. v. Omar Abdel Rahman et al.,* January 30, 1995.

16 FBI SECRET/NOFORN memo: Ramzi Ahmed Yousef: A New Generation of Sunni Islamic Terrorists. NOFORN was a designation indicating no distribution to foreigners. Woodward, *Veil,* p. 418.

17 Author's interview with confidential source.

18 Jim Gomez and John Solomon, "Authorities Warned of Hijack Risks," Associated Press, March 3, 2002.

19 *Washington Post,* September 23, 2001.

20 Lawrence Wright, "The Counter Terrorist," *The New Yorker,* June 1, 2002.

21 "The Man Who Knew," *Frontline,* October 3, 2002.

22 The difference in spelling between the most commonly used form of bin Laden's name, "Osama," and the form used by the FBI and the Justice Department is worthy of note. The variations are a function of transliteration. Norman Goldstein, the stylebook editor for the AP, was quoted as saying, "Arab vowels commonly become A, I or U; E and O don't really exist except for personal preference. And since we're not going to ask Osama bin Laden his preference, Osama—more often than not—is spelled with an "O." Robert K. Elder, "Usama, Osama? Tracking Suspects Spells Confusion." *Chicago Tribune,* October 22, 2001. Note: while the discussion seems somewhat arcane, the variation in Islamic names makes tracking members of al Qaeda (a.k.a. al-Qaida) extremely difficult, especially considering the number of aliases used by terrorists. Even journalists attempting to untangle the Gordian knot differ as to the proper spelling and pronunciation. In this book we have referred to "The Red" as Mahmud Abouhalima, the same spelling used in his federal indictment for the World Trade Center bombing. But in *The War Against America,* scholar Laurie Mylroie spells his last name Abu Halima (loosely translated, "father of Halima").

23 Joint Inquiry Staff Statement, October 8, 2002.

24 Dwyer, *Two Seconds Under the World,* p. 211.

25 Benjamin, *The Age of Sacred Terror,* p. 226, 303–304, 395.

26 Gertz, *Breakdown,* pp. 29–30.

27 Paraphrasing a passage in *The Age of Sacred Terror,* pp. 226–227, in which Daniel

Benjamin and Steven Simon cite Charles Alan Wright, *Federal Rules of Criminal Procedure,* 2nd ed. (St. Paul, Minn.: West Publishing, 1982).

28 Testimony of FBI Agent Michael Rolince FBI before the Joint Inquiry, September 29, 2002.

29 Mylroie, p. 7.

30 Gertz, p. 25.

31 Author's interview with Eve Bucca, February 29, 2003.

30. JOHN DOE NO. 2.

1 Stephen Jones and Peter Israel, *Others Unknown: The Oklahoma City Bombing Case* (New York: Public Affairs, 1998), p. 4.

2 John Kifner, "FBI Seeking 2 in Blast: Search for Bodies Is Slow," *New York Times,* April 21, 1995;

3 Interpol Report, "Regarding: Update of Oklahoma Bombing to Include New Composite Sketch for 'John Doe' Suspect #2. "Marked: Critical Urgent. From: Interpol Washington. To: Secretary General, Interpol. Attention: Anti-Terrorism. Date: May 6, 1995.

4 Don Terry, "In a Kansas Army Town, Report of 2 Men in a Hurry," *New York Times,* April 22, 1995. Tim Weiner, "F.B.I. Struggling to Find Answers in Bombing Case. Search Continues for Second Suspect as the Authorities Try to Fathom Motives," *New York Times,* April 28, 1995.

5 Congressman McCurdy appeared on CNN on April 19, 1995, and reportedly said, "My first reaction when I heard of the explosion was that there could be a very real connection to some of the Islamic fundamentalist groups that have, actually, been operating out of Oklahoma City. They've had recent meetings—even a convention—where terrorists from the Middle East that were connected directly to Hamas and Hizbollah participated. If you look at the nature of the destruction, this looks very similar to the destruction of the Israeli Embassy in Argentina and even the U.S. Embassy in Beirut." CNN, April 19, 1995.

6 *U.S. v. Timothy James McVeigh and Terry Lynn Nichols,* Indictment, August, 1995.

7 Joe Thomas, "Sightings of John Doe No. 2 in Blast Case, Mystery No. 1," *New York Times,* December 3, 1995.

8 James Collins, "The Weight of Evidence: The Case Against McVeigh Is Strong, but the Mess at the FBI and a Babel of Witnesses Make It Vulnerable," *Time,* April 28, 1997.

9 Affidavit of FBI Special Agent Henry C. Gibbons, April 20, 1995.

10 Jo Thomas, "Suspect's Sketch in Oklahoma Case Called an Error," *New York Times,* January 30, 1997.

11 FBI 302, Philip Rojas re: conversation with Abdul Hakim Murad April 19, 1995, by FBI Agent Frank Pellegrino and Secret Service Agent Brian Parr. Transcribed April 20, 1995.

12 *U.S. v. Ramzi Ahmed Yousef et al.,* August 9, 1996, pp. 3953–3954.

13 Ibid., August 9, 1996, p. 3989.

14 Passport of Terry Lynn Nichols. Visa granted November 4, 1994.

15 Marriage contract of Terry L. Nichols and Marife Torres, September 20, 1990, before Judge Rodolfo B. Gandiango. Filed November 21, 1990, Cebu City, the Philippines.

16 *First Deposit National Bank v. Terry L. Nichols,* Motion to Strike.

17 Affidavit of Terry Nichols, April 2, 1992, Re: Notice of Revocation of Signature and Power of Attorney.

18 David Jackson, "Portrait of a Federal Foe," *Chicago Tribune,* May 11, 1995.

19 Jones, p. 123; Lana Padilla with Ron Delpit, *By Blood Betrayed: My Life with Terry Nichols and Timothy McVeigh* (New York: HarperCollins, 1995).

20 In McVeigh's trial the Government argued that Nichols and McVeigh had financed the Oklahoma City bombing by using the proceeds from the robbery of Arkansas gun dealer Roger Moore on November 4, 1994. But evidence later showed that on the day of the robbery McVeigh was at a gun show in Kent, Ohio, hundreds of miles away. Moore alleged that he had been accosted outside of his house at 9:00 or 9:30 A.M. by a man wearing a black ski mask and wielding a gun. Moore said that the man then took him inside the house and singlehandedly tied him up with rope and duct tape before robbing a series of guns, ammunition, coins, and other valuables. In his book *Others Unknown: The Oklahoma City Bombing Case and Conspiracy,* McVeigh's defense counsel, Stephen Jones, questioned how Nichols, who "saw poorly" without his glasses and didn't own contact lenses, could have effected the robbery. According to Jones, Moore was never called by the government as a witness at McVeigh's trial, but at Nichols's trial, when Moore's girlfriend and/or business associate listed one of the guns stolen, Nichols's attorney, Michael Tiger, pointed out that Nichols had, in fact, purchased that same weapon at a gun show two years before—a revelation described by Jones as "a stunning blow to the prosecution." *Others Unknown,* pp. 79, 272, 304.

21 In his own handwriting, fixed with his thumbprint, Angeles wrote: "I certify that Terry Nichols was known to me personally during our meeting w/Abdul Hakim Murad, Wali-Khan + Ahmed Yousef in . . . Davao City in 1991. Note: Terry Nichols introduced himself to me as a farmer." Affidavit of Edwin Angeles. Philippines National Police Station, Basilan, the Philippines, November 3, 1996.

22 The summary was prepared by an investigator for Stephen Jones, who was representing Timothy McVeigh at the time. The summary quotes "excerpts from [the] report" by two agents of the PNP in which Angeles is referred to as #3. But the summary gives different dates for the meeting: "#3 flatly stated the [*sic*] he knows personally Terry Nichols. He met Terry Nichols . . . sometime in 1992 or 1993 at the vicinity of Del Monte Labeling factory in Davao. This was before the New York bombing. #3 said that Terry Nichols introduced himself as a farmer. At that time, #3 said that his companions were Abdul Basit (Yousef), Wali Khan (Shah) and Abdul Hakim Murad." It is unclear whether Angeles himself gave conflicting dates or whether the PNP agents recorded dates that were different from Angeles's sworn affidavit.

23 PNP Debriefing Report Interrogation of Abdul Hakim Murad, February 18, 1995. According to the report Murad was enrolled at the Continental Aeronautical Flying School in Pasay City, Philippines, "where he took his Ground School/Training before going into actual flying."

24 Reeve, *The New Jackals,* p. 136. Angeles was later gunned down by a suspected Abu Sayyaf member in January 1999.

25 Confidential report of Oscar P. Coronel, March 1, 1996, with reference to documents dated January 15, 1996, and February 28, 1996.

26 Summary of Telephone Activity on Daryl Bridges's Account Spotlight Prepaid Card December 7, 1993–April 17, 1995. Prepared August 16, 1996.

27 The only other name was "Tony." *U.S. v. Ramzi Ahmed Yousef et al.* August 26, 1996;

log book, Dona Josefa Apartments, December, 1994–January 9, 1995; obtained by author.

28 Jones, p. 302.

29 Sworn Affadavit of Daisy Yvonne B. Legaspi, Cebu City, October 3, 1996.

30 FBI 302 ALAT Ronald Ward interview with Seraphin Uy, April 28, 1995. Transcribed December 18, 1995.

31 Patricia O'Meara, "Iraq Connections to U.S. Extremists," *Insight,* October 30, 2001.

32 *U.S. v. Timothy McVeigh,* May 12, 1997.

33 Author's interview with Mike Johnston, March 20, 2003.

34 Author's interview with Stephen Jones, May 15, 2003.

35 *V.Z. Lawton et al. v. The Republic of Iraq,* Complaint, March 14, 2002.

36 *V.Z. Lawton et al. v. The Republic of Iraq,* Motion to Dismiss, March 3, 2003. Exhibit phone records.

37 Author's interview with Mike Johnston, March 20, 2003.

38 *U.S. v. Ramzi Ahmed Yousef et al.,* May 21, 1996.

39 Author's interview with Bernie Kleinman, February 3, 2003.

40 Ibid.

41 Author's interview with confidential source.

42 Jim Crogan, "Heartland Conspiracy," *L.A. Weekly,* April 30, 2002; William Jasper, "Terror Trail: WTC, OKC, 9-11," *The New American,* July 1, 2002; Jim Crogan, "The Middle Eastern Connection to Oklahoma City," *Indianapolis Star,* February 17, 2002; Micah Morrison, "The Iraq Connection," *Wall Street Journal,* September 5, 2002; Patricia O'Meara, "Iraq Connections to U.S. Extremists," *Insight,* October 30, 2001.

43 John Kifner, "FBI Seeking 2 in Blast: Search for Bodies Is Slow," *New York Times,* April 21, 1995.

31. THE DEVIL HIMSELF

1 *U.S. v. Ramzi Ahmed Yousef et al.,* August 7, 1996.

2 FBI 302 Interview with Ramzi Yousef, February 13, 1995. Transcribed February 14, 1995.

3 Mohammed Salameh, Mahmud Abouhalima, Mohammed Ajaj, and Nidal Ayyad.

4 *V.Z. Lawton et al. v. The Republic of Iraq,* Motion to Dismiss, March 3, 2003.

5 Ottoway and Coll, "Retracing the Steps of a Terror Suspect: Accused Bomb Builder Tied to Many Plots," *Washington Post,* June 5, 1995.

6 Raghida Dirgham, "Ramzi Yousef Discusses WTC Bombing, Other Activities" *Al Hayat,* translated in FBIS-NES-95-097, April 12, 1995.

7 Author's interview with Raghida Dirgham, March 24, 2003.

8 Russell Watson and Christopher Dickey, "Cracking the Conspiracy," *Newsweek,* February 20, 1995.

9 Anonymous, *Through Our Enemies Eyes,* pp. 140–141. "According to the Director of the Algerian Judicial Police, Mohamed Isouli, bin Laden was a sponsor of Algeria's Islamists—GLA and the Islamic Salvation Front—and helped them 'maintain a genuine network supplying arms and military equipment to the Algerian guerrillas.' "

10 Author's interview with Raghida Dirgham.

11 Joseph P. Fried, "After Five Months, Prosecution Rests in Terrorism Case," *New York Times,* June 28, 1995.

12 *U.S. v. Omar Abdel Rahman et al.,* January 30, 1995.

13 Ibid., February 6, 1995.

14 Ibid., July 26, 1995.

15 Ibid., July 27, 1995.

16 Joseph P. Fried, "Sheik and 9 Followers Guilty of a Conspiracy of Terrorism," *New York Times,* October 2, 1995.

17 Pat Milton, *In the Blink of an Eye: The FBI Investigation of TWA Flight 800* (New York: Random House, 1999), p. 209.

18 Reeve, *The New Jackals,* p. 250.

19 Author's interview with FBI Agent Len Predtechenskis (ret.), December 18, 2002.

20 Joseph P. Fried, "Sheik Sentenced to Life in Prison in Bombing Plot," *New York Times,* January 18, 1996.

21 Douglas Jehl, "Islamic Group Vows Revenge on Americans," *New York Times,* January 22, 1996.

22 James C. McKinley, "F.B.I. Arrests Man in Far East Charged in Plot to Bomb Planes," *New York Times,* December 13, 1995.

23 Author's interview with U.S. Postal Inspector Frank Gonzalez (ret.), January 3, 2003.

24 Greg Miller, Bob Drogin, and Sebastian Rotella, "Arrest Exposes Terrorist Network," *Los Angeles Times,* March 2, 2003.

25 David Johnston, "Major Catch, Critical Time," *New York Times,* March 2, 2003.

26 Tabassum Zakaria, "9/11—Bin Laden Vanished, but Al Qaeda Still Threat," Reuters, August 20, 2002.

27 Alaa Shahine, "Reporter: Al-Qaida Eyed Nuke Plants," Associated Press, September 8, 2002.

28 "The Plot," *60 Minutes II,* October 9, 2002.

29 Baluchi, Urdu, Arabic, and English. Bill Saporito and Tim McGirkk, "Architect of Terror," *Time,* March 1, 2003.

30 Christopher John Farley, "The Man Who Wasn't There," *Time,* February 20, 1995.

31 Miller, Drogin, and Rotella, "Arrest Exposes Terrorist Network."

32 In its final report the Joint Congressional Inquiry found that Mohammed was "a key al Qaeda leader" identified by the U.S. intelligence community as early as 1995, yet there was a failure "to recognize his growing importance in al Qaeda." In fact, the intelligence community "did not anticipate his involvement in a terrorist attack of September 11th's magnitude" even though intelligence about him had been collected over the previous six years. September 23, 2002.

33 Richard C. Paddock and Josh Meyer, "Suspect's Role in '95 Plot Detailed," *Los Angeles Times,* June 7, 2002.

34 Ibid.

35 Terry McDermott, "Early Scheme to Turn Jets Into Weapons," *Los Angeles Times,* June 24, 2002.

36 Terry McDermott, "Agents Saw Mohammed's Stamp Behind Many Plots," *Los Angeles Times,* March 2, 2002.

37 *U.S. v. Ramzi Ahmed Yousef et al.,* 1996; unsealed, January 1998.

38 Author's interview with Samuel Katz, October 1, 2002.

39 Bob Drogin and Josh Meyer, "Alleged 9/11 Mastermind Linked to Hamburg Cell," *Los Angeles Times,* June 6, 2002.

40 Gertz, *Breakdown,* pp. 55–56.

41 James Risen, "C.I.A.'s Inquiry on Qaeda Aide Seen as Flawed," *New York Times,* September 23, 2002.

42 Joint Inquiry Report, September 23, 2002.

43 *U.S. v. Osama bin Laden et al.,* February 6, 2001.

44 Daniel Benjamin, Steven Simon, *The Age of Sacred Terror,* p. 41.

45 *U.S. v. Osama bin Laden et al.,* February 6, 2001.

46 Drogin and Meyer, "Alleged 9/11 Mastermind Linked to Hamburg Cell."

47 Erick Eckholm, "Pakistanis Arrest Qaeda Figure Seen as Planner of 9/11," *New York Times,* March 2, 2003.

32. THE BOMB MAKER AND THE MADE GUY

1 Christopher S. Wren, "Plot of Terror in the Skies Is Outlined by a Prosecutor," *New York Times,* May 30, 1996.

2 *U.S. v. Ramzi Ahmed Yousef et al.,* May 29, 1996.

3 Ibid., May 30, 1996.

4 Ibid.

5 Ibid., June 12, 1996.

6 Ibid., June 18, 1996.

7 Ibid., June 24, 1996.

8 Ibid., August 9, 1996.

9 Lawrence Wright, "The Counter-Terrorist," *The New Yorker,* June 1, 2002.

10 "The Man Who Knew," *Frontline.*

11 Jerry Capeci, "Mobster Gets 40-Year Term," *New York Daily News,* May 9, 1999.

12 Author's interview with Steven Legon, January 20, 2003.

13 Greg B. Smith, "FBI's Chilling Terror Leads on '96 Tapes," *New York Daily News,* January 21, 2002.

14 In the FBI documents relating to the Scarpa undercover operation Bojinka was spelled "Bojinga."

15 Smith, "FBI's Chilling Terror Leads on '96 Tapes."

16 Greg B. Smith, "Terrorist Called Pals on Feds Line," *New York Daily News,* September 24, 2000.

17 Smith, "FBI's Chilling Terror Leads on '96 Tapes."

18 Author's interview with Bernie Kleinman, February 3, 2003.

19 Ibid.

20 Author's interview with Steven Legon.

21 Author's interview with confidential source.

22 See discussion of Appeal decision in Epilogue.

23 Author's interview with confidential source.

33. SHUT IT DOWN

1 Pat Milton, *In the Blink of an Eye: The FBI Investigation of TWA Flight 800.*

2 Paul Gray, "The Search for Sabotage: Investigators Find Possible Evidence That TWA 800 Was Blown Up," *Time,* August 5, 1996.

3 Christine Negroni, "Six Months Later, Still No Answer to TWA Flight 800 Mystery," CNN.com, January 17, 1997.

4 "FBI: Bomb 'less likely' as TWA 800 Crash Cause," CNN.com, November 20, 1996.

5 *In the Blink of an Eye,* p. 219.

6 Ibid., pp. 110, 338.

7 Ibid., p. 210.

8 *U.S. v. Ramzi Ahmed Yousef et al.,* July 18, 1996; Christopher S. Wren, "Judge to Ask Bomb Trial Jury About Prejudice from Crash," *New York Times,* July 23, 1996.

9 Reed Irvine and Cliff Kincaid, "Revealed—Shrapnel Was Found in 89 TWA 800 Victims," *Accuracy in Media.* www.aim.org/publications/media_monitors, June 10, 2002.

10 In her ambitious examination of the TWA 800 crash *In the Blink of an Eye,* reporter Pat Milton explained that "In theory, the NTSB investigation would remain open until a probable cause was identified or new evidence appeared to suggest the cause was criminal. The NTSB now accepted as a given that Flight 800's center fuel tank exploded after a spark was introduced to ignite its volatile vapors. But where had the spark come from?" As of the publication date of Milton's book, the Safety Board was "still studying Flight 800's wires trying to determine if and how a spark or surge of high-voltage energy from a high-voltage wire could have entered the tank through low voltage wiring in the fuel-quantity indicating system that leads into the tank," pp. 338–339.

11 *U.S. v. Ramzi Ahmed Yousef et al.,* August 15, 1996.

12 Author's interview with Supervisory Special Agent in Charge Kenneth Maxwell (ret.), March 29, 2003.

13 Author's interview with confidential source, April 18, 2003.

14 Milton, p. 182.

15 Ibid., p. 210.

16 "As he became convinced that a mechanical failure caused the tank to explode [Dr. Bernard] Loeb [the NTSB's Director of Aviation Safety] became irritated, even angered, by the FBI's frequent statements about not ruling out a missile or bomb. The FBI, he felt, seemed to be perpetuating the notion that terrorism had taken out the plane." Ibid., p. 250.

17 Serge F. Kovaleski, "A Massive Probe, a Grinding Pace: Hundreds of Agents Around Globe Seek to Unravel Mystery of TWA Plane Crash," *Washington Post,* August 6, 1996; Don Phillips, "Blast Has Had Effect on Airline Procedures," *Washington Post,* July 14, 1997.

18 Miller, *The Cell,* p. 170.

19 *U.S. v. Ramzi Ahmed Yousef et al.,* September 5, 1996.

20 Christopher S. Wren, "Jury Convicts 3 in a Conspiracy to Bomb Airliners," *New York Times,* September 6, 1996.

21 Benjamin, *The Age of Sacred Terror,* pp. 237–238.

34. INGENIOUS, DIABOLICAL, AND RUTHLESS

1 "The Trail of Terror," *New York Times,* September 6, 1996.

2 Ibid.

3 Ibid.

4 Author's interview with PNP Col. Rodolfo B. Mendoza, April 19, 2001.

5 *U.S. v. Ramzi Ahmed Yousef et al.,* August 6, 1996.

6 Joint Inquiry Report, September 18, 2002, p. 11.

7 Author's interview with Harry Ellen, February 25, 2003.

8 Mark Flatten, "FBI Entanglement Blocks Charity's Efforts in Gaza," *East Valley Tribune,* July 30, 2001.

9 Letters of endorsement for Harry Ellen (Abu Yusef) from Shoeil Juma al-Gool, September 21, 1999, and Major General Mahmoud Abu Marzoug, Director General of Civil Defense Palestinian National Authority, October 20, 1999.

10 Mark Flatten, "A World of Intrigue: Valley Couple Take on FBI in Tale of Espionage, Betrayal, Romance"; "Documents, Letters Back Fantastic Story of Intrigue," *East Valley Tribune,* July 29, 2001. Ibid.

11 Dana Priest and Richard Leiby, "Phoenix FBI Agent Accused of Naming Terrorism Informant," *Washington Post,* May 24, 2002.

12 Gertz, *Breakdown,* pp. 84–85.

13 Author's interview with Harry Ellen, February 25, 2003.

14 Author's interview with Mark Flatten, February 26, 2003.

15 Author's conversation with Phil Edney of the FBI's Office of Public Affairs, May 8, 2003, in response to a letter requesting an interview with Williams sent to Rex S. Taub, Unit Chief of the Public Affairs Office on April 11, 2003.

16 Mark Flatten, "Could We Have Stopped Attacks? Hindsight Reveals McVeigh, Hanjour Left Clues in Arizona," *East Valley Tribune,* October 14, 2001.

17 Mark Flatten, "Sept. 11 Answers Lurk in Arizona," *East Valley Tribune,* May 26, 2002. "Author of Memo Trained in Valley." Ibid., September 25, 2001.

18 Author's interview with Kris Kolesnik, March 4, 2003.

19 Bill Saporito and Tim McGirkk, "Architect of Terror."

35. RECONNAISSANCE

1 Author's interview with Jacob L. Boesen, September 13, 2002.

2 Ibid., September 14, 2002.

3 Associated Press, May 22, 1997; http://www.pbs.org/wgbh/pages/frontline/shows/knew/etc/cron.html.

4 John Sullivan, "Jury Examines Whether Saudi Contributed to Terrorists Groups," *New York Times,* July 17, 1997.

5 *Frontline,* Hunting bin Laden. http://www.pbs.org/wgbh/pages/frontline/shows/binladen/bombings/warnings.html.

6 On September 15, 1998, six years to the day after El-Hage's friend Mahmud Abouhalima had been subpoenaed by the Feds, he testified before a second grand jury. This time after testifying that he didn't know Osama bin Laden, for whom he'd worked as secretary, he was arrested and charged with perjury. *Frontline,* "Portrait of Wadih El-Hage," http://www.pbs.org/wgbh/pages/frontline/shows/binladen/upclose/elhage.html.

7 Shahine, "Reporter: Al-Qaida Eyed Nuke Plants."

8 Brian Ross, "Preparing for Terror? 1997 Al Qaeda Tape Shows World Trade Center and Other Landmarks," ABCNews.com, March 3, 2003.

9 Andy Soltis, "WTC VID Reveals Planning of Attack," *New York Post,* March 4, 2003.

10 Al Goodman, "Al Qaeda Suspect Filmed WTC," CNN.com, July 16, 2002.

11 Peter Slevin and Walter Pincus, "Attacks Studied Mistakes in Previous Assaults," *Washington Post,* September 13, 2001.

12 David Johnston, "Report Criticizes Scientific Testing at F.B.I. Crime Lab," *New York Times,* April 16, 1997.

13 Benjamin Weiser, "Bomb Trial Judge Tries to Put the Jury at Ease," *New York Times,* August 10, 1997.

14 Benjamin Weiser, "As Trade Center Smoldered, Suspect Watched, Jury Hears," *New York Times*, October 23, 1997.

15 "Prosecutor Argues Yousef Wanted to Kill Thousands: Trade Center Bomb Called Twisted . . . Protest," Reuters, November 4, 1997; Benjamin Weiser, Prosecutor Urges Jury to Convict 2 in Trade Center Bombing," *New York Times*, November 4, 1997.

16 Benjamin Weiser, " 'Mastermind' and Bomber Found Guilty in 1993 Plot to Blow Up Trade Center," *New York Times*, November 13, 1997.

17 www.forensicdentistryonline.com.

18 According to a report by the Congressional Research Service (CRS), Refa'i Taha Musa, the head of the al Gamm'a Islamiya, "serves in [Osama] bin Laden's inner circle as his top lieutenants." Kenneth Katzman, "Terrorism: Near Eastern Groups and State Sponsors 2001," September 10, 2001.

19 Ibid.

20 *U.S. v. Ramzi Ahmed Yousef,* S1293 CR.180 (KTD), January 8, 1998.

21 Author's interview with Eve Bucca, July 16, 2002.

22 Sharon Walsh, " 'Proud' Terrorist Gets 240 Years in N.Y. Bombing," *Washington Post*, January 9, 1998. Larry Neumeister, " 'Apostle of evil' Terrorist Sentenced to Life in Prison," Associated Press, January 9, 1998. Benjamin Weiser, *New York Times*, January 9, 1998.

36. THE DRUMS GET LOUDER

1 Matthew Brezinski, "Bust and Boom," *Washington Post*, December 30, 2001.

2 Joint Inquiry Statement of Staff Director Eleanor Hill, October 8, 2002, p. 16.

3 Gary M. Stern, "Big Apples Blues." *Government Executive Magazine*, May 1, 1999.

4 *U.S. v. Wadih El Hage et al.,* October 7, 1998.

5 *U.S. v. Osama bin Laden,* June, 1998, unsealed November 1998.

6 U.S. Department of State, http://usinfo.state.gov/topical/pol/terror/99129502.htm; Alexander and Swetnam, *Osama bin Laden's al Qaeda: Profile of a Terrorist Network,* Appendix B, p. 1.

7 Steve Fainaru, "Clues Pointed to Changing Terrorist Tactics," *Washington Post*, May 19, 2002.

8 Joint Inquiry Report, September 24, 2002, p. 3; testimony of FBI Director Robert M. Mueller before the Senate Judiciary Committee.

9 Ibid.

10 Joint Inquiry. CNNcom/interactive/us/0205/intelligence.timeline/content..1..html.

11 Gertz, *Breakdown,* p. 17.

12 Miller, *The Cell,* p. 201.

13 Tim Weiner, "Man with a Mission Takes On the U.S. at Far-Flung Sites," *New York Times*, August 21, 1998.

14 *U.S. v. Wadih El-Hage et al.,* October 7, 1998.

15 "The Man Who Knew," *Frontline.*

16 Miller, pp. 140–143.

17 Emerson, *American Jihad,* p. 58.

18 Alexander and Swetnam, *Osama bin Laden's al Qaida: Profile of a Terrorist Network,* p. 39.

19 Author's interview with retired intelligence official.

20 *U.S. v. Osama bin Laden,* June, 1998, unsealed November 1998.

21 Mylroie, *The War Against America.*
22 Author's interview with Richard Swick, December 17, 2002.
23 Author's interview with Diane Bodner Duhig, December 20, 2002.
24 Author's interview with Len Predtechenskis, June 1, 2003.
25 Author's interview with FBI ADIC William A. Gavin (ret.), June 15, 2003.
26 Author's interview with Nancy Floyd, January 8, 2003.
27 Ibid.
28 Author's interview with Len Predtechenskis (ret.), January 10, 2003.

37. AN EGYPTIAN MOLE IN THE FDNY?

1 Author's interview with former Chief Fire Marshal Mike Vecchi, now the FDNY's chief of staff, April 1, 2003.
2 Author's interview with Captain Mike Byrne, FDNY (ret.), August 26, 2002.
3 Ronnie Bucca, *Chronology of Terrorism Incidents and Anniversary Dates,* Week of November 9–15, 1998.
4 Author's interview with Jacob L. Boesen, September 14, 2002.
5 "The Plot," *60 Minutes II,* October 9, 2002; *The Cell,* pp. 241–254.
6 David Kocieniewski, "Leader Arises for Top Post in State Police," *New York Times,* July 30, 1999.
7 Ibid.
8 Stephen Barr, "From Justice Dept. to Jersey, by Way of ATF," *Washington Post,* November 4, 1999. According to the *Post* story, Dunbar was legally able to hold both the state and federal job because of the little known Intergovernmental Personnel Act (IPA), which allows federal employees to take temporary appointments at state agencies, colleges, and think tanks. At the time, 450 federal workers were taking advantage of the program. But Dunbar's job switch, "which drew a few grumbles at ATF," according to the *Post,* was made possible via the personal intervention of Attorney General Janet Reno.
9 Author's interview with Firefighter Tony Tedeschi, Rescue One, July 30, 2002.
10 Bureau of Fire Investigation "face sheet" reports on Ahmed Amin Refai, August 26–September 1, 1999.
11 Author's interview with Fire Marshal Mel Hazel FDNY (ret.), July 18 and September 20, 2002.
12 Author's interviews with FDNY Assistant Deputy Commissioner Kay Woods, July 30, 2002; Mel Hazel, July 18 and September 20, 2002; and Fire Marshal Bobby Greene, July 16 and 30, 2002.
13 Jim Hickey, report on arrest of Mohammed Salameh, *ABC News,* March 4, 1993.
14 Author's interview with Mel Hazel, July 18, 2002.
15 Author's interview with Eve Bucca, February 28, 2003.

38. THE LOST CHANCE IN MALAYSIA

1 "The Man Who Knew," *Frontline.*
2 Khalid Shaikh's participation in the meeting was reported by Maria Ressa, Manila Bureau Chief for CNN, and Yosri Foudra, the al Jazeera reporter who actually interviewed Khalid Shaikh and Ramzi Binalshibh in the summer of 2002. Foudra and Fielding *Masterminds of Terror: The Truth Behind the Most Devastating Terrorist Attacks the World Has Ever Seen,* pp. 129–130.

3 Joint Inquiry Staff Statement, October 8, 2002, p. 22.
4 Michael Isikoff and Daniel Klaidman, "The 9/11 Terrorists the CIA Should Have Caught," *Newsweek,* June 10, 2002. Curt Anderson, "FBI Informant Knew 9/11 Hijackers," Associated Press, July 21, 2003.
5 Author's interview with Supervising Fire Marshal James Kelty, June 21, 2002.
6 Wright, "The Counter Terrorist."
7 *U.S. v. Ahmed Abdel Sattar et al.,* April 30, 2002.
8 After 9/11 Laurie Mylroie, a scholar with the American Enterprise Institute, republished her earlier work *A Study in Revenge* as *The War Against America: Saddam Hussein and the World Trade Center Attacks.* In it she continued to maintain that Saddam Hussein was the primary force behind the al Qaeda–directed attacks. The foreword of the second version was written by former CIA Director Woolsey, who on September 27, 2001, wrote of the 9/11 attack, "as of today Usama bin Laden appears to have been involved, but a key question remains: Did he and his network act alone? . . . The central argument of this brilliant and brave book is that the Iraqi government was key in the planning and implementation of that attack and, more specifically, that Ramzi Yousef was himself an Iraqi intelligence agent."
9 Wright, "The Counter Terrorist."
10 Associated Press, "FBI Agents Are Leaving Cole Probe in Yemen. Progress Is Cited in Investigation, *Washington Post,* November 18, 2000.
11 Joint Inquiry Staff Statement, October 8, 2002, p. 22.
12 *Military News,* www.mdw.army.mil/news/contingency_planning.html.
13 Joint Inquiry Staff Statement summarizing the National Commission on Terrorism's Report, October 3, 2002, p. 5.
14 Michael Elliott, "Could 9/11 Have Been Prevented?" *Time,* August 4, 2002; ibid., "How the U.S. Missed the Clues," May 27, 2002.
15 *Frontline,* http://www.pbs.org/wgbh/pages/frontline/shows/knew/etc /cron.html.
16 CNNcom/interactive/us/0205/intelligence.timeline/ content..1..html.
17 Jim Yardly and Jo Thomas, "For Agent in Phoenix, the Cause of Many Frustrations Extended to His Own Office," *New York Times,* June 19, 2002.
18 Accuracy in Media, http://www.aim.org/publications/aim_report/2002/09.html.
19 *U.S. v. Osama bin Laden,* February 6, 2001.
20 Joint Inquiry Staff Statement, September 24, 2002.
21 *U.S. v. Osama bin Laden et al.,* February 14, 2001; Alexander and Swetnam, *Usama bin Laden's al-Qaida: Profile of a Terrorist Network,* p. 51.
22 Joint Inquiry Staff Statement, September 18, 2002, p. 16.
23 Miller, *The Cell,* p. 287.
24 CNNcom/interactive/us/0205/intelligence.timeline/ content..1..html.
25 Statement of FBI Director Robert S. Mueller III before the Joint Inquiry, September 25, 2002.
26 Flatten, "Could We Have Stopped Attacks? Hindsight reveals McVeigh, Hanjour Left Clues in Arizona."
27 Author's interview with Harry Ellen, February 25, 2003.
28 Josh Meyer, "Suspected Mastermind of Cole Bombing Held," *Los Angeles Times,* May 1, 2002, p. A-2. Joint Inquiry Staff Statement, October 8, 2002, p. 22.
29 Joint Inquiry Staff Statement, September 20, 2002; Gertz, *Breakdown,* p. 305.
30 Ibid., October 8, 2002, p. 22.
31 Author's interview with confidential source.

32 *Frontline,* http://www.pbs.org/wgbh/pages/frontline/shows/knew/etc/cron.html; Elliott, "Could 9/11 Have Been Prevented?"
33 CNN.com/interactive/us/0205/intelligence.timeline/ content..1..html.
34 Barton Gellman, "Before Sept. 11, Unshared Clues and Unshaped Policy," *Washington Post,* May 17, 2002.
35 Ibid., CNN.com/interactive.
36 Elliott, "How the U.S. Missed the Clues."
37 Her admission took place at a White House press briefing on May 16, 2002.
38 Gellman, "Before Sept. 11, Unshared Clues and Unshaped Policy."
39 Ibid., CNN.com/interactive.
40 Gertz, *Breakdown,* p. 83.
41 Joint Inquiry Staff Statement, September 24, 2002.

39. "SOMEDAY SOMEONE WILL DIE"

1 Elliott, "Could 9/11 Have Been Prevented?"
2 Ibid.
3 Benjamin Weiser, "The Terror Verdict: The Organization; Trial Poked Holes in Image of bin Laden's Terror Group," *New York Times,* May 31, 2001.
4 Larry C. Johnson, "The Declining Terrorist Threat," *New York Times* op-ed page, July 10, 2001.
5 "Ashcroft Flying High," CBSNews.com, July 26, 2001.
6 Miller, p. 293.
7 Kate Clark, "Revealed: The Taliban Minister, the U.S. Envoy, and the Warning of September 11 That Was Ignored," *London Independent,* September 7, 2002.
8 Elliott, Ibid.
9 "The Man Who Knew," *Frontline.*
10 Wright, "The Counter Terrorist."
11 Elliott, "How the U.S. Missed the Clues."
12 Joint Inquiry Staff Statement, October 17, 2002.
13 Ibid.
14 Title 50 U.S. Code Chapter 36, Subchapter I Section 1801. Such warrants are granted by a special series of judges when sufficient evidence is presented to establish probable cause that a group is "engaged in international terrorism or activities in preparation thereof."
15 Joint Inquiry Staff Statement, October 17, 2002, p. 17.
16 In the absence of Moussaoui's consent, the FBI agents had to obtain a search warrant to examine the contents of the briefcase. Since the matter involved a foreign national and potential issues of international terrorism, the warrant application had to be processed via a special protocol under the Foreign Intelligence Surveillance Act. (See footnote 14.)
17 Joint Inquiry Staff Statement, October 17, 2002, p. 19.
18 Ibid., September 24, 2002, p. 20.
19 In 2001 President Bush received a daily intelligence briefing memo known as the PDB (Presidential Daily Briefing). Compiled of information from the major intelligence agencies, the memo informed Mr. Bush about a host of international issues. A White House deputy press secretary offered details about the PDB during a media briefing on May 31, 2002. www.usinfo.state.gov/regional/nea/sasia/text/0531wths.htm.

20 Bob Woodward and Dan Eggen, "Aug. Memo Warned of Attacks Within U.S. Bush Frustrated by Lack of Fresh Information," *Washington Post,* May 18, 2002.
21 Ibid. "In one brief mention, sources said, the memo noted that unconfirmed information from British intelligence in 1998 showed that al Qaeda members talked about using an airline hijacking to negotiate the release of imprisoned Muslim cleric Sheik Omar Abdel Rahman, who had been convicted of plotting to blow up New York City landmarks."
22 Greg Miller, "Blunders Numerous Before 9/11," *Los Angeles Times,* September 21, 2002.
23 Yosri Foudra and Nick Fielding, *Masterminds of Terror: The Truth Behind the Most Devastating Terrorist Attacks the World Has Ever Seen* (New York: Arcade Publishing, 2003), p. 140.
24 "Omar Abdel-Rahman Taliban's likely choice," *Frontier Post,* September 10, 2001; Clark, "Revealed: The Taliban Minister, the U.S. Envoy, and the Warning of September 11 That Was Ignored."
25 Miller, p. 293.
26 John Cloud, "The Plot Comes into Focus," *Time,* October 1, 2001.
27 Pat Wingert, Michael Isikoff, and Daniel Klaidman, "Cracking the Terror Code," *Newsweek,* October 15, 2001.
28 Author's interview with Supervising Fire Marshal Jimmy Devery (ret.), June 21, 2002.
29 Author's interview with Fire Marshal Andy DiFusco, June 23, 2002.
30 Author's interview with Jimmy Devery.
31 Jim Dwyer and Ford Fessenden, "Lost Voices of Firefighters, Some on the 78th Floor," *New York Times,* August 4, 2002. Portions of the tape were played for some of the families of FDNY firefighters who battled the South Tower blaze. But the transcripts of the emotionally charged broadcasts have been ordered sealed by the Justice Department so as not to jeopardize pending 9/11-related prosecutions.
32 Slevin and Pincus, "Attacks Studied Mistakes in Previous Assaults."
33 Arthur M. Langer and Roger G. Morse, "The World Trade Center Catastrophe: Was the Type of Spray Fire Proofing a Factor in the Collapse of the Twin Towers?" *Indoor+ Built Environment,* 2001: 10, pp. 350–360.
34 Vincent Dunn, Deputy Chief, FDNY (ret.), "Why the World Trade Center Buildings Collapsed: A Fire Chiefs Assessment." http://www.vincentdunn.com.
35 Jim Dwyer, Eric Lipton, Kevin Flynn, James Glanz, and Ford Fessenden, "Fighting to Live as the Towers Died," *New York Times,* May 26, 2002; "Study Faults Bolts in WTC Collapse," Associated Press, October 27, 2002.

40. THE BLACK HOLE

1 Dwyer and Fessenden, "Lost Voices of Firefighters, Some on the 78th Floor."
2 "Report from Ground Zero," *ABC News* special, September 11, 2002.
3 Author's interview with Fire Marshal Keith O'Mara, August 1, 2002.
4 Author's interview with Firefighter Tony Tedeschi, July 30, 2002.
5 Author's interview with Supervising Fire Marshal Jimmy Kelty, June 21, 2002.
6 Author's interview with Firefighter Tony Tedeschi.
7 "Report from Ground Zero."
8 Author's interview with Detective Bill Ryan, January 10, 2003.
9 Author's interview with Fire Marshal Bobby Greene, July 17, 2002.
10 One of the options FDNY pensioners have is for their checks to go to their widows if

they die. Refai had reportedly selected that option when he filed his retirement papers earlier in the year, but had not provided sufficient information about his spouse; author's interview with Bobby Greene.

11 *U.S. v. Ahmed Abdel Sattar et al.,* April 9, 2002.

12 On February 25, 2002, Byrne was named Regional Homeland Security Coordinator for Washington, D.C.; Associated Press, "Former NYC Firefighter to Coordinate DC Homeland Security," CBS2.com, February 25, 2003.

13 Author's interview with Fire Marshal Bobby Greene, January 6, 2003.

14 Author's interview with Detective Lou Napoli, January 10, 2003.

15 Author's conversation with FBI Agent Tom Callaghan, January 8, 2003.

16 Author's interview with Kay Woods, May 27, 2003.

17 Author's interview with confidential FDNY source, June 10, 2003.

18 Author's conversation with FBI media spokesman Joseph Valiquette, April 15, 2003.

41. OPERATION IRAQI FREEDOM TWO

1 Author's interview with PNP Col. Rodolfo B. Mendoza, April 19, 2002.

2 As previously noted, the PNP had given the U.S. authorities a list with the names of ten men who Murad admitted were engaged in U.S. flight training at the time of his interrogation between January and March of 1995 (Jim Gomez and John Solomon, "Authorities Warned of Hijack Risks," Associated Press, March 3, 2002). In 1996 FBI agents questioned officials at two of Murad's flight schools, but the investigation was unexplainably dropped (Steve Fainaru and James V. Grimaldi, "FBI Knew Terrorists Were Using Flight Schools," *Washington Post,* September 23, 2001).

3 Stephen Barr, "Executive Notes: From Justice Department to Jersey, by Way of ATF," *Washington Post,* November 9, 1999.

4 fbi.gov/libref/executives/damuro.htm.

5 Philip Shenon, "Lawmakers Say Misstatements Cloud F.B.I. Chief's Credibility," *New York Times,* May 31, 2002.

6 Fainaru and Grimaldi, "FBI Knew Terrorists Were Using Flight Schools."

7 Remarks prepared for delivery by Robert S. Mueller at the Commonwealth Club, April 19, 2002.

8 David Johnston "FBI Says Pre-Sept. 11 Call for Inquiry Got Little Notice," *New York Times,* May 9, 2002; "FBI Director's Comments," *New York Times,* May 31, 2002; Statement for the Record of Robert S. Mueller, III, Director Federal Bureau of Investigation on FBI Reorganization Before the Senate Committee on the Judiciary, May 8, 2002. Note: the remarks quoted were not contained in Mueller's prepared text, but came during questioning by the Committee members.

9 Letter from Coleen Rowley, FBI Minneapolis to Robert S. Mueller III, FBI Director, May 21, 2002.

10 Philip Shenon, "Traces of Terrorism: The Warnings," *New York Times,* May 18, 2002.

11 Author's interview with FBI ADIC William A. Gavin (ret.), June 15, 2003.

12 Author's interview with Jim Roth, May 30, 2003.

13 Author's interview with confidential source, April 4, 2003.

14 Joint Inquiry Staff Statement October 1, 2002, pp. 8–9.

15 Josh Meyer, "FBI Falls Short in Assessing Threats to U.S., Report Finds," *Los Angeles Times,* October 2, 2002.

16 Eric Lichtblau and Charles Piller, "War on Terrorism Highlights FBI's Computers

Woes," *Los Angeles Times*, July 28, 2002; Richard B. Schmitt, "FBI's Computer Upgrade Develops Its Own Glitches," *Los Angeles Times*, January 28, 2003.

17 Philip Shenon, "Threats and Responses: A Whistleblower Agent Who Saw 9/11 Lapses Still Faults F.B.I. on Terror," *New York Times*, March 6, 2003; "F.B.I. Agent's Warning," Letter from Coleen Rowley to FBI Director Robert S. Mueller III, *New York Times*, March 6, 2003.

18 Bob Woodward, *Bush at War* (New York: Simon & Schuster, 2002), p. 83.

19 Walter Pincus, "Report Casts Doubt on Iraq–Al Qaeda Connection," *Washington Post*, June 22, 2003.

20 Josh Meyer, "Al Qaeda Feared to Have 'Dirty Bombs,'" *Los Angeles Times*, February 8, 2003.

21 Press Release, "Agency Actions in Response to the National Elevated Alert Level," U.S. Department of Homeland Security, February 7, 2003.

22 John J. Lumpkin, "No Need to Panic Over Alerts," *Associated Press*, February 14, 2003.

23 Richard Simon, "Bush Urges Americans to Be Alert, Stay Calm," *Los Angeles Times*, February 16, 2003.

24 Doyle McManus and Robin Wright, "Is War Necessary? Why Now? Who Agrees?" *Los Angeles Times*, February 16, 2003.

25 Ibid.

26 Remarks of Secretary of State Colin Powell before the UN Security Council, February 5, 2003.

27 Brian Ross, "Weak Link? Radical Islamic Leader Denies Powell's Link Between Al Qaeda and Iraq," ABCNews.com, February 5, 2003.

28 Patterns of Global Terrorism, www.fas.org/irp/threat/terror.

29 "Leaked report rejects Iraqi al-Qaeda link," BBC.com, February 5, 2003.

30 Wafa Amr, "Iraqis Say Anarchy Could Lead to Anti-U.S. Violence," Reuters, May 16, 2003.

31 Neela Banerjee, "Iraq to Import Gasoline from U.S.," *New York Times*, May 7, 2003.

32 Craig S. Smith, "Iraqi Shiites, Jockeying for Power, Preach an Anti-American Sermon," *New York Times*, May 20, 2003.

33 "Doctors Protest Conditions and U.S. Appointee," *Reuters*, May 8, 2003.

34 Patrick Tyler, "Hussein Loyalists Rise Again, Enraging Iraqis," *New York Times*, May 9, 2003.

35 James Dao and Eric Schmitt, "President Picks a Special Envoy to Rebuild Iraq," *New York Times*, May 7, 2003.

36 Alissa J. Rubin and Michael Slackman, "Official Shakes Up Iraq Effort," *Los Angeles Times*, May 11, 2003; Terry Ganey, "U.S. Diplomat Forced Out of Baghdad," *Santa Barbara News Press*, May 11, 2003.

37 Eric Slater, "Death Shadows U.S. Troops in Iraq," *Los Angeles Times*, May 10, 2003; "U.S. Marines Killed in Helicopter Crash," Reuters, May 19, 2003; U.S. Soldier Killed in Ordnance Accident," Associated Press, May 20, 2003; Edmund L. Andrews, "Once Hailed, Soldiers in Iraq Now Feel Blame at Each Step," *New York Times*, June 29, 2003.

38 Monica Davey, "As the Fighting Continues, Some Back Home Wonder 'Why Are People Dying?'" *New York Times*, June 2, 2003.

39 Greg Miller and Terry McDermott, "U.S. Defends Its Role in Iraq," *Los Angeles Times*, July 1, 2003.

40 Reuters, "There Was No Hussein Bunker, CBS Reports," *Los Angeles Times*, May 28,

2003. "Australian Paper Obtains Tape Purportedly Made by Hussein," *Los Angeles Times*, May 8, 2003. Douglas Jehl and David Johnston, "Hussein Is Probably Alive in Iraq, U.S. Experts Say," *New York Times*, June 19, 2003.

41 Dexter Filkins, "Hussein's Son Took $1 Billion Just Before War, Bank Aide Says," *New York Times*, May 6, 2003.

42 Paul Richter and Warren Vieth, "Hussein Clan May Have a Billion Ways to Foment Unrest," *Los Angeles Times*, May 7, 2003.

43 Josh Hendren, "Dangerous Loot South of Baghdad," *Los Angeles Times*, May 22, 2003.

44 David Streitfeld and Mark Fineman, "Bechtel Lands Iraq Contract," *Los Angeles Times*, April 18, 2003.

45 Elizabeth Becker, "Details Given on Contract Haliburton Was Awarded," *New York Times*, April 11, 2003.

46 "Shadow over the Oil Fields," *New York Times*, April 18, 2003.

47 Barton Gellman, "Frustrated, U.S. Arms Team to Leave Iraq," *Washington Post*, May 11, 2003.

48 Melinda Liu, Rod Nordland, and Evan Thomas, "The Saddam Files," *Newsweek*, April 28, 2003.

49 James Risen, "Captives Deny Qaeda Worked with Baghdad," *New York Times*, June 9, 2003.

50 "Graham Just Hints at Impeachment," Reuters. *Los Angeles Times*, July 18, 2003.

51 Steven R. Weisman and Neil Macfarquhar, "Powell, in Riyadh, Sees Signs of Al Qaeda in Series of Explosions," *New York Times*, May 14, 2003; Chris Plante, "U.S. Suspects al Qaeda in Morocco Bombings," CNN.com, May 18, 2003.

52 Josh Meyer, "Al Qaeda May Be Back, and Stronger," *Los Angeles Times*, May 14, 2003.

53 "FBI Warns of Possible Attacks in U.S.," Associated Press, May 20, 2003.

54 Associated Press, "U.S. Examining Quality of Intelligence," *New York Times*, May 22, 2003.

55 Josh Meyer and John Goetz, "War With Iraq; Qatar's Security Chief Suspected of Having Ties to Al Qaeda; interior minister reportedly sheltered terrorists, including 9/11 plotter. U.S. military campaign's headquarters are in the Gulf nation's capital." *Los Angeles Times*, March 28, 2003.

56 Privileged and Confidential Attorney Work Product Memorandum to: OGH From (name redacted), December 5, 1995, Re: Investigation into Terrorism.

57 Author's interview with confidential Senate source.

58 "Report of the Joint Inquiry into the Terrorist Attacks of September 11, 2001—by the House Permanent Select Committee on Intelligence and the Senate Select Committee on Intelligence," p. 3; David Johnston, "Report of 9/11 Panel Cites Lapses by CIA and FBI," *New York Times*, July 25, 2003; John Yaukey, "U.S. Missed 9/11 Warning Signs," Gannett, July 25, 2003.

59 Editorial, "Undercutting the 9/11 Inquiry," *New York Times*, March 31, 2003.

60 Philip Shenon, "9/11 Commission Says U.S. Agenices Slow Its Inquiry," *New York Times*, July 8, 2003.

61 Editorial, "Undercutting the 9/11 Inquiry," *New York Times*, March 31, 2003.

EPILOGUE

1 Eve Bucca, *New York Daily News* op-ed piece, September 5, 2002; Steve Dunleavy, "9/11 Widow Won't Let Bravest Get Axed," *New York Post*, January 13, 2003.

2 Author's interview with Supervising Fire Marshal Jimmy Kelty, April 5, 2003.

3 "Coalition building camp for Iraqi POWS," CNN.com, March 29, 2003.

4 *U.S. v. Ramzi Ahmed Yousef et al.,* U.S. Court of Appeals for the Second Circuit, August Term 2001, Docket Number 98-1041 L.

5 Given his extraordinary insight into Osama bin Laden and the al Qaeda network—at least as it was configured up until he was imprisoned in the late 90s—one would think that Yousef would be a ripe prospect for interrogation; especially given the fact that he faces life imprisonment in solitary. Yet his two lawyers say that other than his visit by the two FBI agents on 9/11, federal prosecutors have never approached them to even inquire about whether Yousef would agree to become a cooperating witness. Author's interviews with Bernie Kleinman, February 3, 2003, and Steve Legon, January 20, 2003.

6 David Johnston with Don Van Natta Jr. "U.S. Officials See Signs of a Revived Al Qaeda," *New York Times,* May 16, 2003.

A NOTE ON SOURCES

1 Pete Yost, "FBI Unit Probes Intercepted Package Case," *Washington Post,* April 23, 2003.

2 Associated Press, "AP Protests Government Seizure of Package Sent From One Reporter to Another," May 13, 2003.

Appendix I: FBI 302
Re: Interrogation of Abdul Hakim Murad,
May 11, 1995

FEDERAL BUREAU OF INVESTIGATION

Date of transcription   5/11/95

On 4/13/95, SA's Francis J. Pellegrino and Thomas G.
Donlon, conducted an interview of ABDUL HAKIM ALI, AKA ABDUL
HAKIM ALI HASHEM MURAD. MURAD was interviewed as he was being
transported from Manila, Philippines to New York as a result of a
sealed indictment issued by the United Stated Federal District
Court for the Southern District of New York. The indictment of
MURAD charged him with Title 18 USC Section 32 Conspiracy to
Destroy U.S. Civil Aircraft. MURAD was advised of the identities
of the interviewing agents and the purpose of the interview.
MURAD was read his rights in English and stated that he
understood. MURAD then read his advise of rights in both English
and Arabic and again stated that he understood. MURAD then signed
the waivers of his rights, witnessed by the interviewing agents.
MURAD agreed to speak to the interviewing agents and provided the
following information in English.

MURAD advised that he arrived in Manila, Philippines on
December 26, 1994, aboard Singapore Airlines which originated in
Dubai, U.A.E., with a stopover in Singapore before arriving in
Manila. MURAD advised that he had received a call in Dubai from
RAMZI YOUSEF (AKA ABDUL BASIT MAHMOUD ABDUL KARIM) in the
beginning of December, 1994. MURAD stated that he was living with
his uncle, SULIMAN AHMED, in Qassais, a small community in Dubai.
Since his uncle does not have a telephone at his residence, the
call came from RAMZI into his neighbors phone, JUMA MURAD (no
relation). MURAD stated that RAMZI requested his presence in the
Philippines without fully elaborating on the purpose, however,
MURAD believed that he would be travelling to the Philippines to
participate in a bombing. MURAD advised that RAMZI sent him
$1,200 to buy the airline ticket.

MURAD stated that he knew that RAMZI was responsible
for the World Trade Center bombing and that he was wanted by the
U.S. authorities. MURAD stated that he had been with RAMZI during
August, 1994, at which time RAMZI was staying at the Embassy
Hotel in Karachi. While in Karachi, MURAD advised that RAMZI
explained to him that he wanted to "blow up" unnamed American

---

Investigation on 4/12-13/95 at Aircraft in Flight   File #

SA FRANCIS J. PELLEGRINO, FBI
by SA THOMAS G. DONLON, FBI   Date dictated 4/19/95

FD-302a (Rev 11-15-83)

airliners by placing explosives aboard the aircraft. MURAD
explained that RAMZI took him to Lahore in September or October,
1994 in order to provide MURAD with training in the use of
explosives and chemicals. MURAD stated that he maintained a
notebook on the formulas and instructions provided to him by
RAMZI. After departing Lahore, he travelled to Karachi and then
on to Quetta, Pakistan. RAMZI proceeded directly to Quetta. When
MURAD arrived in Quetta he stayed at RAMZI's brother's house,
ABDUL MONEEM. MURAD stated that RAMZI was already in Quetta when
he arrived.

       MURAD stated that he left Quetta after about two weeks
and travelled to Layari, Karachi, in late October or early
November, 1994, where he stayed with another of RAMZI's brothers,
ABDUL KARIM MAHMOUD ABDUL KARIM. After leaving Karachi, MURAD
stated that he returned to Dubai where he received a telephone
call from RAMZI during the early part of December, 1994, asking
him to go to the Philippines. After arriving in the Philippines,
RAMZI instructed MURAD to register at the Las Palmas Hotel in
Manila utilizing the alias SAEED AHMED (ph), without displaying
his passport which reflected his true identity.

       MURAD advised that when he arrived in Manila at about
3:45 pm, he took a taxi to the Las Palmas Hotel. When he arrived
at the hotel he checked in as SAEED AHMEN. MURAD stated that
RAMZI, clean shaven, was in the lobby of the hotel at this time.
MURAD advised that he ignored RAMZI while he registered but they
both then proceeded to his room. MURAD stated that when RAMZI
previously contacted him in Dubai, he asked MURAD to bring some
hair dye. MURAD stated that he brought five or six different
Loreal hair colorings. MURAD stated that as soon as they settled
in the in the hotel, he shaved his beard and RAMZI assisted him
in coloring his hair. MURAD advised that he and RAMZI were trying
to disguise their Arabic features while appearing more European
in order to receive less attention. MURAD stated that they left
the hotel around 5:00 pm and returned about 8:00 pm after dining
alone at a local restaurant. That night, RAMZI stayed at the
hotel with MURAD and they engaged in only social conversation.

       On the following day 12/27, MURAD stated that they woke
up approximately 1:00 pm and went to the SM Store at the Shangra
La Mall in Edsa, to purchaser contact lenses for MURAD and Casio
watches to make timers for explosives. MURAD advised that they
did not buy any watches at this time. At about 5:00 pm, MURAD

FD-302a (Rev 11-15-83)

advised that RAMZI received a call on his cellular telephone from
an individual identified by RAMZI, as KHALID, from Qatar, who was
visiting the Philippines. MURAD advised that RAMZI was told that
KHALID had something for him from Qatar, and that KHALID had
arrived in the Philippines a few days earlier. MURAD advised that
he and YOUSEF went to KHALID's apartment in Ermita, but MURAD
could not remember the address, but believed it was on Mabini
Street. MURAD stated that it was his opinion that this was the
first occasion that RAMZI met KHALID based on the way they
introduced themselves. MURAD explained that KHALID gave RAMZI a
handbag that contained chocolate, potato chips, and non-alcoholic
beer. KHALID also gave RAMZI a letter from someone named SALEH.
MURAD stated that KHALID said that he came from Qatar to open up
an employment business to locate Filipinos to work in Qatar.
MURAD said that he and RAMZI stayed about ten minutes and MURAD
never had contact with KHALID again. MURAD described KHALID as
approximately 5'11", thin build, 26 or 27 years old with a beard
and brown hair. MURAD advised that RAMZI stayed with him at the
Las Palmas on the evening of 12/27. Murad stated that he and
RAMZI, after leaving KHALID, spoke of Islam, Islamic wars, the
current position of Arab countries, they purchased Time magazine,
walked on the beach, and watched CNN before going to sleep.

On 12/28, MURAD advised that he checked out of the Las
Palmas Hotel at about 2:00 pm and paid for his stay. He and RAMZI
then went to RAMZI's residence, the Dona Josefa Apartments, 711
Qirino Ave Malate Manila, apartment 603. MURAD advised that later
that same day, ABDUL MAJID came by at about 6:00 pm and stayed
for only about one hour. MURAD advised that MAJID previously
lived with RAMZI in apartment 603 until 12/27, at which time he
moved out in order to allow MURAD to move in. MURAD stated that
it was obvious that MAJID knew what was in the apartment and
RAMZI explained that MURAD always wore gloves in the apartment
since he was frightened of all the chemicals. MURAD described
MAJID as about 165 centimeters, brown complexion, clean shaven,
medium build, black hair, and originated from Saudi Arabia. MURAD
advised that he knew MAJID from Karachi and was surprised to see
him in Manila. MURAD advised that RAMZI told him he was there for
diving lessons. MURAD advised that MAJID lived in Karachi in a
section called Sharafabad where he visited MAJID, who is in the
electronics business, with RAMZI, in April of 1993. MURAD also
advised that MAJID had visited RAMZI when RAMZI was in the Jinnah
Hospital in Karachi in August of 1993. MURAD advised that RAMZI
told him that ABDUL MAJID is just an alias. MURAD also advised

FD-302a (Rev. 11-15-83)

Continuation of FD-302 of ABDUL HAKIM MURAD _____ , On 4/12-13/95, Page 4

that MAJID had a United States visa and was planning to travel to
the U.S. sometime in the near future. MURAD stated that he
thought that MAJID might go to the Richmore Flying School in
Albany, New York, because MAJID seemed interested in obtaining
his pilots license and MURAD suggested the Richmore Flying
School.

MURAD advised that in either July or August, 1993, he
was living in apartment 402 at the Lighthouse Naddi Tower in
Karachi, Pakistan. The apartment was owned by HAJI YOUSEF, a
friend of his uncle. MURAD advised that RAMZI stayed with him
(MURAD) for about one week. While in the apartment, RAMZI was
cleaning lead azide out of a container when it exploded, causing
serious injuries to RAMZI, including blindness in his right eye.
MURAD stated that RAMZI spent a long period of time in the
hospital and then went to his parents house in Iran to continue
to recuperate. MURAD described RAMZI as being very careless which
at times caused problems, including the fire at the Dona Josefa
apartment which resulted in MURAD's arrest.

MURAD advised that when he moved into apartment 603, he
observed chemicals, cotton, timers, and electronic materials.
MURAD advised that he moved into the apartment with RAMZI to
construct bombs. MURAD advised that RAMZI told him at the Las
Palmas Hotel upon his arrival that RAMZI wanted MURAD to place
bombs on some unnamed American airlines. MURAD advised that RAMZI
asked MURAD to assist in determining the proper timing of the
explosive devices because of his aviation background.

MURAD advised that he believed it would be more
advantageous to set the timer 4 days ahead to remove suspicion,
since the authorities would focus on those travelling on the
flight the day of the explosion. MURAD stated that he was going
utilize two carry-on bags. In one bag would be two bottles of
nitroglycerine that were contained in contact lens cleaning
solution bottles, one being 320 milliliters, the other 350
milliliters. In the second bag, MURAD stated he would put the
cotton, batteries, watches and wires, while carrying the
detonators in his shoe. MURAD stated that he and RAMZI discussed
placing detonators in a Parker Pen, in the future, to avoid
airport security. MURAD stated he was going to depart the
Philippines on 1/14/95 and proceed to Singapore. That night he
would get on UA flight 2, which flies from Singapore to Hong Kong
and the on to Los Angeles. MURAD advised that he would place the

FD-302a (Rev 11-15-83)

Continuation of FD-302 of   ABDUL HAKIM MURAD   . On   4/12-13/95. Page   5

bomb on flight 2 on the Singapore to Hong Kong leg. MURAD said
that he would depart the aircraft in Hong Kong, wait until the
next morning, about 8 hours, and then get on United Airlines
flight 1, on the Hong Kong to Singapore leg. MURAD advised that
he would plant the bomb and get off the flight in Singapore.
MURAD stated that he would set the timers to have the bombs
explode in four days. MURAD advised that it was going to cost
about $ 4,000 U.S. dollars to purchase the airline tickets for
the fights he was going to bomb. MURAD stated that he believed
that AMIN LNU, from Yemen, was going to send RAMZI the money.
MURAD stated that RAMZI always had four or five thousand pesos
with him and MURAD believes that the money was coming from AMIN.
MURAD said that AMIN had contacted RAMZI while they were in the
Philippines. MURAD stated that he was unaware of any bank
accounts that RAMZI had, but suggested that the money may have
gone into MAJID's account at the Hong Kong bank.

     MURAD advised that he was unaware of any other
airliners that were currently being targeted. MURAD said that he
does not know what Bojinka means, and never heard of Bojinka
until the Philippine police informed him of the term. MURAD
advised that the CASIO watches that he and RAMZI purchased could
be programmed for up to one year.

     MURAD advised that the explosive devices were comprised
of two bottles of explosive material on which he would place two
timers, two detonators, and two watches on each bottle. One of
the watches would be connected to one nine volt battery, while
the other watch would be connected to two nine volt batteries.
MURAD advised that he and RAMZI purchased five Casio watches, one
was to be used for practice, the other four to construct timers
for explosives. MURAD advised that after his baggage passed
through the x-ray machines at the airport, he would proceed into
the bathroom located in the waiting area in order to mix the
cotton with the nitroglycerine. The mixing was done after passing
through security because the x-ray machine would not detect the
nitroglycerine and cotton separately, however if the components
were mixed before passing through security, the density would
change and be detected. While in the bathroom on the plane, MURAD
advised that he would assemble the wires, batteries and explosive
to the watch whose timer was already set to explode over water.
MURAD would then place the bomb underneath a detachable plastic
piece adjacent to the sink. The bathroom is near the cockpit and
MURAD advised that he and RAMZI were certain that the hull of the

FD-302a (Rev 11-15-83)

plane would rupture and cause chaos in the cockpit. MURAD advised
that he and RAMZI were sure that the explosion would cause the
destruction of the plane and the death of everyone on board the
aircraft.

MURAD stated that he was going to pack Bibles in his
travel bag in order to draw attention away from the bags other
contents, as security personnel would be intrigued by a person
with a Muslim name carrying a Bible. MURAD also stated that he
was going to secrete the detonators in his shoes while wearing a
Christian medal around his neck, and if the metal detector alarm
signaled as he passed through he would blame it on his jewelry.

MURAD advised that MAJID returned to apartment 603 on
the 29th of December, and he, RAMZI and MAJID went to a travel
agent on Adriatico Street where RAMZI and MAJID made reservations
to go diving at Batangas beach. MURAD advised that MAJID may have
made the reservation in his real name. MURAD said that MAJID gave
MURAD a piece of paper from the booking agent and MAJID asked
MURAD to return the following day to collect 2000 pesos from the
agent. MURAD advised that he placed the paper in his pocket
without reading the name. When they returned to the apartment,
MAJID asked for the paper to be returned and MURAD complied.
MURAD stated that RAMZI informed him that the reason MAJID wanted
the paper returned was that MAJID realized he made the
reservation in his real name and did not want MURAD to know his
true identity.

After making the diving reservations, MURAD advised
that he and RAMZI went to a chemical company whose name he could
not recall, and ordered some chemicals. On the following day, the
30th of December, RAMZI and MURAD picked up the chemicals they
purchased the day before. MURAD advised that they purchased one
small carton that contained one two and a half liter bottle of
sulfuric acid, and two big cartons which contained four bottles
each, two of nitric acid and two of sulfuric acid. MURAD stated
that RAMZI paid four or five thousand pesos, in cash, for the
chemicals.

MURAD advised that ABDUL MAJID returned to the Dona
Josefa apartments at about midnight on 12/29/94. MURAD stated
that MAJID wanted someone to accompany him to check his account
balance at the Hong Kong bank in Makati. MURAD said that he went
with MAJID, who told him, after checking the account, that the

FD-302a (Rev 11-15-83)

money MAJID was expecting had not arrived yet. MURAD advised that
he is unaware of the origin of the money, nor does he know the
amount MAJID expected. After leaving the bank, MURAD advised that
he returned to the Dona Josefa apartment and MAJID went home.

⎰ MURAD advised that on either the 28th or 29th of
December, he and RAMZI purchased the CASIO watches that were
needed for the timers at the Shangra La Mega Mall in Edsa in a
store whose name he could not recall. MURAD stated that RAMZI
paid for the watches. MURAD stated that on 12/30/94, RAMZI
instructed him how to modify the Casio watches into timers for
the explosives. MURAD advised that on that afternoon he made two
of the timers, which took about two hours each to construct.

⎰   MURAD stated that MAJID was present at the apartment on
December 30th when he and RAMZI returned from picking up the
chemicals they ordered the day before. MURAD advised that MAJID
stayed with them that evening. MURAD stated that they never
discussed their bombing plans in the presence of MAJID, but MURAD
believed that MAJID must have known something was planned since
MAJID was aware of the chemicals and the electronic components in
the apartment. MURAD stated that MAJID stayed that night at the
apartment because MAJID and RAMZI were going diving and were
leaving early in the morning on 12/31/94. After MAJID and RAMZI
departed on 12/31, MURAD stated that he did some shopping, ate a
late lunch and in the evening he constructed two additional
timers. MURAD advised that RAMZI returned to the Dona Josefa
apartment at about 1:00 pm on 1/1/95, advising him that MAJID had
stayed behind to continue diving.

/   MURAD advised that on 1/2/95 he and RAMZI purchased
wires, clips and batteries at the SM Store, and began to put some
of the electronic components of the explosives together. MURAD
advised that he and RAMZI did not meet anyone the week leading up
to "black Friday", 1/6/95, the day he was arrested. MURAD said
that the last time he saw MAJID was on 12/31/94, and believed
that MAJID was still diving at the time of his arrest.

The week before he was arrested, MURAD advised that he
and RAMZI purchased some heaters (stove top burners),"big
timers", batteries, wires, Bibles, and Catholic jewelry. MURAD
advised that RAMZI told him that he was going to take one burner
and timer to visit the ABU SAYYAF group in the south of the
Philippines, to instruct them on how to mix chemicals, and use

FD-302a (Rev 11-15-83)

Continuation of FD-302 of ABDUL HAKIM MURAD _____ . On 4/12-13/95. Page 8

timing devices and watches for explosives. MURAD said that RAMZI
was going to bring one timer and burner to Algeria, Egypt, and
France, to teach Muslims in those areas how to construct bombs.
MURAD stated that RAMZI had visited the ABU SAYYAF group once
before in Mindaneo during the early part of 1994. MURAD stated
that RAMZI told him that the ABU SAYYAF group would be difficult
to instruct in explosives since their main interest is in the use
of firearms.

          MURAD advised that he and RAMZI woke up about noon on
Friday, 1/6/95, went out for lunch, and did some shopping at the
Harrison Plaza Mall. MURAD stated that they did not meet anyone
that day. MURAD advised that late in the evening of 1/6/95, RAMZI
was burning some chemicals that were no longer needed. MURAD said
that RAMZI became careless, and the burning began to produce more
smoke than he expected. The smoke was very dense so they opened
the front door and windows to allow the smoke out of the
apartment while he and RAMZI exited the apartment to wait for the
smoke to dissipate. MURAD said that the smoke caused some
neighbors to contact the fire department because they believed
there was a fire in the apartment. MURAD stated that he escorted
the fire department to the apartment to show them that there was
no fire. After observing the inside of the apartment the fire
department was satisfied that there was no current danger and
departed. MURAD advised that RAMZI had departed the area when the
fire department arrived. Subsequent to the departure of the fire
department, the police responded to the apartment. MURAD advised
that he let the police into the apartment and assured them that
there was no problem. The officer informed MURAD that he wanted
MURAD to come down to the police station for questioning. MURAD
said that he informed the officer that this was his friend's
apartment and that he would try and contact his friend. The
officer told MURAD to come to the station that night after he
found his friend.

          MURAD advised that he went back to the apartment and
called RAMZI on RAMZI's cellular telephone. RAMZI told him that
he was at the 7-11 store on Mabini street. MURAD advised that he
went to the 7-11 store were he met RAMZI and OSAMA ASMURAI, who
MURAD claims he had not seen in Manila previously. The three then
proceeded to a Kareoke bar were MURAD explained to RAMZI that the
police wanted MURAD to go to the station for questioning. MURAD
stated that RAMZI told MURAD to give him his passports and to go
back to the apartment and retrieve the computer. MURAD gave RAMZI

FD-302a (Rev 11-15-83)

Continuation of FD-302 of ABDUL HAKIM MURAD _____ . On 4/12-13/95. Page 9

his passports and when he returned to the Dona Josefa apartments
he was apprehended by the police in the lobby. MURAD stated that
he tried to escape but fell down on the sidewalk just outside the
apartment complex. MURAD stated that he was taken to the police
station for about 30 minutes, then was taken back to apartment
603. MURAD advised that the police discovered in the apartment,
the computer, the chemicals, electronic components, one completed
pipe bomb and three pipes that were not yet armed. MURAD was then
taken back to the police station by the police.

MURAD advised that after the bombs exploded on the
airlines, credit would be given to the LIBERATION ARMY. MURAD
advised that the LIBERATION ARMY consisted of only him and RAMZI.
MURAD said that RAMZI made up the name in order to make people
believe that the LIBERATION ARMY was a large group of committed
terrorists.

MURAD advised that RAMZI told him in August of 1992
that he (RAMZI) would be travelling to the United States to
commit a bombimg. MURAD advised that when the bomb exploded at
the World Trade Center he was certain that RAMZI was the person
responsible. MURAD advised that he and RAMZI would use the code "
A1168 of the Liberation Army" when claiming responsibility for
terrorist acts. MURAD stated that the "A" was for ABDUL, the
true first name of both MURAD and RAMZI, the first "1"(one)
represented the day he (MURAD) was born 4/1/68, the second
"1"(one) was arbitrary, and the "68" is the year that both he and
RAMZI were born. MURAD advised that when the fire bomb exploded
in the New York City subway in December of 1994, RAMZI called him
and instructed him to telephone various Embassies claiming that
the LIBERATION ARMY A1168 was responsible. MURAD claimed that he
contacted the Omani Embassy in Islamabad, the American Embassy in
Islamabad, and the American Consulate in Karachi.

MURAD advised that RAMZI told him upon his arrival to
the Philippines on December 26, 1994, that he had placed a bomb
earlier that month on the Philippines Airlines flight that
travels from Manila to Tokyo's Narita Airport, with a stopover in
Cebu, Philippines. MURAD stated that RAMZI told him that he only
used a small quantity of explosives as he was testing the timers
and the explosive to insure that it operated as he expected.
MURAD advised that RAMZI would remove the contents of a pill
capsule and replace it with what MURAD believed to be the
explosive "acetone broxide". When purchasing tickets for the

FD-302a (Rev. 11-15-83)

Continuation of FD-302 of ABDUL HAKIM MURAD _____ , On 4/12-13/95 , Page 10

flight, RAMZI utilized an unknown Italian name which he obtained
from the Atlas software stored on his computer. MURAD claims that
RAMZI called him to go to the Philippines after the Philippine
Airline explosion.

MURAD advised that after the World Trade Center bombing
RAMZI travelled to Karachi, Pakistan, were they met on numerous
occasions. MURAD stated that RAMZI told him of his involvement in
the World Trade Center explosion. MURAD said that he never met
AHMED AJAJ and only knows that he entered the United States with
RAMZI and was arrested. MURAD stated that RAMZI "used" the other
individuals that were involved in the Trade Center bombing. MURAD
stated that RAMZI told him that he resided with MOHAMMAD SALAMEH
in New Jersey and he, SALAMEH, ABDUL RAHMAN YASIN, and a
Jordanian were involved the day of the explosion. MURAD said that
he was unsure of the Jordanian's name but believed it might be
something like ISAM, and believes that he has green eyes and
light hair.

MURAD was shown photos of various individuals to
determine whether he could make identifications. MURAD identified
photo number one as an individual by the name of HABIBA, a
Balouchi, from Pakistan, who he never met in the Philippines.
MURAD said that the only time he met HABIBA was at RAMZI's
brother's house, ABDUL MONEEM, in Quetta, in either September or
October of 1994. MURAD said that RAMZI never spoke about HABIBA.

Photo number two was identified by MURAD as OSAMA
ASURMAI. MURAD said that the Philippine police told him that the
man's name was WALI KHAN AMIN SHAH, but MURAD stated that he
never knew him by that name. MURAD advised that OSAMA a was a
Saudi who allegedly lived in Medina, Saudi Arabia. MURAD advised
that he believes that OSAMA has a brother by the name SAKER.
MURAD stated that the first time that he met OSAMA was in ABDUL
MAJID's apartment in Karachi, Pakistan in August of 1994. MURAD
advised that the next time he encountered OSAMA was the day he
was arrested, 1/7/95, at the 7-11 store in Manila, in the company
of RAMZI. MURAD said that OSAMA was angry at the Philippine
government because they arrested his friend and turned him over
to United States authorities. MURAD said that he believed that
OSAMA arrived from Islamabad on 1/6/95.

MURAD was shown photo number three and identified the
individual as ABDUL MONEEM, the brother of RAMZI, who lives in

FD-302a (Rev. 11-15-83)

Continuation of FD-302 of __ABDUL HAKIM MURAD_____ On _4/12-13/95_ Page __11__

Quetta, Pakistan. MURAD advised that he never saw MONEEM in the Philippines. MURAD described Moneem as approximately 31 years old, married, with 3 or 4 children, and is an Arabic teacher in Quetta.

MURAD identified photo number four as RAMZI's brother in law ABDUL SAMAD, who is married to one of RAMZI's sisters, and is currently living in IRAN.

MURAD advised that RAMZI planned to transport some of the chemicals and cotton back to Karachi after they completed their bombing of the U.S. airlines. MURAD said that RAMZI was going to make additional nitrocellulose to commit further acts in the name of his religion. MURAD also advised that the pipe bombs discovered in the apartment at the Dona Josefa were going to be used in an attempt to take the life of Pope John Paul. MURAD advised that RAMZI was going to plant the bombs on the Pope's travel route in Manila, while using a remote control device to initiate the explosives. MURAD stated that he was opposed to any attempt on the life of Pope John Paul because Islamic law forbids the killing of a holy man. MURAD claims that RAMZI was uncertain as to whether the pipe bombs would kill Pope John Paul, but was certain that it would cause enough commotion to be newsworthy. RAMZI was going to credit the attempt on the life of Pope John Paul to the ABU SAYYAF group in an attempt to enhance their stature.

MURAD advised that he was born on 4/1/68 in Kuwait, and his full name is ABDUL HAKIM ALI HASHIM MURAD. MURAD said that his parents still live in Sabahiya, Kuwait. MURAD said that his parents are both Balouchi, from Pakistan, although his mother has OMANI citizenship. MURAD's family and RAMZI's family were acquaintances since both families are Balouchi, and lived in Kuwait at the same time. MURAD stated that he attended a Pakistani school when he was very young and then went to the Aumal- Kura Abu Halifa elementary school in the Ahmadi district of Kuwait. MURAD advised that he then enrolled at the Khalifa Talal Al - Jiry school were he graduated but never attended any college or university.

MURAD advised that he first met RAMZI in a Mosque in Fahaheel City in Kuwait in either 1983 or 1984. MURAD advised that he did not stay in frequent contact with RAMZI while RAMZI attended school in the United Kingdom. MURAD stated that RAMZI is

FD-302a (Rev 11-15-83)

Continuation of FD-302 of ABDUL HAKIM MURAD   . On   4/12-13/95. Page   12

married with two daughters, and believes that they reside in the
Iranian section of Baluchistan. MURAD advised that RAMZI had a
girlfriend in the Philippines who sold perfume at the Harrison
Plaza Mall.

MURAD advised that when the Philippine National Police
questioned him they tape recorded the interviews. MURAD advised
that he does not know MOHAMMAD JAMAL KHALIFA and heard the name
for the first time when it was mentioned to him by the Philippine
Police. MURAD advised that although he never met OSAMA BEN LADIN
he is familiar with the name. MURAD advised that RAMZI told him
that he met the blind Sheik, OMAR ABDEL RAHMAN, on one occasion
at a Mosque in Jersey City, New Jersey. MURAD stated that he was
told by RAMZI that neither Sheik RAHMAN nor SIDDIG ALI had any
involvement with the World Trade Center bombing. MURAD advised
that he did not believe that RAMZI was associated with any
particular group. MURAD advised that he does not know TARIQ RANA
but had heard the name on one occasion from either RAMZI or the
Philippine National Police. MURAD also advised that he does not
know anyone by the name of SALEM ALI or SHEIK MOHAMMAD.

MURAD advised that RAMZI has a friend, who he (MURAD)
also knows, by the name of ABDUL SHAKOOR, who was also born in
Kuwait. MURAD stated that RAMZI met SHAKOOR in Afghanistan in
either 1991 or 1992, while RAMZI was taking six months of
explosive training. MURAD stated that SHAKOOR travelled to
Afghanistan and attended approximately two weeks of training
before departing. MURAD stated that SHAKOOR was a very violent
individual and believed in killing indiscriminately on behalf of
his religion, even if it resulted in the deaths of Muslims. MURAD
stated that RAMZI would never kill a brother Muslim, and their
different views on fighting for their cause resulted in a
strained relationship.

As for any future terrorist plans, MURAD advised that
he and RAMZI discussed the possibility of bombing a nuclear
facility in the United States. They also discussed additional
attacks on American airline carriers such as United and Northwest
Airlines. MURAD stated that RAMZI wanted to bomb El-Al Airlines
but believed that security would be too difficult to penetrate.
The underlying reason for these attacks would be to make the
people of the U.S., and their government, "suffer" for their
support of Israel. MURAD stated that America should remain
neutral regarding the problems of the Middle East. MURAD advised

FD-302a (Rev. 11-15-83)

Continuation of FD-302 of __ABDUL HAKIM MURAD_____ .On __4/12-13/95__.Page __13__

that RAMZI wanted to return to the United States in the future to
bomb the World Trade Center a second time.

     MURAD gave the following information regarding his
family;

Mother: AMINA AHMAD
Father: ALI HASHIM   Working in Kuwait Petroleum Company.
     Parents live in Sabahiya B/1 St. 17 HN 828 Kuwait tel:
     3615585.

Sisters: MAJIDA   Single, living in Kuwait, 28 years old.
     FARIDA   Married living in Ajman City, U.A.E, 23
     years old.
     MANAL   Living in Kuwait, 10 years old.

Brothers: AHMAD   Deceased.
     ANWAR   Single, living in U.A.E, 25 years old.
     ANWAR is working in the Customs office in
     Abu Dhabi, U.A.E.
     KHALID   Single living in the United States 22 years
     old. MURAD advised that KHALID was studying
     in Kentucky but is currently residing with
     his brother's brother-in-law in D.C., whose
     name is ABDUL KHALIQ who is studying
     computer engineering at Georgetown
     University.
     MOHAMMAD   Living in Kuwait, 8 years old.
     ADEL   Living in Kuwait, 3 years old.

     MURAD advised that he has a good friend, KHALID HASSAN,
a Palestinian, who lives and studies dentistry in Cebu,
Philippines. MURAD advised that HASSAN has no connections with
RAMZI and HASSAN was unaware of MURAD presence in the
Philippines.

     At this time the aircraft landed in Alaska for
refueling.

     MURAD advised that on 11/19/91 he left DUBAI and
travelled to London, England for a week of sightseeing. MURAD
stated that prior to going to England, he was in Dubai obtaining
his private pilots license at the Emirates Flying School. MURAD

FD-302a (Rev 11-15-83)

Continuation of FD-302 of   ABDUL HAKIM MURAD   . On   4/12-13/95 . Page   14

advised that his friend, NASIR ALI MUBAREK, who also attended the
Emirates Flying School, had arrived in London a couple of days
prior to MURAD. MURAD stated that he travelled on his Pakistani
passport in which he obtained a single entry, 6 month visa for
the United Kingdom at the U.K. Consulate in Dubai. MURAD stated
that they stayed in Oxford with a woman, whose name he does not
recall, who MUBAREK had met on a previous trip to England. MURAD
said that MUBAREK has relatives in Birmingham, England, and
further advised that MUBAREK does not know RAMZI.

        After approximately one week, they departed London and
proceeded to the United States. MURAD said that MUBAREK flew to
San Antonio, Texas while he travelled first to Washington, D.C.,
on TWA. MURAD stated that he stayed with his brothers brother-in-
law, ABDUL KHALIQ, for a few days then proceeded to San Antonio,
also on TWA. MURAD advised that he and MUBAREK were scheduled,
per their immigration I-20s, to attend school at the Alpha Tango
Flying School at Berne Stages, Texas. MURAD advised that he
obtained a U.S. visa in Dubai that was valid for one or two
years. MURAD advised that his father financed his airfare,
tuition for the flying school, and living expenses while staying
in the Unites States.

        MURAD advised that he obtained his initial Pakistani
passport in 1987 from the Pakistani Embassy in Kuwait. MURAD
stated that since the pages in the passport were exhausted, he
obtained another Pakistani passport at the Consulate in Dubai.
When this passport became full with visa's and stamps, he
obtained a third passport in 1994 from the Consulate in Dubai.
Since none of the passports expired, MURAD advised that he
travelled with all three. MURAD stated that he has no additional
passports in other names or from other countries.

        MURAD advised that he and MUBAREK attended the Alpha
Tango School because their chief instructor at the Emirates
Flying School, RIAZ AHMED, in Dubai, had also attended Alpha
Tango. MURAD advised that many Pakistani's were enrolled at the
Alpha Tango School. One of the instructors at Alpha Tango was a
Sudanese by the name of BAHA ELDIN. MURAD stated that the chief
pilot, HAMED AFZL, arranged for an apartment for MURAD and
MUBAREK in San Antonio. MURAD stated that they did not visit any
Mosque's in San Antonio and they departed after approximately two
weeks because they were unhappy with the facilities at Alpha
Tango.

FD-302a (Rev. 11-15-83)

MURAD advised that he and MUBAREK purchased a Hyundai automobile in San Antonio, Texas, and travelled to the Richmore Flying School, located near Albany, New York. MURAD stated that they drove through New York City and stopped only to purchase a map, and then continued on to the Richmore School. MURAD estimates that it took them three days to drive from San Antonio, Texas, to Albany, New York. MURAD stated that a RICHARD LNU was in charge at the Richmore Flying School which they only attended for approximately two months.

MURAD advised that he departed Richmore to return to San Antonio's Alpha Tango School because the weather in Albany was much too cold. MURAD advised that he attended the Richmore school in January and February of 1992, after which time he departed on TWA, to San Antonio, with MUBAREK remaining at the Richmore School. MURAD said that he attended the Alpha Tango School for the months of March and April, 1992, and stayed with two Pakistani's, RAGIB LNU and NASER LNU, and one Saudi, HASSAN MUBAREK (no relation to NASER). After about two months at the Alpha Tango School he returned to Richmore, first stopping in Washington D.C. to visit with ABDUL KHALIQ for a few days. MURAD advised that MUBAREK met him in Washington D.C., and they proceeded to the Richmore School.

MURAD stated that they attended the Richmore School for about two weeks and departed for North Carolina to attend the Coastal Aviation School in Newburgh, N.C., where they resided. MURAD said that they arrived in North Carolina the end of May or beginning of June, 1992. MURAD advised that MUBAREK obtained his license prior to MURAD, then returned to the Richmore School, while MURAD received his certification on 6/6/92. After MURAD obtained his license MUBAREK returned to North Carolina in order to accompany MURAD to the Richmore School. Prior to returning to the Richmore School, MURAD and MUBAREK visited New York City for one evening. Upon arriving at the Richmore School they met a mutual friend of theirs, ABDULLAH YOUSEF, who they knew from the Emirates School in the U.A.E. After about a week in Richmore, all three proceeded by automobile to California.

In June, 1992, all three attended the California Aeronautics School in Red Bluff, California, which is located three hours north of San Francisco. Both MURAD and MUBAREK were attempting to obtain an instructor rating at the California Aeronautics School. MURAD said that he paid $1,300 to attend the

FD-302a (Rev. 11-15-83)

school, but he departed after two weeks without completing the course. While at Red Bluff, MURAD stayed with an Italian individual known only as MAX, and a Vietnamese individual with American citizenship who MURAD only knew as HEYO (ph). MURAD advised that he alone returned to Dubai after leaving California.

MURAD stated that before reaching Dubai he stayed with an aunt, GUL BIBY, and uncle, SAADI MOHAMMAD for three days in Bahrain. MURAD advised that he then returned to Dubai and resided with his uncle for two months. MURAD stated that he frequently traveled throughout the Gulf States in an attempt to find employment as a pilot. MURAD advised that he obtained a U.S. visa in Muscat, Oman in November of 1992, that was valid until February of 1993. MURAD advised that he wanted to return to California to complete his instructor qualifications since he already paid for the course. MURAD stated that he decided not to return to the U.S. but rather travelled to Karachi in an attempt to obtain employment with Pakistani International Airlines. MURAD advised that he stayed in Karachi from November, 1992 until April, 1993.

MURAD stated that RAMZI contacted him while he was in Dubai in either July or August, 1992. MURAD advised that RAMZI stated that he obtained "chocolate training", when MURAD explained that he did not understand, RAMZI replied "boom". MURAD said he understood this to mean that RAMZI had obtained some training in explosives. MURAD said that RAMZI stated he was going to the United States to find employment, however he was aware RAMZI was going to the States to commit a bombing. MURAD advised that RAMZI did not say when he was planning this travel.

MURAD stated that when he was in Karachi from November 1992 to April 1993, he resided with an individual named ABDUL GHANY, who is unknown to RAMZI. MURAD advised that he obtained a flying license in Karachi from the Pakistan Civil Aviation, file number in Karachi 3815, and license number 1929.

MURAD said that he met RAMZI numerous times in Karachi in April, 1993, at which time RAMZI advised him of his participation in the World Trade Center bombing. MURAD said that RAMZI was staying at the Embassy Hotel in Karachi during this time, and RAMZI felt secure.

FD-302a (Rev 11-15-83)

Continuation of FD-302 of __ABDUL HAKIM MURAD__ _____ . On __4/12-13/95__. Page __17__

      MURAD stated that he departed Karachi in May of 1993 and travelled between Dubai and Kuwait, returning to Karachi in August, 1993, where he again met with RAMZI. RAMZI stayed for a couple of weeks at the Lighthouse Naddi Tower with MURAD, where he had an accident cleaning lead azide from a container which resulted in a serious injury. MURAD stated that RAMZI spent a part of July, and most of August, in the hospital in Karachi. MURAD said that he left Karachi in mid August to attend the Peshawar Flying School, were he resided. MURAD advised that most of the students enrolled in this school originated from the Sudan. MURAD stated that attended the Peshawar School for 22 days where he obtained his instructor rating. MURAD then returned to Karachi to apply for a pilot position at Pakistani International Airlines.

      While in Karachi, MURAD resided at the home of his friend ABDUL GHANY, House Number Y5, Phase 6, Khayabanshabaz. MURAD stated that RAMZI's brother, ABDUL KARIM MAHMOUD ABDUL KARIM advised him that RAMZI had returned to their parents residence in Iranshar, Iran, to continue his recuperation. MURAD said that he stayed in Karachi until November of 1993.

      MURAD stated that he left Karachi at the end of November and proceeded to Dubai were he remained until May, 1994. MURAD stated that he had no contact with RAMZI during this time and believed that RAMZI was still recuperating in Iran. MURAD advised that he was attempting to convert his pilots license to qualify in Dubai, which was a complicated process. MURAD advised that he travelled to Kuwait in June, 1994, to visit with his family, after which he returned to Dubai. In August, 1994, MURAD advised that he went to Karachi and resided with ABDUL KARIM, where he remained there for 15 days.

      MURAD stated that RAMZI came from Manila to Karachi in August, 1994, and stayed at the Embassy Hotel. MURAD explained that RAMZI did not always get along well with ABDUL KARIM and would usually stay at the Embassy Hotel when in Karachi. MURAD advised that RAMZI told him that he travelled around Southeast Asia, i.e. Hong Kong, Singapore, and the Philippines, to find a permanent residence because he believed the FBI was actively searching for him in Karachi. MURAD said that RAMZI concluded that the Manila area was acceptable because the cost of living is reasonable.

FD-302a (Rev 11-15-83)

Continuation of FD-302 of   ABDUL HAKIM MURAD   . On   4/12-13/95. Page   18

       While in Karachi, MURAD advised that RAMZI told him of his desire to bomb unnamed American airlines. MURAD also said that RAMZI wanted to travel to Lahore, Pakistan, to train MURAD in the use of explosives, timers, and Casio watche modifications. MURAD said that RAMZI travelled to Lahore a couple of days prior and they stayed in Lahore for 18 days of training. After completing the training, MURAD returned to Karachi and Yousef travelled to Quetta to visit his brother. MURAD said that he remained in Karachi for about two weeks, then returned to Dubai where RAMZI contacted him in December 1994 requesting MURAD to travel to the Philippines. MURAD advised that when RAMZI asked him to go come to the Philippines he was fully aware that "something was planned".

       MURAD advised that RAMZI spoke to him on one occasion about attacking the U.S. Consulate in Karachi with a "rocket" that RAMZI was going to construct. MURAD explained that RAMZI drew a diagram of this rocket and advised that it would be fired from a park adjacent to a church located across the street from the Consulate. RAMZI never explained how the rocket was going to be fired or when he planned on committing the attack. MURAD said that RAMZI gave no particular reason the U.S. Consulate was the target, but conjectured that it was convenient since RAMZI spent a substantial amount of time in Karachi.

       MURAD advised that he never encountered, nor does he know anything about, MIR AHMED KANSI. MURAD said that RAMZI never spoke of KANZI and he is unaware whether RAMZI ever had contact with KANSI. MURAD also claimed that he did not know who was responsible for the shooting of two Americans in Karachi on 3/8/95, and that he only learned of the attack from the Philippine National Police.

ADVICE OF RIGHTS

YOUR RIGHTS

Place _____
Date _____
Time _____

Before we ask you any questions, you must understand your rights.

You have the right to remain silent.

If you have already made statements to the Philippine authorities, you still have the right to remain silent now.

Nothing the Philippine authorities may have said to you is binding on the United States government, and you should not rely on any promises or representations made to you by those authorities.

Anything you say can be used against you in court.

You have the right to talk to a lawyer for advice before we ask you any questions and to have a lawyer with you during questioning.

If you cannot afford a lawyer, one will be appointed for you before any questioning if you wish.

If you decide to answer questions now without a lawyer present, you will still have the right to stop answering at any time. You also have the right to stop answering at any time until you talk to a lawyer.

WAIVER OF RIGHTS

I have read this statement of my rights and I understand what my rights are. I am willing to make a statement and answer questions. I do not want a lawyer at this time. I understand and know what I am doing. No promises or threats have been made to me and no pressure or coercion of any kind has been used against me. In making this waiver, I am not relying on any promises or representations made to me by the Philippine authorities, nor is this waiver made in response to any pressure or coercion by the Philippine authorities.

Signed _____

Witness: _____

Witness: SA _____, FBI, NYO, 4/12/95

Time: _____

Appendix II: Memo to Orrin G. Hatch
Re: Investigation into Terrorism, December 5, 1995

PRIVILEGED & CONFIDENTIAL/ATTORNEY WORK PRODUCT

MEMORANDUM

TO: OGH

FROM:

VIA: Coodney/Dibbles/Iverson

DATE: December 5, 1995   OK-D   Rec'd 12/7

RE: Investigation into Terrorism

_____

The purpose of this memorandum is to outline several issues
in the area of domestic and international terrorism which we
believe should be the subject of an investigative oversight
and/or hearings by the full Committee. Specifically, we will
investigate the FBI's involvement before, during and after a
terrorist threat and/or attack. This area is particularly
topical in light of the tragic incidents in Tokyo's subway, at
the federal building in Oklahoma City and at the World Trade
Center. Moreover, the increased threat of terrorist activities,
be it nuclear, biological or chemical, is of special interest
considering the upcoming Olympic Games in Atlanta and Salt Lake
City.

The investigation would be two-fold: (1) a review of the
preventative measures currently in place to anticipate and
hopefully prevent such acts; and (2) what mechanisms do we have
in place in the event a terrorist attack does occur. Using the
World Trade Center as an example, we may also want to take a
critical view at what has occurred in the past, what could have
been done to prevent it and what measures have been taken since
that tragedy.[1]

With respect to prevention, we have received information
from a company in Florida which tracks potential acts of
industrial espionage for private companies. On numerous
occasions, while conducting these investigations, the company has
uncovered information relative to potential terrorist (nuclear,
biological and chemical) threats on the United States. In each
instance, the company has contacted the FBI. The company is not
in the business of tracking potential terrorist threats in the
U.S. nor does it want to be. However, the company has offered to
teach the FBI how it collects this information and how the FBI
can identify terrorist activities before they happen. The FBI's

_____

[1]As an aside, much of the good work that was conducted after
the fact at the World Trade Center was that of ATF. If we could
restore some of the lost confidence in ATF by exposing some of
their good work, that would be a bonus.

response is that the technique used by this company "is too difficult to learn" and therefore the FBI is not interested.[2] We propose to investigate whether this scenario is in fact true and what types of measures are being taken to identify and prevent terrorist before they happen.

A good case study on the preventive issue is what the FBI is doing in anticipation of the Atlanta Olympics. In addition to the "terrorist" issues surrounding the Olympics, the Committee will also be looking at the use of HRT at the Atlanta Olympics, as part of continuing oversight stemming from the Waco investigation. This would also ensure some long-range planning with respect to the effectiveness of the FBI in anticipation of the Olympics in Salt Lake City. Specifically, if we can investigate how Atlanta is handled, we may be able to ensure that any problems that do occur will be addressed and resolved before Salt Lake City.[3]

With respect the FBI's involvement after a terrorist event has occurred, the FBI is the lead agency with respect to coordinating rescue efforts and preservation of evidence from a crime scene. The FBI works in conjunction with FEMA, HHS, DOD, American Red Cross and numerous other agencies. The major problem in this arena appears to be the lack of training and equipment in situation that involve nuclear, biological and chemical substances. Specifically, the individuals first on the scene do not have the expertise to handle such complex and multi-faceted attacks. We will want to investigate what the FBI is doing to ensure that the FBI is prepared to handle these situations in case of attack.

Given the increase in terrorist attack in this country coupled with the high visibility associated with hosting the Olympic games, we believe that this issue is timely and will attract positive public as well as press attention. Both NBC and

---

[2]As with any source, we are investigating the background and motivation of this particular company. Regardless of the outcome of that inquiry, the idea of prevention of domestic terrorism is one which clearly desires serious attention.

[3]We have information that some instances, like the World Trade Center, could have been prevented if the relevant agencies had worked in concert with each other in the sharing of information. Simply stated, several different agencies had a small piece of the puzzle. If they had shared with each other, there is at least a strong possibility that they would have identified the World Trade Center as a target before the bombing. As we uncovered in the Waco investigation, the sharing of "intelligence" is lacking among federal law enforcement agencies -- an area which we may want to be more aggressively active in promoting.

60 Minutes have scheduled news stories focusing on the increase
in terrorist activities in the United States and what the
government is doing to protect its citizens. Accordingly, we
believe an oversight investigation in this arena is both
appropriate and imperative.

OPTIONS

X   Continue with investigation

X   Plan hearings

____   Schedule members briefing (may include classified info)

____   Discontinue investigation

____   Other:

INDEX

Salameh, Mohammed (*continued*)
  Kensington Avenue address of,
    140–41
  in 1993 WTC bombing, 116,
    117, 118, 131
  traffic accidents of, 111, 186
  trial of, 201–6
Salem, Emad Eldin Aly Abdou,
    12, 13, 53–59, 98, 102–4,
    106, 112, 113, 134, 141,
    146–47, 150–59, 161,
    172–73, 179, 185–86, 206,
    297, 305
  and Abouhalima's capture, 145,
    147–48
  background of, 54
  "bootleg" tapes of, 162–64,
    165–66, 168, 221, 224, 324
  consent document signed by,
    166
  credibility of, 161
  debriefing of, 68–69
  decision to withdraw, 93–94
  Detroit trip of, 66–68
  mistrust of FBI of, 151
  payment for work by, 150–52,
    170
  polygraphs taken by, 87, 91,
    135
  recordings by, 152–53, 154, 157
  reinstatement of, 136–37,
    150–52
  safe house rented by, 154–55
  timer episode and, 155–56
  undercover work of, 59–63,
    69–71, 82–93, 149, 157–58
  value as asset of, 152
  videos shot by, 64
Santiago, Carol, *see* Brioso,
    Catherine
Sapanara, John, 93

Sattar, Ahmed Abdel, 69, 103,
    156–57, 184, 326, 367, 426
Saudi Arabia, 212, 337
  aid to the Afghan rebels from,
    39
Sawyer Aviation School, 355
Scarpa, Gregory, Jr., 338–40
Schlesinger, Alvin, 65, 83
Schultz, George, 441
Schumer, Charles, 160
Schwarzkopf, Norman H., 47
Sears Tower, 280, 360
Secret Service, 133
Semtex, 190
Senario, Mina, 232–33, 264
Senate, U.S., 3
September 11, 2001 terrorist
    attacks, 1, 4, 5, 12, 13, 29,
    77, 414–23
Serbian Liberation Army, 131
Services Office for the
    Mujahadeen, 40, 41, 52, 56,
    85, 193, 211, 331, 370–71
Shah, Wali Khan Amin, 200, 232,
    233, 236–37, 259, 262, 266,
    297, 303, 326–27, 402
Shahriarfar, Hossein, 192
Shakur, Abdul, 189
Shalabi, Mustafa, 41–42, 43, 44,
    45–46, 52, 56, 100, 193,
    228, 300
  murder of, 16, 49–50, 103, 105
Sharia, 39, 189
Shea, Kevin, 121–23, 127–29,
    178, 249
Shelby, Richard, 3, 405
Sherman, Jim, 60, 88, 89, 93,
    134–35, 172, 377
Sief, Abu, 211, 352
Sig Sauer P228, 95
Simon, Steven, 348